FUNDAMENTALS OF ARGUMENTATION THEORY

A Handbook of Historical Backgrounds and Contemporary Developments

Frans H. van Eemeren
Rob Grootendorst
Francisca Snoeck Henkemans
University of Amsterdam

J. Anthony Blair *University of Windsor*
Ralph H. Johnson *University of Windsor*
Erik C. W. Krabbe *University of Groningen*
Christian Plantin *University of Lumiére Lyon 2*
Douglas N. Walton *University of Winnipeg*
Charles A. Willard *University of Louisville*
John Woods *University of Lethbridge*
David Zarefsky *Northwestern University*

 LAWRENCE ERLBAUM ASSOCIATES, PUBLISHERS
1996   Mahwah, New Jersey

Lawrence Erlbaum Associates, Inc., Publishers
10 Industrial Avenue
Mahwah, New Jersey 07430

Library of Congress Cataloging-in-Publication Data

Fundamentals of argumentation theory : a handbook of historical
   backgrounds and contemporary developments / Frans H. van Eemeren . . .
   [et al.].
      p.   cm.
   Includes bibliographical references and indexes.
   ISBN 0-8058-1861-8. — ISBN 0-8058-1862-6 (pbk.)
      1. Persuasion (Rhetoric). 2. Logic. 3. Reasoning. I. Eemeren,
   F. H. van.
   P301.5.P47F86 1996
   808—dc20   95-53033
                                                              CIP

Books published by Lawrence Erlbaum Associates are printed on acid-free paper,
and their bindings are chosen for strength and durability.

Printed in the United States of America
10 9 8 7 6 5 4 3 2

FUNDAMENTALS
OF
ARGUMENTATION
THEORY

*A Handbook of Historical Backgrounds
and Contemporary Developments*

CONTENTS

PREFACE

In the past decades the study of argumentation has become a field of interest in its own right. Several scholarly societies and associations and various academic journals are devoted to argumentation. A great number of books and articles concentrate on this subject. It is also the focus of attention at many conferences, symposia, and courses. The growing interest in argumentation is an international phenomenon. It is not restricted to one discipline, being apparent in philosophy, logic, linguistics, discourse analysis, rhetoric, speech communication, education, psychology, sociology, political science, law, and many other disciplines. Recently, some multidisciplinary and interdisciplinary approaches to argumentation have also been developed.

Because of the complexity, diversity and rate of developments in the study of argumentation, one might easily lose sight of the ways in which argumentation theory has matured. The authors of this book therefore think that a comprehensive survey of the various theoretical contributions is now worthwhile. *Fundamentals of Argumentation Theory* is intended to serve this purpose. Although it stands to reason that choices had to be made and that not all contributions could be equally accentuated, it essentially describes the historical works that provide the background to the field of argumentation studies and the contemporary developments that make it prosper. All major trends in current research are discussed and all prominent approaches which are (at least partly) accessible in English.

The present volume originates in part with *The Study of Argumentation* (Irvington, 1984), jointly authored by Frans H. van Eemeren, Rob Grootendorst, and Tjark Kruiger, and republished as the *Handbook of Argumentation Theory* (Foris, 1987). Because argumentation theory has advanced considerably since the manuscript for this book was completed (1980), it has been apparent for some time that it was being overtaken by new developments. It became clear that a substantially new study would be needed, and it was decided to write *Fundamentals of Argumentation Theory* with that idea in mind. The first three authors, Frans van Eemeren, Rob Grootendorst, and Francisca Snoeck Henkemans, acted as "writers-in-chief." They wrote *Fundamentals* together with their colleagues Anthony Blair, Ralph Johnson, Erik Krabbe, Christian Plantin, Douglas Walton, Charles Willard, John Woods, and David Zarefsky, all specialists in the field. The resulting book is altogether the authors' joint responsibility.

It goes without saying that a comprehensive book such as *Fundamentals of Argumentation Theory* could hardly be written without the help of a great many others. Various members of the research group for Argumentation and Discourse Analysis of the Institute for Functional Research of Language and Language Use of the University of Amsterdam, the Free University of Amsterdam and the State University of Leiden have been helpful in improving the manuscript. The authors would like to thank Antoine Braet, Petra Boers, Eveline Feteris, Bart Garssen, Janne-Maaike Gerlofs, Susanne Gerritsen, Peter Houtlosser, Agnès van Rees, Maarten van der Tol, Erik Viskil, Shi-Xu, and the associated members of the Erasmus University Rotterdam, Ton van Haaften, Harm Kloosterhuis, and José Plug, for their useful suggestions. They also want to thank Bart Garssen, Peter Houtlosser, and Paul Nagtegaal for their technical and bibliographical assistance.

In addition, the authors were fortunate enough to find a number of their most distinguished colleagues, from various parts of the world, willing to advise them. All of these argumentation scholars read parts of the manuscript; many suggested important corrections and clarifications, some proposed elaborations or additions. Their comments have been crucial in getting the book published in its present form. The authors therefore make a point of emphasizing that their support has been invaluable. As a token of their appreciation, they have listed the names of these generous colleagues.

ACKNOWLEDGMENT

The authors would like to express their gratitude to the following colleagues who have been of help in preparing this book:

William van Belle, Catholic University of Leuven
Marie-Jeanne Borel, University of Lausanne
Dale Brashers, University of Ohio
Georg Brutian, National Academy of Sciences Armenia
Adelino Cattani, University of Padua
Robert Craig, University of Colorado at Boulder
Maurice Finocchiaro, University of Nevada Las Vegas

Alec Fisher, University of East Anglia
James Freeman, City University of New York
Bice Mortara Garavelli, University of Turin
Thomas Goodnight, Northwestern University
Trudy Govier, Calgary
Hans Hansen, Brock University
David Hitchcock, McMaster University Hamilton
Paul van den Hoven, University of Utrecht
Sally Jackson, University of Arizona
Scott Jacobs, University of Arizona
Henry Johnstone Jr., Pennsylvania State University
Manfred Kienpointner, University of Innsbruck
Vincenzo Lo Cascio, University of Amsterdam
Robert Maier, University of Utrecht
Jo Martens, Polytechnic Eindhoven
Sebastian McEvoy, Ecole des Hautes Etudes en Sciences Sociales, Paris
Denis Miéville, University of Neuchâtel
Wim de Pater, Catholic University of Leuven
Robert Pinto, University of Windsor
Marc van der Poel, Catholic University Nijmegen
Igno Pröpper, Free University Amsterdam
Peter Jan Schellens, University of Twente
Harvey Siegel, University of Miami
Tanya Tretyakova, St. Petersburg University
Ineke Vedder, University of Amsterdam
Frank Veltman, University of Amsterdam
Barbara Warnick, University of Washington
Joseph Wenzel, University of Illinois at Urbana-Champaign
Rob Wiche, Association of Universities in the Netherlands
Jaap Wisse, University of Leiden
Harald Wohlrapp, University of Hamburg

With mortals, gold outweighs a thousand arguments.

—*Medea*. In Euripides, *Medea and other Plays*. Trans. and Intr. by
Philip Vellacott. London, England: Penguin, pp. 46, 966.

1

INTRODUCTION

1.1 ARGUMENTATION

Argumentation (or argument) is familiar to all of us. The following three quotations are examples of argumentation:

(a) *Mother to daughter*: Forget about vacationing all by yourself. No way! When your sister was fourteen, we didn't let her go either.

(b) *Tom*: Of course I'm in favor of heavier punishment for drug addicts.
Jim: Why?
Tom: Well, otherwise the problem will get worse and worse.
Jim: How do you mean?
Tom: You know, soon enough the rumor spreads that not much is going to happen, even if you get caught, so they'll all have a go at it.

(c) *Letter to the Editor*: Sir, When consideration is being given to a third television channel could not a way be found round the "advertising break" problem by devoting the new channel entirely to advertising? In that way the present commercial channel could be left free from programme breaks (natural or otherwise), thus satisfying those of us who object to these interruptions while those millions who are alleged to prefer "the adverts" will also be made more happy in their viewing.

Yours faithfully,
E.H. Dare

Nobody will have much trouble in identifying such examples as specimens of argumentation as argumentation is present in virtually all our verbal communication. Both oral and written argumentation are indeed integral parts of our daily routines. We all regularly engage in argumentative practices, when we advance arguments in defense of certain assertions or actions and when we react to arguments put forward by others.

Argumentation is a *verbal* activity, which is normally conducted in an ordinary language (such as English). A speaker or writer, engaged in argumentation, uses certain words and sentences to state, question, or deny something, to respond to statements, questions or denials, and so on.[1] Just as other verbal activities, argumentation may well be accompanied by the use of nonverbal means of communication, such as facial expression and gestures, but not to the extent that the verbal expressions are completely replaced by the nonverbal ones. Without the use of language, there can be no argumentation.

Argumentation is a *social* activity, which in principle is directed at other people.[2] Of course, the social nature of argumentation is most clearly evident in a discourse between two or more interlocutors. All the same, even when people are conferring with themselves, contemplating the pros and cons of their own ideas, their conduct is basically social. For as soon as they start weighing up the various considerations, this amounts to an anticipation of an interlocutor's possible reactions, even if these reactions are only their own. Thus, when people put forward their arguments, they attempt to meet the outspoken or tacit reactions of others.

Argumentation is an activity of *reason*, which indicates that the arguer has given some thought to the subject. Putting forward an argument means that the arguer attempts to show that a rational account can be given of his or her position on the matter. This is not to say that emotions cannot play a part in adopting a position, but that these internal motives, which have been assimilated in the discourse, are not directly relevant as such. When people put forward their arguments in argumentation they place their considerations within the realm of reason.

In the discourse, argumentation always relates to a particular opinion, or *standpoint*, about a specific subject.[3] The need for argumentation arises when opinions concerning this subject differ or are supposed to differ. By itself, holding an opinion is not enough to initiate argumentation. Arguing makes sense only if there is a listener or reader who entertains doubt about an opinion or has a diverging opinion. Argumentation starts from the presumption, rightly or wrongly, that the standpoint of the arguer is not immediately accepted, but is *controversial*.

---

[1]For brevity's sake, we shall usually refer to the participants in an argumentation as speaker and listener when, *mutatis mutandis*, our remarks apply to a writer and a reader as well.

[2]In this general characterization we neither differentiate between addressing an audience consisting of one person and addressing (perhaps over the heads of those officially addressed) a broader audience consisting of a variety of people, nor do we differentiate between speakers or writers speaking only on behalf of themselves and those acting as representatives of others.

[3]Other virtual synonyms of the term "standpoint," used by various authors, are *view*, *viewpoint*, *point of view*, *claim*, *thesis*, etc.

A difference of opinion may be completely overt and explicit—it being clear to all that the interlocutor does not share the arguer's standpoint—but in practice the controversy will often remain covert and implicit. The standpoint itself may also remain obscure. It can vary in firmness, nature, and scope. A standpoint that is presented as absolute ("It is certain that litmus reacts to acid by changing color") is firmer than a more restrained standpoint ("It is likely that not all top sportsmen take stimulants"). A standpoint pertaining to a factual judgment, a claim that a certain state of affairs obtains ("No such journal exists"), is different in nature from a standpoint referring to a value judgment ("This journal is not very good"). And a standpoint referring to all members of a certain class ("All writers are intelligent") has a wider scope than a standpoint referring to only one member ("Jane Austen is an intelligent writer").

Standpoints, hence differences of opinion, can be about all kinds of subjects, from economics, psychology, and politics to sex, entertainment, and the weather. They can be expressed by affirmative or negative "objective" statements, but also by personal judgments, and even by questions and imperatives. Standpoints of any type might give rise to argumentation. A few examples may illustrate the diversity:

(1) Litmus reacts to acid by changing color.

(2) Amsterdam is the capital of the Netherlands.

(3) If you ask me, not all top sportsmen take stimulants.

(4) In my opinion Satie's "Prélude de la porte héroïque du ciel" is superb.

(5) I think one should help one's fellow men in times of need.

(6) Wouldn't it be nicer if people in academic circles were a little more tolerant?

As shown by the examples, a standpoint may be marked as such by the use of phrases like "in my opinion," "I think," and "if you ask me." In ordinary discourse, however, such indicators are frequently absent. Thus, it is perfectly usual to present a standpoint by a statement consisting simply of the utterance of an unmarked (impersonal) indicative sentence, or even by a question. For an utterance to count as the expression of a standpoint, it is crucial that the person involved may be considered to have taken position for or against a certain proposition about the subject of discourse. Standpoints can only play their part in argumentative discourse if the people who advance them are committed to the stands they have taken and can be called upon to defend them.

Argumentation is intended to *justify* one's standpoint, or to *refute* someone else's.[4] In an argumentative justification of a standpoint one is attempting to

---

[4] Of course, people may also have other motives for arguing, such as showing how clever or likeable they are, but these objectives, which can be pursued simultaneously, are secondary.

defend the standpoint by showing that it conveys an acceptable proposition; in an argumentative refutation one is to attack the standpoint by showing that the proposition is unacceptable whereas the opposite, or contradictory, proposition is acceptable.[5] Justifying or refuting a standpoint by way of argumentation, as in advancing standpoints, proceeds by putting forward propositions. In the case of argumentation, however, the *constellation of propositions* has, due to its justificatory or refutatory force, a special communicative function.

In an attempt to justify a standpoint, the constellation of propositions consists of one or more *pro-arguments* ("reasons for"); in an attempt to refute a standpoint, it consists of one or more *contra-arguments* ("reasons against"). In practice, arguers often restrict themselves to putting forward either pro-argumentation or contra-argumentation. In principle, however, these two activities are interdependent: pro-arguments often presuppose certain contra-arguments, and vice versa. They are, in fact, complementary tools for testing the acceptability of a standpoint.

Argumentation is aimed at *increasing (or decreasing) the acceptability* of a controversial standpoint for the listener or reader. The constellation of propositions put forward by the arguer is calculated to achieve that purpose by convincing or persuading the audience. It depends not only on the intrinsic qualities of the arguments whether or not the approbation of the audience will be gained, but also on the audience's qualities in evaluating them. The more sophisticated the audience, the better it can fulfil a critical function in testing the strength of the argumentation for (or against) the standpoint.

In advancing argumentation, arguers submit their arguments to the scrutiny of the audience. In principle, the very act of arguing involves an appeal, for better or worse, to the audience's reasonableness. In a reasonable evaluation, the audience must determine the extent to which the argumentation renders the standpoint acceptable. The appeal to reasonableness would be pointless if the audience were not presumed to evaluate the argumentation as a *rational judge*.[6] In order to comply with this requirement the audience should evaluate the argumentation on the basis of sound standards.

In practice, arguers addressing an audience with a view to justifying or refuting a standpoint will generally presume that there are certain standards available for judging the quality of argumentation. They will also presume that these standards will be applied by the audience in evaluating the argumentation.

---

[5]This is "strong refutation." In "weak refutation" it is sufficient to cast doubt upon the attacked standpoint, without a defense of the opposite standpoint. Weak refutation is not argumentation in the strict sense, though it is an important ingredient of the argumentative process.

[6]A reasonable evaluation of argumentation is optimally based on rational evaluation criteria rather than tradition, prejudice and uncontrolled sentiments. In the evaluation of a rational judge emotions play a (motivational) part only insofar as they have become "rationalized" (and are open to criticism).

Otherwise their argumentation would be futile. Of course, the standards arguers have in mind are not necessarily those of a rational judge, and arguers can be wrong in thinking that the audience shares their standards.

Having thus unraveled the main aspects of the meaning of the word *argumentation*, we can now clarify the argumentation theorists' object of study by providing a general definition. This definition is descriptive in the sense that it is closely connected to the way in which the word argumentation is used in ordinary language. This means, for one thing, that its "process-product ambiguity" is retained. Argumentation refers not only to the process of arguing ("I'm almost through with my argumentation"), but also to the product resulting from it ("The argumentation as it stands is not convincing").

The definition is also stipulative in the sense that it introduces a terminological convention. The meaning given by this convention to the term *argumentation* is more precise than that which is normally assigned to it by ordinary language users. It is not only more explicit, but also more comprehensive. The reason for this being that in this way one obtains a clear common denominator of the subject matter under investigation in the study of argumentation. The specific additional meanings attached to the term argumentation by various argumentation theorists can then be more easily brought into perspective.

The general characteristics of argumentation are then recapitulated in the following definition:

> *Argumentation is a verbal and social activity of reason aimed at increasing (or decreasing) the acceptability of a controversial standpoint for the listener or reader, by putting forward a constellation of propositions intended to justify (or refute) the standpoint before a rational judge.*

1.2 ARGUMENTATION AND LOGIC

The study of argumentation is, by outsiders, often too easily identified with "doing logic." In order to illustrate some of the differences between the problems argumentation theorists are interested in and those currently studied in logic, let us take as our point of departure the following dialogue in colloquial speech:

Dale: Mary said she was going to get beef or cod. Do you know what we're eating tonight?

Sally: No, but if she's already done the shopping it'll probably be in the fridge.

Dale: Well, she rang me about her essay, and she told me then that she's already done the shopping because she wanted to go on working this afternoon.

Sally: I'll have a quick look in the fridge ... It's stacked full. But I can't smell fish, anyway.

Dale: O.K., shall we get some mushrooms to go with the beef?

In this conversation, Dale deduces from what Sally says and does (looking in the refrigerator), and from what Mary told him, that there is beef in the refrigerator. Because Mary has done the shopping and is in the habit of putting the shopping in the refrigerator, Sally and Dale think that the shopping is in the refrigerator. Looking into the refrigerator, Sally does not smell any fish. Both Sally and Dale apparently deduce that there is no fish in the refrigerator. Moreover, Dale concludes that Mary has bought beef because she was going to get beef or cod and has not bought cod. Although Dale does not really state this conclusion, it is clear to Sally that he has drawn it. It is presupposed in his question "Shall we get some mushrooms to go with the beef?"

Although Dale and Sally reach their conclusions through reasoning, they do not engage in argumentation. Their conclusions are arrived at by way of (implicit) deduction. No standpoint is defended by either of them, neither explicitly nor implicitly. At this point, a first and crucial difference between the primary interests of argumentation theorists and those of contemporary logicians is to be mentioned. Argumentation theorists study the way in which people take up standpoints and defend these standpoints, whereas logicians tend to concentrate on the way in which conclusions are derived from premises.

Other differences are connected with the present set-up of logic as the study of formal reasoning patterns and its methodological starting points. These differences can be illustrated by slightly altering our example, so that it involves argumentation. Let us assume that Dale concludes the conversation as follows:

Dale: O.K., as I see it, it is beef tonight, since it was either that or cod and there
           is no fish. Shall we get some mushrooms to go with the beef?

When studying reasoning, modern logicians confine themselves to the "formal validity" of arguments, disregarding the actual reasoning processes and the contextual surroundings in which they take place. Although abstracting from the actual discourse has been highly beneficial to the development of logic, it has been detrimental to the study of argument as envisaged by argumentation theorists. Restricting the study of argument to formal reasoning patterns leads to the exclusion of many important problems of reasoned discourse. Consequently, the discourse as an attempt to justify (or refute) a standpoint before a rational judge cannot be fully dealt with. On the basis of the amended example, it can be shown which methodological abstraction steps are made in formal logic.[7]

The *first* step in the abstraction process makes the study of argument independent of the situation in which the arguments happen to occur. Departing from the literal wording of the conversation or text, a discourse is interpreted

---

[7]This exposition of abstraction steps in formal logic is to a large extent based on Nuchelmans (1976, pp. 173–180).

in such a way that implicit elements are made explicit. In the case of Dale's argument, this would result in something like the following:

Dale: It was either beef or cod. There is no fish. If there is no fish, we are not going to eat cod. Therefore, it is beef tonight.

Part of Sally's reasoning can be rendered as follows:

Sally: If Mary did the shopping, then the shopping is in the refrigerator. Mary did the shopping. Therefore the shopping is in the refrigerator.

The *second* abstraction makes the argument independent of the participants involved, and even of people in general. Regarding every argument as an impersonal linking of premises and a conclusion, what remains to be studied are the connections between the opinion expressed in the conclusion and the justifying propositions that are expressed in the premises.[8] In our example, this can be achieved by omitting Dale and Sally and writing out their statements as depersonalized sentences.

The *third* abstraction involves presenting the argument in standard form. Different wordings of the same information are eliminated so that expressional variants of sentences are formulated in a uniform manner. The indicators *premise* and *conclusion* are added. This produces the following arguments in standard form:

argument 1
premise: We are going to eat beef or we are going to eat cod.
premise: There is no fish.
premise: If there is no fish, we are not going to eat cod.
conclusion: We are going to eat beef.

argument 2
premise: If Mary did the shopping, then the shopping is in the refrigerator.
premise: Mary did the shopping.
conclusion: The shopping is in the refrigerator.

The *fourth* abstraction renders the arguments in such a form that expressions having a special meaning to logicians become more prominent. This concerns, for instance, words that link the sentences to one another such as "or" and "if ... then," and the word "no(t)," which also appears in the example. Individual sentences are abridged while the logically important words "or," "if ... then,"

---

[8]This abstraction is illustrated in definitions of "argument" in logic textbooks. Berger (1977, p. 3), for instance, says that arguments are usually defined by logicians in the first place as lists of sentences, one of which is regarded as the conclusion and the rest as the base for that conclusion.

and "not" are written in full, so that they are clearly differentiated from the "content" part of the sentences composing the argument. It is now immaterial how the arguments were worded in English (or any other language). The sentences may, therefore, be replaced by arbitrary (capital) letters (A, B, C, etc.), as long as the same sentence is represented by the same letter. Logicians call these "abbreviations" *sentence constants*, or *constants* for short. In our example, this abstraction would lead to the following notation:

abbreviations
B: We are going to eat beef.
C: We are going to eat cod.
F: There is fish.
S: Mary did the shopping.
R: The shopping is in the refrigerator.

argument 1
premises: B or C, not F, if not F then not C
conclusion: B

argument 2
premises: if S then R, S
conclusion: R

In the *fifth* abstraction step, the logically relevant expressions are replaced by *logical constants*, thereby translating them into a logical language in which these constants have a standardized meaning.[9] The last reminders of ordinary language in our example, "or," "if . . . then," and "not," are thus removed. The meanings of the logical constants used in these translations are laid down in *propositional logic*, the logic that deals with logical constants of this type. In the language of propositional logic, these logical constants are symbolized as $\lor$ ("or"), $\rightarrow$ ("if . . . then") and $\neg$ ("not").[10] Using the symbol $/\therefore$ to indicate the conclusion, the arguments in our example can then be translated in the following way:

argument 1
$B \lor C$
$\neg F$
$\neg F \rightarrow \neg C$
$/\therefore B$

argument 2
$S \rightarrow R$
S
$/\therefore R$

---

[9]It should thus be clear that much more is involved in translating expressions from natural language into logical constants than in abbreviating sentences by sentence constants.

[10]Other (systems of) symbols for these logical constants are also current. See Schagrin (1968).

The logical constants appearing in this example are: $\neg$ (*negation*), $\vee$ (*disjunction*), and $\rightarrow$ (*material implication*); another important logical constant of propositional logic is $\wedge$ (*conjunction*), the logical "equivalent" of "and." The meanings of these logical constants are much more sharply defined than those of their counterparts in ordinary language. In these definitions, the meanings of the logical constants are generally related to the concept of *truth value*.

Starting from a binary concept of truth value, sentences like "We are going to eat beef" can be either true or false. A sentence constant "A" therefore has two possible truth values: "true" and "false." Two or more sentence constants can be connected to each other with the help of logical constants such as $\vee$ ("or") and $\rightarrow$ ("if ... then"); a sentence constant can also be preceded by the logical constant $\neg$ ("not"). All these cases result in new, compound sentences whose truth value is determined by the truth values of their component sentences and the meanings of the logical constants used in linking them.

In order to examine their influence on the truth value of the sentence (or "proposition"), the meanings of logical constants of this type are, in propositional logic, usually laid down in "truth tables." These truth tables show which truth values a compound sentence acquires on the basis of the possible truth values of its component sentences. The truth value of the compound sentence "We are not going to eat beef," for instance, is *false* if the sentence "We are going to eat beef" is true, and *true* if the sentence "We are going to eat beef" is false.

Translating expressions such as "or" and "if ... then" into the language of propositional logic involves an abstraction from various aspects of the ordinary meaning of these words. In the definition of the logical constant $\rightarrow$, for instance, all sorts of information is ignored that the use of the wording "if ... then" normally provides. The meaning of the logical constant is confined to those aspects of "if ... then" which are relevant to the possible truth values of sentences composed with its help. As a consequence, the translation of "if ... then" by $\rightarrow$ in sentences like "If this man jumps from a tower, then he falls to his death" inevitably leads to a reduction in meaning.[11]

Though this may not be immediately apparent due to the abbreviation of the sentences by sentence constants, even after the fifth abstraction the arguments that are dealt with continue to be specific arguments about a specific topic. Because it is not the logicians' intention to deal with arguments by examining them all separately, a further abstraction step is taken, which is crucial to logical theory.

In the *sixth* abstraction step, individual arguments are interpreted as instances of *argument forms*. Specific arguments about a specific topic are then viewed as particular instances or instantiations of formal constellations of premises and a conclusion. In the notation of these argument forms, instead of the

---

[11]It is, for instance, left out of the account that there is a *causal* relation between the fall and the death.

letters A, B, C, etc. which stand for sentences, the *variables p, q, r*, etc. are used, for which declarative sentences of any kind may be substituted. Because they are not sentences, the variables do not have any truth value; they only become true or false if sentences are substituted for them. This means that individual arguments are treated as "substitution instances" (fillings) of certain abstract reasoning patterns. The two arguments from our example, for instance, can be seen as substitution instances of the following argument forms:

argument form of argument 1
$p \cup q$
$\neg r$
$\neg r \rightarrow \neg q$
$/ \therefore p$

argument form of argument 2
$p \rightarrow q$
p
$/ \therefore q$

As soon as these six steps of abstraction are taken, logicians can set out to fulfil their general aim of distinguishing between *valid* and *invalid* argument forms (and hence, indirectly, between valid and invalid arguments). An argument form is valid (in propositional logic) if none of its substitution instances is an argument with true premises and a false conclusion. All (and only) substitution instances of a valid argument form are valid arguments.[12]

In order to test the validity of an argument, logicians determine whether the argument concerned is a substitution instance of a valid argument form. One method used in this endeavor amounts to a systematic search for a counterexample, which will disprove the validity of the most specific argument form of which the argument is an instance. If a substitution instance of this form is found with true premises and a false conclusion, then not only the argument form but also the argument itself is invalid (in propositional logic).[13] On the other hand,

---

[12]Thus if an argument is valid in propositional logic it is impossible that its conclusion be false whereas its premises are true. It is important to realize that this does not mean that the premises are required to be true. A valid argument may very well have false premises. Valid arguments that do have true premises are usually called "sound," but generally the soundness of arguments is no concern of logicians. On the other hand, logicians study many other types of validity besides those relating to propositional logic. If an argument is not valid in propositional logic it may still be valid in some other (stronger) logic, such as predicate logic, see below.

[13]The validity question can also be approached in another way. To every valid argument there is a "corresponding implication": a true "if . . . then" sentence in which the premises—connected by "and"—are placed after "if" and the conclusion after "then." The corresponding implication itself is not an argument but a sentence, and may therefore be true or false. In a valid argument, the corresponding implication is necessarily true, and a valid argument form must have a corresponding implication form, all of whose substitution instances are true.

if no such substitution instance is found, and the search was truly systematic and complete, then both the form and the argument are valid.

The arguments we have used as our examples are substitution instances of argument forms in which the logical constants ¬ (*negation*), ∨ (*disjunction*), and → (*material implication*) are used. In propositional logic, where the validity of argument forms employing this type of logical constants is examined, it is demonstrated that they are valid. The valid argument form of *argument 2* is called *modus ponens*.

In order to examine the validity of argument forms employing other types of logical constants, logical theories that go beyond propositional logic are required. Arguments whose validity cannot be established in propositional logic may prove to be valid in other logics. One such logic is *predicate logic*, which deals with the use of "quantifiers" such as "all" and "some" in arguments. Amongst other logics that have so far been developed are *modal* logics, examining the logical behavior of words like "necessary" and "possible," *deontic* logic, concentrating on logical constants such as "obliged" and "permissible," *epistemic* logic, studying the logical behavior of words like "know" and "believe," and *tense* logic, investigating the logical effect of temporal references.[14]

This brief account of the various ways in which logicians abstract from argumentative reality in order to pursue their general aim of distinguishing between valid and invalid argument forms should suffice as an introduction to the kinds of problems argumentation theorists are interested in. It illustrates that logicians, rather than studying argumentation as it naturally occurs in everyday discourse, concentrate on abstract premises formally structured by logical constants. In this endeavor, a great many verbal, contextual, situational, and other pragmatic factors that play a part in the communication process are not taken into account, so that the problems of argumentative discourse cannot be adequately dealt with. As is illustrated in the next Section, the study of argumentation ought to contain more than logic currently has to offer.

For the sake of clarity, it should be added that in drawing this conclusion we neither say that the study of argumentation can do without logic altogether nor that the present state of affairs will never change.[15] There are logicians of various types, one being more inclined than the other, to obey the call of argumentative practice. As we shall see, there has already been a tendency among logicians towards broadening their interests in the phenomena of argumentative discourse which have escaped their attention for too long. At the same time, various argumentation theorists attempt to include, in their theories, relevant aspects of logic, in some form or other. For the time being, in view of the many

---

[14]Unlike propositional and predicate logic, these logics are "intensional" logics, since they take into account the effect of nonextensional aspects of meaning.

[15]In itself, there can be few objections to look upon argumentation theory as a branch of logic. In recent times, however, logic has become far removed from argumentative practice and is now largely a matter for specialists with a mathematical or computational background.

complexities involved in studying argumentative discourse, it seems best to aspire to a sensible division of labor, and to regard the study of argumentation as a discipline in its own right nourished by the combined efforts of philosophers, logicians, linguists, (speech) communication specialists, psychologists, lawyers, and others.

1.3   THE STUDY OF ARGUMENTATION

Having defined the subject matter of the study of argumentation, we can now delineate its general objective by distinguishing it from the general objective of (formal) logic. In order to do so, we shall first identify four problem areas in the study of argumentation that can be adequately dealt with only if pragmatic factors are duly taken into account. These problem areas are the following: "unexpressed elements in argumentative discourse," "argumentation structures," "argumentation schemes," and "fallacies."

Argumentation theorists are, broadly speaking, interested in the problems involved in the *production, analysis,* and *evaluation* of argumentative discourse. In studying these problems, they view argumentative discourse in the light of the actual circumstances in which it takes place. In examining argumentative discourse, many argumentation theorists therefore start from a unifying perspective on reasoned discourse which is to provide a general framework for studying the interplay of pragmatic factors.

When communicating with each other by means of reasoned discourse, people observe, as a rule, certain standards that ensure that their communication can serve its purpose. These standards can be summarized in the Principle of Communication, stating that the participants in the communication process should refrain from making any moves which impede the communication proceedings. As long as there is no evidence to the contrary, the interlocutors may be assumed to comply with this principle. The Principle of Communication is implemented by the maintenance of four standards: clarity, honesty, efficiency, and relevance.[16]

In practice it is not at all uncommon that one or more of these standards are violated, but this does not automatically mean that the Principle of Communication has been abandoned. In ordinary communication, apparent violations of the standards are often means of implicitly or indirectly conveying some extra information. People can utilize the standards in order to be ironic, to make suggestions they would not like to state explicitly, to avoid stressing the obvious,

---

[16]The Principle of Communication, introduced by van Eemeren and Grootendorst (1992a), has a similar role and epistemological status as Grice's (1975) Co-operative Principle, from which it is partly derived. According to Kasher (1982), observing the standards inherent in the Gricean Co-operative Principle stems from the compliance with a general Rationalization Principle stimulating the use of effective means (p. 33).

and so on. Even if the standards are occasionally violated without any such intent, there is usually no great harm done.

Argumentation theorists, who deal with argumentative discourse, attempt to gain sufficient insight into the textual and contextual pragmatic factors that play a part in this type of discourse.[17] They must have reasons to support their interpretation of a given discourse in order to justify their analysis. The crucial questions they have to answer are: Under what circumstances do speakers incur a commitment to a statement they did not utter explicitly; and how can implicit and indirect meanings be inferred from the utterances that were literally made? To answer these questions, one must take into account the various general and specific presuppositions entertained by the interlocutors, which constitute the point of departure of the argumentation. In this endeavor, the four standards that implement the Principle of Communication can be useful tools.

In ordinary discourse, no two utterances are ever wholly identical in meaning. A high standard of preciseness is usually only aspired to in certain types of emphatic or formal usage when a speaker wishes to exclude all possible misunderstanding. Explicitness is the exception rather than the rule. Sometimes the communicative function of an utterance becomes clear only after the event, when this function is identified or indicated by one of the participants ("So, that is your standpoint then, eh?," "You have heard my major arguments"), but more often than not no explicit identification will be given, while, moreover, the propositional content of the utterance remains ambiguous.[18]

Fortunately, there are some verbal indicators that specifically refer to standpoints and argumentation, such as "therefore," "hence," "so," "thus," "ergo," and "since," "for" and "because." Some of them, for example "for," are used retrogressively, referring to a preceding standpoint; others, like "so," are used progressively, being followed by the standpoint, and some, like "because," can be used in both ways. The fewer the number of verbal pointers, the more it will be necessary to make use of verbal and nonverbal contextual clues. Usually, some background knowledge of the context and the type of speech event involved, and even some knowledge of the world, will be required to detect these clues and put them to good use. Otherwise, it would, for instance, be hard to tell that in the argument, "You should see that film; there is no cooler apology for crime," first a standpoint is formulated and then a reason in its support.

Confusingly, formulations of standpoints and reasons may be presented in speech acts that are, at first sight, nonassertive, as in "Let's take an umbrella, or

---

[17]In practice, the interlocutors themselves may differ in their interpretations of what the context of the discourse is. Such different interpretations can impede a meaningful exchange. In some cases, the analyst, considering the context from an external perspective, can shed some light on why and where the interpretations diverge.

[18]In many cases, the function and propositional content of certain utterances cannot be determined until the entire speech or text is scrupulously examined, even then the analyst sometimes has to resort to an educated guess.

do you want to get wet?" Taken literally, what the speaker does is to confront the listener with a proposal, accompanied by a question. The (rhetorical) question, however, must be interpreted as a reason to accept the implicit standpoint that the two should take an umbrella. In order to correctly determine the speaker's commitments, one must diagnose this discourse as containing an implicit (and indirect) standpoint defended by an implicit (and indirect) reason: "We should take an umbrella, for we do not want to get wet." In the analysis of such implicitness (and indirectness), and in the justification of this analysis, an important role is usually played by general standards for reasoned discourse and by the context (in its broadest sense) of the specific discourse under analysis.

It is important to realize that standpoints and reasons are functional discourse units that are instrumental in an effort to resolve a difference of opinion. Verbal utterances per se are never standpoints or reasons; they are not standpoints or reasons by nature, but only when they fulfil a specific function in the discourse. They are standpoints or reasons when they serve to express a certain position in a (potential) difference of opinion or to defend a certain position in a context of (potential) controversy. In a dispute, for example, regarding where the Dutch monarch is inaugurated, the (false) statement "The Hague is the *de jure* capital of The Netherlands" may serve to construct an argument ("Because The Hague is the *de jure* capital of The Netherlands, the Dutch monarch is inaugurated in The Hague"), but the same statement can serve as a standpoint if the dispute is about which city is the capital of The Netherlands ("The Dutch monarch is inaugurated in The Hague, therefore The Hague is the *de jure* capital of The Netherlands").

The pivotal points of an argument are often constituted by unexpressed elements, which are only implicitly present in the discourse. This holds in particular for *unexpressed premises* and *unexpressed standpoints*.[19] In the arguments composing ordinary argumentation usually one of the premises is left unexpressed. In some cases, the identification of the elements implicit in enthymematic argumentation is quite simple. It is obvious, for example, that in "Amos is pigheaded, because he is a teacher" the premise that is left unexpressed is "Teachers are pig-headed." In "I am sure that Amos is pig-headed, since all teachers *are* pig-headed," it is just as clear that the unexpressed premise is: "Amos is a teacher."

There are also cases in which the identification of unexpressed premises may cause more problems—usually, because there are several possibilities. In order to determine what the commitments of an arguer are, the analyst must effect not only a logical analysis, based on the validity criterion, but also a pragmatic analysis, based on standards for reasoned discourse.[20] In the logical analysis,

---

[19]Virtual synonyms of these terms, used by various authors, are *implicit, tacit, unstated, hidden* and *suppressed* premises (or *assumptions*) and standpoints (or *conclusions*).

[20]A commitment to some validity criterion is required, but it is open to discussion which criterion is to be preferred. No dogmatic commitment to deductivism is thus implied. Cf. Govier (1987, pp. 81–104). The identification of other unexpressed elements in argumentative discourse than unexpressed premises and unexpressed standpoints is often more complicated since no heuristic tool such as the logical validity criterion is available.

an attempt is made to reconstruct the argument as one having a valid argument form; in the pragmatic analysis, the unexpressed premise that helps to make the argument logically valid is then more precisely defined on the basis of contextual information and background knowledge. The logical analysis is thus instrumental to the achievement of a satisfactory pragmatic analysis.[21]

We illustrate this analytic procedure by an example citing a Dutch politician's retort, at a public meeting, to a colleague, who has just rejected a proposal to legalize abortion:[22]

> You are right to set such store by the sanctity of human life, but you cannot include a 6-week foetus. Speaking as a Liberal, I am amazed by your standpoint. What about the sanctity of the life of the mother who has become pregnant against her will and is unable to give the child the life it has a right to?

Although the politician does not explicitly state his standpoint, we may take it that he defends the standpoint that abortion should be legalized, since his argumentation reacts to the other politician's standpoint that abortion should *not* be legalized, whereas his own reasons seem to indicate the opposite. His second reason is presented by way of a rhetorical question. The premise involved can be reconstructed as "A woman who has become pregnant against her will and is unable to provide for her child should have the right to end her pregnancy." How is this premise connected to the standpoint that abortion should be legalized? Which unexpressed premise is understood to fill the gap between this premise and the standpoint?

First, in a logical analysis the incomplete argument can be made valid by adding the following premise to the argument: "If a woman who has become pregnant against her will and who is unable to provide for her child should have the right to end her pregnancy, then abortion should be legalized." Since this addition is not really informative, the analyst then has to investigate whether the unexpressed premise can be made more informative, making use of the pragmatic data available in the context concerned. Without ascribing any unwarranted commitments to the speaker, the unexpressed premise can, in view of the politician's avowed liberal stance expressed in the preceding sentence, be generalized by relying on the common background knowledge that the Dutch Liberals are staunch legalists. This would lead to the following unexpressed premise: "A right can only be exercised if it is legalized."

---

[21]Taken literally, an argument in which a premise has been left unexpressed is invalid. The premise that is logically required to correct the invalidity may be futile, thus going against the standards for reasoned discourse. If there is no reason to assume that the speaker flouts the Principle of Communication, the analyst should investigate whether there is any pragmatic information available which enables a completion of the argument by a premise which no longer violates this Principle.

[22]The procedure described here is basically that of pragma-dialectics, considered in chap. 10, but it captures problems that are encountered also in other approaches.

In the absence of disambiguating contextual information or background knowledge, the pragmatic identification of unexpressed premises will be hard to accomplish. A logical analysis must then suffice. Otherwise there is a danger that the added premise oversteps the mark, attributing more to the speaker than he or she is actually committed to. With unexpressed standpoints we are on safer ground. Starting from the explicit premises, a logical analysis of the underlying argument usually leads to an unequivocal determination of the conclusion representing the unexpressed standpoint that is being advocated. The following example may serve as an illustration:

> *Arnold*:   Well, she is in love with a student. And affairs between teachers and their pupils always end in trouble. . . .

The conclusion which has been omitted here is: "She will end up in trouble." Arnold, who says that she is in love with a student and that affairs between teachers and students always end in trouble, certainly suggests that conclusion, even though he might subsequently maintain that he had not said as much. Strictly speaking, it could be maintained that Arnold himself is not arguing. Rather he initiates a particular reasoning process in the listener. Although in such cases it is arguable whether or not a standpoint is actually being justified or refuted by means of arguments, it is beyond dispute which conclusion figures as the bone of contention.

Argumentation for or against a standpoint can be simple, but it may also display a more complex *argumentation structure*, depending on how the arguer organizes the defense of the standpoint in view of (manifest or anticipated) doubts and criticisms. The simplest case is that of a *single argumentation*, consisting of just one argument pro or contra the standpoint. Because complex argumentation can always be analyzed as a combination of single argumentations, single argumentation is considered to display the *basic structure* of argumentation. In a typical single argumentation the argument contains, as a rule, one explicit and one unexpressed premise:

> You are a chauvinist, because you are a man.

In this argument, the unexpressed premise is "Men are chauvinists." True, it has been omitted, but that does not mean that it has no part to play; it is a necessary element of the argument, since only if this premise is included does the argument form a complete whole. Although the argumentation structure is not affected by the unexpressed premise, even if it would have been expressed, this unexpressed premise is a constitutive part of the argumentation.

Complexly structured argumentation consists of more than one single argumentation. In such argumentation, several arguments are advanced pro or contra the same standpoint. These arguments can be unconnected, but they may

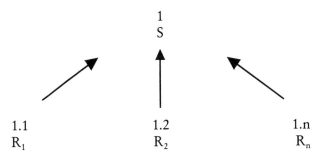

S = standpoint
R_1, R_2, R_3 = reasons such that each
represents a single argumentation

FIG. 1.1.   Structure of multiple argumentation.

also be interdependent. In the first case, the argumentation consists of alternative defenses of the same standpoint and can be structurally characterized as *multiple argumentation*. Here is an example:

> Postal deliveries in Holland are not perfect. You cannot be sure that a letter will be delivered the next day, that it will be delivered to the right address, or that it will be delivered early in the morning.

Multiple argumentation is structurally represented in Fig. 1.1.

In the second case we mentioned, a compound argumentation is created consisting of a chain of arguments that reinforce each other. If the single arguments constituting the chain are "connected in parallel," the arguments being part of a combined attempt to defend the standpoint, the argumentation can be structurally characterized as *coordinatively compound argumentation*. Here is an example:

> This book has literary qualities: the plot is original, the story is well-told, the dialogues are incredibly natural, and the style is superb.

Coordinatively compound argumentation is structurally represented in Fig. 1.2.

If the arguments in the chain are "connected in series," the one supporting the other, the argumentation structure is that of *subordinatively compound argumentation*.[23] Whereas in coordinatively compound argumentation all the argu-

---

[23]Some authors use other terms for characterizing the various argumentation structures, representing similar but not always the same distinctions. Among these terms are *convergent* (for independent or multiple), *linked* (for interdependent or coordinatively compound), and *serial* (for subordinatively compound).

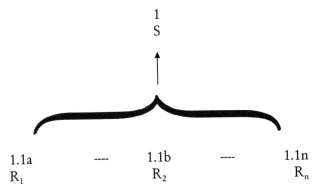

FIG. 1.2. Structure of coordinatively compound argumentation.

ments relate directly to the standpoint, in subordinatively compound argumentation the first argument relates directly to the standpoint, the second to the reason presented in the first argument, which reason now serves as a "substandpoint," and so forth. Here is an example:

> I don't have to invite Carla to my party. She cannot be trusted. Last week she ran off with my friend.

Subordinatively compound argumentation is structurally represented in Fig. 1.3.

A major problem when analyzing complex argumentation is that it is often unclear whether one is dealing with multiple, coordinatively compound or subordinatively compound argumentation. Explicit indications of the argumentation structure in the discourse are generally thin on the ground. As a rule, the analyst will have little more to fall back on than the connectives and other clarifying expressions that are used in the text.[24] Another complication is that various types of argumentation structure may occur together in the discourse, multiple argumentation, for instance, being combined with coordinatively compound argumentation in a subordinatively compound argumentation. A warrantable analysis can usually be achieved only if, among other pragmatic factors, the distinctive features of the type of speech event or text one is dealing with are duly taken into account.

An analysis of the argumentation structure, as it describes the "external organization" of the various arguments, yields insight into the composition of the argumentation as a whole. Argumentation theorists, however, are also interested

---

[24]Certain words and expressions can be (but need not be) indicators of the argumentation structure. Among them are: for multiple argumentation, "by the way," "moreover," "incidentally," "quite apart from," "and then I haven't even mentioned the fact that," and "needless to add that"; for coordinatively compound argumentation, "these two things combined lead to the conclusion that," "when it is also remembered that," "in addition to the fact," and "as well as the fact that"; for subordinative argumentation, "since because," and "because because."

1

S

↑

1.1

R_1

=

SS_1

↑

1.1.1

R_2

=

SS_2

↑

and so forth

FIG. 1.3. Structure of subordinatively compound argumentation.

in the "internal organization" of the individual single arguments, that is, the principles on which these arguments rely in defending the standpoint at issue by means of the premises. These principles are called *argumentation schemes*.

Argumentation schemes relate to the kind of relation established in a single argument between its premises and the standpoint the argument aims to justify or refute. An argumentation scheme characterizes the type of justification or refutation provided for the standpoint.[25] An analysis of the argumentation schemes used in a discourse should produce information as to the principles, standards, criteria, or assumptions involved in a particular attempt at justification or refutation.

It should not be taken for granted that anyone who puts forward an argument is automatically involved in an attempt to logically derive the conclusion from the premises. Yet, in some way or other, a transfer of acceptance from the explicit premise to the standpoint must be aimed at. On this point, so far, formal logic has not much to offer. Modern logicians seem almost unanimous in their concern with formal validity rather than substantive relations between premises and conclusions, concentrating on implications and truth rather than plausible inferences and the transmission of acceptance.[26]

---

[25]Just as logical argument forms, such as *modus ponens*, argumentation schemes are abstract frameworks which can have an infinite number of substitution instances. All substitution instances can, of course, be logically analyzed as involving an argument form of the *modus ponens*-type, but this argument form does not reveal the distinctive features of the various argumentation schemes.

[26]Some promising developments, however, have taken place. See Harman (1986), Cohen (1992) and others on acceptance and belief, Rescher (1976) and others on plausible reasoning, and the recent literature on default logic.

The speaker aims to effect a transfer of acceptance from the premises to the standpoint that makes the listener accept the standpoint. Hence, the speaker attempts to design the argument in such a fashion that it will convince the listener. Take the following argument:

Danielle: Daniel is sure to be concerned about the costs, as he is an American.

When looking for an argument to defend her standpoint that Daniel will be concerned about the costs, Danielle may, for example, have entertained an unfriendly thought like "It is typical of Americans that they are materialistic." From this thought, she may have backed up her standpoint by the argument shown above, the unexpressed premise being "Americans are inclined to care a lot about money." In another case, we might speculate that Danielle, from a thought such as "We are now faced with the same problem as last year," came up with the following argument "The method I propose worked last year, it will therefore work again," the unexpressed premise being "This problem is similar to the one we had last year." And starting from a thought such as "Heavy drinking is bound to cause a hangover," she might have argued "Tom must have a terrible headache, because he has been drinking an excessive amount of whiskey," the unexpressed premise being "Drinking too much whiskey leads to a terrible headache."[27]

By arguing in either of these ways, Danielle is relying on more or less ready-made argumentation schemes: conventionalized ways of displaying a relation between that which is stated in the explicit premise and that which is stated in the standpoint. The internal organization of each single argument can be characterized by the argumentation scheme being employed. One of the problems argumentation theorists are confronted with is to describe these argumentation schemes, to determine how they operate, and to assess their acceptability.

Most often, it is not clearly indicated in the discourse which type of justification or refutation is used. Generally, some interpretation on the part of the analyst is required to identify the argumentation scheme. In the absence of clear markers, speakers sometimes employ certain more or less standardized expressions to indicate a particular argumentation scheme.[28] If the argumentation scheme is not, in some way or other, indicated by the speaker, the analyst has

---

[27]These examples are taken from van Eemeren and Grootendorst (1992a, pp. 94–102). According to these authors, the argumentation scheme employed is in the first example of the "token" type (indicating a symptomatic relation), in the second example of the "similarity" type (indicating a comparison relation), and in the third example of the "consequence" type (indicating an instrumental relation).

[28]Among these markers are such expressions as "X is characteristic of Y," "X is typical of Y," and "X's are essentially Y," for the token type; "X is comparable to Y," "X corresponds to Y," and "X is just like Y," for the similarity type; and "X leads to Y," "X is a means of getting Y," and "Y results from X," for the consequence type.

to detect the implicit *topos* relied on in the argument. For this purpose, the unexpressed premise bridging the gap between the explicit premise and the standpoint must first be identified. This means, again, that the analyst must exploit the pragmatic information contained in the context of discourse.[29]

A final problem area argumentation theorists are interested in, which should be briefly mentioned, concerns the *fallacies*. According to the standard definition, a fallacy is an argument that seems valid but is not.[30] Well-known objections to this definition point out that a great number of the generally recognized fallacies are not arguments and that others are not invalid arguments. Therefore, these fallacies are not covered by the definition.

One explanation why fallacy theorists stuck with this definition, although many fallacies are outside its scope, is that until recently most approaches to the fallacies have been logico-centric in a very restricted way. However, if the old definition is dropped, and fallacies are conceived as discussion moves which damage the quality of argumentative discourse, it is easier to bring to the light what is fallacious about them. For this purpose, a pragmatic approach is required which makes allowances for the communicative and interactional context in which the fallacies occur. If pragmatic knowledge is not taken into account, many of the fallacies cannot be satisfactorily analyzed.

In this endeavor, a set of norms must be developed for distinguishing between acceptable and unacceptable moves in argumentative discourse. The criteria used in deciding whether such a norm has been violated, should also be investigated. For determining in specific cases if these criteria are satisfied, procedural tools are to be designed, involving the use of various kinds of contextual information. As a preliminary to this last enterprise, it must be established if the situation in which a would-be fallacy occurs is indeed within the scope of the norms.

Argumentation theorists are concerned with the problem areas we have just outlined, not only for analytic purposes, but also because the analysis can be instrumental in accomplishing an adequate evaluation of argumentative discourse and may serve as a basis for improving its production. In order to be acceptable for a rational judge, the point of departure of the argumentation as well as its presentational layout should comply with certain soundness criteria. These soundness criteria are validity criteria in a pragmatic sense, relating to all elements that are part of the argumentative discourse, from the premises, whether explicit or implicit, and other constituents of the point of departure of

---

[29]Conversely, in cases where the argumentation scheme is clearly indicated, this scheme is part of the context and can be instrumental in identifying the unexpressed premise. A crucial concept in argumentation theorists' analysis of the pragmatic information available in the context of discourse, is *relevance*, which pertains to the appropriateness of the connections between separate utterances.

[30]See Hamblin (1970, p. 12).

argumentation, to the argumentation structures and the argumentation schemes employed in its presentational layout.

The point of departure of argumentation comprises everything stated as such or implicitly assumed by the speaker or writer. Normally, this starting point will be only partly explicit, the other part being tacitly presupposed in the discourse and in its contextual environment. These presuppositions, pertaining, *inter alia*, to the facts, ideas, values, and standards which play a part in the discourse, are immanent parts of the point of departure. Their propositional content is to be judged for accuracy and relevance, as well as the plausibility and level of endorsement of their functional status as facts, suppositions, or preferences.

The presentational layout of argumentation comprises every move in the argumentative discourse which is instrumental to the justification or refutation of a standpoint. Normally, the structure of the argumentation and the argumentation schemes employed in individual arguments will be indicated only to some extent. Hence, the analyst can make them explicit only by taking account of the contextual clues provided by the way in which the discourse proceeds in its contextual environment. The argumentation structures are to be judged for appropriateness and adequacy, while the argumentation schemes must be judged for suitability and correctness of application.

The soundness criteria of a rational judge are not necessarily identical with those employed by an arbitrary audience. However much the audience may agree with the point of departure and the presentational layout of the argumentation, it may nevertheless fail to meet the requirements applied in a reasonable evaluation. A rational judge will find the argumentation pragmatically valid only if the evaluation of its point of departure and its presentational layout is in both cases positive, so that the argumentation as a whole may be considered sound.[31] It is the first responsibility of argumentation theorists to specify the validity criteria to be applied by a rational judge in carrying out a reasonable evaluation of argumentation with regard to both its point of departure and its presentational layout. The general objective of the study of argumentation can therefore be summarized in the following way:

> The general objective of the study of argumentation is to develop criteria for determining the validity of argumentation in view of its points of departure and presentational layout and to implement the application of these criteria in the production, analysis and evaluation of argumentative discourse.

Argumentation theorists differ in the meanings they assign to the term *valid*. For the most part, these differences relate to the various conceptions of ration-

---

[31]In this endeavor, the term *valid* (and the term *sound*) acquires a pragmatic meaning which accords with the interests of argumentation theorists. In formal logic, of course, the term *valid* has a much stricter meaning. As will be clear from ordinary usage, however, formal logicians have neither been granted a patent for this term nor do they hold the monopoly of its use.

ality or reasonableness taken as starting point in their study of argumentation and to the specific goals aimed for in these studies. In a sense, these studies can all be seen as particular views on what we are to understand by valid argumentation. By these lights, every theoretical contribution to the study of argumentation provides us with a definition of (particular aspects of) pragmatic validity, depending on a specific, usually implicit, conception of rationality.

In order to provide some insight into the nature of the rationality conceptions underlying the various contributions to the study of argumentation, we offer a brief outline of three main conceptions of rationality distinguished by the philosopher Stephen Toulmin (1976) in *Knowing and Acting*. These distinctions may be used as a background for the discussion of several contributions in the present study.

Toulmin differentiates between the philosophical answers given to the question "What is it to have *reasons for* our beliefs or actions?" (1976, pp. vi–vii). He distinguishes a "formal" or "logical" tradition, originating in Plato, an "empirical" tradition, familiar from the eighteenth century and derived from "common sense," and a "critical" or "transcendental" tradition, starting with Kant. These traditions find, according to Toulmin, expression in three different approaches to rationality: a *geometrical*, an *anthropological*, and a *critical* approach. Each of them induces a particular approach to argumentation.

The geometrical approach relies heavily on formal logic. Arguments are regarded rationally acceptable only if they start from true or certain premises that necessarily lead to true or certain conclusions. This amounts to saying that the points of departure of valid argumentation must be indisputable and the arguments must be laid out in a formally valid way. The anthropological approach takes the rationality conception of a specific community as its starting point and bases its judgments on empirical evidence. Argumentation will then be regarded as valid if its point of departure and presentational layout agree with the standards of reasoning consented by the community concerned. The critical approach equates rationality with the functionality of the argumentative procedures used for achieving the aim for which they are designed, leaving aside specific logical or empirical assumptions. A rational judge taking this approach will find argumentation acceptable only if its point of departure and its presentational layout are suitable means for achieving a well-defined aim. In practice, of course, various elements from different approaches can be combined in a single conception of rationality.

A rational judge represents an authority to which the evaluation of argumentation is entrusted. It is debatable whether this authority should consist of an existent person or group of people or should remain an abstract ideal. If the first is preferred, it is assumed that the assessors are people capable of setting aside their own prejudices etc. If the second is preferred, it is assumed that a normative construct can be theoretically devised that is fully adapted to the task of making optimum judgments. Different argumentation theorists have different preferences in the matter. For our present purposes, it is most important to realize that a rational judge can take various shapes.

The various contributions to the study of argumentation differ not only in being founded on different rationality conceptions. They also differ because their specific aims are different; some are entirely *descriptive*, others have an orientation that is primarily *normative*. Descriptive approaches to argumentation aim at a description of those points of departure and presentational layouts that are regarded valid in practice. Normative approaches to argumentation aim at a determination of those points of departure and presentational layouts that are to be regarded valid from an external perspective.

The crucial difference between descriptive and normative approaches to argumentation is that the first type of approach is more empirically based, whereas approaches of the second type have an analytic basis. In practice, approaches of the two types are also often combined, or considered as complementary. If the theorists aims are diagnostic as well as therapeutic, some combination of the two seems to be a prerequisite, for one can only properly embark upon improving the production, analysis, and evaluation of argumentative discourse if one has first made clear what practice one desires to bring about, and how this accords with actual practice.

The study of argumentation has so far not resulted in a universally accepted theory. The state of the art can therefore not be explained by describing one leading theory. It is characterized by the coexistence of a variety of approaches, differing considerably in conceptual breadth, scope of horizon, and degree of theoretical refinement.[32] A fair picture can be given only by a survey of the various contributions, with an emphasis on the most influential and most elaborated. As a consequence, apart from the general proclamation provided in this introduction, a broad perspective in which they are all put in their proper place can hardly be given.

Before discussing contemporary developments which gave shape to the field as it currently is, we pay some attention to its historical background. We begin in chapter 2 with classical analytic, dialectic and rhetoric, which are still highly relevant to present-day argumentation theory. After a brief introduction to Aristotle's logic of the syllogism, we shall deal with the dialectical art of critical debate, the rhetorical art of civic discourse, and Roman-Hellenistic rhetoric.

In chapter 3, we first discuss the Aristotelian heritage in the study of fallacies and the Standard Treatment of fallacies, so that, in spite of the enormous and unavoidable gap, at least some bridge is built between classical antiquity and modern history. We then move to Crawshay-Williams's analysis of controversy and Naess's insights concerning the clarification of discussions. Thus we hope

---

[32]For an illustration of the variety, see, for example, van Eemeren, Grootendorst, Blair, and Willard (1992).

to provide information concerning some substantial contributions to the study of argumentation which, in our opinion, have been unjustly neglected.

In chapter 4, we give a treatment of the New Rhetoric developed by Perelman and Olbrechts-Tyteca. We sketch their rhetorical framework and explain their specific perspective regarding the points of departure of argumentation and about argumentation schemes. In chapter 5, we explain Toulmin's model for argumentation analysis, paying attention to Toulmin's ideas concerning field-invariance and field-dependency and the relation between the form of argumentation and validity. We also mention some applications of his model.

These authors have set the stage for the developments in the study of argumentation that have taken place in the last two decades. Some of these contemporary developments took place in North America, some in Europe and the rest of the world. We start with three chapters dealing with North American developments, followed by three chapters about developments in Europe.

In chapter 6, our survey of the present state of affairs in argumentation theory starts with an exposition of the (re)emergence of Informal Logic, naming its main issues. Then we go on to the educational reform movement called Critical Thinking. In chapter 7, we discuss Communication and Rhetoric as practiced in American (speech) communication departments. We trace the development from debating contests to argumentation studies and give an impression of the social science perspectives on communication and the various contributions to the study of argumentation stemming from an interest in practical philosophy and social and cultural critique.

In chapter 8, the formal treatment of the fallacies is at issue, starting with Aristotle and formal logic. Next the use of formal methods in the study of fallacies is discussed, as exemplified in the Woods-Walton approach. In chapter 9, the discussion of formal approaches to argumentation is continued. Barth's interesting conception of logical validity is explained, as well as the Logical Propaedeutic of the Erlangen School, their dialogue logic, and Barth and Krabbe's Formal Dialectics.

Chapter 10 is devoted to Pragma-Dialectics, expounding van Eemeren and Grootendorst's model for critical discussion, their method for reconstructing argumentative discourse, and their conception of the fallacies as moves which are obstacles to the resolution of disagreements. Some other, language-oriented, approaches to argumentation are discussed in chapter 11. First Anscombre and Ducrot's Radical Argumentativism and their ideas concerning polyphony in argumentative discourse, then the Natural Logic described by Grize and his collaborators and Lo Cascio's argumentative grammar.

Finally, in chapter 12, other more or less recent developments are mentioned that have taken place in the non-English speaking world. Among them are several philosophical and theoretical contributions to the study of argumentation, inspired by the Erlangen School and by Habermas and originating mainly in

Germany, some stylistic and rhetorical studies from Italy and other European countries, particularly on the rhetoric of science, and a number of diverse contributions from scholars active in various countries. Since our study is meant to serve as an introduction to argumentation theory, we have supplemented our extensive list of references with a classified bibliography which may assist those readers who wish to acquaint themselves more thoroughly with a particular subject.

HISTORICAL BACKGROUNDS

2

ANALYTIC, DIALECTIC, AND RHETORIC

Because the sources for modern theoretical thinking on argumentation lie in Greek antiquity, it stands to reason that we begin our survey of the historical backgrounds of argumentation theory with a brief reconnaissance of classical logic, dialectic, and rhetoric. These new disciplines evolved in the 6th and 5th centuries B.C. Then the mythological picture of the world began to change, and attempts were made to account for natural phenomena and the genesis of the world in a rational manner, without appealing to the gallery of the gods.

Before that, the cultural climate in Greek society had been rigid and dogmatic: *kosmos* (nature) and the social order of the *polis* (city-state) were seen as an immutable system ordained by the gods as a reflection of the divine order. For open discussion and argumentation there was no place: "The gods have wished it so." Postulating any other explanation for the world and its creation meant setting oneself against the gods.

When this picture of the world was challenged in the 6th and 5th centuries B.C., other explanations were offered. The existence of everything was, for example, explained by "primordial" principles or laws, such as "the limitless," "the air," "the atoms," or "everlasting numerical relations between the components of the world." These explanations and metaphysical speculations on "everything that exists," or the nature or structure of "the world," differed from, even conflicted with each other. Thus Heraclitus believed that everything was always in constant motion, while Parmenides opined that motion and change were impossible.

At a somewhat later period (chiefly in the 5th century B.C.) questions of direct social significance came to be discussed. Some people believed the social order to be inherent in human nature, while others thought it was the result of agreements, laws, and conventions. Another problem was the question of whether all members of the community should be treated as political equals or whether the cleverest and strongest must simply ensure that power remained in their hands.

All these, and other, opinions regarding the origin of the world and the political order laid claim to truth and acknowledgment by others. The ensuing differences of opinion led to questions like "What actually *is* a 'good' opinion?" and "When can we say that something is true?" Defending a particular opinion now required giving arguments for it, but how was one to determine which argumentation was the best? Is there such a thing as *good* argumentation?

The Greek Sophists were the first to ask these sorts of question. They were itinerant scholars who taught lessons in argumentation and social and political skills. Though also interested in natural philosophy, they were chiefly concerned with ethics, political theory, morality, and theoretical reflection on the episte-mology of these subjects. Some Sophists had rather radical views. Gorgias, for example, was of the opinion that (a) nothing really existed, (b) if anything really did exist it would be "unknowable," and (c) if anything was "knowable" it would be uncommunicable to others. According to this view, everything we see about us is only an illusion. Another well-known point of view was that moral values are relative and subjective. According to this view, in the event of a dispute concerning moral questions one cannot appeal to objective criteria; the most one can do is ensure that one's own opinion is accepted.

Directly related to this view is the Sophist standpoint that, objectively speak-ing, there can be no such thing as good argumentation. If one person convinces another with his arguments, this is because the other person accepts what he says. The first person is, in other words, *agreed to be right*, but that does not necessarily mean that in objective terms he actually *is right*.

The Sophists were excellent orators, and their orations were followed with interest and pleasure. They also organized public debating contests, and would debate for a fee. They had a reputation for being able to argue for any arbitrarily chosen standpoint. One of the earliest examples of their skill at devising argu-ments is the following advice to someone accused of murder. If he is small in stature, he must argue in his defense that it is unlikely that so weak a person committed the crime. If he is of sturdy build, he can argue that it is improbable that so substantial a person did the deed, since he would be suspected straight-away (Guthrie 1971, p. 178).

Because good and convincing oratory was seen as a means towards achieving success in public life, there was widespread interest in the teaching of the Sophists. The democratic system as it existed in Athens for the major part of the 5th century required that an advocate of a particular political measure defended it at public meetings.[1] On such occasions it was naturally more than

---

[1]On the working of this democratic system, see Sabine (1966, pp. 3–21).

helpful to be able to put an argument well. When involved in a legal dispute, too, it was advantageous to be able to defend oneself before a judge.

Two main factors have thus promoted an interest in studying argumentation. First, comparison of the arguments for opposing views on all sorts of subject led to the general query of what is good argumentation. Second, the practice of politics and the law led to the question of what is good, and above all effective, argumentation. This general reflection on argumentation took shape in classical logic, dialectic, and rhetoric.

The theories of classical logic, dialectic, and rhetoric were at their most influential in the finely worked out form given them by Aristotle.[2] Aristotle's logical theory is found first and foremost in the *Prior Analytics* and *Posterior Analytics*. What we now call "logic" was referred to by Aristotle as "analytic." In antiquity, it was often called "dialectic." In the way in which Aristotle uses the word "dialectic," however, it is the theory or art of debate. His dialectic is to be found in the *Topics* and in the *Sophistical Refutations*. The theory of good and convincing oratory, finally, Aristotle discusses in his *Rhetoric*.

Aristotle starts from the assumption that all knowledge, insights, and opinions, in so far as they arise from rational thought, are based on existing knowledge, insights and opinions (*Posterior Analytics* 71a, 1–10). Existing opinions make up the material on the basis of which we can arrive at new opinions with the help of reasoning or arguments (*Prior Analytics* 68b, 14). Aristotle divides the arguments which may be used for this purpose into two sorts: *deductive syllogisms* and *inductive syllogisms*.[3]

In the case of deductive syllogisms, something is asserted or assumed in a number of statements, and from these statements, the premises, there necessarily follows a conclusion. ("Necessarily" means that the conclusion *must* follow from the premises.) In this sort of argument the relation between the premises and the conclusion is such that it is impossible for the premises to be true and the conclusion false. Nowadays, arguments that have this quality are called "deductively valid."

Let us give an example of our own. Suppose there are two premises: "All cities have a city council" and "Paris is a city." From these two premises necessarily follows the conclusion "Paris has a city council." Of course, at a particular moment

---

[2]Aristotle wrote on logic, natural philosophy, biology, metaphysics, political theory, and other subjects. His logical writings were called the *Organon* ("organon" means "tool"): Logic was to be a tool in the service of the sciences and other areas of knowledge. From the *Organon*, we draw on the *Prior Analytics*, *Posterior Analytics*, the *Topics*, and the *Sophistical Refutations*. Aristotle's *(Nicomachean and Eudemian) Ethics* and *Rhetoric* are not part of the *Organon*, but Aristotle defines rhetoric as the counterpart of dialectic (*Rhetoric* 1354 a1).

[3]Aristotle argues (in *Prior Analytics* 68b, 15) that all forms of reasoning can be brought back to the syllogism. In practice, he distinguishes between deduction and induction. In some places, he contrasts (valid) deductive syllogisms and straightforward induction (*Topics* 105a, 14), and he also refers to inductive syllogisms (*Prior Analytics* 68b, 15). We follow him in the latter.

a city may *not* have a city council (the council may just have resigned, for example), but even then the conclusion still follows necessarily from the premises, because *if the premises were true*, then the conclusion would be true also.

In the second sort of argument, inductive syllogisms, specific cases are named in the premises, and from these premises a general conclusion is drawn.[4] One of Aristotle's examples is: "The trained helmsman is the best; the trained charioteer is the best; therefore a trained man is generally the best in his field."[5]

Aristotle distinguishes arguments also according to the purpose they are intended to serve. Arguments designed to achieve absolutely certain and reliable knowledge, he calls *apodictic* or *demonstrative*; arguments calculated to lead to generally acceptable opinions, or points of view, are *dialectical*; and arguments that are primarily intended to convince a particular audience of the correctness of a standpoint, are called *rhetorical* arguments.

For a demonstrative argument it is possible to use either a deductive or an inductive syllogism. The certainty of the premises is passed on to the conclusion by the argument. In a sound deductive demonstration the premises are incontrovertibly true, and so is the conclusion. Such arguments therefore serve as an apodictic ideal of knowledge, particularly of mathematical knowledge.[6]

For dialectical arguments, too, it is possible to use either deductive or inductive syllogisms. The premises of a dialectical argument are generally accepted, or they are acceptable to "the wise," that is, "to all of the wise or to the majority or to the most famous and distinguished of them" (*Topics* 100b, 23). Because the premises are only "generally accepted," the conclusions too are only "generally accepted." Again, the degree of certainty—in this case, acceptability or probability—is transmitted from the premises to the conclusion.

The premises of a rhetorical argument must be chosen so that they have cogency for the audience. By the use of a deductive or inductive syllogism, the conclusion is then also cogent in the eyes of the audience. The audience must *accept* the step from the premises to the conclusion; whether the reasoning is valid by demonstrative or dialectical criteria, is not important. To persuade the audience, then, two conditions must be met: both the premises *and* the inference must have cogency.

Aristotle mentions an interesting example of an argument that is apodictically invalid, but can function well rhetorically: "Someone who is committing adultery

---

[4]Nowadays, inductive arguments are generally understood as arguments in which the premises are calculated to make the conclusion plausible while it is, strictly speaking, possible for the premises to be true and the conclusion false. Aristotle's inductive arguments are covered by this definition, but other arguments, such as reasoning by analogy, are encompassed as well.

[5]See Aristotle's *Topics* 105a, 13–16, where he also defines induction.

[6]In antiquity, mathematics was regarded as representing empirical knowledge. For example, it was considered obvious that parallel lines do not meet, since this can simply be "seen" to be so.

ARGUMENTS	demonstrative	dialectical	rhetorical
objective	certainty	acceptability	persuasiveness
status of the premises	evidently true	acceptable	persuasive to audience
inference	valid	valid	persuasive to audience
theory	logic	dialectic	rhetoric

FIG. 2.1. Aristotle's three sorts of argument and their characteristics.

wears gaudy clothes and loiters in the street at night; this man is wearing gaudy clothes and loiters in the street at night; therefore this man is committing adultery." If the (invalid) connection between the premises is accepted by the audience, this argument can function well on the rhetorical plane.

Apodictic arguments are treated in Aristotle's logical theory, the *Analytics*; dialectical arguments in the *Topics* and the *Sophistical Refutations*; and rhetorical arguments in *Rhetoric*. Before briefly discussing these three theories, we summarize the three sorts of argument and their characteristic features in Fig. 2.1.

2.1   THE ANALYTICAL LOGIC OF THE SYLLOGISM

In his logical theory Aristotle concerns himself chiefly with deductive syllogisms.[7] His definition of a syllogism is so broad that it covers any argument in which a conclusion necessarily follows from two or more premises (*Topics* 100a, 18–25, *Prior Analytics* 24b, 20). Aristotle only deals with the type now known as a "categorical syllogism," which must meet more stringent requirements than the general definition suggests. Here is an example:

(1) All humans are mortal.
(2) All Greeks are humans.
(3) All Greeks are mortal (*conclusion*).

A syllogism consists of two premises (1 and 2) and a conclusion (3). The premises and the conclusion are all *categorical* statements, that is, they relate to categories of entities. In practice, it is also possible to have an argument with more premises or with only one premise, or with premises and conclusions that are not cate-

---

[7]Further extensions of Aristotle's logic, which is now termed *traditional logic*, have a long history.

gorical statements. Just as Aristotle, however, we shall concentrate on syllogisms of the earlier described type.

In a categorical statement a predicate (P) is attributed to a subject (S) by means of the word "is" or "are" (*kategorein* means "to predicate"). In (1), for example, it is said of "humans" (the subject) that they are "mortal" (the predicate). The term which functions as the subject of a statement is known as the *subject term* (in 1 "humans," in 2 and 3 "Greeks"), the term functioning as the predicate being called the *predicate term* (in 1 "mortal," in 2 "humans," and in 3 "mortal").

In (1), the predicate "mortal" is attributed to the subject "humans," that is, *all* humans. The predicate, however, may also have been *withheld* from the subject, or might not be allocated to *all* humans, but only to *some*. In this way, a total of four variants can be distinguished, all of which Aristotle regards as categorical statements. The four variants are:

(1a) All humans are mortal.
(1b) Some humans are mortal.
(1c) No humans are mortal.
(1d) Some humans are not mortal.

In (1a) and (1b) the predicate "mortal" is attributed to the subject "humans," while in (1c) and (1d), by contrast, it is withheld from the subject. The statements (1a) and (1b) are therefore called *affirmative*, (1c) and (1d) *negative*. In (1a) and (1c) the predicate is attributed to *all* humans and in (1b) and (1d) to *some* humans. All-statements are called *universal*, some-statements are called *particular*. The difference between affirmation and denial is a qualitative difference, the difference between all and some a quantitative difference. The medieval abbreviations A, I, E, and O are generally used as indications of "universal affirmative," "particular affirmative," "universal negative," and "particular negative" statements respectively.[8] The examples (1a) to (1d) may thus be identified as follows:

(1a)	universal affirmative	(A)
(1b)	particular affirmative	(I)
(1c)	universal negative	(E)
(1d)	particular negative	(O)

In example (1), both the premises and the conclusion of the syllogism are universal affirmative. It is also possible for a syllogism to contain categorical statements of some other type, and it can also contain a variety of types. It

---

[8]The letters A and I represent the first two vowels in the Latin word *affirmo* (I affirm), the letters E and O the vowels of the Latin word *nego* (I deny).

might, for example, consist of three particular negative statements or two particular affirmative statements (e.g., the premises) and one universal negative statement (the conclusion):

(4) Some humans are not mortal.   (O)
(5) Some Greeks are not humans.   (O)
(6) Some Greeks are not mortal.   (O)   (*conclusion*)

(7) Some humans are mortal.   (I)
(8) Some Greeks are human.   (I)
(9) No Greeks are mortal.   (E)   (*conclusion*)

Using the various possible ways of combining different types of categorical statement, it is possible to indicate the *mood* of a syllogism. This is usually done with the medieval abbreviations A, I, E, and O. The mood of the syllogism (1–3) is thus AAA, that of the syllogism (4–6) is OOO, and that of the syllogism (7–9) is IIE.

Syllogisms, moreover, may be characterized by reference to their *figures*. The figure of a syllogism is determined by the manner in which the subject and predicate terms occurring in the syllogism are divided over the premises and conclusion. To refer to this division, the following terminology is used. The predicate term of the conclusion is called the *major term* of the syllogism, and the premise in which the major term occurs is called the *major premise*. The subject term of the conclusion is the *minor term*, and the premise in which it occurs is the *minor premise*. The term which appears in both of the premises but not in the conclusion is the *middle term*.

The "figure" of a syllogism is determined by the position of the middle term in the major and minor premises.[9] The figure of (1–3), for example, can now be reproduced as follows:

major premise
(1) All *humans* are mortal   *middle term*   major term

minor premise
(2) All Greeks are *humans*   minor term   *middle term*

conclusion
(3) All Greeks are mortal   minor term   major term

In this example, the middle term in the major premise is thus in the position of the subject, and in the minor premise in the position of the predicate. In all, there are four possible combinations for the position of the middle term in the

---

[9]In modern introductions to logic, the "figure" of a syllogism is characterized on the basis of the middle term.

first figure		second figure	
middle term	major term	major term	*middle term*
minor term	*middle term*	minor term	*middle term*
third figure		**fourth figure**	
middle term	major term	major term	*middle term*
middle term	minor term	*middle term*	minor term

FIG. 2.2. The four figures of the syllogism.

major and minor premises. These four combinations correspond to four different figures for the syllogism. Syllogism (1–3) is an example of the *first* figure. Together with the other three figures, this is represented schematically in Fig. 2.2.[10]

The combination of mood and figure produces the *form* of the syllogism. There are many possible combinations, so that there are many forms of syllogism. However, by no means all forms are valid. Syllogism (1–3) (mood AAA, first figure) is valid, but syllogism (4–6) (mood OOO, first figure) and syllogism (7–9) (mood IIE, first figure) are not. Aristotle distinguishes eighteen valid combinations of mood and figure.[11]

Aristotle only treats arguments in which the premises and conclusion all consist of categorical statements. Strictly speaking, arguments with statements known as *singular* statements, which are found in many arguments, fall outside the scope of his theory. In singular statements the predicate is attributed to a subject term that refers to a single individual, not a category of individuals. Examples are premise (11) and conclusion (12) in argument (10–12):

(10) All humans are mortal.

(11) Socrates is a human.

(12) Socrates is mortal (*conclusion*).

Argument (10–12) is the most commonly used example of a syllogism in modern textbooks on logic.[12] It is then either disregarded, or permitted by some artifice, that (11) and (12) are not categorical statements. Usually this amounts to the singular term "Socrates" being considered as a term that refers to a class

---

[10]Aristotle discusses only the first three figures.

[11]These include the subaltern ones (whose medieval abbreviations were *Barbari*, etc.).

[12]According to de Pater, "Socrates is a human" is a categorical statement to Aristotle (cf. his definition). The reasons why such a sentence has no place in Aristotle's syllogistics is (1) that logic is a tool for science, and science concerns *species*, not individuals, (2) it poses problems for conversion, which plays a role in the validity proofs of the syllogisms (personal communication with de Pater, October 20, 1994).

consisting of only one member, Socrates. In this way, the singular statement (11) is reduced to a categorical statement (Kahane, 1973, p. 221):

(11a) All members of the class whose sole member is Socrates are human.

(11b) All things identical with Socrates are human.

This artifice, then, enables us to treat arguments as syllogisms even if they contain noncategorical statements. In order to distinguish these arguments from "genuine" syllogisms, they are sometimes termed *quasi-syllogisms*.

2.2 THE DIALECTICAL ART OF CRITICAL DEBATE

In Greek antiquity, dialectic was the term used to denote a particular argumentative technique in a discussion or debate. For the sake of debate, one of the interlocutors assumes a thesis, deduces from this assumed thesis a conclusion which conflicts with it, and on the basis of this contradiction rejects the thesis. This dialectical argumentation technique is called *reductio ad impossibile* (reduction to the impossible) or *indirect proof*.[13]

In Aristotle's *Topics*, the term "dialectic" has a broader meaning, dialectic being the art of reasoning using premises which are not evidently true. Aristotle examines how these premises can be used as "concessions" in a debate, one party drawing on the other party's acceptance of these premises in discussing the thesis. The premises often consist of generally accepted assumptions, but in any event they must be accepted by at least one of the interlocutors.

Aristotle gives general rules for the conduct of debates. He also describes the manner in which a particular thesis may be attacked or defended, providing a system of possible "moves" which are primarily executed by the opponent, various warnings to the defender to be wary of certain moves, and a list of the psychological tricks that may be used by the attacker and the defender to mislead each other.

The *Topics* reads like a manual for the conduct of a public debating contest held in the presence of an audience. Aristotle, however, finds dialectic also useful as a mental training. If in answering philosophical questions one can find arguments both for and against a certain point of view, the truth will be more expeditiously revealed. Dialectic is thus the art of arguing for and against.[14]

Arguing for and against a standpoint in a debate worked like this. First of all, although the discussion may have seemed to be about specific questions, it was,

---

[13]This technique of argumentation is sometimes also called *reductio ad absurdum*. It is possible to draw a distinction by saying that in *reductio ad impossibile* the conclusion contradicts the accepted premise itself while in *reductio ad absurdum* it conflicts with other true statements.

[14]For a clear and comprehensive study of the influence of Aristotle's *Topics* on neo-classical topical systems, such as that of Boethius, see Stump (1978).

on closer inspection, about general questions. The opponent offered the defender a thesis in the form of a question like "Must this man be punished?" By way of this specific question (and the subsequent questions and answers) a general question was raised, for example, "Is virtue teachable?" The defender could reply in the affirmative or in the negative. Depending on the answer the opponent had in mind, he then had to attack either the thesis "Virtue is teachable" or the thesis "Virtue is not teachable." Arguments pro and contra recurred continually throughout the course of the debate. Once the defender had been committed to a thesis by his answer, the attacker would pose a further question, and so on.

The opening question (the *protasis*), would be in the form "Is S P?" ("S" standing for subject, "P" for predicate). Thereafter the questions would take the form "Is S P or not?" These latter questions (and the answers to them) were the *problemata*. By his reply, the defender again committed himself (now to a *problema*), and because the attacker would not know in advance what the defender's answer would be, assuming that the defender had accepted certain theses and was making use of them, his attack would have to take account both of the *problema* "S is P" and of the *problema* "S is not P."

This makes it somewhat clearer what kind of role generally accepted assumptions play in dialectic. The attacker offers the defender these assumptions if he wishes to elicit a particular conclusion so that he will be able to call on it later. The defender is more likely to commit himself to generally accepted assumptions than to arbitrary ones. The attacker has won when it becomes clear that the defender has accepted theses which contradict each other.

In order to make defenders contradict themselves, attackers can avail themselves of a system of *topoi* (Latin: *loci*): a series of argumentation techniques. The major part of the *Topics* consists of a treatment of such techniques. A *topos* is the "place" from which the attacker can get his arguments. Some translations of the word *topos* stress its "topographic" nature: "place," "argument place," "location," "search formula." A *topos*, however, is also a rule, law, or procedure, and this is what is stressed in other translations of the word *topos*: "argumentation scheme," "argumentation schema," "argumentation technique," "procedure." In order to do justice to both aspects, we translate the term *topos*, following Kneale and Kneale (1962, p. 34), as "move." A further advantage of this translation is that it also calls to mind the association with playing a game and holding a contest, thus underlining the fact that, like a game or contest, a debate can be won or lost.

A move is a tactical aid in setting up an argument for or against a thesis. The argument consists of a conclusion and premises. The move specifies which premises may be used. This is its *selective function*, corresponding to its "topographic" character. Moreover, the move itself is a premise, albeit one of a more fundamental nature than the others. It guarantees the transition from the other premises to the conclusion. This is its *guarantee function*, corresponding to its

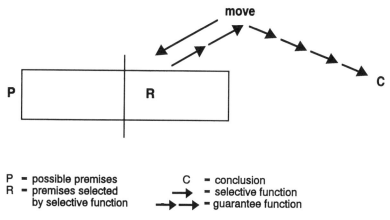

P = possible premises   C = conclusion
R = premises selected   → = selective function
     by selective function   ⇒ = guarantee function

FIG. 2.3.   The selective and guarantee functions of a move.

"rule-like" or "procedural" character. These two functions of the move are shown in Fig. 2.3.[15]

Just like the moves in a game of chess, not every move is suitable for every kind of attack. What sort of move may be made depends on the thesis to be opposed. By looking at the way in which the predicate says something about the subject, Aristotle divides theses into types. A predicate may contain a *definition*, a *property*, a *genus*, or an *accidental attribute* of the subject (*accidens*). In the case of a definition, the predicate indicates the "essence" of the subject (e.g., "Man is a rational animal"); in the case of a property, the predicate is convertible with the subject although it does not express its essence (e.g., "Man is a language-learning animal"); in the case of a *genus*, the predicate is a wide class to which the subject belongs as a *species* (e.g., "Man is a living being"); and in the case of an *accidens*, finally, the predicate refers to an accidental property of the subject (e.g., "Man is brave").

Following on from this classification, Aristotle discusses "definition moves," "property moves," "*genus* moves," and "*accidens* moves." An *accidens* move is one employed as an attack on a thesis in which the predicate expresses an *accidens* of the subject. *Mutatis mutandis*, the same applies to a *genus* move, which is employed in an attack on a thesis whose predicate expresses a *genus* of the subject. And so on.

To clarify the way a move works, let us look at two examples from the *Topics*. In the first, the attacker wishes to arrive at a conclusion in which two contradictory predicates are attributed to the subject ("There is correctness and error in perception"), using a *genus* move and not, for instance, definition. The attacker then has to find a *genus* to which "perception" belongs and to which both of these contradictory predicates apply. Aristotle calls "distinguishing" a *genus* of

---

[15]This figure is, with slight modifications, taken from de Pater (1965).

perception. Because distinguishing can be right and wrong, perception, as a species of distinguishing, can also be right and wrong (*Topics* 111a, 15). The selective and guarantee functions of this move are shown in Fig. 2.4.

Of the possible premises P, the move selects the premises R1 and R2. The selection takes place as follows. There must be one premise (R1) in which the term "perception" (from the conclusion) occurs as a *species* of a *genus* (in this case, distinction). The move does not specify *what genus*, leaving that to the ingenuity of the attacker, but only that there must *be* a *genus*. When the *genus* has been found, the contrary terms from the conclusion are attributed to it. This is how we arrive at premise R2.

In the second example, the attacker must bring about the conclusion that what a particular subject term refers to is more worthy of choice than what a particular predicate term refers to ("Health is more worthy of choice than exercise"). The move amounts to the attacker exploiting the fact that the subject is worthy of choice for its own sake, while the predicate is only a means to an end (*Topics* 116a, 29–31). In that case, the subject is more desirable than the predicate. The two functions of this move are shown in Fig. 2.5.

The first move (Fig. 2.4) is a more general one than the second move (Fig. 2.5): the latter, containing the term "desirable" (or "worthy of choice"), and can only be used in comparing degrees of desirability.

Moves (*topoi*) of the first type have a logical character and are called *general* moves, moves (*topoi*) of the second type are axiological and are called *special* moves. Special moves serve to make value judgments possible. This is illustrated by the following special move:

That which has more favorable consequences is preferable to that which has less favorable consequences.

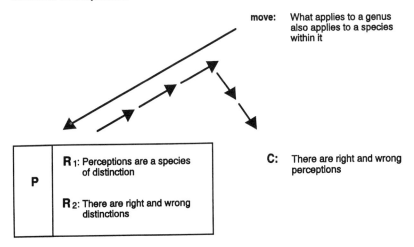

FIG. 2.4. Example of a general move.

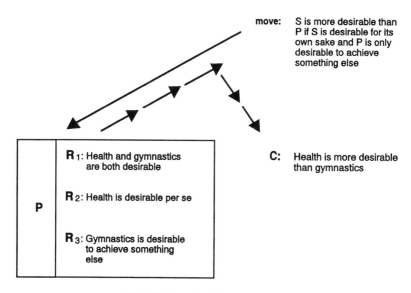

FIG. 2.5. Example of a special move.

An end is more desirable than a means, and the means that best achieves the end is more desirable than the means which achieves the end less well.

How are such moves employed in a debate of the form we have just outlined? In order to clarify this, let us reconstruct a debate in which the attacker (A) uses the move "What is desirable for its own sake is more desirable than what is desirable only to achieve something else" against the defender (D):

(1) A: "Is health more desirable than gymnastics?"

(2) D: "Health is not more desirable than gymnastics."

(3) A: "Is what is desirable for its own sake more desirable than what is desirable only to achieve something else, or not?"

(4) D: "What is desirable for its own sake is more desirable than what is desirable only to achieve something else."

(5) A: "Is health desirable for its own sake, or not?"

(6) D: "Health is desirable for its own sake."

(7) A: "Is gymnastics desirable for its own sake or desirable to achieve something else?"

(8) D: "Gymnastics is desirable to achieve something else."

(9) A: "Is health more desirable than gymnastics, or not?"

(10) D: "..."

It is already clear from the defender's answer to question (3) that the defender is going to contradict himself. Of course, this only happens if the attacker phrases the questions in such a way that the defender does not, at once, realize what the attacker is getting at. Moreover, the defender must answer in such a way that he causes the attacker the greatest possible difficulty.

General issues of this kind, which have more to do with the form of the debate than with the moves themselves, are treated by Aristotle in the final book of the *Topics*. Among other things, he goes into the order of the questions ("for the time being, conceal the purpose of the desired concession"), the sort of concession the attacker must contrive to elicit, and the sort of question which the defender *cannot* avoid answering affirmatively ("someone who refuses to concede a generally accepted universal statement without being able to advance a counterargument behaves improperly").

Just like the players in a game, the participants in a debate can cheat, that is, break the rules by executing wrong or false moves. Aristotle deals with wrong moves in a separate work, the *Sophistical Refutations* (*De Sophisticis Elenchis*)—he regards false moves as characteristic of the Sophists. The *Sophistical Refutations*, however, is not concerned solely with refutations; it also discusses other strategies which may lead to one's adversary losing.

Refutation of one's adversary's argument means that the adversary accepts both the thesis and a statement that conflicts with it. If the attacker can make the defender do this, the attacker has won the debate and the defender has lost. According to Aristotle, the attacker can also win by (1) seducing the defender into stating an untruth or paradox, (2) tricking the defender into making grammatical blunders, or (3) seeing to it that the defender continually repeats himself. In the *Sophistical Refutations*, Aristotle discusses the moves whereby the attacker can achieve these ends. He also deals with the ways in which the defender may react in order not to be driven into a corner by false moves. First he describes how attackers must couch their questions to achieve their objectives, subsequently going on to explain how false moves may be parried by the defender. The false moves Aristotle discusses in the *Sophistical Refutations* have since played an important role in the history of what has later become known as the theory of fallacies (see chap. 3).

2.3 THE RHETORICAL ART OF CIVIC DISCOURSE

Aristotle defines rhetoric as the faculty of discovering the possible means of persuasion in oratory.[16] Classifying the "genres of oratory" according to the circumstances in which a discourse is conducted, he distinguishes three genres: (1) the *genus iudiciale*, (2) the *genus deliberativum*, and (3) the *genus demonstrativum*.

---

[16]As a matter of course, within the framework of this study the history of classical rhetoric can only be traced briefly. For a more comprehensive survey we refer to Kennedy (1994).

The *genus iudiciale* relates to a juridical situation in which speeches are made in favor of a particular judgment. In most cases, the point at issue is whether a past act is to be regarded as lawful or unlawful, or just or unjust. The *genus deliberativum* relates to a political situation in which—as in a council of citizens— speeches are made for or against the expediency of a particular political measure or a course of action. The *genus demonstrativum*, finally, relates to a festive or ceremonial occasion at which a person or thing is praised or condemned. This last genre is also known as the *epideictic* genre.

In all three genres, the audience for whom the discourse is intended is the most important factor to be taken into account. Since the means of persuasion are, in rhetorical practice, characteristically chosen to suit the listeners, Aristotle examines them in relation to the audience. As an example of attuning the means of persuasion to the audience, he mentions that deductive reasoning can best be used in the presence of experts whereas inductive reasoning, because examples are being given, is better suited for a discourse addressed to an unlettered multitude.

Aristotle distinguishes between "inartificial" and "artificial" means of persuasion. Inartificial means of persuasion do not depend on the speaker's skill but are based on preexisting material. Instead of having to make anything up, the speaker can call on laws, documents, statements by witnesses, or confessions by suspects. Artificial means make a demand on the speaker's skill: They are devised by speakers in order to persuade their audience of their own point of view.

Among the artificial means of persuasion, Aristotle distinguishes three categories, depending on whether they make use of *ethos*, *pathos*, or *logos*. *Ethos* (character) is being employed when it is indicated, whether directly or indirectly, that the speaker exhibits practical wisdom, virtue, and good will. In Aristotle's view, this is the most effective means of persuasion, since once an audience trusts a speaker it will also be inclined to accept what the speaker says. *Pathos* (sentiment) is being used when the discourse plays on the audience's emotions. In connection with pathos, Aristotle notes that our judgment tends to be clouded by joy, sorrow, love, or hatred (*Rhetoric* I, ii, 5). When the speaker makes use of *logos*, persuasion is aimed for by way of arguments.

The first two means of persuasion, *ethos* and *pathos*, are nonargumentative, while *logos* is argumentative.[17] The argumentative means of persuasion that the speaker may call to his aid (and to which we confine ourselves here) are deductive syllogisms and inductive syllogisms. Aristotle calls rhetorical deductive syllogisms *enthymemes*, and rhetorical inductive syllogisms *examples*. With

---

[17]Relying on the speaker's trustworthiness, is to Aristotle not necessarily emotional: For someone who has no other means of determining whether something is true, it is reasonable to be persuaded by *ethos*. Aristotle regards all emotions as *pathetic*, even those used solely to elicit the audience's sympathy for the speaker. Cicero considers these kinds of emotion as *ethical*, leaving only the "heavy" emotions under the rubric of *pathos*. *Ethos* is for Cicero an emotional means of persuasion. See Wisse (1989, p. 33).

the help of enthymemes and examples it is possible to defend points of view concerning which other opinions might be held. Rhetorical syllogisms, whether enthymemes or examples, are—like their dialectical counterparts—bound to a particular form of communication, in this case the monologue. In rhetorical deductive syllogisms, premises that are acceptable to the audience are used in an enthymeme to make a point of view acceptable; in rhetorical inductive syllogisms, examples that are acceptable to the audience are used to make a generalization or another (unknown) example plausible.

A speaker who can assume that the audience will automatically accept certain premises as obvious or taken for granted, can do without making these premises explicit. Indeed, it might have a deleterious effect if all the premises were continually set out explicitly.

When setting up an enthymeme, it is first and foremost important that the speaker chooses the right, that is, acceptable, premises. For example, when defending a decision not to take a seat on a committee, one is advised not to say that one cannot be bothered, but, for instance, that the interests of the club are served better by choosing some other candidate.

The premises are grouped by Aristotle according to their degree of acceptability for the audience. He distinguishes among three gradations: certainty, plausibility, and fortuity. An example of a premise that is (or rather *was*) certain for all audiences is "A pregnant woman has had sexual contact with a man"; a premise that is plausible for most audiences is "A father loves his children"; a premise whose acceptability is fortuitous is "An adulterer wears gaudy clothes."

Although premises that are certain are more likely material for demonstrative arguments, they can, if they are available, also be used for rhetorical arguments. The premises that are plausible are the most important to rhetoric. They often contain value judgments ("We must strive after peace"), and may then be used to justify an action or decision. For example, if it is nowadays found plausible that "Cars destroy the living conditions in the city," then this premise can be used to defend the standpoint that "Cars are to be kept out of the city."

If one wishes to defend a standpoint by means of a rhetorical deductive syllogism, then that standpoint must be presented as the conclusion of an enthymeme. But how is one to come by the premises? What plausibilities can one rely on?

Here the speaker is assisted by the rhetorical moves represented by the *topoi*, whose selective function aids the speaker in the choosing of premises. The transition from the premises to the conclusion is then made plausible by the guarantee function of the *topoi*. In Fig. 2.6, this is illustrated by a rhetorical move that can be used in defending the modern standpoint that it is better not to smoke.

In his dialectic, Aristotle discusses general as well as special moves. Some general moves are also discussed in his logic, but there they are treated as logical rules and not formulated in terms of the role they can play in a debate.

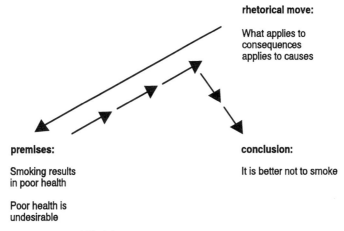

rhetorical move:

What applies to
consequences
applies to causes

premises: conclusion:

Smoking results   It is better not to smoke
in poor health

Poor health is
undesirable

FIG. 2.6. Example of a rhetorical move.

The special moves in Aristotle's dialectic are in the minority. They are, by contrast, the chief subject of discussion in his rhetoric.[18]

2.4 ROMAN-HELLENISTIC RHETORIC

In the Hellenistic Age that followed Aristotle, Greek rhetoric developed further. Only in part, this development was built on Aristotle, the enthymeme being taken over, albeit in an extended form. A more important connection was that with the earlier rhetoric of the Sophists. Viewed from the perspective of argumentation theory, two developments are most notable.

First, due to the tendency to design more detailed classifications, rhetoric became increasingly systematized. Second, an alternative to Aristotle's doctrine of the three means of persuasion was circa 150 B.C. created by Hermagoras of Temnos. In this alternative, *ethos* and *pathos* were seen as mainly pertaining to the introduction and the conclusion of the oration, and *logos* acquired a different content: the doctrine of *stasis*.

In discussing the place of argumentation in the Hellenistic rhetorical system, we cannot make use of Greek-Hellenistic sources, since they have been lost. Instead, we will be guided by the oldest Roman rhetoric handbooks: the anonymous *Rhetorica ad Herennium* (which has been traditionally attributed to Cicero), and *De Inventione*, written by Cicero in his youth.[19] Although these works, dating

---

[18]A parallel between Aristotle's dialectic and his rhetoric is that the false moves which are known as *fallacies* are discussed in both. See chap. 3.

[19]Although *Rhetorica ad Herennium* and Cicero's *De Inventione* are textbooks rather than theoretical works, they are adequate sources for drawing a picture of Roman-Hellenistic rhetoric (see Leeman & Braet, 1987). *De Oratore*, Cicero's later work, would be a less adequate source because it describes Cicero's personal (Aristotelian) views, and these have not been adopted by other Roman rhetoricians. Quintilian's (1920) *Institutio Oratoria* will also not be discussed.

from circa 85 B.C., are written in Latin, they follow the somewhat older Greek-Hellenistic handbooks closely, in particular Hermagoras.[20]

In contrast to what is known about Hellenistic rhetoric, *Rhetorica ad Herennium* and *De Inventione* show a practical interest in *ethos*, *pathos* and *logos*, albeit without making use of these terms and of Aristotle's division, and a continued use of Aristotle's rhetorical moves. The place of the study of argumentation in Roman-Hellenistic rhetoric may best be characterized by connecting together two systems of classification that are fundamental to this rhetorical system as a whole.[21] The first classification relates to the "tasks" (*officia*) speakers must perform before making their speech, the second to the "components" of the speech.

Orators have five tasks to perform before delivering a speech. They must (1) decide what they are going to say (*inventio*), (2) arrange their subject-matter (*dispositio*), (3) choose the right wording or formulations (*elocutio*), (4) learn the speech by heart (*memoria*), and (5) provide the speech with the right intonation, facial expressions and gestures during delivery (*actio*). When arranging their material (*dispositio*), orators divide their discourse into components. The discourse starts with an introduction (*exordium*) aimed at making a favorable impression on the audience and arousing their interest in the subject. Then an account is given of the subject or the facts of the case (*narratio*). The most important part of the speech, the argumentation (*argumentatio*), is often subdivided into two parts: giving evidence for the speaker's own opinion (*confirmatio*) and refutation of the arguments of the opponent (*refutatio*); there can also be a digression (*digressio*). The speech is concluded with a summary and peroration (*peroratio*).[22]

In Roman-Hellenistic rhetoric, the tasks of the orator and the various components of the oration are examined in considerable detail. Complex classifications and subclassifications are being discussed, and individual components from the classification are provided with examples and practical hints. Moreover, the discussion is in many cases linked to the rhetorical genres.

In the *inventio* of the *argumentatio*, the orators examine which means of persuasion are best suited for their particular purpose. Once the means of persuasion have been found, the arrangement of the oration can be determined. Would it, for example, be better to start with weak arguments and then go on to more powerful ones, or the other way around? Should examples be given first that support the defended view, or must this view be supported by enthymemes straightaway? And how should the various arguments be interwoven?

---

[20]In using terms, we shall sometimes deviate from these sources if other terms have become more common.

[21]According to Wisse (1989), the historical situation was, in fact, more complicated than is depicted here because the two systems were used independently.

[22]In *Rhetorica ad Herennium*, the components of the oration only play a part in the *inventio*, which takes place step by step for each component. The *dispositio* only has a role in ordering the arguments in the *argumentatio*. Unlike Hermagoras, the author of *Rhetorica ad Herennium* did not strictly divide the oration into such components as *exordium*, *narratio*, etc. See Wisse (1989, pp. 86–87).

The guidelines provided in the *inventio* are by far the most important and the most detailed. Due to Hermagoras, an alternative is offered here to the Aristotelian approach of *ethos*, *pathos* and *logos*. This alternative concentrates mainly on the methodical search for arguments, albeit that some advice is also offered concerning the use of *ethos* (to bring about benevolence) and *pathos* (to arouse pity or indignation) in the introduction and the conclusion. Basic to this approach is the doctrine of the choice of *status* at the start of the *inventio* (*status* is a Latinization of the Greek *stasis*, which can best be translated into English as "issue"). Although the scope of the doctrine of *status* was thought to be much broader, it has only been elaborated for the *genus iudiciale*, concentrating mainly on criminal court cases, and adopting the perspective of the defendant rather than that of the prosecutor.

The first important step in the *inventio* is, in *Rhetorica ad Herennium* as well as *De Inventione*, that the orator, that is, the defender in a criminal case, reflects on how to respond to the accusation or complaint. In a murder case, for instance, the defender can, according to Hermagoras's doctrine, choose from four kinds of strategy: (a) denying the criminal act concerned (*status coniecturalis*), (b) redefining the act concerned as "manslaughter" (*status definitivus*), (c) appealing to extenuating circumstances such as the need for self-defense (*status qualitatis*), (d) pointing out procedural flaws (*status translativus*). Depending on the *status* chosen by the defender, a certain issue will be central. This choice is not only highly relevant to the parties, but also to the judges, whose judgment must depend on the quality of the arguments put forward by the parties in support of their position concerning the central issue.

The *status* chosen determines the point of departure of the search for arguments. A denial requires other sorts of argument than a procedural defense. A forceful aspect of Hermagoras's doctrine of *stasis* is that Hermagoras offers almost exhaustive lists of matching arguments for all four kinds of issue. In preparing the defense, the orator can decide what could best be put forward in the case concerned.

Rhetorica ad Herennium suggests the following issues to a prosecutor who wants to make plausible that the accused is guilty of the deed he is accused of (*status coniecturalis*): (a) the degree of probability that the accused is guilty (e.g., the motive and the accused's way of life), (b) comparison of the accused with other persons, (c) signs pointing towards guilt (the place and time of the crime, opportunity, chance of success, chance of evading detection), (d) presumed evidence for the guilt of the accused (e.g., his behavior before and after the crime). This example reveals a principal difference between the Hellenistic and Roman-Hellenistic rhetoric as presented in the handbooks and the much more abstract rhetoric of Aristotle.[23] Aristotle's general dialectical moves may be applied to any

---

[23]It is worth noting that Aristotle's topics were further developed by Cicero as part of his rhetorical theory.

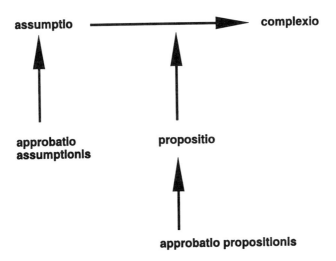

assumptio = accepted starting point or minor premise
complexio = conclusion
approbatio assumptionis = support for the accepted starting point
propositio = justifying principle or major premise
approbatio propositionis = support for the justifying principle

FIG. 2.7.   The epicheirema and its elements.

subject, and his special moves contain some content elements (e.g., the moves relating to cause and effect and to end and means), but not as many, and not as detailed, as the special moves of (Roman-)Hellenistic rhetoric. In (Roman-)Hellenistic rhetoric, the moves are so specific that listing them would amount to giving a more or less systematic *catalogue* of all possible premises. These moves represent, in fact, subject-committed rules: If a particular case arises, the speaker must adduce the arguments belonging to that particular type of case.

The doctrine of the issues and the matching *loci* enabled orators preparing their speech to determine their position and to find their arguments. In order to connect the arguments with the position that was to be defended, and to present this connection in the oration, the Roman-Hellenistic handbooks went back to Aristotle's enthymeme, having it first elaborated into a so-called *epicheirema* (see Fig. 2.7).

An epicheirema, then, is an enthymeme extended with new elements. In *De Inventione*, Cicero gives an example which we illustrate in Fig. 2.8 (I, xxxiv, 58–59).

The choice of elements an orator wishes to use must depend on the audience the orator is going to address. For example, the *propositio* can be left out if it is very obvious. In choosing the premises that must be used to complete the epicheirema, the theory of the *inventio* can be of help by providing a system of *loci* or rhetorical moves.

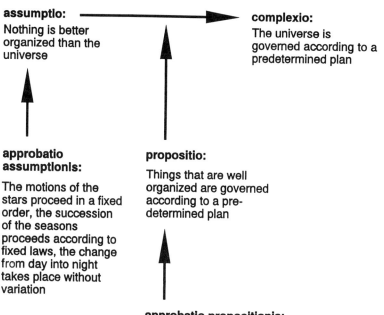

assumptio:
Nothing is better
organized than the
universe

complexio:
The universe is
governed according to a
predetermined plan

**approbatio
assumptionis:**

The motions of the
stars proceed in a fixed
order, the succession
of the seasons
proceeds according to
fixed laws, the change
from day into night
takes place without
variation

propositio:

Things that are well
organized are governed
according to a pre-
determined plan

approbatio propositionis:

A household governed according to a predetermined
plan is better organized than a household governed
without a predetermined plan; the same applies to
an army; the same applies to a ship

FIG. 2.8. Example of an epicheirema.

There have always been critics of rhetoric, also in antiquity: Plato and various later philosophers. Their criticisms pertained to the fundamental objectives of rhetoric, not to any developments within rhetoric. The critics detested the rhetoricians' aim of persuading people of plausible—hence disputable—points of view, instead of searching for the truth. Plato even accused them of persuading people by means of lies. To his way of thinking, rhetoric was only defensible as a vehicle for conveying indisputable knowledge. By condemning the rhetorical practices of his times, he also condemned the essential point of rhetoric: that it lends cogency to views about matters on which more than one opinion is possible.

No growing disrepute of rhetoric, however, was discernable in antiquity. On the contrary, rhetoric became increasingly seen as important. Due to the requirements of social and political practice, the art of oratory was held in high esteem in public life. And although the Roman and Hellenistic writers of practical handbooks, concentrating on the deliverance of effective speeches, leave us in no doubt as to their appreciation of the means of persuasion which Aristotle rubricated as *pathos* and *ethos*, *argumentatio* and the doctrine of *status* were still considered crucial.

The eighteenth-century view that rhetoric was brought in disrepute by the Roman predilection for playing on the audience's emotions, and the heavy emphasis on *elocutio*, seems not correct; it is, in any case, hard to sustain. Some other reasons that have been mentioned for the decline of rhetoric in later times are equally doubtful. In the Renaissance, the part of rhetoric dealing with the theory of the *inventio*, still important in Roman rhetoric, became part of dialectic; however, this shift did not change the character of the theory, just its name. Mainly for practical reasons (the books became too thick), *inventio* and *dispositio* were brought under the label of "dialectic," leaving *elocutio* under "rhetoric."

Because rules for correct usage, a clear style and stylistic embellishments can be very useful, we do not consider this change of object as automatically to the detriment of rhetoric. One of the basic rules of rhetoric is, and has always been, that oratory must make a natural and unaffected impression, and that it should be impossible to tell that any rules have been applied at all. Viewed from a modern as well as a historical perspective, the current criticisms of rhetoric that it is associated only with insincerity and bombast are therefore misplaced.

3

ANALYSIS OF FALLACIES, CONTROVERSY, AND DISCUSSION

Analytic, dialectic, and rhetoric, as developed in antiquity, still provide an important background to contemporary studies of argumentation. Having discussed some of the major concepts in chapter 2, and prior to our discussion of the present state of argumentation theory, we now turn to some historical contributions of a much more recent date. In this endeavor, we shall pay attention to the study of fallacies, the theoretical contributions of Crawshay-Williams and Naess, and the still influential argumentation theories of Perelman and Olbrechts-Tyteca, and Toulmin.

Until the 1950s, the study of argumentation had been dominated by the classical tradition inherited from antiquity, principally rhetoric, and, to a lesser extent, by the developments in modern logic. The attention paid to reasoning in colloquial language found expression mainly in attempts to make rhetorical and logical insights applicable to teaching, without there being any question of theoretical innovations.

A kind of renewed practical interest in argumentation arose in the 19th century, starting in the United States. Since the second half of that century, courses in public speaking and writing were given in schools and universities. The teaching of these courses, in which argumentation plays an important part, has become one of the tasks of the rhetoric and (speech) communication departments (Kinneavy, 1971). It was coupled with a revaluation of rhetoric, seeking help from the classical rhetorical tradition. For many years now, a number of books of the "classical rhetoric for modern students" variety have been available, a well-known example being Corbett (1966). There are also a great many textbooks based on rhetorical insights for instruction in discussion and debate.[1]

---

[1]See the bibliographies of Cleary and Haberman (1964), and Kruger (1975).

Debate has been an important source of argumentation studies. As an alternative to social fraternities and athletics, American colleges and universities began late in the 19th century to start debate competitions. Debating was seen as a pedagogical device, a form of practical training for careers in law, government, or politics. The earliest publications were textbooks to instruct students and coaches in this new activity, the most prominent of which was George Pierce Baker's *Principles of Argumentation* (1895). The early books shared several common features. They were practical how-to-do-it guides informed primarily by their authors' intuition and experience. They were unreflective, in that they treated matters of practice as neither complicated nor problematic. Little attention was paid to the relationship between the *species* debate and the *genus* argumentation. Typically, the instruction was not placed in a context broader than preparation for the contest activity itself.[2]

The renewed practical interest in argumentation has also found expression in introductory textbooks on logic and in popularizing works on logical thinking. The main influences to be discerned in these publications are those of classical dialectic and traditional logic based on classical analytics. Many modern logic textbooks include a separate section on traditional logic, in which attention is paid to the practical application of logic, often in connection with a treatment of the Aristotelian theory of the syllogism and the theory of the fallacies stemming from dialectic. Many authors make room, too, for a discussion of definitions.[3] Usually, the application of logical insights is confined to the translation of argumentation from colloquial language into a logical standard form (e.g., Copi, 1972). The popularizing publications on logical thinking concentrate on everyday reasoning, the main focus of attention being the recognition and avoidance of fallacies.[4]

In the 1950s, some philosophers saw to it that the study of argumentation received new impulses as they advanced ideas that led to a sharp increase in the interest in theoretical thinking on argumentation in various fields and opened up new areas for practical application. None of these philosophers envisaged an absolute break with the classical tradition: they rather attempted to create new perspectives. This applies to Chaim Perelman and Lucie Olbrechts-Tyteca and to Stephen Toulmin, but also to Rupert Crawshay-Williams and to Arne Naess.

According to Henry Johnstone Jr. (1968), who was the first to publish a brief survey of the state of the art in modern argumentation theory, the reevaluation of

---

[2]The earliest textbooks joined rules of oratory, elaboration, and logic (Baker, 1895; Foster, 1908). Later texts focused on recipes for good research, case-building, and refutation (Baird, 1928), concentrating on the "analysis and criticism of predominantly reasoned discourse" (Mills, 1968, p. 5), of "primarily logical appeals" (Freeley, 1966, p. 2). They were claiming to study "the force of the better argument," defining the study of argumentation as a focus on the essentially rational, reasonable, and prudential aspects of discourse, as a method of inquiry, of criticism, of truth-seeking (Pelsma, 1937).

[3]See, for instance, Copi (1972), Kahane (1973), and Rescher (1975).

[4]See, for instance, Fearnside and Holther (1959), Emmet (1960), Michalos (1970), and Beardsley (1975).

the study of argumentation among philosophers was principally due to two of them: Perelman and Toulmin. There can indeed be no doubt that Perelman and Toulmin have been the most influential writers in the field of argumentation in the 1960s and 1970s. Many other authors have drawn inspiration from their works, which were published in the late 1950s, and references to them appear in countless books and articles on the subject. Because of the important role that their ideas have played in the development of the study of argumentation, we regard them as belonging to the historical background of argumentation theory.

Perelman and Olbrechts-Tyteca's "new rhetoric" is an attempt to provide a description of the techniques of argumentation used by people to obtain the approbation of others for their opinions. The new rhetoric amounts to a description of different sorts of audience, an arrangement of premises into different classes, and a catalogue of argumentation schemes that may be used in persuading or convincing an audience. Perelman and Olbrechts-Tyteca formulate their rationality norm for argumentation in terms of the audience for which the argumentation is intended. They equate the soundness of argumentation to the degree of approval that the argumentation receives from the chosen audience.

Perelman and Olbrechts-Tyteca want to create a framework for investigating "nonanalytic" thinking making use of dialectical arguments, as studied in Aristotle's *Topics*, rather than apodictic arguments, as discussed in Aristotle's *Prior Analytics* and *Posterior Analytics*. They examine arguments that may be logically invalid but rhetorically acceptable, that is, convincing or persuasive to an audience.[5] In doing so, they have given dialectic a rhetorical twist, making it accord with the aim of rhetoric laid down by Aristotle.[6]

It is not only in its aim that the new rhetoric corresponds to classical rhetoric and dialectic: in the further elaboration of the theory, too, there are striking similarities. For example, Perelman and Olbrechts-Tyteca's classification of premises for argumentation is the same as Aristotle's, and just as in Aristotle this classification is linked to the extent to which the premises are acceptable to the audience. Another similarity relates to the distinction between two of the new rhetoric's argumentation schemes, which parallels Aristotle's distinction between rhetorical syllogisms, or enthymemes, and rhetorical inductions, or examples.[7] Many

---

[5]Perelman and Olbrechts-Tyteca do not seem to take into account that dialectical arguments are also logically valid, validity having nothing to do with the status of the premises.

[6]The dialogue, essential to Aristotle's dialectic, does not play any effective role in Perelman and Olbrechts-Tyteca's new rhetoric. Neither does the dialectical criterion by which an opinion is acceptable as long as it is proof against the criticism of an opponent.

[7]In rhetorical syllogisms, the argument is based on *accepted* premises, the matter for which is provided by the *topoi* (or *loci*): generally accepted relations in reality, such as "what applies to effects applies to causes"; rhetorical inductions offer the possibility of *generalizing* about reality. Cf. Perelman and Olbrechts-Tyteca's distinction between argumentation schemes "based on the structure of reality" and argumentation schemes "establishing the structure of reality," discussed in our chapter 4.

subtypes of Perelman and Olbrechts-Tyteca's argumentation schemes can be found in the *Topics* (book III).

According to Toulmin, argumentation proceeds along lines analogous to those of legal procedures. In his approach to argumentation, Toulmin, too, turns his back on the logical concept of validity. In his view, formal validity is a criterion that can be applied only to analytic arguments, and in the practice of argumentation such arguments occur but rarely. He presents a model that is intended to be an alternative to the logical approach.

In Toulmin's model, argumentation is placed in the context of a discussion between a speaker and a critical listener. Although the model therefore has some dialectical features, Toulmin's angle of approach is primarily rhetorical. Unlike in dialectic, the acceptability of the claim does not depend on a methodical weighing up of pro-arguments and contra-arguments, the adversary (the critical listener) remains completely passive. Toulmin's model is, in fact, a rhetorical extension of the syllogism which is comparable to the *epicheirema*. Specific criteria for evaluating argumentation are not provided by Toulmin; they are left to the experts in the field to which the argumentation applies.

There is an important difference between Perelman and Olbrechts-Tyteca's and Toulmin's approaches to argumentation.[8] Perelman and Olbrechts-Tyteca's approach is, in principle, purely descriptive, whereas Toulmin's model for describing argumentation is meant primarily as a preparatory instrument for its evaluation. Ultimately, however, Toulmin leaves the assessment of argumentation to the experts in the field to which the argumentation refers.

Naturally, a survey of the state of the art in argumentation theory must pay close attention to such comprehensive and influential approaches as those put forward by Perelman and Olbrechts-Tyteca and Toulmin. We discuss their ideas in chapters 4 and 5 respectively.

We believe that some attention should also be paid to some less familiar, but by no means less fundamental, contributions to argumentation theory. That is why we discuss in this chapter a number of salient points from the works of the philosophers Crawshay-Williams and Naess. The first will be treated in Section 3.3, the second in 3.4.

Crawshay-Williams and Naess, who are also mentioned in Johnstone's brief survey (1968), published their works in the 1940s and 1950s, even earlier than Perelman and Olbrechts-Tyteca and Toulmin. Their ideas evolved quite separately but reveal on closer inspection some degree of kinship. Because Crawshay-Williams' and Naess' ideas are, in a sense, extensions of each other, one

---

[8]The link between Toulmin's model and Perelman and Olbrechts-Tyteca's typology of argumentation schemes is also obvious: most argumentation schemes distinguished in the new rhetoric can be viewed as descriptions of the nature of the justificatory premise which Toulmin calls the "warrant." See chapters 4 and 5.

might even speak of a joint contribution. Both authors are equally concerned with the lucidity of argumentative discussions, and both aim for clarification of the positions taken up in a discussion aimed at resolving a difference of opinion; a clarification to be achieved by a more adequate degree of preciseness of expression. Though neither Crawshay-Williams nor Naess offers a fully-fledged theory of argumentation, both of them have made an original contribution to the development of such a theory.

Naess considers it a precondition for a rational exchange of ideas that the participants in a discussion make clear what exactly is being discussed. Crawshay-Williams opts for a comparable method by emphasizing the need for establishing the exact purpose of the statement that is being discussed. Both allocate a major function to a negotiation between the interlocutors of an agreement about the language usage in discussion, because they assume that differences of opinion can only be resolved when agreement can be reached on the criteria that are to be applied in testing the disputed opinion. They consider it part of the task of the argumentation theorist, or someone similarly interested, to suggest possible criteria of this kind.

In his analysis of controversy, starting from a discussion of the way in which disputed statements are formulated, Crawshay-Williams provides criteria that can help people to resolve their disputes by taking due account of the purpose for which the disputed statements were made. In his view, a difference of opinion can only be resolved when this purpose has been indicated, since only then can it be made clear which criteria should be used to test the statement concerned. It is apparent from this that Crawshay-Williams' insights have dialectical features. The theory of argumentation he had in mind is a dialectical theory about the resolution of differences of opinion.

Naess' views, too, are allied to classical dialectic, for he, too, assumes that differences of opinion should be solved in a critical dialogue, and he also feels that discussions can only follow a rational course if the interlocutors are agreed on the procedures that are to be followed. His contribution to argumentation theory consists in offering tools for achieving these ends. Just as with the dialecticians, according to Naess discussions do not center on the absolute truth of statements, but on their tenability in the light of contra-arguments. One of the methods for improving the quality of argumentative discussions developed by Naess solves a problem raised by Aristotle in his dialectic:

It is useful to have examined the various meanings of a term both with a view to clarity (for a man would know better what he is stating if the various senses in which it can be used had been made clear) and also in order that his reasonings may be directed to the actual thing and not to the name by which it is called. For if the various ways in which a term can be used are not clear, it is possible that the answerer and the questioner are not applying their mind to the same thing. (*Topics* 108a, 18–24)

There is yet a further historical background to modern argumentation theory which deserves mentioning here: the study of the "fallacies," the stereotypes of unsound argumentation. The most outstanding contribution to this study was made by Aristotle, who drew up a list of fallacies which has been the basis of most later studies. Aristotle paid attention to the fallacies in *De Sophisticis Elenchis, Prior Analytics* and *Rhetoric*. We discuss the Aristotelian heritage in the study of fallacies in Section 3.1.

Over the years, Aristotle's original list has been reinterpreted and extended by a great many other authors. The most important extension is the addition of the so-called "*ad* fallacies," a concept introduced by John Locke. During the 19th and the 20th century a large number of *ad* fallacies have been identified. Hamblin (1970), who described the history of the study of fallacies, baptized the treatment of the fallacies generally adopted in the (logical) textbooks of his time the Standard Treatment. This Standard Treatment of fallacies, which is severely criticized by Hamblin, we shall discuss in Section 3.2.

3.1 THE ARISTOTELIAN HERITAGE IN THE STUDY OF FALLACIES

The purpose of the study of fallacies is to describe and classify forms of argumentation that are regarded as incorrect or unsound, and to explain why they are incorrect or unsound.[9] The first to make a systematic study of fallacies was Aristotle (384–322 B.C.). For a long time, his list of fallacies has been the point of departure of the study of fallacies. Over the years it has been extended considerably, and the fallacies he distinguished were often given new interpretations and new definitions, but his ideas are still recognizable in modern treatments.

In his influential book *Fallacies* (1970), the Australian philosopher Charles Hamblin surveyed the history of the study of fallacies since Aristotle and discussed contemporary treatments of fallacies in introductory logic textbooks. The uniformity Hamblin observed in the way in which fallacies were dealt with in these textbooks led him to speak of the *Standard Treatment* of fallacies:

> [. . .] the typical or average account as it appears in the typical short chapter or appendix of the average modern textbook. (1970, p. 12)[10]

---

[9]Throughout this chapter the word *unsound* is used in its colloquial meaning, unlike in logic where it refers to a valid argument with true premises.

[10]Six textbooks are mentioned by Hamblin (1970, p. 13) as the basis for his characterization of the Standard Treatment: Cohen and Nagel (1934), Black (1952), Oesterlee (1952), Copi (1953), Schipper and Schuh (1960), and Salmon (1963, 1984). Among the introductory logic textbooks not mentioned by Hamblin which treat fallacies more or less in line with the Standard Treatment are Beardsley (1950), Fearnside and Holther (1959), Carney and Scheer (1964), Rescher (1964), Kahane (1969, 1971), Michalos (1970), Gutenplan and Tamny (1971), and Purtill (1972). The unanimity in the textbooks is not as striking as Hamblin suggests. For differences within the Standard Treatment of the *argumentum ad hominem*, see van Eemeren and Grootendorst (1993, pp. 54–57).

Due to its use of historical sources and its severe criticism of the Standard Treatment, Hamblin's book, which also contains Hamblin's own theoretical contribution to the study of fallacies, is now a standard work on the subject. Our discussion of the Aristotelian approach to the fallacies and the Standard Treatment relies heavily on Hamblin's work.

Aristotle addresses the fallacies in *De Sophisticis Elenchis*, *Prior Analytics*, and *Rhetoric*. In *De Sophisticis Elenchis* he treats the subject most thoroughly; the *Prior Analytics* contain some additional remarks; and in *Rhetoric* only a selection is discussed from the list compiled in *De Sophisticis Elenchis*. The title *De Sophisticis Elenchis* means "On Sophistical Refutations" or "On refutations as used by the Sophists."[11] This is why fallacies are sometimes called *sophisms*.

Refuting the thesis of one's opponent is one of the ways of winning a debate treated by Aristotle in his dialectic (see Section 2.2). In Aristotle's view, however, the refutations discussed in the *Sophistical Refutations* are only *apparent* refutations, which he sees as typical of the Sophists' way of arguing. The correct moves attackers may use in order to refute the defender's thesis Aristotle discusses in the *Topics*.

The incorrect or false refutations which can be used in a dialectical context Aristotle divides into two groups. The first consists of Sophistical refutations that are dependent on language (*in dictione*), the second of Sophistical refutations that are independent of language (*extra dictionem*). Aristotle then divides these groups of fallacies into altogether thirteen different types, indicating in each case how false moves can be parried by the defender.

The fallacies dependent on language are divided into six types, all connected with the ambiguities and shifts of meaning which may occur in ordinary colloquial language. According to Aristotle, they point to the imperfection of colloquial language. The fallacies that are independent of language he divides into seven types, all of which could also occur if the language were perfect.

Let us take an example of a language-dependent fallacy from Plato's *Euthydemus* dialogue. In this dialogue, two Sophists, Euthydemus and Dionysodorus, take turns to demonstrate their debating skills (*Euthydemus* 275d–276c, see Hamilton and Cairns, 1994, pp. 389–390). Socrates is telling Crito how Euthydemus debates with the young Clinias:

> Well, Euthydemus began something like this, I think.
> Now Clinias, which of mankind are the learners, the wise or the ignorant?
> This was a large question; so the boy blushed, and looked at me in doubt. Seeing that he was troubled I said, My dear Clinias, cheer up and answer like a man, whichever you think, for perhaps it will do you a deal of good.
> Just then, Dionysodorus leaned over me, and whispered in my ear, smiling all over his face, Now look here, Socrates, I prophesy that whichever the lad answers, he will be refuted!

---

[11]In the present study, we shall refer to the English translation of *De Sophisticis Elenchis*.

While he spoke, Clinias made his answer, so I had no chance to warn the boy to take care, and he answered that the wise were the learners.
And Euthydemus said, There are people you call teachers, aren't there?
He agreed.
The teachers are teachers of the learners; for example, the music master and the grammar master were teachers of you and the other boys, and you were learners?
He said yes.
Of course at the time when you were learning, you did not yet know the things you were learning?
No, he said.
Then you were wise when you did not know these things?
Certainly not, he said.
If not wise, then ignorant?
Yes.
So you boys, while learning what you did not know, were ignorant and were learning?
The boy nodded.
So the ignorant learn, my dear Clinias, not the wise as you suppose.
When he said this, it was like conductor and chorus—he signaled, and they all cheered and laughed, I mean Dionysodorus and Euthydemus and their followers.

Euthydemus' rebuttal of Clinias' thesis is directly followed by a rebuttal by Dionysodorus of the thesis that those who learn are the ignorant. In both cases use—or misuse—is made of the ambiguity of the words "wise" ("learned" and "sensible") and "ignorant" ("untaught" and "stupid").

An example of one of Aristotle's language-independent fallacies can also be found in the same Platonic dialogue (*Euthydemus* 298d–299a, see Hamilton and Cairns, 1994, p. 412). The debate is conducted between Dionysodorus and a spectator, Ctesippus:

Just tell me, have you a dog?
Yes, and a very bad one, said Ctesippus.
Has he got puppies?
Very much so, he said, as bad as he is.
Then the dog is their father?
I have seen him myself, he said, on the job with the bitch.
Very well, isn't the dog yours?
Certainly, he said.
Then being a father he is yours, so the dog becomes your father and you the puppies' brother.
Dionysodorus quickly broke in again, that Ctesippus might not get in his retort first. One more little question. Do you beat this dog?
Ctesippus said with a laugh, No mistake, I do, for I can't beat you!
Well then, you beat your own father, the other said.

These examples show that the distinction between language-dependent and language-independent fallacies is not without problems. The fallacy in the dialogue about learning stems from ambiguity, and is thus dependent on language, but in the dialogue about the dog the situation is more complex. The fallacy in the argument "This dog is a father, this dog is yours, therefore this dog is your father," too, appears to be dependent on rather than being independent of language. According to Aristotle, however, this kind of fallacy is caused by an illegitimate shift of an attribute from an accidental property of a subject (*accidens*) to the subject itself, or *vice versa* (*Sophistical Refutations* 166b 28–34, 179a 26–32.). What Aristotle here means by "accidental" is not clear.

Hamblin (1970, p. 85) thinks that Aristotle calls a property *accidental* if the subject and predicate terms of the statement in which the property is attributed to someone or something are not *convertible*. If an accidental property is treated in an argument as if it were a convertible property, a fallacy is created which is independent of language.[12] This can be illustrated by the following invalid argument, taken from Hamblin (1970, p. 85):[13]

(1) Coriscus is different from Socrates.

(2) Socrates is a man.

Therefore:

(3) Coriscus is different from a man.

Premise (2) contains a statement of an accidental property of Socrates, for "Socrates is a man" cannot be converted into "A man is Socrates" since not every man is identical to Socrates. It is uncertain in which way the example must be analyzed. Perhaps one may read premise (1) as attributing "being different from Coriscus" to Socrates, the subject of premise (2). In the conclusion (3) this attribute is applied to "being a man," the accident expressed in premise (2). Thus an attribute ("being different from Coriscus") is shifted from a subject (Socrates) to its accident ("being a man").

The example of the dog presents even more difficulties. What seems to be involved is that the statement "This dog is [a] father" is not convertible, because not all fathers are identical to this dog. Therefore the fatherhood must here be regarded as an "accidental" property, so that the presented conclusion cannot be drawn.

Judging from introductions to logic and popular books on fallacies such as Fearnside and Holther (1959), modern authors have little difficulty with Aristotle's language-dependent fallacies. Clear—albeit not always very realistic—examples of fallacies of ambiguity are given, generally in the form of puns. A frequently recurring example is the following (see e.g., Copi, 1972, p. 93):

(1) Some dogs have fuzzy ears.

---

[12]Cf. also Bueno (1988).

[13]Cf. *Sophistical refutations* 166b 34.

(2) My dog has fuzzy ears.

   Therefore:

(3) My dog is some dog.

Another example is:

(1) After her finals Laura went crazy [with joy].

(2) Crazy people [lunatics] must be locked up.

   Therefore:

(3) Laura must be locked up.

Language-independent fallacies present more problems to modern authors, at least if they want to stick to Aristotle's classification. In some logic textbooks, the difficulty is solved by moving the *accidens* fallacy into the category of language-dependent fallacies (e.g., Cohen & Nagel, 1964). Usually, however, this fallacy is given a non-Aristotelian interpretation. It is then a fallacy because of the application of a general rule, without any modification, to a special case in which accidental circumstances render it inapplicable (see e.g., Copi, 1972, p. 81). The following argument is an example of this fallacy:

> Member of Parliament Giebels is entitled to publish the contents of his conversation with the Queen, since in Holland we have freedom of speech.

In this argument, an appeal is made to the general rule that in Holland freedom of speech applies to everybody. The fallacy arises because the argument ignores the accidental circumstance that this general rule does not apply to a confidential meeting of a Member of Parliament with the Queen.

Several other language-independent fallacies on Aristotle's list have undergone similar changes in modern textbooks, sometimes up to the point of becoming almost unrecognizable. One reason for these changes is undoubtedly the obscurity of some of Aristotle's definitions, an obscurity which is, as it were, an invitation to multifarious reinterpretations. Another reason is that many modern authors have not taken their definitions and examples of fallacies straight from Aristotle but from other authors who, in turn, may themselves not have gone straight back to Aristotle either. In this way, old mistakes may be perpetuated. The treatment of the following fallacy provides an example (Hamblin, 1970, p. 29):

(1) What you bought yesterday, you eat today.

(2) You bought raw meat yesterday.

   Therefore:

(3) You eat raw meat today.

According to De Rijk (1962), in his survey of the treatment of fallacies in 12th-century logic, this example first appears in the *Munich Dialectica*. This argument is usually regarded as belonging to the type of fallacy that is known as *secundum quid* ("in a certain respect"), the second of Aristotle's language-independent fallacies.[14] In the 19th century, De Morgan still considered this example as a *secundum quid*, but the passage in which he discusses *accidens* and *secundum quid* fallacies may easily be read as stating that the example is an *accidens* fallacy. Before De Morgan, no author regarded it as an *accidens* fallacy, whereas following him several writers do (e.g., Cohen & Nagel, 1964, and Copi, 1972).

Even more important than the changing interpretations of the fallacies on Aristotle's list, are, in our opinion, the shifts in perspective in the approaches to the fallacies. In *Sophistical Refutations*, Aristotle places the fallacies in the context of a dialogue in which a thesis is attacked by one person and defended by another.[15] The attacker (or "questioner") tries to refute the thesis of the defender (or "answerer"). In this perspective, fallacies are false moves employed by the attacker in his efforts to refute the defender's thesis. In many modern accounts, the dialectical perspective has been replaced by a monologic perspective. Fallacy theory then deals exclusively with errors reasoners make in their own reasoning, and deals no longer with deceptive maneuvers made by one party trying to outwit the other party.

One of the consequences of the abandonment of the context of debate has been that it sometimes becomes quite obscure why a particular fallacy from Aristotle's list should at all be included in a list of fallacies. Some of his fallacies are intrinsically linked with the dialogue situation. A clear example is the fallacy of *many questions*, which belongs to Aristotle's category of language-independent fallacies.

The *many questions* fallacy occurs when a question is asked that can only be answered by answering at the same time at least one other question that is "concealed" in the original question. The answer to the original question "presupposes," in other words, a particular answer to one or more other questions. By (implicitly or explicitly) forcing someone to answer a question other than the one that is asked the fallacy of *many questions* is committed. The following examples are commonly given as an illustration:

(1) Are you still beating your wife?

(2) When did you stop beating your wife?

A person who answers question (1) as intended, with a simple Yes or No, thereby admits being, or having been, in the habit of beating his wife. This is because (1) contains the following presupposition:

---

[14] In modern terminology, a reinterpreted version of *secundum quid* is referred to as "hasty generalization."

[15] This does not mean that Aristotle thought that fallacies are always dialectical mistakes. See chapter 8.

(1a) You used to beat your wife.

The same presupposition is contained in question (2), but in that case there is also a second presupposition:

(2a) You no longer beat your wife.

Because *many questions* hinges on the dialogue situation, this "fallacy" can only be discussed adequately in a dialectic approach. Asking questions of the *many questions* type can serve to pin down an opponent who fails to spot the treacherous nature of such a question. According to Aristotle, such questions are incorrect ways of making opponents contradict themselves in a debate. This happens, for example, if the thesis that the defender has never beaten his wife is at some point refuted through the No answer of the defender to question (1) of the attacker (of course, the defender is in even deeper water if he answers Yes).

In the type of debate discussed by Aristotle, the defender is therefore allowed to split up such questions into several questions and to answer them separately (*Sophistical Refutations* 181a 36). The defender thereby addresses the dubious presupposition(s) and avoids giving a direct answer to the original question. In the case of question (2), this strategy might lead to these replies:

(2′) I am still beating her.
(2″) I have never beaten her.

Answer (2″) is the best way to parry question (2) if the discussion hinges on whether the defender is or was in the habit of beating his wife. A "direct" answer, such as "Last week," would lead to an immediate and irrevocable defeat in the debate.

It is clear why Aristotle regards *many questions* as incorrect, that is, constitutive of fallacious refutation, in the context of debate. Again, however, it is unclear exactly why he classifies this wrong move in the category of language-independent fallacies. After all, it is precisely the way in which the question is framed that offers the possibility of checkmating one's adversary. The wording of question (1) virtually forces the defender of the thesis to answer Yes, or No, and thus to admit what the opponent tries to demonstrate: that the defender is, or was, in the habit of beating his wife.

3.2 THE STANDARD TREATMENT OF FALLACIES AND BEYOND

The fallacies of Aristotle's list were not only interpreted in various ways in later centuries, the list was also expanded. The most important addition consists of the fallacies known as the *ad* fallacies. Among them, the *argumentum ad hominem* ("argument directed at the man") is the most familiar.

In the study of argumentation, the term *argumentum ad hominem* is nowadays predominantly used in a pejorative sense. It refers to the fallacy of attacking the opponent personally in one way or another, instead of responding to the actual arguments put forward by the opponent in support of a standpoint. There is also a long-standing nonpejorative tradition, however, in which arguing *ad hominem* is regarded as an indispensable for successful argumentation.[16]

It is not quite clear what the 17th-century philosopher John Locke had in mind when he discussed the *argumentum ad hominem* in *An Essay Concerning Human Understanding* (1690/1961).[17] In the chapter "Of reason," he introduces three more types of "*ad* arguments": *ad verecundiam*, *ad ignorantiam*, and *ad judicium*. This gave him the reputation of being the "inventor" of the category of the "*ad* fallacies." Yet he does not explicitly state that he considers the *ad* arguments to be fallacious:

> [. . .] it may be worth our while a little to reflect on *four sorts of arguments* that men, in their reasonings with others, do ordinarily make use of to prevail on their assent, or at least so to awe them as to silence their opposition. (*Essay* IV, iii)

The *argumentum ad hominem* is placed third in Locke's list:

> A third way is to press a man with consequences drawn from his own principles or concessions. This is already known under the name of *argumentum ad hominem*. (*Essay* IV, iii)

The latter remark reveals that Locke does not assume to be introducing anything new. His source for this meaning of *argumentum ad hominem* is not easy to trace.[18] The following example is a modern case of an *argumentum ad hominem* in the Lockean sense:

> How can you say the Casinos in Las Vegas should be closed down? You've always said everyone should be free to decide for himself what to do or not to do.

In the following text fragment two other of the four sorts of argument mentioned by Locke are used, the *argumentum ad verecundiam* ("awe-directed argument") and the *argumentum ad ignorantiam* ("ignorance-directed argument"):

> Of course Beethoven dictated that symphony to Rosemary Brown: in *Playboy* the famous authoress Elisabeth Kübler-Ross recently explained that communication

---

[16]For the Aristotelian roots of the pejorative and the nonpejorative meanings of the term *argumentum ad hominem*, see Nuchelmans (1993).

[17]Cf. Hamblin (1970, p. 41, pp. 158–163), and also Finocchiaro (1974).

[18]Hamblin (1970) claims that Locke is referring to a Latin translation of a passage from Aristotle's *Sophistical refutations* and to several medieval treatises (pp. 161–162). Nuchelmans (1993) sheds more light on this question.

with the dead is perfectly possible. Anyway, nobody has ever proved that dead composers *don't* manifest themselves in this way.

The *argumentum ad verecundiam* is generally described as a misplaced appeal to authority. This does not quite accord with the literal meaning of *verecundia* ("diffidence, awe, shame, embarrassment, modesty"), though it appears to be in line with what Locke intended. With Locke, the *argumentum ad verecundiam* refer to cases in which it is suggested or stated that it would be arrogant of listeners to set themselves up in opposition to the authority to which the speaker appeals in the argument.

It can be reconstructed from Locke's remarks, that an *argumentum ad ignorantiam* relates for him to the burden of proof in a debate: It is an inadmissible way of evading one's duty to give arguments for one's point of view when expressing an opinion contrary to somebody else's. Nowadays the *argumentum ad ignorantiam* is generally regarded as a fallacious appeal to ignorance or lack of proof (as in the earlier example). On the basis of the observed fact that something has not been proven *not* to be the case, it is concluded that it *is* the case.

It must be emphasized, again, that it is not clear whether Locke himself regarded the *argumentum ad hominem*, the *argumentum ad verecundiam* and the *argumentum ad ignorantiam* as fallacious arguments, as is usually done in present-day literature.[19] An example of an *argumentum ad hominem* in the modern non-Lockean pejorative sense is the following:

> The argument that the state may not impose limitations on free speech and thus may not contemplate any curtailment of the cable television explosion has only the appearance of being sound. This reasoning is used by groups with a vested interest in the cable explosion going ahead. It is therefore a false argument.

This is a fallacy, for the *argumentum ad hominem* is not concerned with the facts of the matter and the argument that was given but addresses the motives and background of those who advance an opinion. To put it in the very general terms found in most modern interpretations, an *argumentum ad hominem* is a direct or indirect fallacious attack on the person of one's adversary rather than on the adversary's arguments.

It is difficult to determine when the term *argumentum ad hominem* acquired its pejorative meaning, and from whom. In his discussion of the Standard Treatment, Hamblin (1970) does not tell. The first occurrence known to us is in Sellars (1917); the second in Cohen and Nagel (1934).[20] This is what Sellars says about *ad hominem*:

---

[19]Definitions of the *argumentum ad hominem* that are similar to Locke's can be found in the works of the 19th century British logician Whately, the 19th century German philosopher Schopenhauer, the 20th century American philosopher Johnstone, Jr., and the 20th century Belgian philosopher Perelman. See van Eemeren and Grootendorst (1993).

[20]We owe these references to Hans Hansen (personal communication).

In this fallacy the argument is directed against the character of the man who is the opponent instead of adhering to its proper task of proving the point at issue. (p. 153)

And this is what Cohen and Nagel write:

The *fallacy of the argumentum ad hominem*, a very ancient but still popular device to deny the logical force of an argument (and thus to seem to prove the opposite), is to abuse the one who advances the argument. (p. 380)

In a number of introductory textbooks on logic that appeared between 1950 and 1972, the term *argumentum ad hominem* is used to designate the fallacy of attacking the opponent personally. One of the most influential books in which this occurs is Irving Copi's *Introduction to Logic*, first published in 1953 and reprinted many times (the eighth edition—coauthored by Carl Cohen—was published in 1990).

How is the *argumentum ad hominem* defined in the Standard Treatment? This is what Hamblin (1970) says:

[. . .] an argument *ad hominem* is committed when a case is argued not on its merits but by analysing (usually unfavourably) the motives or background of its supporters or opponents. (p. 41)

Besides being vague, this definition is also atypical of the books representing the Standard Treatment of fallacies. The introductory logic textbooks differ more than Hamblin suggests.[21]

What kinds of argument are in the Standard Treatment identified as an *argumentum ad hominem*? According to authors such as Copi (1953/1972), Kahane (1969/1973), and Rescher (1964), three ways of attacking someone personally can, roughly speaking, be distinguished. Correspondingly, there are three variants of the *argumentum ad hominem*: (1) an *abusive* variant, (2) a *circumstantial* variant, and (3) a *tu quoque* variant.[22]

The *abusive argumentum ad hominem* is a head-on personal attack. By portraying the opponent as stupid, dishonest, unreliable, or indicating otherwise negative aspects, an attempt is made to undermine the opponent's credibility:

Bacon's philosophy is untrustworthy because he was removed from his chancellorship for dishonesty. (Copi, 1972, p. 75)

---

[21]Cf. van Eemeren and Grootendorst (1993).

[22]Unless mentioned otherwise, the examples we give of the three variants are taken from Copi (1972).

The *circumstantial argumentum ad hominem* is an attempt to undermine the opponent's credibility by pointing out special circumstances pertaining to the opponent or by suggesting that the opponent's actions are only out of self-interest, claiming that the opponent's arguments are merely rationalizations:

> A manufacturer's arguments in favour of tariff protection are rejected on the grounds that a manufacturer would naturally be expected to favour a protective tariff. (Copi, 1972, p. 76)

The *tu quoque* (or "you too") *argumentum ad hominem* is directed at revealing an inconsistency in the positions that the opponent has adopted on various occasions. This may be an inconsistency between the standpoint that the opponent now attacks or defends and the standpoint the opponent attacked or defended in the past; or a discrepancy between a standpoint verbally expressed by the opponent and other behavior which is not in accordance with this standpoint. The latter is, for example, the case if someone is guilty of the same practices criticized in the opponent:

> The classical example of this fallacy is the reply of the hunter when accused of barbarism in sacrificing unoffending animals to his own amusement. His reply is to ask his critic, "Why do you feed on the flesh of harmless cattle?" (Copi, 1972, pp. 75–76)[23]

The *tu quoque argumentum ad hominem* is sometimes given a somewhat broader context, not only referring to the opponent's own behavior but also to that of others. This broad variant is mostly employed as a defense against criticism of one's own conduct: others do the same or have done the same. Rescher (1964) gives the following example:

> My client, Councilman Smith, did not act improperly in using an official auto for the commuting between his home and his office. The accuser, Councilman Jones, does this also from time to time, and so does the mayor. In fact, it has been a general practice for all higher officials of this city. (p. 82)

In this example, an inconsistency in the opponent's position is exposed: Jones disapproves of Smith's use of an official car for travelling between home and office but, occasionally, he does exactly the same, and obviously he does not object to the mayor and other higher-ranking civil servants doing this as well.

Although all three variants of the *argumentum ad hominem* are directed against the person and aim at undermining the opponent's credibility, they differ considerably in the way in which this objective is pursued. As a matter of fact, the differences between the three variants are so substantial that there might

---

[23]Copi has taken this example from Whately (1826).

be some justification for regarding them as a separate category of fallacy rather than different variants of the same fallacy.[24]

Since Locke's days, the list of *ad* fallacies has grown considerably. Some well-known newcomers are *ad baculum*, *ad consequentiam*, *ad misericordiam* and *ad populum*. Hamblin (1970) mentions more than twenty new *ad* fallacies (p. 41). Only a few of these are treated in the majority of modern treatments of fallacies.

Other fallacies discussed in the Standard Treatment resemble the Aristotelian categories, although, as mentioned before, there are also significant differences. Instead of distinguishing fallacies *in dictione* from fallacies *extra dictionem*, a distinction is sometimes made between *fallacies of ambiguity* and *fallacies of relevance* (e.g., Copi, 1972).

Fallacies of ambiguity or *fallacies of clearness*, as they are sometimes called, correspond more or less with Aristotle's fallacies *in dictione*. They are caused by *lexical* or *syntactic* ("grammatical") ambiguity (*amphiboly*), or by shifts of *accent*. The fallacy of *amphiboly* is committed when the syntactic interpretation of an ambiguous sentence is surreptitiously changed during the discourse—to the advantage of the speaker's own purpose. Examples of sentences that are syntactically ambiguous are:

Pleasing students can be trying.
They are visiting doctors.

Another (often quoted) example is:

Save soap and waste paper.

The fallacy of *accent* is also founded on a shift of meaning, but here the cause is a shift of stress within the sentence:

We must not direct our action against our *members*.
We must not direct our action against *our* members.

Another example is:

Why did Adam eat the apple?

---

[24]Some authors do indeed treat the *tu quoque* as a separate fallacy, for example, Carney and Scheer (1964, pp. 31–36), and Kahane (1973, p. 236). For Kahane, the term *tu quoque* is another name for the fallacy "two wrongs make a right." He does not make any further subdivision within the *argumentum ad hominem*. What he calls an *argumentum ad hominem* is the same as what Copi and Rescher call the *abusive* variant. Carney and Scheer treat the *abusive* variant and the *circumstantial* variant under the heading of *argumentum ad hominem*.

The differences of meaning resulting from the stress differences can be indicated as follows: (1) stress on *did*: "If not for the reason . . ."; (2) stress on *Adam*: "Rather than Eve"; (3) stress on *eat*: "Rather than save it"; (4) stress on *the apple*: "Rather than the lemon."

Fallacies of relevance dealt with in the Standard Treatment include Aristotle's fallacies *extra dictionem* and the *ad* fallacies already referred to. They are all forms of argumentation that offer no logical justification for the opinion expressed; that is why they are considered "irrelevant." Psychologically speaking, however, they prove to be capable of persuading an audience. Alongside *secundum quid, accidens, many questions, ad hominem, ad verecundiam* and *ad ignorantiam*, this category includes the following fallacies: *begging the question, ignoratio elenchi, non sequitur, post hoc ergo propter hoc, ad baculum, ad misericordiam, ad populum, ad consequentiam*, and *slippery slope*.

Begging the question, also known as *petitio principii* or *circular reasoning*, means that the arguer assumes that what needs to be proven (the question at issue) has already been shown to hold. A simple example is:

God exists, because the Bible says so, and the Bible is God's word.

Ignoratio elenchi ("ignorance of refutation") amounts, in the Standard Treatment interpretation, to an argument that does not address the thesis that happens to be the point at issue, but a totally different opinion attributed, rightly or not, to the other party. Thus a person who doubts whether state-controlled housing projects are a useful means of alleviating the housing shortage may, for example, be opposed by advancing arguments for the thesis that there is a serious shortage of houses. This, however, is not the point at issue.

A *non sequitur* ("it does not follow") is a form of argumentation, similar to *ignoratio elenchi*, in which the arguments that are used and the conclusion that is drawn may in themselves be correct, but the one does not follow from the other. The Dutch author Piet Grijs once gave this absurd example:

The devil painted the world. But he is not allowed to deduct the costs from his taxes. Then his nephew appears, in the year 1982. His nephew has an affair with the prime minister, and that is why the trees turn green again.

As the name suggests, *post hoc ergo propter hoc* ("after this, therefore on account of this") means that just because the one event follows the other temporally the first caused the second. This fallacy is used when it is claimed that the rise in (un)employment which has manifested itself since the new government took office is the result of the new government's policies, when it is in fact perfectly clear that there are other causes.

The *argumentum ad baculum* ("argument with the stick"), the appeal to force, amounts to resorting to the use of threats against an adversary who refuses to accept one's standpoint. The threat may involve physical force, but also other measures. Usually, threats are issued indirectly, sometimes preceded by an emphatical assurance that no pressure is being put upon the listener or reader:

> Of course, I leave it entirely to you to take your stand, but you must realize that we are your biggest advertiser (and if you publish that article about our role in South Africa you can forget about our advertising account).

The *argumentum ad misericordiam* ("pity-directed argument") is a fallacy in which an unjustified appeal is made to the audience's sympathy in order to further one's own interests:

> If you don't improve my grade for this course I will lose my self-esteem and find it difficult to continue with my life.

The *argumentum ad populum* ("argument directed at the people"), sometimes referred to as "mob appeal" or as "snob appeal," appeals to the prejudices of a particular group. This is, for instance, done by contrasting "we" (the speaker and his audience) and "they" (those against whom the discourse is aimed). The following might be an example:

> We all know that the arms race is carefully maintained by the arms manufacturers and that in the final analysis it's just a matter of lining the pockets of a crowd of unscrupulous shareholders.

The *argumentum ad consequentiam* ("consequence-directed argument" or "wishful thinking") is a fallacy in which unfavorable light is cast on a factual thesis by pointing out its possible consequences, without the rightness of the thesis itself being disputed. For example:

> We may suppose no H-bombs will ever hit The Netherlands, for our country is so small that nothing would remain of it. (From a Civil Defense pamphlet issued in the 1960s)

Or:

> God exists, otherwise life would be without hope.

The *slippery slope* fallacy is a special case of *argumentum ad consequentiam*, in which the speculation on unsubstantiated negative consequences is carried to an extreme. This fallacy entails wrongly suggesting that by taking the proposed course one will be going from bad to worse. In discussions about legalizing abortion and euthanasia, this type of argument occurs frequently:

If we start making euthanasia legal, we end up with gas chambers as in Nazi Germany.

Somewhere between the fallacies of ambiguity and the fallacies of relevance, we find the fallacies of *composition* and *division*. The fallacy of *composition* arises when characteristics of the parts are attributed to the whole in order to make a standpoint with respect to the whole acceptable. The fallacy of *division* is the converse. For example:

All the part of the machine are light in weight, therefore the machine is light in weight. (*composition*)
The machine is heavy, therefore all the parts of the machine are heavy. (*division*)

These examples show that properties of the parts are not automatically transferable to the whole, and *vice versa*. Here the words "light" and "heavy" refer to relative properties. As soon as there are enough light parts, they will make the machine heavy.

As already indicated in Section 3.1, Hamblin's (1970) book *Fallacies* is not only important because of its excellent historical overview of the study of fallacies, but also because of its diagnosis of the shortcomings of the Standard Treatment. Hamblin's criticisms are devastating:

[...] what we find in most cases, I think it should be admitted, is as debased, worn-out and dogmatic a treatment as could be imagined—incredibly tradition-bound, yet lacking in logic and historical sense alike, and almost without connection to anything else in modern logic at all. (p. 12)

This quotation illustrates Hamblin's earlier lament:

We have no *theory* of fallacy at all, in the sense in which we have theories of correct reasoning or inference. (p. 11)

According to Hamblin, the shortcomings of the Standard Treatment already reveal themselves in the standard definition of the term *fallacy*:

A fallacious argument, as almost every account from Aristotle onwards tells you, is one that *seems to be valid* but *is not* so. (p. 12)

The problem with this definition is that most fallacies discussed in the Standard Treatment do not fit with it. In fact, only a few formal fallacies fall without any problems under the definition. This applies, for instance to *affirming the consequent*) (affirming the consequent means that from the premises "If A then B" and "B," it is inferred that "A").

The mismatch between the definition and the fallacies in most other cases is sometimes due to the fact that there is no argument; in other cases, the reason is that the argument is not invalid at all. As an example of the former, Hamblin mentions the fallacy of *many questions*, and as an example of the latter the fallacy of *begging the question* (*petitio principii, circular reasoning*). With respect to the fallacy of *many questions* Hamblin (1970) writes:

> [. . .] a man who asks a misleading question can hardly be said to have argued, validly or invalidly, for anything at all. Where are his premisses and what is his conclusion? (p. 39)

And with respect to the fallacy of *begging the question*, he says:

> However, by far the most important controversy surrounding *petitio principii* concerns J.S. Mill's claim that *all* valid reasoning commits the fallacy. (p. 35)

This can be illustrated with an example:

> That is my bicycle, therefore this is my bicycle.

In a debate about whose bicycle it is, this argument is unlikely to have much effect, since the premise only repeats the conclusion. But according to standard logic, the argument as such is not invalid, because it substantiates a (valid) argument form:

> A, therefore A

In many other cases, it would be highly overdoing things if one looked for the error in the invalidity of the argument. This is true for fallacies such as the *argumentum ad verecundiam* and the *argumentum ad populum*, but also for the *argumentum ad hominem*. We can demonstrate this point by referring to an earlier example of an *argumentum ad verecundiam*:

> Of course Beethoven dictated that symphony to Rosemary Brown: in *Playboy* the famous authoress Elisabeth Kübler-Ross recently explained that communication with the dead is perfectly possible.

The "fault" here appears to lie not so much in the form of the argument as in the incorrectness of an unexpressed premise.[25] If this unexpressed premise is made explicit, the argument is not *per se* invalid:

(1) Elisabeth Kübler-Ross has said that communication with the dead is possible.

---

[25]Cf. van Eemeren and Grootendorst (1992a, pp. 60–72).

(2) Kübler-Ross is an authority in the field of occultism: everything she says about it is true.
Therefore:

(3) It is possible that Beethoven dictated that symphony to Rosemary Brown.

This argument has the following form:

(1′) X says that S is possible; this is a statement of type T

(2′) Everything X says about statements of type T is true
Therefore:

(3′) S is possible

If an objection is made to the original argument, it is not so likely that it concerns the form of the argument. It is more likely that its content causes problems. Such an objection would, for example, be "It's easy enough for Kübler-Ross to say things like that" or "Just how does that Kübler-Ross person know so much, then?"

Another example of overdoing things by looking at the validity of the argument is Copi's (1972) illustration of the *abusive* variant of the *argumentum ad hominem*, a head-on personal attack in which the opponent is portrayed as stupid, dishonest or unreliable, thereby undermining the opponent's credibility:

Bacon's philosophy is untrustworthy because he was removed from his chancellorship for dishonesty. (p. 75)

In this example, there is indeed an argument, but its fallaciousness seems to be lurking in the unacceptability of the unexpressed premise (Why should a swindler not have any interesting philosophical ideas?) rather than in the invalidity of the argument. Many examples of the *argumentum ad hominem* are not even presented as arguments which have the form of a premise-conclusion sequence. Granted, some of them could be reconstructed as such without difficulty, but others cannot. Take this example from Schopenhauer's "Eristische Dialektik," written between 1818 and 1830:

Vertheidigt er [der Gegner] z.B. den Selbstmord, so schreit man gleich "warum hängst du dich nicht auf?" [If the opponent defends suicide, one yells immediately "Why don't you hang yourself?"]. (p. 685)

It is not immediately clear what a reconstruction should look like:

(a) Suicide is wrong, *because* you don't hang yourself.

(b) Your defense of suicide is worthless *since* you don't hang yourself.

(c) You are inconsistent *because* you defend suicide but you don't hang yourself.

(d) You should hang yourself *because* you defend suicide.

It is difficult to make a well-founded choice between the alternatives because it is hard to determine what the speaker can be held to. Each reconstruction seems somewhat more absurd than the next.

Here we face, in Hamblin's (1970) words, the problem of "nailing" a fallacy: The accused can quasi-naively maintain that no argument has been advanced. Hamblin describes how that defense could proceed with regard to the use of an *argumentum ad hominem*:

> Person *A* makes statement *S*: person *B* says "It was *C* who told you that, and I happen to know that his mother-in-law is living in sin with a Russian": *A* objects, "The falsity of *S* does not follow from any facts about the morals of *C*'s mother-in-law: that is an *argumentum ad hominem*": *B* may reply "I did not claim that it followed. I simply made a remark about incidentals of the statement's history. Draw what conclusion *you* like. If the cap fits. . . ." (p. 224)

Hamblin's book has provoked various kinds of reaction.[26] In textbooks on logic, initially very little of his criticism of the Standard Treatment can be noticed. In reprints of Copi (1953), Rescher (1964), Carney and Scheer (1964), for example, no attempt was made to deal with Hamblin's objections.[27]

An extreme and unexpected reaction to Hamblin can be found in Lambert and Ulrich (1980). In chapter 3, entitled "Informal Fallacies," the reader will not find a discussion of the informal fallacies but an explanation of why this subject would be better dropped from logic textbooks. Lambert and Ulrich's main reason is that, viewed from a systematic-theoretical perspective, the study of informal fallacies is a futile venture (pp. 24–28). Lambert and Ulrich clarify their drastic step by means of a discussion of the *argumentum ad hominem*, which they define as an attempt to cast doubt on someone's standpoint by bringing that person's reputation into disrepute. They contend that it is impossible to characterize the *argumentum ad hominem* satisfactorily by appealing to its form or to its content. Their general conclusion runs as follows:

> [. . .] until a general characterization of informal fallacies can be given which enables one to tell with respect to any argument whether or not it exhibits one of the informal fallacies, knowing how to label certain paradigm cases of this or that

---

[26]For a critical overview of these reactions see Grootendorst (1987).

[27]Copi states in his Preface to the fourth edition of *Introduction to logic* (1972) that in the chapter on fallacies he made grateful use of Hamblin's critical remarks; however, a closer comparison reveals that, aside from a few minor alterations, Copi strictly adheres to the Standard Treatment.

mistake in reasoning is not really useful for determining whether a given argument is acceptable. (p. 28)

To others, Hamblin's book has been a source of inspiration. Many studies about fallacies refer to his criticism of the Standard Treatment, aiming to develop a better alternative. The post-Hamblin studies differ considerably in their objectives, approaches, methods, emphases, et cetera. Most new theories are still in an embryonic stage, so it is too early to make any balanced judgments. All the same, several interesting developments can be mentioned.

First of all, there is the approach taken by the Canadian logicians John Woods and Douglas Walton. Since 1972, they have made it their task to raise the study of fallacies to a higher level by thoroughly tackling one fallacy after another in a flood of books and articles. Initially, they made mainly use of the theoretical apparatus of their own discipline: logic. Later they were also influenced by pragmatic views, which is particularly apparent in Walton's work.[28] (The Woods-Walton approach is further discussed in chapter 8.)

The second approach to fallacies to be mentioned here is "pragma-dialectics." Inspired by Barth and Krabbe's "formal dialectics" (see chapter 9), the Dutch discourse and argumentation theorists Frans van Eemeren and Rob Grootendorst developed this approach in the early eighties. In pragma-dialectics, a fallacy is defined as a speech act that constitutes a violation of one or more rules for critical discussion, thereby jeopardizing the resolution of a difference of opinion. (The pragma-dialectical approach to fallacies, is treated in more detail in chapter 10.)

A third—and final—renovation we should mention is the recent development of an "epistemic approach" to the fallacies by the American philosophers John Biro and Harvey Siegel. In "Normativity, argumentation and an epistemic theory of fallacies" Biro and Siegel (1992) define the fallacies as epistemic failures of rationality. (The epistemic approach is still in a programmatic state; we shall come briefly back to it in chapter 6.)

3.3 CRAWSHAY-WILLIAMS' ANALYSIS OF CONTROVERSY

An original, though somewhat underestimated, early contributor to the study of argumentation is the British philosopher Rupert Crawshay-Williams (1908–1977).[29] Crawshay-Williams moved in the intellectual milieu of his friend Bertrand

---

[28]The pragmatic turn in Walton's work took place around 1985 with the publication of his book *Arguer's position*. In their discussion of Walton (1987), van Eemeren and Grootendorst (1989) call attention to this shift in Walton's position.

[29]Among those who recognized the importance of Crawshay-Williams' insights to the study of argumentation are Olbrechts-Tyteca (1963), Johnstone, Jr. (1968), and Barth (1974).

Russell, and his publications refer frequently to the affinity between their ideas.[30] After having acquired the reputation of a leading reviewer of gramophone records in the 1930s, in 1947 he published *The Comforts of Unreason*, a brilliantly entertaining study of the motives behind irrational thought, in which attention is paid to "paralogisms" and other fallacies. His main theoretical contribution to the study of argumentation is *Methods and Criteria of Reasoning; An Inquiry into the Structure of Controversy* (1957).[31]

Throughout his work, Crawshay-Williams pays a great deal of attention to verbal misunderstandings as a source of controversy. Under the influence of C.K. Ogden and I.A. Richards, he puts strong emphasis on the role of language in discussions directed towards the resolution of differences of opinion. In *Methods and Criteria of Reasoning*, Crawshay-Williams defines the subject of his investigation as follows:

> This book enquires how we use language as an instrument of reason, and whether our present use of it is efficient. (p. 3)

In the final chapter, he gives a characterization of what he had in mind:

> Indeed I could almost have called it an Introduction to the Theory of Logic and Rhetoric if I could have ensured that the word "logic" would be interpreted not in its specialist (formal deduction) sense but in the lay sense, and the word "rhetoric" *vice versa*, not in the lay sense but in the specialist sense, used by I.A. Richards, of "a persistent, systematic, detailed inquiry into how words work . . . , a study of misunderstanding and its remedies." (p. 261)

Crawshay-Williams starts out from the problem of how controversies come about in a discussion. More in particular, he wants to find out "why certain kinds of theoretical and philosophical controversy are so oddly intractable" (p. 3). Why can such disagreements not always be resolved?

If there is agreement between the defender and the attacker of a given opinion as to the *criteria* according to which the statement concerned is to be tested, says Crawshay-Williams, then it ought not to take long to decide either that (1) the statement is true or false, or that (2) the statement is probably true or probably false, or that (3) it is impossible to determine whether it is true or false because there is not, or not yet, enough evidence available. Very often, however, the disputants cannot reach agreement on one of these conclusions. According to Crawshay-Williams, this is to be explained by their lack of agree-

---

[30]Crawshay-Williams (1970) records their relationship affectionately in *Russell remembered*.

[31]Some of Crawshay-Williams' most significant ideas can already be found in his earlier publications (1946, 1947, 1948, 1951). Cf. also Crawshay-Williams (1968). After his death, he left behind the virtually completed manuscript for a book, *The directive function of language*, which is still unpublished.

ment as to the criteria by which the statement must be tested, and to their failure to realize that this is the point where they disagree. In such a case, there is a fundamental misunderstanding.

Discussions are, as a rule, conducted between two or more members of a group of people which Crawshay-Williams calls a *company*. In order to resolve disagreements between the members of a company about a particular statement, there are three sorts of criteria available: (1) logical criteria, (2) conventional criteria, and (3) empirical criteria.

Logical criteria have to do with the rules for valid reasoning and good argument that are, explicitly or implicitly, accepted by the company.

When using a *conventional* criterion, the interlocutors appeal to other statements about which the company is agreed. This agreement may have been created by accepting definitions, by establishing procedures, or by negotiation. The conventional criteria include, in Crawshay-Williams' (1957) view, also rules that the company implicitly accepts as taken for granted (p. 10). An example of a conventional rule that is generally tacitly accepted in a discussion is that words must not be used in meanings that deviate from common usage in the company. Another example is the logical principle that a statement cannot be simultaneously true and false. As Crawshay-Williams emphasizes, it should be noted that the following rider pertains to implicit conventional criteria:

> Conventions which are not explicit can of course act effectively as criteria only while they remain unanimously accepted in a given company. (p. 11)

For example, in a meeting one may want to assert that the vote which has just been taken is invalid because of a lack of quorum. In order to do so effectively, however, it is required that the company assembled assumes that a valid vote needs a quorum; moreover, it should be possible to back up the prevailing meaning of the term "quorum" by reference to the statutes or to standing orders.

Empirical criteria relate to empirical statements; they are, therefore, not relevant to discussions about other kinds of statement. Empirical criteria comprise an *objective* criterion and a *contextual* criterion (Crawshay-Williams, 1957, pp. 34–36). The objective criterion is that the statement must be in accordance with the facts. The contextual criterion is that the way in which the facts are described must be in accordance with the *purpose* of the statement.

The subject and the predicate of an empirical statement must, according to Crawshay-Williams, always be related to each other with a view to a particular purpose. Because of this inherent connection with a certain purpose, he considers every empirical statement as a *methodological* statement (pp. 5–7).[32] The statement "S is P" is equivalent to the statement "S is P with a view to *purpose*

---

[32]In using the words "method" and "methodology," Crawshay-Williams refers to their "lay" meaning of "the way in which."

M" and, therefore, amounts to the methodological statement "In connection with purpose M it is a good *method* to regard S as something which is commonly known as P."[33]

The purpose of an empirical statement constitutes to Crawshay-Williams (1957) the *context* of that statement:[34]

> I am afraid I must continue to use the words "purpose" and "context" somewhat indiscriminately. As can be seen, what I really need is a word which would cover the range of both notions. (p. 32)

According to Crawshay-Williams, it is only possible to determine whether an empirical statement is true or false if the context of the statement is known. A difference of opinion as to its truth can never be resolved merely by looking at "the facts," that is by applying the objective criterion on its own. It is always necessary to look also at the purpose for which these facts are described. In other words, the contextual criterion must also be applied. Together, the objective criterion and the contextual criterion constitute the *empirical* criterion. This empirical criterion can now be formulated as follows: "Are the facts such that in connection with the context concerned we may say that the statement 'S is P' is correct?"

In practice, the context of a statement is often left unexpressed. In Crawshay-Williams' (1957) opinion, this is one of the main reasons why fundamental misunderstandings arise and discussions fail. Statements whose context has not been expressed and remains obscure to those concerned he calls *indeterminate statements* (pp. 14–17). Here are some examples:

(1) Mozart's music comprises fourteen periods.
(2) A language is a set of sentences.
(3) Neuroses arise through a disturbance of the normal control apparatus.

In order to clear up misunderstandings, Crawshay-Williams provides in *Methods and Criteria of Reasoning* an analysis of discussions concerning indeterminate statements. The misleading aspect of such statements is, in his opinion, that they seem to suggest that one need only look at "the facts" to see whether they are true. In a discussion about an indeterminate statement, those participants who believe that the discussion can be decided by applying the objective criterion are often victims of this suggestion. In spite of adducing all sort of facts

---

[33]Often the form of an empirical statement is more complicated than would appear from "S is P": Some statements, such as "London is bigger than Amsterdam," express more complicated relations. Crawshay-Williams' analysis can be so adapted that such statements can also be formulated "methodologically."

[34]In using the term "context" in this specific way, Crawshay-Williams gives the word "context" a more pronounced meaning than it generally has.

that they suppose to corroborate the disputed statement, they do not succeed in resolving the difference of opinion. A way out of the impasse can only be found if they realize that the discussion parties may be assuming *different contexts* for the statement.

Crawshay-Williams (1957) explains that disagreement about an indeterminate statement can be resolved only if the statement is first made *determinate*: each of the parties must make explicit which context it has in mind. He demonstrates this with the following example:

> Mr. Brown is a schoolmaster standing in a field near to a white line marked on the ground. Jones and Smith are two schoolboys rapidly approaching him from the same direction. Jones crosses the white line at 3:45 p.m. and Smith crosses it half a second later. This, then, is the situation and these are often called "the objective facts." Now how are we going to describe these facts? Are we going to say that Jones and Smith arrived at the same time or are we going to say that they arrived at different times? (p. 22)

The correct answer to this question depends on the purpose the schoolmaster had in mind when he gave the two boys instructions to come to him. If he had only called to them because he wanted them to get him a deck chair, then the obvious thing would be to say that they had arrived *at the same time*. If, on the other hand, he had instructed them to run a race, then one would say that they had *not* arrived at the same time. Thus both the statement "The boys reached the master at the same time" and the statement "The boys did not reach the master at the same time" may be true.

According to Crawshay-Williams, these two empirical statements only *seem* contradictory: in reality, they are complementary. The reason why this is not immediately evident is that in the present form they are indeterminate: the purpose for which they are made has not been indicated. When each statement's purpose is explicitly formulated, it turns out that the statements, instead of being contradictory, complement each other:

(4a) *Statement 1 in indeterminate form:*
The boys reached the master at the same time.

(4b) *Statement 1 in determinate form:*
Viewed with the purpose of comparing the times of arrival to establish whether the boys came as soon as they were called by the master, the boys reached the master at the same time.

(5a) *Statement 2 in indeterminate form:*
The boys did not reach the master at the same time.

(5b) *Statement 2 in determinate form:*
Viewed with the purpose of comparing the times of arrival to establish who has won the race, the boys did not reach the master at the same time.

An obvious objection to this analysis of the example is that "strictly speaking," "in fact," or "in reality," the boys did not reach the master at the same time, since a stopwatch would show a difference of half a second. Such an objection, says Crawshay-Williams, fails to distinguish between *correctness* and *precision* (pp. 111–113). The difference between the two can, again, be illustrated with the help of an example.

Suppose a curtainbuyer measures a window and says it is two meters high, and a carpenter measures the same window and says it is 2.02 meters high. Is the carpenter's description then "really" correct and the curtainbuyer's not? No, the carpenter's description is only more precise (as it should be, for the carpenter's purposes). It is not so that the carpenter's description is "really" correct because it is precise, for it could always be made more precise. Along these lines, even the most precise description available would not "really" be correct: New and better measuring tools would enable us to make the description again more precise, *ad infinitum*.

According to Crawshay-Williams, a description is "correct" if its degree of precision is appropriate to its purpose. Anybody who raises the objection that the curtainbuyer did "not really" determine the measure of the window—or that the boys did "not really" reach the master at the same time—commits the error of making all possible contexts subordinate to a single context: one in which a difference of two millimeters—or half a second—is significant. Thus the objector's own context is declared the *universal* context.

A major source of misunderstanding, says Crawshay-Williams, is to suppose one's own context to equal the universal context, without realizing that the interlocutors have different contexts in mind. This occurs in the following example of a company of people discussing the question of what a language is. One of the interlocutors says:

(6) A language is a set of sentences.

An interlocutor says:

(7) Not so: A language is a means of revealing and unfolding our humanity.

Both interlocutors behave as though their statements are true in a universal context. They therefore find themselves in a disagreement that cannot be resolved by a discussion. To save the discussion, the disputants must make their statements determinate by indicating *in what context* they allocate their preferred predicates to the subject "language." The determinate form of (6) might then look like this:

(6a) In order to study the structure of language, it is a good method to look upon a language as a set of sentences.

In this form, the *methodological* character of the statement is made clear. The context of (6) has now been made explicit, and the statement has thus become determinate.[35] With a little more trouble, the context of (7), too, could be ascertained and formulated, so that the present misunderstanding, and perhaps also the difference of opinion, may be eliminated.

More obstinate problems arise if the discussion is about a *nonempirical* statement. In that case, even though the parties may have indicated the context of their statements, the discussion cannot be decided by looking at the "facts." The empirical criterion is then useless. To what extent can logical and conventional criteria provide the solution?

Crawshay-Williams tackles this question by reference to an example. A company of people are discussing the following question:

(8) Can ethical statements be true or false?

One of the parties answers this question in the negative, advancing the following argument:

(9) a Statements in which no facts are expressed cannot be true or false.
    and
  b In ethical statements no facts are expressed.
    Therefore:
  c Ethical statements cannot be true or false.

The other party answers the question in the affirmative, justifying this by the following argument:

(10) a Ethical statements can be confirmed and denied with the words "true" and "false" respectively; for example: "it is true that peace is good."
    and
  b Statements that can be confirmed and denied with the words "true" and "false" can be true or false.
    Therefore:
  c Ethical statements can be true or false.

---

[35]Cf. the elucidation of the context of the statement "A language is a set of sentences" provided by the grammarians De Haan, Koefoed and Des Tombe (1974): "This postulate may appear banal, but one might equally well have chosen another. For example, language is the medium through which people can communicate [...]. The difference is that the postulate chosen focuses all attention on the form of a language [...], not on what is done with it" (p. 3). It is apparent that these authors do not regard their context as the universal context.

Both argument (9) and argument (10) are valid, so that logical criteria are of no help in resolving the difference of opinion regarding (8). The parties could now start talking about the premises of the arguments, but that would probably not take them much further, since they cannot easily be tested with the help of empirical criteria. If new arguments were put up for (9a), (9b), (10a), or (10b) the discussion would transfer itself to the premises of these new arguments.

In other words, the parties are left with no alternative but to try to reach agreement on (8) by means of the conventional criteria. That is, they will have to negotiate agreements on the meanings in which they are going to use the terms "ethical statement," "true," and "false." In order to resolve the problem, they might decide to define these terms in such a way that either conclusion (9c) or conclusion (10c) is made into an *analytic statement*, which is necessarily true. Crawshay-Williams warns that the parties are not to arrive at some arbitrary decision with regard to the meanings of the terms. As in the case of the empirical criterion, this decision must be based on *contextual* considerations.

The subject of discussion is now no longer (8), but (11):

> (11) Is it sensible to treat ethical statements as statements which can be true or false?

Because, in this formulation, the context has not been indicated, the question is still indeterminate. If the parties go on to formulate the context explicitly, they may then decide, on the grounds of the purpose of (11), whether they wish to regard (9c) as an analytic statement or (10c).

In discussions that cannot be decided by applying empirical or logical criteria, the parties can thus try to resolve their problems by means of conventional criteria. Crawshay-Williams regards it as being of fundamental importance that a sharp distinction be made between, on the one hand, the creation of a convention (agreement, law) when the members of a company come to a decision or a negotiated consensus, and, on the other hand, the contextual considerations of a methodological kind underlying and justifying the decision or the consensus.

Crawshay-Williams (1957) believes that, ultimately, logical rules and laws, too, are valid because they are accepted as such by the members of a company, whether on the basis of an explicit agreement or tacitly:[36]

> The only rules of logical deduction which are formally valid are those which are *accepted* as formally valid. (p. 175)

The fact that logical rules and laws are accepted by the company invests them with conventional validity. This, however, is not enough: they must be rules and laws that have "methodological necessity." According to Crawshay-Williams, the

---

[36]Although, in this respect, logical rules and laws resemble statements like (6) and (9c), the difference remains, of course, that they relate to nondescriptive terms, whereas statements like (6) and (9) are descriptive.

company's decision to confer on them the conventional status of a logical rule or law must be based on contextual considerations of a methodological kind, just like the definitions of the terms "ethical statement," "true," and "false" in (8). Take the fundamental logical principle known as the *law of noncontradiction*:

> (12) No statement can be simultaneously true and false.

The validity of this law depends not only on its explicit or tacit acceptance by the company that makes use of it, but also on its methodological necessity. In fact, the methodological reasons for accepting the law of noncontradiction invest it with its status as a logical law. A "methodological formulation" of (12) might look like this:

> (12a) In order to be able to speak about the world without getting tied up in knots, it is a good method not to treat any statement whatever as simultaneously true and false.

Without any methodological considerations, there would be no reason for the company to accept a given rule as a logical law. Crawshay-Williams (1957) makes clear why this is so by reference to the *law of identity*:

> The law of identity, for example, seems to assert something which no one but a madman could conceivably doubt: if A is not A, then we will all eat our hats in despair. But, of course, the reason why A *simply must* be A is that thinking and communicating by means of symbols would be impracticable otherwise. If we had no wish to think or communicate at all, the reason would disappear. (p. 224)

When told that he or she *must* accept a particular rule as "necessarily true," a skeptic listening to the methodological considerations which have led the company to accept the law can, according to Crawshay-Williams (1957), always say:

> That is perhaps a good reason for your saying that I would be *well-advised* to treat it so. But it still does not explain why you use the word "must." Who *says* I must? (p. 225)

The only possible reply to this is:

> Clearly, it is we—the company concerned—who say it. (p. 225)

Logical validity, then, depends in Crawshay-Williams' view both on the negotiated agreements in a company and on the methodological considerations underlying those agreements. It has, in other words, both a conventional and a contextual basis.[37] When seen in this perspective, general criteria of rationality

---

[37]In contrast to the conventionalist view that logical validity is a matter of agreements about usage, the concept of validity defended here is not arbitrary. Cf. Kneale & Kneale (1962, Ch. X.5).

always rest on two foundations: they must have an "intersubjective" conventional basis and an "objective" contextual basis. It is this clear revelation of the dual basis of rationality criteria that makes *Methods and Criteria of Reasoning* such an important contribution to the fundamentals of argumentation theory.[38]

3.4 NAESS ON CLARIFYING DISCUSSIONS

The Norwegian philosopher Arne Naess, born in 1912, has recurrently paid attention to argumentation and argumentation theory throughout his work. Naess' approach to argumentation is semantic and empirical, stemming from his philosophical attitude. He has the attitude of a skeptic who wishes to bring conceptual and philosophical clarification to existing disagreements, without regarding any particular starting point as *a priori* evident or necessary.

According to Barth (1978, p. 155), Naess has developed from an "anti-apriorist," who took a stand against fixed starting points, into an "a-apriorist," who does not himself use any fixed starting points, not even an anti-apriorist one. Initially, his skepticism was the equivalent of antidogmatism. Now it may be equated with a refusal to commit oneself to particular standpoints in abstract philosophical matters, this refusal leading to an attitude of constant interrogation and searching. Naess' attitude is superbly illustrated by the following passage from a discussion with the British philosopher A. J. Ayer (NOS Dutch television, 1971):

Naess: Up to now a cigarette has always burned when you lit it. The floor never caved in. Food stilled your hunger. But can you deduce from that that things will still be the same in the future? It remains a circular argument, based on something that cannot be proved. A lot of philosophy is looking for answers to questions like that.

The significance of Naess' philosophical attitude and his empirical semantic insights for the study of argumentation is clearly expressed in his article "How can the empirical movement be promoted today? A discussion of the empiricism of Otto Neurath and Rudolph [*sic*] Carnap":[39]

Let us assume that there is some difference of opinion among psychologists and that they want to settle the matter through discussion. A spokesman for [...]

---

[38]Crawshay-Williams' influence on theoretical thinking about argumentation can be clearly noticed in Barth and Krabbe (1982), van Eemeren and Grootendorst (1984, 1992a), and van Eemeren, Grootendorst, Jackson, and Jacobs (1993). For reviews of *Methods and criteria*, see Johnstone, Jr. (1957–1958, 1958–1959), Simmons (1959), Lazerowitz (1958–1959), Eveling (1959), Rescher (1959), and Hardin (1960).

[39]Carnap's first name is misspelt: it is, in fact, Rudolf. Originally, this paper was written in 1937–1939, but important comments were added in 1956 when a German version was made accessible as a mimeographed reprint.

philosophical clarification [. . .] suggests to the participants that they should tentatively adopt certain rules as a technique of discussion and exposition. One of these rules could go as follows:

When a participant makes a statement A whereas someone else states *non-A* and it is unclear in what the difference consists, then both participants are to indicate the conditions—which it must be possible to realize in a research process—under which they would regard A as verified (or corroborated) resp. falsified (weakened). If both would be of the opinion that there are no such conditions, then this is to count as an indication that neither a continuation of the discussion nor additional research would contribute to the elimination of the verbal difference of opinion among them. At the same time it would count as an indication that their verbal disagreement is not connected with any more-than-verbal (*sachliche*) difference of opinion. (Naess, 1992b, p. 140)

Naess goes on to say that the spokesman for philosophical clarification must not act as a "judge," but as a "broker" and a "middleman": this intermediary would have to recommend guidelines for an effective discussion, and these would have to turn out differently depending on the circumstances. Instead of logical-empiricist, pragmatical, or operationalist meaning criteria, "series of discussion models for various situations would emerge" (*loc. cit.*). In this clarificatory work, the views of the broker on the question of what sorts of statement can justly claim to be knowledge would not have to be involved as criteria for evaluation. In other words, his views on cognitive meaningfulness, or regarding the relation between cognitive meaningfulness and testability, need not play a part. According to Naess (1992b), "the aim is to unburden the task philosophically and to soften down the pretensions connected with it." Otherwise, the fact is disguised that "more or less expedient rules for discussion and exposition are quite something else than general criteria for cognitive meaning." (p. 141)

It is conspicuous that Naess takes a disagreement in a discussion as his starting point. The argumentation theorist must not blow up his own yardsticks—for example, particular criteria of meaningfulness—into a single all-embracing criterion. He must confine himself to giving "more or less effective rules for debating and formulating." These rules may vary, depending on the circumstances.

Discussion, or debate, is regarded by Naess (1992b) as a "dialectic" amounting to a form of "systematic intersubjective verbal communication" (p. 138). This verbal communication must be conducted in accordance with certain discussion rules, procedural as well as material. The aim of a dialectic is in the first place to clear up misunderstandings and in the second place to prepare individual standpoints for testing:[40]

In order to characterize what I mean, the word "dialectic" might be preferable, whereby one will have to distinguish between eristics (rhetoric) and dialectics,

---

[40]Naess (1992b) was particularly interested in eliminating nonempirical formulations by way of discussion (p. 111).

between sophistics and philosophical investigation, roughly in the way Aristotle and Plato did. The debate or dialectic constitutes in my terminology a part of the scientific process, namely a systematic intersubjective verbal communication, whereby misunderstandings are eliminated and the various standpoints undergo the necessary precization (*Präzisierung*) so that recommendations for research programs may be subjected to testing. (p. 138)[41]

The dialectic envisaged by Naess is close to classical dialectic:

Understood in this way the *philosophical dialectic* (*dialektikè*) seems to me to be today a new edition [. . .] of the classical dialogue (*dialogos*) in so far as this was [. . .] a method for the joint labor of several philosophers. (p. 138)

In *Interpretation and Preciseness*, published in 1953, Naess fought back against "armchair semantics" as practiced at Oxford (and elsewhere) by developing an *empirical semantics*. He reveals himself to be a radical empiricist, and prefers methods from the social sciences, such as questionnaires and personal interviews, for investigating what is understood by particular expressions in particular circles. The empirical research Naess wants to be carried out is designed to lead to a more precise determination of the statements about which disagreements exist.

Before a disagreement can be resolved, misunderstandings have to be eliminated. In *Communication and Argument*, Naess (1966) therefore provides rules for clearing up misunderstandings.[42] The subject of this book is interpretation, clarification, and argumentation. It is designed chiefly to function as an aid in discussions as they occur in practice, or in their analysis.[43]

One of the central theses of *Communication and Argument* maintains that misunderstandings in a discussion can be eliminated by the participants by *clarifying* or—as Naess (1966, p. 38) calls it—*precizating* their statements. Since "precization" makes use of a domain of possible interpretations of an expression,

---

[41]In English there are no direct translations available for the German noun *Präzisierung* (Norwegian: *presisering*) and the verb *präzisieren*, which are crucial in Naess' work. Taking up a suggestion by Barth in her translations of Naess (1992a, 1992b), we shall make use of two neologisms: (1) *to precizate an utterance or a formulation* means: to make it more precise by replacing it by an utterance of another formulation which eliminates some reasonable interpretations without adding new ones, (2) *a precization (of an utterance or a formulation)* means the outcome of a precizating operation, as well as the operation itself.

[42]*Communication and argument* is the English translation, published in 1966, of a work mimeographed copies of which first appeared in 1941 in Norwegian, *Om meningsytring; En del elementaere logiske emner* (On the expression of opinions: some elementary subjects in logic.) Several editions with the title *En del elementaere logiske emner* have appeared since Naess (1947).

[43]All the same, *Communication and argument* also introduces some useful theoretical insights. After the publication of this book, Naess has only seldom participated in the discussion among argumentation theorists. See, for instance, Naess (1993).

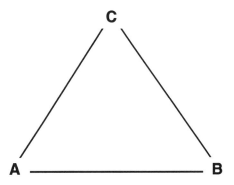

A-entities = linguistic expressions: words, terms, sentences ('formulations')
C-entities = conceptual entities: concepts and statements (propositions)
              expressed in words, terms, or sentences
B-entities = real world entities: objects and states of affairs which are
              referred to by words, terms or sentences

FIG. 3.1. The sign triangle.

it is necessary to explain first how Naess understands the term "interpretation."
He elucidates this concept by reference to the distinction between sentences,
statements, and states of affairs, which was developed by the Stoa (p. 13). This
distinction is often illustrated with the help of the "sign triangle" (see Fig. 3.1).

According to Naess, to interpret is to assign a statement (proposition) to a
sentence ("formulation"). Suppose the sentence uttered is "He came home at 2
o'clock." To this sentence we can either assign a statement to the effect that he
came home at 2 o'clock in the morning, or the statement to the effect that he
came home at 2 o'clock in the afternoon. In either case we interpret the original
sentence. But, because we do not have direct access to C-entities, the statements
we assign to the original sentence must, in turn, themselves be cast in words
(A-entities). That is why Naess, as we shall see, defined the term "interpretation"
so as to refer to A-entities and not to C-entities. Moreover, interpretation is not
a casual, random affair: it takes place in a particular context of (or in relation
to) speaker, listener, and circumstances. This approach too, must be borne out
by the definition of "interpretation."

Naess (1966) suggests the following definition of interpretation: *Sentence U is
an interpretation of sentence T* means the same as *in at least one context, U can*

express the same statement as T (p. 28). Two remarks are in order. First, "reasonable" interpretations, in a given context, must be distinguished from "unreasonable" interpretations. Naess is aware of this and attempts to elucidate the notion of reasonableness in terms of frequency of occurrence in real or imaginable contexts. We cannot describe this attempt here any further, but it is important to note that "reasonableness" admits to having gradations and is, therefore, to be preferred to a notion, such as "correctness," with absolutist connotations (pp. 31–32). Second, in many cases a particular part of a sentence determines differences in the interpretation of the sentence as a whole. In our example, the difference depends on the words "2 o'clock." In order to deal with such complications, Naess (1966, p. 34) provides a second definition of interpretation: *to say that term b is an interpretation of term a means that if b is substituted for a in a sentence T_0, the result will be a sentence T_1 that gives us an interpretation of T_0.*

Inasmuch as real disagreements relate not to sentences but to the statements they express, the interlocutors must ensure that they allocate the right statements to the sentences they use to avoid misunderstandings in a discussion or debate. If the interlocutors have reason to believe that they are not allocating the right statement to a sentence, then they must request, and provide, *precizations.*

Naess (1966, p. 42) points out that precizations should not be confused with *specifications*. A sentence U specifies another sentence T, if U asserts what T asserts but at the same time asserts something *more* about the same subject matter. Unlike a precization, a specification does not add information that serves to identify what is being asserted (i.e., to enable one to know whether to accept or reject the assertion), but merely adds to an assertion that has already been identified.[44]

Naess (1966, p. 39) suggests that precization be defined as follows: *The sentence U is a precization of the sentence T means the same as there is at least one reasonable interpretation of T which is not a reasonable interpretation of U, but there is no reasonable interpretation of U which is not also a reasonable interpretation of T.* A precization is a limitation on the number of statements which may be allocated to a sentence:

---

[44]Depending on the context, a specification for some, may be a precization for others. "She is walking away," for example, may be a specification of "She is leaving us." To those, however, who are tempted to interpret "She is leaving us" as saying that she is dying, "She is walking away" may be purely a precization of "She is leaving us." Although all reasonable interpretations of "She is walking away" are reasonable interpretations of "She is leaving us," "She is leaving us" has at least this one reasonable interpretation of "She is dying" that "She is walking away" has not. "She is walking away" can therefore be seen as a limitation on the number of interpretations which may be allocated to the sentence "She is leaving us," and serves then as a precization.

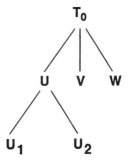

T_0 = sentence serving as point of departure
U, V, W   = interpretation of T_0
U_1 , U_2 = interpretation of U and T_0

FIG. 3.2. U as a precization of T_0.

In Fig. 3.2, V and W are reasonable interpretations of T_0, but not of U. U itself is
a reasonable interpretation of T_0. U_1 and U_2 are reasonable interpretations of U,
but also of T_0. Therefore U is a precization of T_0.

Naess (1966, p. 39) points out that "U is more precise than T" means the same
as "U is a precization of T." From this, it will be apparent that precization is not
an absolute but a comparative concept. Naess also observes that his definition
suppresses two variables that a full definition should contain: one of these
concerns the person for whom the precization is intended and the other concerns the general background of the discussion: *U is more precise than T for a*
person X in context Y.

It is not Naess' intention that the participants in a discussion should continually precizate their expressions or be as precise as would theoretically be
possible; discussion would then become a practical impossibility. Precization
must only take place when there is a need for it: where the disagreement relates
(or may relate) to the fact that different statements might be assigned to the
same sentence. Since in that case the interlocutors have different statements in
mind when they confront the same sentence, there is a merely *verbal* disagreement, no real disagreement. Verbal disagreement makes it impossible to weigh
standpoints against each other.

If a disagreement is (or has become) a *real* disagreement, then the standpoints can, and must, be weighed against each other. In developing a method
for doing this, Naess starts from the dialectical idea that it is important to
establish which standpoint is more *acceptable* than the other (or others). Just
like precization, "acceptability" is a comparative concept: To a person X, or a
group of people X, standpoint T_1 is more acceptable than standpoint T_2.

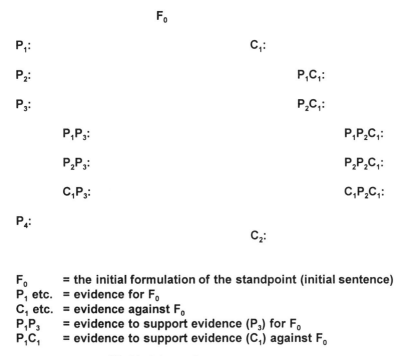

F_0 = the initial formulation of the standpoint (initial sentence)
P_1 etc. = evidence for F_0
C_1 etc. = evidence against F_0
P_1P_3 = evidence to support evidence (P_3) for F_0
P_1C_1 = evidence to support evidence (C_1) against F_0

FIG. 3.3. Scheme of a pro-et-contra survey.

In order to determine which of two conflicting standpoints is the more acceptable, it is necessary to examine both the evidence for and the evidence against those standpoints.[45] Here the link between Naess' thinking and classical dialectic becomes even clearer. In Naess' practical method for evaluating individual standpoints the pieces of evidence both for and against a standpoint are weighed up. In order to acquire proficiency in examinations of this kind, Naess recommends doing exercises in compiling surveys of the available evidence. He differentiates between two sorts of survey: a "*pro-et-contra* survey" and a "*pro-aut-contra* survey."

A *pro-et-contra* survey sums up the most important pieces of evidence that have been advanced, or may be advanced, both in favor of (*pro*) and against (*contra*) a standpoint. All this type of survey contains is what the interlocutors regard as counting for or against a certain standpoint. The dispute is then still undecided, so the survey does not include a conclusion. A *pro-et-contra* survey

---

[45]In this connection, Naess (1966, p. 101) refers to the Greek philosopher Carneades (c. 214–129 B.C.), who believed that there is always something to be said for and against an opinion. According to Naess, absolute certainty is not possible, and for assessing an argumentation it is also not necessary.

is always preceded by a sufficiently precise formulation of the standpoint at issue. There is also an indication of the hierarchical structure of the arguments: complex argumentation is broken down into simple arguments. Figure 3.3 is taken from Naess (1966, p. 108) to illustrate this method.

The *pro-et-contra* survey is the basis on which the separate pieces of evidence (each expressed in a sentence) are weighed against each other.[46] The result of this weighing is expressed in the second survey of the evidence, the *pro-aut-contra* survey (for-or-against survey). This survey contains the evidence which *its compiler regards as* counting in favor of a standpoint or against the standpoint. The standpoint in question is the compiler's conclusion, whether positive of negative, drawn from the evidence. A *pro-aut-contra* survey should not contain any arguments that contradict each other.

Naess pictures a *pro-aut-contra* survey as a tug-of-war between F_0 and not-F_0, the acuteness of the angles in the positions of the various arguments being indicative of the cogency of the arguments: the more cogent an argument is, the more acute the angle.[47] Such a picture is represented in Fig. 3.4.

Whether F_0 wins against not-F_0, that is, whether it is more acceptable than not-F_0, depends on both the "tenability" and the "justifying force" of each piece of evidence on each side.[48] The tenability of a piece of evidence is determined by its truth, correctness, or plausibility. Its justifying force is equal to its *proof potential*, which Naess also calls its *relevance*. Naess (1966, p. 110) gives the following example:

F_0: It will rain tonight.

P_1: The sky is covered with grey clouds.

P_2: The swallows are flying low.

The proof potential of P_1 and P_2 taken together is equal to the certainty of the hypothesis "If the sky is covered with grey clouds and the swallows are flying low, then it will rain tonight."

Naess advises, if possible, to test the tenability of a piece of evidence. As regards proof potential, he distinguishes between *descriptive* theses, in which it is asserted that something is so, and *normative* theses, in which it is asserted that something ought to be so or should be done. In the case of descriptive

---

[46]Especially with public discussions, the compilation of a *pro-et-contra* survey containing *all* the arguments put forward by the parties, including the arguments which are untenable or irrelevant, provides a broad basis for selecting in the *pro-aut-contra* survey the arguments the compiler regards worth considering.

[47]The result of the tugging depending not only on the number of tugs, but also on the effectiveness of the tug-direction, the sharpness of the angles symbolizes the proof potential of the arguments concerned.

[48]The same kind of weighing of evidence for and against will often be required with regard to evidence for evidence, and so on. Thus an intricate web of separate "tugs-of-war" may arise.

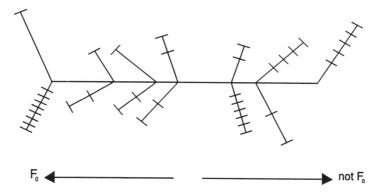

F_0 ←———————   ——————————→ not F_0

FIG. 3.4. The pro-aut-contra survey as a tug-of-war.

theses, the concept of proof potential somewhat resembles that of validity. It is much less stringent, however, if validity is seen as absolute—arguments are either valid or not—and is taken to imply that valid arguments cannot possibly have true premises (the evidence) and a false conclusion (the standpoint) at the same time. Proof potential is, in any case, a comparative concept: A piece of evidence for a descriptive conclusion has more proof potential than another piece of evidence, if the hypothesis that the conclusion is true, given that the first piece of evidence holds, is more certain than the hypothesis that the conclusion is true, given that the second piece of evidence holds.

If the conclusion is normative, the proof potential of the evidence varies in accordance with the desirability of the actualization of the consequences adduced by the evidence. The following example is from Naess (1966, p. 111):

F_0: As long as I study I have to devote all my time to my subject.
      Antithesis: I must set aside some of my working hours for reading poetry.[49]
P_1: I will be earning a steady income a year earlier.
P_2: I shall be a useful member of society a year earlier.
C_1: I shan't be a social success.
C_2: I shall become one-sided.

Each piece of evidence consists of a possible consequence of devoting all one's time to study. So P_1, P_2, et cetera must be understood as hypothetical statements: If I devote all my time to study, I will be earning a steady income a year earlier, and so on. The compiler of this pro-aut-contra survey finds P_1, P_2, C_1 and C_2

---

[49]For the sake of clarity, it is often worthwhile to formulate the alternative of the thesis (F_0) that is being considered: the "antithesis" (not-F_0).

P_1 and P_2, on the one hand, and C_1 and C_2, on the other, depends on the proof potential that, within a particular system of values and norms, can be attributed to the various pieces of evidence. If making money earlier and becoming a useful member of society is regarded more important by the compiler than acquiring a "richer inner life," then P_1 and P_2 have greater cogency to that person than C_1 and C_2.

In practice, the argumentation involved can, of course, be much more complex. One might, for example, have to consider the evidence PP_1 that it would then be possible to buy that nice cottage in the country a year earlier (this enhances the proof potential of P_1), while one might also have to consider the evidence CC_2 that the design of the course of study is itself a guarantee for broad-mindedness (this detracts from the tenability of C_2), and so on.

Besides advice concerning precization, the making of surveys of arguments, and the weighing up of the arguments for and against a standpoint, Naess (1966, pp. 122–132) also provides some rules, or principles, that are designed to promote an adequate exchange of ideas. Among them are—in their "preliminary formulation"—"Keep to the point" and "Do not attribute to your opponent views to which he does not subscribe." Naess precizates these rules according to his own method, and also specifies what counts as a violation of the rules.

The practical significance of *Communication and Argument* for the enhancement of the quality of argumentation is nicely registered by Barth (1978):

> Generations of freshmen at the University of Oslo have had to study this book as prescribed preliminary reading, the only exceptions being dentists and pharmaceutists. For those two professions, and for them alone, verbalized communication was regarded as of secondary significance. (p. 162; our translation)

Naess's influence on the theoretical development of the study of argumentation has been rather limited. Apart from Naess' reviewers Mates (1967) and Johnstone (1968), Barth and Krabbe (1982) and van Eemeren and Grootendorst (1984, 1992a) are about the only argumentation theorists who have explicitly acknowledged the importance of his work.[50]

---

[50]Among the exceptions are the Germans Göttert (1978), Berk (1979), and Öhlschläger (1979).

4

PERELMAN AND OLBRECHTS-TYTECA'S NEW RHETORIC

A highly regarded contribution to the development of a theory of argumentation is made by the Belgian philosopher Chaim Perelman and his compatriot Lucie Olbrechts-Tyteca. Perelman (1912–1984) was professor of logic, ethics and metaphysics at the University of Brussels. Having studied first law and then philosophy, he completed the latter study with a thesis on the German logician Frege. His associate Olbrechts-Tyteca (1900–1987) read social science and economics. They started to do research together into rhetoric and argumentation in 1947.[1]

Perelman and Olbrechts-Tyteca call their theory of argumentation *the new rhetoric*. The idea of developing such a theory was in 1949 announced by Perelman in a lecture. With Olbrechts-Tyteca, he spent 10 years working out this plan. After some programmatic articles and partial studies, in 1958 the two of them published the results of their research in a bulky survey: *La Nouvelle Rhétorique: Traité de l'Argumentation*.[2] (For the reader's convenience, we shall refer to the English translation that appeared in 1969: *The New Rhetoric; A Treatise on Argumentation*).

---

[1]Born in Warsaw, Perelman held his chair in Brussels from 1944 until his death. His argumentation theory is inspired by the Belgian philosopher Eugène Dupréel, whose sociology postulates that social groups form round particular values. Perelman's view of rationality aims to do justice to the diversity of values which characterizes social reality. Together with Dupréel's pupil Olbrechts-Tyteca, he has elaborated this view.

[2]According to Perelman's daughter, Noémi Perelman Mattis, "in their joint work the theoretical armature is entirely Perelman's, the examples were mostly Olbrechts', and they shared the writing." Although devoted friends, "they never let go of a quaint formality in their contacts": after 36 years of collaboration "they still called one another 'Madame Olbrechts' and 'Monsieur Perelman' " (personal recollection, August 12, 1994).

The new rhetoric studies argumentation in ordinary language. It gives a description of sorts of argumentation which can be successful in practice; it is not a normative theory that establishes norms to which the investigators feel argumentation ought to adhere. Methodically, the new rhetoric is in the nature of a phenomenological theory. According to Perelman, it constitutes a reaction to "positivistic empiricism" and "rationalistic idealism" in which important areas of rational thinking, such as legal reasoning, are simply passed by.[3]

During the 1940s Perelman investigated various philosophical questions, particularly concerning the law. His study of the upholding of material law led him to conclude that formal law is possible only if some particular value judgments can be referred to.[4] People can only be treated equally if it is first established what class of people is concerned and what people belong to that class. Certain criteria are required in order to determine whether people are in comparable circumstances; even though they must be as far as possible incorporated into formal rules, ultimately, these criteria are based on value judgments. Value judgments underlying the formal rules might also be that in certain circumstances people cannot entirely or at all be held responsible for their actions and that some people find themselves in a state in which they must be regarded as not responsible for their own actions or that account must be taken of the interests of the defendant as well as those of the community at large when determining the sentence.

According to his own testimony, at this time Perelman adhered to the philosophy of logical empiricism (1970, p. 280). This philosophy did not enable him to account for the use of value judgments. Technically speaking, this meant that they ought to be regarded as unfounded and unjustified.[5] The implication would be that argumentation relying on value judgments is not rational. This implication regarded Perelman as unacceptable: It renders the extremely important concept of a "reasonable decision" meaningless.[6] If the adjectives *rational* and

---

[3]With "positivistic empiricism" Perelman very probably refers to the analytic school of thought generally called logical empiricism or—disregarding any differences—*logical positivism* or *neopositivism*. Logical empiricism is opposed to such philosophical schools as German Idealism and Thomism that believe in a "higher" reality which is by definition inaccessible. It attempts to link the results of empirical research with developments in modern logic, and regards only those statements as cognitively meaningful which relate to the sensorily physical, that is, to things in time and space. According to "rationalism," the only reliable source of knowledge is not experience (as empiricism claims) but reason (or "ratio"). Perelman reacts to a rationalism based on "idealism," that is, one in which reality is reduced to ideas—to what are termed people's "consciousness contents."

[4]Material law is concerned with setting out the citizen's rights and obligations, and lays down regulations. Formal law regulates the manner in which material law is administered.

[5]The problem of deriving "ought" from "is" cannot satisfactorily be solved. For an exposition of this problem, see Searle (1969), and, for a broader discussion, Hudson (1969).

[6]For his distinction between "rational" (the formal applications of rules) and "reasonable" (the use of judgment and common sense), see Perelman (1979b).

reasonable are to be reserved only for statements capable of being verified by empirical observation or of being reached deductively by formal logic, then there is no rational basis for formal law as the systematic application of rules founded on value judgments. Lawyers—like philosophers and other language users—rarely produce perfect formal proof of the theses they advance; rather, they try to *justify* those theses. According to Perelman, such attempts at justification may very well be regarded as rational.[7]

In Perelman's view, argumentation aimed at justification is a rational activity which stands alongside formal argument—it is complementary to it. There is an urgent need of a theory of argumentation that describes the manner in which argumentation takes place—as the complement of formal logic. This theory of argumentation should deal with disputes in which values play a part, disputes that can neither be resolved by empirical verification or formal proof, nor by a combination of the two. The theory would have to show how choices and decisions, once made, can be justified on rational grounds. The new rhetoric of Perelman and Olbrechts-Tyteca is an attempt to create such an argumentation theory.

The method used by Perelman and Olbrechts-Tyteca in developing their argumentation theory is, according to Perelman, very similar to Frege's (1970, p. 281). Frege analyzed mathematical thinking in order to arrive at a theory of logical reasoning. Perelman and Olbrechts-Tyteca investigate philosophical, legal, and other kinds of argumentation in order to arrive at a theory of reasoning with value judgments. Rather than establishing the points of departure and schemes of argumentation *a priori*, they detect them by subjecting cases of successful argument to analysis.

In this endeavor, modern science proved to have few things to offer, but the classical approach to argumentation of Aristotle and his followers has several important similarities to what Perelman and Olbrechts-Tyteca envisaged.[8] This relationship is expressed in the name for their theory, the new *rhetoric*. In

---

[7]This observation led Perelman to seek a logic which makes it possible to argue about values instead of simply letting them depend on irrational choices based on interests, passions, prejudices, and myths. He felt that recent history had provided abundant evidence of what sad excesses can result from the latter attitude. Critical research in existing philosophical literature, however, did not provide a satisfactory solution: "I agreed with the criticisms made by various types of existentialism against both positivist empiricism and rationalistic idealism, but I could find no satisfaction in their justification of action by purely subjective projects or commitments" (1970, p. 281). Instead of elaborating a priori possible structures for a logic of value judgments, Perelman decided to investigate how authors of different schools of thought actually argue about values, in order thus to discover the existing logics of value judgments.

[8]For an autobiographical account of this encounter with classical rhetoric and the development of the new rhetoric, see Olbrechts-Tyteca (1963). Olbrechts-Tyteca also acknowledges Perelman's admiration for C. S. Peirce's ideas concerning a *rhetorica speculativa*, or "objective logic," which studies the transmission of meaning from mind to mind and from one state of mind to another by means of signs.

choosing this name, Perelman and Olbrechts-Tyteca do not react against dialectic: They regard classical rhetoric and dialectic as a single whole. In their view, dialectic is a theory relating to the techniques of argument, rhetoric is a practical discipline indicating how dialectical techniques can be used to convince or persuade people.

In the new rhetoric it is postulated, just as in classical rhetoric, that argumentation is always designed to achieve a particular effect on those for whom it is intended. Thus in both rhetorics the *audience* plays an important part. Arguers unfold their argumentation in order to sway the audience, or to convince them of something. Rhetorically speaking, the soundness of argumentation depends on its success with the audience for whom it is intended.

If argumentation is to have the desired effect, it is very important that the audience should be approached in an effective manner. The techniques used in argumentation must be attuned to the audience's frame of reference. As far as possible, arguers must therefore identify themselves with the audience and make use of existing knowledge, experiences, expectations, opinions, and norms. Perelman and Olbrechts-Tyteca's strong endorsement of this point stamps their theory of argumentation as a rhetorical theory: It is calculated to provide a systematic survey of the knowledge necessary to bring about persuasive effects on the people to whom one addresses oneself in argumentation.

There are also some differences between the new rhetoric and Aristotelian rhetoric. According to Perelman and Olbrechts-Tyteca, the dialectical component of the new rhetoric is so substantial that the theory could also have been called the new *dialectic*. This, however, would have been confusing, as the emphasis in classical dialectic is placed on the parallel with analytic reasoning. Besides, Hegel's later adoption of the term *dialectic*, and the meaning he has given it, might have given rise to serious misunderstandings. There is also a slightly different conception of the object of investigation in the new rhetoric than, say, in Aristotle. Aristotle's rhetoric relates to orations and debates involving large groups of people, or held for a specific purpose, and they are chiefly about political and legal problems. The new rhetoric refers to oral as well as written argumentation, which may be addressed to an audience of any sort and size, and that argumentation can be about any subject whatever.

According to Perelman (1970), the new rhetoric is not merely a theory that describes the practice of nonformal argument. It is also an attempt at creating a framework that unites all forms of "nonanalytic" thinking.[9] A theory of argumentation must make it possible to place different claims to rationality, and a

---

[9]Although Perelman does not define what is meant by "nonanalytic" thinking, it is clear from what he says that he refers to reasoning based on "discursive means of obtaining the adherence of minds" rather than on "the idea of self-evidence" prevailing in modern logic and mathematics.

multiplicity of philosophical systems, in a single theoretical framework. In Perelman's view, the different philosophies are systems of justification for particular ideas. As a rule, philosophers do not offer formal proof of the rightness of their ideas: They try to justify the rationality of those ideas with the help of argumentation. Claiming rationality is not the same as proclaiming the only, ultimate truth, and it should therefore not be equated with it.

Claiming rationality always means claiming the approbation of people—not just of arbitrary people, but of the *ideal* audience. This ideal audience is not an existing reality: It is a thought-construct of the arguer. The ideal audience will look different to different people. The picture people have of the ideal audience will hang together with the historical circumstances in which they find themselves. Some may imagine it as a certain elite corps (e.g., "the forum of scientific researchers"), others might have an overall picture of "the reasonable human being." No existing audience constitutes a generally recognized body for evaluating nonanalytic argument.

A person that claims rationality will have to use argumentation to convince others that this claim is justified. This also applies to the philosopher. In principle, it is the philosopher's own choice which audience he or she wishes to convince with the argumentation. Depending on the philosopher, the choice may be different: One will wish to convince the adherents of a particular school of thought or a few recognized specialists, another will want to convince humanity as a whole. The same goes, *mutatis mutandis*, for other thinkers, such as lawyers. Always, however, is argumentation in *nonanalytic* thinking directed towards convincing people. The new rhetoric is designed to do justice to this essential characteristic. Nonanalytic thinking is, in all its variety, submitted to an analysis, in order to bring about a synthesis between the seemingly conflicting claims different thinkers (and representatives of different thought systems) make to rationality.

Because of the correspondence of soundness criterion for argumentation between the new rhetoric and classical rhetoric, they are open to the same kinds of criticism (cf. chapter 2). Perelman and Olbrechts-Tyteca counter the Platonist criticism of a lacking guarantee for quality by pointing out that arguers are, in principle, free to determine what audience they wish to convince. Thus all arguers can decide themselves what audience they wish to be their norm. If a given audience is regarded as being of insufficient quality, it can always be replaced by another considered more authoritative. Therefore, the criticism of the rhetorical criterion of soundness is, in Perelman and Olbrechts-Tyteca's opinion, no fundamental criticism of the soundness norm, but criticism of a particular choice of a particular audience that is claimed to be universal. In their view, the quality required of argumentation in order to be acceptable, is always a function of the quality of the audience that carries out the evaluation. This relation of dependence is in the criticism of rhetoric not profoundly taken into account.

4.1   THE RHETORICAL FRAMEWORK

Perelman and Olbrechts-Tyteca (1969) define the new rhetoric as "the study of the discursive techniques allowing us *to induce or to increase the mind's adherence to the theses presented for its assent*" (p. 4). The purpose of their research is to give a systematic description of those techniques.

As approval is always connected with people, theses that are approved by one person may not be approved by another, and approval can vary in intensity. Argumentation may make a thesis wholly acceptable, but it may also make it *more* acceptable—it is a matter of degree. A person can agree with something "a hundred percent," but may also agree with it "up to a point." The measure of approval depends on the value judgments of the evaluating audience. That is why the description of argumentation in the new rhetoric starts from the audience.

In the deductions called "valid" in formal logic there is an analytic connection between the premises advanced and the conclusion of the argument. The cogency of the argument depends on it being compelling to anyone who accepts the formal system concerned. Argumentation in ordinary language, say Perelman and Olbrechts-Tyteca, is never immediately compelling. In principle, the symbols used—words and sentences—are polysemous, and the totality of premises may make the conclusion (to a greater or lesser degree) acceptable. There is no question of validity, but of plausibility. The crucial difference between the new rhetoric and formal logic is that in the former the decision as to the soundness of argumentation rests with the audience for which it is intended, while in the latter the criteria for assessing an argument are defined independently of the evaluator.

The concept of an *audience*, crucial to the new rhetoric, Perelman and Olbrechts-Tyteca define as follows: "*An audience is the ensemble of those whom the speaker wishes to influence by his argumentation*" (1969, p. 19). It is important to bear in mind that the picture that speakers (or writers) have formed of their audience is always a construction of their own making. It is the totality of opinions, systematized to a greater or lesser degree, the arguers have formed about the persons they wish to influence with their argumentation.

For argumentation to be successful, the arguer's picture of the audience must as far as possible accord with reality. It is therefore a condition of sound—that is, in this context, effective—argumentation that arguers are in possession of the necessary knowledge concerning those whom the argumentation is to influence, so that they can take advantage of it in the argumentation. The trouble is that in all sorts of ways the audience may be of heterogeneous composition. In oral argumentation, the speaker's construction of the audience will often be subject to change during the argumentation (e.g., under the influence of reactions).

Sound argumentation requires a certain degree of rapport between the speaker (or writer) and the audience. The arguer's train of thought must in some way accord with the audience's way of thinking. In practice, this condition is not always met at once. A speaker must often first gain the audience's attention before it is prepared to attend seriously to the argumentation. As a rule, it is an illusion to suppose that argumentation will speak for itself, and convince the audience by its own merits. With the help of anecdotes, examples, and stylistic devices, the speaker must interest the audience and maintain this interest throughout the argumentation. This can be difficult to achieve, particularly when the speaker has no clear picture of the audience's composition.

The arguer's knowledge of the audience will also have to cover the techniques which can be employed to influence it. All arguers must decide for themselves how far they can and will go in adapting to the audience. The problem of the ethics to be employed in this regard, say Perelman and Olbrechts-Tyteca, cannot be solved by argumentation theory.

Argumentation which may be assumed to be acceptable to any reasonable being, is called *convincing* by Perelman and Olbrechts-Tyteca, and argumentation that meets with approval from one particular person or group, they call *persuasive*. The familiar usage connection of the word "convincing" with creating cogent beliefs and the word "persuading" with moving others to some course of action, they only make indirectly. They say that the distinction between convincing argumentation and persuasive argumentation is determined primarily by the sort of audience for which the argumentation is intended.

Perelman and Olbrechts-Tyteca distinguish between a *particular* audience, consisting of a particular group or person, and a *universal* audience, consisting of all human beings that are considered reasonable. Persuasive argumentation lays claim to approval from a particular audience; convincing argumentation lays claim to approval from the universal audience. As only "concrete" people can be prompted into action, the connection with a particular audience is obvious: Only this audience's approval can manifest itself in practical terms. The universal audience is determined by the idea of reasonable people that the arguer has formed in his or her own mind.[10] Its approval, and the accompanying change in belief, are therefore more a "right" to which the arguer lays claim than a fact.[11]

The picture of the universal audience may vary from arguer to arguer, and from group to group. Sometimes a particular audience can stand for "rationality," thus fulfilling the function of a universal audience. For a person living in

---

[10]According to Olbrechts-Tyteca (1963, p. 12), the universal audience, though transcending the "concrete," does not replace it, but is as close to it as possible. The concept does not occur in classical rhetoric, but is related to the elite audiences and the interlocutor in a dialogue.

[11]Coupling the concepts of convincing and persuading to universal and particular audiences respectively—whose distinction requires insight into the arguer's imagination—means that the distinction between convincing argumentation and persuasive argumentation is imprecise and must remain so. In practice, it will often be difficult to tell where convincing ends and persuading begins, and vice versa.

the Middle Ages, a particular ecclesiastical elite may have been the embodiment of reasonable thinking; a particular group of colleagues may be the universal ("ideal") audience to a modern philosopher; people writing a letter to a newspaper, may perhaps count on its readers being the universal audience ready to concur. Ultimately, the universal audience represents a norm transcending all specific parties.[12] A particular audience can never be more than a fortuitous ("momentary") embodiment of the universal audience.

Arguers must decide for themselves whether they want to regard their audience as an embodiment of the universal audience or purely as a particular audience—in other words, whether they want to convince or persuade. Every particular audience can be treated as the universal audience. Perelman and Olbrechts-Tyteca pay special attention to two cases: audiences that consist of a single interlocutor, and self-deliberations in which arguers constitute their own audiences. Both sorts of audience can also be seen as embodiments of the universal audience. Then the criticism brought forward by the interlocutor and the criticism thought up by the arguer are respectively regarded as representing universal rationality, and their positive validation is appreciated equally.

Self-deliberation may lead to self-criticism and rejecting one's own train of thought as unreasonable. Although the arguer can consider this a matter of convincing rather than persuading, not everyone would agree with that outright. Instead of being regarded as a guarantee that one is addressing oneself to a pure representative of the universal audience, the exceedingly closed nature of the deliberation can just as well be seen as leading to self-deception. In Perelman and Olbrechts-Tyteca's view, argumentation of people trying to come to terms with themselves is, rhetorically speaking, just a special case of argumentation aimed at obtaining the approbation of other people. They observe that the deliberations that people conduct with themselves can best be regarded as deliberations with some other person, who may or may not represent the universal audience.

Argumentation addressed to a single interlocutor or a reader must be regarded as part of a dialogue, even if the other adopts a passive attitude and says nothing in reply. If they are accessible to the arguer, the other's reactions—frowning, nodding, et cetera—will still have to be taken into account. Even with an audience that is totally impassive, the arguer out for success will anticipate possible counterarguments and try to meet supposed objections. Freud, in his *Introductory Lectures on Psycho-Analysis*, thus ascribes all sort of objections to a fictitious opponent and then proceeds to refute them.

If the interlocutor reacts explicitly, perhaps by adducing counterarguments, there is then the beginning of an explicit dialogue. This is consistently the case, for example, in the famous Socratic dialogues, in which the discourse is a string

---

[12]Barbara Warnick considers the term *universal audience* a misnomer: It is neither an actual audience nor really universal (personal communication, November 29, 1994).

of repartee. In these dialogues, the interlocutor may be seen as a representative of the universal audience. Plato, for one, seems to hold the view that the dialogical method leads to the truth. This could not be the case if the other party's objections and approval were to be regarded as fortuitous reactions from a particular and arbitrary audience.

Perelman and Olbrechts-Tyteca make a theoretical distinction—which is not so easily drawn in practice—between heuristic dialogues which they call *discussions* and "eristic" or polemical dialogues which they call *debates*. In a discussion, arguers seek to convince their partners; the interlocutor is treated as an embodiment of the universal audience. In a debate, arguers seek to persuade their partners and the interlocutor is purely seen as a particular audience. Still, without considering them as embodying the universal audience, debaters might very well regard the interlocutors—rightly or wrongly—as representing a larger group: the Episcopalian church, the hockey team, or some other set of people with whom they are involved in a dispute.

As argumentation, according to the new rhetoric, always serves the rhetorical purpose of making a particular opinion (more) acceptable to an audience, the reasons put forward by an arguer must be chosen in such a way that they maximize this rhetorical effect. In a sense, these reasons can be regarded as *rationalizations* created by the arguer in order to justify an opinion in a way satisfactory to the audience.[13] Such rationalizations need not have much to do with why and how the arguer has actually arrived at that opinion (the *causa* of the opinion). The rationalizations are attuned to the audience that is to be convinced or persuaded; they must be, as far as possible, adapted to the specific context in which the argumentation occurs. In a given case, it is quite possible for a judge to come, on the basis of a vague mixture of motives and impressions, to the conclusion that criminal intent lay behind the defendant's actions, but when finding the defendant guilty the judge will shroud this judgment in legal argumentation. An even more obvious example is the defendant's counsel who tries to present the court with acceptable arguments designed to secure an acquittal, while intuitively believing that the client is guilty.

In their study of argumentation, the designers of the new rhetoric are less interested in the arguer "being right" than in the arguer "being put in the right." They equate sound argumentation with effective argumentation, and consider argumentation effective to the extent that it obtains the approbation of the audience for whom it is intended (or, in the case of argumentation directed to the universal audience, to the extent that it may be regarded as deserving such approbation). What counts in evaluating the quality of argumentation, are nei-

---

[13]Perelman and Olbrechts-Tyteca give the term *rationalization* a less specific meaning than currently attached to it under the influence of psychology: In present-day discourse, rationalization usually refers to reasons advanced by people in defense of their behavior or attitude without them being aware that these are not their real reasons (the real reasons being suppressed).

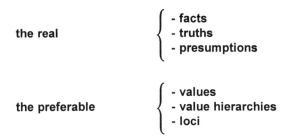

FIG. 4.1. Premises which may serve as points of departure.

ther the formal norms of logic, nor any aesthetic or other norms imposed by the argumentation theorist, but the criteria applied by the people for whom the argumentation is intended, or (in the case of a universal audience) the criteria those people may be deemed to apply.

4.2 POINTS OF DEPARTURE

Perelman and Olbrechts-Tyteca's aim is to provide a survey of argumentation techniques that may be successful in practice. In fact, they do not describe *argumentation techniques* but *argumentation schemes* that they regard to have a certain cogency. These argumentation schemes can only be successfully employed as argumentation techniques if they are attuned to the premises of the evaluating audience. Therefore Perelman and Olbrechts-Tyteca start their account with an exposition of the premises that may serve as the *starting point* or *point of departure* for argumentation.

Perelman and Olbrechts-Tyteca divide premises into two classes: premises relating to "the real" and those that relate to "what is preferable." In premises relating to reality, a claim is laid to recognition by the universal audience. This class of premises comprises facts, truths and presumptions. Premises relating to what is preferable have to do with the preferences of a particular audience. This class comprises values, value hierarchies, and *loci*. See Fig. 4.1.

Facts and *truths* are premises that are treated as not being subject to discussion. Facts are statements about reality which are acknowledged by every rational being and require no further justification. "Madrid is the capital of Spain" and "The earth is round" are examples of facts. What has just been said about facts also applies to truths, but this term is used for more complex systems of connections between facts, such as scientific theories. As soon as facts or truths are presented for discussion, their universal status is at stake and they cease to be facts or truths. The statement "The earth is flat," for example, was for centuries endowed with the status of a fact, but has lost this status due to scientific discoveries. Today, the statement "The earth is round" is treated as a fact.

Presumptions are premises that imply that something is real or actual. They too are regarded as enjoying the agreement of the universal audience. In contrast to facts and truths, however, it is expected, perhaps even assumed, that the supposition involved will at some stage be confirmed. An example of a presumption is the supposition that a person's actions will say something about that person's character. When such a presumption is used as a premise, everyone is taken to agree with it and it is expected that cases will occur which confirm the presumption.[14]

Values are premises that are related to the preference of a particular audience for one thing as opposed to another.[15] They serve as guidelines in making choices: "As personal liberty is very important, I shall vote for the party that will provide more police." Values are also a basis for the forming of opinions: "I prefer grape juice to coke because I like natural products."

In a rhetorical approach to argumentation values play an important role. The arguer not only relies on certain values in order to be able to make a particular choice of one thing as against another, but also in order to justify choices once made in such a way that they are accepted by others. Agreement over values makes a common course of action possible.

The values upheld by a given audience can be used as criteria for determining what that audience will and will not accept. The values adhered to may vary from person to person and from group to group. Sometimes, indeed, it is characteristic of a given audience that it cherishes certain values. The values adhered to also indicate what attitude the audience concerned adopts towards certain aspects of reality. A group of art lovers may thus be distinguished from a group of investors by the fact that for the former beauty is the only criterion to be applied to a building project, while for the latter the only possible criterion is profitability. Values that at first sight appear to be universal, say Perelman and Olbrechts-Tyteca, will lose their universality when they are more precisely defined: Everyone strives after good, but on closer inspection different people have different ideas of what good is.

Value hierarchies are, as a rule, even more important premises in argumentation than the values themselves. The hierarchy composed of the various values adhered to by its members varies from audience to audience more widely than the values themselves. Thus the majority of audiences will probably regard both beauty and profitability as values, but if they have to be weighed against

---

[14]This example of a presumption concerning a person and that person's actions reappears in Perelman and Olbrechts-Tyteca's typology of sorts of argumentation as an argumentation scheme (1969, pp. 296–305).

[15]In linking the distinction between values and facts and truths so strongly to the status of statements for an audience, Perelman and Olbrechts-Tyteca differ from other philosophers who understand facts as actual states of affairs in reality ("In France there are many vineyards") and values as attitudes towards reality ("It is a good thing that there are many vineyards in France").

each other, the preference of one audience will probably be different from that of other audiences. Value hierarchies are often more characteristic of different audiences than are values in themselves. This is what makes our earlier example of the art lovers, the investors, and the building project so much of a caricature: Different sorts of people have all sorts of different values and differ not so much in the values they have as in the way they arrange them in a hierarchy.

Like values, value hierarchies generally remain implicit. Nevertheless the arguer cannot simply ignore the audience's values; however, by presenting one value as subordinate to another, a value hierarchy can be held up to the audience, which accords with the purpose of the argumentation. In doing so the arguer exploits the fact that not all values are adhered to with the same intensity at all times: Sometimes one value will predominate over another and sometimes it will be the other way round. The arguer can try to make the value hierarchy predominate that suits him or her best.

Loci are preferences of a particular audience which are of an extremely general nature and can, without any difficulty, serve as justification for statements made in argumentation addressed to that audience.[16] For example, the argumentation in "You should take the job offer you have rather than waiting for an offer which you may not ever get" can be justified by a *"locus* of the existent": "A bird in the hand is worth two in the bush."[17] According to the new rhetoric, *loci* express a preference for one abstraction rather than another. Thus it may be a *locus* for a particular audience that the enduring is preferable to the transitory. This *locus* is then the basis for the value hierarchy in which friendship is placed above love because friendship is more enduring. *Loci* constitute an extensive store to be drawn on, which is a rich basis for values and value hierarchies.

Perelman and Olbrechts-Tyteca follow Aristotle in distinguishing *loci* of quantity and *loci* of quality. It is a *locus* of quantity we rely on when we state that a particular course of action is to be preferred because then the *most* people would benefit: "The government ought to nationalize all those private estates and parks, then they would be some good to everyone." An appeal to a *locus* of quality is made when it is asserted that a certain course of action must be taken because it is the *best:* "I know that a very great many students can't stand multiple choice tests, but I still think they're a good idea because there is no other way of telling as fast and as reliably whether required knowledge is there."

Facts, truths, presumptions, values, value hierarchies, and *loci* can all serve as points of departure for argumentation. The point of departure of an argumentation always consists of several premises or combinations of premises. These need not always be stated explicitly in advance. In many cases it only emerges during the course of the argumentation, or even on closer examination after-

---

[16]Perelman and Olbrechts-Tyteca prefer the Latin term *loci* to the Greek *topoi.*
[17]We owe this example to Barbara Warnick.

wards, that the arguer is assuming certain premises. Now whether or not the premises of an argument are stated in advance, the argument can only be a success if the audience agrees with the point of departure—or (in the case of a universal audience) may be regarded as being in agreement with it.

The arguer and the audience may disagree about the premises at three levels: (a) the status of premises, (b) the choice of premises, and (c) the verbal presentation of premises. There is a lack of agreement about the status of premises if, for example, the arguer advances something as a fact which the audience still wants to see proven ("You keep assuming that Laura is ill, but is she really?"), or if the arguer assumes a value hierarchy that the audience regards as nonexistent ("Ann can say Bourbon is nicer than Scotch if she likes, but I think all whiskeys are much the same"). There is a lack of agreement about the choice of premises if, for example, the arguer uses facts that the audience does not consider relevant to the argument or would have preferred not to see mentioned ("Of course Harry has been to Indonesia, but what has that to do with what we are talking about?"). Finally, there is a lack of agreement about the verbal presentation of premises if, for example, the arguer is presenting certain facts— acknowledged to be facts and agreed to be relevant—with a slant or in words which have connotations unacceptable to the audience ("You keep referring to terrorists while I should prefer to call them freedom fighters"). In practice, agreement may be lacking on more points at the same time.

The point of departure is of great significance for the argument's success and hence for its rhetorical soundness. In the interests of effective argumentation, arguers are therefore wise to consider carefully what status the audience is likely to accord to certain premises, to select the premises with great care, and to choose their words for the maximum effect.

Arguers must not simply assume values that the audience does not subscribe to, or name facts that the audience regards as immaterial, or use phrasing that the audience will regard as tendentious, since that would place an obstacle in the way of rhetorical success. The point of departure is itself one of the rhetorical tools by which argumentation can be made to succeed. Arguers are perfectly entitled to start from a point of departure to which the audience does not subscribe, but then they must be conscious that this point of departure itself requires supportive argumentation, so that it is no longer a common starting point.

4.3 A TYPOLOGY OF ARGUMENTATION SCHEMES

Following their discussion regarding the point of departure of argumentation, Perelman and Olbrechts-Tyteca consider a number of argumentation schemes. Their survey of the argumentation schemes that prove effective in practice comprises a typology of sorts of argumentation that can be used to make theses (more) acceptable. Perelman and Olbrechts-Tyteca regard these argumentation

$$
\text{argumentation by association} \left\{ \begin{array}{l} \text{-} \quad \textbf{quasi-logical arguments} \\[1em] \text{-} \quad \textbf{arguments based on the} \\ \quad \textbf{stucture of reality} \\[1em] \text{-} \quad \textbf{arguments establishing the} \\ \quad \textbf{structure of reality} \end{array} \right.
$$

argumentation by dissociation

FIG. 4.2. Argumentation schemes as potential techniques of argumentation.

schemes as special species of *loci*: They are general schemes for defending standpoints, and only agreement among the audience regarding their soundness can justify their use in particular cases of argumentation.

Argumentation schemes can only be used effectively as argumentation techniques if they accord with the preferences of the audience that the arguer wishes to move to (greater) approbation, or, in the case of argumentation addressed to the universal audience, with the preferences the arguer attributes to the rational beings that constitute the universal audience. In this sense, the new rhetoric provides a survey of possible techniques of argumentation.

The argumentation techniques envisaged by Perelman and Olbrechts-Tyteca rest on two principles: *association* and *dissociation* (see Fig. 4.2). Association consists in unifying elements into a single whole by bringing together elements which were previously regarded as separate. Dissociation consists in letting existing wholes disintegrate and separating elements previously regarded as a unit. We shall first discuss argumentation on the basis of association.

Argumentation by Association

Every association that has a justifying function puts elements into a particular argumentative relation. An example of an associative relation between a statement and an opinion is saying that it is good to read books because you will learn a lot from them. The previously separate elements that are brought together here are reading books and learning. The use of the word *because* indicates the justificatory function of the statement that you will learn a lot from reading books with respect to the statement that it is good to read books.

Argumentative associations like this can be brought about in different ways. Perelman and Olbrechts-Tyteca's typology is an attempt to chart the various possibilities. It is an inventory of the sorts of relation that can be drawn between particular elements. In the new rhetoric, three sorts of associative relation capable of being made in argumentation are distinguished: "quasi-logical relations," "relations based on the structure of reality," and "relations establishing the structure of reality."

Before looking at each of these sorts of relation, we must point out that the examples we use in our discussion are lifted from the context and situation in which argumentation normally takes place. The advantage is that the interpretations can be adapted to the purpose of the discussion. A disadvantage is that not much attention can be paid to the interaction between arguments and their contextual surroundings, and between the arguments themselves: How does the order in which the arguments are presented influence their effect, how does one argument reinforce another et cetera? Perelman and Olbrechts-Tyteca stress that, in practice, individual arguments are always part of a larger entirety of mutually influencing elements. In their opinion, however, in order to pay proper attention to the synthetic aspects of argumentation an analysis of the individual arguments is required first.

Quasi-Logical Argumentation

Argumentation in which elements are placed in such a relation to each other that the impression is given that the connections are logical is termed *quasi-logical* by Perelman and Olbrechts-Tyteca. In quasi-logical argumentation the illusion is created that there is a relation between the argumentation and the posited opinion just as compelling as between the premises and the conclusion of a logical argument form that resembles it. This suggestion is misleading: The similarity between argumentation and a formal argument is never sufficient to justify the validity claim. Hence the prefix *quasi*: quasi-logical argumentation is only seemingly logical.

Perelman and Olbrechts-Tyteca observe that mathematics and logic have acquired considerable prestige with their strictly formal argument forms. In quasi-logical argumentation, in order to bring about the audience's acceptance of the opinions defended, an attempt is made to make the prestige of mathematics and logic reflect on argumentation in ordinary language. In reality, there are crucial differences between quasi-logical argumentation and the formal demonstrations of logic. Formal demonstration is possible only in isolated and precisely delineated systems in which the terms are established unequivocally. There is no question of this being the case in ordinary language: The language forms that are used often have several meanings, which are not precisely defined and need not be the same for all language users. Important factors in the interpretation of argumentation are the context and situation: Without any context, speech utterances are practically always equivocal. The statement "The socialists want leveling," for example, could mean that the socialists want a reduction in the difference between the highest and lowest incomes, but also that they are in favor of removing differences between people in general. Equal linguistic forms can only be treated equally if they indeed have the same meaning. According to Perelman and Olbrechts-Tyteca, in ordinary language this is seldom or never the case.

In order to give argumentation in ordinary language the appearance of containing valid formal arguments it will always be necessary to carry out certain manipulations. As far as possible, the form of the argumentation must be made to accord with the chosen argument form. The arguments must resemble homogeneous, congruent, and unambiguous premises. This requires a certain reduction or specification of meaning—in the earlier example, for instance, of the word "leveling"—which must be adapted to the purpose of the argumentation. Quasi-logical argumentation exploits the possibilities offered by ordinary language in this regard. The adaptation—which need not be deliberate or conscious—must be as subtle as necessary for the audience to be reached. It is, for example, unlikely that the following quasi-logical argument is subtle enough for our readers: "Crazy people have to be locked up. After her finals Lottie went quite crazy. Therefore Lottie must be locked up."

The use of suitable terms and premises is not enough for quasi-logical argumentation to have the desired effect; it must also be ensured that the audience *recognizes* the form of the argumentation as logical. In order to emphasize the similarity with argument forms from mathematics or logic, speakers and writers will have to do their best to mark the form of their argumentation as clearly as possible. They may do this by stating explicitly that what they are presenting is a logical argument form:

(a) We agreed that those who have doubts must withdraw. Well, Gerard has doubts. So from that it follows that Gerard must withdraw. Doesn't it?

(b) You said you would approve the plan if Jim joined in. Jim is joining in. So it is perfectly logical to conclude that you approve the plan.

In the sense in which Perelman and Olbrechts-Tyteca use this term, these two arguments are certainly quasi-logical. Elements of ordinary language have in such a way been placed in relation to each other as to make it appear as if the connections between them are logical ones. According to Perelman and Olbrechts-Tyteca, the nature and scope of logic fall short of enabling us to deal adequately with such relations in ordinary language; only by artifice is it possible to give the impression that they are logical (or mathematical). In order that speech utterances in ordinary language take on the appearance of formal arguments, human intervention is required. The process of translation involved is not mechanical: Such interventions can always give rise to disagreement, hence requiring new argumentation, so that the compelling nature of the argument is lost. This disagreement may relate to the reductions and specifications of the terms, but also to the operations carried out in order to make the argumentation resemble a logical or mathematical argument form. In the case of example (a), for instance, it might be objected that the doubting Gerard cannot be classed as one who has doubts because, rather than being fundamental, his doubts should be seen as vacillatory; in the case of example (b), it might be objected that the modal aspect of "would" is not fully taken into account—and so on.

Depending on the form that is being imitated, or mimicked, Perelman and Olbrechts-Tyteca divide quasi-logical argumentation into argumentation claiming a logical relation and argumentation claiming a mathematical relation. The first of these subgroups includes arguments in whose justification contradictions, perfect or partial identity, and transitivity play a part, but also arguments relying on the rule of justice, whereby persons or situations of the same sort must be given identical treatment. The second subgroup includes arguments in which relations like "x is part of y," "x is smaller than y," and "x is larger than y" are an important element.

Let us first look at an example in which a logical relation is claimed:

Politician-1: The sanctity of all human life has always been a foremost principle of our party. It would be to go against that principle if we now went along with the proposal before us to legalize abortion. The members of my party in this House will therefore vote against the proposal.

In this example, the sanctity of all human life and the legalization of abortion are presented as *contradictory*; the implication is that to defend *both* things would be a logical inconsistency. This is a form of quasi-logical argumentation: The suggestion is that, logically speaking, maintaining both points of view is untenable and that therefore at least one of the two must be dropped. Although this form of argumentation may appear compelling to some, others may not be convinced, as appears from the following reaction.

Politician-2: You are right to set such store by the sanctity of human life, but you cannot include a 6-week foetus. And what about the sanctity of the life of the mother who has become pregnant against her will and is unable to give the child the life it has a right to?

Genuine logical contradictions can only occur in systems with unambiguously defined terms; they seldom occur in ordinary language. In ordinary language the meanings of the terms are rarely defined unambiguously and enable different interpretations, so that it is usually possible to avoid the charge of logical inconsistency by giving at least one of the terms a different interpretation: "Deliberately ending a human life is indeed murder, but in the case of a 6-week foetus it is not yet a matter of human life." This maneuver is all the more possible because the statements are rarely perfectly explicit and the terms employed are usually defined poorly or not at all. As a rule, then, the charge that someone is making contradictory statements is itself a form of quasi-logical argumentation: The person making the charge pretends to apply logical criteria to the assessment of the argumentation.

The apparent contradictions in ordinary speech can usually be reduced to *incompatibilities*. These incompatibilities resemble contradictions. They occur when two or more statements are made with which one is regarded as unable to agree simultaneously, so that one has to make a choice, not because there is any formal contradiction but because there is a barrier to the simultaneous defense of both in "the nature of things": the way reality is constructed, a human decision, the consequence of principles or values adhered to. Thus the confrontation of different rules of law may lead to incompatibilities. The same applies to a confrontation of moral rules, as becomes apparent, for example, when the rule that one must always tell the truth confronts the rule that one must not cause one's fellow humans unnecessary suffering. Incompatibilities, then, do not depend primarily on attributes of the language system that is being used, but on the views held by the audience. As we see from the abortion debate examples, statements which for one audience are so clearly incompatible that they even appear contradictory may not even lead to an incompatibility for another audience with slightly different moral norms.

Let us now turn to an example of quasi-logical argumentation in which a mathematical relation is claimed:

> The club is bound by certain stipulations and therefore the members are also bound by those stipulations.

In this example it is a matter of a relation between *the whole and its parts*. Here the parts are compared with the whole which comprises them, and the parts are treated as being in a position equivalent to the whole. The only thing that is considered is the quasi-mathematical relation which makes possible an equation between the whole and its parts, so that it is possible to exploit the principle "what applies to the whole also applies to the parts."

Often, the relation between the whole and its parts is approached differently: The whole contains the parts and is therefore regarded as more important than the parts. In this form of quasi-mathematical argumentation, the superiority is assumed of the whole over one, or each, of its parts. The conclusion is then legitimized with "mathematical certainty" by the fact that the whole always contains the parts. Perelman and Olbrechts-Tyteca point out that this form of quasi-logical argumentation is closely related to the *locus* of quantity: The argument constitutes a backing for that *locus* or is itself backed by it. This close relation is expressed in the following example: "You would do better to buy the collected works rather than just *David Copperfield*: It won't cost much more and you'll have all his other books as well."

Argumentation Based on the Structure of Reality

Argumentation in which an attempt is made to justify a thesis by connecting it with certain of the audience's opinions concerning reality, is termed by Perelman and Olbrechts-Tyteca *based on the structure of reality*. In this kind of argumentation there is an appeal to the way in which reality is constructed to bring about a transfer between opinions that the audience already adheres to and the thesis being defended. This type of argumentation draws on the view that the audience has formed of reality.

There is no question of Perelman and Olbrechts-Tyteca adopting an ontological posture when they describe this argumentation scheme. Neither do they try to give an objective description of reality, nor are they talking about their views of the way in which the world is structured: They merely describe the manner in which the *opinions of an audience* regarding the way in which reality is ordered are used by arguers in the development of their argumentation. Whether explicitly or implicitly, certain opinions about reality, or particular relations in reality, are in the argumentation presented as facts, truths, or presumptions which can be used for the justification of theses.

In argumentation based on the structure of reality a relation is drawn between elements already accepted by the audience and the element that the arguer wishes to render acceptable; this relation must conform to the audience's conception of reality. Perelman and Olbrechts-Tyteca distinguish two sorts of relation: *sequential relations* and *coexistential relations*.

Sequential relations are relations that have to do with the order in which the elements occur. Two consecutive events or facts may, for example, be presented as *means* and *end*: "They have achieved their aim: Their criticism has made it impossible for me to write another word." Another way of presenting two consecutive events is as *cause* and *effect*: "Now that they are allowed to have a say it has become total chaos."

A prominent type of argumentation based on a sequential relation is *pragmatic argumentation*. In this type of argumentation a verdict (positive or negative) is presented concerning a certain action by reference to the favorable (or unfavorable) consequences of that action. For example, a positive opinion of a proposed measure can be made plausible by presenting the audience with a picture of its advantageous effects. The value attached to the effect must then be transferred to the event that caused it. This is what happens if someone points out that digging up the road is something to be applauded because at least you can then walk about without constantly being bothered by cars.

Pragmatic argumentation can only succeed if the causal relation between the two elements concerned is evident and the positive value of the consequence speaks for itself, so that both can be accepted purely on the basis of "common sense." Such an argument becomes effective as soon as the connection between the thesis being defended and its favorable consequences are perfectly clear to the audience. When the audience regards it as plausible that the thesis represents a sufficient condition for the acclaimed consequences to actually materialize, the thesis gains acceptability. Other conditions and consequences that might play a part the arguer will as far as possible present as coincidental and unimportant.

Pragmatic argumentation is a special form of argumentation based on the sequential relation between *cause* and *effect*. Cause-and-effect argumentation can also be used where the relation between a particular condition and an effect approved (or disapproved) of by the audience is not immediately evident. One of two events being discussed is then presented as the cause of the other and the second as the consequence of the first. This kind of presentation will, for example, be used if the arguer wishes to convince the audience that a particular event should be disapproved of and knows that the audience already deprecates another event related to it. Then, by stamping the event that is deprecated by the audience as the natural consequence of the event that concerns the arguer, the arguer can try to bring about a transfer of the negative opinion of the consequence to the event that is being presented as its cause. Argumentation of this type occurs, for instance, in the following example: "Some sort of unsavory affair like that one involving the Queen was bound to happen sooner or later: If you put people in an unassailable position you're asking for things like that to happen—so you shouldn't do it."

In the case of argumentation using a sequential relation between *means* and *end*, the connection between one event and the other is presented as one deliberately brought about (or deliberately to be brought about) by human agency. With the help of this type of argumentation a transfer is sought to be realized from the audience's approval (or disapproval) of the means to the end ("You liked preparing the food, so now you should also eat it"), or from the audience's approval (or disapproval) of the end to the means ("The Americans should evacuate the orphans; this will doubtless do their prestige a bit of good").

In coexistential relations, just as in sequential relations, a link is established between two elements in order that a transfer of approval takes place from the accepted to the not yet accepted. Whereas in sequential relations the elements brought together lie in principle on the same plane and are of approximately equal importance, in coexistential relations one element is presented as being more fundamental or as having greater explanatory force than the other. Such a coexistential relation is displayed in "She must be very right wing: You can see it in that pearl necklace," where wearing a pearl necklace is being presented as a clear sign of being fundamentally right wing. In sequential relations it is the order of the elements that is of primary significance, in coexistential relations it is the way in which they are inherently structured.

In one type of coexistential relation a link is drawn between *a person* and *that person's actions*: "That fellow laughs too much for my liking: He must have a superficial character." Another type of coexistential relation hinges on the connection between *a group* and *its constituents*: "That Bloggs fellow must be a pretty unreliable person—he's been a member of the Socialist Party for years." The most general coexistential relation is that between *the essential* and *its manifestations*: "That's what I call real beauty—you can see it straight away in those aristocratic lines."

According to Perelman and Olbrechts-Tyteca, the relation between a person and that person's actions is the prototype of a coexistential relation. It is assumed then that *the person and that person's actions* can be seen as a relative *entity*. The person expresses itself in the actions; the actions are manifestations of the person. Argumentation in which a relation is drawn between a person and that person's actions is designed to bring about a transfer of an opinion held by an audience about a person, to particular actions by that person ("We all know that Adrian is someone who does everything he can to keep the club going: I see his proposal as an extension of that"), or vice versa ("This proposal is calculated to sow dissension amongst us: and if we look at the proposer we therefore know what sort of person we are dealing with").

There is, incidentally, between the person and that person's actions not the same inextricable relation as between *a thing and its attributes*. The relation between a thing and its attributes is, as it were, inherent in the nature of things, while the relation between a person and that person's actions must in principle on each new occasion be reassessed: A person may change to some degree, and the person's image with the audience may be altered by new actions on the part of the person, so that the actions themselves will be evaluated differently. This evaluation will always be based on the audience's picture of reality at the particular time in question.

Another example of a type of argumentation based on a coexistential relation is *argumentation from authority*. This is argumentation in which judgments or actions of a particular person or group are used as evidence for the thesis being defended. By making a connection between the opinion the arguer wishes to defend and the opinion of the same matter that is known (or assumed) to be held by someone whom the audience regards as an authority, arguers hope to bring about a transfer of the value attached to the authority's opinion to their own: "I feel—and Russell feels the same way, as it happens—that one must always first try to understand a text properly before one can start a critical reading of it." The argumentative force of such an argument depends entirely on the prestige vested by the audience in the person or group that is to act as the authority. "That is a good method: I use it myself," is likely to be proportionately more convincing as the speaker enjoys more prestige in the eyes of the audience.[18]

---

[18]Perelman and Olbrechts-Tyteca (1989, pp. 57–58) note that precisely because the rhetorical argument from authority has some value it may be utilized in bad faith. In order to establish this bad faith in another, "we make use of the ensemble of rhetorical methods of argument which permit us to conclude from the acts to the intention."

Argumentation based on a coexistential relation between *the essential and its manifestations* attempts to make a connection between some specific, individual manifestations and something essential, which may also find expression in other events, things, beings or institutions. In the statement "In the Stalinist era Marxism showed its true face," for example, a negative opinion (not explicitly put into words) concerning the Stalinist era is transferred to the essence, Marxism, of which it is claimed to be a manifestation. A related type of argumentation occurs if it is brought to the audience's notice that a certain phenomenon always goes together with something else ("Fat people are always jolly") or that something always has particular features ("Free public transport just means that we shall all be paying for it"). Of course, it applies to all such types of argumentation that they only have a chance of succeeding if the audience acknowledges the value attached to the element serving as *premise* and the relation drawn between the elements to be correct. It can, for instance, only be shown that a certain measure is the expression of a "capitalist" attitude or that a painting is essentially "romantic," if the audience subscribes to the distinctive features attributed by the arguer to the measure or the painting and agrees with the way in which these features are connected with the intended characterization.

Perelman and Olbrechts-Tyteca conclude their discussion of argumentation based on the structure of reality with an account of more complex types of argumentation based on sequential and coexistential relations together. One of these is the *double hierarchy* argumentation. Its point is to defend that a certain hierarchy is well-founded or that some specific element occupies a particular place within the hierarchy.

In double hierarchy argumentation the fact is exploited that hierarchies, apart from being points of departure in argumentation, can themselves also be the subject of discussion. An argument is double hierarchy argumentation if a hierarchical structure is defended by recourse to some other hierarchy (or even to more hierarchies). The hierarchies are then, for instance, presented as being so closely related that the one hierarchy serves implicitly as criterion, or definition, for the other. An example of this can be found in a discussion regarding the ranking of various cooking traditions, when the thesis that the Chinese cooking tradition is superior to other traditions is being defended by pointing out that it is more aesthetic and brings out the flavor of the ingredients better than other traditions.

Argumentation Establishing the Structure of Reality

Argumentation calculated to justify a thesis by drawing connections that structure reality in a particular way, is called argumentation *establishing the structure of reality* by Perelman and Olbrechts-Tyteca. With the intention that it will then accept a thesis which happens to fit into this picture of reality, the audience is presented here with a particular idea of how reality is structured. In argumentation of this kind, elements of reality are linked with one another in such a way that an order is created that is *new* to the audience. The plausibility of the new order then invests the elements adduced in defense of a thesis with a certain plausibility of their own.

Perelman and Olbrechts-Tyteca distinguish two ways of structuring reality. The arguer can resort to a specific case, which is then presented as an example of a particular relation existing in reality. The arguer can also suggest a correspondence, or a similarity, between a structure or relation of facts or events which is already acknowledged by the audience and a structure or relation that the arguer still wishes the audience to accept. Let us look at both these ways of arguing.

Argumentation in which there is an order based on the relation between a particular case and a general rule may take the form of argumentation *by means of example*. A specific case is then taken as the starting point for a generalization about reality. By subordinating the specific case to a generalization, the arguer introduces the audience to a rule. This will only succeed if the audience, while not previously aware of the rule, is acquainted with the example (or at least acknowledges it as correct), and if the audience agrees that it is possible to make generalizations on the basis of such a specific case.

In order for it to be possible to arrive at the introduction of a rule by means of an example, the cases that are to serve as examples must in the opinion of the audience have the status of facts. The moment they are challenged, the generalization is jeopardized. Incidentally, discussion about the status of the cases that are to serve as the starting point for the generalization, can be quite useful if the arguer can easily demonstrate their factual nature. It distracts the attention from the manner in which the generalization is made: "Just clap your hands and you'll see that Tiddles is deaf! That's precisely what I'm trying to get into your head: White cats are always deaf."

If the audience is firmly convinced that the example given is indeed one to be regarded as a fact, this can add to the ease with which the generalization is accepted. The number of examples needed to justify the transformation of the generalization into a rule cannot usually be predicted; the ambiguity of language provides many escape routes. It is often possible to take refuge in *an exception*. Suppose one puts forward an argument by means of example which says that women make better interviewers than men because you only have to look at the interviews by such renowned female interviewers as Oriana Fallacci or Barbara Walters to see that they can get much more out of their subjects than their male colleagues. If someone else then objects that this takes no account of someone like David Frost, one has little option but to call Frost an exception to the rule, assuming that having acknowledged the objection, the generalization can still be maintained.

In argumentation in which reality is structured by means of a specific case, the specific case need not necessarily be an example: It can also be *an illustration* or *a model.* Rather than really creating a new structure of reality, an illustration lends support to a previously established regularity. An illustration that appeals to the imagination can ensure that a rule that has slipped into the background is recalled to full "presence" in the audience's consciousness. The difference between an illustration and argumentation by means of an example lies in the status of the rule or principle concerned: The example is calculated to establish a rule, while an illustration is supposed to reinforce the audience's approval of a rule that is already known and more or less accepted by it. As the distinction hinges upon whether or not the audience recognizes the rule in question already, it is in practice often difficult to ascertain whether an argument should count as an illustration or as an example, as this depends on the context.

Argumentation by reference to a model, say Perelman and Olbrechts-Tyteca, is primarily an attempt to influence the audience's actions. By starting from a generally respected model, the arguer attempts to make the prestige of the model reflect on the behavior that is recommended, in the hope that this will prove sufficient reason for the audience to imitate the model. A model may consist of an idealized contemporary, but may also be a historical figure or a being represented as perfect: "We must render assistance to our fellows; otherwise we do not act in the spirit of Jesus Christ."

In argumentation *by analogy*, an idea concerning the way in which things in the thesis are ordered, is suggested by pointing out a similarity with a structure of things that is not subject to doubt in the mind of the audience. Here an attempt is made to equate the structure of what is being discussed, the *theme*, with the structure of something from quite a different sphere, the *phoros.* The structure of the *phoros* is known to the audience, but not the structure of the *theme.* By suggesting this similarity, a link is created between the relation of facts or events in the thesis and facts or events whose relation is already known, so that the plausibility of the new association is increased. This is what happens if, for example, someone says that from the lack of discipline and the tolerance shown towards immorality in modern western society it is clear that society is on the point of collapsing (= *theme*), because the Roman empire was likewise close to ruin when people lost their sense of order and discipline and were tolerant of immoral behavior (= *phoros*). Schematically analogy argumentation looks like this:

term$_1$ *theme* (moral decline western society) : term$_2$ *theme* (collapse modern western society)
= term$_1$ *phoros* (moral decline Roman empire) : term$_2$ *phoros* (collapse Roman empire)

Examples of analogy are not difficult to find. A striking one, where *phoros* and *theme*—as is characteristic of a prototypical analogy—are taken from different spheres, is that drawn by van het Reve (1977), a Dutch specialist on Russian affairs writing in the 1970s:

One thing that has been too little taken into account is man's capacity for recuperation. Just as an insect can be made resistant to DDT, so can man be made resistant to an ideology, and in the same way: by continuously exposing him to very high doses of it. And just as with the insect, there are at first millions of victims, but as time passes the treatment loses its effectiveness, and you find in the survivors that total immunity which the average Russian intellectual has to Marxism. (p. 8)

Argumentation by Dissociation

Alongside the argumentation techniques just discussed, all of which are based on the principle of *association*, Perelman and Olbrechts-Tyteca distinguish argumentation based on the *dissociation* of elements. The process of dissociation entails the introduction of a division into a concept the audience previously regarded as constituting a single entity. In practice, this means that a concept is differentiated from the concept that it was originally part of. In contrast to association, dissociation renounces an opinion initially accepted by the audience. In cases in which this renouncement serves the justification of an opinion, the dissociation is a technique of argumentation. Here is an example:

> *Christian Democrat politician:* "There is a great need for genuinely Christian political policies."

> *Opponent:* "You wouldn't think so, with all the figures showing dechristianization: The churches are getting emptier."

> *Christian Democrat politician:* "Ah, but that's where you make your mistake: That people go to church less is a sign of secularization, and that is not to be confused with them being less Christian."

Originally, the elements divorced from one another by dissociation constituted— at least, that was the arguer's impression—a unity in the opinion of the audience; they were part of a single concept ("dechristianization"). Dissociation changes this and introduces a differentiation within the original concept. As maintaining the original concept would lead to incompatibilities, the dissociation is presented as unavoidable. The arguer establishes the dissociation terminologically, by placing a new term alongside the old one. Thus a dissociation is completed which serves the arguer's purposes.

Dissociation can take place when the old concept no longer appears to provide an adequate picture of the elements to which it relates. Acknowledgment of a dissociation by an audience is sometimes the result of a series of argumentations and findings. Thus the results of a large number of scientific investigations have made it necessary for Christians to dissociate their concept of truth. The truth of science needs to be separated from religious truth to avoid unacceptable contradictions between, for example, the story of the creation in the Bible and scientific discoveries relating to the origins of the earth.

Perelman and Olbrechts-Tyteca illustrate the need for dissociation by reference to the example of a stick partly in and partly out of the water. To the eye, the stick is bent at the surface of the water, but the observer knows that it is straight—and would, in fact, be able to feel that it is so. From this example, it is clear that what we see does not always accord with what is actually true. Our knowledge of reality therefore, requires us not to simply accept everything we see as reality but to introduce a dissociation between *reality* and *appearance*. In this way, it becomes possible to differentiate between reality as it actually is and the seeming reality that we sometimes observe or think we observe. The consequence of dissociation is that concepts that are no longer adequate are replaced, while new terms are placed alongside the old ones.

Dissociation is a creative process. As such, it is of major importance for all original thought. This may, according to Perelman and Olbrechts-Tyteca, be deduced from the evolution of a whole series of familiar philosophical pairs: subjective/objective, theory/practice, relative/absolute, and so on. Time and time again, thought has been taken a step further by the division of supposed unities into separate concepts. Within the framework of argumentation calculated to elicit an audience's approval of a particular opinion, however, the crucial thing is that the newly introduced dissociation should be acceptable to the audience that the speaker wishes to reach. Whether the dissociation was thought of by the speaker, or has been borrowed from the thinking of others, is of secondary importance. Thus the dissociation of De Saussure's *langue* and *parole* or Chomsky's *competence* and *performance*, even though they did not introduce these distinctions first themselves, can be a useful tool to language teachers wishing to teach their pupils to think about linguistic phenomena in a new manner.

It is important to note that dissociation must not be confused with *opposition to associations*. A refusal to agree to an association implies that one refuses to acknowledge a link introduced between elements that were previously separate. One must then show that the link does not exist and that the elements are not related in the manner suggested, but have been brought together in an incorrect manner. In the case of dissociation, by contrast, one is dealing with something that was regarded precisely as a natural unity or indivisible whole, and a change is proposed which will break up the unity. Thus dissociation means a change in the way the structure of the elements is presented.

To conclude this discussion of argumentation schemes that are, according to the new rhetoric, used in argumentative discourse, we must point out with some emphasis that the argumentation schemes we have analytically separated from one another will, in practice, occur together and will interact, that is, reinforce or weaken each other. In our discussion, they have, as it were, been lifted from a synthetic whole. In fact, Perelman and Olbrechts-Tyteca say, every association implies dissociation, and vice versa: At the same moment that diverse elements are united in a whole by means of association, a dissociation takes place which differentiates these elements from the neutral background of which they were hitherto a part. The two processes are complementary and take place simultaneously. Placing one of the two in the foreground, and shifting into the background whichever one appears at that moment to offer fewer rhetorical possibilities, is a matter of technique.

In practice, different argumentation schemes will occur together, and they may also be jumbled up and combined with each other, the effect of one scheme influencing the effect of the next. Then again, the order in which they are used is a factor that helps to establish the rhetorical soundness of the argumentation. Another factor affecting the soundness is the way a person arguing succeeds in responding to intermediate reactions from the audience. Perelman and Olbrechts-Tyteca observe the influence of these factors but do not otherwise examine them in any depth. They do not describe the manner in which argumentative discourse takes place in practice: the specific roles of the interlocutors, the stages by which a discussion develops, the psychological mechanisms on which the effects of certain argumentation schemes depend, et cetera. The new rhetoric remains a general outline of the basic elements that play a part in rhetorical influencing by means of argumentation.

4.4 PERSPECTIVES

The main ambition of the founders of the new rhetoric was to create a framework for all nonanalytic thinking. Whether Perelman and Olbrechts-Tyteca's ambition has been realized depends, according to their own thinking, largely on the degree of acceptance the conception of rationality promulgated in the new rhetoric has acquired. Perelman and Olbrechts-Tyteca offer a rhetorical concept of rationality in which the soundness of argumentation is equated with the degree to which argumentation is well suited to those for whom it is intended. This means that the soundness of argumentation is, according to this criterion, always related to an audience.

The consequence of Perelman and Olbrechts-Tyteca's soundness criterion is that the norms of rationality that prevail are relative to a more or less arbitrary group of people. Ultimately, there can be as many rationality concepts as there are audiences—or even more, in view of the fact that audiences can change their norms in the course of time. The introduction of the universal audience does not result in any fundamental limitation, the only difference being then that the variation is eventually tied to arguers instead of audiences. Arguers are, after all, free to construct their own universal audience. As they may imagine the universal audience to be an audience with norms of rationality akin to their own, this leaves the standard of rationality as being no less arbitrary.

From this, it can be concluded that Perelman and Olbrechts-Tyteca offer an extremely relativistic standard of rationality. A reminder is appropriate here of the Platonist criticism of rhetoric that striving after approval of people, and the equation of approval with soundness, are barriers in the way of the search for truth. Far from being connected with any form of cynicism, however, Perelman and Olbrechts-Tyteca's relativism springs from their firm belief, inspired by Dupréel, in democracy and philosophical pluralism.[19] They most certainly care about ethics and moral standards. In this connection, it is noteworthy that, besides the distinction between a particular and a universal audience, at several places in *The New Rhetoric* normative elements are introduced, such as the distinction between an eristic debate and a co-operative discussion (1969, pp. 37–39) and that between a personal attack *ad personam* and—inevitably audience-bound—argumentation *ad hominem* (1969, pp. 110–114).[20]

Bearing in mind the far-reaching pretension with regard to nonanalytic thinking that Perelman (1969) attaches to the new rhetoric, the manner in which he turns against "modern formal logic" is curious. Logic is to him an illustrious example of a field which has made important progress thanks to well-directed reflection—in this case, reflection on mathematical thought. Logic, he observes, has gone through "brilliant developments" during the past hundred years, but these developments have resulted in a restriction of the field it covers, "since everything ignored by mathematicians is foreign to it" (p. 10). According to Perelman, argumentation theory must investigate the whole (unordered) field disregarded by logicians, thus encompassing the entire area of nonanalytic thought.

In carrying out this gigantic endeavor, Perelman takes no account of developments in logic—or other disciplines, come to that—which might ease his task. It is not quite clear, for instance, in what way the new rhetoric would deal with the logically valid arguments that occur in ordinary argumentative discourse. They are certainly compelling to those who accept the rationality norms of logic, although Perelman and Olbrechts-Tyteca would point out that ordinary language always leaves room for evading their compelling effect. As there is no reason to keep argumentation that is compelling to an audience out of a true-to-reality typology of argumentation schemes, and their typology hardly allows for an alternative, Perelman and Olbrechts-Tyteca would probably regard logically valid argumentation as quasi-logical argumentation with a pretension to be compelling to the universal audience. Then, however, the prefix "quasi-" could be misleading.

---

[19]See Perelman (1979a) and Kluback (1980).

[20]Giving a wider meaning to the term *ad hominem* than generally adopted in fallacy theory, Perelman and Olbrechts-Tyteca contemplate that argumentation is always addressed to people and must therefore always be *ad hominem*. While the audience might disapprove of arguers carrying out personal attacks, it can hardly find fault with them arguing *ad hominem*.

Anyway, underlying the objective of creating a rhetorical framework for all nonanalytic thinking is a relativism which many philosophers and thinkers find hard to accept. Some will argue that norms of rationality are always, at least partly, defined by a social contract, such as the law, or some other socially bound empirical set of external restrictions. Others will be of the opinion that there are (actual or possible) universal or absolute criteria for rationality or truth. These norms and criteria are not solely dependent on the rationality norms of an audience that is always to some extent fortuitous. It seems too much of an immunization to simply incorporate such views of rationality in the rhetorical system by saying that their adherents have formed their own idea of the universal audience and posit this idea as absolute. Seen from this perspective, it is questionable whether Perelman's ambition of creating a framework for all nonanalytic thinking can be said to be realized.

In *The New Rhetoric*, Perelman and Olbrechts-Tyteca do not closely define the disciplinary scope of the new rhetoric as a field of study compared to other fields. Loosely referring to "argumentation structures" as the subject of investigation of the new rhetoric, they acknowledge that argumentation can also be studied in experimental psychology, but they do not provide a sharper demarcation of the two disciplines.[21] The general aim of the new rhetoric is, they say, to provide a systematic description of the discursive techniques for obtaining approval, or increasing approval, of theses presented to people for their assent. Therefore, the next question is to what extent the new rhetoric does indeed provide such a systematic description.

A problem in answering this question is that *The New Rhetoric*—a bulky volume of 566 pages—covers a vast subject, whose treatment calls for the most precise delineation possible, a clear organization, lucid elaboration and, for the benefit of a proper understanding, a well-organized and comprehensive style of discourse, with recognizable examples. In *The New Rhetoric*, these preconditions are not always met. Although the division of the book into three sections makes a systematic impression, much of the system is lost in the elaboration, which gives no clear insight into the relations between the sections and contains a

---

[21]Recently, Arnold (1986) argued for joining Perelman's theory of argumentation with contemporary psychological theories of practical communication. In the United States, there exists a "limited but active" tradition of research blending rhetorical theory with psychological theory in studying persuasion and rhetoric (p. 38). Much of this persuasion study had been constrained "by the linear-logical-formal image of discourse that Perelman set out to displace." Currently, there is a growing awareness that arguments do not seek adherence of other minds by entailments among facts, premises and conclusions, but by creating and offering "liaisons" (p. 39). The result is "not syllogistic linearity in discourse, but a *web* of discursive symbolization with potentiality for influencing the intensities of cognitions." Arnold, dealing with particular audiences rather than the universal audience, points to some of the ways in which Perelman's work and contemporary psychological and critical studies in persuasion converged "to become mutually supportive and enlarging" (p. 37). In this endeavor, she concentrates on "cognitive approaches" to persuasion.

large number of lengthy digressions. Clear definitions are nowhere to be found, and the explanations that are given are not always equally lucid. In some cases, such as quasi-logical argumentation and argumentation based on the structure of reality, the new concepts are explicitly introduced, while in other cases, such as argumentation which structures reality, they receive no introduction at all. Concise summaries of the main points are lacking and the examples that are given sometimes require careful analysis. In other words, any account of the new rhetoric is based on interpretation.[22]

Concentrating on nonformal argumentation schemes, the new rhetoric provides a description of the connections discovered by Perelman and Olbrechts-Tyteca between certain constellations of statements and increased acceptability of a thesis. Such argumentation schemes, however, can only be used successfully as part of an arguer's argumentation technique if their appropriateness in view of the audience's premises is duly taken into account. It remains unclear how arguers will acquire the knowledge about the audience's premises that is required for this purpose. More importantly, the readers of *The New Rhetoric* can only verify what is asserted in the book by *recognizing*, on the basis of their own experience, the truth of the claims that are made.

The description of argumentation schemes provided in the new rhetoric is systematic to the extent that the schemes are divided up in a typology according to two ordering principles: association and dissociation. Whether the list of argumentation schemes drawn up by Perelman and Olbrechts-Tyteca is meant to be exhaustive is not really clear.[23] It is certain that the classes of argumentation schemes distinguished in the new rhetoric are not (and are not intended to be) mutually exclusive. In a given case, an argument may, for example, be regarded both as quasi-logical argumentation and as argumentation based on the structure of reality. The same goes for certain subtypes of the various classes. It is, for example, sometimes hard to determine whether one is dealing with an example or an illustration. Perelman and Olbrechts-Tyteca may regard all these complications as natural phenomena, which are true to the way in which argumentation is perceived in practice. However inevitable these consequences of Perelman and Olbrechts-Tyteca's approach may be, they are serious drawbacks to those empiricists who would like to put Perelman and Olbrechts-Tyteca's observations to the test.[24]

---

[22]Much of Perelman's later work constitutes an effort to elaborate on the new rhetoric and can be utilized to further its understanding. Cf., for instance, Perelman (1970, 1982).

[23]As Perelman and Olbrechts-Tyteca's compilation of argumentation schemes is based on their analysis of a somewhat accidental collection of argumentations, a natural consequence of their method is that exhaustiveness cannot be claimed automatically for their list.

[24]Some of the problems mentioned here are, in fact, anticipated by Perelman and Olbrechts-Tyteca, but no feasible solutions are offered to those who do not share their theoretical preconception.

When applying Perelman and Olbrechts-Tyteca's typology in analyzing argumentation it is rarely possible for all interpreters to arrive at the same unequivocal interpretation. The poor definitions of the various categories and the lack of clear examples, even though they make it difficult to decide what interpretations are legitimate, can still be regarded as technical imperfections. A more serious problem, however, is that divergent ordering principles have been used in drawing up the typology: quasi-logical argumentation is distinguished on the basis of a formal criterion (does the argumentation display a structural correspondence to a valid logical or mathematical argument form?), whereas argumentation based on the structure of reality and argumentation establishing the structure of reality are both distinguished on the grounds of a content criterion (does the argumentation flow from a particular view of reality, or does it suggest a particular idea of reality?).

With argumentation schemes distinguished on the basis of a content criterion one may wonder how far one can, in the structural sense, still speak of an argumentation scheme. The notion of scheme has been stripped of its formalistic meaning, while the formal connotations remain intact. Then, it is all the more necessary to indicate precisely which sort of cases (with which kind of empirical features) are to be counted as belonging to each of the various argumentation types. The vague content criteria that are provided by Perelman and Olbrechts-Tyteca make this problem hard to solve.

The all-important role that the new rhetoric allocates to the audience, not only as regards the soundness but also as regards the distinction of argumentation schemes, means that the typology is of little use to anyone requiring an unequivocal interpretation of argumentation that is the same for all interpreters. Going by Perelman and Olbrechts-Tyteca's distinctions, one audience can discern argumentation schemes in an argument which are different from those discerned by another—the same can be said for interpreters. The criterion cannot simply be "what determines the effectiveness (i.e., the persuasive effect)?" in a particular case, as neither the audience nor an independent interpreter can know for certain which scheme is responsible for the effect (which is itself often difficult enough to determine). Little is solved by an analysis that sums up all the schemes that *may* be effective in a particular case.

A typology in which a decisive role is played by the audience can only be implemented in practice if it is precisely indicated when, and under which conditions, a particular argumentation scheme can be an instrumental part of an effective technique of argumentation. In theory at least, the interpreters can then determine whether in a given case these conditions have been fulfilled, and decide accordingly in their analysis. In the new rhetoric, no such specification of conditions is given.

Together, the shortcomings in the demarcation of the various sorts of argumentation scheme and in the systematic design of the typology, make it difficult to answer the question as to the degree in which the new rhetoric provides a realistic survey of the argumentation schemes that influence the acquisition of approval of theses. The sorts of argumentation distinguished by Perelman and Olbrechts-Tyteca are indeed closely connected to the topical tradition, and they have a certain "recognizability." This, however, is not a sufficient basis for deducing testable hypotheses regarding the way people persuade and convince one another.[25]

Nevertheless, the new rhetoric's typology of argumentation schemes has been taken up by several authors. Kienpointner (1983, 1992a, 1993), who acknowledges some of the weaknesses of the typology, has added a number of argumentation schemes to the collection described in *The New Rhetoric*. Other authors distinguish argumentation schemes that are similar to Perelman and Olbrechts-Tyteca's.[26] There are also authors who elaborate on specific concepts of argumentation schemes described in the new rhetoric.[27]

Only a few authors have attempted to meet the criticisms of the typology. Warnick and Kline (1992) made an effort to clarify and elaborate the argumentation schemes. After acknowledging some of the criticisms we mentioned, they set out to counter them, ignoring other criticisms in the process.[28] In the *The New Rhetoric*'s scheme system, form and content are indeed fused, they admit, but this fusion, they add somewhat beside the point, does not prevent the schemes from being recognizable to various interpreters.

When examining arguments using Perelman and Olbrechts-Tyteca's system, Warnick and Kline (1992) observe correctly, form and content cannot be separated. Their answer to the typological criticism that Perelman and Olbrechts-Tyteca's system is endangered by the use of inconsistent classification criteria, is that reducing an argument only to its formal features—whose proposal?—would undermine "the *New Rhetoric*'s central purpose of reintroducing culturally recognizable argument features that formal logic has set aside" (p. 5). Reassuringly, they state that most variations can be resolved when they are considered "in the context of the argument situation and in relation to the arguer's intention." According to Warnick and Kline, in their inference structures the schemes make use of culturally accepted commonplaces. True, an effort of reconstruction is often required on the part of the interpreter to make arguments accord with the appropriate form of an argumentation scheme.

---

[25]Judged by strict criteria, the new rhetoric does not offer an empirically relevant theory: any risk of refutation is excluded because it does not give rise to any verifiable predictions.

[26]Seibold, McPhee, Poole, Tanita, and Canary (1981) and Farrell (1986) have made an effort to apply the schemes to argument practices.

[27]See, for instance, Dearin (1982) on quasi-logical argumentation, Measell (1985) on analogy, and Schiappa (1985) on dissociation. Goodwin (1991) extends the concept of dissociation in order to investigate "how distinctions modify the very desiderata by which argumentation itself is understood and assessed, and thus reconstruct social values, hierarchies, and concepts of the real" (p. 141).

[28]They respond to van Eemeren, Grootendorst, and Kruiger (1984).

Warnick and Kline (1992) are amazed about the criticism that Perelman and Olbrechts-Tyteca's examples are not clear: "Even though *The New Rhetoric*'s authors spent over a decade collecting examples from discourse in various fields, their efforts were held to be inadequate" (p. 4). They do agree, however, that the treatment of the schemes in *The New Rhetoric* "does at times lack clarity" (p. 5). They began their study therefore by identifying "as precisely as possible" the features of each scheme as discussed in the writings (not just *The New Rhetoric*) of Perelman and Olbrechts-Tyteca: "Consequently, we were able to construct a substantial set of identifiable attributes for each scheme" (p. 5).

Having thus reviewed the typology of the new rhetoric critically, Warnick and Kline (1992) began investigating the validity of Perelman's argumentation schemes empirically. For this purpose, they developed "detailed coding guidelines identifying the attributes of each scheme category according to descriptions contained in *The New Rhetoric* and *The Realm of Rhetoric*" (p. 12). Unfortunately, as mentioned in a footnote, these guidelines are only available from the authors upon request.

Warnick and Kline (1992) found their scheme system "to be generally complete, since nearly all the arguments could be categorized into at least (*sic*) one of the scheme types" (p. 14). Their conclusion is that the use of thirteen schemes coded by them could indeed be identified by three individuals "with an acceptable level of consistency" (p. 13). Therefore, Warnick and Kline claim to have established that "the schemes recognizably appear in discursive arguments" (p. 2).

Various insights from the new rhetoric have been abundantly used by others, albeit not always in publications that are available in English. In particular, Perelman's work has been a major source of inspiration to philosophers, in spite of their initial denigration of his rhetorical approach.[29] The philosophical assumptions of the new rhetoric have been elucidated by Dearin (1989), a communication scholar. In a philosophical vein, Maneli (1994) sees Perelman's theory of argumentation as "a new social philosophy and a critical instrument for social reform" (p. 115). In Maneli's view, argumentation legitimizes democratic government. Rather than the techniques of argumentation, however, he concentrates on Perelman's concepts of morality, power and authority, law and politics.[30]

Among the scholars that have been inspired by the philosophical perspectives offered by Perelman and the new rhetoric are many jurists.[31] Perelman's ideas concerning the philosophy of law and his views on justice and judicial justification have exercized substantial influence.[32] According to Maneli (1978), the new rhetoric is a good starting point for a rhetorical foundation of legal philosophy. As to Wiethoff (1985), the movement called Critical Legal Studies

---

[29]Cf. Johnstone, Jr. (1993).

[30]We refrain from going further into philosophical studies based on Perelman in which argumentation theory does not play a major part. See, for example, Meyer (1982a, 1986a, 1986b, 1989), and a great many contributions to Haarscher (1993).

[31]For a review of Perelman's theory from a judicial perspective, see Alexy (1978, pp. 197–218).

[32]Cf. Golden & Pilotta (1986), Haarscher and Ingber (1986), and Haarscher (1993).

offers the most likely opportunity for the application of Perelman's philosophy of legal argument.[33]

Golden and Pilotta (ed., 1986) collected various applications of Perelman's insights to the field of law: Haarscher discusses Perelman's ideas concerning justice, Makau his rationality model as an alternative to the mathematical model, and Rieke his theoretical tools for analyzing the legal decision process. In a series of essays collected by Haarscher (1993), many authors concentrate on the implications of Perelman's ideas for legal theory and legal philosophy, while Holmström-Hintikka discusses practical reasoning in law, and Pavcnik points out the importance of a theory of practical reasoning to the study of law.

In North America, Perelman's views of legal argumentation have attracted the attention of scholars in speech communication. According to Makau (1984) and Schuetz (1991), his concept of an audience and his views of argumentative strategies are useful tools for analysis. Makau proves her point by describing the securing of adherence by the Supreme Court from a composite audience consisting of a variety of legal and nonlegal groups. Schuetz analyzes the use of value hierarchies, precedents and presumptions in a Mexican legal process.

A particularly strong influence of Perelman's ideas has emanated from his views on legal argumentation, to which he paid some special attention.[34] In *Logique Juridique; Nouvelle Rhétorique*, Perelman (1976) gave a description of the argumentation techniques that play a role in legal argumentation. In the legal decision process, judges cannot apply the rules automatically. The rules always need to be interpreted first; the reasoned choice involved in this interpretation is based on certain values. According to Perelman, judges attempt to gain the approbation of three different audiences: the legal practitioners (judges and lawyers), the community of law scholars and other interested members of society at large, and the parties involved in the dispute.[35]

When attempting to convince their audience of the soundness of their decision, judges have to show that it is in accordance with certain accepted judicial starting points and argumentation schemes. In attuning the argumentation to the starting points accepted in the legal community, the general legal principles and values, such as equality, can be used as *loci*. These are relatively abstract values, so that they can be interpreted in various ways.[36]

---

[33]For a collection of Perelman's philosophical essays on the concept of justice, see Perelman (1980). Perelman articulated his philosophy of legal argument most clearly in *The idea of justice and the problem of argument* (1963).

[34]From a different perspective, Abbott (1989) explains the influence of judicial reasoning on modern rhetorical thinking.

[35]Starting from Perelmanian criteria, Corgan (1987) proposes an analysis of legal arguments that uses the universal audience as a critical tool.

[36]For nonjudicial uses of Perelman's concept of *loci*, see, for instance, Wallace (1989), who writes about developing a modern system of rhetorical invention, and Cox (1989), who concentrates on a particular *locus*.

By taking certain accepted legal principles as a starting point, consensus can be gained on points that are controversial. Starting from Tarello's (1972) description of methods for interpreting legal rules, Perelman discusses various argumentation schemes that can be used for defending legal standpoints: the argument *a contrario*, the argument *a simili*, the argument *a completudine*, the argument *a coherentia*, the psychological argument, the historical argument, the apagogic argument, the teleological argument, the argument *ab exemplo*, the systematic argument, and the naturalistic argument.

In justifying their decisions in accordance with their legal convictions, judges that have a teleological approach will concentrate on whether a certain goal will be reached by a certain rule or set of rules. Judges favoring a functional approach, in which the law is regarded as a means for attaining the goals intended by the legislator, will concentrate on arguments that represent the intentions of the legislator.

Perelman does not elaborate systematically on how the new rhetoric can be applied to law. He gives, for instance, no description of the way in which, and the circumstances in which, the specific kinds of *loci* constituted by the general legal principles can be effective means of convincing an audience. His treatment of starting points and argumentation schemes is also not really systematic. Which sorts of starting point and which sorts of argumentation scheme play a part in the general legal principles, he does not say. Nor does he describe the relation between the various audiences, starting points, and argumentation schemes in a legal context.

Many argumentation theorists have elaborated on the new rhetoric, applying Perelman's insights to their own areas of interest.[37] Several of them have been attracted to the new rhetoric's conception of an audience, often with a critical eye for its problems. This conception has been adopted as the central focus of attention in various publications, in particular the distinction between a particular audience and a universal audience (in some interpretation or other).

Among the more recent interpretations of the two kinds of audience are those of Golden (1986), Dunlap (1993) and Wintgens (1993).[38] Golden emphasizes the critical use that can be made of the concept of a universal audience, Dunlap relates it to Isocrates' "competing image" of an ideal audience, which embodies the ideals of Greek culture, and Wintgens argues that a better understanding can be achieved of Perelman's view of reasonableness, and what is meant by arguers constructing their audience, by connecting the concept of a universal audience with that of the "generalized other" that is part of the theory of

---

[37]See, for instance, Schiappa (1993) on arguing about definitions, and Koren (1993) on discursivity and argumentation in the French press.

[38]Other studies of the concept of a universal audience are, for instance, Crosswhite (1989), Ede (1989), Fisher (1986), Golden (1986), Ray (1978), and Scult (1985, 1989).

symbolic interactionism developed by the pragmatist Mead.[39] Another interesting connection is discovered by Gracio (1993), who shows that in Gadamer's hermeneutics the relation between rhetoric and philosophy is viewed in terms similar to Perelman's.

Various publications are devoted to the study of fallacies from a rhetorical perspective.[40] A remarkable contribution to this study has been made by Goodwin (1992). He connects the Perelmanian concept of dissociation with Rescher's idea of "distinction' as a "dialectical countermove," and examines then how current arguments against the Standard Treatment of fallacies are underpinned by distinctions that challenge previously formulated distinctions. Crosswhite (1993) uses the distinction between a universal and a particular audience to deal with the problem of the fallacies in a rhetorical fashion. Rather than as violations of "formal" or "quasi-formal" rules, fallacies arise, according to Crosswhite, when the arguer mistakes a particular audience for a universal audience.[41] In order to determine whether an argument is a fallacy, Crosswhite thinks, we first have to know to what audience it is addressed and how it is understood.

Some more topics central to the new rhetoric have been given special attention. We mention just a few, naming only some of the authors that have explored them. Farrell (1986), for one, studied the relation between reason and rhetoric. McKerrow (1982) and Laughlin and Hughes (1986) go into Perelman's position on the rational and the reasonable, as does Rieke (1986), who has been mentioned earlier in the context of judicial justification. McKerrow (1986) focused also on pragmatic justification. Perelman's theory of values is discussed by Warnick (1981) and by Walker and Sillars (1990), and the universal aspects of values by Eubanks (1986). Karon (1989) examined the rhetorical concept of "presence."[42]

---

[39]According to symbolic interactionism, rather than individual and coincidental intentions and reactions, speakers attribute to their interlocutors the intentions and reactions of a "generalized other" who shares the basic rules of their social community.

[40]For a review of Perelman's view of the fallacies, see van Eemeren and Grootendorst (1995a).

[41]There is a resemblance here with Walton's (1992c) "dialectical shifts," albeit that Crosswhite concentrates on audience shifting and Walton on purpose shifting.

[42]Perelman's ideas have been used in so many ways that they cannot all be dealt with here. Nimmo and Mansfield (1986) emphasize their relevance for the study of political communication, and Pilotta (1986) stresses Perelman's alignment with the critical school. Mickunas (1986), to name just one more, discusses Perelman's ideas of justice and political institutions.

5

TOULMIN'S MODEL
OF ARGUMENTATION

The British-American philosopher Stephen Toulmin gained an impressive reputation in the field of argumentation theory with *The Uses of Argument*, in which book he introduces a model representing the "layout of arguments." In many argumentation textbooks, this model has been used for the analysis, evaluation, and construction of arguments. Toulmin's views on argumentation have also been influential at a more theoretical level.

Toulmin was born in England in 1922 and studied mathematics and physics at the university of Cambridge, where he took a doctorate in philosophy. At Cambridge he studied under Wittgenstein and John Wisdom; he studied also in Oxford under Gilbert Ryle and John Austin. During his philosophy studies he came under the influence of the "ordinary language philosophy" developed at Cambridge and Oxford. Toulmin has been professor of philosophy in the University of Leeds. Since 1965 he has held positions in the United States; first at Michigan State University, later at Brandeis University, Massachusetts. Most recently he has been the Avalon Foundation Professor in the Humanities at Northwestern University.

Toulmin has written on a variety of subjects, his first article appearing in 1948. Since then, he has published books and articles on logic, philosophy, epistemology, philosophy of science, the history of science, ethics and meta-ethics. His books include *The Place of Reason in Ethics* (1950), *Human Understanding* (1972), *Wittgenstein's Vienna* (1973, coauthored by Allen Janik), *Knowing and Acting* (1976), and *Cosmopolis* (1990).

A central theme throughout Toulmin's books is the way in which assertions and opinions concerning all sorts of topics, brought up in everyday life or in academic research, can be justified. He is particularly interested in the norms that must be applied in a rational assessment of argumentation in support of such assertions and opinions. Is there one universal system of norms, by which all sorts of argumentation in all sorts of fields must be judged, or must each sort of argumentation be judged according to its own norms?

The Uses of Argument, published in 1958, is the first publication in which Toulmin systematically set out his views on these questions. In the preface to the paperback edition of 1964 (which is unaltered in its many reprints), Toulmin writes that the reactions to the first edition only had strengthened his convictions:

> The reaction which the argument of the book met with from the critics in fact served only to sharpen for me the point of my central thesis—namely, the contrast between the standards and values of practical reasoning [. . .] and the abstract and formal criteria relied on in mathematical logic and much of twentieth-century epistemology. (p. viii)

In *Human Understanding* (1972), he refers to the main issues discussed in *The Uses of Argument*. In a keynote address at the Second International Conference on Argumentation, held in Amsterdam in 1990, he spoke about the same issues, referring retrospectively to "some of these ideas I hinted at thirty years ago or more, when I wrote *The Uses of Argument*" (1992, p. 9). Although the model does not appear in Toulmin's later theoretical work, it can be found in *An Introduction to Reasoning*, a practical textbook written by Toulmin together with Richard Rieke and Allan Janik (1979). Our exposition is based on *The Uses of Argument* (referring to the 1988 paperback edition).

Toulmin's central thesis is that rationality can, in principle, be claimed for every sort of argumentation and that its soundness criteria depend on the nature of the problems at issue.[1] He rejects the view that there are universal norms for the evaluation of argumentation and that these norms are supplied by formal logic. The scope and function of contemporary formal logic is, according to Toulmin, too restricted to serve this purpose.

In Toulmin's opinion, there is an essential difference between the norms which are relevant to evaluating everyday argumentation or argumentation in the various scholarly disciplines, on the one hand, and the criteria of formal validity employed in formal logic, on the other hand. He is convinced that formal criteria are irrelevant to the assessment of argumentation as it occurs in practice. If logic is to serve as a basis for evaluating practical arguments, it cannot remain merely a formal science. In Toulmin's view, a radical reorientation of logic is required.[2]

---

[1]Toulmin (1988) uses the term *soundness* as equivalent with *validity, cogency,* or *strength* (cf. p. 147).

[2]Such a radical reorientation of logic would for Toulmin amount to going back to the Aristotelian roots of logic. He refers several times to the first sentence of the *Prior analytics*, where Aristotle expresses the double aim of logic: Logic is concerned with *apodeixis* (i.e., with the way in which conclusions are to be established), and it is also the—formal, deductive, and preferably axiomatic—science (*episteme*) of their establishment (1988, pp. 2, 177, 187).

Before he arrives at this conclusion, Toulmin turns first to the characteristics of the process of argumentation at the macro-level, then to the structure of argumentation at the micro-level. His ideas concerning the former are discussed in Section 5.1, his ideas concerning the latter in Section 5.2. In Section 5.3, we survey the ways in which Toulmin's model has been applied by others. In Section 5.4, finally, we discuss the merits of Toulmin's view of argumentation and his model; we also draw some conclusions concerning the impact of his main ideas on the study of argumentation.

It is not surprising that Toulmin's radical attack on what he sees as standard formal logic has evoked strong criticism from logicians and other philosophers. They combined their reviews of *The Uses of Argument* often with an almost passionate "defense of logic."[3] We shall not go into the details, but confine ourselves to a general account of Toulmin's ideas of logic.

The view ascribed by Toulmin to logicians is that argumentation can be evaluated by means of universal norms. In his opinion, they hold this view because they mistakenly think that the validity of an argument depends solely on its form. In judging the validity of an argument, the content of the premises is supposed to be irrelevant. It does neither matter what the subject of argumentation is nor what sort of problems it aims to solve. Toulmin calls this view the "geometrical" concept of validity.[4] He illustrates this concept with this example:

All sprinters are runners.
All runners are athletes.
Therefore: All sprinters are athletes.

The argument in the example has the following argument form:

All A are B.
All B are C.
Therefore: All A are C.

This argument form can be visualized by a Euler diagram, in which A, B, and C are each represented by a circle. The premises state that the A circle is part of the B circle and that the B circle is part of the C circle. This is what we see in the left half of Fig. 5.1.

If the drawing in Fig. 5.1 is right, it also illustrates the conclusion "All A is C": It is impossible to make the drawing in such a way that the premises are properly

---

[3]See Abelson (1960–1961), Bird (1959), Castaneda (1960), Collins (1959), Cooley (1959), Cowan (1964), Hardin (1959), King-Farlow (1973), Körner (1959), Mason (1961), O'Connor (1959), Sikora (1959), and Will (1960).

[4]In elaborating on this concept in *Knowing and acting*, Toulmin (1976) compares the geometrical approach to rationality with the "anthropological" and the "critical" approach. See chapter 1 of the present study.

FIG. 5.1. Geometrical form of an argument.

reproduced without the A circle ending up inside the C circle. This is shown in the right-hand part of Fig. 5.1.

In logic, Toulmin (1988) says, "validity" is equated with "formal validity" in this geometrical sense. Formal valid arguments can be said to be "deductively" or "analytically" valid. This means that the conclusion necessarily follows from the premises:

> The only arguments we can fairly judge by deductive standards are those held out as and intended to be analytic, necessary and formally valid. (Toulmin, p. 154)

Toulmin (1988) disagrees with this narrow concept of validity. He allocates a much wider meaning to the term *validity*, arguing that logic must not be an "idealized" discipline closely connected to mathematics, but must evolve into a discipline based on the practice of argumentation and seeking closer ties with epistemology (p. 254).

According to Toulmin, arguments which comply with the logicians' criterion of formal validity cannot be regarded as representative examples of argumentation as it occurs in practice. On the contrary, outside the textbooks of logic and mathematics they are difficult to find. Moreover, the manner in which argumentation takes place in everyday life and in the academic disciplines is in such textbooks left untouched. Judging by the formal validity norm, most arguments that are regarded as acceptable in everyday life or in the academic disciplines must be regarded as invalid. The reason for this is that such arguments are not analytic but what Toulmin calls "substantial."

By calling arguments *substantial*, Toulmin (1988) refers to the fact that in such arguments the conclusion is not contained in the premises: it is not entailed (p. 125). The reason for this is that the premises are of a "logical type" which is different from that of the conclusion. According to Toulmin, many substantial arguments involve "type-jumps" from the premises to the conclusion (p. 167). As a consequence, such arguments are usually formally invalid: their conclusions do not follow necessarily, but at most only probably, from the premises.[5] An example may clarify what he means. The phase of the moon on, say, May

---

[5]This does not mean that Toulmin (1988) thinks that analytic arguments are always formally valid and substantial arguments always formally invalid: "An argument in any field whatever *may* be expressed in a formally valid manner [. . .]. On the other hand, an argument may be analytic, and yet not be expressed in a formally valid way" (p. 135).

24, 2095, can 100 years earlier be predicted by an astronomer making use of observations of the moon up to May 24, 1995. The reasoning the astronomer will use contains a conclusion in which an assertion is made about the future, and premises which relate to the past. Therefore, the premises are of a different logical type than the conclusion. However probable or plausible the astronomer's prediction may be, it will never follow necessarily from the premises.

For anyone who desires to achieve certainty as to the accuracy of the prediction, studying the argument is wasting time: This person must simply wait until the night of May 24, 2095. Similar logical gaps occur in arguments whose conclusions are assertions concerning the past and whose premises contain data taken from the present, or in arguments in which conclusions about the laws of nature are based on particular observations and experiments, or in which an aesthetic judgment is founded on references to such attributes as form and color.

According to Toulmin, those who hold that arguments in which the logical type of the premises is different from that of the conclusion are invalid also think that valid arguments occur only in logic and mathematics and that validity is the supreme criterion of rationality. One consequence of this view is that arguments in academic disciplines which allow for a jump from one logical type to another between the premises and the conclusion are regarded as nonrational or at least less rational than the arguments in logic or mathematics. Toulmin regards this an absurd idea, which is counterintuitive and even dangerous. In addition, he also regards the logical concept of formal validity practically irrelevant to the evaluation of the soundness of argumentation, whether in everyday life or in the academic disciplines.

Formal validity in the logical sense, says Toulmin, is neither a necessary nor a sufficient condition for soundness of argumentation. In his view, for making a rational judgment a requirement of formal validity *in quite another sense* is required. It cannot for all cases of argumentation at the same time be established by means of a universal logical norm what a rational judgment involves. Ultimately, the evaluation criteria depend on the nature of the problem or the kind of problems at issue. In order to achieve a rational assessment, a discussion about whether the summer is going to be hot and dry meteorological criteria need to be applied, not logical criteria. Sound argumentation, that is, argumentation containing arguments that may be called valid in a broader sense, is to Toulmin argumentation conducted in accordance with a formally valid *procedure* and in conformance with the specific soundness conditions of the *field* or *subject* concerned.

The widening of the validity concept Toulmin is arguing for has, in his opinion, farreaching implications for logical research. It is no longer the logicians' task to develop systems of formally valid argument forms without any reference to the fields in which arguments are used. Because the arguments that occur in the various academic disciplines or fields are not analytic but substantial, there will be a difference between the sort of statements making up their premises and the sort of statements occurring in their conclusions. There is, however, no question of an unbridgeable logical gap that makes these arguments automatically defective. Substantial arguments are not imperfect, but for such arguments the analytic ideal is not relevant.

For this reason, Toulmin holds that logicians ought to abandon the criterion of formal validity in the strict sense and should pay more attention to the practical aspects of assessing argumentation outside mathematics, the one field where analytic arguments find their proper place. Logic should amalgamate with epistemology. The epistemological logic thus produced should be devoted to studying the structure of argumentation in the various academic disciplines and sciences in order to discover the qualities and defects of the various sorts of argumentation that are characteristic of different fields.

Instead of starting from an absolute analytic ideal, logicians ought to develop a comparative method, starting from the premise that all sorts of argumentation are in principle equal. The different structures can then be compared and contrasted without one sort being automatically considered superior or inferior to the other. The soundness of argumentation ("validity" in the broader sense) is an "intraterritorial," not an "interterritorial" notion. This means that argumentation must be assessed according to the particular norms which happen to apply adequately to the field to which the argumentation refers. The evaluation criteria must, in other words, not simply be shifted from the one territory to the other. It would be the task of logicians who use a comparative method to identify similarities and differences in the different sorts of argumentation, both in simple and compound argumentation. If differences are found, they must be respected. It is open to anybody so desiring to try to improve the argumentation methods in his or her field of interest, but it is wrong to start from the assumption that there are fields in which *all* methods of argumentation are automatically unsound.

One final implication that Toulmin attaches to his broadening of the concept of validity is that logic will be less of an a priori science and become more empirically and historically oriented. *Empirically oriented* means that logicians start looking at the forms of argument that actually occur in the various fields of science; *historically oriented* means that logic is going to incorporate the history of ideas. According to Toulmin, the great scientific discoveries of the past have changed not only the fields of the discoverers, and our general state of knowledge, but also the ways in which we argue and our norms for good argumentation. If logic were to evolve in this epistemological, comparative, empirical, and historical direction, it could be left to mathematicians to draft abstract formal systems of possible arguments that are cut off from the practice of argumentation everyday life and in the various empirical disciplines.

To Toulmin himself, the implication of the development of a nonidealized practical logic is not necessarily that only specialists who are acquainted with the latest developments in a specific field would be competent to judge the soundness of the argumentation in that field. His intention in presenting his views was chiefly to shift the accent from an exclusive attention to universal evaluation criteria towards a practice in which field-dependent and subject-related considerations are taken into account.

In *The Uses of Argument*, Toulmin's view of logic is a recurrent theme. Ultimately, his objections to logic amount to objections to the concept of formal validity that is used by logicians. His own conception is not only broader, it is also essentially different. The difference concerns the notion of "form." In logic, *form* is a quasi-geometrical concept, while Toulmin regards *form* as a procedural term, which has a similar content as *form* has in legal practice.

According to Toulmin, a geometrical interpretation of *form* leads to a model of argumentation that is too simple, since it fails to do justice to the complexity of argumentation in everyday life and the academic disciplines. A procedural interpretation of *form* can lead to a more adequate model of argumentation, in which the characteristic differences between sorts of argumentation in the wide range of fields to which argumentation may refer are also taken into account.

5.1 FIELD-INVARIANCE AND FIELD-DEPENDENCY

Toulmin (1988) regards argumentation as an attempt to justify a statement or a set of statements. To him, this justifying function of argumentation implies the following. Stating a standpoint regarding a subject means making a claim. A person who puts forward a standpoint lays claim to the audience's belief. Sometimes the audience will already be of the same opinion, sometimes it may simply decide to believe what the arguer says, but there are also cases in which it requires some argumentation in support of the claim (p. 11). The better this demand is met by the arguer, the higher the audience's appreciation of the standpoint. In other words, the degree to which a claim can justifiably be asserted depends on the quality of the argumentation that can be advanced in its support.

The audience always has a right to attack a standpoint by asking for argumentation in its support, and a right to accept the standpoint only if the supporting argumentation is sound, regardless of the nature of the subject matter of the standpoint. Justification may be demanded for any claim that is made, whether the claim concerns a weather forecast by a meteorologist, an accusation of negligence by an employee against his employer, a doctor's diagnosis, a remark by a businessman about the dishonesty of a customer, or a critic's verdict on a painting. Toulmin wonders to which extent argumentation relating to such diverse subjects can be cast in the same mold and to which extent it will be possible to judge argumentation by the same standards. He provides an answer to these questions by comparing argumentation with jurisprudence.

The practice of law, too, is concerned with the justification of statements, and in law courts, too, widely disparate matters may be at issue. The study of jurisprudence concerns itself, *inter alia*, with the legal process, while the study of argumentation demands a characterization of the "rational process" in general. Toulmin regards law actions as a special form of rational discussion, viz. one in which the procedures and rules of argumentation have been institutionalized in a particular way. The evidence presented in judicial proceedings varies from case to case, but also from sort of case to sort of case. For example, a civil action for libel will require evidence of a different sort than a murder charge in a criminal case. However different the cases may be, there will still be clear similarities in the procedure that is followed. Thus there will first be a formulation of the charge or claim, then there will be a stage during which evidence is produced and witnesses are heard, and finally judgment will be given and sentence passed.

According to Toulmin, constant elements like this can be discerned in argumentation in general, while in every case there will also be some variable elements. In order to obtain a better insight into this similarity and variance, it is important to bear the variety of subjects in mind concerning which arguments may arise. An effort should be made to determine what is common to all types of argumentation and what is different in individual types. To this end, Toulmin introduces some technical terms: "logical type," "field of argument," "field-dependent" or "particular" elements, "field-invariant" or "general" elements, "force" (of statements), and "criteria" (for using modal terms and evaluating argumentation).

Toulmin provides no explicit definition of *logical type*, but from his examples one has a fair idea of what he means.[6] He finds that statements like the following are of different types:

(1) The ministers handed in their resignations.
(2) The government is on the way out.
(3) Early elections will probably be held.
(4) The guilty party has behaved improperly.
(5) It is difficult to make out who is responsible. for the crisis.
(6) Measures will have to be taken to avoid a repetition.

Statements of fact relating to the past (1) and the present (2), predictions (3), moral judgments (4), other judgments (5), and opinions regarding a course of action to be followed (6), are in Toulmin's eyes examples of different logical types. The list is not exhaustive. Aesthetic opinions and geometrical axioms, for example, might be added.

---

[6]It is probable that Toulmin made use of the concept of "logical type" introduced by Ryle (1949/1976): "The logical type or category to which a concept belongs is the set of ways in which it is logically legitimate to operate with it" (1976, p. 10). Ryle uses this concept throughout his book, which has been highly influential, so Toulmin may have regarded the concept so familiar that he did not think it necessary to give a definition.

If statements that are to be justified are of the same logical type, and if all of the supporting statements are also of one logical type, Toulmin considers the argumentations concerned to belong to the same *field of argument*.[7] The supporting statements need not necessarily belong to the same logical type as those that are to be justified. A moral judgment ("He is a bad man") may, for instance, have statements of fact adduced in its support ("He beats his mother, he has poisoned his cats, he is a taxdodger").

There are elements that remain the same in all fields of argumentation and elements that differ from field to field. The general features of argumentation that are the same in all fields Toulmin calls *field-invariant*; particular features that are different in each field of argumentation he calls *field-dependent*.

In argumentation, a wide variety of statements can occur. With this fact in mind, Toulmin wonders to which extent the form and soundness of argumentation in different fields of argumentation are field-invariant or field-dependent. In his opinion, just as in jurisprudence, a fixed procedure can be discerned, and *in that sense* argumentation has a general form. This procedure, or form, consists of a number of steps that have to be followed in a fixed order. The order need not necessarily correspond to the various phases in the process of reasoning a person went through before arriving at a particular conclusion. They rather run parallel to the various stages to be discerned in the justification of the conclusion to others.

According to Toulmin, the argumentative procedure starts with the formulation of a problem in the form of a question. The next step involves the listing of possible solutions, setting aside solutions that appear inadequate straight away. The possible solutions are then weighed up against each other. Sometimes this process will lead to one solution emerging as the only right one; in that case, it is called a "necessary" solution. In other cases, a choice has to be made between several possible solutions, "the best" solution being the one that is or appears to be better or more likely than the others. In one field of argumentation it will be more difficult to arrive at a solution which may be termed *necessary* or *the best* than in another. If, for example, moral attitudes or questions of personal taste are involved, finding such a solution can present enormous problems. In all fields of argumentation, however, the steps just described can be distinguished. In this respect, Toulmin says, the procedural form of argumentation is therefore general, or field-invariant.

In the various steps, *modal terms* occur, such as "impossible," "possible," "necessary," and "probable." The function of these terms is to indicate the degree of certainty or confidence with which the statements are made in the step concerned. A solution that emerges as the only possible or only right one

---

[7]The expression "field of argument" is Toulmin's (1988, p. 14). For a proper understanding, it seems better to replace the term *argument* by the term *argumentation*, which is what we shall do.

out of all the possible solutions is called "necessary" or "certain." If the solution is less certain, or if subject to certain conditions, modal terms like "presumably" or "probable" will be appropriate.

To what extent, then, are modal terms field-dependent or field-invariant? Toulmin answers this question by referring to the modal term "cannot" (or "can't"), which can appear, as the following examples show, in a wide variety of contexts:

(1) You can't lift a ton.

(2) You can't get 100,000 people in the Albert Hall.

(3) You can't talk about a horse's "feet."

(4) You can't have an aunt of the male sex.

(5) You can't give him that small a tip—it's not done.

(6) You can't put the cat out in this rain.

In these examples, "can't" sometimes means "be incapable" or "it is impossible" (1–4) and sometimes "ought not" (5–6). Nevertheless, the function of "can't" is in all six examples the same: it eliminates something. The reason for the elimination, however, is in each case different: the limits of human strength (1), the limited capacity of a building (2), a linguistic convention (3), the meaning of a word (4), a social convention (5), a moral rule (6). In all these cases, the modal verb *can* and the logical operator *not* are used to qualify the certainty of a particular statement, though the grounds for the qualification are different in each case. Toulmin (1988) refers to the function of modal words as their *force*: the force of a modal term is the practical point or message it conveys in the context in which it is used.[8] The grounds which justify the use of modal terms he calls the *criteria* for their appropriate use (p. 30).

The force of modal terms is, according to Toulmin, field-invariant, but the criteria that are applied in order to determine whether in a given context a given modal term has been used rightly or wrongly are field-dependent. For example, if we call something *impossible*, we must be in a position to justify this claim by advancing grounds or reasons, but the nature of our justification—relating to the criteria we invoke for judging our use of the term *impossible*—is different in each field of argumentation. Toulmin argues that something like this is true of all modal terms, including "probable."[9]

---

[8]Toulmin also speaks of the "moral" of a modal term, as in the moral of a fable.

[9]Some of the implications Toulmin attaches to this observation relate to semantic and philosophical questions that are not directly relevant here. They pertain to the development of an adequate semantic theory for modal words and to the vigorous philosophical controversy about probability in the 1960s. In that controversy, Toulmin opposed the views on probability put forward by Carnap (1950) and Kneale (1949).

5.2 ARGUMENTATION FORM AND VALIDITY

How does the validity of arguments depend on the mold in which they are cast and how must we view the validity and form of arguments if we are interested in evaluating them? These are the questions asked by Toulmin when he turns to the level of single argumentation known as the micro-level. In answering these questions, he chooses legal argumentation as his example. The model he introduces to represent the layout of arguments is a procedural one, that is, one in which the various functions of the steps that are successively taken are given due consideration.[10] Here too, Toulmin wonders to which extent general, or field-invariant, elements play a part, and to which extent particular, or field-dependent, elements.

The first step in argumentation is the expressing of a standpoint (or assertion, opinion, preference, view, judgment, and so on). A person who expresses his standpoint on a certain matter thereby takes upon himself the duty to defend this standpoint in the event that it should be attacked. In general terms: He must be in a position to justify his opinion if challenged to do so. In Toulmin's terminology, the standpoint put forward and to be upheld is called the *claim* (abbreviated C).

How can a claim that has been attacked be defended? One way of defending it is to point to certain facts on which the claim is based, the *data* (D). The second step in argumentation thus consists of the production of data that support the claim. Naturally, a challenger will not always immediately concede the accuracy of these data. In that case a *preparatory* step on the part of the arguer is required to try to remove the objection.

Even if the data produced are accepted as accurate, a different kind of request may follow. Rather than asking for more data, the challenger may require an account of how the data lead to the claim in question. The third step in the argumentation, then, consists of providing the justification or *warrant* (W) for using the data concerned as support for the claim—for the data-claim relationship. The warrant can be expressed by a general statement referring to a rule, principle, and so on. In principle, this general statement will have a hypothetical form ("if [*data*] then [*claim*]"). The warrant functions as a *bridge* between the data and the claim. In Toulmin's view the warrant can take different forms. It can be very brief:

(1) If D then C.

---

[10]The expression "the layout of arguments" is Toulmin's (1988, p. 94). In the present study, we speak of the "layout of argumentation." Freeman (1991, pp. 3–6), who has made a careful study of Toulmin's insights, agrees with our interpretation that Toulmin's model refers to the procedure of argumentation, not to arguments as a product in the logical sense of a premise-conclusion sequence.

The warrant can also be more explicitly expanded, in various ways. Here are two examples provided by Toulmin (1988, p. 98):

(2) Data such as D entitle one to make claims such as C.

(3) Given data D, one may take it that C.

Toulmin expresses the difference between data and warrant as follows:

> [...] data are appealed to explicitly, warrants implicitly. (1988, p. 100)

According to Toulmin (1988), there is a close relationship between the data and warrants used in any particular field of argumentation:

> The data we cite if a claim is challenged depend on the warrants we are prepared to operate with in that field, and the warrants to which we commit ourselves are implicit in the particular steps from data to claims we are prepared to take and to admit. (p. 100)

So, the warrant is implicitly present in the step from data to claim and, conversely, the nature of the data depends on the nature of the warrant. This does not mean that in practice it will always be easy to recognize statements as data or as a warrant from their grammatical form alone. As Toulmin (1988) admits:

> [...] the distinction may appear far from absolute, and the same English sentence may serve a double function: it may be uttered, that is, in one situation to convey a piece of information, in another to authorise a step in an argument, and even perhaps in some contexts to do both these things at once. (p. 99)

Sometimes, indeed, drawing any sharp distinction will be quite impossible. But this does, of course, not mean that it will be impossible in all cases to distinguish the different *functions* fulfilled by the statements in the argumentation:

> At any rate we shall find it possible in *some* situations to distinguish clearly two different logical functions. (p. 99)

It is now possible to draft a first, simple model of argumentation. We shall do so by reference to an example used by Toulmin, and introduce the questions Toulmin asks to indicate the function of *data* and *warrant*:

Claim (C)	Harry is a British subject.	What have you got to go on?
Datum (D)	Harry was born in Bermuda.	How do you get there?
Warrant (W)	A man born in Bermuda will be a British subject.	

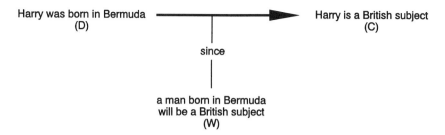

FIG. 5.2. Example of Toulmin's simple model.

This example is schematized in Fig. 5.2.

In this example it is assumed that the warrant is a rule without any exceptions, and that the accuracy of the warrant itself is not at issue. The force of the warrant would be weakened if there were exceptions to the rule, in which case conditions of *exception* or *rebuttal* (R) would have to be inserted.[11] The claim must then be weakened by means of a *qualifier* (Q).[12] A *backing* (B) is required if the authority of the warrant is not accepted straight away.

Thus three auxiliary steps may be necessary in argumentation.[13] Toulmin's extended model of argumentation therefore contains six elements. Let us illustrate these with the same example as the simple model, again using questions to indicate the function of each subsequent statement:

Claim (C)	Harry is a British subject.	What have you got to go on?
Datum (D)	Harry was born in Bermuda.	How do you get there?
Warrant (W)	A man born in Bermuda will generally be a British subject.	Is that always the case?
Rebuttal (R)	No, but it generally is. If his parents are for- eigners or if he has become a naturalized American, then the rule doesn't apply.	
		Then you can't be se definite in your claim, can you?

---

[11]We have used Toulmin's own terminology in describing his model. Other authors sometimes call data "evidence," and conditions of exception or rebuttal "reservation."

[12]A qualifier need not always weaken the claim. As Toulmin says: "Some warrants authorise us to accept a claim unequivocally, given the appropriate data—these warrants entitle us in suitable cases to qualify our conclusion with the adverb 'necessarily' " (1988, p. 100).

[13]In Goodnight (1993) it is argued that a communicative situation may occur in which the step from the backing to the warrant itself stands in need of justification.

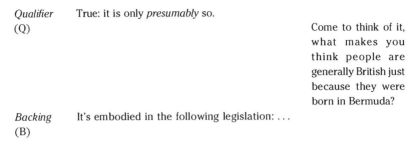

Qualifier   True: it is only *presumably* so.
(Q)

                                                        Come to think of it,
                                                        what makes you
                                                        think people are
                                                        generally British just
                                                        because they were
                                                        born in Bermuda?

Backing   It's embodied in the following legislation: . . .
(B)

This example is schematized in Fig. 5.3.

Of the six elements in the extended model, the claim, the data and the warrant are present in every argument; the rebuttal, the qualifier and the backing need not always occur. That is not to say that the warrant is always explicitly expressed; it can also be implicitly appealed to. This is, in fact, common practice. See for Toulmin's extended model Fig. 5.4.

Whether a backing appears in an argumentation depends on whether or not the warrant is accepted straight away. If it is, then there is no backing, if it is not, then there is. Toulmin (1988) observes that it is not possible to demand a backing for every warrant in a discussion, because that would make practical discussion impossible:

[. . .] unless, in any particular field of argument, we are prepared to work with warrants of *some* kind, it will become impossible in that field to subject arguments to rational assessment. (p. 100)

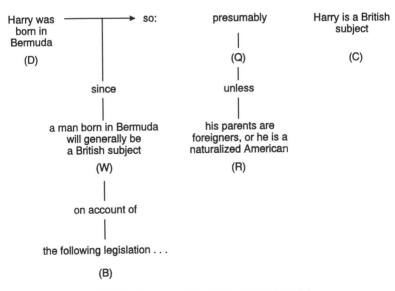

FIG. 5.3. Example of Toulmin's extended model.

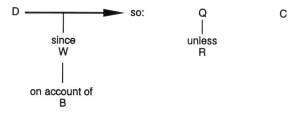

FIG. 5.4. Toulmin's extended model.

And:

> Some warrants must be accepted provisionally without further challenge, if argument is to be open to us in the field in question: we should not even know what sort of data were of the slightest relevance to a conclusion, if we had not at least a provisional idea of the warrants acceptable in the situation confronting us. (p. 106)

Toulmin sees the relation between the occurrence of a condition of rebuttal and the occurrence of a qualifier as follows. Whenever there is a condition of rebuttal, the claim must be weakened by a qualifier. Conversely, however, it is not necessary that there is a condition of rebuttal to the warrant just because there is a qualifier to the claim. It is possible that the warrant contains not an absolute rule but one with an addition such as "in general," without specific exceptions being named. This is the case in the example in Fig. 5.5.

The data in Toulmin's model consist of facts produced in support of the claim. Facts, however, may also have another function in an argumentation. They can be referred to in the backing for the warrant (as in our example), or to confirm or deny that a warrant satisfies the conditions of rebuttal. In the example of Harry (see Fig. 5.3) the warrant may be applied without reservation if additional information about Harry includes such statements as the following:

(1) Neither of his parents were foreigners.

(2) He has not become a naturalized American.

Then the qualifier "presumably" could be removed, since the claim would "necessarily" follow from the data and the warrant.[14] If, on the other hand, the additional information were to indicate that Harry belongs to one of the exceptional categories mentioned in the conditions of rebuttal, this would mean that

---

[14]Cf. Schellens (1979), who observes that in this case R no longer functions as a condition of rebuttal. Instead, there are three data ("Harry was born in Bermuda"; "Neither of his parents were foreigners"; "He has not become a naturalized American") and a complex warrant ("A man born in Bermuda will generally be a British subject unless his parents are foreigners or he has become a naturalized American").

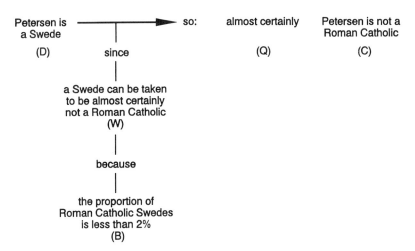

FIG. 5.5. Example of an argument with a qualifier without a rebuttal.

"the general authority of the warrant would have to be set aside" (Toulmin, 1988, p. 101). Consequently, the claim is not successfully defended, at least not on the ground that he was born in Bermuda.

What, now, is the relation between argumentation in Toulmin's model and legal argumentation? It is already apparent from the fact that both in Toulmin's model and in legal argumentation there are steps in the justification of a statement which fulfill various functions in the process of justification and which have to be executed according to the rules of a particular procedure. According to Toulmin himself, however, there are also more specific similarities. For example, the claim corresponds with the indictment by the prosecution in a criminal case, the data with the evidence, and the warrant with the content of the legal rules or stipulations obtaining in the case concerned, while the backing may be compared with the relevant passages in the relevant legal codes or textbooks. In legal matters it may also be necessary, just as in argumentation in general, to discuss the extent to which a particular law or regulation or rule applies in a particular case—whether it need necessarily be applied, or whether particular circumstances make the case an exception, or whether the rule can only be applied in a weakened form.

In Toulmin's model, it is assumed that the data as such are accurate (or in legal terms, that a case has been made out). What does the validity of the argumentation depend on, according to Toulmin? He calls argumentation "valid" if, first, the required procedure has been correctly followed, that is, if the argumentation has been cast in the mold represented in the model, and, second, if the warrant for the step from data to claim is adequate and may be regarded authoritative.

The warrant is adequate if it justifies the step from the data to the claim, thereby guaranteeing the accuracy of the claim, whether or not modified by a qualifier. It is authoritative if it is immediately accepted as such or if it obtains its authority from the backing. According to Toulmin, the warrant is the crucial element in determining the validity of argumentation, for the warrant indicates explicitly *that* the step from data to claim is justified and also *why* this is so.

To what degree does form determine validity? And to what extent are form and validity field-invariant or field-dependent in the Toulmin model? This is what Toulmin (1988) says about the first question:

> Yet one thing must be noticed straight away: provided that the correct warrant is employed, any argument can be expressed in the form "Data; warrant; so conclusion" and so become formally valid. By suitable choice of phrasing, that is, any such argument can be so expressed that its validity is apparent simply from its form [. . .]. On the other hand, if we substitute the backing for the warrant, [. . .] there will no longer be any room for applying the idea of formal validity to our argument. (p. 119)

With respect to the second question, Toulmin's view is that the form of argumentation is field-invariant. Not only legal argumentation, but argumentation from every class of field can in principle be represented in the same form. The validity of argumentation is not, says Toulmin, totally field-invariant but has a field-invariant and a field-dependent aspect. Validity is partly a function of the form (the procedure must have been correctly performed) and in this sense validity is field-invariant. But validity is also partly, and essentially, determined by the warrant, so that ultimately it is field-dependent.[15]

Ultimately, the warrant obtains its authority from the backing, and backings can vary in different fields of argumentation. For example, a backing may refer to particular legal stipulations, as in the Harry example, or to the results of a census, as in the Petersen example; but it may also refer to aesthetic norms, moral judgments, psychological patterns or mathematical axioms. In every field of argumentation it has to be determined which warrants may be regarded authoritative and in what manner they must be backed.

Thirty years after the publication of *The Uses of Argument*, Toulmin (1992) made this comment:

> If I were rewriting the book today, I would broaden the context, and show that it is not just the "warrants" and "backing" that vary from field to field: even more, it is the *forums* of argumentation, the *stakes*, and the contextual details of "arguing" as an *activity*. (p. 9)

By now it should be clear that Toulmin had a conception of the notions of "form" and "validity" and of their relationship which is radically different from the

---

[15]Toulmin's view that validity is ultimately field-dependent implies that in principle every field of argumentation may claim rationality for the argumentation being used. The only condition Toulmin requires is that in the field concerned question there must be accepted and authoritative warrants.

standard view in formal logic, with which he fundamentally disagrees. According to him, the cause of all trouble is the distinction between major and minor premises made in classical syllogistic logic (which Toulmin equates with the modern "logical view").[16] Toulmin finds this distinction misleadingly simple. The functions of the two sorts of premise are, in fact, so different that it is even wrong to place them under the same label of "premise." He gives the following example:

(1) Petersen is a Swede.

(2) No Swedes are Roman Catholics.

   So, certainly

(3) Petersen is not Roman Catholic.

In this syllogism, (1) is the minor premise and (2) the major premise. The major premise conceals, in Toulmin's view, a treacherous simplicity because it can be interpreted either as a warrant (W) or as backing (B). These two interpretations are apparent from the following wordings:

(2a) A Swede is certainly not a Roman Catholic.

(2b) The proportion of Roman Catholic Swedes is zero.

(2a) represents the W-interpretation, (2b) the B-interpretation. The major premise in the syllogism takes no account of the different functions of the warrant and the backing, and therefore contains a hidden complexity. Whether the major premise is interpreted as W or as B, in either case its function is quite different from that of the minor premise, which acts as a datum (D). In the syllogism, the distinction is ignored by using the same term *premise* for both functions.

According to Toulmin, the argument in the Petersen example—minor premise (1), major premise (2), therefore conclusion (3)—is regarded valid in the logical view because of its form. He points out that in the W-interpretation of the major premise (2a) the argument has a formally valid form, but the B-interpretation (2b) presents problems. In the latter interpretation, the argument is clearly not formally valid in the logical sense, even though it is perfectly acceptable, and therefore sound in a broader sense. Toulmin (1988) concludes that the validity of the argument with (2b) as a premise is not really a consequence of its formal properties and that the validity of the argument with (2) or (2a) as a premise can therefore not be a formal matter either:

> Once we bring into the open the backing on which (in the last resort) the soundness of our arguments depends, the suggestion that validity is to be explained in terms of "formal properties," in any geometrical sense, loses its plausibility. (p. 120)

---

[16]For a discussion of classical syllogistic logic, see chapter 2.

According to Toulmin (1988), logicians fail to see this because the "ambiguity" of the major premise conceals the crucial distinction between warrant and backing. Consequently, the fact that the validity of arguments ultimately depends on the backing remains in the dark (pp. 107–122).

The cause of all the trouble, says Toulmin, is the geometrical interpretation of validity prevalent in formal logic. According to this view, an argument is valid if it is a substitution instance of a valid argument form. An argument form is valid if the conclusion is contained in the premises, if it is simply a "formal transformation" of its premises (1988, p. 118). This, in Toulmin's view incorrect, conception flows from the logicians' onesided interest in analytical arguments, which he thinks should not be regarded exemplary for all arguments. Formal validity in the logical sense relates only to the way in which arguments are formulated and has nothing to do with the real sources of validity.

By means of yet another example Toulmin (1988) tries to show that nonanalytic arguments, too, can be valid in his procedural sense (pp. 123–127):

(1) Anne is one of Jack's sisters.
(2) All Jack's sisters have red hair.

So

(3) Anne has red hair.

The major premise (2) can be rewritten as a warrant (2a) and as a backing (2b):

(2a) Any sister of Jack's will (i.e., may be taken to) have red hair.
(2b) Each one of Jack's sisters has (been checked individually to have) red hair.

Toulmin (1988) observes that the backing (2b) includes explicitly the information which is also present in the conclusion (3):

> [...] indeed, one might very well replace the word "so" before the conclusion by the phrase "in other words," or "that is to say." (p. 124)

For this reason, Toulmin calls the argument analytic:

> In such case, to accept the datum and the backing is *thereby* to accept implicitly the conclusion also; if we string datum, backing and conclusion together to form a single sentence, we end up with an actual tautology. (p. 124)

According to Toulmin, the warrant (2a) is only authoritative if, as we are informed in the backing (2b), all Jack's sisters individually have undergone a check as to the color of their hair. But in that case, of course, Anne's hair has also been checked: in other words, the conclusion that Anne has red hair (3) goes no further than what has already been said in the premises.

In nonanalytic arguments—those which Toulmin calls "substantial"—the conclusion does contain new information. This becomes apparent, says Toulmin, if we change the Anne-example as follows (1988, p. 126):

(1')   Anne is one of Jack's sisters.
(2a')   Any sister of Jack's may be taken to have red hair.
(2b')   All Jack's sisters have previously been observed to have red hair.

     So

(3')   presumably, Anne now has red hair.

The conclusion (3') has now been weakened by the qualifier "presumably" because in the meantime Anne's hair may have changed color or she may have lost her hair. It is therefore necessary to make a reservation regarding the warrant (2a'):

(2a")   Unless Anne has dyed/gone white/lost her hair . . .

In this example, the backing (2b') no longer contains exactly the same information as the conclusion, but in Toulmin's view it is still valid because the warrant justifies the step from the datum (1') to the claim (3'), acquiring its authority from the backing (2b'). See Fig. 5.6.

With this example Toulmin claims to have proved that substantial arguments, which he says are by far the most prevalent in practice, can also be valid. He also provides an explanation of why substantial arguments are more common in practice than analytic ones:

> If the purpose of an argument is to establish conclusions about which we are not entirely confident by relating them back to other information about which we have greater assurance, it begins to be a little doubtful whether any genuine, practical argument could *ever* be properly analytic. (1988, pp. 126–127)

Unlike analytic arguments, substantial arguments do make a contribution to the purpose of argumentation as Toulmin sees it. Inasmuch as the conclusions of analytic arguments contain basically the same information as the premises, there is no uncertainty about the information contained in the conclusion. And therefore, says Toulmin, there is no need for an argument at all.

Reference to the examples of Anne, Petersen, and Harry can also illustrate, once more, the field-dependency of the validity of argumentation and arguments. In the Anne example, backing up the warrant requires that the natural (or original) color of all Jack's sisters' hair be established, in the Petersen example a national census would be required, and in the Harry example it would be

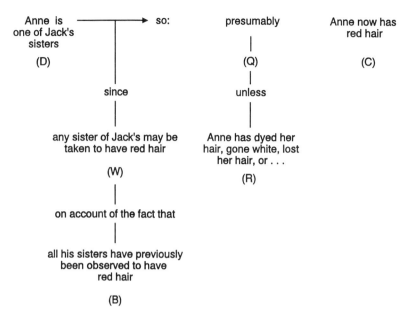

FIG. 5.6. Example of an argument in Toulmin's view nonanalytic but nevertheless valid.

necessary to check the relevant laws. For all these things to be done properly, we should need first a chemist who is not color blind (or a hairdresser with a knowledge of chemistry), then a demographer, and finally a lawyer. The arguments can in principle be equally valid. According to Toulmin, there is no reason whatsoever to regard them as being automatically less rational than analytic arguments, or even to go so far as to call them irrational.

In Toulmin's view, the idea that there are universal criteria of validity can only be upheld if validity is conceived of as a formal property of analytic arguments, as happens in standard logic. Toulmin concludes that it is the reluctance of logic to drop this conception of validity that has made logic insignificant for the evaluation of arguments as they actually occur in practice.

5.3 SOME APPLICATIONS OF THE MODEL

In the reviews of *The Uses of Argument* in the philosophical journals, little or no attention is paid to the model, and the opinions concerning the rest of the book are predominantly negative. For a more positive appreciation we must look primarily beyond the ranks of philosophers.

Several authors have pointed out similarities between Toulmin's model and the syllogism and have discussed the relation between the model and classical rhetoric and dialectic, particularly the concept of *topos* (Bird, 1961; Kienpointner, 1983, 1992a). Others used the concept of warrant in order to classify processes of reasoning (Hastings, 1962; Windes & Hastings, 1969).[17]

Some authors have linked the model with mental processes playing a part in convincing (Cronkhite, 1969; Reinard, 1984; Voss et al., 1993). Other authors examined its applicability to the interpretation of texts (Huth 1975), and literary texts in particular (Grewendorf, 1975); it has also been related to theories of truth and rationality (Gottlieb, 1968; Habermas, 1973, 1981), and to argumentation and communicative action (Kopperschmidt, 1989a). Another group of authors has written about uses of the model for particular forms of argumentation, notably for linguistic argumentation (Botha, 1970; Wunderlich, 1974), dialectic argumentation (Freeman, 1992; Healy, 1987), and legal argumentation (Pratt, 1970; Newell & Rieke, 1986; Rieke & Stutman, 1990).

In some cases, specific elements of Toulmin's views have been taken up, for instance the concept of "argument field." This concept has in various forms been adapted, for example, by authors such as Willard (1983) and Goodnight (1982). The most favorable response, however, the model has received in literature on the skills of arguing, debating, discussing, and speaking. We shall pay some closer attention to this last kind of application of the model in practice oriented articles and books.

Toulmin's model can be found in numerous textbooks on one or more communicative skills. Most of these have appeared in the United States and are inspired, so far as the application of the model is concerned, by Ehninger and Brockriede's *Decision by Debate* (1963). Brockriede and Ehninger's adaptation of Toulmin's model led to its widespread adoption in practical textbooks on argumentation. Other books in which the Toulmin model is used are Richard Crable's *Argumentation as Communication* (1976), Toulmin, Rieke, and Janik's *An Introduction to Reasoning* (1979), and Eisenberg and Ilardo's *Argument; A Guide to Formal and Informal Debate* (1980).[18]

Wayne Brockriede and Douglas Ehninger laid the foundations for their influential textbook on debating in an article published in 1960. They gave an interpretation of the Toulmin model and applied it to the construction of a system for classifying sorts of argumentation. Generally speaking, they endorse Toulmin's criticism of logic and conclude that the Toulmin model is better suited to

---

[17]Hastings (1962) distinguishes among three main processes of reasoning: verbal reasoning, causal reasoning, and direct proof of conclusion. Verbal reasoning, which includes arguments from example, criteria, and definition, is based on accepted symbolic formulations in language and thinking. Causal reasoning includes reasoning from sign, from cause, and from circumstantial evidence; the warrants used in these forms of reasoning are causal generalizations. Direct proof of conclusion includes argument from comparison, analogy, and testimony. Windes and Hastings (1969) present an adapted version of this classification.

[18]The model is also used in several Dutch textbooks, for example, Schellens and Verhoeven (1988).

the description, analysis and evaluation of argumentation than the logic-based methods usually employed in textbooks on argumentation. They see the model as an alternative more in tune with actual practice.

Brockriede and Ehninger interpret Toulmin's model as a *rhetorical* model, which is reflected in their classification of sorts of argumentation. This classification goes back to the Aristotelian tripartition of means of persuasion based on *logos, pathos* or *ethos*. The first type they call *substantive*, the second *motivational*, and the third *authoritative*. The differences between these three forms of argumentation, say Brockriede and Ehninger, must be looked for in the nature of the *warrant* in Toulmin's model. In a *substantive* argument the warrant tells us something about the way in which "the things in the world about us" relate to one another, in a *motivational* argument it tells us something about the emotions, values, desires or motives which can make the *claim* acceptable to the person to whom the argument is addressed, and in an *authoritative* argument it says something about the reliability of the source from which the data are drawn.[19]

Let us now look at an example of each type, taken from Ehninger and Brockriede's *Decision by Debate* (1963). The authors distinguish between various sorts of *substantive* argumentation. An example of the first of these, arguments in which a *causal* relationship is defined, is seen in Fig. 5.7.

Examples of *motivational* argumentation and *authoritative* argumentation are:

Motivational argumentation
Continued testing of nuclear weapons is needed for U.S. military security, therefore continued testing of nuclear weapons is desirable for the United States, since *the United States is motivated by a desire to maintain the value of military security.*

Authoritative argumentation (our own example)
Milton Friedman says that the nation's economy would benefit from a drastic cutting back of government interference. That will probably be true, since Milton Friedman's views on economics are authoritative.

Another attempt to make Toulmin's model applicable in practice, has been made by James Trent (1968). Trent's interpretation of the model resembles Brockriede and Ehninger's, but has been much less influential. Trent treats the Toulmin model as a *syllogistic* model. He refers to some authors (among them Manicas, 1966) who regard the syllogistic nature of the model as a drawback because it renders it unfit for the analysis of nonsyllogistic argument forms, such as *modus ponens*, but Trent does not find this limitation very serious. In his view, the vast

---

[19]Brockriede and Ehninger's definition of substantive, motivational, and authoritative argumentation is slightly different from the classical tripartition into *logos, pathos*, and *ethos* discussed in chapter 2. This is particularly true of authoritative argumentation, classical rhetoric being exclusively concerned with the *speaker's* reliability and good character.

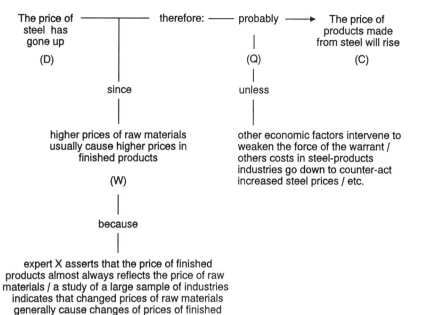

FIG. 5.7. Example of a substantive argument with a causal warrant.

majority of arguments occurring in practice are either syllogistic or can easily be reduced to the syllogistic form.

The great advantage of Toulmin's model, according to Trent, is the emphasis it puts on *material* rather than *formal* validity; this is more in line with everyday practice. Still, he regards the model as incomplete and hence inadequate to evaluate the material validity of arguments. By modifying the model, he tries to remedy this drawback. First, he extends the model by including a backing, a qualifier, and a rebuttal in the data. This makes the model, in his view, more complete and the source of (un)certainty of a claim can be more easily indicated. Second, Trent distinguishes between three groups of argument types, which he calls *epicheiremes*: *selection* epicheiremes, *inference* epicheiremes, and *rhetorical* epicheiremes. In a selection epicheireme, the claim is selected from the backing by the warrant; in an inference epicheireme, it is inferred from data or warrant; and in a rhetorical epicheireme, it is guaranteed by the authority of the speaker.[20]

Trent illustrates the differences between these three categories of epicheiremes by reference to Toulmin's Anne example. Still, it is not quite clear what exactly he has in mind; except perhaps for the inference epicheiremes, which we shall take as our example. See Fig. 5.8.

---

[20]A rhetorical epicheireme resembles Brockriede and Ehninger's authoritative argumentation, which is a rhetorical means of persuasion based on *ethos*.

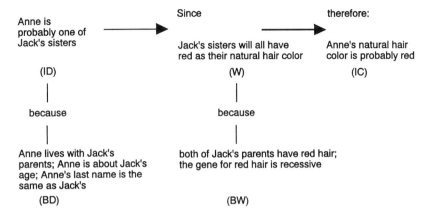

FIG. 5.8. Example of an inference epicheireme.

In this example, the inference claim (IC) cannot be asserted with absolute certainty because there is a qualifier to the inference datum (ID). The uncertainty regarding the datum has its cause in the backing for the datum (BD). The backing for the warrant (BW), however, does allow an absolute warrant.

Trent sees his own extension of the model, but also Brockriede and Ehninger's interpretation of it, as an attempt to bring logic closer to the practice of argumentation. This was also Toulmin's purpose in *The Uses of Argument*, albeit that he argues that a radical reorientation of logic is needed for accomplishing this task. Toulmin's exposition of the model is, in fact, only intended to show that the criteria for evaluating argumentation are ultimately field-dependent. Of course, this does not mean that the model cannot be used as a general model for the analysis of argumentation. Apart from Brockriede and Ehninger, and Trent, many authors have tried to do so, including Toulmin himself in *An introduction to reasoning*, coauthored by Rieke and Janik (1979).[21] In the preface of this textbook, the authors state explicitly:

> The "basic pattern of analysis" set out in Part II of this book [including all the elements of the 1958 model] is suitable to arguments of all types and in all fields.
> (p. v)

It is striking that most authors who used Toulmin's model as a general model for argumentation analysis—again, including Brockriede and Ehninger, Trent, and Toulmin himself 20 years later—ignore the logical ambitions Toulmin intended his model to serve. In most practical textbooks the model is completely isolated from its philosophical starting points.

---

[21]In various reviews of *The uses of argument* it is rightly assumed that Toulmin regards his model as generally applicable. Cowan, for one, writes: "This pattern has, according to Toulmin, the necessary scope to encompass all arguments" (1964, p. 29).

There have been some exceptions, however. In their *Argumentation and the Decision-Making Process*, Richard Rieke and Malcolm Sillars (1975), in surveying some important theories of argumentation, give a brief summary of the wider framework within which Toulmin's view of argumentation is to be placed (pp. 1–24). And in Crable's *Argumentation as Communication* (1976), too, something of this broader context can be found at various places.[22] Yet even in these two books the application of the model is separated from Toulmin's radical views on logic.

Toulmin's philosophical ideas, notably his theses about the field-dependency of argumentation and the epistemological nature of the evaluation of argumentation, have had a considerable influence in another area: the educational reform movement known as Critical Thinking, which is discussed in chapter 6. This influence manifests itself, for example, in the works of John McPeck. In two books, *Critical Thinking and Education* (1981) and *Teaching and Critical Thinking* (1990), McPeck explicitly appeals to the Toulmin conception when arguing that field-independent instruction in the standards of reasoning and argumentation is impossible, for there are no such standards. He agrees with Toulmin that the standards for reasoning and argumentation are a function of the epistemology of the fields or disciplines concerned. The warrants that authorize the moves from data to claims are dependent on the prevailing epistemology. The correct way of learning how to argue about literature or about history is thus to learn the standards of literary criticism or of history. Learning to think critically, McPeck argues, requires learning the epistemology of each field. McPeck's position has been taken up and extended in Weinstein (1990a, 1990b).

5.4 PERSPECTIVES

According to Toulmin, logic has for too long been reluctant to drop its narrow formal conception of validity, which is responsible for the insignificance of logic for the evaluation of arguments as they occur in practice. His chief aim with *The Uses of Argument* was to bring logic closer to argumentation in everyday life and in the academic disciplines. This can only be achieved by way of a radical change in orientation.

Although in the most favorable reviews (e.g., Abelson 1960–1961) there is some sympathy with Toulmin's efforts to improve the applicability of logic, initially his suggestions were not well-received by his fellow philosophers. In most reactions, the course he advocates is rejected. The criticisms mainly concern his ideas on probability (see, for example, Cooley, 1959, and King-Far-

---

[22]This comes as no surprise, since Crable (1976) refers to Toulmin as his "most profound influence" and "a source of challenge and insight" (p. vi).

low, 1973) and the form and validity of arguments (e.g., Castaneda, 1960, and Cowan, 1964).[23]

More recently, several argumentation theorists with a philosophical background, such as Freeman (1985, 1988, 1991, 1992) and Weinstein (1990a, 1990b), have taken Toulmin's ambitions and his model more seriously. They regard his ideas useful contributions to the development of theoretical tools for the analysis and evaluation of argumentation. In citing the influences that have led to the rise of informal logic, Johnson and Blair (1980) note the Toulmin model. With Toulmin—though not always for the same reasons—informal logicians tend to hold that formal logic does not constitute the best, and certainly not the only, tool for analyzing and evaluating argumentation. As we explain in chapter 6, Toulmin's radical critique, and the new perspective on argumentation he provided, was an inspiration to explore this territory with other models and instruments than those supplied by formal logic.

We shall leave the general theoretical implications of Toulmin's radical ideas on logic further undiscussed, and concentrate on the merits of his model.[24] One of the major problems is the vagueness, ambiguity, and sometimes even inconsistency in his use of key terms. An example of vagueness is the term *field of argument*, which he defines by reference to another term, *logical type*. From the examples, one gets the impression that factual statements, moral judgments, and predictions belong to different fields of argument. In his explication of the field-dependency of the backing, however, Toulmin gives the impression that the terms *field of argument*, *topic*, and *discipline* are synonymous. A weather forecast would then belong to a different field of argument (meteorology) than an economic forecast (economics).

More serious is the confusion Toulmin creates in his use of the terms *valid* and *validity*. The word valid is sometimes used in its formal logical sense. More often, however, it appears to be used in a more general sense, meaning something like "sound," "defensible," "well-grounded," "cogent," "good," or "acceptable."[25] A confusing ambiguity is involved in the phrasing of the central question in the chapter in which Toulmin presents his model:

How, then, should we lay an argument out, if we want to show the sources of its *validity*? And in what sense does the *acceptability* or *unacceptability* of arguments dependent on their "formal" merits and defects? (p. 95; our italics)

---

[23]Critical reactions to *The uses of argument* of a more recent date are Hample (1977b), and Healy (1987). More positive about the Toulmin model are Burleson (1979), and Reinard (1984).

[24]It is apparent from Toulmin's later work that his views on logic have become subtler and more refined (e.g., Toulmin, 1976).

[25]Cf. Toulmin (1988, p. 147), where he uses the terms *soundness*, *validity*, *cogency*, and *strength* interchangeably.

The first sentence leaves room for the interpretation that the term *validity* is to be understood in its formal logical sense; the second sentence suggests that validity is equal to acceptability.

Throughout *The Uses of Argument* Toulmin does not clearly differentiate between the formal logical meaning of validity and its general nontechnical meaning. This distinction is important, however, in view of the question whether the "validity of an argument" is field-invariant or field-dependent. Let us look again at the Petersen example, discussed in Section 5.2:

(1) Petersen is a Swede (minor premise).

(2) No Swedes are Roman Catholics (major premise).

(2a) A Swede can be taken to be certainly not a Roman Catholic (W).

(2b) The proportion of Roman Catholic Swedes is zero (B).

    So

(3) Petersen is not a Roman Catholic.

In the formal logical sense, the argument "minor premise (1), major premise (2), therefore conclusion (3)" is valid. Toulmin finds the argument also valid if the major premise (2) is interpreted as a warrant (2a), implying that the validity here too is a matter of validity in the formal logical sense:

> [. . .] provided that the correct warrant is employed, any argument can be expressed in the form "Data; warrant; so conclusion" and so become *formally valid*. By suitable choice of phrasing, that is, any such argument can be so expressed that its validity is apparent simply from its form: this is true equally, *whatever the field of the argument* [. . .]. (1988, p. 119; our italics)

The argument in which the major premise (2) is interpreted as a backing (2b), however, is according to Toulmin not formally valid, but may be sound or acceptable in practice:

> On the other hand, if we substitute the backing for the warrant, i.e., interpret the universal premiss in the other way, *there will no longer be any room for applying the idea of formal validity to our argument.* Any argument of the form "Data; backing; so conclusion" may, for practical purposes, be entirely in order. We should accept without hesitation the argument: Petersen is a Swede; The recorded proportion of Roman Catholic Swedes is zero; So, certainly, Petersen is not a Roman Catholic. (1988, p. 119; our italics)

The implication for Toulmin is then that *therefore* the validity of 1–2a–3, too, cannot be the consequence of *formal* qualities:

> But there can no longer be any pretence that the soundness of this argument is a consequence of any formal properties of its constituent expressions. (1988, p. 120)

And Toulmin concludes:

> Once we bring into the open the backing on which (in the last resort) the *soundness* of our arguments depends, the suggestion that *validity* is to be explained in terms of "formal properties," in any geometrical sense, loses its plausibility. (1988, p. 120; our italics)

In connection with these quotations several observations may be in order.

First, it seems clear that the—general and undefined—terms *acceptable* and *sound*, on the one hand, and the—formal logical and well-defined—term *valid*, on the on the other hand, are turned into synonyms.

Second, from the observation that argument 1–2b–3 cannot be called a formally valid argument because of its form, even though it is sound or acceptable in the practical sense, it cannot be concluded that *therefore* the formal validity of argument 1–2a–3 cannot be due to its formal properties either.[26]

Third, it remains obscure what form the warrant must take in order for the argument to be either formally valid or valid in Toulmin's own, general sense. It might be thought that Toulmin does not actually regard this question as very important, since his only intention is to show that it is, ultimately, the (field-dependent) backing for the warrant—whatever form it may take—which determines the validity or invalidity of an argument. But this is not very likely, because Toulmin himself says that a condition for formal validity of an argument is that the warrant shall be formulated *explicitly* as a warrant and that it shall justify *precisely* the inference concerned.[27] He does not elaborate on the requirements of an "explicit formulation" or a "precise warrant."

Fourth, if we follow Toulmin in his interpretation of validity as broader than formal validity, then it is not so difficult to agree that the validity of argumentation is not entirely a matter for formal logicians and that field-dependent considerations may come into play. In fact, various authors, such as Johnstone (1968) and Manicas (1966), agree with Toulmin's claim that the evaluation of argumentation in everyday and academic life require norms other than those

---

[26]*In this form*, by the way, argument 1–2a–3 is not formally valid in, for example, standard syllogistic logic, propositional logic or predicate logic. The same is true for the argument (1) "Petersen is a Swede," (2a) "A Swede is almost certainly not a Roman Catholic," so (3) "Petersen is almost certainly not a Roman Catholic." This argument does not even become formally valid if the warrant (2a) is interpreted as a major premise: (2) "Almost no Swedes are Roman Catholics."

[27]Toulmin assumes that the function of an argument is to justify a conclusion. Cowan (1964, pp. 32, 43) points out that its function is to supply a lucid *organization* of the material. Only in analytic arguments this objective is realized to the maximum. According to Cowan, Toulmin's substantial arguments can easily be made analytic by making one or more unexpressed premises explicit. The kind of "reconstructive deductivism" promoted by Cowan is criticized by informal logicians. For a discussion of these criticisms and a defense of deductivism, see Groarke (1992).

provided by formal logic and that such other norms cannot be universally established for all argumentation, but are field-dependent.[28] They disapprove, however, of Toulmin's confusing use of logical terms with a clear and fixed meaning. By reinterpreting these terms in such a way that they become useless for logical purposes, Toulmin only obscures, in their opinion, his own worthwhile cause.

Toulmin's model has been widely accepted as a useful model for analyzing argumentation, not so much as a model for its evaluation.[29] In analyzing argumentation in spoken discourse and written texts, the model is frequently used to make its structure more transparent, and to provide a good starting point for its evaluation. To which extent is the model adequate for this task?

Is the model really, as Toulmin claims, a model of the structure of argumentation on the micro-level? If this is to mean that it refers to the smallest unit of argumentation, then we think that this is not the case. By including a backing, Toulmin turned his model from a model of single argumentation into a model of complex argumentation.[30]

In his model, Toulmin assumes that the data are accepted at face value. If this is not the case, he says, then it will have to be made the case by way of a preliminary argumentation. The datum from the one argument will then be the claim in the other. There is absolutely no reason, however, why the same should not apply to the warrant. If a warrant is not immediately accepted as authoritative, then an attempt must be made to remove the objections by means of a new argumentation, in which the warrant from the first argumentation serves as the claim. So, if argumentation contains a backing for the warrant, then there are in fact *two* single argumentations, the one being subordinatively connected with the other.[31]

Is it in practice always possible to differentiate between data and warrants? Toulmin himself admits that this may be sometimes difficult. This problem is caused by the two different characterizations given by Toulmin (1988) when introducing the concepts of data and warrants: (1) data contain specific factual information, while warrants are general, hypothetical, rule-like statements that act as a bridge between claim and data and authorize the step from data to claim (p. 98); (2) data are explicitly appealed to, warrants implicitly (p. 100).

It is emphasized by Toulmin that the key distinction between data and warrant is their different function. Even in combination with other criteria, however, it is in practice often hard to determine which statements are exactly the data

---

[28]Unlike for Toulmin, for some authors the ultimate implication of this view is that only experts in a particular field are competent to evaluate argumentation in that field (e.g., Abelson 1960–1961).

[29]An exception may be Hastings (1962), who formulates critical questions for different sorts of warrants.

[30]For the distinction between single and complex argumentation, see chapter 1.

[31]For the notion of subordinatively compound argumentation, see chapter 1.

and which statement serves as the warrant. We can illustrate this with the example from Fig. 5.2:

Claim (C)   (1) Harry is a British subject.

What have you got to go on?

Data (D)   (2) A man born in Bermuda is a British subject.

How do you get there?

Warrant (W) (3) Harry was born in Bermuda.

In Toulmin's original example, (3) is the datum and (2) the warrant. The inversion which has taken place in the example above is possible because the defender of the claim evidently assumes that the attacker is acquainted with Harry's birthplace and not with the law. Therefore, (3) is initially implicit, while (2) is stated explicitly. Statement (3) is necessary because the attacker's question shows that the defender's supposition is incorrect; the statement now functions as a bridge between (1) and (2). Thus the datum is in this case a general, rule-like statement and the warrant contains specific factual information. And if (2) is understood to be the warrant and (3) the datum, then—in contrast to what the criteria for making the distinction stipulate—the warrant has been explicitly expressed and the datum can remain implicit.

What this example shows is primarily that Toulmin's different characterizations of data and warrants sometimes conflict with each other. If one wants to be consistent, a clear choice has to be made between the characterizations. It is obvious that sticking to the explicit/implicit distinction will not solve anything. It seems preferable to interpret data as containing factual and specific information, and warrants as general and rule-like statements, referring to the argumentation scheme that is used. The latter interpretation is in fact, albeit usually implicitly, favored in most textbooks in which the Toulmin model is used, including in Toulmin, Rieke, and Janik (1979).[32]

Despite these and other problems, Toulmin's model has had a strong impact on practical textbooks dealing with the analysis of—single and complex—argumentation.[33] An important merit of the model is that it draws attention to the argumentation schemes that play a crucial part in argumentation, and to their similarity with the *topoi*. Another merit is its emphasis on the different kinds of backings that are required and the field-dependency involved. A third merit is that—with some modifications—the model, as shown in Freeman (1991), enables

---

[32]For similar objections to the distinction between data and warrants, see Schellens (1979), Johnson (1981), and Freeman (1991, pp. 49–90).

[33]For a survey of practical problems in the application of the Toulmin model to the analysis of argumentative texts, see especially Schellens (1979), who also offers some solutions.

the analyst to give a transparent picture of complex argumentation structures. Of course, this can also be achieved in other ways, but that does not diminish the attraction of the Toulmin model.[34]

A major attraction of Toulmin's model is probably that it explicitly addresses argumentation in everyday situations in ordinary language. Equally attractive is Toulmin's view of the nature of the criteria for evaluating argumentation, his starting point being that in establishing these criteria the supremacy of one particular field of argumentation over others must be rejected. In claiming that each field of argumentation provides in principle the criteria for arriving at a rational evaluation of argumentation pertaining to the field concerned, Toulmin rejects the idea of universal or absolute evaluation criteria.

The idea that the criteria for evaluating argumentation are field-dependent has over the years gained approval. It is, for example, applauded in the works of several American communication scholars, such as Rowland (1981, 1982), Goodnight (1982), and Willard (1983, 1989). Despite the vast body of literature about argument(ation) fields, it is still not quite clear how they are to be defined, how they should be classified, and in which ways the norms of rationality differ in the various fields. All the same, most authors persist in their enthusiasm about the field concept.[35] Zarefsky (1982) expresses their optimism as follows:

> There is a certain temptation to throw up one's hand in the face of conceptual fuzziness and confusion, abandoning the troublesome concept altogether. But the "field" concept has useful purposes to serve. It is a potential aid to explaining what happens in argumentative encounters, to classifying argument products, and to deriving evaluative standards. (p. 203)

Whether the promising potential of the concept of argument field, as introduced by Toulmin, will ever materialize is still an open question. As the discussion of argument fields shows, Toulmin's ideas have been a stimulus to others to embark upon the study of argumentation. It is largely thanks to his work that the interest in argumentation theory has so considerably increased since the 1950s.

---

[34]Cf. Snoeck Henkemans (1992).

[35]See also the special issue of the *Journal of the American Forensic Association* on Argument Fields, edited by Willard (1982), and the sections on argument fields in Ziegelmueller and Rhodes (1981).

CONTEMPORARY
DEVELOPMENTS

6

INFORMAL LOGIC AND CRITICAL THINKING

A forceful movement toward the study of argumentation has been created in North America by a group of philosophers who call themselves "informal logicians." These informal logicians set out to study arguments from a point of view that is different from the formal logicians'.[1] Although a general conception of informal logic has gradually developed that is more or less shared by most informal logicians, it is by no means universally agreed-upon. Some informal logicians have quite a different, or a more limited, conception of informal logic.[2] Others understand it to be simply the nonformal treatment, without formal or symbolic apparatus, of elementary deductive logic.[3] For the purposes of this chapter, we shall take the most common conception of informal logic as canonical.

Initially, the term *informal logic* was primarily used as a rhetorical means of declaring the independence from formal logic of a distinct approach to argument interpretation and evaluation. Today, few logicians, whether formal or informal, see any incompatibility between the two, however much the terminology might suggest otherwise. Hence, informal logic is in some respects an unfortunate term. However, as Woods and Walton (1989) allow, "the expression has taken root and does some responsible semantic work" (p. xxi).

---

[1] For a collection of early papers on informal logic, see Blair and Johnson (1980).

[2] Much earlier, Ryle referred to the "informal logic" of concepts such as pleasure, seeing, and chance when expressing his interest in their implications (1954: Lecture VIII). Informal logic is also used by many as a general label for the study of the "informal" fallacies. Others identify informal logic with critical thinking. This is due to the fact that applied informal logic is frequently used in teaching critical thinking skills.

[3] In this sense of the term, Copi and Cohen (1990) qualifies as an informal logic textbook.

In order to understand what is meant by informal logic, one must look at how this term is used in the history of the subject over the last quarter of the century. If logic is understood in the broad sense as the philosophical study of the norms of reasoning, informal logic is a branch of logic. It is the branch that takes argumentation as its focus, particularly the argumentation of nontechnical everyday discourse and discourse about issues in the *polis*. The informal logic approach is philosophical, because of its conceptual and normative orientation.

Informal logic theory is devoted to analysis of the concepts used in argument interpretation and evaluation. It critically elaborates and defends the norms appropriate to these two practical activities. On the one hand, its concern is normative in that it seeks to develop procedures, standards, and criteria for the interpretation, evaluation, criticism, and construction of arguments in which due account is taken of logical merit, or cogency. On the other hand, informal logic also partakes of the recent trend against *a priorism* in philosophy: It takes practice to be the starting point and the end point of theory. One of the definitive features of informal logic has, in fact, been its insistence on taking as its point of departure the natural language argumentation of the "market place" and the political arena, as found typically in newspapers and magazines, but also in nonfiction books and essays. In this respect, it contrasts with the *a prioristic* application of deductive calculi to the contrived arguments typical of some applications of formal logic to natural language.

Informal logic also belongs to philosophy by virtue of its subject matter. The problems it deals with, such as the nature of deduction and induction and the distinction between them, the justification of beliefs and other commitments, and the nature and legitimacy of analogical reasoning and arguments, have been traditional philosophical issues in epistemology and the philosophy of logic since Aristotle.

Both informal and formal logic are concerned with what their practitioners call "arguments," but the term *argument* has different denotations in the two fields. In this sense, the subject matters are different. The arguments as studied by informal logicians are historical events, expressed in natural languages, and are inherently *social, dialectical,* and *pragmatic* in nature.

The arguments informal logicians are interested in are *social* in at least two respects. First, they are the constituents of a complicated, multifaceted social practice; they are, among other things, the means whereby members of social groups identify disagreements or negotiate agreements and consensus. Second, these arguments occur against a background of shared meanings, values, and problems or controversies. They are also, in at least two respects, *dialectical*. Usually, they are part of an actual or anticipated back-and-forth exchange, and in this way they are interactive. Moreover, when such exchanges are dialogues, each intervention builds upon its predecessors. In either case, the proponent argues from the beliefs or commitments of the audience or respondent, whether these are just supposed or are stated, and the proponent must respond to objections to the standpoint he or she is advancing, whether those objections be anticipated or stated explicitly in a respondent's dialectical turn. Finally, rather than being purely semantic or syntactic events, the arguments are *prag-matic*, because their meanings are a function of purposive contexts. As Grice (1975) has made clear, they cannot be understood apart from their interlocutor's intentions and a rich fabric of contextual rules and understandings. We discuss Grice's "Co-operative principle" shortly, but in general his point is that communication requires the assumption that speakers and writers try to be relevant, accurate, and as complete as the occasion requires, other things being equal.

In contrast, the arguments studied by formal logicians are decontextualized sets of sentences or symbols viewed in terms of their syntactic or semantic relationships. Formal logicians map systems of patterns of implication-relationship that authorize valid deductive inferences among subsets of such sentences. In the process, they abstract from any particular arguer, audience, purpose—or any other features of contexts in which actual people draw, or invite others to draw, inferences. As to the connection between formal and informal logic, suffice it to say that it is an assumption of informal logicians that not all the inferences made or invited in actual arguments are correctly modeled as (intended) deductive entailments. Even if they were, informal logicians maintain, actual arguments have other important logical properties besides their inference patterns.

This chapter also deals with critical thinking. As a term of art, *critical thinking* traces back to Dewey's (1909/1991) idea of "reflective thought": "Active, persistent, and careful consideration of any belief or supposed form of knowledge in the light of the grounds that support it, and the further conclusions to which it tends" (p. 6). Critical thinking was the label Glaser employed in the early 1940s to advocate an educational reform theme (1941). By the 1970s, it emerged as a focal point of an educational reform movement in the United States. This movement had (and has) as its objective the development of a reflective, critical attitude of mind, together with the skills deemed necessary to implement it effectively, as the centerpiece of the primary school, high school, and postsecondary educational curricula.

As contrasted with informal logic as a branch of a particular discipline (logic) and partly defined by its subject matter (arguments), critical thinking refers to an attitude of mind whose application knows no disciplinary boundaries. Any topic that engages the intellect or the imagination may be examined from a critical thinking perspective. Thus, rather than denoting a theory or a discipline, critical thinking denotes a set of dispositions and attitudes.

There is a straightforward explanation of the tendency to treat the terms *critical thinking* and *informal logic* as coextensive. In the early 1970s there emerged a "new" logic course, launched by several text books that introduced a novel syllabus for the standard university-level introductory logic course in the United States and Canada. Most of these texts shared the following three features: They aimed to foster critical thinking; they did so by teaching the analysis and critique of arguments; and they taught methods of argument analysis and evaluation other than those developed for formal logic.[4] Informal logic connects centrally with the last two features. Because the educational goal of critical thinking was sought by using the perspective and methods of informal logic as the means, and because this combination continues to this day, it is understandable that informal logic and critical thinking are widely taken as equivalent.[5]

Still, it is good to remember that there are importantly different referents for these two terms. Trudy Govier (1987) argues that critical thinking and informal logic should be distinguished, because thinking can be critical without using or issuing in arguments. One can think critically about things other than arguments (e.g., art), and use other critical methods besides argument in doing so (pp. 237–241). An implication of Govier's distinction is that critical thinking has wider scope than informal logic. In order to engage in critical thinking, one will have to be able to appraise many different kinds of intellectual product, whereas informal logic is particularly focused on the realm of argumentation. When assessing the wide range of intellectual products, the critical thinker will profit from training in informal logic, but from much else besides (see Johnson, 1989).

6.1 THE (RE)EMERGENCE OF INFORMAL LOGIC

In order to understand informal logic, one needs to have a sense of the type of logic instruction in the United States and Canada to which it was a reaction. We begin our account at mid-century.

By 1950, in North American universities and colleges for undergraduates there were roughly three levels of logic instruction, and corresponding textbooks. Expert-level textbooks, aiming at graduate students specializing in logic or mathematics, covered second order calculi, set theory, recursive function theory, theory of models, and various nonstandard logical systems. Advanced textbooks, written primarily for advanced philosophy students, were by and large introductions to elementary symbolic or mathematical logic, covering sentential logic and the first order predicate calculus. Typical of the introductory logic textbooks, designed for the only logic course most undergraduates would take, is Irving Copi's classic *Introduction to Logic* (1953). Its latest (8th) edition (1990) has three parts, dealing with language, deduction, and induction. The book covers a wide range of different

---

[4]See Kahane (1971), Thomas (1973), Scriven (1976), Johnson and Blair (1977), Weddle (1978), and Fogelin (1978).

[5]Other factors have contributed to the confusion. Both the terms *informal logic* and *critical thinking* have their origins in programs of educational reform, with overlapping, albeit different, focuses. Many of the important theorists have feet in both camps, and some of them have tended to use the terms as if they were interchangeable. There also exists an organization called the Association for Informal Logic and Critical Thinking (AILACT), which suggests something natural and acceptable in their juxtaposition.

topics, such as uses of language, different sorts of definition, informal fallacies (briefly), introductory class logic, the propositional calculus, proof theory, quantification theory, inductive analogy, Mill's methods, scientific explanation and testing, probability theory, and legal reasoning.[6]

The philosophers who began to develop informal logic, some of whom were themselves logicians, received their own logic education from these courses. For this generation of American and Canadian philosophers, logic proper meant symbolic or mathematical logic. Informal logic emerged as a reaction primarily to the standard introductory level course, but also to the presumption of most logicians at the time that symbolic logic instruction has ready and useful application to the analysis and evaluation of the arguments of daily life.

The development of informal logic was spearheaded by three textbooks, the first being Howard Kahane's *Logic and Contemporary Rhetoric: The Use of Reason in Everyday Life* (1971, 2nd edition 1976).[7] To understand how Kahane's text came to be, his own words in the introduction are helpful:

> Today's students demand a marriage of theory and practice. That is why so many of them judge introductory courses on logic, fallacy and even rhetoric not relevant to their interests.
>
> In class a few years back, while I was going over the (to me) fascinating intricacies of the predicate logic quantifier rules, a student asked in disgust how anything he'd learned all semester long had any bearing whatever on President Johnson's decision to escalate again in Vietnam. I mumbled something about bad logic on Johnson's part, and then stated that Introduction to Logic was not that kind of course. His reply was to ask what courses did take up such matters, and I had to admit that so far as I knew none did.
>
> He wanted what most students today want, a course relevant to everyday reasoning, a course relevant to the arguments they hear and read about race, pollution, poverty, sex, atomic warfare, the population explosion, and all the other problems faced by the human race in the second half of the twentieth century. (1971, p. v)

In other words, Kahane wanted logic to be useful in the analysis of argumentation in public discourse. Although he was already the author of a successful formal logic textbook (1969, 2nd edition 1973), he held that formal logic was not well-suited for that purpose.

What stands behind Kahane's concern that logic be relevant in this way? The background is furnished by cultural developments during the previous decade in North America. At that time, many students had taken an increasingly radical

---

[6]Non-North American readers must keep in mind the relatively open admissions policy of most universities and colleges in the United States and Canada. Hence, a book such as Strawson's *Introduction to logical theory*, designed as "a general introduction to logic" (1952, p. v), would have been used in an advanced logic course in the United States or Canada.

[7]These were not traditional textbooks in the sense of being works that distilled and presented to students the established knowledge of the field. They were really "handbooks"—instructional for argument analysis and evaluation, introducing numerous theoretical innovations.

political stance—not only towards the university. In the United States, some had been actively involved in the antisegregation civil rights movement of the early 1960s; some belonged to the "radical"—that is, mildly social-democratic—student-power groups; and many more were active through the mid and late 1960s in the anti-Vietnam War protest movement on campuses. Student protest was not confined to political and social issues. Within the university, students were demanding that their courses relate to their needs as citizens. Kahane's text can be seen as one type of pedagogical response to that demand. Kahane takes a traditional subject like logic and makes it *relevant*.

Kahane's text helped to change the focus of logic instruction in North America. He did this by taking what had until then been but one section of the traditional introductory logic course, the part on fallacies, and making that the core of his approach. In so doing, he was tapping the historical roots of Aristotle's *De Sophisticis Elenchis* rather than his *Prior Analytics*, the tradition in logic that became known as fallacy theory.

Kahane made fallacy, not deductive validity, the primary tool of argument criticism. He did more than this, however, for he attempted to breath new life into the fallacy tradition. He expurgated such "hoary" old fallacies as *amphiboly* and *accent*, which, he thought, deceive no one. He added new fallacies to the traditional list, so that one will find not only *ad hominem* but also "provincialism," not only *ad verecundiam*, but also the "red herring," not only hasty generalization but also "suppressed evidence."

In order to show the relevance of logic for the affairs of daily life, Kahane replaced the traditional chapters on scientific method and causal reasoning with chapters on the mass media (advertising and the news media). He also did something novel: Instead of using contrived invented examples of arguments, or examples taken from philosophy or other academic sources, he illustrated his theory, and stocked his exercises, with specimens from current newspapers and magazines dealing with the political and social issues of the day.

Kahane's text was thus an important breakthrough. Although he himself did not use the term, Kahane paved the way for the informal logic movement. His was not, however, the only challenge issued to the conventional assumptions about logic tuition as found in logic texts. In 1973, Stephen Thomas published *Practical Reasoning in Natural Language*. With some indebtedness to Beardsley's *Practical Logic* (1950), which in certain respects is a precursor of these 1970 texts, Thomas's book represents an approach to the teaching of argument evaluation quite different from both Beardsley's and Kahane's.

First, Thomas, following Beardsley, placed heavy emphasis on the task of clearly laying out the structure of the argument. He interpreted the organization of the support for the standpoint being defended (or the premises for the conclusion) and the manner in which the arguments are grouped in providing that support. This feature was absent from Kahane's text. Thomas devoted two long chapters to it, far more attention than given in any other text. What is the more striking is that he provided an interpretive apparatus which makes no reference at all to the traditional argument forms of formal logic, such as *modus tollens*, "disjunctive syllogism" and so on. Thomas thereby contributed to informal logic by showing how the internal structure of arguments can be analyzed without employing the traditional notion of logical form.

Second, Thomas introduced a new, stretched sense of validity as his criterion for inferences in arguments. He contends that arguments vary in the strength of the premises' support for the conclusion from zero (where the premises are irrelevant), at one extreme, to maximum strength (where the premises logically entail the conclusion), at the other extreme. According to his proposal, reasoning should be regarded as "valid" if the truth of the premises would guarantee *or make extremely likely* the truth of the conclusion.

Third, Thomas had the first discussion of the Principle of Charity in an informal logic text, thus bringing pragmatic considerations into the interpretation of argumentation. The Principle of Charity has been given various formulations.[8] For Thomas (1973) it is formulated as follows: "If a passage contains no inference indicators or other explicit signs of reasoning *and* the only possible argument(s) you can locate in it would involve obviously bad reasoning, then categorize the discourse as '*non*argument' " (pp. 15–16).

Finally, like Kahane, Thomas had an eye firmly on the sorts of issues that are likely to come up in the world beyond the classroom and academia.

The final pioneering book that must be mentioned in this discussion of first generation informal logic texts is Michael Scriven's *Reasoning* (1976), which is important for several reasons. For one, since Scriven was the most prominent philosopher of the early authors, his writing an informal logic text helped to legitimize this new approach. Like the others, he eschewed teaching the apparatus of formal logic in a course with the goal of teaching argument analysis and evaluation. He contended that learning formal logic has little transfer to these goals. He argued that insisting on translating natural language arguments into the symbolic notation called for by formal logic entails questionable translation practices, such as distorting the meanings of texts in order to force them to fit the available possible schema. And he held that in any case the task of translation has costs outweighing any possible benefits. It takes far longer to produce an, at best, dubious symbolization in order to apply the apparatus of formal logic to evaluate the validity of the argument's inferences than it would take to evaluate the argument in the first place using other methods.

As an alternative to symbolization and testing for validity, Scriven proposed a 7-step method of argument analysis: (1) clarification of meaning (of the argument and its components), (2) identification of conclusions (stated and un-

---

[8]See, for instance, Scriven (1976, pp. 71–72), Grice (1977, pp. 1–11), Lambert and Ulrich (1980, p. 60), and Johnson and Blair (1993, p. 11). It is worth noticing that they all subscribe to a view of the Principle of Charity that is to some extent at variance with that of Davidson (1971).

stated), (3) portrayal of structure, (4) formulation of assumptions (the "missing premises"), (5) criticism (a) of the premises (given and missing) and (b) of the inferences, (6) introduction of other relevant arguments, (7) overall evaluation of this argument in the light of (1) through (6).

Like Thomas, Scriven treated deductive entailment as the strongest extreme in a continuum of degrees of support that the grounds offered to support the claim may provide. He extends Thomas's method of tree diagrams, employing the convention of using numbers to represent assertions, by adding a placement in argument diagrams for assertions that "point the other way," that is, provide reasons for opposing the conclusion. This convention permits diagramming what Scriven and others call "balance of considerations" arguments, namely arguments such as those about public policy questions, in which reasons for and against the conclusion are considered and balanced in arriving at a conclusion.

Scriven was the first author to discuss at length the ethics of argument analysis, offering a new formulation of the Principle of Charity in the process. For Scriven (1976), the Principle of Charity "requires that we try to make the best, rather than the worst, possible interpretation of the argument we're study-ing" (p. 71). That is, we should impute the best argument for the conclusion, consistent with what is said. This is a more inclusive principle than Thomas's, for it goes beyond deciding when an argument is present and applies to choices between possible alternative interpretations of what is identified as argumenta-tion.[9] Scriven extends the scope of the Principle of Charity beyond argument interpretation to argument criticism. He takes it to proscribe "taking cheap shots," "nit picking," and "setting up a straw man." It is for him partly an ethical principle, not merely an instrumental rule for accurate or reliable interpretation.

Scriven further distinguishes between what he calls "strong" and "weak" criticism, and recommends emphasizing the latter. Weak criticism can be readily answered by relatively minor emendations to the argument; strong criticism gets to the heart of the argument, and cannot be met without abandoning its main thrust. Furthermore, Scriven's text contained the first discussion of the "principle of discrimination" in producing a critique of an argument, namely the rule that the critic should proportion the critique to the gravity of the logical offense. Like Kahane, he draws his examples and exercises from arguments about the lively issues of the day, newspaper editorials, and advertisements.

In our view, the textbooks by Kahane, Thomas, and Scriven, all of them still widely used, are the first generation of informal logic texts. They each broke new ground. They also prefigured the remarkable divergence in approaches of later texts. Their only main points of agreement were that they all targeted actual

---

[9]In a similar vein, van Eemeren and Grootendorst started from the Principle of Charity in reconstructing unexpressed premises and in developing such strategies as "maximally argumentative interpretation" and "maximally argumentative analysis" (1984, pp. 117, 125–126; 1992a, pp. 49, 81).

contemporary arguments, and minimized the recourse to formal apparatus so characteristic of formal logic texts, or even of global paradigm introductory logic texts.

The development of informal logic can be observed by going beyond these three first generation texts, and examining those of the second and third generation. Among the textbook authors that followed the first generation are Ralph Johnson and Anthony Blair (1977). They borrowed heavily from Kahane, but also modified and extended his ideas, and added novel features of their own. Govier (1985), in turn, borrowed from and modified Johnson and Blair, besides adding her own independent contributions. Damer (1987), Seech (1987), and Freeman (1988) similarly adapted and extended Govier and Johnson and Blair.[10]

At the start of the informal logic movement, there was in philosophy no set body of informal logic theory to fund the textbooks. In some respects, this fact served the movement well: It forced authors, as they gradually broke away from the perspective of their own training in formal logic, to deal with the phenomena—actual arguments—with a fresh eye, and to discover the numerous problems requiring theoretical analysis. These problems belong in three groups.

The problems of the first group have to do with the identification of argument in discourse. What in general constitutes argument? What are the identifying features of the presence of argument in a text? How are unclear cases to be dealt with? How is the argumentation in the text to be separated from the nonargumentative features or portions of the text?

The second group of problems pertain to the analysis of the identified argument. How are arguments to be individuated? What is the most accurate and perspicuous way to portray the patterns of support in an argument? What are the possible connections between individual (or atomic) argument bits that go to make up an overall argumentative presentation or case for a position being defended?

The third set of theoretical problems have to do with the logical evaluation of the argument. What are the criteria for a cogent argument? Are general criteria available? What is a fallacious argument? What are the defining conditions of each particular fallacy? Does a critique in terms of fallacies exhaust possible argument criticism? Is fallacy identification the best, or even a useful, tool for argument evaluation?

The questions listed indicate the extent of the problematic, but the list is not exhaustive. The attempt to teach informal logic, and to write textbooks for the courses, soon led many philosophers to tackle the theoretical questions that thereby arose. In doing so, many found theoretical inspiration in other, earlier works. We shall mention some of the more significant ones.

---

[10]A preliminary attempt to study the development in the several dozen textbooks that have emerged was made by Johnson and Blair (1980).

Some informal logicians turned to Toulmin's *The Uses of Argument* (1958) and Perelman and Olbrechts-Tyteca's *The New Rhetoric* (1958, English transl. 1969), not so much for theoretical details as for general orientation and affirmation. As the informal logic turn was not greeted with universal interest or approval by the philosophical community, and went against the grain of their own logical training, early proponents found confirmation of the legitimacy of their enterprise most welcome.[11] (*The Uses of Argument* and *The New Rhetoric* played that confirming role.) Their authors were internationally respected philosophers, who had, 15 years earlier, likewise challenged formal logic's ability to illuminate and evaluate actual argumentation.

So far as doctrine goes, Toulmin's model—data-warrant-backing-qualification/rebuttal-claim—was not picked up by informal logicians the way it was by the argumentation branch of the speech communication community. Instead, it was the spirit of Toulmin's approach to argumentation that was influential: Be sensitive to context; be empirical rather than *a prioristic*; expect differences in standards in different domains.

Similarly, the influence of *The New Rhetoric* by Perelman and Olbrechts-Tyteca was by way of certain general features of their approach rather than its details. Informal logicians were particularly attracted by Perelman's view of the "framework of argumentation," with its relegation of the domain of formal logic to demonstration *in contrast to* argumentation, its emphasis on the importance in argumentation of the speaker and the audience, the distinction of truth-oriented discussion from victory-oriented debate, and the idea that individual deliberative reflection can be argumentative in character. In contrast, Perelman's list of argument schemes, and their classification, have received little attention.

Nicholas Rescher's *Plausible Reasoning* (1976) and *Dialectics* (1977) had a more direct theoretical influence on some informal logicians. John Woods and Douglas Walton (1982) used Rescher's method of plausibility screening in handling conflicting advice from authorities in their treatment of *ad verecundiam* arguments.

In *Dialectics*, Rescher dipped back into the scholastic tradition in order to borrow and revitalize the "disputation model" of argumentation. He regarded the disputation model as a counter to the Cartesian model. Rescher's disputation model emphasizes "the communal and controversy oriented aspects of rational argumentation and inquiry," whereas the Cartesian model is solipsistic, for it supposes an isolated reasoner building chains of proofs constructed from undisputed truths.

Rescher's modeling of dialectical argumentative exchanges has been influential, as has his associated account of burden of proof.[12] With regard to the

---

[11]McGraw-Hill, Scriven's publisher for another, profitable text of his, would not initially publish *Reasoning*. Initially, Johnson and Blair met the same fate at the hands of formal logic oriented reviewers with *Logical self-defense*.

[12]See Blair and Johnson (1987).

former, his model makes room for cautious and provisoed initial assertions, alongside the standard categorical opening statements, in dialectical exchanges. That leads, in turn, to a richer inventory of dialectical countermoves.

Rescher's burden of proof analysis implies that a proponent carries a variety of changing commitments during a dialectical exchange. From his close analysis of the patterns of dialectical interchange, Rescher draws analysis of the dialectical tools of burden of proof, presumption and plausibility. He makes a distinction between the probative burden of initiation which rests with the party who initiates by asserting, and the evidential burden, which may shift from proponent to respondent during the exchange. Intimately connected with any account of burden of proof will be a doctrine about presumption, namely about what may be taken as standing in the usual, normal, customary course of things. The need to identify how presumption works in different contexts leads Rescher to a discussion of plausibility, which he regards as the crucial determinant of presumption. He discusses the notions of "evidential weight," "intrinsic plausibility," the authoritativeness of "expert testimony," and of "broad consensus." All of these topics have been taken up in subsequent informal logic literature.

Hamblin's now-famous study of the fallacy tradition, *Fallacies* (1970), caught the attention of the Canadian philosophers Woods and Walton, who were persuaded by its condemnation of the state of fallacy theory. They decided to set about meeting the challenge this critique entailed.[13] Woods and Walton's series of articles, providing rigorous analyses of individual fallacies (1989), were noticed by informal logicians using fallacy as a critical tool. Their work also alerted other informal logicians to Hamblin's monograph.[14] In the analyses of particular fallacies Woods and Walton's approach is methodologically eclectic. Without any *a prioristic* methodological assumptions, they bring to bear existing theories, whether formal or not, such as intuitionistic logic, relatedness logic, plausibility theory, graph theory, aggregate theory, among others.

Finally, we should list three authors whose work in other areas has had an influence on the development of informal logic: Carl Wellman, John Wisdom, and Paul Grice.

Wellman (1971), argues in his monograph on ethical reasoning, *Challenge and Response*, that there is a species of ethical reasoning that is neither deductive nor inductive, which he terms "conductive" reasoning. Conductive reasoning occurs when someone draws a conclusion about some individual case nonconclusively from one or more premises about the case, and without appeal to other cases (p. 52). Govier (1980a) was the first to point out that Wellman's conductive reasoning could well have a counterpart in argumentation.

---

[13]The scholarly work on the theory of fallacies and on individual fallacies has since proliferated: Hansen's (1990) bibliography cites over 140 articles published in this area since 1970.

[14]In turn, informal logicians' interest in their work, brought Woods and Walton in touch with the informal logic movement. They published their own textbook in 1982.

Wisdom (1957/1991), in what are known as the Virginia lectures, set out what he termed "case-by-case reasoning." In case-by-case reasoning, inferences may be drawn regarding a particular case by a kind of analogy from similar cases that is neither deductive nor inductive. Govier (1980b), again, drew attention to the implications of Wisdom's work for the interpretation and evaluation of argumentation. She notes four kinds of context in which Wisdom thought case-by-case reasoning is necessary: inferences from the presence of a property in a paradigm case to its occurrence in a less clear case, inferences involving the truth or the significance of metaphysical statements, inferences made in trying to resolve borderline cases, and inferences from criteria which are not explicit enough to permit deductions.

The influence of the third of these thinkers, Grice, depended especially on his article "Logic and Conversation" (1975) in which he set out rules codifying the presuppositions of discourse.[15] Grice's account of the tacit rules of conversation has particularly influenced informal logicians' thinking about the interpretation of arguments.[16] According to Grice, ordinary (informative) discourse is governed by what he calls the Cooperative Principle, and its conversational maxims.[17] An apparent flouting of the maxims when both interlocutors are mutually aware of what they are doing may create a "conversational implicature." Grice is thus able, for example, to account for innuendo: saying one thing, but implying just the opposite. Together, the notions of the Cooperative Principle, the conversational maxims, and conversational implicatures provide a theoretical basis for explaining the interpretations of argumentative texts. Grice's account also led to further issues. For example, how is this sense of relevance to be understood? When is there evidence enough to satisfy the rules of Quality?

Wellman, Wisdom, and Grice have influenced the work of informal logicians, such as Govier, Woods and Walton, Johnson and Blair, and Tindale. Other philosophical influences are manifested in the writings of different informal logicians, perhaps the greatest of which is that exercised by the later works of Wittgenstein (1953, 1969).

6.2   THE MAIN ISSUES IN INFORMAL LOGIC

The main theoretical problems that have characterized informal logic relate to the analysis and the evaluation of argumentation. The first set of issues concerns

---

[15]This article is, in fact, an independently published part of Grice's 1967 William James Lectures. For the complete lectures, see Grice (1989, pp. 3–143).

[16]Fogelin went so far as to reprint Grice's article in his textbook (1978).

[17]Grice (1989, pp. 26–27) distinguishes four conversational maxims: Quantity (be as informative as the current purposes of the exchange require, no more, no less), Quality (do not say what you believe is false or what you lack adequate evidence for), Relation (be relevant), and Manner (be perspicuous).

the interpretation and "reconstruction" of argumentation in a text and how to comprehend and to display the structure of the argumentation. These issues include the handling of unexpressed premises, diagramming conventions, and the ethics of argument interpretation. Another—interrelated—set of problems relates to the nature of argument and argumentation. What types of arguments are there? How is the concept of argument best understood? By what standards, and according to what theory, should one evaluate arguments?

The turn informal logic made to actual arguments forced theorists to face up to the ill-organized, incompletely stated, wandering-off-topic arguments found normally in written and spoken discourse. With the exception of Fogelin (1978), informal logicians have tended not to address the complex theoretical issues arising from the attempt to explain how we manage to interpret such discourse, leaving this task to linguists, speech communication theorists, and philosophers of language. The advice found in textbooks about how to identify the argumentation embedded in natural language discourse has been *ad hoc*, and not theoretically developed. Instead, assuming that the argumentative components of the discourse can be identified, informal logicians have focused their attention on how to lay out the sentences playing argumentative roles in such discourse with the goal in mind of evaluating the argument.

As noted, Toulmin's model had little sway until recently on informal logic. Beardsley's (1950) diagramming convention, with its distinction between "convergent," "divergent," and "serial" arguments, was more influential. According to Beardsley, an argument is convergent if several independent reasons support the same conclusion; it is divergent if the same reason supports several conclusions; and serial if it contains a statement that is both a conclusion and a reason for a further conclusion. Thomas (1973) added the concept of a "linked" argument: "when a step of reasoning involves the logical combination of two or more reasons" (p. 36). Scriven (1976) added symbolizing negative support, in order to diagram "balance of considerations" arguments. Johnson and Blair (1977) adapted Scriven's diagramming method to longer arguments, representing groups of statement with a single symbol. Later texts have modified and amplified these basic approaches. A handful of texts attempt to modify their diagramming techniques to handle suppositional reasoning, the reasoning that is so important for hypothesis formation and testing, but most ignore it.[18]

The variations among notations are not, as a rule, significant. It is worth noting, however, that the general diagramming practice among informal logicians has been to isolate individual assertions and their relationships in a way that mirrors the practice of logicians tracing deductive entailments. In our opinion, this close resemblance to the diagramming of deductive relationships in formal logic is an indication of the enduring influence of formal logic training.

---

[18]The exceptions are Thomas (1986, pp. 216ff.), Fisher (1988a, pp. 82ff.), and Freeman (1991, pp. 212ff.).

Recently, the conceptions of argumentation structure underlying such diagramming have come under critical scrutiny. For example, there is an unresolved ambiguity as to whether each unit in the diagram should be, as such, a distinct premise or an argument, that is, a set of premises. The "linked" structure seems to capture sets of premises working jointly, whereas the "convergent" structure seems to capture different lines of argument. Snoeck Henkemans (1992), applying the Amsterdam pragma-dialectical argumentation theory of van Eemeren and Grootendorst, argues that conceiving arguments as dialogical discussions aimed at dispute resolution permits the removal of these and other unclarities. Recently, Yanal (1991) and Conway (1991) also discussed the linked-convergent distinction. Yanal argues that it is really a distinction between when there is one argument and when there are more; Conway argues that there is no satisfactory way to distinguish between the two categories (on the assumption that they refer to alternative ways of structuring single arguments).

One of the first attempts to join the old formal logic and the new informal logic is to be found in Fisher's, *The Logic of Real Arguments* (1988a). Fisher adopts two of the premises of the informal logic movement and welds them onto two premises retained from formal logic. From informal logic he takes the need to focus on actual arguments rather than contrived ones. Indeed, he extends this development by taking under the scope arguments from Malthus on economics, John Stuart Mill, and Karl Marx. This is an important modification of the practice of focusing on shorter and less intellectually demanding arguments. Fisher also adopts from informal logic a modified form of the tree diagram approach to display the macrostructure of arguments. For microstructure as well as for his theory of evaluation, he turns to formal deductive logic. He makes use of propositional logic to interpret microstructure; and he retains the ideal of soundness when evaluating argumentation. Fisher (1988a) adds another interesting modification: as an evaluative tool, he introduces what he calls "The Assertability Question": "What argument or evidence would justify me in asserting the conclusion C?" (p. 131). Fisher also developed an extended and intricate analysis of suppositional reasoning.

An ambitious attempt to resolve such difficulties systematically is James Freeman's *Dialectics and the Macrostructure of Arguments* (1991). Freeman undertakes a revision of the Toulmin model by rejecting Toulmin's data-warrant-backing distinction as applicable to arguments as artifacts, and by adding a dialectical dimension to the model. He provides a dialectical analysis and justification for the distinctions between premises, modalities, rebuttals, and conclusions and their structural relationships. His claim is that his model is sufficiently complete and comprehensive to apply to any possible argument, and moreover captures the structure of the arguments to be found in real life.

Attention to the structure of actual examples of argumentation has invariably been accompanied by the attempt to account for "assumptions," or "hidden," "missing," "suppressed," "tacit," "unexpressed," or "unstated" premises.[19] If an arguer clearly intends one statement to support another, but in fact it does not, there is a presumption that the arguer expected the listener or reader to have understood as read some additional proposition(s) that, when added to the initial statement, enable the entire set to be relevant, or to provide stronger support. Aristotle's enthymemes are an instance.

The treatments of missing premises in the literature reveal a variety of overlapping assumptions about the problem and approaches to the problem. Singly or in combination, they can entail variations in the missing premise that is supplied. For one thing, a decision has to be made as to which argument is under scrutiny. Some theorists focus on the argument given, or intended, by the arguer, with the attendant problems of interpretation. Others focus on the argument in relation to the person deciding whether to believe or act on its conclusion, and then seek to interpret it in terms of how well it supports that claim. Another decision has to be made as to the norms to be followed in reconstructing the argument. Some hold that the missing premise should produce a valid entailment between premises and conclusion. These "deductive reconstructionists" can be subdivided into the "deductive chauvinists," who regard any argument as necessarily deductive in intent, and the "methodological deductivists," who regard deductive reconstruction as a way of avoiding the difficulties of other reconstruction strategies or as particularly illuminating (or both). Others contend that pragmatic considerations should be determinative. What was the author's intended meaning? What makes the inference most plausible? What could the arguer have known or believed? What can the arguer have known or believed that his or her audience knew or believed? Or should these and other factors be combined, using an informal weight and sum decision procedure? In the informal logic literature about the questions surrounding the problem of missing premises, there is no widely accepted unified set of answers to these questions.[20]

The foregoing areas of discussion and controversy might be classified as belonging under the heading of interpreting arguments. Unsurprisingly, there have been numerous further discussions of this issue. The viability of Toulmin's paradigm has been much discussed, as have general principles of argument interpretation, including topics in the ethics of interpretation such as the Principle of Charity.[21]

Let us suppose that the structure of the argument has been laid out, giving as plausible a reconstruction as possible, and turn to the theoretical problems of the evaluation of argumentation. Now arises the question: "How good is this argument?" In order to answer this question without recourse to formal logic's ideal of soundness (true premises and a deductively valid implication), the development of an informal logic theory of evaluation is required.

---

[19]Even this list of the labels to be found in the literature is not exhaustive.

[20]See Hansen's (1990) index entry. Textbooks are another source.

[21]Hansen (1990) lists 33 articles under his Index entry for "argument interpretation."

Historically, one option has been to use some version of fallacy theory; we shall discuss that option first. One important feature of a good argument, this theory holds, is that it will be free of fallacy, so that the presence of a fallacy is a *prima facie* weakness in the argument. The problem with this intuition is that there is little consensus about how precisely to shape the theory of fallacy and use it for critical purposes. The framework to be discussed here is one that has been widely adopted. According to this approach, an argument must satisfy the criteria of *relevance, sufficiency* and *acceptability*; a fallacious argument is one that violates one or more of these criteria.[22] The three criteria for a good argument, each of which we shall briefly discuss, can be reproduced in the "RSA-Triangle," introduced by Johnson and Blair (1994, p. 55). See Fig. 6.1.

There is no widely accepted informal logic account of "probative relevance," the relevance of premises for conclusions. This is not surprising, since, until recently, relevance has received little attention from informal logicians, and from philosophers in general.[23] Grice (1989, p. 27) identifies relevance as one of the governing assumptions of conversational communication, but his account does not provide any theoretical enlightenment as to the nature of relevance. From another perspective, Sperber and Wilson (1986) have the most definitive account to date, but being broadly focused on communication, it does not settle the question of the nature of probative relevance (Woods, 1992b).[24]

A useful contribution has been Walton's (1989a) distinction between "local" and "global" relevance (p. 78). Local relevance is the relevance of the premises offered in a single argument; global relevance is the relevance of a proposition to the issue under discussion.

John Biro and Harvey Siegel (1992) have objected that treating relevance as a separate criterion is wrongheaded, since "sufficiency" already presupposes "relevance": if premises satisfy the sufficiency requirement, they must be relevant. However, this point does not show that relevance and sufficiency are not distinct. A set of premises can be relevant to a conclusion without providing sufficient support for it. For example, the fact that Ivo is qualified and experienced is relevant to the conclusion that Ivo should be hired, but it is not sufficient, since Inga may be even more qualified and experienced. Moreover, it is arguable that certain fallacies exhibiting failures of relevance, such as "straw man" or "red herring," can be identified only if relevance is considered as a separate requirement.

---

[22]This account first appears in Johnson and Blair (1977), and later, with varying terminology, in Govier (1985), Damer (1987), Freeman (1988), Little, Groarke and Tindale (1989), and Seech (1993).

[23]Cf. Bowles, who analyzes propositional relevance in terms of probability (1989, 1990, 1991).

[24]As can be seen in van Eemeren and Grootendorst (1992c), which includes most of the papers from a conference on relevance at McMaster University, the variety of approaches to the problem is as noteworthy as is the lack of consensus about them.

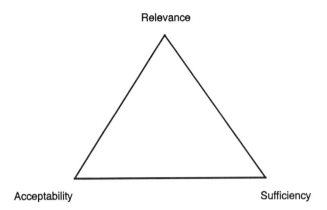

FIG. 6.1. The RSA-triangle: The criteria for a good argument.

Of the three criteria, *sufficiency* has so far attracted the least amount of sustained discussion. It is clear, though, that no one seriously believes that anything like an algorithm for sufficiency will ever be available. The question whether the premises provide sufficient evidence for the conclusion has three dimensions. First, there is the question of whether the appropriate types of evidence are being presented. Second, the question is whether, within each type, enough evidence of that kind is provided. Third, there is the issue of "dialectical sufficiency": Does the arguer deal with the appropriate kinds of objection?

A local-global distinction applying to sufficiency can parallel the one for relevance. Local sufficiency would be the adequacy of the arguments for a particular conclusion. Global sufficiency would apply to the adequacy of the case for a point of view, all things considered, within a wider argument.

The criterion of "acceptability" is the informal logicians' counterpart to the truth requirement in the formal logicians' doctrine of soundness. Influential in this respect was Hamblin, who argued that truth is an inappropriate criterion for the premises of arguments because it is neither sufficient nor necessary. Truth is not sufficient, because a premise could be true but not known to be true. Truth is not necessary, because in many arenas the very idea of truth is questionable. Hamblin's argument was not unlike that of the deconstructionist: The idea of truth presupposes an impossible God's eye position from which to view matters.

Many informal logicians have adopted acceptability as a requirement. According to this requirement, the premises of an argument should be acceptable to the arguer, the audience to whom the argument is directed, and generally to the critical community in which they are situated (see Blair & Johnson, 1987, pp. 48–53). For example, in arguing that Ronald Reagan was responsible for the financial problems facing the California educational system in the early 1990s, a critic writing in *The New York Times* stated in 1992, "When Ronald Reagan became governor in 1976 he began siphoning money out of what was then the country's finest public education system." While the two claims in this statement may well be true, the arguer owed her readers a defense of them, given their controversial nature and the 16-year elapse of time between the claim and the events it alleges. Without such defense, the critic's premise would be held to fail the acceptability requirement (see Johnson & Blair, 1993, pp. 76–77). In other words, the acceptability requirement assigns the burden of proof. Johnson (1990a, 1990b) reviews the reasoning by which Hamblin dismisses alethic and epistemic criteria and argues for dialectical criteria. Johnson contends that Hamblin's arguments against alethic and epistemic criteria are seriously flawed, and that Hamblin's own proposal for dialectical criteria is not without its own problems.

Now we shall pay some attention to the viability of fallacy theory, together with the issue of the nature of fallacies and the analysis of individual fallacies, one of the three main areas of controversy in informal logic connected with fallacies. In *Fallacies*, Hamblin (1970) issued a challenge to logicians to rebuild the theory of fallacy, which was taken up by Woods and Walton by providing studies of a great many individual fallacies, including *begging the question, ad hominem, ad verecundiam*, and *false cause*. These papers, collected in Woods and Walton (1989), helped convince many that the fallacies provide a legitimate object of inquiry.

In the early 1980s, two influential articles, building on Hamblin, challenged the viability of fallacy theory. Maurice Finocchiaro (1981) criticized the accounts of fallacies found in textbooks (in the spirit of Hamblin but looking at a different selection). He suggested that the very charge of fallacy is more often than not a creation of the critic, usually resulting from uncharitable interpretation. Finocchiaro argued that the fallacy approach stresses negative instead of positive evaluation, thereby illustrating an important orientation in the theory of evaluation. Gerald Massey (1981), the second challenger, also criticized textbook accounts of fallacy, arguing that there cannot be a logic of fallacies. His argument is based on the standard definition of fallacy given by Hamblin that a fallacy is an argument that appears to be valid but is not. Massey argued that since there cannot be a theory of invalidity, it follows that there cannot be a theory of fallacy.[25]

In defense of fallacy theory, Govier (1982) argued that the challenges raised by both Finocchiaro and Massey make important but undefended assumptions about the theory of argumentation. Massey moves uncritically from the claim that there is not a formally adequate method for deciding invalidity, to the claim that there is not any theoretically adequate method. Moreover, invalidity is neither a necessary condition for fallaciousness (begging the question is a fallacy despite arguments in which it occurs being valid) nor yet a sufficient condition (because there are nondeductive fallacious arguments also).

Govier acknowledges that Finocchiaro "moves us from formalism and deductivism" and that he is right in pointing out both the sloppiness of some textual

---

[25]Still later, a somewhat different challenge came from Hintikka (1989). He argued that, instead of seeing fallacies against the background of inference and argument, they should be seen within the context of the highly structured form of discourse practiced in the Lyceum in which questions were asked in a dialogical setting according to certain rules. Hence it is mistaken to represent fallacies as incorrect inferences or arguments.

treatments of fallacy and the often uncharitable nature of critics' interpretations of arguments. Yet she does not believe this amounts to the claim that there are no common incorrect arguments. Indeed, Finocchiaro's critique supposes that at least once fallacy does exist: the straw man.

Johnson (1987) argues against some of the traditional points raised against fallacy theory, such as that the ways of going wrong are infinite, and hence that there can be neither a theory of fallacy nor a reliable classification of fallacy. Johnson (1989) contends that Massey's position rests on a questionable conception of fallacy: Hamblin's definition is much too subjective to be helpful, since what appears valid to A may not appear valid to B. Moreover, Massey's assumptions about what an adequate theory must look like are biased against informal logic.

Recently, Woods (1992a) has offered a defense of fallacy theory which treats fallacies as "idealized symptoms of misperformance of rational skills necessary for human survival" (pp. 30–31). Fallacies are "snares and delusions." Their identification may serve as a launching pad for deeper theoretical inquiry.

We conclude that, at this point in the debate, the objections directed at fallacy theory, however challenging, have in any case not been sufficiently persuasive either to cause the abandonment of the fallacy approach or to dissuade theorists from the attempt to give better accounts of fallacy theory in general and of the individual fallacies in particular.

Another main bone of contention among those sympathetic to fallacy theory concerns the nature of fallacy, and indeed the nature of fallacy theory itself. There is no single conception of fallacy to which all those interested in this topic can pledge allegiance. Until recently, the most frequently quoted definition was Hamblin's. The last few years have witnessed significant developments in the understanding of fallacy.

Van Eemeren and Grootendorst (1984, 1992a), in their pragma-dialectical approach, see fallacies as procedural violations of the rules for critical discussion (see chapter 10). After repeating the standard charge that fallacies are not always fallacious, Willard (1989) opines that "it is permissible to conceptualize the rules standing behind each fallacy more as *topoi* than as restrictions" (pp. 235–236). Johnson (1989, p. 416) suggests that Hamblin's definition be replaced by a more generic and less formalistic account: A fallacy is a pattern of argument that occurs frequently and violates the requirements of good argumentation. Walton (1992a) largely agrees with the pragma-dialectical approach. He now understands fallacy as "a technique of argumentation that may in principle be reasonable but that has been misused in a given case in such a way that it goes strongly against or hinders the goals of dialogue" (p. 18).

On one point, there is an emerging consensus about fallacies: It is now generally conceded that patterns of argument once considered uniformly fallacious are, in fact, fallacious in only some cases.[26] Most would agree that the *ad*

---

[26]See Walton (1987, pp. 3–4, 1989a, p. 154) and Blair and Johnson (1991, pp. 38–39).

hominem argument is not always fallacious.[27] For example, attacking a witness's credibility in a legal trial, or challenging the motives behind a celebrity's product endorsement, can be nonfallacious argument strategies. The defining characteristics of a pattern or type of argument are therefore to be distinguished from the defining conditions of the fallacious occurrences of that pattern. It seems as well, also for other reasons, that there has been a trend to shift away from defining fallacy in terms either of deceptive intent or of apparent validity. No single alternative has replaced the earlier conception.

As regards fallacy theory, some argue for a unified theory that is not tied exclusively to logic (Willard, 1989). Woods (1992a) thinks that a proof theoretic treatment is a powerfully illuminating tool worth trying for. A unified theory might be impossible, he believes.

As to the study of individual fallacies, we mentioned already the series of articles by Walton and Woods in the 1970s. Particular attention has, so far, been given to *ad hominem, tu quoque, ad verecundiam,* and *begging the question (petitio principii, circular arguments).* In the journal literature, many of the other traditional fallacies have also been subjected to analysis and discussion.[28] There is little unity to these discussions.

Recently, Walton has published several monographs on individual fallacies: *ad hominem* (1985a), *begging the question* (1991), and *slippery slope* (1992b). His approach may be characterized as both dialogical and pragmatic. It is dialogical because fallacies are seen as violations of dialogical rules. It is pragmatic because the fallacies are not viewed as violations of either semantic or syntactic criteria (Walton, 1992a).

Although the fallacy approach has been dominant, other approaches to the task of argument evaluation have been developed. Scriven, for example, takes what might be called a "natural language" approach. On pedagogical grounds, he opposes the use of fallacies for the purpose of argument criticism, contending that doing so requires building into the argument-identification process all the skills that are needed anyhow for analysis. According to Scriven (1976), this turns fallacy criticism into a formal approach with a tricky diagnostic step (p. xvi). Scriven maintains that natural language contains a rich critical vocabulary that is sufficient for critical purposes. Among the terms belonging to that vocabulary are *reason, evidence, conclusion, thesis, relevant, sufficient, inconsistent, implication, presupposition, objection, assumption, ambiguous,* and *vague.* Scriven's method of evaluation is to raise the questions embedded in his 7-step method cited earlier. Another version of Scriven's approach, incorporating the idea of "conductive adequacy," is developed by Hitchcock (1983).

Then there are those who make use of Toulmin-type theories and envisage informal logic as applied epistemology. Toulmin and his followers take the view

---

[27]Some hold that naming non-fallacious argument schemes using labels associated with fallacies is confusing; the alternative, if the descriptive value of such labels is to be retained, is to use such locutions as "*ad hominem*-type arguments."

[28]See Hansen's (1990) bibliography.

that the important standards of good argument are specific to a particular field or discipline (see Toulmin, Rieke, & Janik, 1979). McPeck (1981) and Weinstein (1990b) think the important standards for an argument are furnished by the epistemology of its field. Battersby (1989) argues that epistemological norms, not rules of logic, constitute the philosophical core of informal logic. He sees a close theory-application parallel between informal logic and applied ethics; hence, informal logic should be called "applied epistemology."

John McPeck (1981) uses a parallel argument to show that critical thinking is essentially applied epistemology. The middle ground position between the "all standards are field-dependent"-view and the "important standards are field-invariant"-view (shared by some fallacy theorists) is occupied by Siegel (1988). Like Toulmin, Siegel argues that there are significant field-invariant and field-dependent standards. For example, while there is a general requirement of sufficient evidence, what evidence is sufficient for a court's finding of guilty or not guilty in a murder trial is different from what is sufficient for a pharmaceutical company's finding of efficacy and absence of harmful side-effects in its trials with a new drug.

Mark Weinstein (1990a) argues that a central task of informal logic is to develop an account of how acceptability is transmitted from premises to conclusions. He feels that "the assessment of the strength of support premises afford conclusions can only be [made] when the domain within which the argument is presented is taken into account" (p. 123). Then we are engaged in applied epistemology, by which he means "the study of the epistemologies in use in the various domains of human understanding in order to ground the assessment of arguments as they occur within them" (p. 123).

More recently, Pinto (1994) has argued that informal logic is tied to epistemology because judging the acceptability of an arguments's premises and the suitability of its inferential link *both* involve epistemic considerations, and both judgments are ingredients of argument appraisal from the point of view of informal logic.

It seems clear that there is an important epistemological dimension to informal logic, but the focus of these arguments on this aspect overlooks its pragmatic aspects. Controversially, this focus relies in some cases on the identification of logic with formal deductive logic. Anyhow, there continue to be divisions among informal logic theorists regarding the kind of normative theory that should be used in evaluating argumentation.

6.3 CRITICAL THINKING

Although we argued that critical thinking should not be identified with informal logic, and is not restricted to the realm of argumentation, yet in much of the literature argumentation is taken as central to the task of critical thinking. In this section, we outline the main theoretical positions that have been adopted.

In an early paper, a pioneer of the critical thinking movement in the United States, Robert Ennis (1962), set out one of the first careful elaborations of critical thinking. He has been refining his position ever since.[29] Critical thinking, Ennis holds, "is reasonable and reflective thinking that is focused on deciding what to believe or do" (1989, p. 1). In his view, the clarification and analysis of arguments and the assessment of their premises and inferences are necessary and major ingredients in critical thinking, but they are not sufficient (Ennis, 1989, Appendix). In order to be able to teach them and test for them, he describes in operational detail the critical thinker's component abilities and dispositions.

Ennis regards arguments as having "deductive," "inductive," or "evaluative" inferences. His approach to argumentation is perhaps the most tolerant, since it is compatible with most other theories. When the time comes, it can accommodate in a straightforward manner any new developments from informal logic that bear on argument interpretation and evaluation.

Another critical thinking theorist, McPeck, has, by his persistent criticisms, challenged informal logicians to clarify their views, thus launching a vigorous debate. Several theorists whom McPeck has attacked contend that McPeck misconstrues their positions.[30]

In an influential paper, Richard Paul (1982) distinguishes between "weak sense" critical thinking and "strong sense" critical thinking. Weak-sense critical thinking refers to the ability to criticize arguments in order to attack one's opponent and defend one's own standpoint. Strong-sense critical thinking is the capacity to question positions and arguments with a view to exposing their assumptions, as well as one's own unexamined values, in order to get closer to the truth of the matter—even if doing so in the light of a full and open examination of all the relevant arguments requires the abandonment of a cherished position.

Paul criticized standard informal logic courses for teaching primarily weak-sense critical thinking, and advocated revising the syllabus so as to teach strong-sense critical thinking. The sort of argument evaluation entailed by strong-sense critical thinking, he argued, requires a broader analysis than that typical of the fallacy approach. It includes an examination of potential counter-arguments to one's views and arguments, but also an investigation into one's own biases and the integrity of one's conduct, examining its consistency with one's avowed beliefs. Paul (1989) contended that character traits such as a disposition to openness and self-examination are necessary for strong-sense critical thinking. More recently, he has articulated a set of intellectual virtues (humility, courage and so on) which he identifies as crucial for critical thinking in the strong sense (pp. 119–121).

---

[29]For a fairly recent formulation, see Norris and Ennis (1989, pp. 1–25).

[30]See Govier (1983, p. 170), Paul (1985, p. 39), Siegel (1985, pp. 61–72), and Blair and Johnson (1991, p. 37).

In part, Paul was calling for the very dialectical approach to argument interpretation and critique that was suggested by Rescher (1977), and has been emphasized by Barth (1985a) and Walton (1989a), while van Eemeren and Grootendorst (1984, 1992a) incorporated it into their pragma-dialectical theory of argumentation. Nowadays, this view of argumentation enjoys widespread acceptance. But Paul was also recommending a kind of moral commitment that, while perhaps commendable in itself and arguable as an educational ideal, is not essentially connected to argumentation theory or informal logic.

McPeck (1981, 1990) has been an early and vigorous critic of informal logic and the standard approach to critical thinking, which he appears to regard as very closely related (Blair & Johnson, 1991, p. 37). Following in Toulmin's wake, McPeck holds that any interesting standards for evaluating an argument will be a function of the standards of knowledge, or justified belief, in whatever domain of knowledge the conclusion belongs to. He therefore denies that fallacy theory, or any other general theory, can provide a basis for assessing the cogency of arguments.

Siegel (1988) argues that a critical thinker is one who is "appropriately moved by reasons" (p. 34). Accordingly, "a critical thinker must be able to assess reasons and their ability to warrant beliefs, claims and actions properly" (p. 34). The principles governing the assessment of reasons, according to Siegel, are of two types: "subject-specific" principles—the sort McPeck claims are the only interesting ones—and "subject-neutral" principles. The latter consist of logical principles, both formal and informal. Siegel (1988) sees no reason to regard one or the other type of principle as more basic. He suggests that although formal argumentation may rarely be encountered in everyday discourse, it constitutes an "ideal type" of argument. Formal reasoning patterns such as the disjunctive syllogism provide the most compelling reasons possible for accepting a proposition (p. 26).

In Siegel's perspective, informal logic supplies some, but not all, of the necessary theory for application by the critical thinker. His views may thus be seen as an attempt to combine Paul's emphasis on the need for a certain outlook or orientation (which Siegel calls "the critical spirit" and which Paul identifies with intellectual virtues) and McPeck's concern for the recognition of discipline-specific principles. Siegel situates these factors within the wider context of epistemological concerns, the need for theoretical justification of critical thinking as an educational ideal, and the demands of rationality theory.

Like McPeck, Weinstein tends to regard critical thinking and informal logic as interchangeable. As we noted in our discussion of Toulmin-type theories of argument assessment, Weinstein (1990a, 1994) holds that informal logic should in effect become applied epistemology. In this light, he advocates the study of the epistemologies of the disciplines, for he thinks the important standards of argument cogency will turn out to be discipline-specific. Unlike McPeck, however, he does not regard this fact as a barrier to informal logic's relevance, but as an opportunity for its expansion. Informal logic will be necessary for critical thinking, because it will supply the criteria for the assessment of the reasoning and arguments that are, at least, a necessary element of critical thinking.

Matthew Lipman, at least as well known for his role as founder of the world-wide Philosophy for Children movement, has tendered a definition of critical thinking as "skillful, responsible, thinking that facilitates good judgment because it (1) relies upon criteria, (2) is self-correcting, and (3) is sensitive to context" (1988, p. 39). Presumably, arguments are one kind of thing that will be subjected to critical thinking so conceived, and such thinking tends to produce good arguments. Lipman's view of the relation of critical thinking and informal logic is like Govier's: the two will overlap, but are distinct.

Reviewing all these theories, Johnson (1992) argues that there are important limitations in the theoretical work done thus far. First, none of these theories makes plain the force of the term *critical* in the expression *critical thinking*. Ennis's widely cited definition seems to be a definition of skillful thinking, but it is not evident what in his definition the word critical points to. Second, Johnson argues, critical thinking belongs to a *network of related terms*, including also "problem solving," "metacognition," "decision making," and "higher order cognitive skills." The precise relationships have yet to be sorted out in any detailed way. Johnson calls this "The Network Problem," and argues that at present there is no viable solution to it in any theory of critical thinking.

Another point of disagreement among the theorists is whether or not critical thinking should be defined so as to include dispositions. Missimer (1990) has explicitly argued that any such definition of critical thinking is misguided. The majority of theorists, however, continue to hold that dispositions are necessarily part of critical thinking. Here Paul (1990) and Siegel (1988, 1993) represent the dominant view.

6.4 PERSPECTIVES

Informal logic is seen by its practitioners as a distinct domain of logic, a domain primarily defined by its subject—argumentation—and its purpose—the development of analytical and normative tools for the analysis of argumentation and the assessment of its logical merits. The nature of informal logic, as well as its present shape, are explained by its origins in, and its development from, a movement to reform introductory logic instruction, on the one hand, and the interest in revivifying fallacy theory on the other. Among the main theoretical issues discussed in the informal logic literature are the nature and structure of argument, fallacies and fallacy theory, the critique of arguments and the evaluation criteria involved, and the connections with related fields.

As a domain of study, informal logic is rich in raw materials. So far, with a few exceptions, informal logicians have largely concentrated on articulating the exigencies their enterprise is to meet and the ensuing objectives. There has been as yet not an attempt to produce a united foundational theory. Some hold that, in order to tackle the problems informal logicians set out to deal with, a more consistent theoretical framework needs to be worked out. Others' meta-theoretical views leave them untroubled by this lacuna. In any case, on many of the issues there is a burgeoning literature that can be instrumental in shaping such a framework, and in developing some overall, unifying theories. For the time being, we have to conclude that informal logic consists of the sum of its promising parts.

Critical thinking as an intellectual habit and educational ideal is related to informal logic but different. Although the two cannot be identified, the theory of informal logic is essential to the exercise of much critical thinking. Critical thinking theorists generally acknowledge that the ability to analyze and evaluate arguments is of crucial importance to critical thinking, however defined. Ideally, the theory generated by informal logicians therefore feeds an ability that is central in critical thinking.

As for its aims, the critical thinking movement can only be applauded. Some critics, however, find the aims of Paul to be overambitious, seemingly presupposing that critical thinking is a cure for all sources of irrationality.[31] By overemphasizing personal responsibility for reasonableness, they argue, the restrictions that lie beyond any individual's personal control can easily be overlooked, which may in turn lead to a disillusionment that is harmful to the ideal of reasonableness.

Informal logicians have moved well beyond their original pedagogical orientation, as is evident from their work on fallacy, the nature and structure of argumentation, argument criticism, and the borderline between informal logic and related fields. They now find themselves confronting a wide variety of theoretical issues. After having searched for theoretical antecedents in the early years of the movement, they have stimulated various sorts of cross-fertilization with dialogue logic, pragma-dialectics, speech communication, and rhetoric.

The connections between dialogue logic and informal logic are evident in the work of Walton (1984, 1985a). Walton's own interest in exploring this area may be traced back to Hamblin. Another important source in the development of dialogue logic is the work of Barth, which is discussed in chapter 9.[32]

Barth (1992, pp. 667–668) situates the emergence of dialogue logic within the wider philosophical context and traces its role in the development of the theory of argumentation. She sees the emergence of dialogue logic as a result of the rejection of foundationalism connected with the Deductive-Nomological Para-

---

[31]According to Paul (1987, pp. 381–382), strong-sense critical thinking instruction can help us "to break down our irrational ego and to develop our rational self." The "intellectual art of stepping outside of our own systems of beliefs" should become "second nature to us" in order to recognize "argumentation" and "argument analysis" as "profoundly essential to our role as moral agents and as potential shapers of our own nature and destiny." For a critique of the critical thinking aims advocated by Paul and his associates, see van Eemeren (1988, pp. 39–41).

[32]For the emergence of dialogue logic, see Barth (1986, 1992).

digm, according to which logic was to be the science that would serve mathematicians in the analysis of strengths and weaknesses of deductive-nomological systems. Dialogue logicians seek to present and justify rules according to which a dialogue can be carried on in a rational fashion. Some make use of formal and mathematical models, and in that respect dialogue logic and informal logic part company. Here the collaboration between Walton and Krabbe (1995), himself a student of Barth's, is interesting.

Still to the degree that texts and conversations in natural language can be represented now as an argument, now as a dialogue, it appears that dialogue logic and informal logic are different approaches, each largely governed by a normative interest. The dialogue logician assigns to logic the task of prescribing rights and duties in the transaction of a rational dialogue. The informal logician assigns to logic the task of developing the criteria or standards for use in the evaluation of arguments. Obviously these are cognate endeavors.

Another important source for the recent development of informal logic is the pragma-dialectical approach to argumentation of van Eemeren and Grootendorst. This approach is discussed in chapter 10, so here we merely mention its general connection to informal logic. As Snoeck Henkemans (1992) shows with regard to the structure of argumentation, fallacy theory is not the only part of pragma-dialectics that has direct application to informal logic. Because pragma-dialectics offers not only a unified theory of fallacy, but a fully articulated theory about the function and structure of argumentation in general, it presents a challenge to informal logicians to either locate their work in terms of the pragma-dialectical outlook, show that there is a gap in that outlook which informal logic fills, or identify mistakes or shortcomings in the pragma-theoretical theory.

Another body of theory with clear implications for informal logic is the work of American argumentation and rhetoric theorists in the field of (speech) communication, discussed in chapter 7. Communication theorists have written about the nature of argument, fallacies, and argument analysis.[33] Especially the empirical work of researchers in these areas may have connections with informal logic, but there is interesting conceptual analysis as well. The little explored connection between rhetoric and informal logic, finally, has been addressed by Wenzel (1987).[34]

---

[33]See, for example, Brockriede (1975) and O'Keefe (1977) on the nature of argument, Ulrich (1992) on fallacies, and Burleson (1979) and Hample (1992) on argument analysis and criticism.

[34]For evidence of the overlap, see Cox and Willard (1982b), and Benoit, Hample, and Benoit (1992).

7

COMMUNICATION AND RHETORIC

As explained in chapter 3, the study of argumentation in the tradition of speech communication began in the United States with the publication of debate textbooks in the late nineteenth century. Debating was seen as a pedagogical device, a form of practical training for careers in law, government, or politics; argumentation more generally was seen as a body of citizenship skills. Argumentation, the texts held, is critical to democratic processes; its pedagogy is a path towards enfranchising a mass public for democratic participation.

This original rationale was broaded during the 1970s with the rise of consensualist theories of truth. The idea that claims are most trustworthy when they are confirmed by the consensus of a defined community puts a premium on the rationality (or defensibility) of the means by which communities achieve consensus. These means increasingly came to be seen as intersubjective or social, so the ideas of argument and argumentation acquired a new prominence—in studies of science and technology, science policy, and the sociology of knowledge, and in studies of decision making and policy formation.

In the early years of American speech communication, argumentation often was defined by reference to the *conviction–persuasion duality*, an idea the textbooks had appropriated from Enlightenment rhetorical theorists such as Campbell, Whately, and Priestly. Under the influence of what was called "faculty psychology," the human mind was divided into discrete functions or domains; reason and emotion were dichotomized, and even seen as hostile forces contending for supremacy. Convincing was considered to be rational, persuading irrational. "Conviction" thus labeled beliefs acquired by logical reason and "persuasion" beliefs that came from emotional appeals.

In an early American journal essay on argumentation—one of only a handful so specifically focused between 1890 and 1960—Mary Yost (1917) challenged this dualism by arguing that psychologists had abandoned it in favor of more holistic views of mind. Logic and emotion cannot be separated, Yost argued, they are interdependent cognitive processes. Perhaps due to her influence, the dualism underwent an important change in the textbooks. Some texts merely hedged the dualism, concentrating primarily on "rational appeals" addressed to the reason, considering "psychological appeals" as secondary (e.g., Winans & Utterback, 1930). In an Aristotelian turn reinforced by attitude theory, many texts defended the dualism as a normative goal, not as a psychological fact: Emotion must be felt because it is natural, but it is best disciplined by reason.[1] The idea, then, was to minimize procedural flaws and rule violations, wishful thinking, suppression of evidence, biases, personal attacks, and, insofar as they are inappropriate, emotional appeals. Reason was to be an end-in-itself *and* a means for protecting discourse from the worst excesses of persuasion. This revision of the dualism, and its pairing with attitude theory, had one side effect that preoccupied American argumentation scholars during the end of the 1970s. It was a debate about the meaning of the term *argument*.

The early textbooks defined argument as primarily logical discourse. Devoted to the judgment of arguments by their logical soundness, many took Aristotle's practical syllogism as the model, or his treatment of argument from example. Later texts, influenced by structural linguistics and analytic philosophy, took an even more formalist view, holding that logic, language, and reasoning are impersonal, *a priori*, and context-free. Meanings, as well as the soundness and fallaciousness of claims, lie in linguistic structure, so the idea was to boil human expressions down to their essences, to reduce abstractions, for instance, to concrete expressions that are themselves "mirrors" of nature (Rorty, 1979). Argumentation, on this view, was to be a procedure for correcting incorrect expressions, for solving disputes by finding and fixing mistakes in reasoning.

By the 1970s, this vision had been largely discredited. Formalism had been challenged in many fields for its sterility, its irrelevance to the social contexts of discourse, to how people actually think, speak, and argue, and for its epistemological hubris in seeking a universal commensurating language (Anderson & Mortenson, 1967). This challenge reflected Toulmin's (1958) call for the study of *arguments-in-use*, "the actual forms of argument current in any field." The field of logic was to pursue a "confessedly empirical" program of studying how arguments work in real contexts.

Currently, the study of argumentation in American speech communication is the province of rhetorical theorists and critics, students of public discourse, analysts of conversation, scholars of interpersonal communication, facilitators

---

[1]Attitude theory described affective and cognitive elements as open to conscious "balancing."

of negotiation, and teachers and directors of contest debate. Its most obvious common features are the dethronement of formal logic as the paradigm case of reasoning and the corollary insistence that argumentation relates to audiences and fits squarely within the rhetorical tradition.

Where do argumentation studies in speech communication stand at the moment? The literature is rich, but the question is where it is going. Largely, the argumentation scholars concerned seem not to be working from a clear and common perspective. There is a growing call for greater coherence in argumentation studies. Without that, it is hard to anchor the burgeoning literature or to indicate how one line of inquiry relates to another. We describe the state of the art in a four-part schema. Because it is uncertain that this arrangement would be shared by others, it is to some extent idiosyncratic.

We start from a root concept of argumentation studies earlier proposed by the American speech communication scholar David Zarefsky (1995). Zarefsky believes that argumentation should be regarded as "the practice of justifying decisions under conditions of uncertainty." His definition has four key elements.

First, argumentation is a *practice*. It is a social activity in which people engage. In the course of this practice, they make and examine texts, which are to be studied as products of the practice. Argumentation, however, is not a practice that can be easily isolated from other practices. It has no unique subject, and people who engage in argumentation are also doing other things. They may not even recognize what they are doing as argumentation. Argumentation is not only something people naturally do, it is also something analysts make use of in examining with a critical attitude all kinds of social practices. The view of argumentation as practice contrasts strongly with a view of argumentation as textual or logical structure.[2]

Second, argumentation is a practice of *justifying*. The word "justifying," standing in contrast to the word "proving," is critical. It expresses the recognition, inspiring the dethronement of the analytic ideal, that the outcomes of argument cannot be certain. On the other hand, neither are they capricious or whimsical. They are supported by what the audience would regard as good reasons warranting belief or action. To say that a claim is justified immediately raises the question, justified to whom?

Several answers can be given to this question, depending on the situation. Claims can be justified for oneself, for one's family or friends, for the particular audience present on the occasion, for a broader audience defined by some special interest, for the general public, and for an audience of people from diverse cultures. The question then becomes whether the practical meaning of *justify* varies among these different audiences and whether the process of justification is different as well.

---

[2]The notion that argumentation can be seen as a point of view is developed more fully in Zarefsky (1980).

Much of the literature on argument "fields," "spheres," and "communities," as well as discussions of what counts as "evidence" for claims, can be seen as addressing the basic question, justified to whom? In any case, this question immediately calls attention to the fact that argumentation is *addressed*. It is a practice that occurs in the context of an audience, not *in vacuo*. Since it is concerned with the nexus between claims and people, it clearly is a rhetorical practice.

Third, argumentation is a practice of justifying *decisions*. Decisions involve choices, for if there were only one alternative there would be nothing to decide. But decisions also presuppose the need to choose. The alternatives are perceived as being incompatible. Making a decision is like standing at the proverbial fork in the road. One cannot stand still, one cannot take both forks, and one cannot be sure in advance which fork will prove to be the right path.

Sometimes decisions are bound to a particular moment in time. Each of the nations in the European Union, for instance, had to decide at a particular moment whether to approve the Maastricht treaty, just as the United States Congress had to decide whether to ratify the North American Free Trade Agreement. These decisions were accompanied by attempts to justify one decision or another. Sometimes, a decision evolves over a long period of time, and the process of justifying the decision is likewise longitudinal. For many years now, we have witnessed an ongoing controversy about whether the national or the global economy should be the unit of analysis for policy choices. From a longer term perspective, Maastricht and NAFTA might be seen as moments in that ongoing controversy.

Decisions involve choices, but they are not always so final that they obliterate the alternative not taken. The same forks in the road may present themselves repeatedly, even if in slightly altered guise. In the United States, for example, the controversy about how best to pay for health care is largely a reenactment of arguments that go back 60 or 80 years, even though various specific decisions have been made along the way. The minority position is seldom vanquished completely; it may come back and win another day. Recognizing this fact, decisions should respect all of the proffered alternatives, even if only one is selected at a given time.

Fourth, argumentation is the practice of justifying decisions *under conditions of uncertainty*. The need to make choices when not everything can be known is the defining feature of rhetorical situations. We might have to act in the face of incomplete information; the universe affected by the decision might be so large that only a sample could be considered; or the decision might depend on other choices or outcomes that cannot be known. Alternatively, the situation may be uncertain because of an inferential gap between data and conclusion. The data might be factual whereas the conclusion is a matter of belief, value, or policy; or perhaps the information relates to present conditions whereas the decision involves predictions for the future. For whichever reason, people argue to justify decisions that cannot be made with certainty. Hence, according to the American communication scholars, for this reason as well argumentation is situated within the realm of rhetoric, not of apodeictic proof. This does not mean that outcomes are irrational, but rather that they are guided by rhetorical reason. Warrants are evoked from the cumulative experience of a relevant audience, not from a particular structure or form.

This conception of argumentation helps to organize the branches of the study of argumentation in communication and rhetoric, giving greater coherence to an otherwise disparate and diffuse field. It encompasses argumentation from "the personal" to "the cultural" and it has descriptive and normative dimensions. The major research traditions we shall distinguish in the next Sections can be grafted onto this conception.

The first tradition we describe (in Section 7.1) is that of competitive debate, an important source of inspiration to the study of argumentation in American speech communication. Next we discuss (in Section 7.2) the development of social science perspectives on communication and their infusion of the study of argumentation with empirical approaches and methods. Then we pay (in Section 7.3) some attention to contributions to our current understanding of argumentation originating in practical philosophy and social and cultural critique. In this way, our survey of research traditions in communication and rhetoric illustrates the plurality that makes the study of argumentation in American speech communication rich and diverse.

7.1 FROM DEBATE TO ARGUMENTATION STUDIES

Argumentation studies in American speech communication sprang from modest roots. Late in the nineteenth century, as an alternative to social fraternities and athletics, American colleges and universities began competition in debate. The earliest publications were textbooks to instruct students and coaches in this new activity. These books shared several common features. They were practical how-to-do-it guides informed primarily by their authors' intuition and experience. They were unreflective, in that they treated matters of practice as neither complicated nor problematic. They paid little attention to any relationship between the *species* debate and the *genus* argumentation. Typically, they did not place their instruction in a context broader than preparation for the contest activity itself.

Subsequent generations of textbooks, in the early and middle years of this century, had many of the same characteristics, but with two important qualifiers. First, they became more sophisticated in their analyses. They could rely on a growing body of experience that both codified conventional categories and permitted more textured and nuanced discussion. Second, they began to make connections with classical rhetorical theory, particularly with the concepts of common topics, issues, *stasis*, and *logos*, *ethos*, and *pathos* as modes of proof. They also revived Bishop Whately's nineteenth-century treatment of presumption and burden of proof. Still, they retained an emphasis on practice that was fairly straightforward, without reflection on its goals, methods, and underlying assumptions. In retrospect, debate during those years can be characterized as dominated by the "stock issues" paradigm, being modeled on formal logic and courtroom oratory.[3] At the time, a term such as *stock issues paradigm* would have seemed meaningless, because that was all there was. Alternative perspectives largely escaped consideration.[4]

The literature on debate beginning in the early 1960s represents a series of departures from this tradition. Perhaps most influential was the publication of *Decision and Debate* by Douglas Ehninger and Wayne Brockriede (1963). At least in embryonic form, this book offered a broader perspective of the debate activity. Debate was seen as a means of making decisions critically. It was described as fundamentally a cooperative rather than competitive enterprise. And it incorporated the model of argument that Toulmin (1958) had set out in *The Uses of Argument*, 5 years before (see chapter 5). By emphasizing this model as a diagram, Ehninger and Brockriede may have reinforced a formalistic understanding of reasoning.[5] But by focusing explicitly on "warrants," "qualifiers," and "rebuttals," they undercut the analytic ideal of argument as applied formal logic. Inferences were seen as fallible and conclusions as uncertain, and the warrants authorizing inferences were seen as coming not come from logical form but from the substantive beliefs of an audience.

Subsequently, theorists of debate began to explore alternatives to the received tradition. In the late 1960s and early 1970s, many pages of the *Journal of the American Forensic Association* (now *Argumentation and Advocacy*) were filled with articles on alternative patterns of case construction—the comparative advantage affirmative case, the goals/criteria case, the alternative justification case—as well as essays identifying underlying consistencies amid these seeming differences.[6] The counterplan, a negative debate strategy traditionally dismissed as weak, was revived and given theoretical anchor.[7] Writers began to focus attention on the underlying nature and goals of the process of debate itself,

---

[3]Stock issues are the issues that the affirmative side in a debate has to address in defense of the proposition.

[4]Among the exceptions are Weaver and Burke, who take a more general view of rhetoric and communication. For a brief overview of their positions, see Foss, Foss, and Trapp (1991), and Enos and Brown (1993).

[5]Charles Willard (1976) has argued that the process of diagramming arguments fundamentally misunderstands the mix of discursive and nondiscursive elements in argument and gives too much credence to formal structure.

[6]See, for example, Fadely (1967), Chesebro (1968, 1971), Lewinski, Metzler, and Settle (1973), and Lichtman, Garvin, and Corsi (1973). An essay questioning distinctions is Zarefsky (1969).

[7]See, for example, Kaplow (1981).

believing that emerging differences about theory and practice really reflected different root assumptions about debate. The late 1970s and early 1980s saw essays explicating different paradigms or models of debate—the policy-making model, the hypothesis-testing model, the game-theory model, the critic-judge model, and the *tabula rasa* model, for example. The traditional perspective on debate, now renamed "the stock-issues model," took its place among these alternatives.[8]

In hindsight, this literature is not so important for its explicit content. Many of the disputes engaging debate theorists were esoteric, and many of the controversies now seem passé, not because they were solved but because they were outgrown. Rather, this phase of the debate literature is significant because it shows how conventional wisdom was rendered problematic through the imagination of alternatives. This is an important step toward developing a more reflective, self-conscious, and critical understanding of argumentation.

One of the major recent trends is to stress the links between debate and argumentation in general. Recognizing that debate is a specific application of more general principles (e.g., John Dewey's view that an educated public could debate public policy issues), educators began to develop courses in argumentation theory and practice that were not geared specifically to debate.[9] These courses involved larger numbers of students in the understanding of argumentation theory. To meet the needs of such courses, a new kind of textbook emerged, such as Rieke and Sillars' (1975) *Argumentation and the Decision-Making Process*, Warnick and Inch's (1989) *Critical Thinking and Communication*, and Branham's (1991) *Debate and Critical Analysis: The Harmony of Conflict*. Even books oriented primarily towards debate, such as Patterson and Zarefsky's (1983) *Contemporary Debate*, often portrayed debate as a derivative of general argumentation.[10]

The linkage between debate and argumentation in general has been pursued in both directions. Not only has debate drawn from an understanding of argumentation; it also has contributed to it. To be sure, even 50 years ago one could find critical studies of legislative or political debate. Often, however, these were either simply descriptive studies or attempts to apply the principles of contest debate to situations they did not fit. Recent literature has been far more sophisticated. In 1979, Thomas Goodnight (1980) delivered a paper on "the liberal and the conservative presumption," demonstrating that presumption was not just an arbitrary concept or a tie-breaking rule but a substantive concept, according

---

[8]Representative articles include Lichtman and Rohrer (1980), and Zarefsky (1982). See also the special forum on Debate Paradigms in *Journal of the American Forensic Association 18* (Winter, 1982).

[9]Cf. Dewey (1916).

[10]The relationship between debate and argumentation was explicitly acknowledged in 1974 when the National Developmental Conference on Forensics defined forensic activities as laboratories for investigating the argumentative perspective on communication.

to which one could distinguish political positions and understand political disputes. More recently, Goodnight (1991) has drawn attention to the dynamics of controversy. Controversy can be described as debate conducted over time, without *a priori* rules, boundaries, or time limits. Scholars trained in debate have employed this understanding of controversy to provide new insight on cultural and political disputes, especially related to military policy and international relations.[11]

We have dwelt at such length on the contributions of contest debate to the field of argumentation for several reasons. First, debate is still too often seen as something of an academic stepchild rather than as an evolving intellectual tradition with far broader implications. Second, many of the leading American scholars of argumentation were introduced to the subject through contest debate and found it an important influence on their subsequent work. Third, the case of academic debate illustrates very well a recurrent pattern in the speech communication discipline. Rather than being driven by grand theories tested through application, the discipline has tended to construct theories as needed to explain or to solve problems encountered in practice. And fourth, debate is both a pedagogy for and a continuing test of Dewey's belief that public policy issues can be researched and debated by a "public" composed of nonexperts.

7.2 SOCIAL SCIENCE PERSPECTIVES ON COMMUNICATION

We do not want to give the impression that the study of argumentation in communication and rhetoric derives directly or singly from competitive debate. Among the other founding traditions in American speech communication are the social science perspectives on communication. The discipline has always stood on the boundary between the humanities and the social sciences, drawing on the methods and research traditions of both. Even in the early years, the journals included articles whose lineage traced to classical rhetoric and others whose ancestry was traced to the 18th and 19th century beginnings of psychology. Often the tension between humanities and social sciences has led to a healthy dialectic; occasionally it has led to an unholy academic war.

Social science studies of communication received a significant boost from the World War II studies of persuasion and attitude change.[12] During the 1950s and 1960s they assumed greater prominence in, and sometimes came to domi-

---

[11]See, for example, Dauber (1988) with regard to the nuclear strategic doctrine, and Ivie (1987) with regard to American foreign policy.

[12]Carl Hovland, who conducted such studies during World War II, then returned to Yale University to establish the Yale Communication and Attitude Change Program. Among its research publications are Hovland, Janis, and Kelley (1953), Hovland (1957), Hovland and Janis (1959), Hovland and Rosenberg (1960), and Sherif and Hovland (1961).

nate, American departments of speech communication. The social science tradition brought at least three major influences to communication studies. First, it emphasized descriptive and empirical, rather than normative, studies. Instead of focusing on an ideal of what communication should be, it sought to describe communication as it actually is. Second, it sought to produce testable statements about communication in general, rather than shedding insight on particular significant cases. It was more concerned with prediction than with retrospective explanation. Because case studies were important only as they contributed to generalizations, it was not necessary or useful to study the "great speakers." Indeed, it might be better to study everyday interactions among ordinary people. These interactions were more likely to yield general theory than would the study of what by definition was an exceptional or atypical case. Third, and directly related to this last point, the social science approach deemphasized formal oratory and public address in favor of studying interpersonal communication, group discussion, and bargaining and negotiation.

Social science perspectives were brought to bear on argumentation studies beginning in the 1970s, predominantly by a group of scholars then located at the University of Illinois and united by their commitment to constructivism. In an influential essay, Daniel O'Keefe (1977) distinguished between two different senses of argument: argument$_1$, referring to texts and products, and argument$_2$, referring to ongoing processes. Argument$_2$ is "a case in which a person makes a claim and overtly expresses a reason (or reasons) for that claim" and "both the claim and the overtly expressed reason(s) [must be] linguistically explicable—which is not to say linguistically explicit" (O'Keefe, 1982, p. 13). Thus, "just as one feature of promises is that they are conveyed in acts of promising, so one feature of arguments, is that they are conveyed in acts of argument-making" (p. 16).

The distinction between arguments$_1$ and arguments$_2$ challenged the assumption that the first of these senses was somehow the more foundational. By way of this distinction, Daniel O'Keefe attempted to clarify a dispute between those who insisted on the importance of nondiscursive elements in argument (Willard, 1976) and those who insisted that any element of an argument must either be linguistic or linguistically explicable (Burleson, 1979, 1980; Kneupper, 1978, 1979). Charles Willard had argued not only that argument diagrams were poorly suited to psychological processes but that they were also inadequate for describing messages: They could not represent irony, ambiguity, and other nondiscursive aspects of messages. Defenders of diagramming argued that Willard's point carried to its logical conclusion made important elements of arguments unanalyzable. O'Keefe's distinction suggests that arguments$_1$ are diagrammable while arguments$_2$ are best studied as instances of communicative acts. Though arguments, O'Keefe argued, may trade upon multiple modes of communication, verbal and nonverbal, and different motives, including discourse organization and relational considerations, they are best defined by appeal to paradigm cases, meaning the most clear-cut, uncontroversial cases. To explain to an alien what a *table* is, we would not show the alien a French Provincial convertible table-chair with a built-in television. We would select the simplest, most straight-forward table, from which we might then turn to more "borderline" cases.

At about the same time, Charles Willard was beginning the work that would lead to a constructivist theory of argumentation, developed in his books *Argumentation and the Social Grounds of Knowledge* (1983), *A Theory of Argumentation* (1989), and *Liberal Alarms and Rhetorical Excursions* (1995).[13] Willard defined argumentation as an interaction in which two or more people maintain what they construe to be incompatible claims. He urged researchers to explore what actually takes place in such interactions.

Starting in the 1960s, a "psychological turn" away from formalism occurred among linguists and communication theorists. In that period, it was a common assumption that meanings are in people, not in things. Although this slogan may seem overstated or even mistaken today, it must be appreciated as a reaction to formalism. Only genetics, went the objection, is a priori; and *nothing* is context-free. Logic, "like reality, truth, and meaning, does not exist independent of the listener" (Delia, 1970, p. 141). So arguments "are not in statements but in people" (Brockriede, 1975). They are psychological phenomena, for it is the arguer's cognitive system that controls the meaning and therefore the outcomes of arguments (Hample, 1977a, 1977b, 1978, 1979a, 1979b, 1980, 1981). The best model of what arguments are is Aristotle's *enthymeme*. This rhetorical syllogism differs from logical syllogisms in that its "substance," its premises, are not certainties but probabilities, opinions believed by audiences. And these premises need not be fully stated, for the orator should not waste time saying what is obvious; the listeners will fill in the missing parts.

A fruitful aspect of the psychological turn was the cognitive-developmental perspective, which focuses on argument as a skill or competency, developed progressively and employed much like other cognitive skills, such as language comprehension, problem solving, and moral reasoning.[14] Paraphrasing Burleson (1983, p. 597), the main claims of this perspective can be summarized as follows: (1) reasoning *uses* underlying cognitive structures, (2) cognitive structures are clustered in content domains, (3) because people differ in cognitive development (their cognitive structures differ) their performances (for instance, arguing) will systematically differ, (4) these individual differences affect the nature and sub-stance of the arguments people make, and (5) individual differences in reasoning processes affect the outcomes of argumentative interactions.

A promising cognitive-developmental line of empirical study is the focus on children's arguments, in which children are not simply viewed as incompetent adults. According to Barbara O'Keefe and Pamela Benoit (1982), "premature

---

[13]His view was first set out in Willard (1978a) and a series of subsequent articles.
[14]See Clark and Delia (1976, 1977, 1979), Burleson (1981), Jackson (1983), Kline and Woloschuk (1983), and Yingling and Trapp (1985).

assumptions of developmental difference are quite dangerous, as the recent history of developmental psychology will attest" (p. 154). They emphasize that a great deal of research has been done "to show that young children can in fact do perfectly well many things Piaget (and others) have claimed they are incompetent to do" (p. 154).

Barbara O'Keefe and Pamela Benoit are among those who study how individuals develop argumentative competence, focusing on argumentation as a set of acquired skills.[15] If we know more about how and when these skills normally are acquired, we can design more effective pedagogy and training. In a somewhat related research program, Dominic Infante has explored the distinction between argumentative competence and skills, on the one hand, and argumentativeness as a personality trait, on the other.[16]

O'Keefe and Benoit (1982) concluded from their study of children's arguments that "it is precisely in borderline cases that a given attribute of arguments is likely to be displayed most clearly." "Attending solely to paradigm cases," they say, "can blind the analyst to the operation of multiple attributes and processes" (p. 161). It appears that disputes may be conducted in a variety of modes, that verbal exchanges are one such mode and that different modes of dispute may be employed, concurrently or successively within the same dispute. Thus, *argument*, in ordinary usage, is "an intrinsically fuzzy concept that can be appropriately applied to a wide range of activities" (p. 157). Where some researchers might be inclined to see fuzziness as a predicament, to be solved by increasingly precise definitions and distinctions, O'Keefe and Benoit advocate seeing fuzziness as a fact to be explained.[17]

Aside from the successes of the developmental perspective, the psychological turn was short lived. Few American theorists would endorse it today without severe modification, for the prevailing view is that argument is a distinctively *public* process. The point is not that reasoning and other psychological processes are unimportant, but that arguers are actors on a public stage, their performances are publicly available. If argumentation is the practice of justifying decisions, then the focus of attention is on justifications (public acts) rather than on psychological processes involved in reaching a decision. The enthymeme, indeed, thanks to Lloyd Bitzer and others, came to be seen as a communicative act—rhetorical proof being a joint creation of speaker and listener.

One impetus for this emphasis on argument as public had to do with the difficulty of analyzing psychological processes. Toulmin's diagram, for instance, was poorly suited to recreating the creative reasoning by which arguers produce

---

[15]See, for example, Benoit (1981, 1983b), and O'Keefe and Benoit (1982).

[16]Infante's bibliography is lengthy. A representative example of his research is Infante (1981).

[17]On these grounds, Willard (1989) continues to argue that once a conversation becomes an argument, anything used as a communication vehicle in the interaction is relevant and conceivably indispensable to argument analysis.

arguments or the inferential processes by which listeners form meanings and reach conclusions (Willard, 1976, 1978b). Another catalyst was the growing emphasis on the idea of communicative acts as public features of conversational argument. For Sally Jackson and Scott Jacobs (1982), argument is a kind of language game "played within other language games—negotiating the outcome of a request, issuing and receiving complaints, attacking and defending assertions" (p. 207). Jackson and Jacobs (1982) see the meaning of discourse acts much as George Herbert Mead saw *gestures*—as "a phase of a social act that finds its completion in the response of another organism" (p. 211). The result is an "ongoing process of mutual adjustment" that is neither purely psychological nor purely sociological. It is social because arguers, like all other interactants, play by, or are held accountable to, publicly-available rules.

Exploring what actually takes place in argumentative interactions, Jackson and Jacobs initiated an ongoing program for studying argumentation in informal conversations.[18] They have tried to understand the reasoning processes individuals actually use to make inferences and resolve disputes in ordinary talk.[19] Their work in discourse analysis has over the years drawn closer to the pragma-dialectical perspective of van Eemeren and Grootendorst, with whom they collaborated on *Reconstructing Argumentative Discourse* (1993).

A related trend in the empirical investigation of argumentation is the studying of argument in natural settings. Unlike the debate contest or the courtroom, these settings are usually informal and unstructured. School board meetings, labor-management negotiations, counseling sessions, public relations campaigns, and self-help support groups are some of the highly varied settings in which argumentation has been studied.[20] The goal of such studies is to produce "grounded theory," that is a theory of the specific case. Of course, recurrent patterns observed in such cases also contribute to a more general understanding of argumentation.

An influential *message-centered* theory has been proposed by Barbara O'Keefe (1988). O'Keefe distinguishes between three different logics of message design, which reveal systematic differences in the assumptions people make about communication—about what it is, what it can do, and how it works. The differences are manifested in the use of systematically different communication-constituting concepts (different implicit theories) that yield different patterns of message organization and interpretation, each "associated with a constellation of related beliefs: a communication-constituting concept, a conception of the functional possibilities of communication, unit formation procedures, and principles of coherence" (p. 84). O'Keefe terms these design logics *Expressive, Conventional,* and *Rhetorical.*

---

[18]See Jackson and Jacobs (1989). For other studies of conversational argument, see also Craig and Tracy (1983).

[19]See, for example, Jackson and Jacobs (1980, 1982), Jacobs and Jackson (1981, 1982, 1983, 1989).

[20]An example of such studies is Putnam, Wilson, Waltman, and Turner (1986).

The *Expressive Design Logic* assumes that language is a medium for expressing thoughts and feelings. Communication is a process in which one expresses what one thinks or feels so that others can know what one thinks or feels. According to O'Keefe (1988), successful communication is clear expression, messages being repositories for meaning independent of context. Expressives thus impress us as being rather literal in their creation and understanding of messages: "they fail to appreciate that in communication, the process of expression can be made to serve other goals," and "they interpret messages as independent units rather than as threads in an interactional fabric, and so seem to disregard context" (p. 84). The Expressive thinks that "the only job a message can perform is expression" (p. 84). "The idea that messages might be systematically designed to cause particular reactions is alien (and possible reprehensible) to the Expressive communicator [. . .]. There are two (and only two) possible relations between speaker intentions and messages: the message can express the speaker's current mental state fully and honestly, or the message can convey some kind of distortion of the speaker's current state—a lie or an edited version of the whole truth" (p. 85). This desire to conduct communication as "full and open disclosure of current thoughts and feelings," leads to a concern for "the fidelity of messages, and to anxiety about deceptive communication" of message function. Characteristically, pragmatically pointless content, for example, expressive messages contain lengthy expressions of the speaker's wants, even if the listener has already heard them or can do nothing about them, redundancies, noncontingent threats, and insults. The "semantic and pragmatic connections between Expressively generated messages and their contexts and among elements within Expressive messages tend to be idiosyncratic and subjective rather than conventional and intersubjective. When one asks of an Expressive message, why did the speaker say this *now*, the obvious answer is generally: because the immediately prior event caused the speaker to have such-and-so reaction or to make such-and-so private mental association, and the speaker then said what he or she was thinking" (p. 86).

The *Conventional Design Logic* assumes that communication is a game played cooperatively, according to socially conventional rules and procedures. The Conventional view thus subsumes the Expressive: Language is a means of expressing propositions, "but the propositions one expresses are specified by the social effect one wants to achieve" (p. 86). One accommodates to conventional methods, as, for example, speech act theory suggests. Conventional communication is constituted by cooperation. One plays the game, obeys the rules, and fulfills one's obligations. Competence is a matter of appropriateness: One succeeds insofar as one occupies the correct position in a situation, and uses one's conventionally designed resources for obligating the interlocutor, behaves competently as a communicator, and is dealing with an equally competent and cooperative interlocutor. "Conventional messages generally have some clearly identifiable core action being performed that is easily characterizable as a speech act. The elements of such messages are generally mentions of felicity conditions on the core speech act, the structure of rights and obligations that give force to the speech act being performed, or the mitigating circumstances or conditions that would bear on the structure of rights and obligations within the situation (e.g., excuses). Just as the connections among message elements involve classic pragmatic coherence relations, the connections between messages and their contexts display a Conventional basis for coherence. In contrast to Expressive messages, which are characteristically psychological and reactive in their relation to their context, Conventional messages bear a conventionalized and rule-following relation to context. If one asks of a Conventional message, why did the speaker say this *now*, the answer is generally that this is the normal and appropriate thing to say under the circumstances" (p. 87).

The *Rhetorical Design Logic*, finally, assumes that "communication is the creation and negotiation of social selves and situations." In this logic, one's conventional knowledge is subsumed within a view of selves and situations as mutable rather than fixed. One sees meaning in terms of "dramaturgical enactment and social negotiation." Information about the subtleties of verbal behavior is constantly relevant to message planning and interpretation: "knowledge of the ways in which communicative choice and language style convey character, attitude, and definitions of the situation is systematically exploited to (on the one hand) enact a particular social reality and (on the other hand) provide 'depth interpretation' of received messages" (p. 87). The function of Rhetorical messages is negotiation. Different speakers can adopt different voices and thereby talk different realities: "The one thing Rhetorical message producers must accomplish in a social situation is the achievement of a consensus regarding the reality in which they are engaged, coming to employ a common descriptive vocabulary and finding a common drama in which to play. Reaching such a consensus anchors meaning and renders a sense of communication achievable" (p. 88). This puts a premium on interpersonal harmony and consensus. It values careful listening, psychological analysis, and adaptation to others in the creation of intersubjective understandings. "Their use of communication is dominated by the goals they want to achieve or facilitate and so messages are designed toward effects rather than in response to the actions of others" (p. 88). Rhetorical messages thus display a characteristic pattern of content and structure: We expect to find "elaborating and contextualizing clauses and phrases that provide explicit definitions of the context," a definite sense of role and character "through manipulation of stylistic elements in a marked and coherent way," and "classically 'rational' arguments and appeals designed to persuade the hearer that the speaker's symbolic reality is true or correct (but not legitimate or powerful or conventional)" (p. 88).

Rhetorical messages have characteristic connections to context. They are proactive rather than reactive. "If one asks of a Rhetorical message, why did the speaker say this *now*, the answer is generally: because they wanted to pursue such-and-such a goal. Similarly, if one asks of a rhetorical message, what connects all these elements as a common theme, the answer is generally: these elements can be interpreted as steps in a plan or as moments in a coherent narrative or as displays in a consistent character (and usually all of these). In short, the internal coherence of rhetorical messages derives from the elements being related by intersubjectively available, goal-oriented schemes" (O'Keefe, 1988, p. 88).

Differences among the design logics are manifested most strikingly when people need to manage multiple, even conflicting goals, for example, cases where one wants to criticize yet offer face protections to another person. The Expressive believes that the purpose of communication is the clear expression of thoughts, so the rule is, be tactful—edit the message or be less than frank. The Conventional will be polite by using off-the-record communications and conventional politeness forms such as apologies, hedges, excuses, and compliments (Brown & Levinson, 1978). The Rhetorical assumes that communication creates situations and selves; the solution: be someone else, by transforming one's social self or identity, by taking on a different character in social interaction. The rhetorical solution is create a new drama, or new characters, so as to minimize the conflict of interest (O'Keefe, 1988, p. 88).

7.3 PRACTICAL PHILOSOPHY AND SOCIAL AND CULTURAL CRITIQUE

Let us now turn to another trend affecting argumentation studies in American speech communication: the recovery of practical philosophy. This theme harks back to the classical concept of *phronesis*, practical wisdom in a given case. Practical wisdom was divorced from analytic knowledge and formal logic during the 17th century. The intellectual history of the disappearance and rediscovery of practical philosophy are described by Stephen Toulmin (1992).

Toulmin himself is a major figure in the recovery of *phronesis*, especially with the publication of *The Uses of Argument* (1958) and *Human Understanding* (1972). The other major figure in this recovery is Chaim Perelman, with *The New Rhetoric* (co-authored with L. Olbrechts-Tyteca, 1958/1969). Both Toulmin and Perelman were surprised to discover far more interest in their work among speech communication scholars than within their own disciplines.

Toulmin's model, discussed in chapter 5, was adapted as a way to understand and systematize informal reasoning. His other concept that strongly influenced argumentation scholarship was that of "field." In *The Uses of Argument*, Toulmin (1958, p. 14) said only that arguments belong to the same field if their data and conclusions are of the same logical type, without explaining what that meant. In *Human Understanding*, he described fields as "rational enterprises," which he equates with intellectual disciplines, and explored how the nature of reasoning differed according to whether the discipline was compact or diffuse. This treatment led to vigorous discussion about what defined a "field of argument": subject matter, general perspective or world-view, or the arguer's purpose, to mention a few of the possibilities.[21]

The study of arguments-in-use took a more populist turn when Wayne Brockriede and Douglas Ehninger adapted Toulmin's argument diagram to the study of arguments by ordinary people. This may have prompted a broadening of Toulmin's emphasis as well, for he later coauthored a textbook devoted to "practical reasoning as it occurs in daily use" (Toulmin, Rieke, & Janik, 1979, p. 16).

The concept of fields of argument, however defined, encouraged recognition that the soundness of arguments was not universal and certain, but field-specific and contingent. This belief was another step in undermining the analytic ideal and resituating argument within the rhetorical tradition. Instead of asking whether an argument was sound, the questions became "Sound for whom?" and "Sound in what context?" Some feared that the only alternative to formal validity was vicious relativism, according to which any argument must be deemed sound if some person could be found to accept it.[22] This concern was allayed as research on argument fields demonstrated the role of cumulative experience in shaping one's perspective and the durability and predictability of a field's standards of judgment.

The idea of argument fields is notoriously vague (see Zarefsky, 1982). It functions, from author to author, synonymously with "rhetorical communities," "discourse communities," "conceptual ecologies," "collective mentalities," "disciplines," and "professions." The core idea is that claims imply "ground," and that the grounds for knowledge claims lie in the epistemic practices and states of consensus in knowledge domains. We thus interpret advocates' positions by inferring the backgrounds they presuppose: the traditions, practices, ideas, texts, and methods of particular groups (Dunbar, 1986; Sillars, 1981). If someone says that "physical processes are characterized by extreme sensitivity to starting conditions," and the field theorist concludes that the claim takes its meaning from Chaos Physics, a specific, concrete imputation is being made to a definite group.

This idea goes back to Wittgenstein (1953), who says that the builder and his helper speak of trowels and mortar in a language game that is "complete in itself." One is socialized into language games by acquiring their endemic myths, conventions, rules, moves, and substantive beliefs. These elements get their meanings in their uses. Thus Toulmin (1958, 1972) proposed that people organize their affairs around pragmatically incommensurable bodies of knowledge. As we saw earlier, he was thinking chiefly of the differences across academic disciplines, but the idea of a field of knowledge can be extended as well to social movements, families—indeed human groups of any sort.

---

[21]These questions are explored in Zarefsky (1982), and the essays that follow this article in the same journal issue.

[22]This concern is explored and answered in Booth (1974).

But as Wittgenstein saw, the language games of epistemic interest are often interdependent with other games. Willard (1995) focuses on fields as "organizations." The organizational view emphasizes relationships among games. Where bricklayers speak of trowels and mortar—the local focus of an argument field—public problems and projects span many lines, so the organizational theorist would add that the carpenters speak of joists and studs, the electricians speak of wire and outlets, the architects speak of aesthetics and use, the cost-accountants speak of cost per square foot, the inspectors speak of building codes, and the contractor speaks of man-hours, material, transportation, and subcontracts. Getting a building up is thus a matter of coordinating multiple discourses, and an instructive parallel for modern epistemic problems. Organizational problems turn on complexity, scope, and design. We have big science (the Hubble telescope, the Supercollider), big agencies (NASA), big problems (the environment), big environments (Federated Europe), big programs (the shuttle) and big projects (the human genome). The problems posed by such bigness are not outside infections that invade epistemic projects: they are integral to the knowledge itself.

Field theorists are fascinated by arguments because they are interested in the effects of controversy on reasoning, speech, public knowledge, organizational change, and upon further interactions. Their concern is partly with the internal coherence of discourse domains, with understanding how and why claims within them are able to pass as knowledge, and with how knowledge is used in policy formation and decision making in social entities of all kinds. But field theorists have a broader concern for interfield discourse and the behavior of field actors in public spheres beyond their borders. Their assumption is that, just as a nation's domestic and foreign policies are interdependent, a field's internal constitution is its basis—good or bad—for external communication.

Unlike poststructuralists and Marxists, most field theorists do not see fields as hermetically sealed, deterministic "iron cages" (in Max Weber's terms). They hold instead that interfield discourse is remarkably commonplace. Fields are no islands (though some act as if they were); every field functions on multiple levels, across multiple borders; and most complex fields are bounded at their peripheries by subfields, rebel enclaves, as it were, where the pull of the paradigm cases at the field's center wanes, and new ideas, including ones imported from outside fields, can be entertained. Their borders are porous and hazy, and their actors are less likely to be concerned about clarifying them. Once again, in other words, fuzziness is a fact.

The term *field*, of course, is a metaphor for the location of arguments. Other metaphors have also been used. Ray McKerrow (1980), for example, has written of "argument communities." He emphasizes that shared values, common personal bonds, and argument evaluation are mutually reinforcing.

Thomas Goodnight has preferred the use of the term *spheres*, emphasizing more general and all-encompassing categories. The focus of argument spheres is owed mostly to his work, which can be seen as bringing Frankfurt School cultural analysis into argument theory.[23] Goodnight's focus on spheres of argument provides a method for discriminating between different sources of doubt. All argument, he believes, arises from uncertainty.

By *sphere*, Goodnight (1982) means "the grounds upon which arguments are built and the authorities to which arguers appeal" (p. 216). "Ground" does not mean "reason," "proof," or any other foundationalist idea. Goodnight uses "argument" to mean interaction based on dissensus, not serial predication, so the *grounds* of arguments lie in doubts and uncertainties. Goodnight distinguishes three spheres of argument: "the personal," "the technical," and "the public." His triad stresses differences between arguments whose relevance is confined to the arguers themselves, arguments whose pertinence extends to a specialized or limited community, and arguments that are meaningful for people in general.

The three spheres are omnibus rubrics for "the manners in which disagreements can be created and extended" (1982, p. 220). They thus differ from field theory, in which "ground" functions in a more foundationalist way. Where field theory plots conventional epistemic structures, Goodnight's triad is a blueprint imposed upon motives for conserving disagreements. The *personal sphere* arises in relatively private, etiquette-ruled, and (usually) unpreserved conversation. The *technical sphere* labels discourse guided by the field-specific ideals, norms, and expectations of expert communities. And the *public sphere* arises when disagreements have consequences that transcend the private and technical spheres. Goodnight wants to devise a "creative tension" among the three spheres that might yield a new basis for criticism.

Goodnight's organizing concern is that the public sphere "is being steadily eroded by the elevation of the personal and technical groundings of argument" (p. 223). We have lost not only the time and space for public discourse, we have lost the art of deliberation. The elevation of the personal sphere means that people are no longer citizens. They have escaped to privatism, celebrating personal lifestyle over civic responsibility. Here we hear the voices of Tocqueville, Richard Sennett, and Jürgen Habermas: The deliberative arts have been suffocated by base and degenerate institutionalized communications, the manipulative languages of public relations and advertising, that masquerade as deliberative discourses. In the words of Goodnight (1982): "As arguments grounded in personal experience (disclosed by averaging opinion) seem to have greatest currency, political speakers present not options but personalities, perpetuating government policy by substituting debate for an aura of false intimacy" (pp. 224–225).

Even worse is the dominance of technical discourses. Where Dewey viewed technical discourses with more hope than skepticism, Goodnight, like Habermas, holds that the public sphere is co-opted by technical specialism and the disciplinary control of knowledge (Lyne, 1983). In this way, Goodnight's work has

---

[23]See Goodnight (1980, 1982, 1987a, 1987b).

sparked a recent focus on fusion discourse—cases in which technical argument intrudes upon (or is harmed by) public discourse.[24] This is a story of necessary evils. A complex world requires specialism and the languages of technique, but instrumental rationality has also brought us to the nadir of human possibility: Auschwitz, environmental disaster, starvation, and—looming over them all—the prospects of a nuclear coda to history. The problem is that, while technical knowledge has burgeoned, it is uncertain that the general knowledge necessary to govern a Republic has become any more refined (Goodnight, 1982, p. 224).

As general knowledge has been increasingly subordinated to specialism and technical expertise, "issues of significant public consequence, which should present live possibilities for argumentation and public choice, disappear into the government technocracy or private hands. As forms of decision making proliferate, questions of public significance themselves become increasingly difficult to recognize, much less address, because of the intricate rules, procedures, and terminologies of the specialized forums. These complications of argument hardly invite the public to share actively the knowledge necessary for wise and timely decisions" (1982, p. 225). Thus Goodnight arrives at a populist thesis: The public has been disenfranchised by modes of argument that favor specialism or expertise. His project dovetails with efforts to revitalize the "public sphere," that metaphorical place in which people transcend their personal interests and guide themselves by a sense of the common good.[25]

Perelman and Olbrechts-Tyteca's *The New Rhetoric* has proved more difficult to digest. Many of its ideas, discussed in chapter 4, have not been plumbed by argumentation scholars, and some, such as the construct of the universal audience, have been shown to be problematic in application. Several of Perelman's ideas, however, have permeated argumentation scholarship. Let us briefly highlight four.

First, the concept of *loci*, akin to the "topics" in classical rhetoric, has been used as a way to understand sources of argument. Second, the treatment of *figures* and *tropes* has made clear that they are not just ornaments applied after an argument is constructed, but that they themselves have the argumentative function of strengthening or weakening presence, that is, the salience of an idea or topic. Third, the concepts of association and dissociation, especially the latter, illustrate the role of definitions and stipulations in advancing or retarding arguments. And fourth, the distinction between "the rational" and "the reasonable" has, like Toulmin's work, helped to displace formal logic as the paradigm of reasoning and instead to position it as a particular, and highly limited, case.

Toulmin and Perelman have probably had more far-reaching impact on argumentation studies than other philosophers, but they are not unique in their interest or concern. Legal philosophers such as Gottlieb and Rawls have, just

---

[24]Cf. Balthrop (1989), Biesecker (1989), Birdsell (1989), Dauber (1989), Holmquest (1989), Hynes (1989), Peters (1989), and Schiappa (1989).

[25]For a collection of papers devoted to spheres of argument, see Gronbeck (1989).

as Perelman, explored reasoning about the nature of justice, and by extension about other abstract values.[26] And Henry W. Johnstone, Jr., has written provocatively about the relationship between argumentation and selfhood. To engage in argumentation, he writes, is to accept risk—the risk of being proved wrong and of having to alter one's belief system and self-concept. But the very act of person-risking proves to be person-making, constitutive of one's sense of self.[27]

In the late 1960s, Robert Scott (1967) wrote an influential essay, "On viewing rhetoric as epistemic." Objecting to the view that the processes of discovering and expressing truth are distinct, he maintained that rhetorical discourse itself is a means of determining truth. His work contributed further to the emerging belief that truth is relative to argument and to audience. It stimulated studies of what sorts of knowledge are rhetorically constructed and how arguing produces knowledge. Proposed answers have included the claim that all knowledge is rhetorical and hence that there are no transcendent standards. An intermediate position is taken by Thomas Farrell (1976), who distinguishes between technical and social knowledge, maintaining that it is the latter that is achieved rhetorically.[28] There is also the more limited position that there is objective knowledge but that argumentation is only one of the means of discovering it.[29]

Although not specifically intended by Scott, one consequence of the rhetoric-as-epistemic perspective has been to foster studies of rhetoric within academic disciplines. More than about any other disciplinary cluster has probably been written about the rhetoric of science.[30] The popular conception being that the hard sciences—the empirical analogue of formal logic and mathematics—yield certain knowledge, it seems easier to establish that rhetoric is a part of other ways of knowing if it could be demonstrated that even to the hard sciences there is a significant rhetorical component. But there also have been studies of rhetoric in economics, sociology, medicine, statistics, business, history, religion, and other disciplines.[31]

---

[26]See Perelman (1963), Gottlieb (1968), and Rawls (1971).

[27]This view is developed in Johnstone (1959), Natanson and Johnstone (1965), and Johnstone (1970), and modified in Johnstone (1983). For a discussion of the modified position, see Heeney (1995). For an example of Johnstone's early influence on argumentation scholarship, see Ehninger (1970).

[28]See also Farrell (1993).

[29]For examples of these positions, see Brummett (1976), Cherwitz and Hikins (1983), and also the Forum Section of the *Quarterly Journal of Speech 76* (February, 1990), consisting of an exchange of essays by these same writers.

[30]See Prelli (1989), Gross (1990), and the special issue on the rhetoric of science of *The Southern Communication Journal*, edited by Keith (1993).

[31]For examples of such studies, see McCloskey (1985), Kellner (1989), Hunter (1990), and Simons (1990). This line of inquiry received a powerful boost from the 1984 conference on The Rhetoric of the Human Sciences at the University of Iowa, the subsequent formation of the Project on Rhetoric of Inquiry (Poroi) at that institution, and the series of books on rhetoric in the human sciences published by the University of Wisconsin Press. See Nelson, Megill, and McCloskey (1987).

Another force that has shaped the nature of argumentation studies within speech communication is the interest in *social and cultural critique*. Although it usually is not characterized this way, the work of Walter Fisher (1987) is an example. Fisher began with an attempt to flesh out the meaning of "good reasons," the rhetorical equivalent of formal deduction. He found that good reasons often take the form of narratives, and has gone so far as to claim that story telling is a defining aspect of the human condition. Traditionally, story telling has been excluded from the category of reasoning, because of what Fisher calls the "rational world model" of knowing. The result, he believes, is systematically to privilege certain kinds of claims over others. In his example of the nuclear debate, it is scientific claims that are preferred over moral claims.

It is not Fisher's primary purpose to do so, but his work points to the nexus between argumentation and power. It is power, whether political, social, or intellectual, that permits one to stipulate what sorts of claims "count" in any argumentative situation. Power enables those who hold it to impose a partial perspective as if it were holistic—the definition usually given for the term *hegemony*. The most recent wave of argumentation studies seeks to explore and expose the tendency of power to foreclose discourse, and it seeks emancipation by opening up alternatives. This project focuses on marginalized arguers and arguments, and is given impetus by the widespread concern for matters of race, gender, and class.

The intellectual underpinning of argument-as-critique is "postmodernism," a pattern of thought that began in architecture and has spread through much of the arts, humanities, and social sciences.[32] There are many varieties of postmodernism, but the central core seems to be the denial that there are any verities or standards of judgment, and the claim that what passes for such standards really is socially constructed. In its rejection of the analytic ideal and the location of argument in communities, this perspective is in some measure consistent with the others we have discussed. But it goes on to argue that only *a part* of the relevant community has defined the standards, then hegemonically imposed them on the whole. The goal of critique is thus to shed light on this practice and to promote emancipatory potential by posing alternatives.

At least two different implications of the postmodern project can be suggested. The more extreme is the denial that there can be any such thing as communal norms or standards for argument. On this view, the principal goal of the project is to celebrate difference and insist that it is "difference all the way down." The other implication is more optimistic. If communal standards have been defined by only the powerful interests in a group, then the goal of argument-as-critique is to expose this practice and to suggest alternatives, so that those who were excluded or marginalized can be brought into the process of

---

[32]For the implications of postmodernism for argumentation, see several of the essays in McKerrow (1993).

deliberation and more inclusive and meaningful norms can be developed. This view fosters empowerment of the marginalized, not in order to tear a community apart but to bind it more closely together. The question, then, is "Should the public sphere be expanded or disbanded?"

7.4 PERSPECTIVES

In American speech communication, the controversies about the nature of argument have largely disappeared from the journals. Not because any of the issues were settled, but because each camp is more or less tending its own garden. Some theorists still see arguments basically as discursive units of proof, textual artifacts, open to diagramming. Other theorists focus on argument-as-interaction[33]—a matter of conversational repair,[34] relational maintenance and repair,[35] or, rather differently, of epistemic and decision-making motives.[36] There are others who focus on argument in groups and organizations.[37] Still others are continuing an enduring focus on legal argument, partly because jurisprudence is a popular metaphor, and partly because legal proceedings offer a promising laboratory for empirical studies of opposition.[38]

Most textbooks on argumentation, much like their early predecessors, continue to be speaker-centered. Their paradigm case is the public speaker framing a message intended for an audience. Their content, in the main, consists of recipes and rules for research, case-building, audience and issue analysis, and refutation. There are also audience-centered texts, but they are not as psychological as that label once implied. An influential case in point is the textbook by Rieke and Sillars (1984), who say that "the ultimate test of argumentation is whether or not people adhere to the claims made by the arguers" (p. 8).

Where economic and mathematical models of decision making seek concrete, impersonal measures of value and utility, in Rieke and Sillars's view, the assumption behind argumentation is that "people make decisions under varying personal and group constraints" (p. 23). Thus, "probability in decision-making does not mean calculation of past frequencies. Probability in argumentation means the extent to which people are willing to commit themselves to a decision and the extent to which they authorize others to hold them responsible for their decisions" (p. 23). This approach, they say, differs from the theories that stress

---

[33]Cf. Benoit (1981, 1983a, 1983b), Benoit and Benoit (1987), Newell and Adams (1985), and Trapp (1983).

[34]Cf. Jacobs and Jackson (1981, 1982, 1983).

[35]Cf. Brockriede (1972, 1974, 1975, 1977).

[36]Cf. Willard (1978a, 1983, 1987, 1989).

[37]Cf. Hirokawa and Scheerhorn (1985).

[38]Cf., for instance, Toulmin (1958, 1972), Sheppard and Rieke (1983), Snedaker and Schuetz (1985), Werling and Rieke (1985), and Riley, Hollihan, and Freadhoff (1987).

an arguer's adherence to rules. The term *argumentation* refers to "the whole process of advancing, rejecting, and modifying claims while 'argument' refers to a single claim, an assertion without support, or a claim with support" (pp. 8–9).

Central to Rieke and Sillars's (1984) theory is a distinction between general and specific argumentation. The historical ancestors of this distinction are Aristotle's contrast between general and special topics and Toulmin's distinction between field-invariant and field-dependent claims. General argumentation draws upon commonly shared knowledge of the sort any adult is expected to have. Special argumentation, draws upon beliefs, assumptions, and methods shared within specific communities. Claims adapted to these specialized audiences are field-dependent. Rieke and Sillars discuss such fields as law, religion, business, scholarship, and politics.

As we have sketched, alongside all these developments, some new concerns have arisen. They are fostered by the study of debate, social sciences perspectives on communication, practical philosophy, and social and cultural critique. Among other innovations, they have led to the study of argumentation in social interaction, a revival of message-centered theories, new turns in the theory of argument fields and a new focus on spheres of argument.

Cox and Willard (1982a) regard the self-conscious examination of its assumptions, rationales, and methods as the first sign of a discipline's maturity.[39] When viewed in this way, the burgeoning literature on argumentation reflects favorably on American speech communication's achievement of that goal. In our view, however, a prerequisite of maturity is a modicum of consensus around core concepts and definitions that permit coherent discussion and shape the theorizing and the research questions. When seen in this light, the situation is less positive.

Starting from Zarefsky's (1995) root concept of argumentation studies, several issues can be distinguished on which research in communication and rhetoric needs to focus. We mention some issues, connected with the research traditions in American speech communication just described, which are suggested by the provisional definition explained at the beginning of this chapter. The questions concerned can be clustered around elements of the definition.

A first set of issues relates to the fundamental role of an audience or community as a validating agent. Given that argumentation occurs within fields, how can it occur *across* fields? How do interfield disputes come about and how do arguers, in practice, transcend field boundaries? Willard (1989, 1995) has made a beginning effort to address these questions, but more attention to them is required. Other questions concern the relationship between argument fields and the public sphere. Is "the public" just another field? Or is "the public" an *alternative* to argument fields? What then determines its boundaries? What conception of the public is appropriate for dealing with a world characterized

---

[39]Cf. Cox and Willard (1982b).

increasingly by cultural diversity and globalism, yet tainted by the confusion of icons, images, staged events, and spectacles?

A second set of issues emanates from the concept of justifying. What do audiences count as justification? How does this view develop, and how does it change over time? How do (or should) listeners proceed upon the threshold level of justification? When and how does this threshold level change? When is controversy healthy for a society, so that the threshold will be high, and when is it unhealthy, so that relatively little would be needed in order to count as justification? How does the possession or absence of power affect what decisions need justification and what counts as justification for them? More generally, how can a commitment to the practice of justifying decisions coexist with the pursuit and attainment of power?

Other issues could be clustered around elements of the definition, but these examples should suffice for illustrating its potential for stimulating inquiry as well as classifying it. It is a view of argumentation which places value in the idea of a "marketplace of ideas" in which claims compete for justification, the perfect market being a "universal audience" as envisioned by Perelman or the "ideal speech situation" as seen by Habermas. Because a person, group, or society determines by means of argumentation, through the practice of justifying decisions, what is to be regarded as right, argumentation is also presumed to have epistemic properties. In our view, community standards should therefore be regarded as a source of validation, rejecting the extreme postmodern view that there are no common bonds and that it is "difference all the way down." In this way, argumentation is firmly placed within a speech communication tradition of studying communication and rhetoric by focusing on how messages affect people rather than on discourse in the abstract.

8

FALLACIES AND FORMAL LOGIC

This chapter examines the role of formal logic in the analysis of fallacies and illustrates the main background of the substantial contribution to the study of the fallacies made by the Canadian logicians John Woods and Douglas Walton. Its broader object is to judge whether, or to what extent, a logical system is capable of throwing the fallacies into sharp and systematic focus. This question is part of an even broader one: Are formal logics good theories of natural language argumentation?

In considering this last question, by way of an introduction to the problems involved, we shall first go back to the concept of *fallacy* and its historical antecedents. After a brief recapitulation of the relevant aspects of Aristotle's concepts of fallacies and formal logic, we turn to some criticisms of Aristotle's logic and to the alternative offered by modern propositional logic. In explaining the use of formal methods in fallacy theory, we shall then have set the stage for the Woods–Walton approach.

The Woods–Walton approach to the fallacies is pluralistic, formalistic and, in a general sense, pragmatic. In discussing two examples of this approach, while avoiding a technical exposition, some idea is given as to its substance and its link with informal logic. Using the kind of formal analysis typical of the Woods–Walton approach, which consists in applying concepts of formal dialectical systems, the Aristotelian theme of refutation is then revisited.

As shown in chapter 3, we owe the concept of fallacy to Aristotle. The *Sophistical Refutations* opens with an invitation:

> Let us discuss sophistical refutations, i.e., what appear to be refutations but are really fallacies (*paralogisms*) instead. (165b, 8–9)

Refutations are a kind of syllogism, or deduction. A syllogism rests on certain statements such that they necessarily involve, through what has been stated, the assertion of something other than what has been stated (165a, 1–2). A refutation is a special case of a syllogism: a syllogism accompanied by a contradiction of a given thesis (165a, 3–4). Sophistical refutations are arguments that appear to be refutations but are not in fact. They are special cases of faulty syllogisms, that is, arguments that seem to be syllogisms but are not in fact, or syllogisms whose conclusions merely appear to contradict a given thesis. As Aristotle says:

> [t]hat some things are syllogisms, while others seem to be so but are not, is evident.[1]
> (164a, 23–24)

The evidence of Aristotle's total text suggests the following definitions:

> **Def SophRef:** An argument is a *sophistical refutation* if and only if it appears to be a refutation but is not.

> **Def Ref:** An argument is a *refutation* if and only if it is a syllogism whose conclusion is the contradictory of a given thesis.

> **Def Syll:** An argument is a *syllogism* if and only if its premises necessitate its conclusion; the argument contains no superfluous or redundant premises (i.e., no proper subset of the premises necessitates its conclusion); its conclusion does not repeat a premise; and there is more than one premise.

Evidently there are two ways in which a would-be refutation can fail to be a genuine refutation. First, it can be an argument that appears to be a syllogism but is not in fact. Second, it can be a syllogism in which, appearances to the contrary, the correctly derived conclusion fails to be the contradictory of the thesis in question.

Aristotle says flatly that sophistical refutations are arguments that appear to be refutations "but are really fallacies [*paralogisms*] instead." He also mentions as fallacies merely apparent geometrical proofs and merely apparent enthymemes (*Topics* 101a, 5ff. and *Rhetoric* 1402b, 26, respectively). This suggests that fallacies are a genus of which sophistical refutations are a species.

Apparently, it is characteristic of fallacies that they are arguments which only resemble certain kinds of good argument. This can be expressed in the following definition:

---

[1]Faulty syllogisms are not syllogisms of a particular kind. Rather a faulty syllogism is an argument having a property which *precludes* its being a syllogism. Faulty syllogisms are like fool's gold rather than like false propositions. False propositions are still propositions, but fool's gold is not gold of any kind.

Def Fal: A fallacy is something that appears to be a good argument of a certain kind but is not in fact a good argument of that kind.

By these lights, there are several ways in which an argument might be fallacious. Its premises may fail to necessitate its conclusion, even though it appears that they do; it may contain an unnoticed redundancy among its premises; its conclusion may, in disguised form, repeat one of its premises; it may also fail to be a demonstration, that is, a syllogism from first principles; it may be a contentious argument, that is, an argument whose premises merely seem to be reputable; it may be a specious enthymeme; and so on.

As we have seen in Section 3.1, Aristotle distinguishes two basic types of sophistical refutation. Under the category of those that depend on language, Aristotle identifies the six fallacies of *equivocation* (or *ambiguity*), *amphiboly*, *composition*, *division*, *accent*, and *figure of speech*. In contrast are fallacies that are independent of language, a further seven: *accident, secundum quid, ignoratio elenchi, petitio principii, consequent, non-cause as cause* and *many questions*.

Some writers have insisted that some of Aristotle's own examples are best understood as inherently *dialectical* mistakes. There is an interesting contention as to whether this was Aristotle's own view of the matter. Hintikka (1987) holds that all of Aristotle's fallacies are essentially, or dominantly, violations of rules of question-and-answer games. Hamblin's (1970) view is that Aristotle's examples are better thought of in this way, but that Aristotle himself probably did not do so. In any case, a good many present-day writers firmly support the dialectical interpretation of fallacies.[2]

If we accept the interpretation of fallacy as something that appears to be a good argument of a certain kind but is not, there will be fallacies that appear to be good dialectical arguments but are not—where a dialectical argument is an argument from dialectical premises and a dialectical premise expresses an opinion that is either widely held or endorsed by experts or by "the wise." These will be merely apparent dialectical syllogisms. For it to be true of all fallacies that they are, or involve, dialectical violations, it would have to be true that all arguments that merely appear to be good do so because they look like dialectical arguments but fail to satisfy a condition on good dialectical arguments. It is clear that Aristotle did not think that this condition was in fact met (*Topics* 101a). So there is reason to resist a dialectical interpretation of Aristotle's concept of fallacy.

Of course, it is always open to the theorist to use the word "dialectical" in a somewhat different way. We might characterize a dialectical argument as an exchange between two parties in which an attempt is made to settle a dispute

---

[2]See Hamblin (1970, pp. 65–66, chap. 8), Barth and Martens (1977), Mackenzie (1979a), Walton (1984, 1989b), Hintikka (1987, pp. 211–238), Woods and Walton (1989, chaps. 1, 2, 3, 5, 10, 11, 15, 19), Walton and Krabbe (1995), and John Woods and Hans V. Hansen, *From dialogue to axiom: The logic of sophistical refutations*, in preparation.

in a reasonable way.[3] For this to be a fruitful notion, it is unnecessary to determine whether or not Aristotle would have endorsed it, and immaterial if it happened that he did not. It is open to the theorist to tailor a notion of fallacy to the present conception of dialectical argument. On some such tailorings, fallacies in this present sense may always be dialectical violations of the rules governing dialectical arguments, also in this present sense.

All the same, to Aristotle belongs the distinction of having originated the long history of fallacy theory in the Western intellectual tradition, and to him, too, is owed the persistently influential idea of a fallacy as a mistake in argument that seems not to be a mistake. Aristotle, however, offers no well-developed theory of the fallacies, but a rather loosely explicated taxonomy and an introduction of names that bear its classificatory burdens. Aristotle describes many of his fallacies as inherently syllogistic or logical errors, and even the most forceful exponent of the view that fallacies are basically dialectic improprieties is prepared to concede that many fallacies have an illogical dimension to them, and that some fallacies are difficult to interpret as anything other than logical errors. If so, a theory that accounts for such fallacies would be a theory of logic as Aristotle, with impressive power, worked out in the *Prior Analytics*. Unfortunately, the *Prior Analytics* sheds no theoretical light on even the logical fallacies of the *Sophistical Refutations*.

The *Prior Analytics* is the first great work of logic. Though it resembles Euclid's axiomatization of plane geometry, the *Prior Analytics* surpasses the *Elements* in systematic power. There are three respects in which this is so. First, Aristotle's logic is a theory of deductive arguments in general, whereas the *Elements* is not a theory of proof but a series of actual proofs for geometrical figures.[4] Second, Aristotle developed a strategy of proof by logical form.[5] Third, Euclid is not able to show that his system is complete, that is, that every truth of plane geometry is provable by methods set out in the *Elements*; Aristotle came close to proving that every example of correct syllogistic reasoning reduces to a small subset of syllogisms made special by the fact that they are *self-evidently* correct.[6]

Aristotle's account of logical forms and his attempted demonstration of the completeness of his system fit together intimately. We shall briefly review his case for completeness and, in so doing, we can see how the doctrine of logical form is

---

[3]See, for instance, the pragma-dialectical theory of argumentation, discussed in chapter 10.

[4]The assertion that Aristotle's logic is a theory of deductive arguments in general requires a slight correction. The *Prior analytics* was designed to give a complete theory of the very large class of deductive arguments known as categorical syllogisms. Aristotle was well aware that certain kinds of hypothetical reasoning and modal reasoning, for example, exceed the scope of his account. See Lear (1980).

[5]There is in Aristotle's Greek no expression for "logical form," but there is little doubt about his implicit subscription to that notion.

[6]Aristotle's attempt is found at *Prior analytics* I, 23; it is known, however, that his proof can be repaired. See Corcoran (1972). Corcoran showed the completeness of Aristotle's logic for the case of more than two premises. Each valid syllogistic argument admits of a deduction using only perfect syllogisms and conversions, and most often the methods of indirect proof.

indispensable to it. It is worth remembering that Aristotle nowhere employs the term "completeness" as a technical concept of his logic. He speaks instead of "perfectibility." Aristotle notices that a certain small number of arguments are self-evidently syllogisms (*Prior Analytics* 24b, 22–25). These Aristotle calls "perfect syllogisms"; they are syllogisms of the "first figure" (see chapter 2).

Aristotle's considerable insight is that any syllogism is reducible to a perfect syllogism: A syllogism which is self-evidently correct. Any argument reducible to a perfect syllogism is itself a (categorical) syllogism; any putative syllogism that is not reducible to a perfect syllogism, is not a (categorical) syllogism. The assertion that all categorical syllogisms are perfectible is a sweeping claim.[7]

Aristotle had in mind a notion of syllogisms in the broad or generic sense, which he sketches in the *Topics* and *Sophistical Refutations*. Syllogisms in the broad sense are the subject of the definition, **Def Syll**, noted earlier. A syllogism in the broad sense, then, is any deductively correct argument with premises—more than one and none redundant—whose conclusion does not repeat a premise. Aristotle's perfectibility claim is that every such argument is reducible to a perfect syllogism. Aristotle recognizes that the number of syllogisms in the broad sense is very large, probably infinite. They are vastly too numerous for exhaustive identification and inspection one by one.

How, then, does Aristotle know of them all that they reduce to perfect syllogisms? It is largely a matter of form. At *Prior Analytics* (I, 4–7, 23), Aristotle investigates the possible forms of two sentence combinations which share a middle term. The three figures arise from the positions which the shared middle term can occupy in the two sentences: predicate of one and subject of the other, predicate of both, or subject of both. In each figure, each sentence exhibits one of four possible forms, and this makes for sixteen possible combinations or forty-eight in all. Concerning each of the forty-eight combinations it may be asked whether some sentence other than the two follows of necessity from them. Aristotle shows that in fourteen cases there is a syllogism, in four a perfect syllogism, and in the remaining ten a syllogism reducible to a perfect syllogism. He then argues (in chapter 23) that every syllogism must be in one of the three figures.

We may now illustrate the ideas of logical form with respect to an example of a perfect syllogism:

(1) All humans are mortal.

(2) All Greeks are humans.

(3) Therefore, all Greeks are mortal.

As we have explained in chapter 2, in order to identify the logical form of this syllogism, it is necessary first to identify the logical forms of its constituent

---

[7]See Lear (1980, p. 10).

propositions. The formal vocabulary for syllogisms we use for this purpose is comprised of what later logicians would call "logical particles":

(a) the present indicative plural of the copula, "to be," that is, the word *are*
(b) uninterpreted *schematic* letters which stand in for general terms: A, B, C, etc.
(c) *quantifier* expressions: "all," "no(ne)," and "some"
(d) the *negation-sign*: not (for predicate negation)

We next define the set of basic propositional forms as concatenations of expressions constructible out of items from the formal vocabulary which satisfies the following assigned order:

$$Q(\pm T)\# \; are \; \#\pm T/$$

In this, Q is a quantifier expression, T and T/ are schematic letters, # is the symbol for concatenation, "are" is the copula, $+T = T$, and $-T = $ not-T, and similarly for $+T/$ and $-T/$. Thus our rule produces the following propositional forms, among others:

*All A are B.
*No A are B.
*Some A are B.
*Some A are not B.[8]

Aristotle identifies these four forms, which he calls the "(basic) forms of categorical propositions," as central to his purposes. It is easy to see that, in our example, the form of the syllogism displayed is just the result of replacing the general terms

---

[8]Other examples are: "All not-A are not-B," "Some B are not-C"; "No not-C are B"; "Some B are not-not-A." Strictly speaking, the schema $Q(\pm T)\#$ *are* $\#\pm T/$ does not quite determine the set of Aristotle's propositional forms. For the specification to be exact, it is necessary to speak of each of the four types of propositional form as generated from a unique "logical particle" as follows: "a _, _," for propositions of the form "All _ are _"; "e _, _," for "No _ are _"; "i _, _," for "Some _ are _"; and "o _, _," for "Some _ are not _." Thus a basic propositional form is the result of filling the blanks in a logical particle with schematic letters A, B, C, etc. standing for general terms such as "man," "bank," "square," "good," etc. We see that the $Q(\pm T)\#$ *are* $\#\pm T/$-scheme permits propositions such as "All not-not-mules are mules" which, for technical reasons, wrecks Corcoran's (1972) completion of Aristotle's perfectability result. On the present alternative scheme, the offending proposition is blocked by two considerations. One is that it distinguishes the embedded *not*s of the logical particles "e _, _" and "o _, _" from the *not*s of term complementation (e.g., "*non*flammable," "*non*stick"); and the second is that Aristotle seems not to countenance unrestricted term-complementation as in "non-non-flammable." Thus the logical particle-scheme precludes propositional forms allowed by the $Q(\pm T)\#$ *are* $\#\pm T/$-scheme which, once allowed, would upset the completeness theorem.

"Greeks," "human(s)," and "mortal" with the schematic letters, A, B and C. Thus the form of this syllogism is itself a sequence of propositional forms:

(1) All B are C.
(2) All A are B.
(3) /∴ All A are C.

Aristotle's formal insight was that any argument got from this syllogistic form by uniform replacement of schematic letters by general terms was itself a syllogism. Any argument exhibiting that form is a syllogism and is so in virtue of its having that form. Aristotle was able to show that all arguments of the sort he was interested in investigating have logical forms in the sense of our present exposition.

   We have taken this detour into the *Prior Analytics* in quest of an answer to the following question. Given that some of Aristotle's fallacies are logical mistakes, and given that the *Prior Analytics* is Aristotle's mature logical theory, what does the *Prior Analytics* have to tell us about the thirteen types of fallacy, anyhow about those that are inherently or dominantly logical errors? The answer is: nothing much. To see that this is so, consider the following logical form:

(1′) No B are C.
(2′) All A are B.
(3′) /∴ No A are C.

This is a syllogistic form: Any argument resulting by uniform substitution of its schematic letters is itself a syllogism. We may take it that no such argument commits a syllogistic or logical fallacy. But consider this example:

(1*) No corporate entities are lips of rivers.
(2*) All banks are corporate entities.
(3*) Therefore, no banks are lips of rivers.

Now, of course, "bank" is ambiguous in English as between "corporate entity" and "lip of a body of water." If "bank" in (1*)–(3*) is interpreted in the first way, the resulting argument is a syllogism. On the other hand, if we interpret "bank" in the second way, the argument remains a syllogism (even though, of course, premise (2*) is not true). But what if we interpreted "bank" in the first way in premise one and in the second way in the conclusion? Doing so would be tantamount to saying that the logical form of (1*)–(3*) is not (1′)–(3′), but rather:

(1**) No B are C.
(2**) All A are B.

(3**) /∴ No D are C.

This new form (1**)–(3**) is no syllogism; in fact, it is said to commit the "fallacy of four terms." Indeed, we may say that for any syllogism in which three general terms occur, if one of the three terms were taken ambiguously, then the argument on that interpretation would have a faulty logical form and would commit the fallacy of four terms.

It is useful here to call to mind Aristotle's basic idea of a fallacy as an argument which appears to be a syllogism but is not in fact. This may lead us to believe that the ambiguity fallacy is that of supposing an argument to have a correct form when it in fact has an incorrect form. In our example, the present suggestion comes to this: The argument (1*)–(3*) commits the fallacy of ambiguity because it is taken to have, say, the correct form (1′)–(3′) whereas in fact it has the incorrect form (1**)–(3**). This is an interesting suggestion, but it does not give a satisfactory solution to our problem of showing how Aristotle's thirteen fallacies are formal properties of arguments. Of course, the ambiguity of "bank" means that (1*)–(3*) is also formally ambiguous, depending on whether "bank" is taken unambiguously throughout. If so, it has a correct form; if not, it has an incorrect form. We cannot say, however, that the fallacy of ambiguity is a property of either form. It cannot be a property of the first form, since the first form is a syllogism. And although the second form exhibits the fallacy of four terms, there is nothing ambiguous about it. That is, the formal fallacy of four terms is not an ambiguity fallacy. Thus it is incorrect to say that ambiguity fallacies are defects of logical forms. The ambiguity fallacy is not a fallacy of ambiguous form.[9]

The ambiguity fallacy is particularly instructive. If a fallacy of ambiguity is committed in a natural language argument, then there is a fallacy-making property, ambiguity, which the argument has but which none of its logical forms has. This enables us, by contrast, to construct a precise definition of "formal fallacy":

Def ForFal: An argument A commits a *formal fallacy* (in the strict sense) if and only if A has *F* as its logical form, *F* is a fallacious form, and A inherits the fallacy from *F*.[10]

---

[9]Ambiguity fallacies are well discussed in Finocchiaro (1980, pp. 427–428).

[10]The idea of a fallacious form introduces a complication. Forms may be said to be logically transparent structures, evocative of the old saw, "What you see is what you get." What this means is that argument forms are such that, for the most part, if they are not syllogistic forms, they will not appear so. It is for this reason that logicians have long held that one way to clarify a natural language argument, that is, to avoid being misled by its appearances, is to specify its logical form. On the other hand, if there are such things as fallacious forms that appear to be syllogistic forms but are not in fact, it is inefficient to test a natural argument for fallaciousness by trying to determine whether it has a fallacious form. For if a fallacious form is one which appears to be syllogistic but is not, what is the good of specifying such a form in an attempt to discover whether an argument, whose form it is, itself appears not to be a nonsyllogism? Though an important complication, it is enough for present purposes that we note it.

If Aristotle's thirteen fallacies do not satisfy the conditions of **Def ForFal**, then they are not formal fallacies.[11] But what is true of Aristotle's thirteen may not be true of other arguments. That is, there may be (and indeed are) other arguments that fail to be syllogisms simply because of the logical forms that they instantiate. As we have seen, any argument form made up of three propositions having a total of four schematic letters is a nonsyllogistic form; and any natural language argument having that form will fail to qualify as a syllogism. Other examples come quickly to mind. An argument form with only negative premises is a nonsyllogistic form; and an argument form with no universal premises will likewise fail to be a syllogism (*Prior Analytics* 41b, 6ff.). Moreover, many (nonsyllogistic) arguments of the following form will be logically incorrect:

> If X then Y
> Y
> Therefore X

The same applies to many arguments of the following form:

> If X, then Y
> Not X
> Therefore, not Y

In the logical tradition that ensued from Aristotle, these were all identified as fallacious forms.

Thus we have the formal fallacy of four terms, the formal fallacy of deriving a claim from only negative premises, the formal fallacy of deriving a conclusion from nonuniversal premises, the formal fallacy of affirming the consequent, and the formal fallacy of denying the antecedent. So it needs to be said with some emphasis that the definition **Def ForFal** is not empty. The definition specifies a set of what later logicians have called "fallacies," and which are a matter of possessing what might also be called fallacious forms. Let us speak of these further fallacies as "post-*Sophistical Refutation*" fallacies. Then we may say that whereas an argument that commits a post-*Sophistical Refutation* fallacy commits a formal fallacy in the sense of **Def ForFal**, an argument that commits an original Sophistical Refutation type of fallacy does not. So the answer to our question whether there are formal fallacies is Yes, but they do not include Aristotle's original thirteen.

Even though the fallacy of ambiguity, for example, does not qualify as a formal fallacy in the sense of **Def ForFal,** it would be a mistake to conclude that it is a fallacy that has nothing whatever to do with the idea of logical form. It can be seen that various arguments commit the fallacy of ambiguity when the only interpretation under which all their constituent propositions are true is an

---

[11]For the purposes of this chapter, we have restricted ourselves to showing that the fallacy of ambiguity does not satisfy the conditions of **Def ForFal**.

interpretation that assigns a logical form which commits, not an ambiguity fallacy, but the fallacy of four terms. This suggests that at least some of Aristotle's original thirteen fallacies, and many others besides, are *formally explicable*, even though they are not themselves formal fallacies. Here, too, a general definition presents itself:

> **Def ForExp:** An argument A commits a *formally explicable fallacy* of type *T* if and only if there is at least one logical form *F* that enters into the *explanation* of how A comes to commit fallacy *T*, and yet *F* need not itself exhibit *that* fallacy.

According to **Def ForExp,** the ambiguity fallacy of the *Sophistical Refutations* is a formally explicable fallacy, but not a formal fallacy. For, again: If an argument A is taken in a term-ambiguous way, then its logical form commits the fallacy of four terms. But that fallacy is not itself an ambiguity fallacy, since logical forms are entirely free of ambiguity.

We now see the truth of the claim that the *Prior Analytics* is not a theory of fallacies. Aristotle has no instructions in the *Prior Analytics* for analyzing his list of thirteen sophisms in such a way that they come out clearly marked either as formal fallacies in the strict sense or as fallacies that are formally explicable. This sets the stage for an important development in the history of fallacy theory. It is the idea that fallacies, by and large, are not formal entities, but informal. With the distinction in mind between formal fallacies in the strict sense and formally explicable fallacies, it is possible to mark a further distinction between extreme and moderate informalists in the theory of fallacies:

> S is an informal fallacy theorist in the extreme sense to the extent that he or she holds that fallacies are neither formal fallacies nor fallacies that are formally explicable.

Whereas,

> S is an informal fallacy theorist in the moderate sense to the extent that he or she holds that many or most fallacies are formally explicable, but are not formal fallacies in the strict sense.

8.1   FORMAL METHODS IN FALLACY THEORY

It attests to the considerable power of Aristotle's logic as a theory of syllogistic reasoning that it has endured, with emendations and improvements of commentators ancient and modern, even into the present century. Even so, there have been various criticisms over the centuries, two of which bear telling here. The one is implicit in writings of the Stoic logicians, who recognized valid forms of argument not recognized by Aristotle which they codified in systems of "propositional logic."[12]

Another criticism comes, in mature form, much later. It is repeated in modern systems of quantificational logic, originating with Frege and Peirce, and the team of Whitehead and Russell.[13] On this view, Aristotle's theory is open to the technical objection that the *Prior Analytics* overconstrains the categorical propositions out of which syllogisms are constructed. It should also be said that systems of propositional logic and modern quantificational logic attempt to do what Aristotle never did, namely, to give an explicit theoretical articulation of the notion of necessitation. We deal with this last point first.

Aristotle's logic is a theory of deductive reasoning (*syllogismos* is translated both as "deduction" and as "reasoning"). Reasoning is codified in syllogisms and, as we have seen, a multipremised argument is a syllogism if and only if:

(a) its premises necessitate its conclusion

(b) it contains no redundant premise, and

(c) its conclusion repeats no premise

It is customary for modern logicians to characterize an argument as valid if and only if it satisfies (a), independently of whether it satisfies (b) and/or (c). Thus a valid argument is an argument whose premises taken together necessitate its conclusion. There is no reason to think that Aristotle would not have accepted this suggestion. In standard systems of modern logic, an argument is valid if and only if its premises are inconsistent with the negation of its conclusion. This, in turn, depends on a definition of inconsistency: P is inconsistent with Q if and only if there is no interpretation on which P and Q are both true.[14]

Modern logicians have been entirely justified in their efforts to define validity (or conclusion-necessitation), and it may be said that, in this, they have met with considerable success. Preoccupied with validity, they have tended to think of an episode of reasoning as deductively successful just when it is valid or when it is valid and its premises are true. This is a preoccupation in which Aristotle's two further conditions, (b) and (c), seem entirely to have dropped out of the picture.

That this is so matters in two important ways for anyone seriously proposing modern logic as a formal theory of real-life argument. The first point is that all circular arguments are valid. The second is that all valid arguments are "monotonic," that is, that if _ is a valid argument so, too, is the result of arbitrarily augmenting_'s premises as many times as you like. Thus, on the modern definition of validity, the following argument is a perfectly good argument, *logically* speaking, even though it is plainly circular:

---

[12]An accessible account of stoic logic can be found in Mates (1953).

[13]See Frege (1967), Peirce (1992), and Whitehead and Russell (1910–1913).

[14]Cf. Tarski (1956, pp. 409–420).

The cat is on the mat.
So, the cat is on the mat.

And take the following valid argument as a starting point:

All men are mortal.
Socrates is a man.
Therefore, Socrates is mortal.

Then the following argument is also valid, hence perfectly good, logically speaking:

2 is the only even prime number.
Socrates is a man.
Henry the VIII was fussy.
Paris is the capital of Texas.
Some men are not mortal.
Socrates is a woman.
Cervantes is a man.
All men are mortal.
Therefore, Socrates is mortal.

Now whatever we may think of Aristotle's logic overall, he would have steadfastly refused each of these two examples. He would have insisted that neither is a syllogism and that to confuse their validity with their being syllogisms is itself a kind of fallacy. The first example he would have rejected because it is circular, the second would have been refused, for one thing, on grounds of premise-irrelevancy. And it would seem that, each time, Aristotle's complaint would be justified.

A third difference between Aristotle's syllogisms and arguments that modern theorists pronounce good "logically speaking," is implicit in our second example. Its premises are inconsistent since "All men are mortal" contradicts "Some men are not mortal" (and "Socrates is a woman" entails that he is not a man). In modern logic, however, any argument having inconsistent premises is guaranteed to be valid. Let the propositions P and not P be the premises of an argument whose conclusion is Q. Then, since P and not P are inconsistent, so is the trio of propositions P, not P and not Q, which latter is the conclusion's negation. Whereupon, by our definition of validity, "P, not P, therefore Q" is a valid argument.

In Aristotle's logic, on the other hand, it is a derivable condition on syllogisms that they do not have inconsistent premises.[15] The modern logician can repair

---

[15]For let our argument be <A, not-A, therefore B>. By an operation called "conversion," this argument is equivalent to <A, B, therefore A>, in which the conclusion repeats a premise. Hence the latter is not a syllogism, and since the property of being a syllogism is closed under conversion, neither is its converse. The inconsistently premised argument <A, not-A, therefore B> is not a syllogism.

some of this damage by strengthening the validity requirement, replacing it with soundness, that is, by requiring that all premises be true. This would take care of the inconsistent-premises problem, but not of the prior two problems.

Another complaint against Aristotle's logic is that it requires its admissible terms to be restricted to those denoting nonempty sets. This makes it impossible to recognize, for example, the following argument as a syllogism:

> All unicorns are single-horned.
> Fred is a unicorn.
> Therefore, Fred is single-horned.

As against this, modern logicians are inclined to the view that the inferences of logic should be valid entirely topic-neutral, that is, valid independently of their subject matter. The necessity to require that terms denote sets of actual referents offends against this stricture.

It is clear that not every valid argument of a natural language has a syllogistic form. Consider, for example, the argument:

> (1) The stone is an emerald.
> (2) If the stone is an emerald then it is green.
> (3) Therefore, the stone is green.

It is obvious that this argument is valid. That is, it is in no sense possible both that its premises are true and its conclusion is false. It is also true that our argument is a syllogism in Aristotle's broad sense of that term, since it satisfies **Def Syll**. What is not true is that it is a syllogism in virtue of its possession of a syllogistic form. It does not have a syllogistic form. For one thing, its constituent statements are not all categorical subject–predicate propositions. Premise (2) is a compound of such propositions linked by the connective "if . . . then." Yet the "if . . . then" connective is not to be found in Aristotle's list of the logical particles.

Other examples of good arguments that have no syllogistic forms are producible at will. For example, the following argument is trivially valid:

> (a) Harry is bald and Sarah is married.
> (b) Therefore, Sarah is married.

Premise (a) is a compound of categorical propositions linked by the connective "and," but "and" is not one of Aristotle's logical particles.

Although not valid in virtue of their possession of syllogistic forms, the question naturally arises as to whether our arguments might not owe their validity to their possession of other kinds of logical form. The answer is that they do, and it is the principal business of the branch of logic known as propositional logic to show that this is so. Propositional logic originated with the Stoics, but it was not until the present era that it was brought to mature completion. In this section, we can only give an elementary account of such a logic.

As with the account of syllogistic forms, we begin by specifying a set of logical particles. They are the propositional connectives "it is not the case that," "and," "or," "if . . . then," "if and only if," together with the atomic propositional letters p, q, r, s, p1, p2, p3, etc. We next define the *propositional forms* of propositional logic as follows:

S1: If "A" is an atomic propositional letter, then A is a propositional form.

S2: If A and B are propositional forms, so too are

It is not the case that A
It is not the case that B
A and B
A or B
If A then B
A if and only if B.

S3: Nothing else is a propositional form.

The set of propositional forms is to be the smallest set fulfilling conditions S1 and S2. With this set now specified, it is possible to characterize the notion of a (propositional) argument form. An argument form is any finite sequence of propositional forms. Thus the following are argument forms:

(i) p and q
(ii) If q then r
(iii) Therefore r
[a] s if and only if q
[b] If q then r
[c] s
[d] Therefore, r

The argument form (i)–(iii) can be seen, for example, to be a logical form possessed by the natural language argument in which "Harry is bald" is put for p, "Sarah is married" for q, and "Harry is happy" for r:

(i*)   Harry is bald and Sarah is married.
(ii*) If Sarah is married then Harry is happy.
(iii*) Therefore, Harry is happy.

Similarly, [a]–[d] is a logical form of the following argument:

[a*] Peter is clever if and only if Eveline is also clever.

[b*] If Eveline is clever, then the Dean is content.

[c*] Peter is clever.

[d*] Therefore, the Dean is content.

In standard versions of propositional logic, considerable attention is paid to the logical particles "it is not the case that," "and," "or," "if . . . then," and "if and only if." In contradistinction to the logical particles of Aristotle's formal syllogisms, the logical particles of propositional logic are expressly defined. Thus "it is not the case that A" is true if and only if A is false, hence false if and only if A is true. "A and B" is true if A and B are both true, and is false otherwise. "A or B" is true when A is true or B is true, and is false otherwise. "If A then B" is always true, except where both A is true and B false. And, "A if and only if B" is true just when A and B are both true or A and B are both false, and is false otherwise. From these definitions it is easy to see that in propositional logic compound propositions are true or false depending only on whether their contained "atomic" propositions are true or false.

We say that truth and falsity are the "truth values" of propositions. In every case, the truth value of a compound proposition of propositional logic is uniquely determined by, or is a function of, the truth values of its atomic propositions. In view of this, the logical particles of propositional logic have come to be known as "truth functional connectives," and propositional logic is called *truth functional logic* or *the logic of truth functions*.

We can now define validity in propositional logic:

Def Val: An argument form of propositional logic is *valid* if and only if every assignment of truth values to its atomic propositional letters for which the premises are true is an assignment for which the conclusion is true.

The logic of propositions is a distinct advance upon Aristotle's formal syllogistic in a number of related respects. First, construed as truth functions, the logical particles of propositional logic are explicitly definable. Second, the concept of argument validity is also explicitly definable. Third, it is always possible to determine whether a propositional argument form satisfies **Def Val**. Further, because it is always possible to make these determinations correctly, mechanically and in a finite number of operations, the concept of validity is said to be *decidable* in propositional logic.

Propositional logic as a logical system is sound and complete with respect to validity; that is, every argument form that the logic pronounces valid is valid (soundness of the system), and moreover every valid form is a form that the logic recognizes as valid (completeness of the system).

The truth functional definition of the connectives of propositional logic appears to take certain liberties with the meanings of those connectives as they occur in actual English usage. For example, by the definition of "if . . . then," any conditional proposition whose antecedent (or "if"-part) is false and whose consequent (or "then"-part) is true will be declared true. On this definition, for instance, the following conditional proposition will be true, whereas that would seem to be the last thing that it is in fact:

If Paris is the capital city of Texas, then 2 is the only prime number.

Similarly, the definition of "if and only if" provides that, for example, it is true that "Caesar crossed the Rubicon if and only if Morris J. Starsky used to live in Ann Arbor, Michigan," since both constituent propositions are in fact true. But this, too, is a statement that hardly strikes us as correct.

In order to accommodate this difficulty, propositional logic proposes the following solution. Instead of saying that the truth functional definitions correctly define the English connectives just as they occur in ordinary usage, it proposes that ordinary language (English in this case) be augmented by five new technical terms or neologisms for which it is stipulated that our five truth functional definitions are indeed correct. Thus, instead of the English constructions "it is not the case," "and," "or," "if . . . then," and "if and only if," it is stipulated that the definitions are correct when applied to their counterpart neologisms ¬ (for "it is not the case"), ∧ (for "and"), ∨ (for "or"), → (for "if . . . then"), and ≡ (for "if and only if"), and further that it now be made explicit that the new terms ¬, ∧, ∨, → and ≡ *replace* their ordinary language counterparts in the set of logical particles of propositional logic.

At this point, it will be helpful to introduce some further technical terms of propositional logic. The words *conjunction* and *disjunction* are ambiguous. In one meaning they are, respectively, names for the connectives ∧ and ∨. In another meaning, they are the sentences formed by the attachment of ∧ and ∨, respectively, to constituent pairs. Similarly, we have ¬, or the negation-connective, which when prefixed to a sentence "A" produces its negation, or ¬A; →, or the conditional-connective, which flanked by "A" and "B" in that order produces the conditional sentence "A→B"; and ≡, or biconditional-connection, which when flanked by "A" and "B" produces the biconditional sentence "A≡B."

We have seen that the connectives ¬, ∧, ∨, →, and ≡ have counterparts in ordinary English (respectively, "not," "and," "or," "if . . . then," and "if and only if"). If the connectives would mean the same as their counterparts in English, our standard logic would turn out to be a decidable theory for a large class of ordinary English statements and for the class of all arguments constructible from them. In short, propositional logic would seem to be a good theory for a large part of English.

On the face of it, however, this hope seems destined to frustration. As we have observed, it seems that → does not mean "if. . .then" and that ≡ does not mean "if and only if." By the definition of →, a false proposition implies every proposition; but, again, it is greatly to be doubted that, for example, "If Paris is the capital of Texas then 2 is the only even prime" is a true sentence of English. Similarly, though "A≡B" is true for any pair of true "A" and "B" and any pair of false "A" and "B," it cannot be said that "Caesar crossed the Rubicon if and only if Morris J. Starsky used to live in Ann Arbor, Michigan" is a true sentence of English.

Conjunction and disjunction also require scrutiny. It is easy to show that ∧ is commutative, that is, that "A∧B" and "B∧A" always have the same truth value. But with respect to the *English* connective "and," it may be doubted whether "Harry punched Roscoe and Roscoe fell to the ground" has the same truth value as "Roscoe fell to the ground and Harry punched Roscoe." Similarly, whereas it is provable that ∨ obeys the rule of Addition, viz. A → A∨B, for any "B" whatever, it seems to some native speakers that the *English* connective "or" does not. It may be that "Harry punched Roscoe" is true, but some English speakers will deny that "Harry punched Roscoe or the successor of any number is a number" *follows* from this, or even that it is true.

It may be, of course, that the arguments against the equivalence of ∧ and ∨ with "and" and "or" are answerable, but we need not pursue the possibility.[16] It suffices to show that each of the connectives of English has a meaning such that it obeys the *falsification* condition on its truth functional counterparts. Thus whenever "A→B" is false, so, too, is "If A then B"; whenever "A≡B" is false, so, too, is "A if and only if B"; whenever "A∨B" is false, so is "A or B"; and so on. It may also sometimes be the case that "If A then B" or "A if and only if B" are false when "A→B" and "A≡B" are true, but it cannot be the case that they are true where their counterparts are false. If the present claim is true, it matters. For it is then possible to show for a large class of English arguments that they are indeed valid if their truth-functional counterpart arguments are valid.

Now this will strike some as clearly wrong. Take the following argument:

Harry punched Roscoe and Roscoe fell to the ground.
Therefore, Roscoe fell to the ground and Harry punched Roscoe.

Why would we think that this argument is valid just because the argument below is valid?

Harry punched Roscoe ∧ Roscoe fell to the ground.
Therefore, Roscoe fell to the ground ∧ Harry punched Roscoe.

The former argument certainly is not valid if its occurrences of "and" are implicitly occurrences of "and *then*" or "and *next*" or "and *as a result*," or some

---

[16]For suggestions that support this equivalence, see Grice (1975), and Woods (1967, pp. 357–368).

such thing. What are we to make of these "temporalized" or "causally-loaded" conjunctions? If they are understood as adverbially qualified "bare" conjunctions, their attribution here would seem to be contextually specified. That is, the meaning of "Harry *punched* Roscoe" and "Roscoe *fell to the ground*," together with the causal principle that being punched often causes people to fall down, seems to call for that construal. On the other hand, we might see "and then" as a stand-alone connective in which there is no occurrence of the (bare) "and," and take this as suggesting that the "ands" of our Harry–Roscoe argument are contextually specified as temporalized or causally loaded counterparts, as suggested before.

Viewed in this perspective, the following argument form, too, is a valid argument form:

$p \rightarrow q$
$\neg q$
Therefore, $\neg p$

It seems quite wrong, however, to judge the following argument as valid:

> If baby cries then we will hug her.
> We don't hug her.
> So baby is not crying.

Here is an argument in which the expression "if . . . then" does not express a direct consequences-relation between crying and hugging. It is questionable how this "if . . . then" is to be interpreted. Whatever the details might be, it seems quite clear that interpreting it thus is a matter of the interpretation of the sentences it flanks. Whatever the precise meaning of "if . . . then," it certainly will not do as an interpretation of the "if . . . then" of, for example, "If the match is struck, then the match fires."

So here, too, we have a case in which the interpretation of a connective is fixed, or anyhow influenced, by the meaning of the flanking simple sentences, together with contextual principles such as "Hugging babies often stops their crying," "People often hug their babies to stop them crying," and "Some unhugged babies cry." Such examples are a plain embarrassment for our present claim that the connectives of English obey the Falsification Principle.

What is required to restore the Principle is a supplementary condition on English sentences and on arguments constructed out of them. This further condition is that sentences and arguments of English be held to a requirement of strict context-insensitivity. This, the *Context-Insensitivity Principle*, is a condition on which the present claim about the falsification condition has a good chance of being true. Its truth is abetted by a further condition, the *Tenselessness Principle*, which provides that the interpretation of English connectives owes nothing to the tenses of flanking sentences.

We now have the means to clarify the claim that each of the English connectives has a meaning for which the Falsification Principle is acceptable. This means that when sentences embedding the English connectives do so in fulfillment of the Principles of Context-Insensitivity and Tenselessness, the Falsification Principle is true.

With these things said, consider any class of simple declarative sentences, true or false, of English. Extend that class to include all sentences constructible from sentences of the former class with the aid of the English connectives, and nothing else, consider now any English argument A constructed out of sentences of this extended class and nothing else. Let A* be its counterpart argument in our logical system in which the English connectives are replaced by their "corresponding" truth functional connectives. A* is valid just in case there is no assignment of truth values to its simple sentences which makes the premises true and the conclusion false. Since the sentences of A obey the falsification condition for their counterparts in A*, any assignment that makes a compound sentence of A* false likewise makes its counterpart in A false. Let it be the case that no assignment makes all the premises of A* true and its conclusion false. Then A* is valid. So, too, is A, its English counterpart. For suppose the opposite. Then there will be an assignment which makes all of A's premises true and its conclusion false. For any such assignment, at least one of its counterpart premises in A* will be false. But this is impossible: The English connectives obey the falsification condition on the logical connectives, so that would mean that one of A's premises would be false as well. Because there is no way for the premises of A* to be true and its conclusion false, at least one premise of A* is false for all assignments in which its conclusion is true. But A cannot fail to be valid unless its counterpart of that false premise of A* is true; and this cannot be. Hence any English argument constructed in the ways lately examined is valid if its truth-functionally counterpart argument is valid.

An example will make this clear. Let A be the following argument:

(1) If Toronto is the capital of Ontario then 17 is an infinitesimal.
(2) But 17 is not an infinitesimal.
(3) Therefore, Toronto is not the capital of Ontario.

This is its interpreted counterpart A* in propositional logic:

(1*) (Toronto is the capital of Ontario) $\rightarrow$ (17 is an infinitesimal)
(2*) $\neg$ (17 is an infinitesimal)
(3*) Therefore, $\neg$ (Toronto is the capital of Ontario)

It is easy to see that there is no assignment of truth values to "Toronto is the capital of Ontario" and "17 is an infinitesimal" that makes the premises of A* true and the conclusion false; so A* is valid. Thus every assignment making its conclusion false makes at least one of its premises false. Turning now to the English argument A, we might suppose that premise (1) is *false independently of* the truth values of its constituent sentences. If so, then there is no assignment making the conclusion false which makes the premises all true. So A is valid. It is valid even where (1) is false whenever (1*) is true.

Although any English argument constructible in the ways we have been considering is valid if its counterpart truth-functional argument is valid, the implication does not hold for invalidity. That is, there are English arguments constructible in these ways which are valid even though their logical forms are invalid. So it is not true that an English argument is invalid if its logical form is invalid.[17] Hence the property of invalidity is not decidable in the class of our English arguments by the procedures that are decidable for validity in the class of their counterpart arguments. This is easily demonstrated. Let B be the following argument:

(a) Figure f is a square.

(b) Therefore, figure f is a rectangle.

Its logical form B* is:

a: p

b: Therefore, q

Although B* is transparently invalid, B is considered to be valid since the conclusion is entailed by the premise. We may say, then, that in the class of English arguments presently in question validity is quasi-decidable under the procedures we have described.

So far we have developed some basic ideas of propositional logic, but nothing that has been said about them has shed any new light on what a formal fallacy might be, except to say that a formal (propositional) fallacy just is any argument whose propositional form satisfies **Def ForFal**. Moreover, in as much as propositional logic concentrates on argument validity at the expense of premise-consistency, premise-nonredundancy and conclusion noncircularity, it will have to be acknowledged that propositional logic is a less good theory of ordinary language argumentation than syllogistic logic is. Whatever we may think of the formal logic of syllogisms as a theory of fallacies, it is hardly likely that formal propositional logic will do conspicuously better in that same regard. Much the same is also true of the modern logic of quantification, which is an improved theory of quantifiers combined with the truth functional connectives of propo-

---

[17]For a discussion of this issue and related issues, see Woods (1995) and Finocchiaro (1994).

sitional logic.[18] In as much as our objective in the present chapter is to explore the success that a formal logic will have as a theory of fallacies, there is little that quantification theory will add to the concept of a formal fallacy. Here, just as in syllogistic logic and propositional logic, formal fallacies all satisfy the basic definition **Def ForFal**.

A much more interesting question is to what extent a formal logic (whether syllogistic, propositional, quantificational, or some other sort) serves as an efficient test of the fallaciousness, or nonfallaciousness, of real-life arguments as they occur in actual human give-and-take. To this, there is a common answer, that is, an answer that cuts across the differences between syllogistic, propositional, and quantificational logic. The answer is that a formal logic will be a good theory of the fallaciousness and nonfallaciousness of actual arguments to the extent that (a) at least some fallacies are either formal or formally explicable and (b) that there is a theoretically satisfactory way of specifying an actual argument's logical form in such a way that (a) is seen to be true of it.

It is easy to show that ordinary arguments do not correctly reveal their logical form unless they satisfy what might be called the *Principle of Semantic Inertia* as applied to their simplest constituent statements. We have already said that the following argument is valid even though it has an invalid form in propositional logic:

(a) Figure f is a square.

(b) Therefore, figure f is a rectangle.

Similarly, the following argument is a syllogism in the broad sense even though its form, having four terms, is not a syllogistic form:

---

[18]For the purposes of this chapter, it is not necessary to develop an account of modern quantificational logic. Even so, it might be helpful to specify the logical particles of quantification theory. They are the logical particles of propositional logic, $\neg$, $\wedge$, $\vee$, $\rightarrow$, and $\equiv$, and the propositional letters p, q, r, s, p1, p2, etc., supplemented by: *schematic letters* for *predicate terms*: F, G, H, I, F1, F2, . . . ; *variables* for individuals: x, y, z, x1, x2, . . . ; and the *quantifier expressions* $\forall$ (read "for all") and $\exists$ (read "there is at least one"). Propositional forms constructible from the logical particles include: $\forall x(Fx \rightarrow Gx)$ (read "for all individuals x, if x satisfies predicate F then x satisfies predicate G"); $\exists x(Hx \vee Ix)$ (read "there is at least one individual x such that either x satisfies predicate H or x satisfies predicate I"). Both propositional and quantificational logic are called *standard* or *classical*. There also exist systems of logic, both propositional and quantificational, in which certain classical principles fail. Intuitionistic logic is a case in point. In the classical systems of propositional and quantificational logic, the following two propositional forms are logical truths, that is, true in every model:

$p \vee \neg p$
$\forall x(Fx \vee \neg Fx)$

Both instantiate the classical law of excluded middle. But in intuitionistic logic the law of excluded middle admits of exceptions. We make mention of intuitionistic logic here to anticipate a brief reference to it below.

(c) All coats have sleeves.

(d) Some coats are scarlet.

(e) Therefore, some red things have sleeves.

The same kinds of difficulty are easily also shown for arguments in relation to their modern quantificational forms. The Principle of Semantic Inertia is designed to avert such problems. The Principle says:

> Let A be any English argument whose validity is to be tested by exposure of its logical form (whether in syllogistic, propositional, quantificational, or some other system of formal logic). Then the atomic constituents of A must be *semantically inert*. That is, they must not be logically inconsistent with one another, and they must neither imply nor be implied by one another.

It is obvious on inspection that our sample arguments violate this Principle. In argument (a) - (b), the atomic statement "Figure f is square" implies "Figure f is a rectangle" by entailment; and in argument (c) - (e), the atomic term "scarlet" also implies the atomic term "red." Similarly, the argument (f) - (g) is considered to be a valid argument (because (f) is an inconsistent premise), even though it has an invalid propositional form:

(f) This square is a triangle.

(g) Therefore, 2 is the only even prime.

The crux of the present difficulty is that it is impossible to determine by formal means whether or not the Principle of Semantic Inertia is satisfied by any pair of atomic constituents of English. Thus whether an argument is invalidated, or validated, by its logical form cannot be decided until its logical form is specified. But its logical form cannot be specified in ways relevant to the task at hand until it is decided whether Semantic Inertia is satisfied. This latter cannot be decided formally. Hence, whether an argument is formally valid is not itself an entirely formal matter, paradoxical as it may sound. By the same token, whether a real-life argument commits a formal fallacy is never entirely a formal matter.[19]

We might say that the necessity to determine whether the Principle of Semantic Inertia is satisfied imposes on the theorist the requirement to have ready to hand a "logic" of implication and inconsistency for atomic constituents. Such a logic cannot be a formal logic, but without it we lack appropriate theoretical guarantees as to what the logical form of a real-life argument "really" is. In a word, the theorist needs an "informal logic" in order to make formal logic work as a logic of real-life argumentation.

This leaves the logical theorist oddly positioned. Informal logic, as discussed in chapter 6, has attracted two quite different kinds of critical opinion. One is

---

[19]A similar conclusion is readied by Finocchiaro (1994).

that it does not and could not exist, that the expression *informal logic* is an oxymoron.[20] The other is that informal logic is a perfectly legitimate discipline, but that it has not yet been worked out in a theoretically satisfactory way.[21] Both these answers matter considerably for any serious fallacies project.

Consider the class of fallacies that theorists have been interested in. As explained in chapter 3, they are either formal fallacies or informal fallacies such as the so-called "*ad*-fallacies." If they are informal fallacies, they would seem to be the province of informal logic. But, if the first criticism is correct, informal logic does not exist and, if there are any informal fallacies, they cannot be discovered by logic. On the other hand, if the second criticism is correct and if there are informal fallacies which it is the business of informal logic to uncover, it may be *possible* to do so, but it has not yet been figured out how to do it in a theoretically satisfactory way. However, if the fallacies in question are *formal* fallacies, then it may be possible to identify them *within* a system of formal logic, but it is not possible to identify them within real-life arguments without the aid of informal logic. And here, too, the two criticisms recur: Either the needed informal logic is impossible or it is not yet known how to construct it. Consequently, either it is impossible to construct a theory of formal fallacies for real-life arguments, or it is possible but not yet known how to do so in a satisfactory way.

Whatever we decide, overall, to make of the criticisms we just mentioned, there is reason to think that, in two respects, they are too harsh. It is true that there exists to date no fully developed and generally received theory of informal logic on a par with the several systems of formal logic, but as research over the past two decades or so attests, efforts are underway to construct theories of informal logic rich enough to expose complexities in real-life argumentation which standard systems of formal logic would have little or no chance of handling (see chapter 6). Moreover, informal logicians would be quick to resist any suggestion that a good system of informal logic must be at parity with standard theories of formal logic. It may be that the complexities and subtleties of real-life arguments, faithful representations of which it is a major part of the informal logic program to provide, are the very things that preclude eventual demonstrations of such things as soundness and completeness in informal logic. And if these requirements are simply not realistic for a theory of real-life argumentation, prospects for informal logic would seem to improve considerably.

There is a second respect in which the criticisms would seem to be too harsh. If it were a justified complaint that there is little or no place in any theory that deserves the name of logic for the analysis of fallacies, it would be difficult to see (a) how the illogical aspects of fallacies could be recognized and dealt with

---

[20]Thus Hintikka (1989, p. 4).

[21]There is a further sort of informal logic in which it is attempted to appraise arguments for which the principle of context-insensitivity is *suspended*. Such theories are important, but they, too, have not yet been worked out in satisfactory ways.

in any kind of effectively theoretical way; and (b) how their theoretical treatment (however it might be proceeded with) could exhibit features that would qualify as "formal" in *any* sense of the word.

There is much in the contemporary research program to suggest that such criticisms are indeed unrealistically severe. Two contemporary developments deserve mention. In one of these developments, it is proposed that if an appropriate new kind of formal logic were contrived, then it would be possible to analyze at least a good many fallacies as both violations of logic and, concurrently, as violations exhibiting certain sorts of logical forms. Logics of this type are called *dialogue logics* or systems of formal dialectic or, in some variations, *interrogative logics*.[22] Formal dialectic is the subject of chapter 9, so it is unnecessary to expound its features here. Suffice it to say that theorists who subscribe to formal dialectical approaches tend to resolve textual ambiguities in the *Sophistical Refutations* in such a way that Aristotle's thirteen fallacies (and many more besides) turn out to be dominantly dialectical rather than syllogistic errors.

8.2 THE WOODS–WALTON APPROACH

A contemporary development that is rather difficult to characterize briefly is the so-called *Woods–Walton Approach*. This approach is exhibited in a series of articles coauthored by the Canadian logicians John Woods and Douglas Walton in the period 1972–1982, and in a number of independently authored articles and books published during this time and thereafter. Woods and Walton explained their approach of the fallacies in a textbook entitled *Argument: The Logic of the Fallacies* (1982) and collected many of their joint papers in *Fallacies: Selected Papers, 1972–1982* (1989).

Woods and Walton do not take a fixed position on whether fallacies are inherently logical as opposed to dialectical. It is, in fact, their view that the answer will vary depending on the fallacy in question. Nevertheless, there is a common methodological theme in all their writings which may be summarized as amounting to the following convictions: (1) fallacies are usefully analyzed using the structures and the theoretical vocabulary of various logical systems, including systems of dialectical logic, and (2) whatever the details of the deployment of such structures and theoretical vocabularies, successful analyses of at least a great many fallacies will have features that qualify those analyses as formal in some sense of that word.

In their analysis of fallacies, Woods and Walton draw upon Hamblin's dialectical concepts of commitment sets and retraction as methodological tools. Thus

---

[22]See especially Hamblin (1970, chap. 8), Barth and Martens (1977), Mackenzie (1979a), Barth and Krabbe (1982), Walton (1984, 1989b), Woods and Walton (1989, chaps. 2, 3, 10, 11, 19), and Hintikka and Bachman (1991). For a dialectical approach to the theory of argument that is neither formal nor logical, see van Eemeren and Grootendorst (1984, 1992a).

their analysis of fallacies is formally oriented, but also dialectical. Besides these two themes, certain other features of their approach stand out, and they recur with enough frequency in their writings to be typical.

Woods and Walton are *pluralists* about the fallacies. History has endowed a great many rather different things with the name of "fallacy." In Woods and Walton's opinion, it makes no more sense to suppose that they must all be given a common analysis than it does to suppose that all diseases should be given the same diagnosis and treatment. This being said, they tend to organize the many fallacies they have recognized in their writings into three grades of *formality*.

First, there are those fallacies, such as the fallacy of four terms, which are formal fallacies in the strict sense, that is, fallacies that satisfy **Def ForFal**. At the next grade of formality come those fallacies such as the fallacies of ambiguity that are not, in the strict sense, formal fallacies, but which satisfy **Def ForExp**, and so are fallacies whose commission is made explicable, in part, by reference to logical forms. In fact, our analysis, pages ago, of the ambiguity fallacy may be taken as typical of the Woods–Walton formal approach at this second grade. Much more prominently realized in their work is a third grade of formality which we have not yet met with in this chapter. To this, we now turn with a definition of formal analyzability:

> **Def ForAnal:** A fallacy F is *formally analyzable* to the extent that its analysis introduces concepts which are described, in whole or part, by employing the technical vocabulary and/or the formal structures of a system of logic or other sort of formal theory.

In English, *formality*, it is well to note, is a multiple-ambiguous word. All sort of things and situations count as formal, from "formal evening," to "formal speech," and all the way to theories of logical form. There is "good form" in tennis, and telling off-color jokes is considered "bad form" in polite society.[23]

The concept of formality that gives sense to **Def ForAnal** is approximately this. Sometimes a definition is said to be formal when it is exact, explicit, general, and rigorous. So, for example, the definition of the successor of any number n as the number $n + 1$ would qualify as formal in this present sense. Similarly, a theory could be said to be a "formal theory" to the extent that its definitions were formal, and its assertions were explicitly and rigorously demonstrated. Especially significant would be those theories, such as number theory, or set theory, whose sets of theorems are up to infinitely large, but which are nonetheless finitely axiomatizable. For such a thing to be true, it is standardly the case that axioms are given by way of finite numbers of *axiom schemata*.

Two examples of the formal analyses typical of the Woods–Walton approach are mentioned here. In several chapters of *Fallacies: Selected Papers*, Woods and

---

[23]Cf. chapter 9, note 12.

Walton analyze the logical structure of dialectical arguments that satisfy the "no-retraction rule" as arguments that have the property of *cumulativity*. Cumulativity is analyzed, in turn, as a certain kind of "Kripke-structure," introduced by Saul A. Kripke (1965) in his "Semantical Analysis of Intuitionistic Logic I." Woods and Walton show that the fallacy of *petitio principii* cannot be committed in such structures, that is, that the formally analyzable property of cumulativeness precludes the *petitio*.[24]

In another example, Woods and Walton set out to show that the analysis of the fallacies of *composition* and *division* rests on a good theoretical account of the part–whole relation. This assumption seems a reasonable one, in as much as these fallacies involve incorrect inferences from properties of wholes to properties of their parts, and from properties of parts to properties of the wholes of which they are parts. In *Fallacies: Selected Papers*, these authors show that neither ordinary set theory nor a standard deviation from it known as "mereology" will suffice for the correct analysis of composition and division fallacies. A better bet, they think, is a formal theory of the part–whole relation, known as "aggregate theory," as developed by Tyler Burge.[25]

The two examples illustrate the general conception of formality that enters into the work of Woods and Walton at the third grade. With it, comes an updated definition of an informal fallacy theorist. We recall that an informal theorist in the extreme sense is one who holds that fallacies are neither made so by possession of fallacious logical forms nor explicable by specifying a fallacious logical form which a given fallacious argument would have under a certain interpretation of it. An informal theorist in the moderate sense is one who denies that most fallacies are formal fallacies in the strict sense but who grants that many fallacies are formally explicable. We now meet with another breed of informal theorist, whom we might call an "informal theorist of grade three":

S is an *informal theorist of third grade* to the extent that he or she holds that many fallacies, while not formal fallacies in the strict sense and not formally explicable, are nevertheless formally analyzable at the third grade of formality.[26]

8.3   A DIALECTICAL ANALYSIS OF REFUTATION

For another example of a formal analysis of the third grade, which is dialectical in nature, we return to the Aristotelian notion of refutation, which was the concern of the beginning of this chapter. In order to illustrate the third grade

---

[24]See, in particular, Woods and Walton (1989, chaps. 10 and 19).

[25]See Woods (1980), Woods and Walton (1989, chap. 8), and Burge (1977, pp. 97–118).

[26]Corresponding to this moderate breed of informal theorist, there is, of course, an extreme informal theorist who holds that no fallacy is either a formal fallacy in the strict sense, or is formally explicable, or is formally analyzable. This definition would seem to be empty; we mention it here as a limiting case of informality in fallacy theory.

of formal analysis, we use the Woods–Walton approach of applying concepts of formal dialectical systems.[27] Showing that refutation can be captured in a dialectical system with commitment sets and retraction, enables us to illuminate the dialectical aspect of the Woods–Walton approach.

Sometimes, at least, a failed refutation will be a fallacy. It falls to a good theory of fallacies not only to specify this range of cases but also to give a satisfactory definition or analysis of the *concept of refutation*. Bearing in mind that a refutation is always a refutation of something, it is important to remember that any valid argument derives the contradictory of the negation of its own conclusion. Why, then, is not every valid argument a refutation of that very proposition? It is more in keeping with common sense to think of a refutation as the derivation of the contradictory of some *given* proposition forwarded in a context of interpersonal disputation as *the* thesis at issue. Call this thesis T. Then no argument, no matter how impeccable, would be a refutation *of* T unless its validly derived conclusion were not-T. What, then, is the structure of a refutation of T in a dispute between the proponent P of T, and the would-be refuter A of T?[28]

A constructs a refutation of T by asking P questions the answers to which are premises for A in an emerging syllogism which, once completed, concludes with not-T. Now either T *itself* is a premise in this emerging argument or it is not. If it is, and the argument is valid, then since the argument is a *syllogism*, T is not a superfluous premise. This being so, the remaining premises (minus T) do not necessitate the conclusion not-T; that is, those premises together with T constitute a consistent set. On the other hand, since the original argument is valid, then the set of its premises together with T is an inconsistent set. But the former set is identical to the latter set. Hence, the supposition that T is a premise in its own refutation leads to an inconsistency, and must be rejected. So we make the contrary assumption, namely that T is not a premise of any syllogism that refutes it. But this leaves us in the unattractive situation in which we must explain how it comes to pass that the following is the case:

(a) although T is *stated* by P, and

(b) although all of A's *premises* must be statements of P,

nevertheless

(c) all of P's statements *except T* are available as premises for A.

---

[27]The present illustration of the Woods–Walton approach at the third grade formality is not based on Woods and Walton's published writings, but rather on Woods, *Aristotle's earlier logic*, in preparation.

[28]It might be thought that the present account presents an overly narrow specification of Aristotelian refutations. Why must it be the case that an argument refutes a thesis T only if T and the argument's conclusion are contradictories, that is, such that exactly one is true and exactly one is false? It would seem that an argument is also a refutation of T when its conclusion and T are contraries, that is, such that they could not both be true, although they could both be false. For our purposes here, it is unnecessary to decide these issues.

In what does this exception consist? It consists in the satisfaction by A's syllogism of the following formal rules of dialectical logic:

> **Premise Selection Rule:** In any dispute D between P and A in which A constructs a refutation R of P's thesis T, let Σ be the set of P's statements in D. Then for all σεΣ, σ is a premise of R only if σ is subject to the no-retraction rule.
> **No-Retraction Rule:** With P, A, D, R and Σ as above, σ *once stated* by P cannot subsequently be retracted by P.

It is entirely straightforward to show that T itself is uniquely placed in not being subject to the no-retraction rule. If it were, then once stated, it could not be retracted. But if it could not be retracted, it could not be refuted either (or, more carefully, given up for its having been refuted). On the other hand, it is easy to see why P's other statements should be subject to the no-retraction rule. If they were not, then any P could make any (self-consistent) T *irrefutable* by the simple expedient of retracting any prior statement (except T) otherwise available to A as a premise in a successful derivation of not-T.

Thus we now have an *analysis* of the concept of refutation, itself embedded in the concept of sophistical refutation, which many theorists take to be indispensable to the analysis of certain fallacies. That analysis is:

> **Def Refutation:** R is a refutation by A in D of a thesis T of P if and only if R is a syllogism, the set of P's statements in D, P1 ... , Pn are R's premises, T εΣ, P1, ...Pn εΣ, T is not a premise of R, and R's conclusion is not-T.

Def Refutation itself counts as formal in the sense of **Def ForAnal**. In particular, it makes use of the technical term *syllogism* in defining *refutation*. Not only is syllogism a technical term in a system of logic, but the logic in question is a theory of formal syllogistic structures. We have it, then, that any analysis of any fallacy that turned on the concept of refutation would turn on a concept whose own analysis, via **Def Refutation**, places the total analysis in the third grade of formality. This result is a typical Woods–Walton result in that it defines a concept of practical usefulness in the analysis of fallacies using the fundamental concepts of formal dialectical systems as the tools of analysis.

8.4 PERSPECTIVES

The present chapter introduced a general conception of what constitutes a system of formal logic. With that conception, it is possible to consider the extent to which a standard system of logic succeeds as a theory of natural language argument for a certain range of target properties, such as validity and consistency. This is a broad question that constrains a narrower one: To what extent do such logics serve as theoretical accounts of fallacies?

We have seen, in answer to the first question, that standard logics do not readily, or reliably, apply to natural language arguments just as they come. Fruitful application requires that real-life arguments be considerably tidied before they are engaged by the formal mechanisms of logic. The tidying up is governed by Principles such as Semantic Inertia and Context-Insensitivity, whose fulfillment is not determinable by the logics in question. This leaves a gap between the formalism of logic and the din and swirl of actual argumentative speech and text.

In view of the gap, it is not surprising that standard logics have best met with success as theories of highly stylized natural discourse, such as mathematics and mathematical physics, to which the Principles of Semantic Inertia, Context-Insensitivity (and Tenselessness, too) have a reasonably ready application. Even so, this has not stopped logicians from extending their formal apparatuses in ways designed to capture features of natural language speech that the standard systems are obliged to ignore. Prominent among such attempts are formal analyses of indexical expressions and adverbial constructions.[29] Whatever the success of these elaborations, it remains true that formal logic has only a limited application to natural language argument, even when it is borne in mind that the properties that is seeks to illuminate are already a highly restricted set, that is, the *deductively* explicable properties of argument.

If this answers the broader question of the applicability of standards logics to real-life argument, it also answers the narrower question of their applicability to the fallacies that crop up in natural discourse. As we have seen, some fallacies, such as denying the antecedent and affirming the consequent, can be seen as instances of invalid logical forms. Most of the fallacies that have interested theorists over the centuries cannot be analyzed in this way. Thus the applicability of logic to fallacy theory meets with a twofold encumbrance. First is the general slackness of fit between logic and natural argument with respect to those properties that admit of construal by way of logical forms. Second is the fact that, apart from this general slackness, most of the fallacies are not in any direct way matters of logical form. That is, most fallacies, whether Aristotle's sophistical refutations or those that engage the interest of subsequent and contemporary theorists, do not manage to satisfy the definition, **Def ForFal** (see p. 220).

If a theory of fallacies counted as formal only if its target fallacies satisfied **Def ForFal**, then it could be said at once that most of fallacy theory is not formal. However, as we have seen, there is reason to countenance at least three grades of formality that a theory might exhibit. A theory exhibits the first grade of formality when, in the spirit of **Def ForFal** itself, its target properties are instances of logical forms. A theory exhibits the second grade of formality when, like theories in which fallacies are formally explicable, its target properties can be explained in ways that call for mention of logical forms of which the target

---

[29]For the former, see Montague (1974); for the latter, see Davidson (1980).

properties are not simple instantiations. Theories at the third grade of formality are theories whose key concepts are formally analyzable, that is, analyzable using the vocabulary and concepts whether of a system of logic or some other technical system, but not in ways that compel the employment of logical forms in the analyses. Systems of formal dialectic, in the manner of Hamblin, Barth and Krabbe, and in some respects Woods and Walton, are theories exhibiting the second grade of formality. Theories of third grade are perhaps most evident in the overall work of the latter two authors.

The formal character of the Woods–Walton approach has its obvious attractions at the level of *theoretical* analysis. But it has been questioned whether it is an approach that is particularly "user-friendly" when it comes to the mundane business of spotting a fallacy in ordinary, everyday argument and giving a quick and easy diagnosis of how it came to be committed. This being so, some critics have held that the Woods–Walton analyses are too technical and too theoretical for effective use by the layman in the day-to-day business of argument appraisal.[30]

It remains an open and interesting question as to how useful theories of second and third grade are in the analysis of real-life arguments. Judgments of utility, of course, follow upon the theorist's interests. It would be true to say that if a theorist is interested in a body of argument from the point of view of the standard fallacies, that fallacy theories of the second and third grade (and where applicable, of the first grade, too) will answer to that interest. But it would not be true to say that a theoretical analysis and appraisal of a body of argument *requires* that it be attended to from the perspective of the traditional fallacies.[31]

That this is so poses another important question: With what frequency in serious real-life argument is there likely occasion to invoke the results of a theory of fallacies? Or, more simply, with what frequency are the traditional fallacies committed in real-life argument? It is an important question, and an open one.[32]

---

[30]See van Eemeren and Grootendorst (1992a). But see also Krabbe (1992, p. 477): "It would be a misrepresentation of the Woods and Walton approach to say that in this approach one assigns one logic (one logical system) to each traditional fallacy. [...] The authors do not present a unified theory of fallacies, nor do they seem to aspire to achieve such a theory. All the same, these papers display a remarkable coherence as they are all products of the typical Woods and Walton approach in which the same formal systems are used again and again in the context of different fallacies." As Krabbe points out, these recurring systems are Hintikka's epistemic logic, Hamblin's formal dialectic, and Kripke's semantics for intuitionistic logic.

[31]There exist very careful analyses of real-life arguments in which there is little occasion to invoke consideration of the fallacies. A case in point is Finocchiaro's (1980) book-length examination of Galileo's arguments in *Dialogue concerning the two chief world systems*, in which, for all the reservations the analyst might have about the adequacy of the argument, there is little occasion to apply the insights, however deep they may be, of a theory of the fallacies.

[32]As regards the contention about the frequency with which certain probabilistic fallacies are committed by ordinary reasoners, see Nisbett and Ross (1980), Kahneman, Slovic, and Tversky (1982), and Cohen (1986). See also Finocchiaro (1980), Jason (1986), Secor (1987), and Jason (1989).

It is sometimes argued that Woods and Walton try to use formal methods of logic to analyze the kind of argument forms associated with the fallacies, and that therefore there is no "pragmatic" component in their analyses. From the very beginning (1972), however, the Woods–Walton approach, while it has been influenced by the methodology of formal logic, was also open to the dialectical concept of argument propounded by Hamblin (1970). For all their sympathy with Hamblin's idea that analyzing the fallacies would be considerably facilitated by placing arguments in a dialogue context, Woods and Walton acknowledged the problem that Hamblin's own idea of a dialogue framework was not defined clearly, exactly, and explicitly enough to study the fallacies in that context.[33] Accepting Hamblin's basic idea of the dialogue structure of argument, and exploiting it systematically in their papers, Woods and Walton do not fix on any *one* type of dialogue structure as exclusively the right normative framework for arguments. Like Hamblin, they leave it open that there could be several kinds of framework of this type. Whereas their approach is rightly classified as pluralistic, it is not rightly classified as nonpragmatic if this means that the framework of dialogue of an argument is excluded as a factor in its evaluation.[34]

The Woods–Walton approach arose in a climate of formal logic dominance, and their work on the fallacies, at times, reflects that dominance in addressing questions of specific logical forms of argument as part of the analysis. Even so, there is no encouragement in this body of work of the idea that an adequate analysis of a fallacy consists merely in the specification of the logical form of arguments that commit the fallacy. Overall Woods and Walton (1982) emphasize the theoretical importance of characterizing fallacies as features of arguments in actual use, exemplified by their fondness for Case Studies such as the contention that once raged over the Shroud of Turin (pp. 91–93).

The Woods–Walton approach is formalistic in a deeper and more revealing sense in its decision to construe a dialogue-context of argument as a formalizable structure. Following Hamblin, Woods and Walton think of a dialogue structure as a kind of formalistically definable structure, with constants and variables, of the sort that logicians are familiar with. But they hold that there could be many of these structures, without there being a unique right one, or even any finite list of right ones. Woods and Walton claim that there could be a plurality of right ones, and they distinguish, just as Aristotle did in *Sophistical Refutations* (165b, 1 - 165b, 3), a plurality of different kinds of argument used in a discussion, and a plurality of kinds of fallacy.

---

[33]Hamblin's main dialogue system was left open-ended. He said vaguely that its purpose was to be "information-oriented," but he made no attempt to define "information" in any precise way.

[34]In linguistic pragmatics, the word *pragmatic* refers, more specifically, to the theoretical study of the contextual and situational conditions for performing speech acts in verbal communication and interaction, whether argumentative or other. Since speech act conditions are not explicitly taken into account, the Woods–Walton approach is not pragmatic in this sense.

In practice, the Woods–Walton approach admits many different contexts in which an argument could be used. In theory, it requires that all these contexts or frameworks should be definable under the general rubric of a structure of dialogue where the participants, moves, locations, commitments, and other factors that define the dialogue exchange, are defined in clear and precise ways acceptable to logicians. Thus the Woods–Walton approach is formalistic in a deeper and more revealing sense of aiming to construe a dialogue-context of argument as a formalizable structure.

Perhaps the most telling criticism of formalistic methods comes from Scriven (1976):

> [. . .] the fallacies generally turn out not to be fallacies—unless one builds into the identification process, and hence into the labels, all the skills needed for analysis without the taxonomy of fallacies. In that case one has made it a formal approach, and the encoding (i.e., diagnosing) step has become the tricky one. (p. xvi)

Scriven's point is that the theoretical neatness of a formal description of a fallacy (such that all and only those arguments fitting the description commit the fallacy) is purchased at the price of messiness about whether the formal description actually applies to a given argument. It is significant that Scriven makes a similar point about false precision of proof techniques of formal logic when used to evaluate arguments in natural languages. The significance of this further claim is that it makes it possible to see the point about formal approaches to fallacies as a special case of it.

There is little doubt that Scriven has noticed something important. To see that this is so, we return briefly to the propositional calculus and to the question whether it enables us in any really helpful way to take the measure of real-life arguments forwarded in natural speech. As we saw, propositional logic can function as a test of only a limited range of argument properties (such as validity) for only a limited range of rather simple natural language arguments. Even so, for propositional logic to do those limited jobs correctly, it is necessary to constrain its choice of natural language arguments to those that fulfill the Principles of Context-Insensitivity and Semantic Inertia. If these Principles are not invoked, then the pronouncements the logic makes on a natural language argument have nothing even close to a guarantee of being right. On the other hand, whether a natural language argument does indeed satisfy the Principles of Context-Sensitivity and Semantic-Inertia is not a question that formal logic can answer. This leaves the theorist with two broad options. One is to make the judgments about the validity of natural language arguments *nonformally*, that is, without recourse to any notion of logical form. The other option is to make judgments of context-insensitivity and semantic inertia nonformally, and then, having done so, make determinations of validity formally. But this leaves an interesting question: If judgments of context-insensitivity and semantic inertia can be handled nonformally, why can judgments of validity not also be made nonformally? Or, in blunter terms, what is the use of formal logic for the appraisal of natural language arguments?

There is little question that, at times, Scriven has the Woods–Walton approach to fallacies in mind when he makes these criticisms. There is not much justification for doing so. As we have seen, there is nothing in the third grade of formal analysis that qualifies for Scriven's disapproval, and it is this third grade of formality that typifies the work of Woods and Walton. In what is obviously a caricature, we could distinguish two kind of formalists about fallacies of natural language argument. Formalists of the first kind seek efficient formal rules for determining whether an argument commits fallacy F1 or F2 or F3, and so on. On the other hand, formalists of the second kind want an analysis of the concept of F1, the concept of F2, and so on, and want it even though the analysis may not significantly improve their powers of *detection* with respect to those fallacies. Crude as it is, our caricature enables us to make a useful point about Scriven's criticism. When directed against the first kind of formalists, it is a weighty objection; when directed against the second kind of formalists, it largely misses the point.

9

DIALOGUE LOGIC
AND FORMAL DIALECTICS

In this chapter, we discuss the dialogue logic proposed by the German logician and philosopher Paul Lorenzen, and the ensuing theory of argumentation known as *formal dialectics*, developed by the Dutch logicians and philosophers Else Barth and Erik Krabbe. We think it more profitable to explain one type of theory within the much wider realm of dialogue theory in some detail than to give a survey of current developments. In trying to do justice to all, we would then do justice to none.

Dialogue theory encompasses various types of descriptive and formal studies, aimed at various purposes, on the structure of dialogues. Some of these studies are linguistically oriented, others are closer related to philosophy and logic; many avail themselves of whatever is useful from either discipline. In order that the reader shall be aware of the existence of these alternative approaches, we mention briefly two other strands of research that are particularly of interest for the theory of argumentation.

First, there are Jaakko Hintikka's (1968) language games, which are logically structured in a way that makes them very similar to Lorenzen's dialogue logic. Their motivation, however, is semantical rather than dialogical. Later developments in what is now called Game Theoretical Semantics bring out the difference even more clearly.[1] Studies into the logic of questions and into the logic of information-seeking dialogues, which are related to Game Theoretical Semantics, are certainly of interest for a further development of argumentation theory.[2]

---

[1] Cf. Saarinen (1979), and Hintikka and Kulas (1983).

[2] Cf. Hintikka's study of information-seeking dialogues (1981), Hintikka and Saarinen (1979), and Hintikka and Hintikka (1982). On the logic of questions ("erotetic logic"), see Åqvist (1965, 1975), and Hintikka (1976). Carlson's (1983) contribution to discourse analysis is another relevant example of a study related to Game-Theoretical Semantics.

Second, there is Charles Hamblin's (1970) "formal dialectic." The term *formal dialectic*, which was later adopted by Barth and Krabbe, was in fact introduced by Hamblin. According to Hamblin (1970), the "study of dialectical systems can be pursued *descriptively*, or *formally*," but in his opinion "neither approach is of any importance on its own; for descriptions of actual cases must aim to bring out formalizable features, and formal systems must aim to throw light on actual, describable phenomena" (p. 256). Hamblin's own systems of formal dialectic bring out many interesting features of discourse (1970, 1971). They differ from the Lorenzen approach (and the related Hintikka approach) in that they do not yield a concept of logical validity. For this reason, it might be better not to call these systems, even though they set a paradigm for formal dialogue theory "systems of dialogue *logic*." As may be clear from their use by Woods and Walton, the Hamblin type systems constitute very important tools in fallacy theory. Further development of such systems was undertaken by Jim Mackenzie in a number of papers, whereas Krabbe and Walton (1995) aim at an integration of the Lorenzen and the Hamblin approach.[3]

Lorenzen's insights that are most significant for the development of the study of argumentation, he worked out in collaboration with colleagues and students at the university of Erlangen, West Germany. The group round him, including Kuno Lorenz, Wilhelm Kamlah, and Oswald Schwemmer, is therefore sometimes called the "Erlangen School." Its activities are not confined to logic but extend to the philosophy of science, ethics, mathematics, and the social sciences.

The insights of the Erlangen School regarding argumentation are most clearly expressed in Kamlah and Lorenzen's *Logische Propädeutik; Vorschule des vernünftigen Redens* (1967), Lorenzen's *Normative Logic and Ethics* (1969), and his *Lehrbuch der konstruktiven Wissenschafstheorie* (1987), and Lorenzen and Schwemmer's *Konstruktive Logik, Ethik und Wissenschaftstheorie* (1975).[4] *Dialogische Logik* by Lorenzen and Lorenz (1978) is notable as a document of the development of logical theory within the Erlangen School because it contains a collection of the authors' earlier publications.

Ever since the appearance of Aristotle's *Prior Analytics* logicians have been chiefly concerned with formal aspects of the validity of deductions, pushing the actual activity of arguing in discussions gradually into the background. Accord-

---

[3]Mackenzie's papers include (1979a, 1979b, 1981, 1985, 1989, 1990). For the influence of Hamblin, see our chapter 8, especially Section 8.2. Cf. Woods and Walton (1982). Barth and Martens (1977) were also influenced by Hamblin, but their major analysis uses Lorenzen's conceptual apparatus. Walton (1985b) edited and introduced a special issue of *Synthese* on the Logic of Dialogue.

[4]A second edition of Kamlah and Lorenzen's *Logische Propädeutik* appeared in 1973 (transl. as *Logical propaedeutic: Pre-school of reasonable discourse* (1984)), Lorenzen and Schwemmer's *Konstruktive Logik Ethnic und Wissenschaftstheorie* (Constructive Logic, Ethics, and Philosophy of Science) first appeared in 1973. (The German title of *Lehrbuch der konstruktiven Wissenschaftstheorie* can be translated as Textbook of constructive theory of science.)

ing to Lorenzen and his associates, this has made logic evolve into a discipline increasingly divorced from the practice of argumentation. By now, it seems to have very little or no direct relevance to discussions in colloquial language. The activities of the Erlangen School are calculated to counteract this trend.

Logische Propädeutik was one of their first contributions in this direction. Containing proposals for standardizing linguistic usage, this book aims to provide "the building blocks and rules for all rational discourse" (1973, p. 13). *Konstruktive Logik, Ethik und Wissenschaftstheorie*, "an elementary school of technical and practical rationality" (1975, p. 5), and *Lehrbuch der konstruktiven Wissenschaftstheorie* are intended as a sequel to these "preparatory grades in the School for Rational Discourse."

The moving spirit behind formal dialectics, based on Lorenzen's dialogic logic, is Else Barth, until 1993 professor of philosophy at the University of Groningen, the Netherlands. She studied first with the Norwegian philosopher Arne Naess, then with the Dutch philosopher and mathematician Evert Willem Beth. Barth regards herself, *inter alia*, as a critical rationalist who builds on the ideas of, chiefly, these two masters.[5]

Barth's contributions to analytic philosophy range from intensional logic and feminism to argumentation theory and empirical logic, including the study of the logical foundations of philosophical systems. In this chapter, we shall confine ourselves to her involvement with argumentation theory. Together with Erik Krabbe, she has formulated a formal dialectic theory of argumentation in a book called *From Axiom to Dialogue*.[6]

As we said before, the expression "formal dialectic" was coined by Hamblin (1970). He used it to denote "the setting up of simple systems of precise but not necessarily realistic rules, and the plotting of the properties of dialogues that might be played out in accordance with them" (p. 256). Hamblin was himself the first to try to design such systems of formal dialectics (pp. 253–282). Barth and Krabbe's formal dialectics, however, is not primarily based on Hamblin's proposals, but on Lorenzen's work.

The development of Lorenzen's insights relating to the dialogical definition of logical constants is of historical significance because they signal the initiation of a pragmatic approach to logic. Building on the "semantic tableau" method introduced by Beth, Lorenzen proposed a method of using what he calls "dia-

---

[5]In an interview, Barth declared: "I am in favour of rational criticism, or critical rationalism. [. . .] criticism is a long way from any urge to lay down ultimate foundations. A 'criticist' merely lends trust to ways of looking at things that have so far stood up to the severest form of criticism—and what's more, that trust can be rescinded. [. . .] So there is neither a fixed starting point nor a Utopia. Consistent criticists see much social salvation in constantly putting everything up for discussion—including logic."

[6]See Barth and Krabbe (1982, chaps. 3, 4). Other relevant publications include Barth (1982, 1985b), Barth and Martens (1977), Barth and Martens (1982), and Krabbe (1978, 1982a, 1985a, 1985b, 1986, 1988).

logic tableaux" to determine in what cases a critical discussion about a particular thesis can be won or lost.[7]

Lorenzen set himself the task of taking the connectives and other logically important nonreferring words, and defining them by describing the ways in which they are used in a dispute: in a discussion between people who disagree about something. As explained by Barth (1980):

> So Lorenzen set himself to analyze the intersubjective use of non-referring elements of language (the *structure giving* elements) as they appear in the interaction between a speaker and a *critical* listener—not just a passive or amenable listener prepared to allow himself to be swept along by a *rhetor*, but one who adopts a critical attitude and puts it into words. (p. 45; our translation)

According to Barth (1980), the great significance of the dialogic definition of logical constants achieved in this way, is that Lorenzen thereby demonstrates that modern logic is "essentially" pragmatic:

> First, he has very explicitly introduced man—the language user—into logical theory, so that logic—modern logic—appears in a new, pragmatic garb. Second, he has also shown that man was already there in that logic, albeit not clearly visible to one and all [. . .]. (p. 46; our translation)

9.1 BARTH'S CONCEPTION OF LOGICAL VALIDITY

Before we turn to dialogic logic and formal dialectics, we shall discuss a contribution of Barth's which pertains to the very foundations of argumentation theory. In an inaugural lecture dating from 1972, Barth gives, building on the ideas of Crawshay-Williams, a dual precization of "logical validity."[8] In so doing, she puts forward some insights that are of major significance for the assessment of rationality conceptions.

Barth is concerned with the authority and character of logical laws and rules. In research into the fundamentals of logic, various attempts have been made, from a variety of philosophical perspectives, to provide "foundations" for logic, or to "justify" logic. According to Barth, all these attempts were doomed to fail from the outset because the problem had been wrongly defined: It was always erroneously assumed that there is some unique "thing" called "logic." Moreover,

---

[7]The semantic tableaux method is explained in Beth (1969, Section 1–3). In a letter of August 17 1959, Lorenzen wrote (in German) to Beth: "If one defines the way to make use of the logical particles in an obvious way, and if one then writes out the dialogues, then—with unessential transpositions—exactly your tableaux make their appearance."

[8]Unfortunately, this publication is not available in English; however, a translation of its most crucial section can be found in Barth and Krabbe (1982, pp. 19–22).

all these attempts to provide foundations for logic were themselves based on logic: The principles to be justified were the same as those to which an appeal was made during the justification.[9]

The word *logic* does not refer to any properly defined doctrine or theory, but to a field of study which accommodates a large number of theories. The problem, then, is not how to justify each of these theories singly or collectively, but how to determine whether there are particular reasons for preferring a particular one of these logical systems to any, some, or all of the others. Just like other theories, a logical theory is not *absolutely* correct or incorrect: There is a comparative relation between different logical systems, the one system being better or not better than the next, and thus to be preferred or not to be preferred. Thus we are not confronted with a "Begründungsproblem" (justification problem) but with a "choice problem" (Barth, 1972, pp. 9–18).

This view is directly related to the ideas of Naess and Crawshay-Williams. The question immediately called to mind is what sorts of reason one would have to make the comparison turn to the advantage of one of the logical systems being compared. According to Naess, when such a comparison is being made, one's starting point should be taken from the context in which the comparison is made. This means that the choice of a logical system must be in some relation to the purpose that system and the systems with which it is being compared, are supposed to serve. As Crawshay-Williams puts it, this choice must be made on "methodological" grounds.

The question, then, is to what purpose or purposes a logical system must be suited. Barth adopts Russell's suggestion that logical systems should be regarded as proposals for solving puzzles or problems. What are the problems of logic? Barth believes that a logical system must make it possible to distinguish between correct and incorrect deductions and must solve so-called "logico-intellectual language problems." A logico-intellectual language problem is defined by Barth (1972) as "a problem consisting in the construction of a linguistic fragment, such that a certain intellectual need is met while at the same time one should try to achieve the principal aim of theoretical logic" (p. 14; our translation).[10] The principal aim of theoretical logic is, in Barth's view, the solving of problems of validity; this is something sought after in all logical systems.

The logical validity of an argument depends on the meanings and positions of the "logical constants" used in the argument. The meaning allocated to a

---

[9]According to Barth (1970), anyone who chooses this path ends up in the "Münchhausen trilemma" (see Albert, 1975). She issues a plea for the abandonment of the "comprehensively critical rationalism" advocated by philosophers like W. W. Bartley and Hans Lenk, who thought that everything can be subjected to criticism except "logic." Instead, she favors a truly "all-embracing rationalistic criticism" implying that logical principles and precepts can also be subjected to criticism (p. 17).

[10]Cf. Barth and Krabbe (1982, p. 20).

logical constant in a logical system—its definition—is part of that system. But what is the logico-intellectual language problem for which the definition of a particular constant would constitute a solution? Let us take the definition of *negation* as our example. The primary problem in this connection would be the following: How must the logical constant *not* ($\neg$) be defined in order to make it possible to draw a distinction between correct and incorrect deductions in so far as this correctness depends on the use of *not*?

One solution to this problem is to define the word *not* as follows: The addition of this logical constant to a true statement produces a false statement, and the addition of this logical statement to a false statement produces a true statement. This is only one of the possible solutions to this logico-intellectual language problem: others are also conceivable (and have been proposed). Other logico-intellectual language problems, too, may admit a plurality of solutions. If a proposed solution indeed solves the problem as set, then it is "adequate in relation to this problem." Because a problem can have more than one adequate solution, the question arises on what grounds one should prefer the one solution to the other or others. Barth takes the view that two sorts of consideration underlie this choice: considerations relating to *objective* validity, and considerations relating to *intersubjective* validity.

Considerations of "objective" (or *problem-solving*) validity amount to the following. A logical system or principle is "objectively better" than another system or principle, if and only if there is at least one logico-intellectual language problem for which that system or principle is adequate and the other is not while there is no such problem for which the converse is true. A system or principle that is better than all other competing systems or principles is "objectively valid." Thus the statement form "——is objectively valid" can be regarded as a (first) precization of "——is logically valid." Problem-solving validity accords with Crawshay-Williams's criterion of methodological necessity, and is, in view of its comparative nature, susceptible of gradation.

Considerations of "intersubjective" validity entail the following. Not every language user has to be convinced once and for all of the adequacy of a particular solution for a particular logico-intellectual language problem. This means that precizating logical validity as objective (or problem solving) validity is not sufficient. The second precization that is required Barth calls intersubjective or *conventional* validity. According to this precization, a logical system or principle is sanctioned by a "logical convention" if and only if the members of a well-defined "company" have committed themselves explicitly to that system or principle by a certain type of written declaration to that effect. Barth (1972) regards the statement form "——is at present a conventional principle of a company" as a "second philosophically important clarifying reformulation [precization]" of "——is logically valid" (p. 16; our translation). Conventional validity corresponds to Crawshay-Williams's conventional criterion, and is, in view of its dependence on the acceptance by a company, *time-dependent*.

It will be apparent that in practice one will hardly ever find a logical system or principle that meets the foregoing conditions and deserves to be termed *conventionally valid*. More often than not, there is no "well-defined company" and there is no declaration set out in a signed document. At the best of times it may be possible to find some texts that, though they fall short of giving us signed declarations, nevertheless permit us to deduce that for a particular but imprecisely defined group of people certain principles appear to have the status of conventions. Barth (1972) refers in such cases to "logical semi-conventions" and "semi-conventional principles" having "semi-conventional validity" (p. 16).

We thus find that, according to the dual precization proposed by Barth, the normative strength of the logical systems and principles hitherto commonly accepted draws on two different sources: (1) problem solving (or objective) validity and (2) (semi-)conventional (or intersubjective) validity. According to Barth (1972), both problem-solving validity and conventional validity are necessary conditions, but it is only jointly that they constitute a sufficient condition for being able to arrive at "the optimal course of monological and dialogical acts of language" (p. 17; our translation).

Precizating "logical validity" in terms of a notion of "problem validity," susceptible of gradation, and a time-dependent notion of "conventional validity" leads to the point of view that no absolute value can be attached in advance to any logical system or principle. It also leads to the view that a totally relativistic standpoint implying that the value of a logical system or principle depends exclusively on the evaluating audience or company, is to be rejected. Starting from the three approaches to rationality Toulmin distinguishes in *Knowing and Acting*, the approach chosen by Barth (following in the footsteps of Naess and Crawshay-Williams) can best be characterized as a *critical* approach. Although Barth's exposition relates to logical validity, it also provides a useful starting point for precizating the rationality norms pertaining to the assessment of argumentation. Clearly, the same dual precization is then fully applicable.[11]

Applying this critical conception of rationality to the study of argumentation, means that any preconceived idea of universal rules for argumentation has to be abandoned. Rather than as being absolute and timeless, argumentation rules are then seen as more or less adequate to the task of solving the problems they are supposed to solve, and their jurisdiction is confined to the company that, at a particular time, is prepared to adhere to them. In order to judge the adequacy of a system of rules proposed in the study of argumentation it will, therefore, be necessary to consider which problems this system can solve and whether the rules involved are acceptable to a company of (potential) interlocutors.

---

[11]In van Eemeren and Grootendorst (1984) it is argued why Barth's conception of rationality is better suited to the study of argumentation than that of Toulmin or Perelman.

9.2 THE LOGICAL PROPAEDEUTIC OF THE ERLANGEN SCHOOL

The basic assumption on which the logical propaedeutic of the Erlangen School is built is that, in order to prevent them from speaking at cross purposes in interminable monologues, the interlocutors' linguistic usage in a discussion or conversation must comply with certain norms and rules. Only when they share a number of fixed postulates with respect to linguistic usage, they can conduct a meaningful discussion. The logical propaedeutic is aimed at constructing an "ortholanguage" (Lorenzen & Schwemmer, 1975, p. 24) that enables interlocutors to engage in a meaningful process of argumentation.

The proposed ortholanguage is constructed from scratch (*ab ovo*). In order to explain how it is to be so constructed, however, one may take advantage of such everyday usage as language users are already accustomed to, and, to some extent, the ortholanguage is a reconstruction of ordinary colloquial language.[12] Kamlah and Lorenzen start the construction of their ortholanguage at what they regard as the basic units of verbal communication: *elementary statements* ("Elementaraussagen"). From here they arrive at the standardization of *complex* or *compound statements*, in which *logical constants* play an important role. We give only a general and selective outline of their proposals, concentrating chiefly on the standardization of logical constants.

Elementary statements are indispensable for speaking to other language users, and they are used by speakers of all natural languages. The statement "William is a dog" is an example of an elementary statement. In it, a so-called *predicator*, "dog," is attributed to an object identified by the proper name "William." In the statement "William is not a dog," by contrast, the predicator "dog" is withheld from the object "William." This, too, is an elementary statement, just as are the statements "William sniffs at Betsy" and "William does not sniff at Betsy," in which the predicator "sniff at" is attributed to or withheld from two consecutive objects. An elementary statement, then, is one in which a predicator is attributed to, or withheld from, one or more (consecutive) objects.

Kamlah and Lorenzen (1973) propose the following standardization of the forms of elementary statements (p. 34ff):

(a) $x_1(,x_2,\ldots,x_n) \, \varepsilon \, P$

(b) $x_1(,x_2,\ldots,x_n) \, \varepsilon' \, P$

---

[12]Kamlah and Lorenzen (1973) want to construct the ortholanguage in a joint effort with its potential users. This is a crucial element of "constructivism." It is carried through by starting from operations mastered by all language users and used by them "immer schon" (all along), and by putting forward proposed systematic normalizations for these operations.

In this standardized form, $x_1, \ldots, x_n$ are variables for proper names, P is a predicator variable, ε is an abbreviation of the Greek ἐστίν ("is") and ε' an abbreviation of its negation ("is not"). Substitution of proper names and predicators for the relevant variables in this statement form, which is not confined to any particular language, produces an elementary statement. Notice that not all sentences express statements, but only those that can be asserted or denied (p. 30). Thus imperatives and questions may be put into sentences, but they are not statements. An elementary statement, then, is simply a statement by which it is asserted (case a) or denied (case b) that a particular predicator belongs to a particular object or to particular consecutive objects.[13]

The use of proper names makes elementary statements independent of the particular context of discourse in which they are uttered, a feature which makes them suited for scientific usage. For, proper names take the place of *ostensive* (or *deictic*) *acts*, which are by contrast entirely dependent on context. If one wishes to attribute a particular predicator, for example, "dog," to an object, one may do so by pointing at the object and saying: "That is a dog." However, it is also possible to give the object a name, for example, "William," and then to say: "William is a dog." Thus, the proper name "William" replaces the demonstrative pronoun "that" and renders the ostensive act superfluous.

Although it is possible in principle to assign a proper name to anything to which a predicator can be attributed, in practice this is not feasible; neither is it necessary. For this reason, alongside proper names, use is made of *definite descriptions*, which generally consist of a small group of words and, like proper names, refer to one thing only. Instead of the proper name "William," for example, one might use the definite description "the animal at the lamp-post." It is immediately apparent from this example that replacing a proper name by a definite description makes the language user more dependent on the context of the discourse, though it is possible to minimize this dependence.

Obviously, it is of paramount importance for a meaningful discussion that the predicators occurring in elementary or other statements be used in the same way by all the interlocutors. A common method of teaching language users to use predicators correctly is to give examples and counterexamples: "That is a dog, that is not a dog but a cat, that is not a dog but a cow," and so on. This method, which is extremely common in primary language acquisition, is called "introduction by means of examples" (1973, p. 29).

But not all predicators can be introduced by means of examples and counterexamples. In particular, this is not possible in the case of abstract predicators ("Abstraktoren") like "fact," "concept," and "meaning." We shall not discuss this in greater depth here, but merely observe that such predicators are often used

---

[13]Obviously, this concurs with notations from predicate logic: $P(x1, \ldots, xn)$ and $\neg P(x1, \ldots, xn)$. But the second type of statement is considered to be complex (not elementary) in predicate logic.

differently by different interlocutors. This could happen even in the case of nonabstract predicators, and therefore it is necessary to achieve a more precise standardization of the use of predicators in general, in order to eliminate the possibility of talking at cross purposes. To this end, explicit agreements must be negotiated to guarantee the correct, consistent, and unambiguous use of predicators.

Predicators whose introduction is effected by means of explicit agreements are called *terms* ("Termini") of the ortholanguage. Making use of those terms that are already available, it is possible to introduce new terms by means of *definitions*. These consist of two or more *predicator rules* (Kamlah & Lorenzen, 1973, p. 73). A predicator rule indicates that it is legitimate to move from one given elementary statement to another. The standardization effected by predicator rules can be illustrated as follows:

(a) $x \, \varepsilon \, \text{dog} \Rightarrow x \, \varepsilon \, \text{mammal}$

(b) $x \, \varepsilon \, \text{dog} \Rightarrow x \, \varepsilon' \, \text{mollusc}$

Expressed dialogically, this means that it is established that whoever asserts a substitution instance of "$x \, \varepsilon \, \text{dog}$," for example, "William is a dog," may neither dispute a corresponding substitution instance of "$x \, \varepsilon \, \text{mammal}$," for example, "William is a mammal" (case a), nor a given substitution instance of "$x \, \varepsilon' \, \text{mollusc}$," for example, "William is not a mollusc" (case b).

In the case of a definition, two or more predicator rules are combined in such a way that defining can be regarded as a form of abbreviating. Moreover, these definitory predicator rules are combined into one compound predicator rule that may be read either from left to right or from right to left. To clarify this, let us take another example.

Just now we described terms as predicators introduced by means of explicit agreements. The use of the term "term" can now be standardized as follows (the conjunction mark $\wedge$ indicates that two predicator rules have been amalgamated and the sign $\Leftrightarrow$ shows that the rule can also be read in reverse direction (1973, p. 79):[14]

$x \, \varepsilon \, \text{term} \Leftrightarrow x \, \varepsilon \, \text{predicator} \wedge x \, \varepsilon \, \text{explicitly agreed}$

On this basis, the definition of "term" reads as follows (the sign $\leftrightharpoons$ indicates that this is a definition):

term $\leftrightharpoons$ explicitly agreed predicator

---

[14]Here we adopt the symbols for logical constants used by Kamlah and Lorenzen, because they wish the symbolic notation to express the mirror-image relation existing between conjunction and disjunction (in their terminology *Adjunktion*).

By explicit agreements on usage, the formulation of predicator rules, and the introduction of new terms by means of definitions, a standardization of the use of predicators is to be effected. This will bring about that those language users who are acquainted with the standardization and adhere to it will use the predicators occurring in their discussions correctly, consistently, and unambiguously. The first and most fundamental condition for the success of a discussion has thus been fulfilled.

Another condition, however, is that the interlocutors can agree as to the manner in which the *truth* of elementary sentences can be established: The interlocutors must ensure that they reach agreement as to whether a predicator, which is clear enough by itself, is or is not *rightly* attributed to, or withheld from, a particular object. In order to establish the truth value of an elementary statement, it must be checked whether the predicator does or does not belong to the object.

This check, however, cannot be entrusted to just any language user: It must be carried out by *expert and rational* speakers (1973, p. 119). "Expert" here means that the language users concerned are competent to carry out the relevant check in a correct manner. "Rational" means that they will display an open attitude both towards their interlocutors and towards the objects discussed, and will not in any event allow themselves to be guided purely by emotions, habit and tradition. Kamlah and Lorenzen (1973) summarize their verification procedure as follows:

> If every other person who shares my language, and who is expert and rational, would, after suitable checks, apply the predicator "*P*" (or a synonymous predicator) to an object, then I too am entitled to say "this is *P*" (in which case the predicator "*P*" belongs to that thing). If this condition is fulfilled, then I may say further: "the statement 'this is *P*' is true" (in which case the predicator "true" belongs to that statement), or alternatively: "the assertion 'this is *P*' is justified." (pp. 119–120; our translation)

When competent language users have carried out the proper check in the appropriate manner, and this check has led to a unanimously positive judgment, one is justified in describing the elementary statement as *true*. This does not mean, however, that an elementary statement to which, at a particular moment, no one happens to agree could not be true. The absence of agreement may, after all, be the result of a lack of necessary facilities for carrying out the required checks. Thus an (elementary) statement may be perfectly true even though there is nobody, or not yet anybody, prepared to confirm it. Of course, it *is* only true if someone in a position to carry out the proper checks in the correct manner would, if he actually did carry them out, be obliged to endorse it (p. 124).

Kamlah and Lorenzen (1973) call this verification procedure, which depends on the carrying out of suitable checks by competent language users, the "interpersonal verification" of statements. They regard it as a "general framework" within which verification of elementary statements ought to take place (pp. 121, 125). The particular methods and techniques used in the checks may vary considerably from case to case, and they may change radically during the course of time. Interpersonal verification is thus not itself a "method" of determining the truth value of elementary statements, but a universal and constant procedural principle, serving as a general guideline.

Interpersonal verification is concerned exclusively with elementary statements. Complex statements, however, can also be put forward, attacked and defended in a discussion; indeed, generally speaking, they are more common. The truth value of such statements can only be established after an analysis has determined the manner in which they are composed of elementary statements: Complex statements must first be decomposed. This requires an understanding of the principles that play a part in their composition.

Complex statements are constructed from elementary statements by means of *logical constants*, which Kamlah and Lorenzen call *logical particles*: connectives ("Junktoren") and quantifiers ("Quantoren"). Establishing the truth value of complex statements therefore demands a standardization of the use of logical particles. To this end, Kamlah and Lorenzen use a method introduced by Lorenzen as early as 1958.[15] They introduce the logical particles dialogically, an approach quite different from that of a definition using truth values, which is the customary procedure in classical propositional logic. In order to effect a dialogical introduction of logical particles, Kamlah and Lorenzen formulate rules for the use of these particles in a dialogue.

The dialogical method makes full use of the fact that human language usage is chiefly directed towards a listener or listeners. If the listener reacts, then a dialogue has been initiated. Statements are not posited as true or false "just like that": they are asserted or disputed in front of an interlocutor who may act as an *opponent* or as a *proponent* of the same statements (1973, pp. 158–159). A dialogical definition of logical particles (connectives and quantifiers), therefore, is to provide an indication of what course the dialogue must take to justify or refute the statements constructed by means of these particles.

We shall discuss briefly how logical particles are defined in the logical propaedeutics (1973, pp. 159–160), confining ourselves to the connectives:[16]

(1) "and"   - *conjunction*

(2) "or"   - *disjunction* (in Kamlah and Lorenzen terminology: "Adjunktion")

(3) "if...then" - *implication* (in Kamlah and Lorenzen terminology: "Subjunktion")

---

[15]See Lorenzen and Lorenz (1978) for the original articles on the subject.

[16]From a constructive point of view, the dialogical definition of quantifiers is actually the essential part of the enterprise, because their alleged semantic definitions make no sense to the constructivist. For illustrative purposes, we prefer to concentrate on the connectives.

(4) "not"   - *negation*

Conjunction ($\wedge$)

Suppose a speaker acts as the proponent of the thesis $A \wedge B$, that is, he asserts the conjunction $A \wedge B$. Another speaker, who acts as the opponent of this thesis, is then entitled to choose either of the two component statements and cast doubt on its veracity. If the proponent is unable to defend this statement, then the opponent wins, and this outcome is definitive. If, however, the proponent parries the attack by a successful defense of the attacked component statement, then he wins, but not definitively, since the opponent is still entitled to undertake a second attack. If in the first round the opponent unsuccessfully attacked (say) A, he may now attack B. If the second attack succeeds, then the opponent wins (definitively); and if the proponent succeeds in parrying this second attack too, by successfully defending the attacked statement B, then *he* wins, this time definitively.

Disjunction ($\vee$)

Suppose a speaker acts as the proponent of the thesis $A \vee B$, that is, he asserts the disjunction $A \vee B$. The opponent of this thesis is then entitled to attack the complex statement by casting doubt on all of it at once. The proponent may now choose one of the two component statements and attempt to defend it. If he succeeds, he wins, and in this case he at once wins definitively. If his defense fails, he loses, but at this stage he does not lose definitively, since he can still substantiate his statement in a second round of defense, if he produces a successful defense of the other component statement. If this second defense is undertaken and succeeds, the proponent wins after all, and then the outcome is definitive; if the second defense fails as well, the proponent loses definitively.

The symbolic notations $\wedge$ and $\vee$ reflect the fact that in several respects conjunction and disjunction are dialogic mirror images one of the other. In the case of a conjunction, the choice of the component statement to be defended is up to the opponent; in the case of a disjunction, it is up to the proponent. In the case of a conjunction, the proponent needs two rounds to reach a definitive victory while he has to lose only one round in order to lose definitively; in the case of a disjunction, the converse is true: Now the opponent needs two rounds for a definitive win, and the loss of only one round is enough to bring about the opponent's definitive defeat.

Implication ($\rightarrow$)

Suppose a speaker acts as the proponent of the thesis $A \rightarrow B$, that is, he asserts the implication $A \rightarrow B$. The opponent of this thesis is then entitled to attack this statement by casting doubt on all of it at once. If he does so, he is himself obliged to assert A. The proponent of the thesis $A \to B$ is now in turn entitled to attack A, and the opponent is obliged to defend A. If the proponent does indeed cast doubt on A and the opponent fails to defend A successfully, then the proponent wins the entire dialogue, and the outcome is at once definitive. If, on the other hand, the opponent succeeds in his defense of A, then the proponent must go on to assert and defend B. If this defense succeeds, the proponent wins definitively, but if it fails, he loses, and definitively so.

Thus in the case of an implication, too, the dialogue may consist of two rounds. However, in the case of conjunctions and disjunctions one of the two parties always has to persist through two rounds of the same kind in order to win: In the case of a conjunction, the proponent has to defend a statement twice in order to achieve definitive victory, and in the case of a disjunction, the opponent has to persist through two rounds of the proponent's defense in order to achieve definitive victory. If in the case of an implication the dialogue runs to two rounds, then the parties have to put up a defense in only one round each: In the first round the opponent defends a statement (A) and in the second the proponent defends a statement (B). In both rounds the proponent has a chance of definitive victory, whereas the opponent can achieve definitive victory only in the second round.

Negation ($\neg$)

Suppose a speaker acts as the proponent of the thesis $\neg A$, that is, he asserts the negation $\neg A$. To attack the assertion $\neg A$, the opponent is to contradict the proponent and assert A. If the opponent subsequently succeeds to defend A successfully, then he obtains a definitive victory. If, on the other hand, the opponent is unable to defend A successfully, then he loses and the proponent of the thesis $\neg A$ wins definitively.

On the strength of these definitions of logical connectives Kamlah and Lorenzen (1973) formulate the rules for the use of "junctors" which are listed in Fig. 9.1. These rules lay down the right to assert or dispute a particular statement

	asssertion	attack	defence
conjunction	$A \wedge B$ $A \wedge B$	L(eft)? R(ight)?	A B
adjunction	$A \vee B$ $A \vee B$	? ?	A B
subjunction	$A \to B$	A?	B
negation	$\neg A$	A?	-

FIG. 9.1. Rules for the use of connectives.

in a dialogue in a particular manner. They may therefore be regarded as a dialogical definition of these logical particles (p. 210).

If the proponent in a dialogue uses a conjunction, the opponent can choose from two possible lines of attack: $L?$ and $R?$. If the proponent uses a disjunction that is attacked by the opponent, he has the choice of two possible lines of defense: A and B. Once an implication has been attacked, the proponent may, instead of offering a defense of B, opt for a counterattack on A. And finally, whenever the attacked statement is a negation, the proponent has no direct line of defense against this attack. In that case, he has no alternative but to carry out a counterattack.

The rules for using connectives have a decomposing effect.[17] This means that a dialogue that contains statements that are composed by means of connectives will always, after a finite number of moves, lead to the assertion of elementary statements. For, inspection of the rules shows that every statement that occurs in some attacking or defending move must have occurred as a component statement (or substatement) of one of the original assertions. This means that the interlocutors must know how a decision can be taken regarding the right to assert an elementary sentence, before they can determine whether a defense was successful, and hence before they can determine who has finally won the dialogue.

Moreover, in order to be able to determine in what cases the proponent of a compound statement can conclude the dialogue with victory, it is necessary to have more detailed rules for the conduct of dialogues. Rules are needed to indicate which statements may be attacked at any particular moment, and which may be defended, and whose turn it is to move. Kamlah and Lorenzen (1973) distinguish three different sets of rules, and hence three different types of dialogue game. Here we discuss only the rules of the type of game they call the "constructive dialogue game" (pp. 213–215).[18]

Starting Rule

The proponent starts by asserting a thesis; the partners in the dialogue take turns to move.

General Dialogue Rule

The proponent attacks one of the statements put forward by the opponent or defends himself against the opponent's most recent attack; the opponent

---

[17]This is a feature they share with the rules for semantic tableaux.

[18]Besides the constructive dialogue game, Kamlah and Lorenzen present the "strictly constructive" and the "classical" dialogue game. The Erlangen School generally prefers the constructive variant.

attacks the statement made by the proponent in the preceding move or defends himself against the proponent's attack in the preceding move.[19]

Winning Rule

The proponent wins if he successfully defends an attacked elementary statement or if the opponent fails to defend an attacked elementary statement.

These rules for the constructive dialogue game refer to so-called "material" dialogues. That is to say, ultimate victory depends on the successful defense of an elementary statement. In classical logic, however, sometimes the truth or falsity of a compound statement can be established without any need to bother about the truth values of the component elementary statements. This is the case with logical truths (*tautologies*) and logical falsities (*contradictions*), since their truth or falsity is not dependent on the contents of the component statements, but on the *statement form* of which such a compound statement is a substitution instance.

Similarly, some compound statements can be defended in a dialogue, no matter whether their elementary components can be successfully defended. It suffices to make sure that each elementary statement is first defended by the opponent, before the proponent (of the original compound statement) needs to present a defense. In that case the proponent can simply copy the defense given by the opponent. Let, for instance, A be an elementary statement and let the proponent assert the compound statement $A \rightarrow A$. Then the opponent is the first one to present a defense of A. If he fails, the proponent wins definitively. If he succeeds, there is to be a second round. But in this round the proponent has to present a defense of A, and all the proponent needs to do to assure a definitive gain is to copy the successful defense presented by the opponent in the preceding round. According to Kamlah and Lorenzen, a statement is to be called *(constructively) logically true*, if and only if the proponent can guarantee that, ultimately, he will have to defend only some elementary statement that has been asserted by the opponent at some earlier stage (p. 220).

Constructive logical truth (and constructive logical falsity) can be established in dialogues in which statement forms ("formulas") take the place of statements. This gives rise to a "formal" dialogue. To make formal dialogue possible, one has to change the general dialogue rule and to stipulate that the proponent is prohibited, when defending a formula, from attacking any elementary formulas; the opponent, however, may attack elementary formulas, but then the proponent has no defense. The winning rule must also be modified. So the rules of the formal (constructive) dialogue game are as follows (1973, p. 221):

---

[19]Obviously, this rule may block the occurrence of several rounds pertaining to one and the same assertion, for instance two attacks, by O, on "$A \wedge B$." This is only to say that a *definitive* loss or win may need more than one dialogue.

General dialogue rule of constructive formal dialogue games:

1. The proponent may attack only one of the compound formulas put forward by the opponent, or he may defend himself against the opponent's last attack.

2. The opponent may attack only the statement made by the proponent in the preceding move, or he may defend himself against an attack in the proponent's last move.

Winning rule of constructive formal dialogue games:

The proponent wins if he has to defend an elementary formula already put forward by the opponent.

Together with other rules, including those for the use of logical particles, these various sets of rules for dialogue constitute attempts at an adequate standardization of argumentative linguistic usage. The rules jointly determine how a dialogue between the proponent and the opponent of a thesis ought to progress.

Before the dialogue proper starts, the opponent may advance certain "hypotheses," but the proponent then has the right to hold the opponent to these, and may make use of this right by attacking the hypotheses in his defense of his thesis. In that case the opponent's hypotheses effectively function as the premises of an argument whose conclusion appears in the dialogue as the proponent's thesis (1973, p. 223).

As may be seen from the rules, each interlocutor's contribution must always be a reaction to some earlier move by his adversary (except for the very first move, of course). The proponent formulates the thesis, after which the opponent attacks it, possibly but not necessarily starting from certain hypotheses. The proponent defends himself against the attacks of the opponent and in so doing may make use of the opponent's hypotheses. The opponent consistently attacks all statements advanced by the proponent in defense of his thesis. The rules of the game determine not only whose turn it is, but also what moves are legitimate and when one of the two parties has won the dialogue game—and who the winner is.[20]

The logical propaedeutic makes a first contribution to designing an adequate apparatus that is to enable joint deliberation on the truth of statements. The rules proposed can be used by interlocutors who have jointly set themselves the target of using verbal means in a dialogue to resolve a dispute about an opinion. All along, it has been tacitly assumed that the interlocutors agree on the purpose of the discussion. In practice, however, this is quite often not the case. A more encompassing theory of argumentation must, therefore, not only provide the technical means to conduct discussions in a context of agreement on objectives and norms for discussion, but also means to discuss these very objectives.

---

[20]Therefore, dialogue games are games in the sense of mathematical game theory. The same holds for Barth and Krabbe's systems of formal dialectics (Section 9.3).

In this connection, it is relevant to point to the books mentioned as sequels to the logical propaedeutic. Kamlah and Lorenzen (1973, p. 231) regard their logical propaedeutic as a "preparatory course" in logic ("logische Vorschule") for a "practical main course" ("praktische Hauptschule"). The practical complement of the logical propaedeutic is provided with a foundation in Lorenzen and Schwemmer's *Konstruktive Logik, Ethik und Wissenschaftstheorie.*

Practical knowledge is needed to eliminate possible sources of conflict and to constructively resolve existing conflict situations relating to purposes and norms. Lorenzen and Schwemmer regard it as the task of ethics to lay down principles of conflict resolution, to the extent that a resolution can be achieved by verbal means and in a teachable fashion. Ethics, they believe, should study the principles of arguing for or against particular objectives (1973, pp. 150–151).

9.3 BARTH AND KRABBE'S SYSTEMS OF FORMAL DIALECTICS

Barth and Krabbe's (1982) formal dialectics provide systematic foundations from the point of view of conflict resolution for a number of rules for formal and material dialogues drawn up by Kamlah and Lorenzen (chaps. 3, 4). They dub their rules the *formal$_3$ rules* of formal dialectics.[21] By a formal$_3$ dialectics they understand a system of rules for the conduct of discussions aimed at the resolution of conflicts about avowed opinions (1978, p. 341; 1982, p. 55).

The *formal$_3$ rules* of formal dialectics comprise both rules for the use of logical constants in attack and defense, and general rules and norms for discussion.[22] The rules for using logical constants (particles), Barth and Krabbe call *formal$_2$ rules.* Formal dialectics consists of a large number of formal$_3$ rules among which the rules for using logical constants (formal$_2$ rules) find their place. This explains why Barth and Krabbe refer to their systems sometimes as "systems of formal$_3$ dialectics."

Just like the logical propaedeutic of the Erlangen School, formal dialectics treats argumentation as a dialogic process. Two roles are distinguished: the role

---

[21]Barth and Krabbe (1978, pp. 340–341) justify the use of the indices with the term *formal* to differentiate between different meanings of formal: "we write:

(a) "formal$_1$" where the word "formal" relates to Platonist forms or ideas [. . .];

(b) "formal$_2$" where the word "formal" relates to syntactic forms;

(c)"formal$_3$" where the word "formal" relates to courses of action or procedures which take place according to a system of rules." (Cf. also 1982, Section 1.3.) In the present context, two other senses of "formal" are important (Krabbe, 1982a, p. 3). When Hamblin (1970, p. 256) contrasted "formal dialectic" with "descriptive dialectic," the term "formal" was used to denote the nonempirical, or even the normative (formal$_4$). A fifth sense (formal$_5$) occurs where "formal dialogue games" are contrasted with "material dialogue games." In games of the first type, the participants use formulas that remain uninterpreted, except for the logical constants; in games of the second type, they make use of meaningful statements, some of which can be verified or falsified by extradialogical means.

[22]Formal$_3$ dialectic systems may very well be material in the sense that the language used in dialogues consists of meaningful statements, and not of formulas.

of proponent and the role of opponent. Argumentation is the totality of moves made by the interlocutors taking part in the discussion in their argumentative roles as proponent and opponent. The rules presented in formal dialectics lay down what moves are permissible in a discussion, in which circumstances a proponent has successfully defended a thesis, and in which circumstances an opponent has successfully attacked one.

The rules of formal dialectics thus standardize discussions. In that sense, formal dialectics may be said to be a *formal* theory of argumentation; and it is to emphasize the special meaning that the term "formal" has in this context that Barth and Krabbe give it a distinguishing index (formal$_3$). The term *dialectics* as used by Barth and Krabbe refers to theory of discussion.[23] Formal dialectics is designed to provide a *critical dialogic* system of rules. It gives not just one system of rules, however, but several. Like Kamlah and Lorenzen, Barth and Krabbe distinguish three main alternatives for a system of regulations of dialogue, and they discuss nonmaterial (purely formal) variants (using formulas) and material variants (using interpreted statements) of each of these. We shall confine ourselves here to the nonmaterial variant of the constructive alternative.[24]

The rules of formal dialectics relate to discussions the purpose of which is to resolve conflicts (or disputes) concerning opinions which have been put forward by one or more of the interlocutors ("avowed opinions"). The point at issue in a dispute in which the Proponent *P(aul)* and the Opponent *O(lga)* are the parties is a statement *T* which was asserted by *P* and attacked by *O*. *T* is the initial thesis of the discussion. *O* may also have made one or more statements expressing a standpoint starting from which *O* challenges *P* to defend *T*. These statements constitute *O*'s set of concessions, abbreviated *Con*; they correspond to the opponent's "hypotheses" in Kamlah and Lorenzen's logical propaedeutic. What is at stake in the discussion is whether or not, in the light of *Con*, *T* is to be accepted.

The language user who has taken upon herself the role of *O* tries systematically to demonstrate that, on the basis of *Con*, it is not necessary to accept *T*, and the language user who has assumed the role of *P* tries systematically to show that it is. Thus the role of *O* entails the persistent *attacking* of *T*, and the role of *P* the consistent *defense* of *T*. Therefore—in contrast to what is most commonly experienced in actual discussions—*O* has no thesis of her own to defend, and *P* has nothing to attack (unless *P* defends a statement of his own by means of a "counterattack" against an attack by *O*).

---

[23]Care must be taken to ensure that no confusion arises between the meaning of the term *dialectics* in "formal dialectic(s)," and the deviant meaning given to the word dialectic by Fichte and Marx. Until the 17th century, "dialectica" was (with some interruptions) the usual name for logic. See Scholz (1967, p. 8).

[24]Besides a "constructive" dialectic, Barth and Krabbe discuss "minimal" dialectic and "classical" dialectic. The constructive and classical dialectics correspond to the similarly named dialogue games of Kamlah and Lorenzen.

This distribution of roles implies that the rules of formal dialectics formulated by Barth and Krabbe are restricted to what they call "simple" or "pure" conflicts. Conflicts in which both language users have a thesis to defend, they term *mixed* (1982, p. 56). For one type of mixed conflict ("mixed conflicts under complete opposition"), they propose a material system of formal dialectics (1982, Section IV, 5.2). This system does not belong to one of the main types mentioned before.

The rules of formal dialectics lay down the manner in which O may attack T, the manner in which P may defend T, the circumstances in which one of the two parties wins, and who the winner is. We shall not list all the rules formulated by Barth and Krabbe—there are more than thirty of them—but will confine ourselves to a concise survey.

Formal dialectics consists of five different sorts of rule, each of which serves a different purpose. For each sort we shall indicate the norm-giving purpose, after which we present a number of rules that indicate a way to comply with this norm. These five sorts of rule are preceded by a number of "elementary" rules and are rounded off by rules establishing "victory and defeat."

Elementary Rules

The *first* elementary rule says that there are language users who assume the roles of P and O. In the simplest case, one language user assumes the role of P and another the role of O. However, it is also possible for one language user to take on the roles of both P and O, or for two or more language users to take on the same role. If, on the other hand, no language users can be found who are prepared to fulfil the roles of P and O, then no discussion falling within the scope of formal dialectics can take place. Of course, some other sort of discussion may ensue instead, such as one serving as an opportunity for the interlocutors to provide one another with information, but only if there are language users who voluntarily take upon themselves the roles of P and O will the rules of formal dialectics apply.

The *second* elementary rule clarifies the roles of P and O. According to this rule, O should adopt the dialogue attitude of "contra-position" with regard to any statements of P's and the attitude of "pro-position" with regard to her own statements. P is to adopt pro-position with regard to his own statements and a neutral position with regard to the statements of O. Contra-position with regard to a statement S implies an unconditional right to attack S, pro-position implies a conditional obligation to defend S, and neutral position implies neither of these. This means that O may attack any statement of P's and that P must defend his own statements as soon as they are attacked by O. P may not attack O's statements, except by way of defense through counterattack. By these definitions the asymmetry of the roles of P and O, a characteristic of simple or pure conflicts, is established.

The *third* elementary rule states that there are two ways of defending a statement S once it has been attacked: protective defense (*pd*) and counterattack (*ca*). A counterattack must therefore be seen as a "defending move," which means that it may be carried out by *P*, who by the terms of the second elementary rule would otherwise not be allowed to attack *O*'s statements.

The *fourth* elementary rule adds a rider to this, viz., that all attacking and defending moves must relate to statements, and that the range of words and syntactic forms that can be used in an admissible attack or defense is to be functionally determined by the syntax and wordings of the statement attacked or defended. Whether a certain move is permissible, Barth and Krabbe state, shall depend on what has been said, and not on intentions, beliefs, et cetera. They call this the *Principle of (verbal) Externalization of Dialectics* (1982, p. 60).

The *fifth*, and final, elementary rule lays down the consequences of violating one or more of the rules of formal dialectics. If either of the parties does anything or says anything which according to the rules of formal dialectics is not one of the permitted moves and which is detrimental to the other party's interests, the other party may withdraw from the discussion without thereby losing it. The party guilty of the violation then forfeits all its rights in the discussion and can even, if desired, be censured as "irrational with respect to the present dialectic situation." The importance of this rule, according to Barth and Krabbe, is that it makes it risky to make irrelevant remarks in a discussion by, for example, changing the subject or advancing an *argumentum ad hominem*, or to insult the other party, threaten him, deprive him of his liberty, or cause him actual physical harm.

The nonelementary rules of formal dialectics are grouped to correspond to the various requirements that the system is intended to meet, namely that the system be "systematic," "realistic," "thoroughgoing," "orderly," and "dynamic." We review these requirements one by one, indicating what they entail and what sort of rules Barth and Krabbe formulate in order to implement them.

Systematic Dialectics

The norm for a systematic dialectics is that *P* shall always have a chance to defend a statement by another statement once it has been attacked. Compliance with this norm is achieved by making the defense progress step by step. Every intermediate thesis is therefore treated as a "conditional" defense of the previous intermediate thesis. This implies that if an intermediate thesis can in some way be defended unconditionally, the preceding ones, and ultimately the initial thesis, will, retroactively, be unconditionally defended as well.

In order that discussions may proceed step by step, they are divided into chains of arguments. These are to be compared to the different rounds in the dialogue games of Kamlah and Lorenzen. For instance, distinct attacks, by *O*, on parts of a conjunction would belong to distinct chains of arguments. These chains of arguments are then subdivided into local discussions with local theses. A new local discussion starts off with each new attack by *O*, the statement attacked being its local thesis, whereas the set of local concessions comprises all concessions present in the chain. Each local discussion is, in a sense, a dialogue in its own right, centred upon its own local thesis. Local discussions, finally, are subdivided into stages (turns to speak).

Realistic Dialectics

The gist of the norm for a realistic dialectics is that P should, in certain cases, have an opportunity to successfully complete the unconditional defense of a statement that has been attacked. A rule to implement this, which P may in favorable circumstances avail himself of, states that a local thesis can be defended unconditionally by means of an appropriate *Ipse dixisti!* remark. An appropriate *Ipse dixisti!* remark consists of the utterance of the words "*Ipse dixisti!*" ("You said it yourself!") by P as soon as O concedes the local thesis, that is, the statement most recently attacked by O, or, conversely, as soon as O attacks a statement made by P which O herself conceded at an earlier stage of the same chain. The consequence of an unconditional defense of a local thesis by P is that O forfeits the right to continue the discussion *in the same chain of arguments*, and this means that O has lost that chain.

Thoroughgoing Dialectics

The norm for a thoroughgoing dialectics is that P must be given an opportunity to defend his local thesis in all possible ways, and that O must have a chance to attack P's thesis in all possible ways. This norm is effected by means of rules enabling either party to abandon a lost or hopeless chain of arguments in order to start a new chain. Losing a chain, therefore, does not automatically mean loss of the entire discussion, since according to the rules of thoroughgoing dialectics O can try various lines of attack, and P can try various lines of defense. However, opening a new chain must always be preceded by the abandonment (forced or voluntarily) of an old chain, which means that that chain is irrevocably lost.

Orderly Dialectics

The norm for an orderly dialectics is that at every stage in the discussion both parties' rights and duties must be clearly and accessibly defined. (Notice that the preceding rules leave it undetermined *how long* certain dialogue attitudes, rights, and duties are to remain in force.) This aim is achieved by taking advantage of the segmentation of each chain of arguments into a series of successive local discussions and by restricting the rights and duties arising out of P and O's dialogue attitudes (see the second elementary rule) to these local discussions, instead of regarding them as applying to the discussion as a whole. As soon as a new local discussion begins, the rights and duties of its predecessor become void. As we said before, a new local discussion arises whenever O

attacks one of P's statements; the newly attacked statement is then the new local thesis of the new local discussion. However, O's preexisting concessions continue to apply.

Dynamic Dialectics

The norm for a dynamic dialectics is that the rules of formal dialectics must further the revision and flux of opinions. One rule to implement this stipulates that an inevitable result should be reached as quickly as possible. To achieve this, one should see to it that the rights of the parties to start new chains, and the length of chains, local discussions, and stages be limited. In other words, it is to be avoided that the parties have a chance to repeat themselves needlessly and thus needlessly prolong the discussion. To achieve this the following rules are proposed:[25]

(1) If at a particular point the discussion can continue on more than one path (i.e., if various chains of arguments are possible), each path may only be taken once.

(2) A statement (utterance) by P may, within a particular chain of arguments, not be made a local thesis by an attack by O more than once.

(3) A local thesis may not be repeated by P in the same chain, as long as O has not granted any additional concessions in that chain.

(4) A counterattack of one particular sort may not be carried out on a statement more than once in the same local discussion.

(5) Stages may not contain more than one utterance of one sentence.

Two other rules intended to implement the same norm are:

(6) The only structural operators which may be used are those whose "meaning in use" is clearly established, that is, those operators of which it is clear how sentences containing them can be attacked or defended.

(7) The operators must be defined decomposingly.

To meet the requirements stated in (6) and (7), Barth and Krabbe include one (and only one) formal$_2$ rule in their formal dialectics. This rule consists of Kamlah and Lorenzen's particular rules for the use of each junctor, which Barth and Krabbe (1982, p. 87) call the "strip rules for logical constants" (see Fig. 9.1). The forms of attack laid down there may be used both for O's attacks and for P's counterattacks.[26] The forms of defense indicate how a statement that has been attacked may be defended protectively (see the third elementary rule above).

---

[25]We do not quote these rules literally, but summarize what they amount to.
[26]With the exception of the rule for atomic statement, which cannot be used for P's attacks.

Winning and Losing Rules

As we saw in realistic dialectics, P wins and O loses a chain if P makes an appropriate *Ipse dixisti!* remark. Another way of losing a chain is to *use up* the rights that the party in question has in that particular chain. When one has to make a move, but all possibilities to execute an attack or a defense have been exhausted, the chain is lost (and won by the other party). A chain that is won by one party (and lost by the other) is called "completed."

If P succeeds in winning a chain according to the rules of formal dialectics, this does not automatically mean that he has won the discussion as a whole, nor, therefore, that he has successfully defended the initial thesis. Only if the chain won by P is the *last completed* chain in a terminated discussion, P has won the entire discussion and successfully defended the initial thesis T against O's attack. If, on the other hand, P loses the last completed chain, then O has successfully refuted T, and P has lost the discussion as a whole.

Sometimes P or O may have a "winning strategy." This means that the party concerned can select each of its moves in such a way that, whatever moves its adversary makes, *every chain* will be concluded with a victory for this party. If P has a winning strategy with regard to T in the face of O, who attacks T from *Con*, then we may say that T "follows logically from *Con*." Surely, it does not follow that T is *true*, for if that is to follow the statements in *Con* must also be true. If P has a winning strategy with regard to O, regardless of whether O makes concessions or not and regardless of what concessions, then T is called "logically true" (on the strength of the dialectic system concerned). P then has a winning strategy with regard to *any* opponent and *all possible* lines of attack or criticism (Barth & Martens, 1977, pp. 83–84).

To give an idea of how a discussion develops according to the rules of (a nonmaterial variant of) formal dialectics, let us look at a simple example of a discussion between O(lga) and P(aul) that is presented in Fig. 9.2.

Explanatory Remarks

(1–3)—The initial situation is shown above the line. P defends the thesis $A \rightarrow C$, the initial thesis, and O attacks it from a position given by $A \rightarrow B$ and $B \rightarrow C$, the initial concessions. This is the "initial conflict." The language user who has assumed the role of P holds that the initial thesis has to be accepted by O (given O's initial concessions), and the language user who has adopted the role of O disputes this.

(4)—In 4 the discussion opens with a move by O. O is the only one who can make a move, since P is neutral towards the statements made by O as concessions; (given that his own thesis has yet to be attacked) P does not have anything to defend. O is in contraposition with regard to P's thesis, and is thus entitled to attack it. According to the "strip rules for logical constants," O can do so in

	O	P
1.	A → B	
2.	B → C	
3.		A → C
4.	(?)A/3	
5.		C\4
6.	C?/5	
7.		(?)A/1
8.	B\7	
9.		(?)B/2
10.	C\9	
11.		!(6,10)

FIG. 9.2. A discussion according to the rules of formal dialectics.

only one way: by uttering *A* as a concession. *(?)A/3* means that *A* is put forward as an attack on the statement made by *P* in 3.

(5)—We have now reached a situation in which a statement by *P* has been attacked. Since *P* is in pro-position with regard to that statement, *P* is obliged to defend it. In 5 *P* opts for a protective defense, which according to the "strip rules" makes him assert *C*. *C\4* means that *C* is put forward as a protective defense against an attack launched by *O* in 4. However, *P* might also, in 5, have launched a counterattack against one of *O*'s concessions on lines 1 and 2. *P* could, in a nonmaterial dialogue, not have attacked the concession on line 4, since it is atomic (logically simple). Only *O* may attack atomic statements. For the sake of clarity and simplicity, we have shown only one of the three possible lines of defense. (*P* can also win selecting either of the other two.)

(6)—In 5, *P* made a new statement, and since *O* has nothing to defend, all *O* can do is attack this statement. *C?/5* means that an attack is being launched against the elementary (atomic) statement made by *P* in 5.

(7)—According to the rules of (nonmaterial) formal dialectics, there is no protective defense against an attack on an atomic statement, so that in 7 *P* has to switch to a counterattack. As a target of this attack *P* chooses *O*'s first concession, but *P* could also have chosen the second one. That way, too, he would have been able to ensure victory.

(8)—We have now, for the first time, reached a situation in which one of *O*'s statements stands attacked, and that gives *O* a right to defend it protectively. But *P* has also, in 7, made a new statement, and that gives *O* a right to attack.

If O were to attack this new statement A, however, that would immediately lead to her losing the chain, because she would be attacking a statement, which she herself put forward in 4. She therefore opts for the first possibility (so we shall assume).

(9)—In 9 P carries out a counterattack on O's second concession.

(10)—O has been pinned down by P's move in 9. She may defend her second concession protectively by conceding C, or she may attack B, the statement made by P in 9. In either case she loses: In the first case, which we have displayed in our example, because she is then positing a statement which she attacked in her most recent attack, viz., move 6, whereas in the second case she would lose because she would be attacking a statement made by herself in 8. (See "Realistic Dialectics" on p. 267.)

(11)—P concludes the chain with a win by making an appropriate "*Ipse dixisti!* remark" on the basis of O's moves in 6 and 10.

9.4 PERSPECTIVES

As we announced at the outset, we have treated only one of the main types of (purely) formal dialectics: constructive dialectics. Barth and Krabbe also discuss two other types: minimal dialectics and classical dialectics. Moreover they present a material system for mixed conflicts as well as a number of formal and material variants of each type of system. More importantly, they have been able to show the completeness of various of their dialectic systems (minimal, constructive, and classical) in terms of equivalence to extant systems of formal deduction or logical semantics.[27]

Barth and Krabbe (1982) do not claim, however, that with their formal dialectics they have produced a " 'complete," ready-for-use theory of argumentation" (p. 307). The relationship between argumentation theory and logic they characterize as follows:

> The subject called "Logic" corresponds to that part of the Theory of Argumentation that studies systems of language-invariant formal₃ dialectic rules and language-dependent formal₂ dialectic rules based on (formal₂) syntactical rules. (p. 75)

One of the first extensions they regard necessary relates to the formal$_2$ rules. In *From Axiom to Dialogue* (1982) they confine themselves to Lorenzen-rules for using conjunction, disjunction, implication, and negation. Since Lorenzen and his associates had already introduced rules for quantifiers—the dialogical intro-

---

[27]This equivalence is a purely extensional one: in each case it is proved that whenever T follows logically from *Con* in terms of winning strategies, T follows from *Con* in some extant deductive or semantic system. This does not mean that dialectics, deduction theory and semantics are equivalent for all purposes.

duction of quantifiers was, in fact, one of Lorenzen's original concerns—only a small step was needed, as Krabbe (1982b) has shown, to integrate rules for quantifiers with the other rules of formal dialectics.

The integration of modal logic, studied too by the Erlangen school, is more complicated. In "Noncumulative dialectical models and formal dialectics" (1985a) and "A theory of modal dialectics" (1986) Krabbe has proposed a number of systems and proved their completeness. According to the proponents of formal dialectics, the formal$_2$ apparatus should also be extended with rules for other logical constants, such as articles.

An adequate theory of argumentation, Barth and Krabbe echo Naess, ought to pay attention to questions of interpretation, definition, and clarification ("precization") relating to "contensive" (content-presenting) words like "Man," "Freedom," and "Revolution." Other important topics are, in their opinion, fallacies, "mixed" discussions (for which they proposed one material system), and discussions between more than two parties. More attention should also be paid to the regulation of "material moves" such as ostensive moves and experimentation (1982, p. 308).

In connection with the study of fallacies, Barth and Krabbe (1978, p. 340) point to the distinction between what they call "first order rules" and "higher order rules." The formal$_3$ rules that we discussed earlier are first order rules; the higher order rules are supposed to be "discussion-promoting" rules, but Barth and Krabbe (1982) do not elucidate this concept. Instead, they give a (not particularly clear) example: "Don't abuse the other party!" (p. 75).

A cautious start has since been made by van Eemeren and Grootendorst (1988, pp. 287–288) to elaborate the idea of higher order rules—or, better, conditions. In *Reconstructing Argumentative Discourse*, van Eemeren, Grootendorst, Jackson, and Jacobs (1993, pp. 30–36) describe first-order conditions as representing constitutive elements of a code of conduct aimed at the resolution of disputes, and second-order conditions as referring to the "discussion-minded" attitudes and intentions of the arguers presupposed by the code. Still higher order conditions are required to enable the arguers to claim the rights and responsibilities associated with the argumentative roles defined by the code. In these authors' view, the third-order conditions relate to political ideals such as nonviolence, freedom of speech, and intellectual pluralism as well as to practical constraints and resources for empowering critical discussion. It is clear, however, that much has still to be done before a system of higher order conditions can emerge that is as refined, precise, and ordered as the systems of first order rules formulated by Barth and Krabbe.

Barth and Krabbe's formal dialectics, and the philosophical ideas of Barth, have been a source of inspiration for further research, not only by themselves, but by various other argumentation theorists as well. Barth herself, together with Martens, used the method of dialogue tableaus, even before formal dialectics had been fully developed, as a tool for analyzing fallacies, notably *argumen-*

tum ad hominem (Barth & Martens, 1977). Grootendorst (1978) chose formal dialectics as the point of departure of his analysis of this fallacy. He concluded that the rules of formal dialectics do indeed exclude arguing *ad hominem*, but, in his opinion, no satisfactory analysis of this rhetorical move can be offered unless formal dialectics is supplemented with higher-order rules.

Unfortunately, Grootendorst's article is only available in Dutch, as are several relevant publications by Wiche. In Wiche (1983), for one, Barth's insights are used to interpret "generic" statements like "The Swede is no racist" in which, instead of terms such as *all* or *some*, the definite article is used to characterize a certain gender or "sort." Wiche (1988) also ponders on the differences between a formal discussion and argumentative discussions. In his opinion, in order to provide feasible tools for analyzing argumentative discussions, dialogic logic, as it is, needs to be amended.

Van Eemeren and Grootendorst (1984, 1992a) started from Barth's conception of rationality in studying argumentation. In developing their "pragma-dialectical" approach to argumentation, they made use of many insightful distinctions propounded by Barth and Krabbe (see chapter 10). They observe that, just as in the dialogic logic of the Erlangen School, the situation that is taken as point of departure in formal dialectics is different from the ordinary starting point in argumentation. In argumentative discourse, initially one person advances a standpoint on which doubt is cast by another. Then, the arguments are advanced, followed by a possible critical response, and so on. The dispute is resolved when the standpoint is accepted by the other person on the basis of the arguments advanced by the arguer, or when the standpoint at issue is abandoned by the arguer as a result of the other's critical response.

The initial situation adopted by Barth and Krabbe in their standardization of dialogues represents a stage in the resolution of a dispute that does not arise until after the arguments of the arguer in defense of the arguer's standpoint have been advanced, and the arguer and the other decide to examine together whether this standpoint is tenable on the assumption that the arguments are acceptable. This means that they set out to check whether the conclusion contained in the standpoint indeed *follows* from the premises contained in the argumentation. The person addressed in the argumentation has then agreed to act as "opponent" and to do so while having the arguer's argumentation as a "concession" added to his or her own commitments.[28]

---

[28]In ordinary discourse, it is highly unlikely that this rather artificial situation will arise in the initial stage, but it can, of course, be created later on in the discussion if so desired. Therefore, van Eemeren and Grootendorst (1984) included a method corresponding with Barth and Krabbe's device for use in a later stage of the resolution process. This method, incorporated in what they call the "intersubjective reasoning procedure," is part of a whole series of evaluation procedures (p. 16). For a different point of view, see Krabbe (1988), where the initial situation of formal dialectics is interpreted as a natural starting point.

10

PRAGMA-DIALECTICS
AND CRITICAL DISCUSSION

Pragma-dialectics is an argumentation theory developed by Frans van Eemeren and Rob Grootendorst in the Speech Communication Department of the University of Amsterdam. Currently, van Eemeren and Grootendorst are members of the Institute for Functional Research of Language and Language Use. Together with their colleagues, they are engaged in a program for Argumentation Theory and Discourse Analysis concentrating on pragma-dialectical and rhetorical analysis of argumentative discourse. Among the other participants are Antoine Braet, Eveline Feteris, Bert Meuffels, Agnès van Rees, and Francisca Snoeck Henkemans.

In the 1970s, van Eemeren and Grootendorst, inspired by Karl Popper's critical rationalism, began to study argumentation as a means of resolving differences of opinion. The general objective they had in mind was to develop a code of conduct for argumentative discourse. Theoretically, they aimed for a sound combination of linguistic insights from the study of language use and logical insights from the study of critical dialogue. As the former study generally is known as (linguistic) "pragmatics" and the latter as (philosophical) "dialectics," they have labeled their approach to argumentation *pragma-dialectics*. In developing pragma-dialectics, van Eemeren and Grootendorst made use of Austin and Searle's speech act theory, Grice's logic of ordinary discourse, Lorenzen's dialogue logic, and Barth and Krabbe's formal dialectics.

Van Eemeren and Grootendorst's most important publications in English are *Speech Acts in Argumentative Discussions* (1984), *Argumentation, Communication, and Fallacies* (1992a), and (together with Sally Jackson, and Scott Jacobs) *Reconstructing Argumentative Discourse* (1993). In *Speech Acts in Argumentative Discussions* the theoretical background of the pragma-dialectical approach to argumentation is explained, together with its philosophical and methodological starting points. In *Argumentation, Communication, and Fallacies* an elaborated version of the pragma-dialectical theory is provided, concentrating on argumentative discourse as linguistic communication and fallacies as violations of the rules for critical discussion. *Reconstructing Argumentative Discourse* explores the connections between a normative model for disagreement resolution and empirical reality of argumentative practice by developing analytic tools for reconstructing argumentative discourse in the light of the critical ideal.

The treatment of pragma-dialectics in this chapter shall be based primarily on these three books. First, we outline the research program, explaining its general starting points. In Section 10.1, we describe the pragma-dialectical model for critical discussion, summarizing the rules for argumentative discourse aimed at resolving a difference of opinion. In Section 10.2, we pay attention to the empirical investigation of argumentative practice and to the operations involved in an analysis of argumentative discourse aimed at reconstructing all relevant elements. In Section 10.3, we discuss the fallacies that can occur in the process aimed at resolving disagreement, distinguishing not only the obstacles to a resolution traditionally known as fallacies but also other obstacles. In Section 10.4, finally, some further theoretical contributions, as well as some applications of pragma-dialectical insights into argumentative practice, are mentioned.

According to van Eemeren and Grootendorst, argumentation is a phenomenon of verbal communication which should be studied as a specific mode of discourse, characterized by the use of language for resolving a difference of opinion. The quality and possible flaws of argumentation are to be measured against criteria that are appropriate for the purpose of such discourse. Because the study of argumentation should encompass the descriptive as well as the normative dimensions of argumentative discourse, it is to be construed as a special branch of linguistic pragmatics in which both dimensions are methodically integrated.

The study of argumentation can neither be based unilaterally on idealization nor can it be based merely on observation.[1] Both the limitations of nonempirical idealization, exemplified in the regimentations of modern logics, and the limitations of noncritical observation, exemplified in the descriptions of contemporary linguistics, need to be systematically overcome. They can only be transcended with the help of a coherent research program in which normative and descriptive approaches are so closely interwoven that they become integrated.

The pragma-dialectical research program is designed to achieve this integration. On the one hand, the program is based on the assumption that a philosophical ideal of critical rationality must be developed and, grounded in this ideal, a theoretical model for argumentative discourse in critical discussion. On the other hand, the program starts from the assumption that argumentative

---

[1]Cf. the views of protagonists of purely normative or purely descriptive approaches such as Biro and Siegel (1992) and Willard (1983, 1989), respectively.

reality must be investigated empirically, so that an accurate description is acquired of the actual processes of argumentative discourse and the factors influencing their outcome. Subsequently, the normative and descriptive dimensions of argumentative discourse must be linked analytically together by a methodical reconstruction of actual argumentative discourse from the perspective of the projected ideal of critical discussion. Finally, the practical problems of argumentative discourse thus discovered must be diagnosed systematically and how they can be tackled methodically in education must be determined. The research program therefore includes a philosophical, a theoretical, an empirical, an analytical, and a practical component.[2]

In the pragma-dialectical research program, argumentation is approached with four basic metatheoretical premises. These premises are metatheoretical, or methodological, in the sense that they concern how one ought to set about studying argument. Each premise represents a point of departure from other contemporary approaches. The premises are the basis for integrating the descriptive dimension of argumentation as an actual phenomenon of argumentative discourse with the normative dimension of argumentation as an essential ingredient of critical discussion. According to these methodological starting points, the subject matter under investigation is to be "externalized," "socialized," "functionalized," and "dialectified."[3] Let us see what these starting points amount to.

First, *externalization*. Pragmatically, argumentation presupposes a standpoint and at least the potential for opposition to that standpoint. It involves more than just a process of personal reasoning, and more than just a situation in which two parties happen to hold incompatible viewpoints. In order to find out whether or not their opinions will be accepted, people put their standpoints to public certification, submitting their reasoning to public scrutiny in argumentative discourse. Channeled by a system of public commitment and accountability, the beliefs, inferences, interpretations, and so on, which underlie argumentation (or any other discursive activity) are expressed or projected in the discourse. Whereas the motives people may have for holding a position might be different from the grounds they offer and accept in its defense, what they can be held committed to is not so much their actual position, but the position they have expressed in the discourse, whether directly or indirectly.[4] For that reason, any efforts to reduce argumentation to a structure of attitudes and beliefs, or a process of reasoning, are inadequate. The study of argumentation should not

---

[2]For a more elaborated version of the five "estates" of this research program, see van Eemeren (1987a, 1994).

[3]For a detailed exposition of these methodological starting points, see van Eemeren and Grootendorst (1984).

[4]It is, of course, important to find out to what extent and in which ways *internal* reasoning and *external* argumentation diverge, and what frustration this divergence causes, but these questions can only be asked (and methodically answered) if the two concepts are kept separate.

concentrate on the psychological dispositions of the people involved in an argumentation, but on their externalized—or externalizable—commitments.[5]

Second, *socialization*. In approaches merely concerned with argument "as a product," arguments typically are seen as an externalization of individual thought processes, abstracting structural elements of reasoning such as "major premise," "minor premise," and "conclusion" from the communicative process in which they occur.[6] The central question then becomes one of assessing whether and how these elements hold together in order to validate the arguer's position. But argumentation does not consist in a single individual privately drawing a conclusion: It is part of a discourse procedure whereby two or more individuals who have a difference of opinion try to arrive at agreement. Argumentation presupposes two distinguishable participant roles, that of a "protagonist" of a standpoint and that of a—real or projected—"antagonist." It reflects the collaborative way in which the protagonist in the fundamentally dialogical interaction responds to the—real or projected—questions, doubts, objections, and counterclaims of the antagonist. This is why in the study of argumentation, rather than in an individualist perspective, argumentation should be put in the social context of a process of joint problem solving.[7]

Third, *functionalization*. Argumentation often is described in purely structural terms, not only in formal and informal logical approaches to arguments, but also in studies of fallacies and practical argumentation. Structural descriptions have much to recommend them, but they tend to ignore the functional rationale of the structural design of the discourse. Argumentation has the general function of managing the resolution of disagreement. It arises in response to, or anticipation of, differences of opinion, and particular lines of verbal justification are contrived to realize this purpose in a particular case. The need for argumentation, the requirements of justification, the structure of argumentation all are adapted to the opposition, doubts, objections and counterclaims that have to be met, and this is reflected in the speech acts advanced. For this reason, in describing and evaluating argumentation the purpose for which argumentation

---

[5]In this respect, externalization is at odds with those rhetorical approaches that refer to presumed psychological states of arguers and their audiences in an attempt to explain the effectiveness of argumentation.

[6]For the distinction between approaches viewing argument as a process, a product, and a procedure, see Wenzel (1980). The logical approaches to argumentation traditionally concentrate on argumentation as a product, directing their attention primarily towards the validity of arguments in which from one or more premises a conclusion is derived.

[7]As explained in chapter 5, Toulmin's (1958) position seems to travel part of the distance towards this perspective on argument, in seeing each element of an argument as a response to a possible challenge or query. But the characteristic questions he associates with each element ("What do you have to go on?", etc.) serve merely as an explanation of how the argument hangs together. As explained in chapter 4, Perelman and Olbrechts-Tyteca's (1958) concept of "universal audience" offers an abstract description of opposition, but without any serious commitment to a collaborative involvement of two parties in argumentation.

is put forward in the conduct of argumentative discourse is to be duly taken into account. The study of argumentation should therefore concentrate on the function of argumentation in the verbal management of disagreement.[8]

Fourth, *dialectification*. Argumentation is appropriate for resolving a difference of opinion only if it is capable of accommodating the relevant reactions of a critical antagonist. Discourse and conversation analysts generally restrict themselves to describing argumentation as it occurs, without regard for how it ought to occur if it is to be appropriate for resolving a difference of opinion. A theory of argumentation, however, must be attentive to a set of critical standards for a discussion aimed at resolving a difference of opinion. This can be achieved by viewing argumentation as part of a critical discussion governed by a valid dialectical procedure for resolving differences of opinion. A dialectical procedure for critical discussion is valid depending on how efficient and efficacious it is in furthering the resolution of disagreement, excluding fallacious moves and being intersubjectively acceptable to the parties.[9] A valid dialectical procedure makes it possible to determine whether the argumentative discourse as it is conducted can be instrumental in resolving a difference of opinion.[10] In the study of argumentation, argumentative discourse should therefore be viewed from the perspective of a dialectical procedure for critical discussion.[11]

In the pragma-dialectical approach to argumentation, externalization, socialization, functionalization, and dialectification of the subject matter under investigation is realized by making use of pragmatic insights from discourse and discourse analysis and dialectical insights from critical rationalist philosophy and dialogue logic. Argumentative discourse is described in terms of the pragmatic functions and structures of the speech acts performed in the verbal interaction

---

[8]This functional perspective, concentrating on the ways in which language is used for achieving certain communicative and interactional purposes, is lacking in most logical approaches to argumentation, whether formal or informal.

[9]In the terminology of Barth and Krabbe (1982, pp. 21–22), a discussion procedure which fulfills these requirements may claim "problem solving validity" and "(semi-)conventional validity." See Section 9.1.

[10]Committing oneself to a dialectical approach to argumentation does not mean that only those exceptional cases are being analyzed in which there is 100% rational and reasonable discussion. It means defining the conditions for critical discussion, distinguishing between principles and practices, between rules and regularities, so that one can see when, how, and why ordinary argument deviates from the critical ideal.

[11]The purpose of a dialectical approach, viewing argumentation as a "systematic management of discourse for the purpose of achieving critical decisions" (Wenzel, 1979, p. 84), is to establish how discussions should be carried out systematically in order to critically test standpoints. The dialectical procedure for critical discussion incorporates the product-oriented and process-oriented approaches to argumentation. In order to avoid the dangers of absolutism and relativism inherent in, respectively, the (logical) "geometrical" and the (rhetorical) "anthropological" traditions in the philosophy of good reasoning, the dialectical approach to argumentation joins the "critical" tradition. For a characterization of these traditions, see Toulmin (1976).

between the participants, and its acceptability is judged by referring to a set of rules for critical discussion aimed at resolving a difference of opinion (van Eemeren & Grootendorst, 1984, pp. 7–18). In developing the pragmatic insights required for this endeavor, reference is made primarily to Austin (1962), Searle (1969, 1979) and Grice (1975). Fundamental dialectical insights are gained from Popper (1972, 1974), Albert (1975), Crawshay-Williams (1957), and Barth and Krabbe (1982).

Externalization is achieved by identifying the specific commitments created by the performance of argumentative speech acts in a certain context of disagreement. Argumentation is aimed at convincing another person, who does not yet agree with a standpoint, of its acceptability. Within a speech act perspective, the notions of acceptability and disagreement can acquire a concrete meaning. Rather than treating "accepting" and "disagreeing" as internal states of mind, these notions can be externalized in terms of discursive activities. Acceptance can be conceptualized as the performance of a preferred response to the arguable act. Disagreement expresses itself in argumentative discourse in an opposition among speech acts interlocked with a common activity. Starting from these externalizations, being convinced can be seen as an undertaking of the commitments entailed by the speech act whose acceptance is the verbal expression of this undertaking.[12]

Socialization is achieved by identifying the participant roles of people involved in argumentative discourse in the collaborative context of an interaction between two or more discussants. The performance of a speech act presupposes a set of preconditions for whose satisfaction the speaker can be held accountable. If the speech act perspective is extended to the interactional level of the argumentative discourse, the speech acts that are performed will be seen to display the ways in which positions, and "cases" in support of positions, are developed and given meaning through the collaborative work of interlocking argumentative roles. Starting from this socialization, the roles of protagonist and antagonist of a standpoint can be assigned to participants performing certain types of speech act.

Functionalization is achieved by identifying the identity and correctness conditions of the speech act complex of argumentation and the other speech acts involved in argumentative discourse. By realizing that argumentative discourse occurs through speech act performances—and in response to speech act performances—it becomes clear which "disagreement space" is involved in argumentation.[13] A specification of what is "at stake" can be gained by organizing the analysis of argumentative discourse around this context of disagreement, paying close attention to the identity and correctness conditions the speech acts concerned may be deemed to have in view of their communicative function and interactional

---

[12]For a general discussion of the relation between the illocutionary act of making an argument and the perlocutionary act of convincing, see van Eemeren and Grootendorst (1984, pp. 47–74) and Jacobs (1987, pp. 231–233).

[13]The term *disagreement space* is introduced in Jackson (1992, p. 261).

purpose. Starting from this functionalization, it can be determined which role the various speech acts may have in resolving a difference of opinion.

Finally, dialectification is achieved by regimenting, in an ideal model for critical discussion, the exchange of speech acts aimed at resolving a difference of opinion. The ideal model can serve as a point of reference when analyzing and evaluating argumentative discourse. The notion of a critical discussion amounts to an adaptation of conceptions of rational and cooperative activity to the restricted domain of relevance provided by the goal of resolving a difference of opinion according to the merits.[14] The construction of such an idealized activity type, designed to model the systematic exchanges of resolution-oriented argumentative moves, defines the nature and the distribution of the speech acts playing a part in a critical discussion.[15] Starting from this dialectification, the speech acts performed in actual argumentative discourse can be screened for their role in resolving a difference of opinion.

10.1 A MODEL FOR CRITICAL DISCUSSION

In order to clarify what is involved in viewing argumentative discourse as aimed at resolving a difference of opinion, the theoretical notion of a critical discussion is given shape in an ideal model specifying the various stages in the resolution process and the verbal moves that are instrumental in each of these stages. The principles authorizing these moves are accounted for in a set of rules for the performance of speech acts. Taken together, these rules constitute a theoretical definition of a critical discussion.

We first need to realize that resolving a difference of opinion is not identical with settling a dispute, the point of settling a dispute being that a difference of opinion is brought to an end. A dispute may be settled by relying on the arbitration of a third party, such as an umpire, a referee, or a judge. A difference of opinion is resolved by argumentative discourse only if the parties involved have reached agreement on whether or not the disputed opinion is acceptable. This means that one party has either been convinced by the other party's argumentation, or the other party, realizing that its arguments cannot stand up to the first party's criticisms, withdraws the standpoint.[16] An exchange of arguments and criticisms

---

[14]For a more elaborate exposition, see van Eemeren and Grootendorst (1984, pp. 7–18).

[15]In some respects, the idealization involved in the notion of a critical discussion is comparable to the way in which Searle's (1969) "felicity conditions" can be seen as an idealized model of a speech act type, and to the way in which Grice's (1975) Cooperative Principle and "conversational maxims" provide an idealized model of conversational practice.

[16]A critical discussion reflects the Socratic dialectic ideal of a rational testing of any form of conviction, not only of statements of a factual kind but also of normative standpoints and value judgments (cf. Albert, 1967). In a Popperian vein, starting from the fallibility of all human standpoints, the methodological concept of critical testing is elevated to the guiding principle of problem solving. Of course, the ideal of critical discussion can also be a helpful point of departure in investigating how disputes are settled or can be settled.

leading to a joint conclusion is crucial to resolving a difference of opinion. That is why a dialectical procedure for resolving differences of opinion is pivotal to the pragma-dialectical notion of a critical discussion.

In a critical discussion, the parties involved attempt to resolve their difference of opinion by reaching agreement about the acceptability or unacceptability of the standpoint at issue. They do so by finding out whether or not this standpoint is defensible against doubt or criticism. The dialectical procedure for resolving differences of opinion by way of critical discussion is a procedure for exploring the acceptability of standpoints. In a critical discussion, the protagonist and the antagonist of a particular standpoint try to establish whether this standpoint is tenable in the light of critical responses.[17] For this purpose, the dialectical procedure for critical discussion should deal not only with (inference) relations between premises (or "concessions") and conclusions, but should cover all speech acts which play a part in exploring the acceptability of standpoints.

Analytically, four stages can be distinguished in the process of resolving a difference of opinion. They correspond with four different phases an argumentative discourse must pass through, albeit not necessarily explicitly, in order to be adequate for resolving a difference of opinion. These stages are therefore incorporated in the ideal model of a critical discussion. The four stages are labeled the "confrontation" stage, the "opening" stage, the "argumentation" stage, and the "concluding" stage.

In the *confrontation stage*, a difference of opinion presents itself through an opposition between a standpoint and nonacceptance of this standpoint. In argumentative discourse, this stage corresponds with the phase where it becomes clear that there is an opinion that coincides with—real or projected—doubt or contradiction, so that a disagreement, or potential disagreement, arises. If there is no confrontation of views, then there is no need for critical discussion.

In the *opening stage*, the protagonist and the antagonist in the dispute are identified and their initial commitments—substantive, procedural, and otherwise. The protagonist undertakes the obligation to defend the standpoint at issue, while the antagonist assumes the obligation to respond critically to the standpoint and the protagonist's defense.[18] In argumentative discourse, this stage corresponds

---

[17]In line with Popperian critical rationalism, dialectical approaches place great emphasis on the consequence of the fact that a statement and its negation cannot both be true at the same time: one of the statements must be withdrawn. The testing of statements is then equated with the detection of contradictions (cf. Albert, 1975, p. 44). Cf. the dialectical method proposed by Barth and Krabbe (1982), discussed in chapter 9, for establishing whether a thesis is tenable in relation to certain concessions by determining if maintaining the thesis leads to contradictions. A method corresponding to this device is included in van Eemeren and Grootendorst's "intersubjective reasoning procedure" (1984, p. 169).

[18]The role of antagonist may coincide with the role of protagonist of another—contrary—standpoint, but this need not be so. Expressing doubt regarding the acceptability of a standpoint is not necessarily to adopt a contrary standpoint of one's own. If a contrary standpoint is adopted by the other party, the difference of opinion is no longer "nonmixed," but "mixed." Cf. van Eemeren and Grootendorst (1992a, pp. 13–25).

with the phase where the parties manifest themselves as such and determine whether there is sufficient common ground (shared background knowledge, values, rules) for a fruitful exchange of views. It only makes sense to undertake an attempt to eliminate a difference of opinion by means of argumentation if such a starting point can be established. If there is no opening for exchanging views, then having a critical discussion is of no use.

In the *argumentation stage*, the party that acts as the protagonist methodically defends the standpoint at issue against critical responses of the antagonist. If the antagonist is not yet wholly convinced of all or part of the protagonist's argumentation he or she elicits new argumentation from the protagonist, and so on. As a consequence, the protagonist's argumentation can vary from very simple to extremely complex, so that the argumentation structure of one argumentative discourse may be much more complicated than that of the next.[19] In argumentative discourse, the argumentation stage corresponds with the phase in which one party adduces arguments in order to overcome the other party's doubts about the standpoint, and the other party reacts to those arguments. Adducing argumentation, and judging its merits, is crucial to resolving a difference of opinion. If there is no argumentation or no critical appraisal of this argumentation, then there is no critical discussion.

In the *concluding stage*, the protagonist of a standpoint and the antagonist determine whether the protagonist's standpoint has been successfully defended against the critical responses of the antagonist. If the protagonist's standpoint needs to be withdrawn, the dispute has been resolved in favor of the antagonist; if the antagonist's doubts have to be retracted, it has been resolved in favor of the protagonist. In argumentative discourse, the concluding stage corresponds with the phase in which the parties draw conclusions about the result of the attempt to resolve a difference of opinion. If the parties do not agree on the outcome of their discussion, then the critical discussion has not led to a resolution of the difference of opinion.

After the concluding stage has been completed, that particular critical discussion of the standpoint at issue is over. But this does not mean that the same parties cannot embark upon a new critical discussion. This new discussion may relate to quite another difference of opinion, but it may also relate to an altered version of the same difference, while the discussion roles of the participants may switch or remain the same. In any event, a new critical discussion then begins, going through the same stages, from confrontation to conclusion. Although the argumentation stage, because of its crucial role in the resolution process, is sometimes identified with the whole critical discussion, for conducting a critical discussion the other stages are equally indispensable.

---

[19]For an analysis of the different types of complex argumentation that can arise in this way, varying from "multiple" argumentation to "coordinatively compound" and "subordinatively compound" argumentation, see van Eemeren and Grootendorst (1992a, pp. 73–89) and Snoeck Henkemans (1992).

In a critical discussion, the protagonist and the antagonist of the standpoint at issue not only go through all four stages of the resolution process, they must also observe at every stage the rules of a dialectical procedure which is instrumental in resolving the difference of opinion. In *Speech Acts in Argumentative Discussions*, van Eemeren and Grootendorst (1984) introduced a proposal for a dialectical procedure in the form of a code of conduct for critical discussion. They specified this code of conduct by stating the rules that are constitutive for a critical discussion in terms of the performance of speech acts.[20] By defining a critical discussion in this way, a heuristic, analytical and critical framework is created for dealing with argumentative discourse.

In its heuristic and analytical functions, the ideal model for critical discussion is a tool for dealing with the interpretation problems that arise when it is not clear what kind of speech act has been performed in argumentative discourse. The ideal model provides a clear indication of what to look for in the argumentative discourse and gives the analyst a point of reference when determining what would be the most appropriate analysis.[21] In its critical function, the model provides a set of norms for establishing the extent to which the actual discourse deviates from the course that would be most conducive to the resolution of the dispute.

In elucidating the pragma-dialectical rules for critical discussion, we restrict ourselves here to the simplified, nontechnical version of the rules introduced by van Eemeren and Grootendorst in *Argumentation, Communication, and Fallacies*, where a succinct recapitulation is given of ten basic principles, the "Ten Commandments" of critical discussion (1992a, pp. 208–209):[22]

Rule (1)   Parties must not prevent each other from advancing standpoints or from casting doubt on standpoints.

Rule (2)   A party that advances a standpoint is obliged to defend it if asked by the other party to do so.

---

[20]A full exposition of the pragma-dialectical rules for critical discussion can be found in van Eemeren and Grootendorst (1984, pp. 151–175).

[21]In some institutionalized contexts, certain expectations regarding the organization of the discourse may already be created by background knowledge of formal or informal procedures and other conventions (cf. Feteris, 1989). Knowledge of the conventions pertaining to legal proceedings, scholarly dissertations, political debates, policy documents, and so on, can thus be a useful supplement to the guidance provided by the ideal model. Often, insight into the proceedings of the discourse and the kind of speech acts that can and cannot be expected to occur can also be furnished by knowledge of the text genre involved and indications from the verbal and nonverbal context, or by general or specific background knowledge.

[22]It is worth noting that observance of the rules can only constitute a sufficient condition for resolving a difference of opinion in conjunction with the fulfillment of the appropriate "higher order" conditions pertaining to the attitudes and dispositions of the discussants and the circumstances of discussion. See van Eemeren, Grootendorst, Jackson, and Jacobs (1993, pp. 30–35).

Rule (3)   A party's attack on a standpoint must relate to the standpoint that has indeed been advanced by the other party.

Rule (4)   A party may defend a standpoint only by advancing argumentation relating to that standpoint.

Rule (5)   A party may not disown a premise that has been left implicit by that party or falsely present something as a premise that has been left unexpressed by the other party.

Rule (6)   A party may not falsely present a premise as an accepted starting point nor deny a premise representing an accepted starting point.

Rule (7)   A party may not regard a standpoint as conclusively defended if the defense does not take place by means of an appropriate argumentation scheme that is correctly applied.

Rule (8)   A party may only use arguments in its argumentation that are logically valid or capable of being validated by making explicit one or more unexpressed premises.[23]

Rule (9)   A failed defense of a standpoint must result in the party that put forward the standpoint retracting it and a conclusive defense of the standpoint must result in the other party retracting its doubt about the standpoint.

Rule (10) A party must not use formulations that are insufficiently clear or confusingly ambiguous and a party must interpret the other party's formulations as carefully and accurately as possible.

Further clarification may be provided by illustrating in which way the various rules can assist in the resolution of a difference of opinion.

Rule (1) is designed to ensure that standpoints and doubt regarding standpoints may be freely advanced. A difference of opinion cannot be resolved if it is not clear to the parties involved that there actually is a difference and what this difference involves. During the confrontation stage the difference of opinion is made explicit, which should offer the parties ample opportunity to express their positions. Both the advancing and doubting of a standpoint are therefore, without reservation, formulated as a basic right.

Rule (2) is intended to ensure that advanced and doubted standpoints are defended against critical attacks. A difference of opinion cannot be resolved if the party who advanced a standpoint is not prepared to take on the role of protagonist of this standpoint. This willingness is vital in preventing the discussion from foundering during the opening stage. A person who advances a stand-

---

[23]Although many (but not all) logicians use "valid" to mean "deductively valid," in the study of argumentation—and in pragma-dialectics—the term *valid* is used in a broader sense (cf. Section 1.2). Some commitment to a clear criterion of validity is required, but this does not automatically lead to a dogmatic commitment to "deductivism."

point has automatically acknowledged an obligation to defend the standpoint, if required to do so.

Rules (3) and (4) are designed to see that attacks and defenses in the argumentation stage are correctly linked to the original standpoint of the protagonist. A difference of opinion cannot be resolved if the antagonist is in fact attacking a different standpoint, or if the protagonist defends a different standpoint later on. A true resolution of a difference of opinion is not possible if the central issue is distorted by the antagonist or protagonist. Rule (4) is also meant to ensure that defense of standpoints takes place only by means of argumentation. A difference of opinion cannot be truly resolved if the protagonist resorts to rhetorical devices in which *pathos* or *ethos* take the place of *logos*.

Rule (5) ensures that implicit elements within the protagonist's argumentation also are examined critically. A difference of opinion cannot be resolved if a protagonist tries to withdraw from the obligation to defend an unexpressed premise, nor can it be resolved if the antagonist tries to exaggerate the scope of the unexpressed premise. To resolve the difference of opinion, the protagonist must accept responsibility for implicit elements in his or her argumentation, and the antagonist, when attempting to reconstruct what is concealed, should try to establish the exact extent of this responsibility.

Rule (6) is aimed at ensuring that the starting points of a discussion are used properly in attacking and defending standpoints, so that argumentation can lead to a resolution of a difference of opinion when the conduct of the discussion shows this to be a consequence of the commitments of the parties involved. The protagonist must not present something as a common starting point when in fact it is not, while an antagonist should not deny something being part of the common starting point when in fact it is.

Rule (7) is aimed at ensuring that an argumentation can lead to a resolution of a difference of opinion when a protagonist and an antagonist agree on a method of testing the soundness of arguments which are not part of the common starting point. The argumentation scheme employed in the protagonist's argumentation must then be suitably selected and correctly implemented.[24]

Rule (8) is aimed at ensuring that an argumentation can lead to a resolution of a difference of opinion only if the reasoning underlying the protagonist's argumentation is valid. When the reasoning is valid, the defended standpoint follows logically from the premises which are used, explicitly or implicitly, in the protagonist's argumentation. If not all premises are actually expressed, the unexpressed premises that are concealed in the argument must be made explicit.[25]

Rule (9) is aimed at ensuring that the protagonist and the antagonist ascertain in a correct manner what the result of the discussion is. A difference of opinion

---

[24]For the pragma-dialectical concept of argumentation schemes as dialectical tools, their typology, and the relevant reactions to their use, see van Eemeren and Grootendorst (1992a, pp. 94–102).

[25]For an analysis of unexpressed premises and the logical and pragmatic tools to make them explicit, see van Eemeren and Grootendorst (1992a, pp. 60–72).

is truly resolved only if the parties agree in the concluding stage whether or not the attempt at defense on the part of the protagonist has succeeded. An apparently smooth-running discussion may still fail if the protagonist wrongly claims to have successfully defended a standpoint or even wrongly claims to have proved it true, or if the antagonist wrongly denies that the defense was successful or even claims the opposite standpoint to have been proven.

Rule (10) is aimed at preventing misunderstandings as a result of unclear, vague, or ambiguous formulations. A difference of opinion can be resolved only if one party does not misinterpret the speech acts performed by the other party. Misunderstandings can lead to a spurious dispute or result in a pseudosolution. Problems in formulation and interpretation may arise at all stages of a discussion; they are not linked to any particular stage.

In order to make such a dialectical procedure for critical discussion pragmatically meaningful, it must be specified which speech acts at the various stages can contribute to the resolution of a difference of opinion. There are five types of speech act that can be performed in argumentative discourse.

The first type consists of the assertive speech acts, known as *assertives* for short. The prototype is an assertion by which the speaker or writer guarantees the truth of the proposition being expressed: "I assert that Chamberlain and Roosevelt have never met." However, assertives relate not only to the truth of propositions but also to their acceptability in a wider sense. In some assertives the chief concern may not be the truth, but the justness of the speaker or writer's opinion concerning the event or state of affairs that is being expressed in the proposition: "Baudelaire is the best French poet." Other examples of assertives are supposing, denying, and conceding.

In principle, all assertives can occur in a critical discussion. They can express the standpoint that is at issue, be part of the argumentation in defense of that standpoint, and be used to establish the conclusion. In establishing the conclusion, it can emerge that the standpoint can be upheld, so that the standpoint is repeated, but it may also have to be retracted. Someone who upholds his position can make this clear by saying, for example, "I uphold my standpoint." Although an assertion is the prototypical assertive, the advancing of a standpoint or argumentation also can be accomplished by the performance of assertives such as stating, claiming, assuring, guaranteeing, supposing, and opining. The commitment to a proposition expressed in a standpoint or argumentation can be very strong, as in the case of a firm assertion or statement, but it may also be fairly weak, as in a supposition.[26]

The second type of speech act consists of the directive speech acts or *directives*. The prototype is an order, which requires a special position of the speaker or writer *vis-à-vis* the listener or reader: The utterance "Come to my

---

[26]In argumentative discourse, many speech acts are, in fact, performed implicitly or indirectly, and other speech acts than assertives may serve as standpoints or premises, which may create serious problems for reconstruction. See Section 10.2.

room" can only be an order if the speaker is in a position of authority over the listener, otherwise it is a request or an invitation. A question is a special form of request: it is a request for a verbal act—the answer. Other examples of directives are forbidding, recommending, begging, and challenging.

Not all directives can occur in a critical discussion: Their role must consist of either challenging the party that has advanced a standpoint to defend that standpoint, or requesting argumentation to support it. A critical discussion does not contain unilateral orders and prohibitions. Neither can the party that has advanced the standpoint be challenged to do anything else other than give argumentation for the standpoint—a challenge to a fight, for example, is out.

The third type of speech act consists of the commissive speech acts or *commissives*. These are speech acts by means of which the speaker or writer undertakes a commitment *vis-à-vis* the listener or reader to do something or refrain from doing something. The prototype of a commissive is a promise by which the speaker or writer explicitly undertakes to do or not do something: "I promise you I won't tell your father." The speaker or writer can also undertake a commitment about which the listener or reader may be less enthusiastic: "I tell you that if you walk out of here now you will never set foot in this house again." Other commissives are accepting, rejecting, undertaking, and agreeing.

Commissives fulfill the following roles in a critical discussion: (a) accepting or not accepting a standpoint, (b) accepting or not accepting argumentation, (c) accepting the challenge to defend a standpoint, (d) deciding to start a discussion, (e) agreeing to take on the role of protagonist or antagonist, (f) agreeing on the rules of discussion, and, if relevant, (g) deciding to begin a new discussion. Some of the required commissives can only be performed in cooperation with the other party (for example f).

The fourth type of speech act consists of the expressive speech acts or *expressives*. These are speech acts by means of which the speaker or writer expresses his or her feelings about something by thanking someone for something, revealing disappointment, and so on. There is no single prototypical expressive. An expression of joy might be "I'm glad to see you're quite well again," hope is echoed by "I wish I could find such a nice girl friend," and irritation resounds in "I'm fed up with you hanging about all day." Other expressives include commiserating, apologizing, regretting, and greeting.

Expressives play no direct part in a critical discussion. This does not mean that they cannot affect the course of the resolution process. If we sigh that we are unhappy with the discussion, we are expressing our emotions, which distracts attention from the resolution of the difference of opinion, but may nevertheless have some significance.

The fifth type of speech act consists of the declarative speech acts or *declaratives*. These are speech acts by means of which a particular state of affairs is called into being by the speaker or writer. That is to say, the mere performance of the speech act creates a reality: If an employer addresses one of his employees with the words "You're fired," he is not just describing a state of affairs to him but he actually makes the words a reality. A subtype of the declaratives, which is not bound to a specific institutionalized context, consists of the *usage declaratives*, which refer to linguistic usage. Their main purpose is to facilitate or to increase the listener's or reader's comprehension of other speech acts. Among the examples are definitions, precisations, amplifications, and explications. The speaker or writer uses these speech acts to indicate how a speech act that may be unclear to the listener or reader is to be interpreted.

With the exception of the usage declaratives, declaratives do not play a role in the resolution of a difference of opinion, due to their dependence on the authority of the speaker or writer in a certain institutional context. At best, they can lead to a settlement of a dispute. Usage declaratives, which require no special institutional relationship, enhance the understanding of speech acts and can thus fulfill a useful role in a critical discussion. They can occur at any stage of the discussion (and they can be requested at any stage). At the confrontation stage, they can unmask a spurious dispute, at the opening stage, they can clarify uncertainty regarding the rules of discussion, at the argumentation stage, they can prevent effects of premature acceptance or nonacceptance, and so on.

The speech acts that can play a role in a critical discussion are listed in Fig. 10.1.

10.2 RECONSTRUCTING ARGUMENTATIVE DISCOURSE

In order to be able to evaluate argumentative discourse adequately, an *analytic overview* is required of all aspects of the discourse that are crucial for the resolution of the difference of opinion. In an analytic overview of the argumentative discourse, the following points need to be attended to:

(1) the standpoints at issue in the difference of opinion
(2) the positions adopted by the parties, their starting points and conclusions
(3) the arguments adduced by the parties
(4) the argumentation structure of the arguments
(5) the argumentation schemes used in the arguments

An analytic overview of an argumentative discourse displays the nature of the difference of opinion ("single nonmixed," "multiple nonmixed," "single mixed," "multiple mixed"), the distribution of roles among the participants ("protagonist," "antagonist"), the premises that make up their arguments and their conclusions ("expressed," "unexpressed"), the argumentation structures ("single," "multiple," "coordinatively compound," "subordinatively compound"), and the argumenta-

stage	role speech act in resolution
	ASSERTIVES
confrontation	expressing a standpoint
argumentation	advancing argumentation
concluding	upholding or retracting of standpoint
concluding	establishing the result
	COMMISSIVES
confrontation	acceptance or non-acceptance, upholding of non-acceptance of standpoint
opening	accepting of challenge to defend standpoint
opening	deciding to start discussion; agreement on discussion rules
argumentation	acceptance or non-acceptance of argumentation
concluding	acceptance or non-acceptance, upholding of non-acceptance of standpoint
	DIRECTIVES
opening	challenging to defend standpoint
argumentation	requesting argumentation
confrontation-concluding	
	requesting for a usage declarative
	USAGE DECLARATIVES
confrontation-concluding	definition, precisation, amplification etc.

FIG. 10.1.   Distribution of speech acts in a critical discussion.

tion schemes ("token," "similarity," "consequence").[27] Analyzing the difference of opinion entails identifying the points at issue in the discourse; analyzing the distribution of participant roles entails identifying the positions adopted with respect to these propositions; analyzing the premises and conclusions making up the arguments entails identifying the arguments which are explicitly, implicitly or indirectly adduced; analyzing the argumentation structures entails identifying the relations between the arguments advanced in favor of a standpoint; analyzing the argumentation schemes entails identifying the way in which the premises support a standpoint in each of the arguments.

---

[27]For a more detailed exposition of the components of an analytic overview and their constitutive elements, see van Eemeren and Grootendorst (1992a, pp. 93–95).

The points included in an analytic overview are of direct relevance to the evaluation of the argumentative discourse. If it is unclear which difference of opinion is the subject of discussion, there is no way of telling whether the difference has been resolved. If it is unclear which positions are adopted by the parties, it will be impossible to tell in whose favor the discussion has ended. If implicit or indirect premises and conclusions are not taken into account, certain arguments may be overlooked so that the evaluation is incomplete. If the structure of argumentation in favor of a standpoint is not exposed, it cannot be judged whether the various arguments advanced in defense of a standpoint constitute an adequate and coherent whole. If the argumentation schemes employed in supporting standpoints are not recognized, it cannot be determined whether the link between the premise and the standpoint is equal to criticism.

In practice, the question of whether, and to what extent, an oral or a written discourse is argumentative is not always easy to answer. Sometimes the discourse, or part of it, is presented explicitly as argumentative. Sometimes it is not, even though it has an argumentative function. There may also be cases in which the discourse is not at all argumentative, at least not primarily. Some kind of determination criterion is required. The most suitable criterion seems to be whether or not argumentation is advanced in the discourse, so that the discourse, or at least part of it, serves to overcome the addressee's—real or projected—doubt regarding a standpoint and to resolve a difference of opinion.[28] A discourse can be justifiably analyzed as argumentative (albeit not necessarily *in toto*) if, and only if, the speech act of argumentation is performed, whether directly or indirectly.[29]

Generally, in ordinary argumentative discourse much remains implicit. Not only is there seldom any mention of a common starting point or discussion rule, but also other structural aspects of the resolution process are often not indicated.[30] Because they are considered self-evident, but also for less honorable reasons, certain indispensable elements of the resolution process are left unexpressed, including the exact nature of the disagreement, the division of roles, the relation between the arguments put forward in defense of a standpoint, the

---

[28]It is good to realize that the doubt anticipated in argumentation can be purely imaginary, as when a speaker or writer envisages the possible reception of a standpoint by a skeptical listener or reader.

[29]For an account of the speech act definition of 'argumentation', see van Eemeren and Grootendorst (1984, pp. 39–46, 1992a, pp. 30–33).

[30]The implicit and unclear way in which the various stages of a critical discussion often seem to appear in argumentative discourse, distorted and accompanied by diversions, should neither give rise to the premature conclusion that the discourse is deficient nor to the superficial conclusion that the ideal model of critical discussion is not realistic. The former is contradicted by pragmatic insights concerning the communication rules governing ordinary discourse, the latter by dialectical insights concerning the process of resolving differences. Cf. van Eemeren and Grootendorst (1984, chap. 4, 1987; 1992a, chap. 5), and van Eemeren, Grootendorst, Jackson, and Jacobs (1993, chap. 3).

way in which the premises are supposed to support the standpoint, and even some of the premises. They usually are, sometimes in other disguises, concealed in the discourse and have to be recovered in the analysis.

Analyzing argumentative discourse amounts to interpreting it from a theoretical perspective. This means that the interpretation is guided by a theoretically motivated model that provides a point of reference for the analysis. As a consequence of the adoption of such a theoretical perspective, specific aspects of the discourse are highlighted in the analysis. An analysis of argumentative discourse undertaken from a pragma-dialectical perspective starts from the ideal model of a critical discussion and summarizes, in an analytic overview, those elements of the discourse that are relevant to resolving a difference of opinion.[31] Such an analysis is "pragmatic" in viewing the discourse as essentially an exchange of speech acts; it is "dialectical" in viewing this exchange as a methodical attempt to resolve a difference of opinion.

A pragma-dialectical analysis is aimed at reconstructing all, and only, those speech acts that play a potential part in bringing a difference of opinion to an adequate conclusion. In accomplishing a systematic analysis, the ideal model is a valuable tool. By pointing out which speech acts are relevant in the consecutive stages of the resolution process, the model has the heuristic function of indicating which speech acts have to be considered in the reconstruction. Speech acts that are immaterial to the resolution process are to be ignored, implicit elements are to be made explicit, indirect speech acts are to be restated as direct speech acts, and inadvertent deviations from the resolution path are to be righted.

The reconstruction of argumentative discourse involved in a pragma-dialectical analysis entails a number of specific analytic operations.[32] These operations are instrumental in identifying the elements in the discourse which may play a part in resolving a difference of opinion. They amount to the systematic performance of four types of transformation: deletion, addition, permutation, and substitution. Each type of transformation represents a particular way of reconstructing part of the discourse in terms of a critical discussion. In the transformations, the various verbal moves as they appear in the discourse are interpreted in the light of the pragma-dialectical objective.[33]

---

[31]Naturally, other kinds of analysis can be envisaged. Things that remain out of sight when the discourse is viewed from one perspective appear relevant from another. A (Freudian) psychological analysis, for example, would, in many cases, produce interesting results which are not acquired by means of a pragma-dialectical analysis. However, one kind of analysis need not necessarily preclude the other. The same discourse may very well be analyzed from different perspectives, though one is well-advised not to let the various perspectives unknowingly interfere.

[32]For the pragma-dialectical reconstruction process as it was originally proposed, see van Eemeren (1986). Cf. Blair (1986) for some comments.

[33]For an account of the transformations executed in a pragma-dialectical analysis of argumentative discourse, see van Eemeren and Grootendorst (1990), and van Eemeren, Grootendorst, Jackson, and Jacobs (1993, chap. 4).

The transformations are connected with a selective idealization of the discourse. They do not necessarily reconstruct the discourse in the way it actually works for the participants, but serve as analytic tools for the externalization of the participants' commitments that should be taken into account in an evaluation of the discourse, so that its merits and demerits can be more easily detected. Due to the transformations, the discourse as it appears—in the form it has been written down or can be transcribed—and the discourse as it has been reconstructed may differ in several respects. Depending on the transformations that are involved, these differences can be characterized with the terms "deletion," "addition," "permutation," and "substitution."

The transformation of *deletion* entails identifying the elements of the discourse that are immediately relevant to the process of resolving the difference of opinion, and then omitting elements that are irrelevant to this purpose, such as elaborations, immaterial interruptions, and sidelines. Any unnecessary repetitions that occur in the text, which merely repeat the same message in a slightly different wording, are also omitted. This transformation, in other words, amounts to the removal of information that is redundant, superfluous, or otherwise not relevant for the presumed goal. Only elements that are relevant for a critical discussion are to be recorded in the analysis.

The transformation of *addition* entails a process of completion which consists of supplementing the given discourse with those elements immediately relevant to the resolution of the dispute but left implicit. In such cases, something is added that is not explicitly present in the discourse. This transformation is partly a matter of making elliptical elements and presuppositions explicit and partly a matter of completing implicit moves, such as unexpressed premises. The supplementation might also include ascribing doubt about the original standpoint to someone who advances a contrary standpoint. All elements that are relevant for a critical discussion are to be recorded in the analysis.

The transformation of *permutation* entails the ordering or rearranging of elements in the original discourse in such a way that the process of resolving the difference of opinion is set down as clearly as possible. In a pragma-dialectical analysis, the elements that are directly relevant to the resolution of the difference are recorded in the order that is most suitable for the evaluation of the discourse. Unlike a purely descriptive record, the analysis need not necessarily follow the order of events in the discourse. Sometimes, the actual chronology can be retained; often some rearrangement is called for to reflect the resolution process. Starting from the various stages distinguished in the ideal model of a critical discussion, overlap between different stages, anticipatory moves and references to earlier stages are readjusted. Argumentative moves that are included in the confrontation, and confrontational elements that are postponed to the conclusion, are, for instance, put in their proper place. In the analysis, all elements that are relevant for a critical discussion are to be recorded in the most enlightening order.

The transformation of *substitution* entails an attempt to produce a clear and explicit presentation of elements that can be instrumental in resolving the difference of opinion. Ambiguous or vague formulations are replaced by well-defined and more precise standard phrases, and different formulations of elements with the same function are represented by the same standard phrase. Different formulations of the same standpoint, for example, are recorded by one standard formulation, and conventional rhetorical questions which function as arguments are recorded as such. This process of translating elements from the discourse into standard phrases results in a uniform notation of elements that have the same function in a critical discussion, substituting pretheoretical formulations of colloquial speech with theoretically motivated formulations in the language of pragma-dialectics. In the analysis, all elements that are relevant for a critical discussion are to be recorded in an adequate way.

For an illustration of the reconstruction of implicit elements, we take a closer look at the transformation of substitution. This transformation accomplishes, for example, the replacement of an implicit standpoint by an explicit standard formulation.

In speech act theory, it is a recognized fact that in ordinary discourse the communicative—or, as Searle calls it, "illocutionary"—force of a speech act is not, as a rule, explicitly expressed. In many cases, this does not present much of a problem. The listener or reader is sometimes clearly directed to the desired interpretation by means of verbal indicators such as "since" or "therefore." In the absence of such indicators, both the verbal and nonverbal context often provide sufficient clues. Indirectness, however, can pose a problem. The following piece of discourse can serve as an example:

Let's take a cab. You don't want to be late for the show, do you?

When carrying out a resolution-oriented reconstruction, the analyst would say that this is argumentation, but where is the standpoint and what constitutes the argumentation? The standpoint is to be found in the first sentence, and the second contains argumentation. However, the first sentence clearly has the communicative force of a "proposal," and the second that of a "question," and a reconstruction should take this into account. How can the attribution of the function of a standpoint to the first sentence, and that of argumentation to the second, be justified?

As speech act theory has demonstrated, performing a proposal presupposes that the speaker believes it to be a *good* proposal. According to the "felicity conditions" for the performance of a proposal, the speaker wants it to be accepted by the listener, otherwise the proposal would be pointless. One way to get the proposal accepted, would be to show that it is in the listener's interest. By asking rhetorically whether the listener wants to be late for the show, the speaker indirectly provides a possibly conclusive reason for the listener: The speaker knows very well that the listener does *not* want to be late (assuming the unexpressed premise that not taking a cab would cause this unwanted effect). By adding the rhetorical question to the proposal, the speaker tries, in advance, to resolve a potential dispute.

This explains how the speaker's proposal can be transformed into the standpoint that it is wise to take a cab, and the rhetorical question into the argument that otherwise they will be late for the show (which is undesirable). Although much more could be said about this reconstruction, it suffices to show the merits of a pragmatic perspective in helping to get the transformation of substitution carried out properly. Without speech act theory, no satisfactory explanation can be given.

It should be noted that there is an important difference between the reconstruction of the standpoint on the one hand and the reconstruction of argumentation on the other. In the first case, the utterance of the speech act has only one communicative force: it is, firstly and lastly, a proposal. In the second case, however, the utterance of the speech act has two simultaneous forces: its primary force is assertive ("If we don't take a cab, we will be late for the show—and you don't want to be late"), and its secondary force is directive (asking a question). It is only in the second case that the speech act is "indirect" in the strict sense (cf. Searle, 1979, pp. 30–57).[34]

If argumentation is partly implicit, as in the cab example, then it is necessary to take the dialectical aspects into account, making use of insights from logic. The missing elements can only properly be identified in a transformation of addition by starting from the explicit elements and then reconstructing the argument concerned so that it becomes logically valid.[35] It is not always easy to see exactly what needs to be added to an incomplete argument, whether the missing element is the conclusion or a premise; usually, there are several possibilities.

In determining which premise may be considered to have been left unexpressed, the pragma-dialectical approach not only uses the logical validity criterion but also the pragmatic communication rules.[36] If nothing other than what is expressed literally is taken into consideration, leaving a premise unexpressed appears to be a violation of a communication rule.[37] However, this is only so at first sight. The violation can be corrected by treating the unexpressed premise as

---

[34]There is also a difference between the two cases in the degree of "conventionalization." The rhetorical question is, as such, highly conventionalized, whereas the "indirectness" of the proposal is not. Only in a well-defined context can "indirectness" be detected and correctly interpreted. See van Eemeren and Grootendorst (1992a, pp. 56–59).

[35]It is still an open question exactly which validity criterion is preferred, but a (tentative) commitment to some validity criterion is in this endeavor required. Cf. footnote 23 of this chapter.

[36]For an exposition of the communication rules based on a synthesis of the Gricean maxims for complying with the Cooperative Principle and Searlean conditions for the performance of speech acts, see van Eemeren and Grootendorst (1991, pp. 156–160, 1992a, pp. 49–55).

[37]In Gricean terms, it appears to be a violation of the Quality maxim.

a special sort of indirect speech act which is implicitly conveyed by the argument. In order to decide whether a would-be unexpressed premise can be assumed to belong to the speaker's commitments, the analyst must determine what the speaker can be held accountable for on the basis of what the speaker has said. Otherwise, something might unjustly be attributed to the speaker. In many cases, the context will allow the analyst to attribute more precise commitments to the speaker than suggested by a purely logical approach concentrating on validity. Something may, for instance, have been said earlier in the discourse which makes it clear that the speaker takes responsibility for more than the speaker is committed to on the grounds of what is actually expressed in the argument.[38]

It is, of course, crucial to a pragma-dialectical analysis of argumentative discourse that the proposed reconstructions are indeed justified. The reconstructions should be faithful to the commitments which may be ascribed to the participants on the basis of their contributions to the discourse.[39] In order not to "overinterpret" what may be implicit in the discourse, the analyst must be sensitive to the communication rules, the details of the presentation, and the contextual constraints inherent in the speech event concerned. So as to go beyond a naive reading of the discourse, empirical insights concerning the way in which oral and written discourse are conducted will be beneficial.[40] The analyst's intuitions can be augmented by the results of empirical research varying from qualitative phenomenology to quantitative measuring.

Empirical research in pragma-dialectics concerns the management of differences of opinion both in informal situations and in more institutionalized contexts. It relates directly to the earlier described theoretical framework and is aimed at describing and explaining the way in which people produce, identify, and evaluate argumentative discourse. The research issues range from the principles that organize argumentative practice, to the cognitive processes and discourse structures that play a part in producing and interpreting argumentative discourse and the factors accounting for individual differences in argumentative competence.

For various reasons, argumentative reality does not always resemble the ideal of a critical discussion.[41] According to the ideal model, for example, in the

---

[38]A general procedure for an analyst wishing to determine, starting from the "logical minimum," the "pragmatic optimum" of what has been left unexpressed in an argument is explained in van Eemeren and Grootendorst (1992a, chap. 6).

[39]Only in exceptional cases, when interpreting a move as a potential contribution to the resolution process is the only charitable option left, an unsustained reconstruction may, "for reason's sake," be warranted. See van Eemeren (1987b).

[40]For a brief survey of the diverging approaches to the analysis of discourse and their empirical basis, see van Eemeren, Grootendorst, Jackson, and Jacobs (1993, pp. 50–59).

[41]This may be due in part to the fact—suggested by empirical research—that argumentative discourse can have (social and relational) meanings and functions other than resolving differences of opinion. Of course, these other functions may co-exist with the function of resolving differences of opinion, in which case the ideal of critical discussion would be relevant even when these other functions occur.

confrontation stage antagonists of a standpoint must state their doubts clearly and unambiguously, but in practice doing so can be "face-threatening" for both parties. It also creates a potential violation of the "preference for agreement" which governs normal conversation.[42] The first questions that have to be answered empirically therefore center around the way in which differences of opinion are handled in practice. How do people express their differences of opinion? How do they try to resolve them? How do they try to prevent certain disputes from arising? How do they try to settle them? Which strategies do people employ in managing their disagreements?[43]

As van Eemeren, Grootendorst, Jackson, and Jacobs have shown in *Reconstructing Argumentative Discourse*, several empirically grounded claims can be made concerning the function, structure, and content of argumentative exchanges. A primary empirical grounding for these claims comes from ethnographic evidence. Other sources are found in comparative information about discourse in general and about conventional structures and strategies of discourse. In the standard pattern of confrontation, for instance, the confronter first isolates and targets an assertion made by the confronted, subsequently questioning the confronted in a way that elicits premises which can later be seen to contradict the original standpoint. Often, the confronter then presents the obvious inconsistency expressly in a kind of "punchline" (say, a rhetorical question) that is designed to get the confronted to back down from the original standpoint (1993, pp. 39–44).

In cases of dialogue, another source of empirical grounding may come from various cues that indicate how the participants themselves understand the argumentative force of the discourse. Pauses, fillers ("uh" or "well"), cut-offs and restarts are all characteristic vocal features of an orientation towards "dispreferred" turns in conversation.[44] Reflexively organized cues as to how the participants perceive what is going on are an important source of empirical evidence. None of the sources of information about what is being argued works alone, and all need to be interpreted against some knowledge of the cultural background of the speech event concerned and a trained intuition with respect to the conduct of argumentative discourse. The acceptability of any particular reconstruction of a discourse depends, ultimately, on its overall coherence, its accountability to the details of the text, and its consistency with other information regarding the particular case, regarding how related cases of this type work, and regarding how discourse in general is known to function.

---

[42]For an analysis of "strategies for threatening face," see Benoit (1985); for "face-saving mechanisms," see Brown and Levinson (1978, 1987). For the Preference for Agreement Principle, or Presumption of Agreement, see Schegloff, Jefferson, and Sacks (1977) and Pomerantz (1984).

[43]Cf. Jacobs (1989).

[44]Cf. Heritage (1984, pp. 265–280), Levinson (1983, pp. 332–336), and van Eemeren, Grootendorst, Jackson, and Jacobs (1993, chap. 3).

Another source of empirical information that pragma-dialectics brings to bear on justifying reconstructions consists of the results of experimental research. An important question that is currently being investigated is the extent to which people are capable of recognizing argumentation. It is to be expected that implicit and indirect argumentation is more difficult to recognize than explicit and direct argumentation.

Experiments carried out so far suggest that verbal indicators of argumentation significantly facilitate the ease of recognition, whereas indirect presentations indeed pose more problems, especially in the absence of sufficient contextual clues (van Eemeren, Grootendorst, & Meuffels, 1989). In undertaking empirical research into argument identification, one must first ensure that the subjects of the experiment understand what is meant by "argumentation." As a preliminary to the research concerning factors influencing the ease of recognition in argument identification, several feasibility studies were carried out.

In order to measure the ease with which argumentation can be identified, van Eemeren, Grootendorst, and Meuffels (1984) first tested the suitability of their measuring instruments, concentrating on "single" argumentation, in which one argument in defense of a standpoint is articulated. The conceptual validity of their argumentation concept was proven by the fact that in 95% of the cases submitted to the subjects the items were correctly identified as argumentation.

Undergraduate students were requested to indicate whether or not a number of discourse fragments contained argumentation. If so, they were to underline the argument. Four factors presumed to influence argument recognition were systematically varied: (a) topic "highly charged" or not, (b) standpoint "marked" or not, (c) "argumentation indicator" present or not, (d) standpoint preceding the argument or following it.

Two different replications of this research were carried out to examine the precise effects of the various factors chosen as variables (van Eemeren, Grootendorst, & Meuffels, 1985). The first consisted of a repeat of the pencil and paper test, varying the experimental subjects with younger subjects at a lower educational level. This replication was undertaken to countermand the ceiling effects in the previous test. In the second replication, a different instrument of measurement was used, concentrating on the analysis of decision time.

Of the four variables manipulated, the influence of the presence of argumentation indicators on the recognition of argumentation, especially of indicators "in the broader sense," such as "owing to" and "on the basis of," proved to be the strongest effect. The absence of such an indicator slows down or hinders the identification of argumentation—in some cases considerably. Marking the standpoint only facilitates the identification of argumentation if no argumentation indicator is present. In the other case, the indicative function of marking the standpoint is, as it were, overruled by the presence of the argumentation indicator. In a "retrogressive" presentation, with argumentation following the standpoint, as in the case of "because," identification turns out to be easier than

in a "progressive" presentation, with the standpoint following the argumentation, as in the case of "therefore." A highly charged topic was (unlike what social
psychology seems to suggest) a factor without any significant effect.

Following this research, attention was paid to the clues for the recognition
of indirect argumentation provided by the verbal presentation of the discourse.
In the interpretation of indirect argumentation (and in implicit argumentation
in general), contextual indication proved to play a major part, assisting the
interpretation of the communicative force of utterances by having a clarifying
effect. As argumentation normally takes place within a more or less defined
context—artificial test situations being the exception—serious problems of interpretation, generally speaking, only arise in an "undefined" context devoid of
helpful pointers.[45]

In the empirical tests concerning the identification of indirect argumentation,
the students serving as experimental subjects were confronted with fragments
of discourse consisting of items half of which, in a "split-plot design," were
supplied with a definite context, and half of which were not. Both contained an
equal number of direct and indirect arguments, with or without an argumentation indicator. All defined contexts serving as independent variables were such
that a literal interpretation, though perfectly possible, would be unsatisfactory.
As expected, the communicative force of direct argumentation proved to be
easier to recognize than that of indirect argumentation. In the latter case, the
subjects needed some extra information in order to know that something more
was meant than what was literally expressed. As the tests show, a well-defined
context provides this information.[46]

10.3 FALLACIES IN RESOLVING DISAGREEMENT

When an analytic overview has been compiled on the basis of a justified reconstructive analysis, a suitable point of departure has been created for an evaluation
of the discourse. A pragma-dialectical evaluation of argumentative discourse is
aimed at determining the extent to which the various speech acts performed in
the discourse can be instrumental in resolving a difference of opinion. In order to
achieve this goal, the evaluation needs to make clear which discussion moves
hinder or obstruct a critical discussion.

---

[45]Van Eemeren and Grootendorst (1992a, chap. 5) have argued that the degree of
conventionalization required in the verbal presentation of indirect speech acts in order to
interpret them properly, is inversely proportional to the required degree of definition of the
context in which they occur.

[46]The fact that with direct argumentation defining the context does not have this influence
suggests some confirmation of van Dijk and Kintsch's (1983) contention that language users
who have to determine the communicative force of verbal utterances, in the first instance, take
refuge in so-called "linguistic strategies." All nonlinguistic factors mentioned by Clark (1979) as
affecting the interpretation of indirect speech acts are incorporated in a defined context.

In principle, each of the ten discussion rules quoted in Section 10.1 constitutes a distinct standard or norm for critical discussion. The performance of any speech act constituting an infringement of one or more of the rules, whichever party performs it and at whatever stage in the discussion, is a possible threat to the resolution of a difference of opinion and must therefore be regarded as an incorrect discussion move. In the pragma-dialectical approach, fallacies are analyzed as such incorrect discussion moves in which a discussion rule has been violated. A *fallacy* is defined then as a speech act which prejudices or frustrates efforts to resolve a difference of opinion, and the use of the term *fallacy* is thus systematically connected with the rules for critical discussion.[47]

In the pragma-dialectical approach, when fallacies in argumentative discourse are discussed, the discourse is treated as if it were aimed at resolving a difference of opinion. In practice, a discourse will hardly ever be completely resolution-oriented—nor, for that matter, completely nonresolution-oriented. For a realistic appreciation of the scope of the pragma-dialectical approach to fallacies, it is important to note that the norms provided by the rules for critical discussion apply only when, and insofar as, the discourse concerned is indeed aimed at resolving a difference of opinion.[48] It is not always self-evident whether or not this is the case; often, however, it is clear or can be plausibly assumed. A discourse can only be fully and methodically screened for fallacies if it first is analyzed adequately by determining the extent to which it can be reconstructed as a critical discussion.[49]

When it comes to the detection of fallacies, the pragma-dialectical analysis proceeds in a number of steps. An utterance must first be interpreted as a particular kind of speech act. After it has been established that the speech act concerned has indeed been performed in a context of discourse aimed at resolving a difference of opinion, it must be determined whether the performance of this speech act agrees with the rules for critical discussion. If the speech act proves to be a violation of one of the norms pertaining to a particular stage of the resolution process, the kind of violation must then be determined. Which specific criterion for satisfying the norm has not been met? Only after this question has been answered can it become clear which fallacy has been committed.

---

[47]The exposition in the remainder of this Section is based, sometimes literally, on van Eemeren and Grootendorst (1995b).

[48]The pragma-dialectical identification of fallacies is always conditional: A discussion move may be regarded as a fallacy only if the discourse is correctly interpreted as aimed at resolving a difference of opinion.

[49]Even a discourse which is clearly argumentative will in many respects not correspond to the ideal model of a critical discussion—or at least not directly, explicitly, and completely. The discourse can only be evaluated adequately if it first has been determined accurately what it actually conveys. In many cases, the why's and wherefore's of divergent forms of argumentative reality can be explained easily with the help of some empirical insight.

A considerable number of things can go wrong in resolving a difference of opinion by argumentative discourse. We turn our attention to some of the most important violations of the rules for a critical discussion. The list of violations van Eemeren and Grootendorst provided in *Argumentation, Communication, and Fallacies* is by no means complete, but it gives an impression of the great variety of fallacious moves that might be detected in the various stages of an argumentative discourse that has been analyzed as a critical discussion (1992a, pp. 93–217).

Rule 1 can be violated—at the confrontation stage—in various ways, both by the protagonist and the antagonist. A party in the discussion can impose certain restrictions on the standpoints that may be advanced or called into question; a party can deny a certain opponent the right to advance a certain standpoint or to criticize a certain standpoint. Violations of the first kind mean that certain standpoints are in fact excluded from the discussion or that particular standpoints are declared sacrosanct, so that the opponent is prohibited from casting doubt on them and they are rendered immune to criticism. Violations of the second kind are directed to the opponent personally and aim at eliminating the opponent as a serious partner in the discussion. This may be done by putting pressure on the opponent, threatening that person with sanctions (*argumentum ad baculum*), or by playing on the opponent's feelings of compassion (*argumentum ad misericordiam*), but also by discrediting the opponent's expertise, impartiality, integrity, or credibility (*argumentum ad hominem*).[50]

Rule 2 can be violated—at the opening stage—by the protagonist by *evading* or *shifting the burden of proof*. In the first case, the protagonist attempts to create the impression that there is no point in calling the standpoint into question, and no need to defend it, by presenting the standpoint as self-evident, giving a personal guarantee of the correctness of the standpoint (special variant of *argumentum ad verecundiam*) or immunizing the standpoint against criticism. In the latter case, the protagonist challenges the opponent to show that the protagonist's standpoint is wrong (special variant of *argumentum ad ignorantiam*) or that the opposite standpoint is right.

Rule 3 can be violated—at all stages—by the protagonist or the antagonist. In a discussion concerning a "mixed" difference of opinion (in which both parties have a standpoint to defend) this can be done by imputing a fictitious standpoint to the other party or distorting the other party's standpoint (*straw man*). The first effect can be achieved by emphatically advancing the opposite as one's own standpoint or by creating an imaginary opponent; the second by taking utterances out of context, by oversimplification (ignoring nuances or qualifications), or by exaggeration (absolutization or generalization).

Rule 4 can be violated—at the argumentation stage—by the protagonist in two ways: first, by putting forward argumentation that does not refer to the standpoint

---

[50]Cf. van Eemeren and Grootendorst (1995b).

under discussion as advanced at the confrontation stage (*irrelevant argumentation* or *ignoratio elenchi*); second, by defending the standpoint using nonargumentative means of persuasion. Among the latter moves, are playing on the emotions of the audience (special variant of *argumentum ad populum*), and parading one's own qualities (special variant of *argumentum ad verecundiam*). If the audience's positive or negative emotions (such as prejudice) are exploited, *pathos* replaces *logos*; for this reason, such violations of Rule 4 are sometimes called *pathetic fallacies*. If protagonists attempt to get their standpoints accepted by the opponent just because of the authority they have in the eyes of the audience due to their expertise, credibility, integrity, or other qualities, *ethos* replaces *logos*; for this reason, such violations of Rule 4 are sometimes called *ethical fallacies*.

Rule 5 can be violated—at the argumentation stage—by the protagonist by *denying an unexpressed premise* or by the antagonist by *distorting an unexpressed premise*. In denying an unexpressed premise ("I never *said* that"), the protagonist in effect tries to evade the responsibility assumed in argumentation by denying a commitment to an unexpressed premise that is correctly reconstructed as such. Antagonists are guilty of the fallacy of distorting an unexpressed premise if they have produced a reconstruction of a protagonist's unexpressed premise that goes beyond the "pragmatic optimum" to which the protagonist can actually be held, given the verbal and nonverbal context of the discussion.

Rule 6 can be violated—at the argumentation stage—by the protagonist's falsely presenting something as a common starting point or by the antagonist's denying a premise representing a common starting point. By falsely presenting something as a common starting point, the protagonist tries to *evade the burden of proof*; the techniques used for this purpose include falsely presenting a premise as self-evident, enveloping a proposition in a presupposition of a question (*many questions*), concealing a premise in an unexpressed premise, and advancing argumentation that amounts to the same thing as the standpoint (*petitio principii*, also called *begging the question* or *circular reasoning*). By denying a premise representing a common starting point, the antagonist in fact denies the protagonist the opportunity of defending his standpoint *ex concessis*, which is a denial of a *conditio sine qua non* for all successful argumentation.

Rule 7 can be violated—at the argumentation stage—by the protagonist by relying on an inappropriate argumentation scheme or using an appropriate argumentation scheme incorrectly. The various violations can be classified according to the three main categories of argumentation schemes: *symptomatic* argumentation of the "token" type, where there is a relation of concomitance between the premises and the standpoint ("Daniel is an actor [and actors are typically vain], so he is certainly vain"), *comparison* argumentation of the "similarity" type, where the relation is one of resemblance ("The measure I would like to take is fair, because the case we had last year was also dealt with in this way [and the one case is similar to the other]"), and *instrumental* argumentation of the "consequence" type, where the relation is one of causality ("As Tom has been drinking an excessive amount of whiskey [and drinking too much alcohol leads to a terrible headache], he must have a terrible headache").[51]

Symptomatic argumentation is being used incorrectly if, for instance, a standpoint is presented as right because an authority says so (special variant of *argumentum ad verecundiam*) or because everybody thinks it is right (populistic variant of *argumentum ad populum* and, as such, also a special variant of *argumentum ad verecundiam*), or if a standpoint is a generalization based upon observations which are not representative or insufficient (*hasty generalization* or *secundum quid*). Comparison argumentation is being used incorrectly, if, for instance, in making an analogy, the conditions for a correct comparison are not fulfilled (*false analogy*). And, finally, instrumental argumentation is being used incorrectly if, for instance, a descriptive standpoint is being rejected because of its undesired consequences (*argumentum ad consequentiam*); a cause–effect relation is inferred from the mere observation that two events take place one after the other (*post hoc ergo propter hoc*); or it is unjustifiably suggested that by taking a proposed course of action one will be going from bad to worse (*slippery slope*).

Rule 8 can be violated—at the argumentation stage—by the protagonist in a variety of ways. Some logical invalidities occur with a certain regularity and often are not recognized immediately. Among them are violations that have to do with confusing a necessary condition with a sufficient condition (or *vice versa*) in arguments with an "If . . . , then . . ."-premise (*affirming the consequent, denying the antecedent*); other violations amount to erroneously attributing a (relative or structure-dependent) property of a whole to its constituent parts or *vice versa* (*fallacies of division* and *composition*).

Rule 9 can be violated—at the concluding stage—by the protagonist concluding that a standpoint is true merely because it has been successfully defended (*making an absolute of the success of the defense*) or by the antagonist concluding from the fact that it has not been proved that something *is* the case, that it is *not* the case, or from the fact that something has not been proved *not* to be the case, that it *is* the case (*making an absolute of the failure of the defense* or special variant of *argumentum ad ignorantiam*). In making an absolute of the success of the defense, the protagonist commits a double error: first, the unjustified status of established fact, the truth of which is beyond discussion, is ascribed to the common starting points; secondly, in doing so, a successful defense is erroneously invested with an objective rather than intersubjective status. In making an absolute of the failure of the defense, the antagonist commits a double error as well: first, the roles of antagonist and protagonist are confused; second, it is mistakenly assumed that a discussion must always end in a victory for either a positive or a negative standpoint, so that not having the positive standpoint

---

[51]For a discussion of the three main categories of argumentation schemes, and their many subcategories, see van Eemeren and Grootendorst (1992a, pp. 94–102).

automatically means adopting the negative standpoint, and *vice versa*, ignoring the possibility of entertaining a "zero" standpoint.[52]

Rule 10 can be violated—at all stages—by the protagonist or the antagonist by taking undue advantage of unclarity (*fallacy of unclarity*) or of ambiguity (*fallacy of ambiguity, equivocation, amphiboly*). Various sorts of unclarity can occur: unclarity resulting from the structuring of the text, from implicitness, from indefiniteness, from unfamiliarity, from vagueness, and so on. Again, there are various sorts of ambiguity: referential ambiguity, syntactic ambiguity, semantic ambiguity, and so on. The fallacy of ambiguity is closely related to the fallacy of unclarity; it can occur on its own but also in combination with other fallacies (such as the fallacies of *composition* and *division*).

An overview of different kinds of violation of the rules for critical discussion is given in Fig. 10.2. This brief overview may suffice to show that the pragma-dialectical analysis of the traditional fallacies as violations of the rules for critical discussion is more systematic than the Standard Treatment discussed in chapter 3. Instead of being given *ad hoc* explanations, all the fallacies are understood as falling under one or more of the rules for critical discussion. Fallacies that only were lumped nominally together in the traditional categories are either shown to have something in common or they are clearly distinguished. Genuinely related fallacies that were separated are brought together. Distinguishing two variants of the *argumentum ad populum*—one a violation of rule 4, the other of rule 7—makes clear, for instance, that these variants are in fact *not* of the same kind. Analyzing one particular variant of the *argumentum ad verecundiam* and one particular variant of the *argumentum ad populum* as a violation of the *same* rule 7 makes clear that if viewed from the perspective of resolving a difference of opinion these variants *are* of the same kind.

The overview reveals that the pragma-dialectical approach makes it possible to analyze so far unrecognized and unnamed "new" obstacles when resolving a difference of opinion: *declaring a standpoint sacrosanct* (violation of Rule 1), *evading the burden of proof* by *immunizing a standpoint against criticism* (violation of Rule 2) or *falsely presenting a premise as self-evident* (violation of Rule 6), *denying an unexpressed premise* (violation of Rule 5), *denying an accepted starting point* (violation of Rule 6), *falsely presenting something as a common starting point* (violation of Rule 6), *making an absolute of the success of the defense* (violation of Rule 9), and so on.

Rather than considering the fallacies as belonging to an unstructured list of nominal categories which happen to have been inherited, as in the Standard Treatment, or considering all fallacies to be violations of one and the same (validity) norm, the pragma-dialectical approach differentiates between a variety

---

[52]For the notion of a zero standpoint, involving only doubt on the part of the antagonist and not a contra-standpoint, see van Eemeren and Grootendorst (1984, pp. 78–81, 1992a, pp. 15–16).

Violations of Rule 1 by protagonist or antagonist at the confrontation stage (ad baculum, ad hominem 1 [direct personal attack, abusive], ad hominem 2 [indirect personal attack, circumstantial], ad hominem 3 [tu quoque, ad misericordiam]):

a   *With reference to standpoints:*
  - banning standpoints
  - declaring standpoints sacrosanct
b   *With reference to opponent:*
  - putting pressure on other party by playing on feelings of compassion or threatening with sanctions
  - making personal attack on other party by depicting party as stupid, bad, unreliable, and so forth (casting suspicion on party's motives, pointing out an inconsistency between party's ideas and deeds in past and/or present)

Violations of Rule 2 by protagonist at the opening stage (shifting the burden of proof 1, shifting the burden of proof 2, ad ignorantiam 1, ad ignorantiam 2):

a   *Evading the burden of proof*
  - presenting standpoint as self-evident
  - giving personal guarantee of correctness of standpoint
  - immunizing standpoint against criticism
b   *Shifting the burden of proof*
  - in nonmixed dispute: antagonist must show that standpoint is wrong
  - in mixed dispute: only the other party must defend standpoint

Violations of Rule 3 by protagonist or antagonist at all discussion stages of mixed discussions (straw man):

a   *Imputing fictitious standpoint to other party*
  - emphatically advancing the opposite as one's own standpoint
  - referring to the views of the group to which someone belongs
  - creating an imaginary opponent
b   *Distorting other party's standpoint*
  - taking utterances out of context
  - oversimplifying (ignoring nuances or qualifications)
  - exaggerating (absolutization or generalization)

Violations of Rule 4 by protagonist at the argumentation stage (ad populum 2, ignoratio elenchi [irrelevant argumentation]):

a   *Argumentation does not refer to standpoint under discussion*
  - using irrelevant argumentation
b   *Standpoint is defended by nonargumentative means of persuasion*
  - playing on audience's emotions
  - parading one's own qualities

Violations of Rule 5 by protagonist or antagonist at the argumentation stage:

FIG. 10.2. *(Continued)*

a *Denying an unexpressed premise* (by protagonist)
b *Magnifying an unexpressed premise* (by antagonist)

Violations of Rule 6 by protagonist or antagonist at the argumentation stage (many questions, petitio principii [begging the question, circular reasoning]):

a *Falsely presenting something as a common starting-point* (by protagonist):
  - falsely presenting a premise as self-evident
  - enveloping a proposition in a presupposition
  - concealing a premise in an unexpressed premise
  - advancing argumentation that amounts to the same thing as the standpoint
b *Denying a premise representing a common starting-point* (by antagonist):
  - casting doubt on an accepted starting-point

Violations of Rule 7 by protagonist at the argumentation stage (ad populum [populistic fallacy, variant of ad verecundiam 1], ad verecundiam 1, ad consequentiam, false analogy, post hoc ergo propter hoc, secundum quid [hasty generalization], slippery slope 1):

a *Choosing inappropriate argumentation scheme*
  - choosing inappropriate symptomatic argumentation
  - choosing inappropriate comparison argumentation
  - choosing inappropriate instrumental argumentation
b *Using an appropriate argumentation scheme incorrectly*
  - using symptomatic argumentation incorrectly
  - using comparison argumentation incorrectly
  - using instrumental argumentation incorrectly

Violations of Rule 8 by protagonist at the argumentation stage (affirming the consequent, denying the antecedent, composition, division):

a *Confusing necessary and sufficient conditions*
  - necessary condition is treated as sufficient
  - sufficient condition is treated as necessary
b *Confusing the properties of parts and wholes*
  - relative or structure-dependent property of whole is ascribed to part of whole
  - relative or structure-dependent property of part of whole is ascribed to whole

Violations of Rule 9 by protagonist or antagonist at the concluding stage (ad ignorantiam 2):

a *Making an absolute of defense's success* (by protagonist):
  - concluding that standpoint is true merely because it has been successfully defended
b *Making an absolute of defense's success* (by antagonist):
  - concluding that standpoint is true merely because the opposite has not been successfully defended

FIG. 10.2. *(Continued)*

305

Violations of Rule 10 by protagonist or antagonist at all stages of discussion (ambiguity)

a   *Taking undue advantage of unclearness*
- using structural unclearness
- using implicitness
- using indefiniteness
- using unfamiliarity
- using vagueness

b   *Taking undue advantage of ambiguity*
- using referential ambiguity
- using syntactic ambiguity
- using semantic ambiguity

FIG. 10.2.   Overview of violations of rules for critical discussion.

of functional norms. A whole series of other norms besides logical validity are taken into account, depending on the rule which has been violated.

10.4   PERSPECTIVES

In principle, the pragma-dialectical rules for critical discussion provide all the norms that play a role in resolving a difference of opinion. They amount to 10 different norms, which cover all fallacies that can be committed in argumentative discourse. Most logico-centric approaches to argumentation make use of only one norm, formal validity (in one sense or another).

Analyzing the fallacies systematically from a well-defined theoretical perspective is also promoted in formal dialectics, envisaging a theory of argumentation as a finite set of production rules for generating rational arguments (see chapter 9). According to Barth and Martens (1977), all (and only) arguments that can be generated by these rules are rational arguments. One important difference between formal dialectics and pragma-dialectics is that the pragma-dialectical rules are not formulated as production rules for generating rational arguments, but as constraints on the process of resolving differences of opinion. Another difference is that the pragma-dialectical rules are not primarily about the use of logical constants in a formal dialogue, but about the performance of speech acts in all stages of a critical discussion.

In logico-centric approaches to fallacies the problems of interpreting ordinary argumentative discourse are usually ignored or discounted as being due to infirmities of natural language. No distinction is generally made between norms that define the various types of fallacy and criteria for deciding whether a certain verbal move is to be regarded as an instance of a particular type of fallacy. Interpretation problems caused by the implicitness and indirectness of ordinary discourse are not systematically taken into account.

In order to classify the various problems arising in interpreting, analyzing and evaluating argumentative discourse, van Eemeren and Grootendorst (1992b) proposed a taxonomy of "relevance" in which this concept is differentiated along three dimensions: "object," "domain," and "aspect." With the help of this taxonomy, the problems of relevance can be more systematically dealt with.[53]

Relevance in argumentative discourse is notoriously difficult to define, particularly in sequences of speech acts by alternating speakers. This is partly so because speech acts are generally not directly relevant to prior speech acts, but to the purposes and plans constructed by these speech acts in the discourse; the difficulty is also partly caused by the demand for responsiveness in ordinary discourse, which allows for the initiation of structurally subordinate goals and plans, the temporary suspension of current concerns, the initiation of new purposes upon closure of old purposes and shifts in metapurposes.[54]

Defining relevance as a functional interactional relation between certain elements of a discourse provides some of the conceptual tools that are necessary for dealing adequately with relevance. As soon as the communicative and interactional goals behind a speech act can be specified, it depends on what can make a difference, one way or another, to the accomplishment of those goals what counts as a relevant response.[55] Of course, a relevant reaction is not necessarily a fitting reaction, let alone the reaction that most closely meets the speaker's wishes or expectations.

Starting from the pragma-dialectical concept of relevance, van Rees (1989, 1992a) has sought to apply this concept to interpreting and analyzing specimens of argumentative discourse. Focusing on problem-solving discussions, she tried to establish whether the purposes of this type of discourse, as laid out in normative handbooks, are sufficiently in accordance with the purposes of critical discussion to warrant a pragma-dialectical reconstruction (van Rees, 1992b). She also used descriptive models for this kind of discourse in order to investigate the extent to which actual problem-solving discussions conform to these ideals (van Rees, 1991). More recently, van Rees has shown how the actual reconstruction of problem-solving discussions as a critical discussion can be accounted for by using insights from speech act theory, discourse analysis and conversation analysis (1994a, 1994b, 1995a), and, conversely, how the pragma-dialectical framework may be useful in interpreting the function of an ordinary discourse phenomenon such as repetition (1995b).[56]

---

[53]This is illustrated by van Eemeren and Grootendorst (1992b, pp. 153–156) for the *argumentum ad hominem.*

[54]Experimental research (Jackson, Jacobs, & Rossi, 1987) has shown that the judged relevance of conversational replies is a function of the directness with which the reply addresses the underlying goals.

[55]The analyst's interpretive strategy implies that a discourse which may or may not be conceived of as a critical discussion is conceived of as such. This strategy can be seen as a normatively specialized version of applying the Gricean presumption of cooperation in generating implicatures.

[56]Verbiest (1987) gives a systematic description of how disputes arise in informal conversations, combining insights from pragma-dialectics with insights from conversation analysis. The absence of elements representing the confrontation stage, and the fact that one conversational

Another pragma-dialectical contribution to the analysis of argumentative discourse is made by Snoeck Henkemans (1992). In *Analysing complex argumentation*, she shows that multiple and coordinatively compound argumentation result from differently oriented dialogical exchanges aimed at resolving a difference of opinion. Coordinative argumentation, consisting of the advancing of additional arguments, results from an attempt to remove the opponent's doubt or criticism concerning the sufficiency of the argumentation. If the coordinative argumentation is used in a direct defense, it is "cumulative"; if used in an indirect defense, it is "complementary." Due to their function with regard to the sufficiency of the argumentation, the arguments are in both cases interdependent. In multiple argumentation, the arguments advanced in defense of the same standpoint are independent, because they are separate attempts to defend the standpoint, the one being motivated by the (potential) failure of the other.[57]

Recently, Snoeck Henkemans (1995a, 1995b) embarked upon a research project concerning the influence of stylistic properties of argumentative discourse on its comprehensibility and acceptability. She aims for a further integration of linguistics and argumentation theory enabling her to describe and classify the verbal means for indicating communicative and interactional functions.[58] In this endeavor, she concerns herself with relational argumentation indicators "in the narrow sense," for example, "because" and "for," which can mark argumentation structures, counterarguments, and concessions, and with indicators "in the broad sense," for example, "my reasons for this are" and "I do not agree with this view," which are used by arguers to express their position in the confrontation stage and to indicate how their contributions in other stages should be interpreted.

Feteris (1989) used the pragma-dialectical theory to reconstruct the way in which argumentative discourse is conducted in the context of law.[59] In order to determine the resemblance between the procedures used in settling legal disputes and the code of conduct for critical discussion, she analyzed the rules laid

---

element may represent several stages of the discussion, can be explained through the concept of "face management strategy" and the Principle of Politeness. Verbiest's study shows that there is an important parallel between the (normative) pragma-dialectical model of confrontation and confrontation in conversations. See also Newell and Stuttman (1983). For the problem of reconstructing indirect speech acts in ordinary argumentative discourse, see Slot (1994).

[57]Snoeck Henkemans indicates three kinds of clues that can be instrumental in reconstructing the argumentation structure: pragmatic clues in the way the arguer has presented the standpoint, dialogical clues in references to criticism, and dialectical clues following from the assumption that the arguer observes the procedural norms for critical discussion.

[58]In the same pragma-dialectical vein, Houtlosser (1994) analyzed the speech act of "advancing a standpoint," Koetsenruijter (1994) proposed a strategy for reconstructing the confrontation stage, and Gerritsen (1994) provided a defense of "deductivism" in reconstructing unexpressed premises.

[59]For the role of the judge in Dutch civil proceedings, see Feteris (1987, 1993a); for the legal procedural rules as additional rules for promoting the resolution of disputes, see Feteris (1990, 1993b); and for the problems of reconstructing judicial discussions, see Feteris (1991). Feteris, *Rationality in legal argumentation*, provides a general overview of theoretical approaches to legal argumentation (to be published).

down in the procedural codes of Dutch civil and criminal law as rules for accomplishing a reasonable solution of a dispute. Differences between the two could be explained by the specific judicial requirements prevailing in a legal context.[60]

In addition to their use in reconstructing argumentative discourse, pragma-dialectical insights have been brought to bear in providing guidelines for the construction of argumentative texts (van Eemeren & Grootendorst, 1994b).[61] The pragma-dialectical procedure for rewriting an argumentative text aims to ensure that the revised text is a demonstrable improvement of the original text by taking feedback from the primary text systematically into account. The main problem is how relevant information can be presented as comprehensibly and acceptably as possible, and there the ideal model of a critical discussion can serve, again, as a methodological starting point. On the basis of an analytic overview of an argumentative text, or serving as a plan for writing such a text, an argumentative text can be (re)written is such a way that its comprehensibility and acceptability is not diminished by redundancy, implicitness, disarrangement, or lack of clarity.[62] In this endeavor, four "presentation transformations" must be performed on the analytic overview, which "mirror" the reconstruction transformations. They roughly correspond to the following questions:

(1) what can be left out? ("presentational deletion")

(2) what should be added? ("presentational addition")

(3) which rearrangements should be made? ("presentational permutation")

(4) which reformulations must be made? ("presentational substitution").

In various pragma-dialectical projects, empirical research has recently been undertaken in order to establish to what extent the recognition of argumentation is facilitated, or hampered, by certain factors in the presentation.[63] Van Eemeren, Grootendorst, and Meuffels (1989) have reported on their investigations concerning the skill in identifying argumentation of 14-year-olds in secondary school.

---

[60]Other pragma-dialectical projects are aimed at integrating insights from argumentation theory and legal theory regarding the standards for reasonable argumentation in a judicial context. These projects aim for a systematic and coherent overview of the procedures and argumentative techniques applied in contexts of law, and the insights used to analyze and evaluate legal argumentation. Examples are Kloosterhuis' (1994) study of the problems involved in the analysis and evaluation of reasoning by analogy in legal argumentation, and Plug's (1994) study of the argumentation structures employed in the justification of judicial decisions.

[61]For an application of the pragma-dialectical approach to oral argumentation, see Berkenbosch and Braet (1994) on the use of critical questions connected with argumentation schemes in debate.

[62]Slot (1993) contributed to this project by studying the clues a writer can provide in order to facilitate the recognition and interpretation of rhetorical questions conveying a standpoint or argumentation. Viskil (1994) provided a useful tool for clarifying the meaning of argumentative discourse by constructing standard paraphrases of different types of definition for unclear or unknown terms.

[63]Most reports regarding these investigations are in Dutch. For a publication in English, see Jungslager (1994).

Can they recognize argumentation without having received any systematic instruction? To what extent is the identification of argumentation an independent skill rather than one based on such cognitive intellectual skills traditionally known as "verbal comprehension" and "general reasoning"?

After having been given an explanation of the concepts of "argumentation," "argument," and "standpoint," a relatively large proportion of second formers in a lower stream of comprehensive school could not identify simple argumentation, whereas a large majority of third formers could.[64] The progress made in "identifying argumentation" is considerably greater than that in "verbal comprehension" and "general reasoning." Grasping the concept of argumentation appears to be a matter of "yes or no": Argumentation is either understood as such or it is not. Although the skill in identifying argumentation is related to other intellectual skills, it has a relatively independent status.

The results of this research indicate that, unless specific education is provided, one should not expect students to gain insight into the concept of argumentation, let alone skill in distinguishing complex argumentation. Moreover, the results cast doubt on the effectiveness of that type of argumentation education among 14-year-olds in a lower stream of comprehensive school (unless, perhaps, a lot of time is spent on it).

Van Eemeren, de Glopper, Grootendorst, and Oostdam (1995) also investigated the performance of students in identifying unexpressed premises and argumentation schemes.[65] The results of two pencil and paper tests clearly indicate that unexpressed "major" premises and "nonsyllogistic" premises are, in the absence of disambiguating contextual information, more often correctly identified than unexpressed "minor" premises. Argumentation schemes of the "consequence" type are more often correctly identified than "token" argumentation, but not more frequently than "similarity" argumentation. Sizable individual differences were found in the identification of unexpressed premises and argumentation schemes. The individual differences are, to a substantial degree, correlated with school type, which indicates that they are related to differences in more general cognitive capabilities.[66] Obviously, these results of empirical research are interesting in their own right; in pragma-dialectics, however, they are primarily turned to account in developing educational methods for moving argumentative practice towards the theoretical ideal of critical discussion.

The pragma-dialectical approach to argumentation is an attempt to integrate a commitment to empirically adequate description with a critical stance towards argumentative practice. The primary theoretical device used to achieve this integration is a model for critical discussion aimed at resolving a difference of

---

[64]In Dutch secondary school education students follow different programs (from vocational to academic) according to their general cognitive skills and achievements.

[65]For empirical research concerning the use of argumentation schemes in response to arguments, see Garssen (1994).

[66]For empirical research into problems with writing argumentative texts in secondary school, see Oostdam, de Glopper, and Eiting (1994).

opinion. In this model, the rules and regularities of actual discourse are brought together with normative principles of goal-directed discourse. The model of a critical discussion is an abstraction, a theoretically motivated system for ideal resolution-oriented discourse. It provides a framework for the interpretation and reconstruction of actual argumentative discourse and for the evaluation of argumentative conduct. Thus it can serve as a standard for guiding the improvement in the practice of argumentation.

Rather than serving as a merely Utopian ideal, this model of a critical discussion can provide people who wish to resolve their differences by means of argumentative discourse with general and vital guidance for their conduct.[67] In part, the rules for critical discussion will correspond to norms they have already internalized. The claim that these rules are acceptable is not based on metaphysical necessity, but on their suitability to do the job for which they are intended: the resolution of disputes. The acceptability of the rules cannot be derived from any external authority or sacrosanct origin, but should rest on their effectiveness when applied. Since the acceptability of the rules is to be judged by the extent to which they appear successful in solving the problems they are designed to solve, the rationale for accepting the rules can, philosophically, be characterized as "pragmatic."[68]

Which sort of people will be willing to adopt the discussion attitude required by the rules, thus providing them with conventional validity? They will be people who accept doubt as an integral part of their way of life and use criticism towards themselves and others in order to solve problems by trial and error.[69] They use argumentative discourse as a means to detect weaknesses in viewpoints regarding knowledge, values and objectives, and eliminate these weaknesses where possible.[70] Such people, being opposed to protectionism with regard to viewpoints and to the immunization of any kind of standpoint against criticism, will reject all fundamentalistic "justificationism" (*Letztbegründung*).[71]

---

[67]Although resting on different philosophical starting points, Habermas' (1971) ideal of consensus in a speech situation of communication unimpaired by power relations is in some respects not dissimilar to the pragma-dialectical ideal, albeit that the driving forces of progress are according to pragma-dialectics intellectual doubt and criticism, leading to a continual flux of opinions, not consensus.

[68]This kind of pragmatism can be seen as "utilitarian" in some sense. See van Eemeren and Grootendorst (1988).

[69]Provided that the appropriate "higher order" conditions, referred to in note 22 of this chapter, are satisfied.

[70]In this respect, pragma-dialectics connects with formal dialectics, described in chapter 9. The use of the term *dialectic* points to this agreement in general objective, whereas the use of *pragma(tic)*, instead of *formal*, points to the differences in orientation.

[71]Justificationism, whatever its make, can never escape from the *Münchhausen-trilemma* (Albert, 1975, p. 13). Usually, the process of *Begründung* is at some point abandoned and a certain starting point is rendered immune to criticism, serving as an *a priori* or even a dogma of reasonableness. The geometrical approach leads to a form of justificationism to which Albert refers to as "intellectualism," the anthropological approach to "empiristic" justificationism.

11

LANGUAGE-ORIENTED APPROACHES TO ARGUMENTATION

Although this volume concentrates on studies of argumentation that are accessible to speakers of English, some attention is also paid to important contributions that are only partly available in English. Among the new approaches to argumentation that have emerged in languages other than English in the last decades, there are several that are language–oriented. These approaches, primarily presented in Romance languages, are surveyed in this chapter.

First, we discuss the linguistic approach to argumentation, propounded by the French linguists Ducrot and Anscombre, which is known as Radical Argumentativism (Sections 11.1 and 11.2). Then, we give a brief survey of some basic insights from Natural Logic, an alternative to formal logic developed at the Swiss Centre de Recherches Sémiologiques by Grize and his associates (Section 11.3). In addition, we sketch the outlines of an argumentative grammar as expounded by the Italian-born linguist Lo Cascio (Section 11.4).

Since the early 1970s, Oswald Ducrot and Jean-Claude Anscombre have been developing their linguistic approach to argumentative discourse. A crucial characteristic of their position is that they regard "argumentativity" as being a general feature of all language use, whereas it is generally seen as a distinctive feature of a specific form, or mode, of discourse.[1] A further notable characteristic

---

[1]According to Meyer (1986b), rather than to show simply that language is used to argue and to convince, Ducrot and Anscombre's aim is "to demonstrate *how* natural language *indicates* a conclusion; suggests, implies, promotes or presupposes it without stating it *explicitly in words*" (p. 95).

is that Ducrot and Anscombre's theory is exclusively descriptive. Their objective is to describe the syntactic and semantic features of sentences that play a role in the argumentative interpretation of these sentences, not to develop any evaluation criteria for argumentation.[2] Ducrot and Anscombre's approach has been highly influential in the French-speaking world; only lately has it become somewhat better known among other argumentation theorists.[3]

Ducrot and Anscombre have shown that the presence of certain words can provide the sentences in which they occur with an orientation that is intrinsically argumentative. This orientation predetermines these sentences to serve in support of particular types of conclusion rather than others. The orientation towards particular types of conclusion does not completely determine which conclusions are eventually defended in the argumentation: language opens the possibility for certain ways of talking, but it is the people that do the talking who decide how they are going to make use of these options. In addition to the linguistic component, Ducrot and Anscombre, also distinguish a rhetorical component in the theory they envisage, but leave it rather sketchy.

Since the 1960s, Jean-Blaise Grize and the other members of his school study what they prefer to call natural logic, as opposed to formal logic (and, at least terminologically, to informal logic). Like Ducrot and Anscombre, the natural logicians are not interested in developing criteria for evaluating arguments: They want to describe the "logic" of ordinary argumentative discourse in a nonnormative, "naturalistic" way. Their approach is partly based on epistemological insights developed by Piaget, and makes reference to the theoretical framework of Ducrot and Anscombre. The influence of Aristotle, and that of Perelman, can be discerned in their concern with speakers adapting the presentation of their arguments to the knowledge and values of the audience in order to meet the conditions of plausibility and acceptability. More generally, their influence manifests itself in the natural logicians' concentration on the *dispositio* of the argument.

In order to do justice to the presentational aspects of argumentative discourse, the natural logicians opt for studying argumentation as a discursive phenomenon. The logic of argumentative discourse is not restricted to deduction, however, this does not mean that argumentative discourse is without form. According to the natural logicians, the forms *schematized* in argumentative discourse are connected with the purposes of the speakers, the things they are referring to, and the situation in which the discourse takes place. Their aim is to study the operations involved in the *construction* of such schematizations.

---

[2]The role of such features in interpretation processes is investigated empirically by Bassano (1991) and Bassano and Champaud (1987a, 1987b, 1987c).

[3]Cf. Lundquist (1987), Nølke (1992), van Eemeren and Grootendorst (1994a), Verbiest (1994), Snoeck Henkemans (1995a, 1995b), and Zagar (1995).

Since these schematizations are designed to modify the state of knowledge of the audience, the natural logicians' approach to argumentation is, basically, epistemological. In their own view, natural logic is, in its present state, "a programme in which nothing is definitive" (Borel, 1989, p. 45). According to Borel (1989), Natural Logic takes an intermediate position between two extremes: logic and rhetoric (p. 36). Natural logic can be seen as a logical approach in that it concentrates on the *forms* of arguments; it can be seen as a rhetorical approach because of its emphasis on the situational (contextual and referential) aspects of argumentation. It can also be seen, one might add, as (pragma-)linguistic, in view of its combination of the two. An argument is studied in a context of situated argumentative discourse by taking account of the syntactic and semantic properties of the language in which it is formulated.

During the last three decades, there is also a growing interest in argumentation in Italy, mainly in its philosophical and rhetorical aspects (see chapter 12). Under the influence of Perelman and Olbrechts-Tyteca (1958), argumentation has been studied as a way of using language for influencing people, manipulative or otherwise.[4] Many Italian scholars of argumentation adhere to the Toulminian idea of each field of thought requiring a different type of discourse. Recently, a language-oriented approach to argumentation has been proposed by Vincenzo Lo Cascio which connects with the Chomskyan idea of generative grammar.

The argumentative grammar envisaged by Lo Cascio responds to the current interest in paying more attention to argumentation in linguistic education. All speakers need to develop the competence to make their reasoning explicit in an effective way. In order to teach argumentation successfully, more knowledge is required of the learning processes and phases which play a part in acquiring argumentative competence in the mother tongue and in learning a second language.

In Lo Cascio's opinion, it is important that speakers choose the most effective "profile" in their argumentative encounters and give their argumentative message an appropriate linguistic form. Therefore, every speaker should have the linguistic competence to produce well-formed argumentative messages and to discover the textual organization of the argumentative messages of others. In order to be able to evaluate the textual organization of argumentative discourse, and to detect its persuasive and manipulative power, an understanding is required of how argumentative discourse works.

---

[4]The Italian translation of Perelman and Olbrechts-Tyteca's (1958) study of the new rhetoric appeared in 1966; it was introduced by the philosopher Bobbio. Its publication led to an immediate revival of the philosophical, sociological and semantic reflection on argumentation. In the words of Eco (1987): "I remember the impact that [...] Perelman and Olbrechts-Tyteca's book had upon us: the field of argumentation, including that bound to philosophy, is that of the plausible and the probable" (p. 14).

11.1   ANSCOMBRE AND DUCROT'S RADICAL ARGUMENTATIVISM

Ducrot and Anscombre have expressed their ideas in a great many publications, almost exclusively in French. The main outlines of their approach are sketched in Ducrot's *Les Echelles Argumentatives* (1980) and *Le Dire et le Dit* (1984), and in *L'Argumentation dans la Langue* by Anscombre and Ducrot (1983). Ducrot and Anscombre are calling their approach Radical Argumentativism because every form of language use has, in their view, an argumentative aspect. They have reached this radical position regarding the argumentative function of language in stages. Initially, they concentrated on describing linguistic indicators of argumentative relations in natural discourse.[5]

In their early work, Ducrot and Anscombre examined verbal *connectives* such as "therefore," "consequently," and "for." Later on, they broadened their analysis to include other types of connectives such as "but" and "and." Traditionally, these particles have been analyzed as introducing relations between states of affair, but, according to Ducrot and Anscombre, they have a similar argumentative value as the generally recognized indicators of argumentative relations.

Anscombre and Ducrot consider as argumentative all utterances that lead the listener or reader, often implicitly, to a certain conclusion. Starting from this view, they conclude that argumentation is not limited to a particular type of intellectual activity. Instead, they regard it as a permanent feature of the use of language. A case in point are such connectives as "and" and "but": rather than being restricted to argumentative contexts, they are used in all types of discourse.

All the same, their use is in a specific way argumentatively constrained: "and" for instance, cannot be used to connect two premises with inconsistent orientations. Under normal circumstances, an utterance like (1) sounds odd:

(1) Go see that movie: It is poorly directed and very well acted.

"But," however, would fit in perfectly.

In a further stage of the development of their approach, Anscombre and Ducrot extend their analysis to other lexical items: *operators* such as "little," "a little," "almost," "barely," and "hardly." Their fundamental idea is that through such operators argumentative values enter into the semantic structure of the sentence. These operators provide sentences with an orientation toward a certain type of conclusion that cannot be deduced merely from the informative content of the sentences concerned.

---

[5]Anscombre and Ducrot describe the evolution in their work in "Argumentativity and informativity" (1989).

This point is illustrated by examples (2), (3), and (4):

(2) (a) There were twenty people.

 (b) So the party was a success/

 (b′) So the party was a failure.

(3) (a) There were *almost* twenty people.

 (b) So the party was a success.

(4)*(a) There were *barely* twenty people.

 (b) So the party was a success.

In example (2), no argumentative operator is being employed. The statement "There were twenty people" (2a) may just as well be used to argue for the success of the party (2b) as for its failure (2b′). It depends on the context and the norms for a successful party, whether there being twenty people can be considered as an argument for the success of the party or for its failure. As soon as an argumentative operator is introduced, this situation changes. In (3), the statement that there were "almost" twenty people (3a) can be interpreted as an argument for the success of the party; in (4), however, the statement that there were "barely" twenty people (4a) cannot be considered to support this conclusion (unless the speaker is being ironical, but then the speaker's intended conclusion is just the opposite of the literal conclusion).

The presence of operators such as "almost" and "barely" has an influence upon the argumentative orientation of the utterance in which they occur that is absent in "neutral" utterances without them. Their use orients the listener or reader towards a certain type of conclusion: a negative conclusion in the case of "barely," a positive conclusion in the case of "almost." This orientation cannot be deduced merely from the quantitative information provided by these operators.

Since "almost twenty" means less than twenty, whereas "barely twenty" means twenty or more, the argument that there were "almost" twenty people would, viewed merely from a quantitative point of view, provide weaker support for the conclusion that the party was a success than the argument that there were "barely" twenty people. If the number of people present at the party would be decisive for its success, then using "barely" in the argument supporting the conclusion would have led to a stronger argument than using "almost": more than "almost," "barely" directs the listener or reader to this desired quality of quantity. In fact, however, just the opposite happens to be the effect of these operators. Evidently, the quantitative information provided by these operators does not determine the way in which they are used argumentatively: There is some extra meaning attached to these operators which transcends their purely informative meaning in the quantitative sense. An extra positive "evaluative" aspect appears to be associated with the use of "almost" and an extra negative "evaluative" aspect with the use of "barely." This evaluative aspect Ducrot and Anscombre call "argumentative."

Currently, Anscombre and Ducrot have taken up a more radical stance. They no longer believe that the afore-mentioned operators introduce argumentative values into otherwise purely informative, or neutral, sentences. In their present view, argumentativity is already inherent in sentences without operators.

At the sentence level, linguistic predicates such as "to be expensive" in "This restaurant is expensive," or "to work" in "John worked more than Peter," always provide an argumentative orientation. These predicates are associated with certain sets of argumentative principles, comparable to the Aristotelian *topoi*. According to Anscombre and Ducrot (1989), describing an object as "expensive" rather than "cheap," instead of merely providing information on its price, involves a choice for applying *topoi* regarding the value of expensiveness as compared to cheapness (p. 80). Calling something expensive may, for instance, invoke the *topos* "The less expensive a thing is, the better deal it is," or its converse, "The more expensive a thing is, the less a good deal it is." A *topos* always entails a correspondence between two dimensions of gradation of a nonnumerical kind.

Topoi authorize the drawing of certain conclusions in a particular speech community. Thus, in a context where the *topoi* "The more expensive a restaurant is, the less recommendable it is to go there" and "The less expensive a restaurant is, the more recommendable it is to go there" apply, calling a restaurant expensive will amount to advancing an argument for not going there, whereas calling it cheap may be considered as an argument for the opposite conclusion.

Conclusions that can be drawn on the authority of certain *topoi* may be left unstated. If conclusions have been made explicit in the discourse, it depends on the *topoi* that are invoked whether or not the specific discursive sequences containing that conclusion will be well-formed. Under normal circumstances, the following sequence of statements sounds rather strange:

(5) * This restaurant is expensive: You should go there.

This sequence might be well-formed, however, in a context where *topoi* apply such as "The more expensive the restaurant is, the better the quality of the food" or "The more expensive the restaurant is, the more impressive it is." The latter *topos* may, for instance, apply in a context where it is important to make a good impression and the addressee will be impressed by the fact that the recommended restaurant is an expensive one.

As we have mentioned, in the current stage of Anscombre and Ducrot's theory argumentativity is not considered to be introduced by argumentative operators. In Anscombre and Ducrot's view, the *topoi* are immanent in the meaning of the predicates, and through the *topoi* argumentative values already enter the sentences as they "initially" are. Nevertheless, the argumentative operators do still play a role, albeit the more restricted one of specifying in what way the *topoi* are to be applied.

First, the argumentative operators can provide information as to whether the "direct" *topos* is to be invoked, which can be schematized as "The more x, the more y," or the "converse" *topos*, which can be schematized as "The less x, the less y." How this may work, can be shown with the help of the sentences (6a) and (6b):

(6a) Peter worked a little.

(6b) Peter worked little.

When the sentences (6a) and (6b) are interpreted, it has to be established first which *topos* should be selected. The set of *topoi* associated with the use of the predicate "to work" includes *topoi* such as "The more someone has worked, the more praise he deserves" and "The more someone has worked, the more tired he is." Assuming that the first *topos*, "The more someone has worked, the more praise he deserves," does apply, it then needs to be established whether the direct *topos* or the converse *topos* should be selected. This is where the argumentative operators come into play. In 6a, "a little" instructs us to select the direct *topos*: that Peter worked a little can be seen as an argument for the conclusion that he deserves to be praised. In 6b, "little" points to the converse *topos*: that Peter worked little may be regarded as a reason for not praising him.[6]

Second, the argumentative operators can provide information regarding the "argumentative force" of an utterance. In (6a), "a little" locates Peter's work at the bottom of the scale (or gradation) of work. The conclusions drawn from (6a) will have to be related to an equally low position on the same scale. Under normal circumstances, (6a) would be followed by a conclusion like "We must give him a little something," not by "He deserves a big reward." Things change if the speaker provides additional arguments such as "The weather is unbearably hot" or "He has recently undergone a severe operation." Through such additions the speaker increases the argumentative force of the utterance, thus authorizing a "stronger" conclusion.

11.2 POLYPHONY IN ARGUMENTATIVE DISCOURSE

Crucial to Anscombre and Ducrot's analyses of different types of sentence connectives is the concept of *polyphony*, or "many-voicedness."[7] According to the polyphonic theory, every piece of discourse, even if it consists of just one sentence, contains a dialogue, whether explicit or implicit. As a consequence, in the utterance of a sentence more than one standpoint can be expressed at

---

[6]For a more detailed analysis of the difference between the examples given in (6a) and (6b), see Anscombre and Ducrot (1989, pp. 90–91), where a Law of Weakness is postulated.

[7]Anscombre and Ducrot's concept of polyphony stems from Bakhtin, who introduced it in literary theory. A detailed explanation of the polyphonic theory is given in Ducrot (1984, chap. 8).

the same time, and no single speaker can, at the same time, be held responsible for all the (sometimes contradictory) viewpoints that are being expressed.

This can be illustrated with the help of an example of a sentence with a negation:

(7) This wall is not white.

According to Anscombre and Ducrot, this sentence entails a dialogue with a (silent) second "voice" that maintains, or at least believes, (8):

(8) This wall is white.

This second "voice" is revealed by analyzing (7) as structurally containing two (incompatible) viewpoints:

(a) This wall is white.
(b) Viewpoint (a) is incorrect.

In support of this analysis of sentences containing a (polemic) negation, Ducrot (1984) refers to the fact that a negative statement can be followed by the expression "on the contrary," as in: "He is not nice, on the contrary, he is detestable" (1984, pp. 216–217). The expression "on the contrary" must refer to the positive statement "He is nice" and not to the negative statement "He is not nice." Both the positive viewpoint ("He is nice") and its rejection must therefore be present in the negative sentence.

In order to account for the possibility that different voices are speaking in one and the same utterance, Anscombre and Ducrot make a three-fold distinction. First, there is a *speaker* or *writer* ("sujet parlant"): the actual producer of the utterance, the physical person who is doing the speaking or writing. Second, there is a *locutor* ("locuteur"): the source that is responsible for the words that are spoken in (a certain part of) an utterance, often referred to in the utterance by the personal pronoun "I" (or a similar linguistic marker).[8] Third, there is the *enunciator* ("énonciateur"): the character that presents a perspective on the points of view or attitudes referred to by a locutor without the locutor being accountable for these views or attitudes.[9]

---

[8]The difference between the "speaker" and the "locutor" can be illustrated with the help of an example. Mary says: "Peter said I don't know what to do." In this example, the speaker, Mary, and the locutor referred to by "I," Peter, are different people.

[9]The role of the enunciator, too, can be illustrated with the help of an example. Suppose a speaker narrating someone else's experiences at an airport waiting impatiently for the arrival of his girl friend: "First a man in a black hat comes out, then a group of teenagers, followed by two rather fat ladies, and then—at last—Joan appears." In this example, the words "at last" cannot be attributed to the (uninvolved) reporting locutor, but they represent the perspective of an enunciator who expresses the waiting person's relief at finally seeing his girl friend.

Through the enunciator, the speaker or writer can introduce a certain view on what is being said by a locutor, whether this locutor is someone else or the current speaker or writer. This view may not be directly attributed to the locutor, because it originates from an independent character, the enunciator. In this way, a distant view can be presented on a locutor's points of view or attitudes without the locutor who is associated with these points of view or attitudes being responsible for this view. According to Ducrot (1984), the distinction between the speaker or writer, the locutor and the enunciator resembles the distinction made in literary theory between the author of a novel, the narrator and the character whose point of view or perspective determines the way in which the narrated events are presented (pp. 206–208).

Anscombre and Ducrot's analysis of the connective "but" provides a good example of the way in which they use the notion of polyphony in their linguistic descriptions. In these descriptions, they combine the notion of polyphony with the concept of *topos*.

In propositional logic, "but" means precisely the same as "and." It is, of course, recognized by logicians that an additional feature of "but" is that it implies a contrast or opposition between the two conjuncts it connects, but this observation has no influence on the truth conditions of the sentence. From a purely logical point of view, the meaning of the sentence "P, *but* Q" is exhaustively analyzed by the equivalence in (9):

(9) The sentence "P *but* Q" is true if and only if "P" is true and "Q" is true.

In Ducrot and Anscombre's (non-truth functional) analysis of "but," an attempt is made to capture the nature of the opposition implied by "but" more precisely than it is captured in the logical analysis. In a sentence like (10), it is clear that the opposition cannot simply be that between [P] and [Q]:

(10) This restaurant is expensive [P], but good [Q]

The opposition cannot simply be that there is a contradiction between the properties "being expensive" and "being good" when applied to a restaurant, since there is no contradiction. In (10), according to Anscombre and Ducrot's view, "but" indicates an opposition between two opposite conclusions that are authorized by the following two *topoi*: "The more expensive a restaurant is, the less advisable it is to go there" and "The better a restaurant is, the more advisable it is to go there."[10] In (10), "but" refers to an opposition between two conclusions:

[10]In an ordinary (unmarked) context, these two *topoi* seem the most suitable. Of course, in some other context other *topoi* might be relevant.

C1 "It is not advisable to go there" (a conclusion drawn from [P])

and

C2 "It is advisable to go there" (a conclusion drawn from [Q])

According to this analysis, P and Q are arguments for two opposite conclusions. However, "but" not only indicates a contrast, so the analysis is not yet complete. A further important characteristic of the construction "P, *but* Q" is that the conclusion *that can be drawn from* Q is the one the arguer wants to endorse. Thus, the presence of the word "but" ensures that the conclusion based on the first part of the sentence is the opposite of the conclusion based on the second part, and it also ensures that the latter is considered stronger. The argument Q carries more weight for the arguer than the argument P. In our example (10), the arguer may be considered to defend the conclusion "It is advisable to go there," which is supported by Q.

In polyphonic terms, the analysis of a sentence like (10) runs as follows. A speaker who says "P, *but* Q" stages four enunciators (Ducrot, 1990, pp. 68–69):

— an enunciator E1, who adopts the point of view expressed in P ("This restaurant is expensive")
— an enunciator E2, who adopts the point of view expressed in Q ("This restaurant is good")
— an enunciator E3, who argues from P to a conclusion C ("It is not advisable to go there")
— an enunciator E4, who argues from Q to a conclusion not-C ("It is advisable to go there")

The locutor agrees with E1 and E2, disassociates himself (or herself) from E3, and associates himself (or herself) with E4.

This analysis makes it also possible to explain the difference in meaning between the sentences (11) and (12):

(11) This restaurant is expensive, but good.
(12) This restaurant is good, but expensive.

In the case of (11), the sentence can be followed by "You should go there." In the case of (12), under normal circumstances this does not result in a well-formed discursive sequence. The reason is that (12) would normally be seen as support for the opposite conclusion: "You should not go there."

In carrying out such analyses and explaining their theoretical basis, Ducrot and Anscombre have a lot to offer to the study of argumentation. Ducrot and

Anscombre may be primarily interested in describing the syntactic and semantic features playing a role in the argumentative interpretation of sentences, but their linguistic approach provides argumentation theorists with most valuable insights, in particular regarding the argumentative function of various operators and connectives.[11]

Starting from these insights, a methodical exploration can be undertaken of the verbal clues for identifying standpoints and arguments and for analyzing the structural aspects of complex argumentation. Snoeck Henkemans (1995a), for example, gives an account of the way in which connectives such as "even" and "anyway" may serve as indicators of "coordinative" (or "linked") and "multiple" (or "convergent") argumentation structures that is partly based on the analyses of Anscombre and Ducrot.

Ducrot and Anscombre's polyphonic and topical analyses of connectives such as "but" and concessive expressions such as "although," have established the ground for more detailed analyses of counterarguments, refutations, and concessions. Moeschler and de Spengler (1982), but also Apothéloz, Brandt, and Quiroz (1991) and Quiroz, Apothéloz, and Brandt (1992), are among those who have carried out such analyses starting from insights gained from the works of Ducrot and Anscombre.

11.3   GRIZE'S NATURAL LOGIC

The theory of natural logic, originating in the Centre de Recherches Sémiologiques of the University of Neuchâtel, Switzerland, has been propounded as an alternative to formal logic in the analysis of argumentation. This theory has been developed since the late 1960s by the Swiss logician Jean-Blaise Grize, his colleagues Marie-Jeanne Borel, Denis Miéville, Denis Apothéloz, and others.[12] Grize, born in 1922, was a collaborator of the epistemologist and psychologist Jean Piaget; in 1960 he became professor of logic at the University of Neuchâtel, and director of the Centre. Since 1965, his work has centered on the logic of ordinary argumentative discourse.[13]

---

[11]Cf. Ducrot et al. (1980) and Anscombre and Ducrot (1983) for detailed analyses of expressions such as "even" (*même*), "anyway" (*d'ailleurs*), "at least" (*au moins*), and "but" (*mais*).

[12]See Grize (1982), Borel, Grize, and Miéville (1983), Borel (1989), and Maier (1989).

[13]According to Gomez Diaz (1991), the development of natural logic has proceeded through three stages. The aim of the first stage was to develop a logic of thought which runs parallel to, and is grounded in, the psychology of intelligence (Psycho-logic, 1958–1976). In the next stage, a sociological orientation is given to the theory (Socio-logic, 1978–1980). In the third stage, the affective aspects of argumentation are accounted for by moving into semiology (Semio-logic). Thus natural logic incorporates the three components that are, according to Grize, common to all discourse: the cognitive component, the social component, and the affective component (pp. 123–124).

As is true of informal logic, the main motive for developing natural logic was dissatisfaction with formal logic.[14] According to natural logicians, it is evident that the logic used in argumentation is not that of deduction alone. Also, formal logical evaluation of argumentation requires a reconstruction which is often far removed from the argument as it was presented. A (formal) logical reconstruction of an argument involves a reduction of the argument to an abstract logical standard form, requiring more often than not the reordering of elements in the text, the addition of implicit elements, and many other transformations. According to Grize (1982), there is no *a priori* justification (nor an *a posteriori* justification, for that matter) for reducing argumentation to mere (deductive) reasoning (p. 186).

The way an argument is presented should not be seen as arbitrary. Its convincingness may just as much, or even more, depend on its presentation as on the abstract reasoning patterns underlying it. In order to do justice to the presentational aspects of argumentation, Grize proposes to study argumentation as a discursive phenomenon. In this endeavor, he opts for an approach that deviates in a number of ways from that of formal logicians.[15]

A first difference is that natural logic purports to be dialogical, not monological. Unlike in formal logic, in natural logic the communicative situation in which argumentation is put forward is not disregarded: Each argumentative discourse is seen as a proposal made by a speaker to a listener in a specific situation.[16] In order to get their proposals accepted by their listeners, speakers either have to present their premises as facts, or, if they are not accepted as facts, provide more argumentation in support of them. In formal logic, by contrast, the premises are regarded as hypothetical or axiomatical; it is not the logician's task to establish their truth.

A second difference, pertaining to the semantics of argumentative discourse, is that the "objects" of argumentative propositions are neither meaningless, nor "empty" as they are in formal logic, nor axiomatically determined beforehand. In discursive texts, the objects that are being talked about—which traditional logicians call the "subjects"—have a more or less well-defined meaning before they are referred to in the text (Grize, 1986, pp. 49–50, Borel, 1992). Associated with these objects is a set of properties, of relations with other objects, and of actions which can be performed with the objects. An object like "key," for

---

[14]Natural logicians prefer the term *natural logic* to *informal logic* since they consider the latter term a *contradictio terminorum*. The term "informal logic" is, in their view, misleading because it suggests that ordinary argumentative discourse is without form (Borel, 1989, p. 38). By using the term "natural logic," natural logicians want to emphasize that logic belongs to the domain of (naturalized) epistemology rather than normative science.

[15]The description of the main differences between formal logic and natural logic serves at the same time as a (contrastive) definition of natural logic.

[16]Although there are some differences in the process of interpreting written texts, what is being said here about speakers and listeners applies, *mutatis mutandis*, equally to writers and readers.

instance, may be taken to have the properties "being made of iron" and "being light," while it will generally not have the properties of "being gaseous" or "being even." The object "key" can be related to other objects such as "lock" and "pocket," but not to an object like "cloud." And an action one can perform with a "key" is "turn" it, but not "subtract" it. A speaker who constructs an argumentative text makes use of the properties that the listener, presumably, already associates with the objects concerned.[17] Not all the properties of an object, however, are predetermined. As the text proceeds, step by step, the objects are given a more precise meaning, new connections are established between them and other objects, and they are otherwise enriched and expanded.

A third difference between natural logic and formal logic is that it takes into account that the aim of argumentation is not, as in formal proofs, to transfer the truth of the premises of the argument to the conclusion, but to gain the listener's approval or acceptance of the conclusion. What is at issue in the discourse is not truth, but plausibility. The argument should therefore be presented in such a way that it fits in with the listener's representations of the world.[18]

Argumentative discourse is by no means without form. According to natural logicians, speakers perform specific operations in order to produce an argumentative text that exhibits a *schematization* of a form adapted to the situation and fitting with their purposes. The objective of natural logic is to study the operations involved in the "construction" of such argumentative schematizations.

According to natural logicians, the schematization a speaker (A) proposes in an argumentative discourse to a listener (B) is a symbolic construction concerning a specific case presented interactively through a text in a given language in a given situation (Borel, 1989, p. 38). The choice for a specific schematization depends on A's aims, but also on the information available to A about B's knowledge, opinions and preferences, A's assessment of the relation between A and B, and A's own knowledge and opinions about the theme of the discourse. In order to refer to the different types of situational knowledge the speaker brings to bear, Borel, Grize, and Miéville (1983) make use of the term *representation*.

It is up to B to reconstruct A's symbolic construction. In this reconstruction, B is helped by textual indications; traces of the activity of schematizing are always to be found. It is due to the use of specific verbal means that certain "images" of the speaker, the theme and the listener emerge in the schematization. These images are produced by the schematization. The speaker's representations belong to the domain of the *production process*; they represent a certain knowledge of the necessary conditions for successful communication.

---

[17]Of course, when speaking metaphorically, all kinds of properties can be ascribed to objects which they do not normally have.

[18]A deduction or formal proof is seen by natural logicians as nothing more than an instance of this general concern to present an argument in such a way that it can gain the approval of the listener.

According to Grize, in order to account for the notion of schematization, a model of communication is required which is not that of a simple transmittance of information. B can only arrive at a reconstruction of A's schematization by performing more or less similar operations as A performed in constructing the schematization. Since B has to play an active role in the reconstruction process, there is no guarantee that the schematization reconstructed by B is identical to the one proposed to him by A (Borel, Grize, & Miéville, 1983, pp. 99–100). If B's reconstruction is more or less identical with the construction intended by A, the natural logicians speak of a "resonance" between the listener's reconstruction and the speaker's construction.

The communication model required to capture the notion of "schematization" is presented in Fig. 11.1. The term *schematization* is ambiguous: On the one hand, it refers to the *product* of the construction process (the schema); on the other hand, it refers to the *process* or activity of schematizing (Borel, et al., 1983, p. 54). According to natural logicians, the ambiguity is not a disadvantage. On the contrary, it is precisely because of this ambiguity that it becomes possible to link the operations involved in the construction of a text to the organization of the text as a product.

Every text contains traces of the activity of schematizing (Borel, et al., 1983, pp. 55–57). What the natural logicians mean by such "traces" can be illustrated by presenting their analysis of an example. For this purpose, we make use of a fragment of a propaganda text aimed at convincing the reader of the fact that no violence is committed by the state in Argentina:

This is not all. In every country in the world each year thousands of people disappear: 10.0000 per year in France who do not inform their relatives at all. A similar

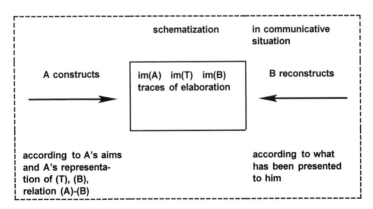

A = speaker / writer
B = listener / reader
T = theme
im = image

FIG. 11.1. Communication model for capturing the notion of schematization.

situation exists in Argentina, where people have simply abandoned their homes, profiting from the chaos and confusion, in order to start a new life elsewhere, for strictly personal reasons [translated from P.F. de Villemarest, *Les stratégies de la peur*].

Taken at face-value, this text is built up around a rule and two facts: people disappear here (in France), in Argentina and everywhere else, and for the same reasons (Borel, et al., 1983, p. 55). An analysis of the text schema by way of an activity of schematization, however, opens the possibility to point at other phenomena.

First, why does the writer introduce France while he could just as well have chosen a different country? From this choice, we may infer that the text is written for a reader who is French. The text therefore refers to a fact that is known to a reader living in France. As soon as this point has been acknowledged, the discourse can no longer be seen as enumerating "true" and neutral facts. Knowing that it is a normal situation in France that people disappear, the reader may conclude that a similar situation might exist in other countries, such as Argentina. Thus the text establishes a relation between different "facts" (the situation in France and that in Argentina) which might produce either an inductive inference on the part of the reader (if this situation exists here, why not elsewhere) or an analogy (Argentina is not very different from France).

Second, why does the writer put so much stress on a specific reason for disappearing (wanting to start a new life)? There are other reasons for disappearing, in France too, such as being the victim of a murder (or having committed one). Here, the values adhered to by the reader are supposed to guarantee the transition from the one fact to the other: Irresponsible people who perturb their families you can find everywhere; this being the case in France, it will *a fortiori* be the case in Argentina.

The text as a whole is constructed in such a way as to prevent the reader from coming to an opinion that is different from the writer's. The writer anticipates the reader's reactions by evoking in the schematization the reader's knowledge of the normal order of things in the reader's own society and the values associated with it. At the same time, the supposedly neutral presentation of the facts is deliberately chosen to silence a reader who might have a different opinion on this issue. Although the form of the text is neutral, it is clear that a polemic situation is presupposed.

A schema, or "schematization," has a number of properties. It reports specific facts that are relevant to the speaker's aim. It can be adapted to a specific listener. It has its own structure, and should therefore be seen as a type of "micro-universe" or symbolic construction. It accentuates specific aspects, masking the unavoidable side-effect of partiality inherent in selecting and constructing a schema.

Traces of that which is left out by the speaker will, nonetheless, always be present. Even a speaker who deliberately leaves certain elements implicit, or presents the information in a specific way to prevent the listener from coming up with specific questions or objections, can not do so without, at the same time, showing to be doing so.

In order for a schematization to be successful, that is, in order to get the listener to adhere to the position advocated by the speaker, a specific operation must be performed in the schematization by the speaker: the operation of neutralizing the fact that the speaker is taking a certain *position*. The speaker can perform this operation by camouflaging the relative character of the schematization. The discourse should be presented in such a way to the listener that it looks as if the information represented is objective and absolute. A schematization can be effective only if the speaker manages to incite the reader to take what Grize calls a "realistic" attitude towards what is being proposed (Borel, Grize, & Miéville, 1983, p. 76).[19] This attitude is the counterpart of a "polemic" or "critical" attitude since it prevents the listener from becoming aware that information that is presented as objective and absolute is, in fact, subjective and relative.

Whether or not the speaker succeeds in invoking a realistic attitude in the listener, depends on the *discursive coherence* of the schematization. It is this coherence which enables the listener to reproduce (at least to some extent) the schematization the speaker has produced.[20] There are three conditions for discursive coherence.

First, the discourse must be *receivable*. The listener should be able to recognize that someone has said something in an identifiable form in order to retrieve the information from what is said and to acknowledge the style in which it was formulated as appropriate for the occasion. Second, the discourse must be *plausible* (or should have verisimilitude, cf. Aristotle's concept of "eikos"). The world that is presented in the discourse should be conceivable, its objects should be identifiable and the relations between these objects should correspond to the listener's idea of reality. Third, the discourse must be *acceptable*. Whereas the plausibility of the discourse refers to the domain of facts, the acceptability has to do with the values that are presented in the discourse. The listener should be able to identify with these values.

---

[19]According to Borel, Grize, and Miéville (1983, p. 75), Grize borrowed the concept of "realistic attitude" from Piaget (1923, p. 68), who considers this attitude to be characteristic of the stage of "egocentrism" in the child's development of thought. In this noncritical or precritical stage, children do not differentiate between their own perspective of the world and that of other people and therefore take their own perspective as the only and true one. The concept of "realistic attitude" parallels Quine's concept of "proliferation of ontologies" and the Marxist concept of "reification."

[20]A discourse is coherent if it invokes a suitable schema in the listener (Borel, Grize, & Miéville 1983, pp. 76–77). This interpretation of coherence is influenced by Piaget's definition of the more general concept of "action scheme." An action scheme is an abstract, nonperceptible form in which the generalizable properties of a particular action are assembled, and which makes it possible to repeat an action or to apply it to new situations (Piaget & Beth, 1961, p. 251).

In constructing a schematization, a speaker performs a number of "logico-discursive" operations. Natural logic distinguishes among three main types of operation: (1) operations of *determination*; (2) operations of *justification*; (3) operations of *configuration* (Grize, 1982, pp. 174–177; Borel, 1989, pp. 39–41, 1991, pp. 46–49).

The operations of determination are general and elementary. They pertain to the qualification of the objects referred to in the discourse (the subjects or topics). Exemplifications of such operations of determination are the objectual operations that introduce, or open up, (preexisting) classes of objects, and subsequently enrich these classes by adding new objects to them. Other exemplifications are the operations of predication which ascribe particular properties, or relations, to objects. There are also operations of restriction, such as the introduction of quantifiers, which mark off the boundaries of the speaker's responsibility for the predication, and operations of modality, which indicate the type of responsibility the speaker is willing to take for the predication.

The operations of justification embody all the speaker's discursive activities aimed at getting the listener to accept or believe what is proposed by the speaker by producing reasons to believe it. Among these operations are those that present the way in which objects are determined as irrefutable, those that enable the speaker to be relieved of the responsibility for his or her determinations by taking recourse to an authority, and those that support one type of determination by another (any type of argument).

The operations of configuration are situated at the interpropositional level. Examples of such operations are repetition, the elimination of (apparent) contradictions and tautologies, analogy, and examples.[21] Argumentation (or explanation) involves the performance of a certain combination of such operations of configuration.

As becomes clear from their description of the various operations involved in constructing a schematization of argumentative discourse, the natural logicians' approach to argumentation can be characterized as *epistemological*. A schematization aims at achieving some form of modification of the listener's state of knowledge. Such a modification can only come about if the speaker is able to establish a relation between that which is known and accepted by the listener and that which is new or not yet accepted by the listener.

A speaker may want to modify a listener's state of knowledge for didactic reasons, but also for polemic reasons. In the former case, an explanation is required of the speaker; in the latter case, argumentation. An operation of analogy, for instance, can establish a correspondence between objects from two different

---

[21]The natural logic account of the operations of configuration is, in fact, rather vague. For some examples of the operation of eliminating contradictions, see Grize (1982, pp. 176–177, 191–192). For an application of the logico-discursive operations to reasoning by analogy and reasoning by examples, see Denis Miéville in Borel, Grize, and Miéville (1983, III).

domains, thus authorizing a transfer of properties from the one object to the other. The result of this transference of properties can be a modification of the listener's knowledge concerning a particular concept, or a change in his or her opinions.

Natural logicians opt for a descriptive approach of argumentative discourse. They are not interested in developing criteria for distinguishing between "good" and "bad" arguments. Although their aim is to expose the "logic" of argumentative texts, without assuming any *a priori* normative concepts, such as "truth" and "validity," Grize and his colleagues are aware of the fact that some theoretical framework is required in order to identify the operations involved in the construction of argumentative texts (Borel, et al., 1983, p. 220). Not only are the operations themselves not directly observable as such, but some preliminary theoretical notions are also indispensable in order to observe anything at all. The concepts of "schematization" and "logico-discursive operation" are intended to serve this purpose.

Two important limitations of natural logic as it has developed so far are that the analysis of argumentative discourse is, in spite of the natural logicians' purported ambitions, restricted to nondialogical situations, and that the descriptions are restricted to discursive strategies that are potentially effective, without making any empirical claims as to when these strategies are effective in practice. Natural logicians concentrate on investigating the way in which an argumentative schematization is built up by a speaker in a monologue, taking situational aspects into account, but neglecting in their investigations the way in which a speaker can respond to objections put forward by an interlocutor in an explicit dialogue. They have refrained from undertaking any empirical research as to which discursive strategies are precisely effective in practice, and under what circumstances.

11.4 LO CASCIO'S ARGUMENTATIVE GRAMMAR

Lo Cascio (1991) proposes a grammar that accounts for the linguistic organization of argumentative discourse.[22] Starting from the assumption that argumentative discourse, as a form of language use, is governed by a set of underlying syntactic rules, Lo Cascio aims to construct an argumentative grammar that links together clauses, or chains of clauses, which have a specific function in the discourse. In some respects, these syntactic rules of the grammar are language-specific.

Speakers who aim to persuade their audience about the truth or acceptability of a standpoint can shape their messages in various ways. The different ways of organizing an argumentative message linguistically Lo Cascio calls "profiles." Every speaker of a language has to learn not only how to form the profiles allowed

---

[22]This proposal is in line with the traditional Italian interest in the relation between language and persuasion. Cf. chapter 12.

by the language, but also how to use them properly in communicative situations. The uses of profiles are regulated by pragmatic rules. According to Lo Cascio, real argumentation always takes place within the "scenario" of a pragmatic framework.

Lo Cascio's main concern is the syntactic and functional form, or structure, of monological argumentative discourse, the verbal presentation of argumentation. The generative textual grammar he envisages defines the syntactic rules, categories, and linguistic conditions underlying well-formed argumentative texts and profiles. In this endeavor, starting from the Toulmin model, Lo Cascio proposes a set of *categorial and formation rules* for textual argumentative profiles. The hierarchical level of the categories and the arrangement of functional categories such as "data," "warrants," and "claims" in argumentative chains, is made explicit in the formation rules. The rules for forming argumentative chains are based on general principles such as *linear disposal, hierarchy,* and *binding at distance.*

After determining the categories that can play a role in an argumentative text, Lo Cascio defines their hierarchical status, making a distinction between "main" categories and "secondary," or "optional," categories. He then defines the syntactic tools that are available for properly enchaining these categories, and formulates rules that establish the order in which these categories can appear.

Speakers can give different directions to the information they provide, according to the topic concerned and the importance they want their statements to have. Compare, for instance, examples (1) - (3):

(1) He was breaking the law, because he was on the wrong side of the road.

(2) Since he was on the wrong side of the road, he was breaking the law.

(3) He was breaking the law (*O*), since he was on the wrong side of the road (*A1*) and he had no lights on (*A2*).

(1) can be interpreted as having the structure Opinion-Argument, (2) as having the structure Argument-Opinion, and (3) as having the structure Opinion-Argument1 + Argument2. Compare (2) also with (4):

(4) He was on the wrong side of the road, thus he was breaking the law.

These two sentences have the same argumentative structure, but in (4) the opinion is marked by the illocutionary indicator "thus," whereas in (2) the premise, or argument, is marked by "since."

The choice of argumentative linear order, and the choice of simple or complex profiles, is a pragmatic one, but the well-formedness of the employed chains is determined by a set of rules that a speaker of a specific language must acquire in order to decode and produce argumentative texts properly. In profiles, two main principles are to be distinguished: *order* and *hierarchy.* Consequently, in chain formation, and profiles, too, two directions are to be distinguished: *horizontal direction* (order) and *vertical direction* (hierarchy and expansion). The connection between elements that belong to the same profile is sensitive at the horizontal or vertical axis, and restricted by some binding conditions.

The *obligatory categories* in an argumentative text are the "opinion" (*O*), and the "justification" or support (*JS*), which is composed of an argument (*A*) and a "general rule" (*GR*). Together, *JS* and *O* form the complex node "argumentation" (*ARG*). *JS* can consist of a single argument (*A*), but also of more than one argument, which can, in turn, be supported by a subjustification. In other words, the argumentation can be simple or complex, and can have a multiple or a pyramidal structure.

An argumentative text *ARG* can thus present an order either of type (5) or of type (6):

(5) [$_{ARG}$ *O-A*]
(6) [$_{ARG}$ *A-O*]

If the text begins with a statement, the listener will expect the presentation of at least one *A*. If a text begins with the presentation of some data or arguments, the listener will expect some conclusion (*C*), or an opinion which serves as thesis (*O*). Each of the two components of *ARG* can be introduced by an argumentative indicator, that is, a connector such as "because," "since," "thus," or "as," indicating the pragmatic function of the clause or set of clauses. The lexicalization of the argumentative indicator is not obligatory, whereas the explicitization of both components *A* and *O* is.

The third obligatory argumentative component is the "warrant," the general rule (*GR*) which allows that an argument can be considered as a good support for a thesis. This component is obligatory only at deep structure level, and is thus semantically always implied, but does not need to be mentioned or lexicalized in the text.

Configurational rules could then be the following: *ARG* is a minimal argumentative text and *O* an opinion that is supported by a justification, or justificatory category, *JS*, which is composed of an argument *A*, and a general rule *GR*, which allows that *A* can be proposed as argument for *O*. *GR* determines the semantic area: the ideological scheme or schedule from which the argument has been taken. The minimal argumentative structure is the following:

(7)

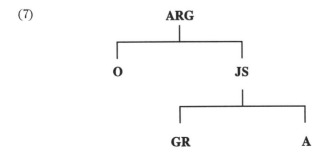

The linear order in the structure does not exclusively determine in what way the statements must appear at the surface level. This has to do with principles of control. In the configurational proposal, *O* is the *head* of the node *ARG* and controls *JS*, while *GR* is the *controller* of *A*. Since more than one argument can be given in support of an opinion, the grammar needs to postulate a higher node *JS'* which represents the maximal projection of the argumentative justification, and represents a justificationary set which can consist of one or more *JS*. Each argument is, according to Lo Cascio, supported and justified by a different general rule. Consequently, in a well-formed argumentative text the same general rule can appear no more than once. Therefore, Lo Cascio proposes the following structure:

(8)

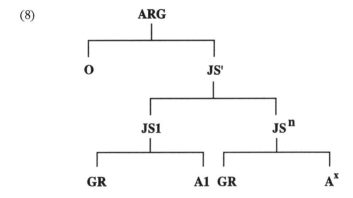

The grammar is recursive. Every argument, or subargument, can be expanded in a subargumentation such that the node *A* can be rewritten as *ARG*, on the condition that the new *O* is coindexed with the *A* of the superior *ARG* and, in turn, supported by an argument *A2*. Take the following complex argumentative text:

(9) This book has no literary qualities (*O*) because its style is defective (*A1*). The dialogues sound artificial (*A2*).

This text can be interpreted as follows:

(9a)

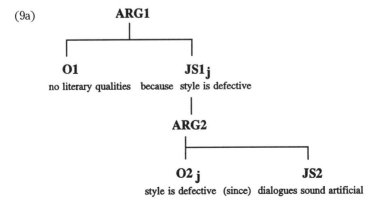

As can be seen, *A1* is expanded in argumentative subtext *ARG2*, where the statement from *A1* has the function of an opinion which is supported by the argument *A2*; this is why *A1* and *O2* are coindexed. *A2* is not an argument for *O1*. The same holds in (10):

(10) John cannot be Mary's killer *because* he is her father and *because* he is a quiet person *since* he always smiled at her.

The smiling data will support only the statement that John is a quiet person, not the primary statement that John has not killed Mary. (10) has the following structure:

(10a)

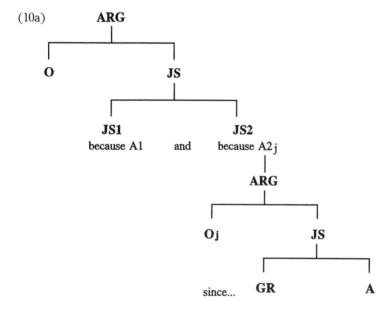

Since every statement, or set of statements, with an argumentative function can be introduced by an "illocutionary" indicator or argumentative connector, Lo Cascio proposes that every category be rewritten as marked by an illocutionary indicator functioning as a specifier, called *Ind*, and a statement or enunciation, or set of enunciations, called *E*.

Optional categories are the "qualifier" (*Q*), which is the modal marker, and the "backing" (*B*), the authorizing source of the information. Both have the function of *specifiers*. To every *A* or *O*, or even *GR*, a qualifier can thus be added in the form of a modal verb, a modal adverb or some other modal form. The "backing" (*B*) functions as support, as source or guarantee, for the *GR*, the general rule. *B* is introduced by illocutionary indicators like "as stated by" and "as X has said."

Three other optional categories are to be considered as adjuncts to the argumentative high node *ARG*, and have a counterargumentative value, that is, function as "reinforcers," "rebuttals," and "alternatives."

To every argumentation an utterance, or sequence of clauses, can be added which is marked by a connective of the "although"-type. This category, which Toulmin does not consider, Lo Cascio calls *reinforcer* (RE). Compare (11), (12), and (13):

> (11) I think he will come, although he is ill, because he loves you.

> (12) Although he is ill, I think he will come because he loves you.

?? (13) I think he will come because he loves you, although he is ill.

This category presents, in other words, a possible counterargument, thus a *JS*, which could lead to an opinion different from, and opposite to, the one preferred and mentioned in the argumentative text. But the possible counterargument given in the "although"-sentence is not considered strong enough by the arguer. This category "reinforces" the validity of the main argumentation. The distribution of this category with respect to the other argumentative categories, *O* and the preferred *JS*, is free. It cannot intervene within the node *JS*, which holds the argument(s) for *O*, since it is a category that belongs to another argumentation, which could be characterized as a negation of the claim sustained by the main argumentation. So a structure with an *RE* can be interpreted as follows:

(JS1) → O1 although JS2 (which is not strong enough and could imply ¬O1)

The category called *rebuttal* (*R*) presents a possible alternative claim, without clearly expressing which opinion is preferred. Toulmin's "rebuttal" represents a possible counterargumentation that could lead to an alternative opinion or conclusion than the one preferred. This category is presented by indicators such as "unless"; it can share an argument, or an opinion, or data, with the first argumentation:

> (14) The digital revolution cannot be turned back, unless a revolution blinds us to the charms of an earlier milieu.

The rebuttal must be considered as a separate *ARG*, with some link with the *ARG* of which it is a rebuttal, or better a reservation, but not a negation. Therefore, Lo Cascio's grammar includes a final maximal projection of *ARG* called *ARG″*, which covers the rebuttal argumentation. The node *ARG″*, dominating both *ARG′* and *R(ARG)*, accounts for the fact that there must be an obligatory link between *ARG′* and *(R)ARG*.

The *reinforcer*, introduced by "although," on the contrary, is a subcategory of *ARG'*, because it does not propose another *O*, but recognizes the same *O*, head of the *ARG* to which it belongs. Conversely, *rebuttal* requires and leads to another *O* and is a way to express doubt about an argumentation, or it is a stylistic tool for performing an indirect speech act, by proposing as secondary an argumentation which should, ultimately, be taken as the true, or as being the preferred one. A structure with a *rebuttal* would be interpreted in the following way:

(15) (JS1) → O1 unless JS2 (which implies O2 ≠ O1)

The third adjunct category in Lo Cascio's grammar is the *alternative* (AL), which is presented by markers such as "but," "nevertheless," and "however," and presents an opposite claim that appears to be stronger than the earlier defended claim. The alternative presents another opinion, or argument, chosen in the first round, as a reconsideration of the validity of the preceding argumentation. It can therefore not precede, but must follow an earlier argumentative text. Unlike a reinforcer or a rebuttal, an alternative cannot open an argumentative text:

(16) He has no money; nevertheless I think that he will buy a business class ticket to Rome.

In (16), the clause "I think that he will buy a business class ticket to Rome" expresses a conclusion that is contrary to the conclusion that would be expected after the mentioning of the fact that he has no money. In an example like (17), the clause "He has no money" represents a counterargument which triggers a claim different from the one represented by the sentence "He will buy a business class ticket to Rome," but which remains undefined:

(17) I think he will buy a business class ticket to Rome; nevertheless he has no money.

The adjunct categories are, somehow, in the nature of being counterargumentation. They propose alternative arguments and another possible opinion, or claim, instead of the one supported by the main argumentation. These categories are graduated as far as their counterargumentative power is concerned. If the categories remain undefined, or nonovert, an inferential activity is required in order to detect them. This inferential work is regulated by specific rules. With "alternative," the structure would be interpreted as follows:

(JS1) → O1 nevertheless JS2 (which implies O2 ≠ O1)
JS1 (→ O1) nevertheless O2 (because JS2)

Since the linear disposition of the argumentative categories and components is not arbitrary, a set of rules and conditions on position and distribution is needed, which allows for the production of well-formed argumentative profiles. Restrictions on succession, combination, and distribution can be imposed by the nature of the categories concerned, by their hierarchical position or by the (linguistic) nature of the argumentative indicators. General and Universal principles, such as "subjacency" or "logical coherence," can also regulate the well-formedness of argumentative textual profiles.

Normally, the set of arguments in support of a claim must be presented as a whole. In other words, the following kind of schemes are to be expected:

(18) $[_{\mathrm{ARG}}[\mathrm{A\text{-}A\text{-}A^n}] - [\mathrm{O}]\ ]$

(19) $[_{\mathrm{ARG}}[\mathrm{O}] - [\mathrm{A\text{-}A\text{-}A^n}]]$

But, according to Lo Cascio, not the following kind of schemes:

(20) $^*[_{\mathrm{ARG}}\ [\mathrm{A\text{-}\ A\ [O]\ \text{-}A^n}]]$

In monological texts, categorial discontinuity is not allowed, whereas more freedom can be found in dialogical texts. The ill-formedness of (20) is due to a very general principle which regulates the argumentative order, and which is an example of the subjacency condition. We do not find schemes where categories are disposed at random. Argumentative categories cannot be extracted from their higher dominating node. Subelements dominated by the same node must stay together and can move only within, and not outside, their maximal projection node domain. The same can be said for a profile as (21):

(21) $^*?$ A-O-A

In (21), the chain dominated by the node *JS* would be interrupted by the presence of the category *O*. So, if a text starts with an *A* and continues with an *O*, we cannot expect more *A*'s which would be considered as arguments for the thesis already mentioned. Neither could we have a chain where a qualifier would be far from its scope. If we have a qualifier for *A*, we cannot have a chain of the following type:

(22) $^*?$ A1 & A2 $-$ O $\mathrm{Q_{[A1]}}$

In a sentence such as (22a), "probably" can, unlike in (22b), not be seen as a qualifier of the argument "He is ill":

(22a) Since he is ill, and he hasn't enough money, probably, he will not come.

(22b) Since he is probably ill, and he hasn't enough money, he will not come.

There are argumentative texts that do not show *Ind* at the surface level. See, for instance, example (9), where the subargument "The dialogues sound artificial" has a nonovert indicator. But a node *Ind* must always be considered present in every structure and node, even if it is *empty* because it holds the necessary information for the entire argumentative chain.

As a matter of fact, in a node *ARG* not every node *Ind* can be lexicalized. There are some very strict rules for lexicalization of *Ind*. Consider, for instance, the cases in which the *ARG* structure in the following examples is not correct:

* (23) Thus John cannot be Mary's killer: He is her father.

(24) He is her father, thus John cannot be Mary's killer.

?* (25) John cannot be Mary's killer because he is her father, and since he is a quiet person, he always smiled at her.

? (26) John cannot be Mary's killer because he is her father, and since he is a quiet person since he smiled indeed always at her.

* (27) John cannot be Mary's killer since he is her father and since he is a quiet person since he always smiled at her/he smiled indeed always at her.

(28) John cannot be Mary's killer since he is her father and since he is a quiet person: He smiled indeed always at her.

Therefore, (29) is not acceptable on the ground of a lexicalization restriction upon illocutionary indicators:

* (29) thus *O-[A-Q]-GR*

An argumentative chain could in fact be ill-formed because of the wrong use of an illocutionary indicator or because of the presence of too many indicators:

* (30) thus *O-A*
* (31) because *A* thus *O*
* (32) because *A* and since *A-O*
* (33) *O* hence *A1* and because *A2*

This means that the function of *O* and *A* cannot be marked at the same time. *O* can be marked only in a structure *A-O*, but never in a structure *O-A*. The choice of the first *Ind* in an argumentative chain determines the choice of the other illocutionary indicators.

Restrictions on chain formation can have a *semantic* or a *syntactic* nature. The syntactic restrictions are determined by conditions upon the use of illocutionary indicators and by subordination rules. The semantic restrictions can be based on logical structures or coherence in text formation.

Now a set of rules can be formulated which underlie the formation of well-formed argumentative structures and profiles. Conditions on chain formation take into consideration basic principles such as linear order (constituents must be properly ordered, that is, sequential notions such as left, right, adjacent, and boundary hold), hierarchy (hierarchical level X, X', X''), and structural relations (head, domination).

The following *lexical rules* are proposed by Lo Cascio:

(a) Only one of the obligatory categories at the surface level, that is, either
    A or O, can be marked by a lexicalized illocutionary indicator *Ind*.
    This is a kind of rule of lexical *alternation*:

    (34a) A thus O

    (34b) Since A-O; but:

    (34c) *Since A-*thus* O

(b) Functional category O never admits a lexicalized Ind_O if it is employed in
    a profile of the type O-JS, i.e., if it starts the argumentative chain.
    Cf. (35) *Thus O-A

(c) A lexicalized *Ind* introducing O can be admitted only in a profile JS-O, on
    the condition that JS has not already been marked by any *Ind* for A.

    (36a) $A1$ and $A2$ hence O

    (36b) *Because $A1$ and $A2$ hence O

(d) If a profile has more than one A, and the A's are going to be marked by
    a lexicalized indicator *Ind*, then at least the first A must be marked by
    Ind. If the other is to be lexicalized, then the procedure is cyclic from left
    to right for the right-branching languages.
    Thus:

    (37) O - since $A1$ and since $A2$; or

    (38) O - since $A1$ and (since) $A2$; but:

    (39) *O - $A1$ since $A2$

(e) The rule of alternance must be applied only to A and O. As a matter of
    fact, other categories contained in the node ARG' can be marked by a
    lexicalized *Ind*, even if either A or O is already marked by a lexicalized
    Ind. So GR can be marked and C and RE as well.

Cf. (40a) Although Ax, O - because $A1$ and because $A2$

    (40b) O -, although Ax, because $A1$ and $A2$

    (40c) Since A-O - thus C

    (40d) A - thus O - therefore C

(f) (Counterargumentative) adjunct categories such as R, RE and AL gener-
    ally require overt *Ind*.

Lo Cascio proposes also a *sequential rule* (g) and a *rule of deletion* (h):

(g) The first lexicalized indicator of the argumentative chain determines the proper choice of the other indicators. The syntactic structuring, and the decision about the structure of a complex argumentative text, also determine the choice and the use of the indicators. The control is cyclic and goes from right to left in right-branching languages.

(h) It is possible to delete every argumentative marker of obligatory categories. In that case, the reverse of the "sequential rule" holds, namely that deletion must go from right to left (in right-branching languages) and is cyclic. Adjunct categories generally do not allow deletion of functional markers.

12

OTHER SIGNIFICANT
DEVELOPMENTS

A number of other contributions to the study of argumentation must be mentioned, besides the approaches to argumentation discussed so far. These contributions stem from argumentation theorists from various parts of the non-Anglophone world and are often less familiar to a broader circle of argumentation theorists. Some of them are not part of a fully fledged research program, being more limited in scope. To conclude our survey, we shall briefly discuss several of these contributions.

All over the world, argumentation is studied by scholars from various disciplinary backgrounds. Some approach argumentation philosophically, generally adopting a normative perspective; some approach argumentation rhetorically, usually with the purpose of analyzing argumentative practices; still others approach argumentation linguistically, aiming for a description of functional uses of discourse. Several topics in the study of argumentation are studied by divergent approaches. Among them are relevance, argumentation structures, unexpressed premises, argumentation schemes, the cognitive processing of argumentative discourse, the stylistic aspects of argumentation, the acquisition and teaching of argumentative skills, and the use of argumentation in special fields. On each of these topics a vast amount of articles and books have been published by a great number of authors.

In this chapter, we shall give an overview of approaches to argumentation which stem from different countries and disciplinary backgrounds, primarily published in other languages than English. We concentrate on the most influential approaches, preferably by authors at least some of whose publications are available in English. In Section 12.1, we discuss some philosophical contributions to the study of argumentation developed in continental Europe. In Section 12.2, we pay attention to several approaches with a rhetorical background. In Section 12.3, a series of contributions to the linguistic approach to argumentation is briefly reviewed. In Section 12.4, finally, some studies of argumentation in special fields are noticed. In order to give a general idea of the study of argumentation outside America and Western Europe, some information is included about argumentation theory in Eastern Europe, Russia, and China.

12.1 PHILOSOPHICAL APPROACHES

In continental Europe the interest in argumentation has been steadily increasing since the early 1970s. Mainly building on philosophical traditions, several important contributions to the study of argumentation have been made. Compared with Anglo-Saxon argumentation studies, these contributions are generally more philosophical in nature and less practically oriented. Two newly developed traditions have been most influential: the dialogue logic of the Erlangen School and Jürgen Habermas' theory of communicative rationality.

We have already discussed the dialogue logic of the Erlangen School in chapter 9. Its influence is manifested, for example, in the philosophical work of the *Hamburger Arbeitsgruppe Argumentationstheorie*, directed by Harald Wohlrapp of the University of Hamburg.[1] Wohlrapp (1977) has modified the views of the Erlangen School by introducing insights from Kuhn and Feyerabend, from action theory and from Hegelian Dialectics.[2] In his view, argumentation is not to be seen primarily as an instrument for conflict resolution but as a way of theory formation, characteristic for Occidental culture. In order to bridge the gap between objective truth and subjective acceptability, Wohlrapp (1995) developed a conception of "Gültigkeit," a validity notion applying to theses rather than reasoning patterns (pp. 289–291). An arguer can arrive at a stage in which a thesis may be regarded "valid" by taking account of the objections of the other party and answering these objections with arguments and precizations, so that the thesis can no longer be practically objected to.

Geert-Lueke Lueken (1991, 1992, 1995) proposed an argumentative solution to the incommensurability problem caused by the radical differences between theories, paradigms, and world views. He argues that the problem, though serious, does not present a threat to the rationality of scientific argumentation. Such a threat arises only if rationality is exclusively connected with a particular system of rules. Proponents of incommensurable theories can never reach consensus in a rule-guided reasoning game ("Begründungsspiel"). Lueken (1991) therefore recommends an "anticipatory practice," consisting in a type of "mutual

---

[1]See Wohlrapp (1987, 1990, 1991), Lueken (1991, 1992, 1995), Mengel (1991, 1995), and Volquardsen (1995).

[2]See also Wohlrapp (1987, 1991).

field research." The participants in the discussion should attempt to learn as much as possible about each other's form of life, mutually assuming the roles of teacher and student and taking note of even seemingly unimportant details, without imposing their own cognitive categories and standards on others (pp. 248–249). Taking up suggestions from the Erlangen School, Lueken suggests techniques that participants can employ, in order to teach each other how to use and interpret their language.

The second influential philosophical tradition is inspired by Habermas' approach to communicative rationality (1971, 1973, 1991).[3] Habermas' work belongs to a stream of philosophy often referred to as *Diskurstheorie*. It takes a stance against all kinds of relativism. The sources of this stream, originating in the Neomarxist "Frankfurter Schule," are Habermas and Karl Otto Apel.

In the normative model of argumentation in an "ideal speech situation" developed by Habermas, the conditions are specified which must be fulfilled for a discussion to result in a well-founded, rational consensus ("Begründeter Konsens").[4] · Three levels of communicative rationality are distinguished, each of them having its own critical standards. At the logical level, argumentation is evaluated as a "product" by applying logical and semantical rules: Speakers may not, for instance, contradict themselves and their use of linguistic expressions must be consistent. At the dialectical level, argumentation is evaluated as a "procedure" aimed at achieving consensus: Pragmatic rules that are applied are, for instance, that speakers should be sincere and prepared to defend themselves against attacks. At the rhetorical level, argumentation is evaluated as a communicative "process": The conditions that have to be fulfilled are, for example, that free participation in the discussion is not limited by external factors. In practice, the ideal speech situation will never be completely realized, but the basic assumptions of ideal communicative action and argumentation are implicitly anticipated. According to Habermas, they can therefore serve as a critical standard for judging everyday argumentation.[5]·

A prominent theoretical approach to argumentation influenced by Habermas is that of Josef Kopperschmidt, professor of speech communication. Kopperschmidt studied rhetoric in Tübingen with Walter Jens, and is an advocate of the rehabilitation of classical rhetoric. Using insights from rhetoric, but also from speech act theory, text linguistics, and the theory of Habermas, he has developed a comprehensive normative theory (Kopperschmidt 1976a, 1978, 1980,

---

[3]The *Journal of the American Forensic Association* once (1979, Vol. 16, no. 2) devoted a special issue to Habermas' critical theory and its theoretical and practical implications.

[4]Apel (1988) regards the argumentative situation as the "transcendental-pragmatic condition" of all rational speech activity. Since it implies the material ethical norm that people should not "instrumentalize" each other, it can be seen as the basis of ethics.

[5]Further elaborations of Habermas' theory of communicative rationality, the dialogue theory of the Erlangen School, and their practical implications are given in Berk (1979) and Gerhardus, Kledzig, and Reitzig (1975).

1987, 1989a).[6] In his work on argumentation, Kopperschmidt attempts to bridge the gap between abstract theory and argumentation analysis and practice. He sees rhetoric as a subtheory of the theory of communicative competence. It is an important aim of the study of rhetoric to develop rules for a felicitous and successful performance of persuasive speech acts which can be used to resolve controversies concerning practical matters and norms for action. An important task for argumentation theorists is, according to Kopperschmidt (1995), to supply means for meeting the growing need for consensus (especially in politics). Rejecting the "absolutism of truth," he argues that this ideal should be replaced by the ancient rhetorical ideal of rational consensus.

Another German philosopher who has developed a systematic perspective on argumentation is Christoph Lumer.[7] Lumer's (1990) epistemical approach aims to integrate epistemic rationality and normative pragmatics. The rationality of argumentation is, in his view, not merely based on the norms applying to formal deductive reasoning, but also on those described in probability theory and decision-making theory.[8] Lumer formulates validity, soundness and adequacy conditions for the evaluation of different types of everyday argument; among the argument types he discusses are generalizations, and interpretive, epistemological and practical arguments.

Michel Meyer's theory of *problematology* embodies a philosophical approach to argumentation stemming from the French-speaking world (Meyer, 1982b, 1986a, 1986b, 1988). It was developed in the early 1980s out of dissatisfaction with formal logic.[9] Meyer, a former student of Perelman's at the Free University of Brussels, aims to solve a number of philosophical problems.[10]

According to Meyer's problematology, every utterance can be used for two purposes: to express a question (or "problem"), and to give an answer (or "solution"). A question is "an obstacle, a difficulty, an exigency of choice, and therefore an appeal for a decision" (1986b, p. 118). Since all discourse, from phrase to text, can serve the double function of expressing problems and presenting solutions, any piece of discourse can mark the question as well as the solution.

---

[6]Kopperschmidt also wrote a substantial number of articles on the history of rhetoric and the analysis and evaluation of political speeches (1975, 1976b, 1977, 1989b, 1990a). He edited books on rhetoric as a theory of the production of texts and the influences of rhetoric in other disciplines (1990b, 1991).

[7]A further example of an epistemological approach to (philosophical) argumentation is provided by Lauth (1979).

[8]For an English publication in which Lumer's norms are described, see Lumer (1988).

[9]Dascal gives a description of the planning skills involved in proving the validity of an argument in deductive logic. He argues that the key strategy of the process of proving, "working backwards," is not easy to impart to students of all ages. He reports on an experiment carried out to test the hypothesis that students of logic and mathematics who also receive training in movement self-awareness, analysis, and stepwise control will develop more easily a higher level of achievement (Dascal, Dascal, & Landau, 1987).

[10]For a philosophical contribution based on Meyer's insights, see Carrilho (1992).

Once a solution to a specific question is presented, the question it means to resolve is generally no longer explicitly referred to. For the answerer, the answer is only an answer, but for another party it may be a problem. This other party may regard the answer as not constituting a real answer because it does not resolve the question it intended to resolve or because it raises new questions.

In order to understand an answer properly, one should be able to identify the question it is supposed to answer. According to Meyer (1986b), "the meaning of an answer is its link to a specific question" (p. 127). This can be illustrated with the statements "John is not married" and "John is single." These statements are semantically equivalent if they are both answers to the question "What is John's civil state?"; if they should be solutions to the problem "Make a sentence of three words," however, these statements are no longer equivalent. In Meyer's words: "The meaning of the statement depends not on the statement alone, but on the question to which it must correspond" (p. 127).

In Meyer's view, the function of argumentative discourse is to provide an answer to a specific problem in a specific context. On the other hand, argumentation can also be seen as "problematizing" an answer; that is, as the recognition of the question contained in a given answer. Final answers are not to be expected, because they can only be provided in the formal language of a formal logic in which there is no room for doubt or contradictory propositions. In nonformal reasoning there is no guarantee whatsoever that a question that is posed will not remain an open one.

In problematology, there is room only for a nonformal logic, governing what Meyer (1986b) calls "nonconstraining reasoning" (pp. 130–131). Consequently, he claims, argumentation pertains to the theory of questioning. Argumentation refers to the possibility of making the answers that are given problematic. The addressee, to whom the argument (i.e., the answer) is directed, reestablishes a link between the argument and the (implicit) question, and thereby creates the possibility of different answers to the same question. Thus, any solution or argument proposed by an arguer will remain problematological: There is no guarantee that the solution will be accepted by the other party (p. 132).

In the former Soviet Union, the philosophical fundaments of argumentation theory are investigated in the search for a new perspective, starting from classical rhetoric.[11] For many years, there has been a specific interest in the analysis of the structure of philosophical argument, primarily in the *Yerevan School of Argumentation*, directed by Georg Brutian, professor of philosophy at the University of Yerevan. The Yerevan School regards the logical component of argumentation as the most important.

---

[11]Although the study of argumentation in Russia (and the rest of the former Soviet Union) dates back to much earlier, it was not until the mid 1980s that philosophers and linguists recognized argumentation as a separate field of study which allowed for an integration of previously separate trends of research in communication and philosophy. The dramatic changes in the political and social life of Russia towards an open society were an important factor in this development.

Although philosophical argumentation is a central theme in the work of Brutian (1979) and his collaborators, they have also published works on theoretical problems in the theory of argumentation and on argumentation analysis (Brutian 1991, 1992, 1993). Brutian and Narsky (1986) compiled a number of theoretical contributions on what they call Argumentology, which they see as a special field of philosophical study. Chuyeshov (1993) lays out the theoretical and historical foundations of Argumentology. Alekseyev (1991) and Markov (1993) emphasize the crucial role of language in argumentation and deal with problems of understanding and interpreting arguments.

12.2 RHETORICAL APPROACHES

The rhetorical approach to argumentation has been highly influential in some parts of Europe, particularly in Italy, France, and Germany. Until 1990, the study of argumentation in Italy concentrated mainly on rhetorical aspects, including the stylistic aspects of argumentative language use. Argumentation was primarily studied as a form of manipulation through language, which was being investigated in such specific contexts as politics and advertising or as a stylistic device in poetry and narration. The interest in rhetorical figures and stylistics was stimulated by the Italian translation of Lausberg's rhetorical work in 1969 and the Group μ's *Rhétorique Générale* in 1970.

A major part of the publications concentrated on explaining the function of rhetorical devices: the creation of new categories by establishing a connection between different elements of reality or between terms belonging to different domains. Barilli (1969), Segre (1985), and Valesio (1980) testify to this particular interest. Until the late 1960s, rhetoric was either studied as the art of linguistic cosmetics or as the art of persuasion. According to Genette (1969, p. 202), the view that rhetoric is artificial and manipulative is characteristic of our age.

Valesio (1980) argues that this conception of rhetoric is not tenable. In his opinion, every statement is rhetorically marked; there are no neutral statements. Rhetoric is therefore at the base of all linguistic behavior. It is difficult, if not impossible, to make a clear division between rhetoric and linguistics. According to Valesio, everything that is structured as a discourse and is (at least in part) grammatically acceptable, is rhetorical. Any spontaneously produced discourse that is intelligible within the code of a given natural language is therefore a proper subject for rhetorical analysis.

In Italy, in the 1990s, four important contributions to the study of argumentation were made: Mortara Garavelli's (1990) comprehensive introduction into rhetoric, Adelino Cattani's (1990) study of modes of arguing, discussing the revaluation of rhetoric as a theory of discourse and an instrument for describing argumentative practice, Marcello Pera's (1991) analysis of rhetoric and science, and Vincenzo Lo Cascio's (1991) grammar of argumentation, discussed in chapter 11.

In *The Discourses of Science* (English translation, 1994), Pera, professor of philosophy at the university of Pisa, attempts a reformation of rhetoric and dialectic in order to find new ways of understanding reasoning in science. In his opinion, the logical ideal model of scientific method is untenable. He attacks the standard philosophies of science as well as the new philosophies: in linking scientific rationality to methodological rules, both sides are mistaken. He proposes to overcome the tension between normative and descriptive philosophies of science by focusing on the rhetoric involved in the construction and acceptance of scientific theories. Science is not just an interchange between nature and the observer, but a three-way interaction between nature, the investigator, and a questioning audience or community. Through the process of attacking and defending, displayed in a context of dispute, this community determines what science is.

Pera (1994) makes a distinction between "scientific rhetoric," that is, "those persuasive forms of reasoning or argumentation that aim at changing the belief system of an audience in scientific debates," and "scientific dialectics," "the logic or canon of validation of those forms" (p. 58). In order to acquire a clearer picture of what scientific rhetoric amounts to in practice, he examines the uses of argumentation in Galileo's *Dialogue*, Darwin's *Origin*, and the "big-bang steady state controversy" in cosmology. From his analysis, Pera draws the conclusion that scientists resort primarily to rhetoric in the following scientific contexts:

1. when attempting to make the choice of a new methodological procedure acceptable,
2. when arguing for a specific interpretation of a methodological rule,
3. when attempting to overcome objections concerning the application of a rule to a concrete case,
4. when justifying a starting point,
5. when attributing a positive degree of plausibility to a hypothesis,
6. when criticizing or discrediting rival hypotheses, and
7. when rejecting objections against a hypothesis.

In formal logic, arguments *by themselves* are examined in order to determine whether they are valid, but according to Pera (1994) it should be established whether they are correct or incorrect in a debate, that is in specific situations for specific audiences. In a debate, an argument is submitted to certain constraints or debating rules which determine which moves are permitted and prohibited. It is the task of scientific dialecticians to formulate such rules for scientific arguments. The rules of scientific dialectics are of two types: rules for conducting a debate, disciplining the type of exchange allowed between the interlocutors, and rules for adjudicating a debate, determining the points bestowed on each side and the awarding of victory (pp. 121–126).

The proponent launches the debate by saying "I state S." The opponent's answer can either consist of admitting or denying S, or of a request to provide reasons for S. If the proponent provides the requested reasons, there are four countermoves available to the opponent: casting doubt on the inferential link between the proponent's thesis and the reasons advanced, rejecting the thesis by denying the reasons which are adduced, challenging the proponent to prove that the main thesis is compatible with other reasons that have already been admitted by the proponent in the debate, or performing a counterattack. The proponent always has the right to withdraw the thesis. In many respects, Pera's approach is thus similar to the pragma-dialectical approach to argumentation discussed in chapter 10.

The study of rhetoric has also been flourishing in other parts of Europe. In France, it has been propagated by Olivier Reboul, who in 1991 wrote a philosophical and practical introduction to rhetoric. This introduction deals with the history of rhetoric, rhetorical strategies and figures as well as with the distinctions between various types of argument. According to Olivier Reboul (1988), argumentation has a number of rhetorical properties that distinguish it from demonstrative proof: It is conducted in ordinary language and directed at an audience, its premises are at best plausible, and its inferences are not compelling. Dialectics is for Reboul (1990) the intellectual instrument of rhetoric, in distinction to the emotive means of persuasion.

Crucial figures in German rhetoric are Walter Jens and Gert Ueding, who are coeditors of a Rhetorical Yearbook (*Rhetorik. Ein internationales Jahrbuch*).[12] Currently, Jens and Ueding are also editing a historical dictionary of rhetoric; the first two volumes of this *Historisches Wörterbuch der Rhetorik* appeared in 1992 and 1994. In addition, Jens has made a series of contributions to the study of political rhetoric and the history of rhetoric (1983). Ueding published, together with Bernd Steinbrink (1994), an introduction to rhetoric based on the classical tradition, with a short survey of the history of rhetoric from antiquity to the 20th century.

A well-known representative of speech communication (*Sprechwissenschaft*) among the German authors on rhetoric and argumentation is Helmut Geissner.[13] Geissner developed a theory of oral communication based on insights from semiotics, linguistics, and the rhetorical tradition (1978, 1988a, 1988b). He has also been concerned with the critical evaluation of rhetorical practice, taking a less normative stance than Kopperschmidt because he is afraid of "idealizing away" the actual restrictions of dialogical and argumentative ability.[14]

---

[12]For the history of rhetoric in Germany from the 16th to the 20th century, see Schanze (1974).

[13]Methods for teaching oral communication are developed in Geissner (1986a); Geissner (1986b) presents methods for teaching rhetorical communication. Another German speech communication scholar, Gutenberg, has contributed to the discussion of rhetoric, dialectic and truth (in English, Gutenberg, 1987).

[14]An English survey of Geissner's theoretical concepts can be found in Geissner (1987).

The argumentation theorists from German-speaking countries have also made a number of contributions of another type, drawing from several sources: classical rhetoric and dialectic, the Toulmin model, and discourse analysis. The Toulmin model, for instance, has inspired argumentation theorists concerned with the analysis of the structure of arguments (Huth, 1975; Settekorn, 1977; Göttert, 1978; Quasthoff, 1978).[15] Some attempts have been made to integrate Georg Henrik von Wright's concept of a practical syllogism with Toulmin's model, for example by Schwitalla (1976) and Völzing (1979), who provide a complex extension of Toulmin's model. Some other argumentation theorists have argued for a reduced Toulmin-model, consisting only of three categories: data, warrant ("Schlusspräsupposition") and claim (Öhlschläger, 1979, 1980; Kienpointner, 1983).

The Austrian Manfred Kienpointner (1992a) contributed to the analysis of argumentation at the micro-level in offering a comprehensive typology of argumentation schemes.[16] The typology combines the ancient topical tradition, particularly Aristotle's *Topics*, with modern approaches such as Perelman and Olbrechts-Tyteca's, Hastings', Schellens', van Eemeren and Kruiger's, and Govier's. This typology is applied by Kienpointner to a corpus of oral and written argumentative discourse.[17]

In the Netherlands, rhetoric has been actively promoted by Antoine Braet. In Braet (1984), he emphasized the importance of the classical theory of status for modern argumentation studies. He gives a historical overview of the classical variants of the theory by Hermagoras of Temnos, Cicero, Quintilian and Hermogenes, followed by a comparison of the classical theory of status with the theory of "stock issues," underlying American "academic debate," and with the rules for the distribution of the burden of proof in Dutch criminal law.[18]

Another Dutchman, Peter Jan Schellens, has proposed a typology of argumentation schemes that is partly based on Hastings (1962). Schellens (1985, 1987) distinguishes four main types of argumentation: (1) argumentation based on regularity, (2) argumentation based on rules, (3) pragmatic argumentation, and (4) unconditional argumentation. For the subtypes of each main type of argumentation he formulates a set of critical questions.

---

[15]Only a few studies tackle the overall structure, or macrostructure, of argumentative texts. Then the argumentation structure is always captured in complex diagrams of the interrelations between the single arguments that make up the argumentative complex. See Deimer (1975), Grewendorf (1975, 1980), Klein (1980), Frixen (1987), and Kopperschmidt (1989a).

[16]English surveys of this typology, and some examples, are given in Kienpointner (1987, 1992b).

[17]In this connection two influential German textbooks are worth mentioning: Walther (1990), which describes formal and informal schemes and principles of philosophical argumentation, and also provides a great number of authentic examples from philosophical texts, and Schmidt-Faber (1986), the most practical German textbook and probably the most complete.

[18]In Berkenbosch and Braet (1994) an approach to academic debate is described, which is based on the pragma-dialectical theory of argumentation.

Initially, the application of insights from the theory of argumentation in The Netherlands focused primarily on the analysis and evaluation of argumentative texts. Van den Hoven (1984) outlined a procedure for writing a (formal) review of an argumentative text. He developed a model for analyzing the text, and for evaluating the relations established between the premises and the conclusion. Van den Hoven (1987) discusses some limitations of dialectical discussion as a problem-solving strategy.

In China, argumentation as we understand it has not been advocated much, let alone as a subject of scholarship. However, there exists a strong tradition of argumentation in China, which can be traced back to Taoism, Confucianism, Buddhism, and other philosophies and religions. Dominant modes of argumentation used in this rhetorical tradition are arguments from authority, from analogy, by example, and so on. In contrast to Western rhetoric, Chinese rhetoric in both its traditional and contemporary senses is not concerned with ways of finding reasons and arguments, but purely with "figures of speech," with the question of "how to write beautiful phrases or sentences" rather than persuasion.

During the Cultural Revolution (1966–1977), a new mode or genre of speech emerged, reminiscent of the orations in ancient Greece. The red Guards and members of different Revolutionary fractions argued in speeches and in writing (Big Character Posters) against all traditional authorities, criticizing everyone except Mao Ze Dong. Prior to and during those years, scholarship in general and theory of argumentation in particular were devoted to the practice of revolutionary argumentation. Since then, little work of any substance has been done on argumentation. Argumentation has been a topic for instruction rather than research. In textbooks for university students, it is treated as a genre of discourse, parallel to lyrics, narration, description, and, conversation. Argumentation is generally defined as a speech or writing activity in which a view is advanced on the basis of factual data and logical inferences. Various techniques are advised for pro- and contra-argumentation: exemplification, citation, comparison, analogy, counterattacks on views or data, etc.[19]

A Chinese author currently working in The Netherlands is Shi-Xu, who analyzes argumentative and explanatory strategies in the discourse of expatriate Chinese intellectuals. Shi-Xu (1992) outlines a social–cognitive model of argumentative and explanatory discourse. He uses this model in identifying the social representations underlying argumentation and explanation in data taken from interviews with Chinese expatriates. In Shi-Xu (1995), the role of cultural attitudes is examined by analyzing a variety of argumentative and explanatory strategies in these interviews.

---

[19]Sources for tracing research in argumentation in China are the academic journals run by universities or state research institutes, such as *Chinese Social Sciences, Chinese Language, Foreign Language Teaching and Research*, and *Journal of Foreign Languages*. Sporadically, short papers appear which deal with the effectiveness of persuasion in writing. Some interest in the analysis and evaluation of argumentation as a scholarly activity has been brought about by the Chinese translation of van Eemeren and Grootendorst (1992a).

12.3 LINGUISTIC APPROACHES

A considerable amount of argumentation studies have been undertaken which are part of the newly developed pragma-linguistic tradition. Argumentation studies inspired by speech act theory, conversation analysis, and discourse analysis started in Germany in the early 1970s with the study of argumentative dialogues and speech acts like "to argue," "to explain," and "to prove."[20] These studies are often strongly influenced by Toulmin and Habermas. They usually start from a corpus of written or spoken argumentative texts and aim for empirical descriptions. In this endeavor, the formalisms provided by modern logic are seldom used (notable exceptions being Metzing 1975, Wunderlich 1980, and Heidrich 1982).[21] Recently, Walter Kindt started a project on the formal analysis of argumentation in natural language at the University of Bielefeld (1988, 1992a, 1992b).

A method for describing argumentative discourse based on pragmatic stylistics was developed by Herbig (1992), who tested his method empirically. Sandig and Püschel (1992) edited a volume on styles of argumentation. The theoretical framework of the studies concerned is constituted by speech act theory and conversation analysis, "text-internal" stylistics (propositional, prosodic and illocutionary aspects) and "text-external" stylistics (emotional, competitive, cooperative, gender-specific, political, intercultural dimensions). Rehbein (1995) favors a linguistic approach to argumentation in which pragmatic, historical, and cognitive insights are implemented. He analyzes the use of complex referential expressions in argumentative discourse.

Linguistic studies influenced by conversation analysis tend to concentrate on conflict management in dialogue and conflict-solving strategies. Psychological and sociological approaches are then often combined with research techniques and concepts from conversation analysis, such as turn taking (Schwitalla, 1987). As is shown by Schwitalla, argumentation is not only a means to solve conflicts, but also serves to maintain consensus and confirm group identity.[22]

At the university of Geneva, the research group of the *Unité de Linguistique Française*, an important group of Francophone Swiss pragma-linguists, has, since the beginning of the 1980s, devoted itself to giving pragmatic descriptions of French markers (pragmatic connectives, modal adverbs, illocutionary verbs) within a general model of discourse structure. The group includes Auchlin, Egner, Luscher, Perrin, Moeschler, (Anne) Reboul, Roulet, Schelling and de Spengler. Their pragmatic studies are influenced by speech act theory, Anscombre and

---

[20]Öhlschläger (1979) discusses "to argue," Strecker (1976) "to prove," Klein (1987) a whole group of speech acts, such as "to confirm," "to explain," "to infer," and "to justify." Apeltauer (1978) provides a survey of sequences of speech acts, moves and strategies in debate and discussion (cf. also Zillig, 1982).

[21]A special mention should be made of Berger's (1988) work on verbal and nonverbal clues of irony in argumentation.

[22]The development of argumentative skills from early childhood is described by Völzing (1981), surveyed in English in Völzing (1987).

Ducrot's theory of argumentation, and Goffman's symbolic interactionalism. Recently, making use of Sperber and Wilson's theory of relevance, a cognitive component has been added to the "Geneva model" for discourse analysis.

An essential characteristic of the Geneva approach is that speech acts are not examined in isolation, in constructed examples, but in their relations with other speech acts in a discourse. For this purpose, material is used from real-life conversations. The Geneva model distinguishes between different levels of the discourse, describes the relations between these levels, and indicates which linguistic markers may be indicative of the various relations. The main contributions to the development of the model have been made by Antoine Auchlin (1981), Jacques Moeschler (1985), and Eddy Roulet (1989; Roulet, Auchlin, Moeschler, Rubattel, & Schelling, 1985). The organizational aspects of discourse that have been captured so far, are: its hierarchical and functional structure; the sequencing principles or rules governing its production; and the interpretive rules governing the connecting of utterances (Moeschler, 1989c, p. 243). Roulet extended the dialogical model to make it suitable for the description of monological discourse.

Working within the framework of this discourse model, several authors have given detailed analyses of markers of argumentative relations.[23] Roulet et al. (1985) provide detailed descriptions of the syntactic, semantic and pragmatic properties of different types of connectives: markers of conversation structure, argumentative connectives, markers of counterargumentation, markers of causal relations, and markers of reevaluations. In Moeschler (1982) it is attempted to characterize the speech act "refutation" typologically, describing the conditions that govern its use, the linguistic markers of refutation, and the place and function of refutations in conversation. More recently, Moeschler (1989a, 1989b) investigated the problem of argumentative coherence from the perspective of Sperber and Wilson's relevance theory. Anne Reboul (1988) confronts Ducrot's theory of argumentative *topoi* with Sperber and Wilson's relevance theory, and Anne Reboul (1989) discusses their solution to the baldness-paradox. Jean-Marc Luscher (1989) contrasts Ducrot's analysis of "d'ailleurs" ("anyway") with an analysis of this operator based on Sperber and Wilson.[24]

Recent studies of argumentation in Sweden also make use of pragmatic insights or from a combination of such insights with perceptions from artificial intelligence.[25] Viveka Adelswärd (1987, 1989) brought conversation analysis to

---

[23]See also Egner (1989) and Jayez (1989).

[24]The French researchers Bassano and Champaud combine a linguistic approach to argumentation based on Anscombre and Ducrot with a cognitive approach in order to carry out a number of empirical studies of the interpretation of utterances with argumentative operators and connectives by children and adults (Bassano, 1991; Bassano & Champaud, 1987a, 1987b, 1987c). Brassart (1990, 1991, 1992) has empirically investigated the development of children's capacity to produce complex argumentative (and counterargumentative) texts.

[25]There is an important critical thinking tradition in Sweden. Some of the classics among the textbooks are Fredriksson (1969), Walton (1970), and Andersson and Furberg (1974). In his influential *Att luras utan att ljuga* (1980), Ryding gave a Gricean reinterpretation of classical rhetoric.

bear in analyzing the argumentation in institutionalized contexts such as job interviews, interviews with conscientious objectors (1991), and discourse in the courtroom (Adelswärd, Aronsson, & Linell, 1988).

Cornelia Ilie (1994) aims to provide a pragmatic framework for the identification, description, and interpretation of rhetorical questions as they occur in everyday English. She develops a typological classification of rhetorical questions and identifies the main pragmatic factors determining their discursive functions in political speeches. By giving a systematic interpretation and evaluation of their argumentative functions, Ilie attempts to account for the argumentativeness of rhetorical questions. From her analysis, she draws the conclusion that rhetorical questions fulfil three major functions in political speeches: the manipulation of opinion by defending the speaker's position or attacking the opponent's position; the facilitation of the storage of the speaker's message in the audience's memory; and the creation or maintenance (by way of irony, sarcasm, etc.) of a sense of togetherness between the speaker and the audience, and the induction or reinforcement of negative attitudes towards political opponents.

Richard Hirsch (1987, 1989, 1991) developed an artificial heuristic model of the expression, evaluation, and revision of belief structures in interactive argumentation. According to the model, argumentation occurs when (some feature of) a belief conflicts with or is incompatible with some other belief. This initiates a search for a resolution of the conflict or an elimination of the incompatibility. Hirsch illustrates his model by analyzing cases of belief revision in the course of interactive argumentation.

The Danish linguist Lita Lundquist studies argumentation from the perspective of text linguistics. Apart from two monographs on text coherence (1980) and text analysis (1983), she published several articles in which she shows that the argumentative constraints posed by particular words and expressions at the sentence level, as described by Anscombre and Ducrot, can be helpful in explaining argumentative relations at the macro-level of argumentative texts (Lundquist, 1987). According to Lundquist (1991), Anscombre and Ducrot's concept of "polyphony" can be used to establish a criterion for determining whether a particular discourse may be considered argumentative.[26]

In Eastern Europe, the Hungarian László Komlósi studied discourse structure, coherence, and argumentation in political discourse. Komlósi and Knipf (1987) discuss the function of argumentative schemes in discourse. The authors claim that the explanatory, coordinative, and negotiative strategies underlying argumentation are motivated by intrinsic human dispositions termed *assimilation* and *accommodation* by Piaget. Komlósi (1991) reports on a case study of the changes in the paradigm of political discourse during the transition from single-party dominance to a pluralistic political practice.

---

[26]Grinsted (1991), another Danish linguist, analyzed differences between Danish and Spanish negotiation styles within the framework of conversation analysis. Vincent Fella Hendricks, Morten Elvang-Gøransson, and Stig Andur Pedersen (1995) provide an example of a Danish approach based on the theory of Al-logics.

The Slovenian Olga Kunst-Gnamus studies argumentation within a pragmatic framework. In Kunst-Gnamus (1987), a distinction is made between the "argumentative relation" between certain elements of an argumentative text and the "persuasive relation," which is not part of the argumentative text but results from a felicitous choice of argumentative text within a particular context. Kunst-Gnamus (1991) investigates the rationality of everyday discourse, and concludes that natural speech is structured in a contradictory way. In order to be effective, it must simultaneously appeal to the interlocutor's emotions and comply with the interlocutor's rational or logical standards.

Antoinette Primatarova-Miltcheva is a Bulgarian author who published work on counterargumentation and concessive relations in argumentative discourse (1987). More recently, Primatarova and Nedeltchev (1991) attempted to explain why argumentative discourse failed to acquire a regular place in Bulgarian political public life.

Studies of argumentative discourse undertaken by Russian scholars include research into such topics as text genre and argumentation structure (Dolinina, 1992), pseudo-argumentation as a form of speech manipulation (Sentenberg & Karasic, 1993), and other types of neorhetorical analyses of discourse with a special emphasis on linguistic problems.

Argumentation theory is now part of the curriculum of students and post-graduates majoring in logic, philosophy, and linguistics.[27] Scholars from the University of St. Petersburg have played an active part in this development. Nowadays, Russian scholars cooperate with their American colleagues in organizing debating tournaments in Moscow, St. Petersburg, and Voronez, which mark the beginning of a growing interest in cross-cultural research into argumentative strategies (Berkov, 1986). Argumentation is also studied by Russian logicians examining logical problems from an epistemological perspective. They address these problems in the context of a descriptive theory of argumentation aimed at identifying premises, propositions, arguments, and fallacies. Recently, some attempts have been made to add a pragmatic component to the descriptions (Baranov, 1990, and Yaskevich, 1993).

12.4 ARGUMENTATION IN SPECIAL FIELDS

Argumentation in special fields has been a topic of common interest. Among the fields which have been studied are literary criticism, judicial argumentation, and political discourse. Several German authors have paid attention to the role of rhetoric in *literary criticism*, showing how categories of ancient rhetoric can be used for the description and interpretation of literary texts.

---

[27]The Russian translation of van Eemeren and Grootendorst (1984, 1992a) has been an impetus to the broadening of scale in the study of argumentation in Russia.

In this endeavor, Heinrich Plett (1975) not only used ancient figures of speech classifications, but also insights from semiotics and text linguistics, thus establishing a new typology of stylistic devices. Manfred Beetz (1980a, 1980b) aimed to show the influence of classical rhetoric and logic on Baroque literature. He also published works on the modifications of the notion of argument (*argumentum*) in rhetorical treatises from the 17th and 18th centuries (Beetz, 1985). The categories of ancient rhetoric are used by Johanna Brandt (1986) to describe the structure of argumentative dialogues in Seneca's tragedies. Siegfried Schmidt (1976) argues for a more empirical, objective, and argumentative literary science. Literary science should not claim its own methodology, but comply with the general scientific norms for rational argumentation and empirical testing. Eike von Savigny (1976) investigated which types of argument are used by literary scientists in motivating their interpretations of poetry, and which rules are used in weighing up the arguments.

The studies of *judicial argumentation* are either influenced by logical and normative schools of thought or by rhetorical and relativistic approaches. The first studies take up the work done in deontic logic and in normative approaches such as those developed by the Erlangen School and Habermas. The second studies follow the tradition of ancient dialectic and rhetoric. A useful overview of research concerning legal argumentation is given by Neumann (1986), who critically discusses contributions from various theoretical backgrounds.

Robert Alexy (1978, 1989) provides an outstanding example of a highly elaborated normative model of legal argumentation. He takes up standards of validity in deontic logic as well as discourse principles of Habermas and the Erlangen school. The central aim of his work is to determine how normative judgments, such as the decisions of judges, can be rationally justified. Alexy formulates a set of general rules for practical discussions about norms and values. He subsequently applies these rules to judicial argumentation.[28]

Hubert Rodingen (1977, 1981) represents the group of scholars inspired by rhetoric (see also Ballweg, 1989; Sobota, 1990a, and, in English, 1990b). Rodingen benefits from the revival of ancient topics and rhetoric that started with the works of Viehweg (1974) and Perelman and Olbrechts-Tyteca (1958). Seibert (1977, 1981, and, in English, 1987) is not only influenced by rhetoric, but also by pragmatics. Struck (1971, 1977) provided a list of different types of standard arguments in law, based on insights of Viehweg.[29]

A number of publications deal with the role of argumentation in *political discourse*. The relations between ideology, the mass media, and argumentation are studied by a research group at the University of Vienna (see Wodak et al.,

---

[28]Other normative logical approaches to judicial argumentation can be found in Tammelo (1969, 1978), Weinberger (1970), Rödig (1976, 1980), Yoshino (1978), and Koch (1980).

[29]Other representatives of this group are Ballweg and Seibert (1982), Horn (1967, 1981), and Schreckenberger (1978).

1990). Using linguistic, psychological and sociological methods, they analyze a corpus of texts consisting of editorials, television interviews, and recordings of street interviews. The analysis is aimed at detecting and describing antisemitic tendencies in Austrian political discourse before and after the election of President Kurt Waldheim.

Kalivoda, a member of the Institute of General Rhetoric in Tübingen and one of the coauthors of the *Historisches Wörterbuch der Rhetorik*, published a book on the structures and processes of political argumentation (1986). As background for an empirical analysis of debates in the first Prussian parliament in Berlin in 1847, he uses classical rhetoric, modern argumentation theory, and historical studies.

In Sweden, Evert Vedung studied manipulation and deception in political discourse (1982, 1987). When analyzing political deception, he argues, we should not focus on the content of messages, but rather on the acts by which this content is communicated. In Vedung's opinion, the rules for evaluating reasoning may be a useful starting point for appraising the verbal conduct of politicians. Vedung (1987, p. 357) proposes some basic rules for evaluating argumentation, and uses these rules to evaluate a number of cases of political reasoning.

Another Scandinavian publication worth mentioning here is *Rationale Argumentation* by the Norwegians Føllesdal, Walloe, and Elster (German translation, 1986), in which the types of arguments most common in the social sciences, physics, and the humanities are analyzed and compared. In Finland, Sonja Tirkkonen-Condit examined argumentation from a cross-linguistic perspective. In Tirkkonen-Condit (1985), she discusses some problems involved in translating argumentative texts from English into Finnish. In Tirkkonen-Condit (1987), she compares the results of a pilot study concerning the location of the main thesis in Finnish newspaper editorials with its location in British newspapers.

CLASSIFIED BIBLIOGRAPHY

Classical Analytic, Dialectic, Rhetoric
Aristotle 1924, 1925a, 1925b, 1928a, 1928b, 1928c, 1928d; Cicero 1949, 1954; Kennedy 1994; de Pater 1965; Quintilian 1920; Wisse 1989

Traditional Fallacies, Crawshay-Williams, Naess
Aristotle 1928c, 1928d; Barth & Krabbe 1982; Barth & Martens 1977; Beardsley 1959, 1975; Black 1952; Bueno 1988; Carney & Scheer 1964; Cleary & Haberman 1964; Cohen & Nagel 1934, 1964; Copi 1972; Copi & Cohen 1990; Crawshay-Williams 1946, 1947, 1948, 1951, 1957, 1968, 1970; van Eemeren & Grootendorst 1984, 1988, 1989, 1993; van Eemeren, Grootendorst, Jackson & Jacobs 1993; Emmet 1960; Eveling 1959; Fearnside & Holther 1959; Finocchiaro 1974; Freeley 1966; Grootendorst 1987; Guthrie 1971; Hamblin 1970; Hardin 1960; Johnstone 1957–1958, 1958–1959, 1968; Kahane 1973, 1976; Kneale & Kneale 1962; Kruger 1975; Lambert & Ulrich 1980; Lazerowitz 1958–1959; Locke 1690/1961; Mates 1953; Naess 1947, 1966, 1992a, 1992b, 1993; Nuchelmans 1993; Oesterle 1952; Olbrechts-Tyteca 1963; Pelsma 1937; Rescher 1959, 1975; de Rijk 1962; Salmon 1984; Schopenhauer 1818–1830; Sellars 1917; Simmons 1959; Whately 1848

Perelman and Olbrechts-Tyteca
Abbott 1989; Arnold 1986; Corgan 1987; Cox 1989; Crosswhite 1989, 1993; Dearin 1982, 1989; Dunlap 1993; Ede 1989; van Eemeren & Grootendorst 1995a; Eubanks 1986; Farrell 1986; Fisher 1986; Golden 1986; Goodwin 1991, 1992; Gracio 1993; Haarscher Ed., 1993; Haarscher & Ingber Eds., 1986; Hudson 1969; Johnstone 1993; Karon 1989; Kienpointner 1993; Kluback 1980; Koren 1993; Laughlin & Hughes 1986; Makau 1984; Maneli 1978, 1994; McKerrow 1982, 1986; Measell 1985; Mickunas 1986; Nimmo & Mansfield 1986; Olbrechts-Tyteca 1963; Perelman 1963, 1970, 1976, 1977, 1979a, 1979b, 1980, 1982; Perelman & Olbrechts-Tyteca 1958, 1969, 1989; Pilotta 1986; Ray 1978; Rieke 1986; Schiappa 1985, 1993; Schuetz 1991; Scult 1985, 1989; Tarello 1972; Walker & Sillars 1990; Warnick & Kline 1992; Wiethof 1985; Wintgens 1993

Toulmin
Abelson 1960–1961; Bird 1959, 1961; Botha 1970; Carnap 1950; Castaneda 1960; Collins 1959; Cooley 1959; Cowan 1964; Crable 1976; Ehninger & Brockriede 1963; Freeman 1985, 1988, 1991, 1992; Goodnight 1982, 1993; Grewendorf 1975; Hample 1977b; Hardin 1959; Healy 1987; Johnson 1981; Johnstone 1968; King-Farlow 1973; Kneale 1949; Kopperschmidt 1989a; Körner 1959; Manicas 1966; Mason 1961; McPeck 1981, 1990; Newell & Rieke 1986; O'Connor 1959; Pratt 1970; Reinard 1984; Rieke & Sillars 1975; Rieke & Stutman 1990; Rowland 1981, 1982; Ryle 1976; Schellens 1979; Sikora 1959; Snoeck Henkemans 1992; Toulmin 1950, 1958, 1964, 1972, 1976, 1988, 1990, 1992; Toulmin & Janik 1973; Toulmin, Rieke & Janik 1979; Trent 1968; Weinstein 1990a, 1990b; Will 1960; Willard Ed., 1982; Windes & Hastings 1969; Zarefsky 1982; Ziegelmueller & Rhodes Eds., 1981

Informal Logic and Critical Thinking
Battersby 1989; Biro & Siegel 1992; Blair 1986; Blair & Johnson 1987, 1991; Eds., 1980; Bowles 1989, 1990, 1991; Conway 1991; Damer 1987; van Eemeren 1988; van Eemeren & Grootendorst 1984, 1992a; Eds., 1992; van Eemeren, Grootendorst, Blair & Willard Eds., 1992; Ennis 1962, 1989; Finocchiaro 1981; Fisher 1988; Ed., 1988; Fogelin 1978; Freeman 1988, 1991; Govier 1980a, 1980b, 1982, 1983, 1985, 1987; Hamblin 1970; Hansen 1990; Hintikka 1989; Hitchcock 1983; Johnson 1987, 1989, 1990a, 1990b, 1992; Johnson & Blair 1980, 1993, 1994; Kahane 1971, 1973; Lambert & Ulrich 1980; Lipman 1988; Little, Groarke & Tindale 1989; Massey 1981; McPeck 1981, 1990; Missimer 1990; Norris & Ennis 1989; Paul 1982, 1985, 1987, 1989, 1990; Pinto 1994; Rescher 1976, 1977; Scriven 1976; Seech 1987, 1993; Siegel 1985, 1988, 1993; Thomas 1986; Ulrich 1992; Walton 1987, 1989a, 1990, 1992a; Walton & Krabbe 1995; Weddle 1978; Weinstein 1990b, 1994; Wellman 1971; Wisdom 1991; Yanal 1991

Communication and Rhetoric
Anderson & Mortenson 1967; Balthrop 1989; Benoit 1981, 1983a, 1983b; Benoit & Benoit 1987; Biesecker 1989; Birdsell 1989; Booth 1974; Branham 1991; Brockriede 1972, 1974, 1975, 1977; Brummett 1976; Burleson 1979, 1980, 1981, 1983; Cherwitz & Hikins 1983; Chesebro 1968, 1971; Clark & Delia 1976, 1977, 1979; Cox & Willard Eds., 1982; Craig & Tracy Eds., 1983; Dauber 1988, 1989; Delia 1970; Dewey 1916; Dunbar 1986; van Eemeren, Grootendorst, Jackson & Jacobs 1993; Ehninger 1970; Ehninger & Brockriede 1963; Fadely 1967; Farrell 1976, 1993; Fisher 1987; Goodnight 1980, 1982, 1987a, 1987b, 1991; Gronbeck Ed., 1989; Gross 1990; Hample 1977a, 1977b, 1978, 1979a, 1979b, 1980, 1981; Hirokawa & Scheerhorn 1985; Holmquest 1989; Hovland Ed., 1957; Hovland & Janis Eds., 1959; Hovland, Janis & Kelley 1953; Hovland & Rosenberg Eds., 1960; Hunter Ed., 1990; Hynes 1989; Infante 1981; Ivie 1987; Jackson 1983; Jackson & Jacobs 1980, 1982; Jacobs & Jackson 1981, 1982, 1983, 1989; Johnstone 1959, 1970; Kaplow 1981; Keith Ed., 1993; Kellner 1989; Kline & Woloschuk 1983; Kneupper 1978, 1979; Lewinski, Metzler & Settle 1973; Lichtman, Garvin & Corsi 1973; Lichtman & Rohrer 1980; Lyne 1983; McCloskey 1985; McKerrow 1980; McKerrow Ed., 1993; Natanson & Johnstone Eds., 1965; Nelson, Megill & McCloskey Eds., 1987; Newell & Adams 1985; O'Keefe, B. 1988; O'Keefe, B. & Benoit 1982; O'Keefe, D. 1977, 1982; Patterson & Zarefsky 1983; Peters 1989; Prelli 1989; Putnam, Wilson, Waltman & Turner 1986; Rieke & Sillars 1975, 1984; Riley, Hollihan & Freadhoff 1987; Schiappa 1989; Scott 1967; Sheppard & Rieke 1983; Sherif & Hovland 1961; Sillars 1981; Simons Ed., 1990; Snedaker & Schuetz 1985; Trapp 1983; Wallace 1989; Warnick & Inch 1989; Werling & Rieke 1985; Willard 1976, 1978a, 1978b, 1983, 1987, 1989, 1995; Winans & Utterback 1930; Yingling & Trapp 1985; Yost 1917; Zarefsky 1969, 1980, 1982, 1992, 1995

Fallacies and Formal Logic
Barth & Krabbe 1982; Barth & Martens 1977; Burge 1977; Cohen 1986; Corcoran 1972; Finocchiaro 1980, 1994; Hamblin 1970; Hintikka 1987, 1989; Hintikka & Bachman 1991; Jason 1986, 1989, Kahneman, Slovic & Tversky Eds., 1982; Krabbe 1992; Kripke 1965; Lear 1980; Mackenzie 1979a; Mates 1953; Nisbett & Ross 1980; Peirce 1992; Scriven 1976; Secor 1987; Tarski 1956; Walton 1984, 1989b, 1991, 1992b; Walton & Krabbe 1995; Whitehead & Russell 1910–1913; Woods 1967, 1980, 1992a, 1995; Woods & Walton 1982, 1989

Dialogue Logic and Formal Dialectics
Barth 1972, 1980, 1982, 1985b; Barth & Krabbe 1978, 1982; Barth & Martens 1977; Barth & Martens Eds., 1982; van Eemeren & Grootendorst 1984, 1988, 1992a; van Eemeren, Grootendorst, Jackson & Jacobs 1993; Grootendorst 1978; Hamblin 1970, 1971; Hintikka 1968, 1973, 1976, 1981; Hintikka & Hintikka 1982; Hintikka & Kulas 1983; Hintikka & Saarinen 1979; Kamlah & Lorenzen 1967, 1973, 1984; Krabbe 1978, 1982a, 1982b, 1985a, 1985b, 1986, 1988; Lorenzen 1969, 1987; Lorenzen & Lorenz 1978; Lorenzen & Schwemmer 1975; Mackenzie 1979a, 1979b, 1981, 1985, 1989, 1990; Saarinen Ed., 1979; Walton 1985b; Walton & Krabbe 1995

Pragma-Dialectics
Blair 1986; van Eemeren 1986, 1987a, 1987b, 1994; van Eemeren, de Glopper, Grootendorst & Oostdam 1995; van Eemeren & Grootendorst 1984, 1987, 1988, 1990, 1991, 1992a, 1992b, 1994b, 1995b; van Eemeren, Grootendorst & Meuffels 1984, 1985, 1989; van Eemeren, Grootendorst, Jackson & Jacobs 1993; Feteris 1987, 1989, 1990, 1991, 1993a, 1993b; Garssen 1994; Gerritsen 1994; Houtlosser 1994; Jackson, Jacobs & Rossi 1987; Jacobs 1987, 1989; Jungslager 1994; Kloosterhuis 1994; Koetsenruijter 1994; Oostdam, de Glopper & Eiting 1994; Plug 1994; Rees 1989, 1991, 1992a, 1992b, 1994a, 1994b, 1995a, 1995b; Slot 1993, 1994; Snoeck Henkemans 1992, 1995a, 1995b; Verbiest 1987; Viskil 1994

Language-Oriented Approaches
Anscombre & Ducrot 1983, 1989; Apothéloz, Brandt & Quiroz 1991; Bassano 1991; Bassano & Champaud 1987a, 1987b, 1987c; Borel 1989, 1991, 1992; Borel, Grize & Miéville 1983; Ducrot 1980, 1984, 1990; Ducrot et al. 1987; van Eemeren & Grootendorst 1994a; Gomez Diaz 1991; Grize 1982, 1986; Lo Cascio 1991; Lundquist 1987, 1991; Maier 1989; Meyer 1986b; Moeschler & de Spengler 1982; Nølke 1992; Quiroz, Apothéloz & Brandt 1992; Snoeck Henkemans 1995a, 1995b; Verbiest 1994; Zagar 1995

Other Significant Approaches
Adelswärd 1987, 1988, 1991; Adelswärd, Aronsson & Linell 1988; Alekseyev 1991; Alexy 1978, 1989; Andersson & Furberg 1974; Apel 1988; Apeltauer 1978; Auchlin 1981; Ballweg 1989; Ballweg & Seibert Eds., 1982; Baranov 1990; Barilli 1969; Bassano 1991; Bassano & Champaud 1987a, 1987b, 1987c; Beetz 1980a, 1980b, 1985; Berger 1988; Berk 1979; Berkenbosch & Braet 1994; Berkov 1986; Braet 1984; Brandt 1986; Brassart 1990, 1991, 1992; Brutian 1979, 1991, 1992, 1993; Brutian & Narsky Eds., 1986; Carrilho 1992; Cattani 1990; Chuyeshov 1993; Dascal, Dascal & Landau 1987; Deimer 1975; Dolinina 1987; Egner 1989; Follesdal, Walloe & Elster 1986; Fredriksson 1969; Frixen 1987; Garavelli 1990; Geissner 1978, 1980, 1986a, 1986b, 1987, 1988a, 1988b; Genette 1969; Gerhardus, Kledzig & Reitzig 1975; Grewendorf 1975, 1980; Grinsted 1991; Gutenberg 1987; Habermas 1971, 1973, 1988, 1991; Hastings 1962; Heidrich 1982; Herbig 1992; Hirsch 1987, 1989, 1991; Horn 1967, 1981; van den Hoven 1984, 1987; Huth 1975; Ilie 1994; Jayez 1989; Jens 1983; Kalivoda 1986; Kienpointner 1983,

1987, 1992a, 1992b; Kindt 1988, 1992a, 1992b; Klein, J., 1987; Klein, W., 1980; Koch 1980; Komlósi 1991; Komlósi & Knipf 1987; Kopperschmidt 1975, 1976a, 1976b, 1977, 1978, 1980, 1987, 1989a, 1989b, 1990, 1995; Kopperschmidt Ed., 1990, 1991; Kunst-Gnamus 1987, 1991; Lausberg 1969; Lauth 1979; Lo Cascio 1991; Lueken 1991, 1992, 1995; Lumer 1988, 1990; Lundquist 1980, 1983, 1987, 1991; Luscher 1989; Markov 1993; Mengel 1991, 1995; Metzing 1975; Meyer 1982b, 1986a, 1986b, 1988; Moeschler 1982, 1985, 1989a, 1989b, 1989c; Neumann 1986; Öhlschläger 1979, 1980; Pera 1991, 1994; Plett 1975; Primatarova-Miltcheva 1987; Primatarova-Miltcheva & Nedeltchev 1991; Quasthoff 1978; Reboul, A., 1988, 1989; Reboul, O., 1988, 1990, 1991; Rehbein 1995; Rödig 1976, 1980; Rodingen 1977, 1981; Roulet 1989; Roulet, Auchlin, Moeschler, Rubattel & Schelling 1985; Ryding 1980; Sandig & Püschel Eds., 1992; Savigny 1976; Schanze Ed., 1974; Schellens 1985, 1987; Schmidt 1976; Schmidt-Faber 1986; Schreckenberger 1978; Schwitalla 1976, 1987; Segre 1985; Seibert 1977, 1981, 1987; Sentenberg & Karasic 1993; Settekorn 1977; Shi-Xu 1992, 1995; Sobota 1990a, 1990b; Strecker 1976; Struck 1971, 1977; Tammelo 1969, 1978; Tirkkonen-Condit 1985, 1987; Ueding & Jens Eds., 1992, 1994; Ueding & Steinbrink 1994; Valesio 1980; Vedung 1982, 1987; Viehweg 1974; Volquardsen 1995; Völzing 1979, 1981, 1987; Walther 1990; Weinberger 1970; Wodak et al. 1990; Wohlrapp 1977, 1987, 1990, 1991, 1995; Wunderlich 1980; Yaskevich 1993; Yoshino 1978; Zillig 1982

REFERENCES

Abbott, D. (1989). The jurisprudential analogy: Argumentation and the new rhetoric. In R. D. Dearin (Ed.), *The new rhetoric of Chaim Perelman. Statement & response* (pp. 191–199). Lanham, MD: University Press of America.

Abelson, R. (1960–1961). In defense of formal logic. *Philosophy and Phenomenological Research, 21*, 333–346.

Adelswärd, V. (1987). The argumentation of self in job interviews. In F. H. van Eemeren, R. Grootendorst, J. A. Blair, & Ch. A. Willard (Eds.), *Argumentation: Analysis and practices. Proceedings of the Conference on Argumentation 1986* (pp. 327–336). Dordrecht/Providence: Foris Publications, PDA 3B.

Adelswärd, V. (1988). *Styles of success. On impression management as collaborative action in job interviews*. University of Linköping: Linköping Studies in Arts and Science, 23.

Adelswärd, V. (1991). The use of formulations in the production of arguments. A study of interviews with conscientious objectors. In F. H. van Eemeren, R. Grootendorst, J. A. Blair, & Ch. A. Willard (Eds.), *Proceedings of the Second International Conference on Argumentation* (Organized by the International Society for the Study of Argumentation at the University of Amsterdam, June 19–22, 1990) (pp. 591–603). Amsterdam: Sic Sat, 1A/B.

Adelswärd, V., Aronsson K., & Linell P. (1988). Discourse of blame: Courtroom construction of social identity from the perspective of the defendant. *Semiotica, 71*, 261–284.

Albert, H. (1967). *Traktat über kritische Vernunft* [Treatise on critical reason]. Tübingen: Mohr.

Albert, H. (1975). *Traktat über kritische Vernunft* [Treatise on critical reason] (3rd ed.). Tübingen: Mohr.

Alekseyev, A. P. (1991). *Argumentacia, pzonaniye, obsheniye* [Argumentation, knowledge, communication]. Moscow.

Alexy, R. W. (1978). *Theorie der juristischen Argumentation. Die Theorie des rationalen Diskurses als Theorie der juristischen Begründung* [A theory of legal argumentation. The theory of rational discourse as theory of legal justification]. Frankfurt am Main: Suhrkamp.

Alexy, R. W. (1989). *A theory of legal argumentation. The theory of rational discourse as theory of legal justification* [Translation of: *Theorie der juristischen Argumentation. Die Theorie des rationalen Diskurses als Theorie der juristischen Begründung*. Frankfurt am Main: Suhrkamp, 1978]. Oxford: Oxford University Press.

361

Anderson, R. L., & Mortenson, C. D. (1967). Logic and marketplace argumentation. *Quarterly Journal of Speech, 53*, 143–151.

Andersson, J., & Furberg, M. (1974). *Språk och påverkan: om argumentationens semantik* [Language and practice: The semantics of argumentation] (1st ed. 1966). Stockholm: Aldus/Bonnier.

Anscombre, J.-C., & Ducrot, O. (1983). *L'Argumentation dans la langue* [Argumentation in language]. Liège: Pierre Mardaga.

Anscombre, J.-C., & Ducrot, O. (1989). Argumentativity and informativity. In M. Meyer (Ed.), *From metaphysics to rhetoric* (pp. 71–87). Dordrecht: Kluwer.

Apel, K. O. (1988). *Diskurs und Verantwortung* [Discourse and responsibility]. Frankfurt am Main: Suhrkamp.

Apeltauer, E. (1978). *Elemente und Verlaufsformen von Streitgesprächen* [Elements and proceedings of disputations]. Ludwigsburg.

Apothéloz, D., Brandt P.-Y., & Quiroz, G. (1991). Champ et effets de la négation argumentative: Contre-argumentation et mise en cause [Domain and effects of argumentative negation: Counterargumentation and calling into question]. *Argumentation, 6*, 99–113.

Åqvist, L. (1965). *A new approach to the logical theory of interrogatives. I: Analysis.* Uppsala: Filosofiska föreningen.

Åqvist, L. (1975). *A new approach to the logical theory of interrogatives. Analysis and formalization.* Tübingen: Narr.

Aristotle. (1924). *Rhetoric.* W. D. Ross (Ed.). Oxford: Clarendon Press.

Aristotle. (1925a). *Eudemian ethics.* W. D. Ross (Ed.). Oxford: Clarendon Press.

Aristotle. (1925b). *Nicomachean ethics.* W. D. Ross (Ed.). Oxford: Clarendon Press.

Aristotle. (1928a). *Prior analytics.* W. D. Ross (Ed.). Oxford: Clarendon Press.

Aristotle. (1928b). *Posterior analytics.* W. D. Ross (Ed.). Oxford: Clarendon Press.

Aristotle. (1928c). *Sophistical refutations.* W. D. Ross (Ed.). Oxford: Clarendon Press.

Aristotle. (1928d). *Topics.* W. D. Ross (Ed.). Oxford: Clarendon Press.

Arnold, C. C. (1986). Implications of Perelman's theory of argumentation for theory of persuasion. In J. L. Golden & J. J. Pilotta (Eds.), *Practical reasoning in human affairs. Studies in honor of Chaim Perelman* (pp. 37–52). Dordrecht: Reidel.

Auchlin, A. (1981). Réflexions sur les marqueurs de structuration de la conversation [Reflections on the markers of conversational structure]. *Etudes de Linguistique Appliquée, 44*, 88–103.

Austin, J. L. (1962). *How to do things with words.* Oxford: Clarendon Press.

Baird, A. C. (1928). *Public discussion and debate.* Boston: Ginn.

Baker, G. P. (1895). *Principles of argumentation.* Boston: Ginn.

Ballweg, O. (1989). Entwurf einer analytischen Rhetorik [Outlines of an analytical rhetoric]. In H. Schanze & J. Kopperschmidt (Eds.), *Rhetorik und Philosophie* (pp. 229–247). München: Fink.

Ballweg, O., & Seibert, T. M. (Eds.). (1982). *Rhetorische Rechtstheorie. Zum 75. Geburtstag von Theodor Viehweg* [A rhetorical theory of law. On the occasion of Theodor Viehweg's 75th birthday] . Freiburg: K. Alber.

Balthrop, V. W. (1989). Wither the public sphere? An optimistic reading. In B. E. Gronbeck (Ed.), *Spheres of argument. Proceedings of the Sixth SCA/AFA Conference on Argumentation* (pp. 20–25). Annandale, VA: Speech Communication Association.

Baranov, A. N. (1990). *Linguisticheskaya theoriya argumentacii* [Linguistic theory of argumentation]. Moscow.

Barilli, R. (1969). *Poetica e retorica.* Milano: Mursia.

Barth, E. M. (1972). *Evaluaties* [Evaluations]. Inaugural lecture as professor of logic, University of Utrecht, Friday 2 June. Assen: Van Gorcum.

Barth, E. M. (1974). *The logic of the articles in traditional philosophy.* Dordrecht/Boston: Reidel.

Barth, E. M. (1978). Arne Naess en de filosofische dialectiek [Arne Naess and philosophical dialectics]. In A. Naess, *Elementaire argumentatieleer* (pp. 145–166). Baarn: Ambo.

Barth, E. M. (1980). Prolegomena tot de studie van conceptuele structuren [Prolegomena to a study of conceptual structures]. *Algemeen Nederlands Tijdschrift voor Wijsbegeerte* [General Dutch Journal of Philosophy], *72*, 36–48.

Barth, E. M. (1982). A normative-pragmatical foundation of the rules of some systems of formal₃ dialectics. In E. M. Barth & J. L. Martens (Eds.), *Argumentation: Approaches to theory formation. Containing the contributions to the Groningen Conference on the Theory of Argumentation, October 1978* (pp. 159–170). Amsterdam: John Benjamins.

Barth, E. M. (1985a). Empirical logic, a new field: Bioprograms, logemes, and logics as institutions. *Synthese, 63*, 375–388.

Barth, E. M. (1985b). Two-phase epistemology and models for dialogue logic. *Philosophica, 35*, 69–88.

Barth, E. M. (1986). Philosophical logic in the Netherlands after 1940. Poznan: *Ruch Filozoficny.*

Barth, E. M. (1992). Dialogical approaches. In M. Dascal, D. Gerhardus, K. Lorenz, & G. Meggle (Eds.), *Sprachphilosophie/Philosophy of language. An international handbook of contemporary research. Vol. I* (pp. 663–676). Berlin/New York: Walter de Gruyter.

Barth, E. M., & Krabbe, E. C. W. (1978). Formele₃ dialectiek: instrumenten ter beslechting van conflicten over geuite meningen [Formal₃ dialectics: Instruments for the resolution of conflicts of avowed opinions]. *Spektator, 7*, 307–341.

Barth, E. M., & Krabbe, E. C. W. (1982). *From axiom to dialogue. A philosophical study of logics and argumentation.* Berlin/New York: Walter de Gruyter.

Barth, E. M., & Martens, J. L. (1977). Argumentum *ad hominem*: From chaos to formal dialectic. The method of dialogue tableaus as a tool in the theory of fallacy. *Logique et Analyse, 20*, 76–96.

Barth, E. M., & Martens, J. L. (Eds.). (1982). *Argumentation. Approaches to theory formation. Containing the contributions to the Groningen Conference on the Theory of Argumentation, October 1978.* Amsterdam: John Benjamins.

Bassano, D. (1991). Opérateurs et connecteurs argumentatifs: une approche psycholinguistique [Operators and argumentative connectives: A psycho-linguistic approach]. *Intellectia, 11*, 149–191.

Bassano, D., & Champaud, Chr. (1987a). La fonction argumentative des marques de la langue [The argumentative function of discourse markers]. *Argumentation, 1*, 175–199.

Bassano, D., & Champaud, Chr. (1987b). Fonctions argumentatives et informatives du langage: le traitement des modificateurs d'intensité *au moins, au plus* et *bien* chez l'enfant et chez l'adulte [Argumentative and informative functions of language: The use of intensifiers (*at least, at the most* and *well*) by children and adults]. *Archives de Psychologie, 55*, 3–30.

Bassano, D., & Champaud, Chr. (1987c). Argumentative and informative functions of French intensity modifiers *presque* (almost), *à peine* (just, barely) and *à peu près* (about): an experimental study of children and adults. *Cahiers de Psychologie Cognitive, 7*, 605–631.

Battersby, M. (1989). Critical thinking as applied epistemology. *Informal Logic, 11*, 91–100.

Beardsley, M. C. (1950). *Practical logic.* Englewood Cliffs, NJ: Prentice-Hall.

Beardsley, M. C. (1975). *Thinking straight. Principles of reasoning for readers and writers* (4th rev. ed., 1st ed. 1950). Englewood Cliffs, NJ: Prentice-Hall.

Beetz, M. (1980a). *Rhetorische Logik. Prämissen der Deutchen Lyrik im Übergang vom 17. zum 18. Jahrhundert* [Rhetorical logic. Premises of German lyric at the transition from the 17th to the 18th century]. Tübingen: Niemeyer.

Beetz, M. (1980b). Disputatorik und Argumentation in Andreas Gryphius' Trauerspiel Leo Armenius [Disputation and argumentation in Andreas Gryphius' tragedy Leo Armenius]. *Zeitschrift für Literaturwissenschaft und Linguistik, 38/39*, 178–203.

Beetz, M. (1985). Argumenta. Stichpunkte zu ihrer Begriffsverwendung, Systematik und Geschichte in der Rhetoriktheorie des 17. und frühen 18. Jh. [Arguments. Their conceptual use, organization and history in the theory of rhetoric in the 17th and early 18th century].

In J. Kopperschmidt & H. Schanze (Eds.), *Argumente-Argumentation. Interdisziplinäre Problem-zugänge* (pp. 48–60). München: Fink.

Benoit, P. J. (1981). The use of argument by preschool children: The emergent production of rules for winning arguments. In G. Ziegelmueller & J. Rhodes (Eds.), *Dimensions of argument. Proceedings of the Second Summer Conference on Argumentation* (pp. 624–642). Annandale, VA: Speech Communication Association.

Benoit, P. J. (1983a). Characteristics of arguing from a social actor's perspective. In D. Zarefsky, M. O. Sillars, & J. Rhodes (Eds.), *Argument in transition. Proceedings of the Third Summer Conference on Argumentation* (pp. 544–559). Annandale, VA: Speech Communication Association.

Benoit, P. J. (1983b). Extended arguments in children's discourse. *Journal of the American Forensic Association, 20,* 72–89.

Benoit, P. J. (1985). Strategies for threatening face: Mitigating and aggravating bids and rejections. In J. R. Cox, M. O. Sillars, & G. B. Walker (Eds.), *Argument and social practice: Proceedings of the Fourth Summer Conference on Argumentation* (pp. 604–618). Annandale, VA: Speech Communication Association.

Benoit, W. L., & Benoit, P. J. (1987). Everyday argument practices of naive social actors. In J. W. Wenzel (Ed.), *Argument and critical practices. Proceedings of the Fifth SCA/AFA Conference on Argumentation* (pp. 465–473). Annandale, VA: Speech Communication Association.

Benoit, W. L., Hample, D., & Benoit P. J. (Eds.). (1992). *Readings in argumentation.* Berlin/New York: Foris Publications, PDA 11.

Berger, F. R. (1977). *Studying deductive logic.* London: Prentice-Hall.

Berger, L. (1988). Sprechsprachliche Argumentation und Ironie [Everyday argumentation and irony]. In W. Brandt (Ed.), *Sprache in Vergangenheit und Gegenwart. Beiträge aus dem Institut für Germanistische Sprachwissenschaft der Philipps-Universität Marburg* (pp. 184–195). Marburg: Hitzeroth.

Berk, U. (1979). *Konstruktive Argumentationstheorie* [A constructive theory of argumentation]. Stuttgart/Bad Cannstatt: Frommann-Holzboog.

Berkenbosch, R., & Braet, A. (1994). The heuristic use of argumentation schemes in academic debate. In F. H. van Eemeren & R. Grootendorst (Eds.), *Studies in pragma-dialectics* (pp. 232–237). Amsterdam: Sic Sat, 4.

Berkov, V. F. (1986). *Vzaimodeistviye lectora i slyushatelya* [Interaction between the lecturer and the audience]. Moscow.

Beth, E. W. (1969). *Moderne logika* [Modern logic] (2nd ed., 1st ed. 1962). Assen: Van Gorcum.

Biesecker, B. (1989). Recalculating the relation of the public and technical spheres. In B. E. Gronbeck (Ed.), *Spheres of argument. Proceedings of the Sixth SCA/AFA Conference on Argumentation* (pp. 66–70). Annandale, VA: Speech Communication Association.

Bird, O. (1959). The uses of argument. *Philosophy of Science, 9,* 185–189.

Bird, O. (1961). The re-discovery of the topics: Professor Toulmin's inference warrants. *Mind, 70,* 534–539.

Birdsell, D. S. (1989). Critics and technocrats. In B. E. Gronbeck (Ed.), *Spheres of argument. Proceedings of the Sixth SCA/AFA Conference on Argumentation* (pp. 16–19). Annandale, VA: Speech Communication Association.

Biro, J., & Siegel, H. (1992). Normativity, argumentation and an epistemic theory of fallacies. In F. H. van Eemeren, R. Grootendorst, J. A. Blair & Ch. A. Willard (Eds.), *Argumentation illuminated* (pp. 85–103). Amsterdam: Sic Sat, 1.

Black, M. (1952). *Critical thinking: An introduction to logic and scientific method* (2nd ed., 1st ed. 1946). Englewood Cliffs, NJ: Prentice-Hall.

Blair, J. A. (1986). Comments on Frans van Eemeren: "Dialectical analysis as a normative reconstruction of argumentative discourse." In *Text, 6,* 17–24.

Blair, J. A., & Johnson, R. H. (1987). Argumentation as dialectical. *Argumentation, 1,* 41–56.

Blair, J. A., & Johnson, R. H. (1991). Misconceptions of informal logic. *Teaching Philosophy, 14,* 35–52.

Blair, J. A., & Johnson, R. H. (Eds.). (1980). *Informal logic. The first international symposium.* Point Reyes, CA: Edgepress.

Booth, W. (1974). *Modern dogma and the rhetoric of assent.* Indiana: University of Notre Dame Press.

Borel, M.-J. (1989). Norms in argumentation and natural logic. In R. Maier (Ed.), *Norms in argumentation. Proceedings of the Conference on Norms 1988* (pp. 33–48). Dordrecht: Foris (PDA 8).

Borel, M.-J. (1991). Objets de discours et de représentation. *Languages, 25,* 36–50.

Borel, M.-J. (1992). Anthropological objects and negation. *Argumentation, 6,* 7–27.

Borel, M.-J., Grize, J.-B., & Miéville, D. (1983). *Essai de logique naturelle* [A treatise on natural logic]. Bern/Frankfurt/New York: Peter Lang.

Botha, R. P. (1970). *The methodological status of grammatical argumentation.* The Hague: Mouton.

Bowles, G. (1989). Favorable relevance arguments. *Informal Logic, 11,* 11–19.

Bowles, G. (1990). Propositional relevance. *Informal Logic, 12,* 65–77.

Bowles, G. (1991). Evaluating arguments: The premise-conclusion relation. *Informal Logic, 13,* 1–20.

Braet, A. (1984). *De klassieke statusleer in modern perspectief. Een historisch-systematische bijdrage tot de argumentatieleer* [The classical theory of status: A historical and systematic contribution to argumentation theory]. Groningen: Wolters-Noordhoff.

Brandt, J. (1986). *Argumentative Struktur in Senecas Tragödien. Eine Untersuchung anhand der "Phaedra" und des "Agamemnon"* [Argumentative structures in Seneca's tragedies. A case study of "Phaedra" and "Agamemnon"]. Hildesheim: Olms.

Branham, R. J. (1991). *Debate and critical analysis: The harmony of conflict.* Hillsdale, NJ: Lawrence Erlbaum Associates.

Brassart, D. G. (1990). Le développement des capacités discursives chez l'enfant de 8 à 12 ans. Le discours argumentatif écrit (étude didactique) [The development of discursive capacities of 8 and 12 year old children. Written argumentative discourse (a pedagogical study)]. *Revue Française de Pédagogie, 90,* 31–34.

Brassart, D. G. (1991). Les débuts de la rédaction argumentative. Approche psycholinguistique et didactique [The first attempts at argumentative editing. A psycho-linguistic and pedagogical approach]. In M. Fayol (Ed.), *La production d'écrits: De l'école maternelle au collège. Actes du colloque organisé par le Laboratoire d'Etudes des acquisitions et du développement de l'Université de Bourgogne, la MAFPEN de l'Académie de Dijon, le CRDP de Dijon, décembre 1990* (pp. 95–122). Dijon: CRDP.

Brassart, D. G. (1992). Negation, concession and refutation in counterargumentative composition by pupils from 8 to 12 years old and adults. *Argumentation, 6,* 77–98.

Brockriede, W. E. (1972). Arguers as lovers. *Philosophy & Rhetoric, 5,* 1–11.

Brockriede, W. E. (1974). Rhetorical criticism as argument. *Quarterly Journal of Speech, 60,* 165–174.

Brockriede, W. E. (1975). Where is argument? *Journal of the American Forensic Association, 11,* 179–182.

Brockriede, W. E. (1977). Characteristics of arguments and arguing. *Journal of the American Forensic Association, 13,* 129–132.

Brown, P., & Levinson, S. C. (1978). Universals in language usage: Politeness phenomena. In E. Goody (Ed.), *Questions and politeness: Strategies in social interaction* (pp. 56–311). Cambridge, England: Cambridge University Press.

Brown, P., & Levinson, S. C. (1987). *Politeness: Some universals in language usage.* Cambridge, England: Cambridge University Press.

Brummett, B. (1976). Some implications of 'process' or 'intersubjectivity': Postmodern rhetoric. *Philosophy and Rhetoric, 9,* 21–51.

Brutian, G. A. (1979). The nature of philosophical argumentation. *Philosophy & Rhetoric, 12,* 77–90.

Brutian, G. A. (1991). The architectonics of argumentation. In F. H. van Eemeren, R. Grootendorst, J. A. Blair, & Ch. A. Willard (Eds.), *Proceedings of the Second International Conference on Argumentation* (Organized by the International Society for the Study of Argumentation at the University of Amsterdam, June 19–22, 1990) (pp. 61–63). Amsterdam: Sic Sat, 1A/B.

Brutian, G. A. (1992). The theory of argumentation, its main problems and investigative perspectives. In J. Pietarinen (Ed.), *Problems of philosophical argumentation* (Reports from the Department of Practical Philosophy Kätytánnöllisen Filosofian Julkaisuja. Vol. 5) (pp. 5–17). Turku: University of Turku.

Brutian, G. A. (1993). Logic of argumentation. The Perelman view: Pros and cons arguments . In G. Haarscher (Ed.), *Chaim Perelman et la pensée contemporaine* (pp. 293–305). Bruxelles: Bruylant.

Brutian, G. A., & Narsky, I. S. (Eds.). (1986). *Philosophical problems of argumentation* (in Russian). Yerevan.

Bueno, A. A. (1988). Aristotle, the fallacy of accident, and the nature of predication. *Journal of the History of Philosophy, 26,* 5–24.

Burge, T. (1977). A theory of aggregates. *Nous, 11,* 97–118.

Burleson, B. R. (1979). On the analysis and criticism of arguments: Some theoretical and methodological considerations. *Journal of the American Forensic Association, 15,* 137–147.

Burleson, B. R. (1980). The place of nondiscursive symbolism, formal characterizations, and hermeneutics in argument analysis and criticism. *Journal of the American Forensic Association, 16,* 222–231.

Burleson, B. R. (1981). A cognitive-developmental perspective on social reasoning processes. *Western Journal of Speech Communication, 45,* 133–147.

Burleson, B. R. (1983). Interactional antecedents of social reasoning development: Interpreting the effects of parent discipline on children. In D. Zarefsky, M. O. Sillars, & J. Rhodes (Eds.), *Argument in transition. Proceedings of the Third Summer Conference on Argumentation* (pp. 597–610). Annandale, VA: Speech Communication Association.

Carlson, L. (1983). *Dialogue games: An approach to discourse analysis.* Dordrecht: Reidel.

Carnap. R. (1950). *Logical foundations of probability.* Chicago: University of Chicago Press.

Carney, J. D., & Scheer, R. K. (1964). *Fundamentals of logic.* New York: Macmillan.

Carrilho, M. M. (1992). *Rhétoriques de la modernité* [Modern rhetorics]. Paris: Presses Universitaires de France.

Castaneda, H. N. (1960). On a proposed revolution in logic. *Philosophy of Science, 27,* 279–292.

Cattani, A. (1990). *Forme dell'argomentare: il ragionamento tra logica e retorica* [Forms of arguing: logical and rhetorical aspects of reasoning]. Padova: Edizioni GB.

Cherwitz, R. A., & Hikins, J. A. (1983). Rhetorical perspectivism. *Quarterly Journal of Speech, 69,* 249–266.

Chesebro, J. W. (1968). The comparative advantages case. *Journal of the American Forensic Association, 5,* 57–63.

Chesebro, J. W. (1971). Beyond the orthodox: The criteria case. *Journal of the American Forensic Association, 7,* 208–215.

Chuyeshov, V. I. (1993). *Teoretiko-isotricheskiye osnovaniya argumentologii* [Theoretical and historical foundations of Argumentology]. St. Petersburg.

Cicero. (1949). *De inventione. De optimo genere oratorum. Topica.* M. Hubbell (Ed.), Loeb Classical Library, 386. London: Heinemann.

Cicero. (1954). *Rhetorica ad herennium.* H. Caplan (Ed. and Trans.), Loeb Classical Library, 403. London: Heinemann.

Clark, H. H. (1979). Responding to indirect requests. *Cognitive Psychology, 11,* 430–477.

Clark, R. A., & Delia, J. G. (1976). The development of functional persuasive skills in childhood and early adolescence. *Child Development, 47,* 1008–1014.

Clark, R. A., & Delia, J. G. (1977). Cognitive complexity, social perspective-taking, and functional persuasive skills in second- to ninth-grade children. *HCR, 3,* 128–134.

Clark, R. A., & Delia, J. G. (1979). Topoi and rhetorical competence. *Quarterly Journal of Speech, 65,* 187–206.

Cleary, J. W., & Haberman, F. W. (1964). *Rhetoric and public address: A bibliography 1947–1961.* Madison, University of Wisconsin Press.

Cohen, L. J. (1986). *The dialogue of reason.* Oxford: Clarendon Press.

Cohen, L. J. (1992). *An essay on belief and acceptance.* Oxford: Clarendon Press.

Cohen, M. R., & Nagel, E. (1934). *An introduction to logic and scientific method* (1st ed.). London: Routledge & Kegan Paul.

Cohen, M. R., & Nagel, E. (1964). *An introduction to logic and scientific method.* London: Routledge & Kegan Paul.

Collins, J. (1959). The uses of argument. *Cross Currents, 9,* 179.

Conway, D. A. (1991). On the distinction between convergent and linked arguments. *Informal Logic, 13,* 145–158.

Cooley, J. C. (1959). On Mr. Toulmin's revolution in logic. *Journal of Philosophy, 56,* 297–319.

Copi, I. M. (1953). *Introduction to logic.* New York: Macmillan.

Copi, I. M. (1972). *Introduction to logic* (4th ed.), New York: Macmillan.

Copi, I. M., & Cohen, C. (1990). *Introduction to logic* (8th ed.). New York: Macmillan.

Corbett, E. P. J. (1966). *Classical rhetoric for the modern student* (3rd ed.). New York: Oxford University Press.

Corcoran, J. (1972). Completeness of an ancient logic. *Journal of Symbolic Logic, 37,* 696–702.

Corgan, V. (1987). Perelman's universal audience as a critical tool. *Journal of the American Forensic Association, 23,* 147–157.

Cowan, J. L. (1964). The uses of argument—an apology for logic. *Mind, 73,* 27–45.

Cox, J. R. (1989). The die is cast: Topical and ontological dimensions of the *locus* of the irreparable. In R. D. Dearin (Ed.), *The new rhetoric of Chaim Perelman. Statement & response* (pp. 121–139). Lanham, MD: University Press of America.

Cox, J. R., & Willard, Ch. A. (1982a). Introduction: The field of argumentation. In J. R. Cox & Ch. A. Willard (Eds.), *Advances in argumentation theory and research* (pp. xiii–xlvii). Carbondale, IL: Southern Illinois University Press.

Cox, J. R., & Willard, Ch. A. (Eds.). (1982b). *Advances in argumentation theory and research.* Carbondale, IL: Southern Illinois University Press.

Crable, R. E. (1976). *Argumentation as communication: Reasoning with receivers.* Columbus, OH: Charles E. Merill.

Craig, R. T., & Tracy, K. (Eds.). (1983). *Conversational coherence.* London: Sage.

Crawshay-Williams, R. (1946). The obstinate universal. *Polemic, 2,* 14–21.

Crawshay-Williams, R. (1947). *The comforts of unreason. A study of the motives behind irrational thought.* London: Routledge & Kegan Paul.

Crawshay-Williams, R. (1948). Epilogue. In A. Koestler, E. L. Woodward, et al., *The challenge of our time* (pp. 72–78). London: Routledge & Kegan Paul.

Crawshay-Williams, R. (1951). Equivocal confirmation. *Analysis, 11,* 73–79.

Crawshay-Williams, R. (1957). *Methods and criteria of reasoning. An inquiry into the structure of controversy.* London: Routledge & Kegan Paul.

Crawshay-Williams, R. (1968). Two intellectual temperaments. *Question, 1,* 17–27.

Crawshay-Williams, R. (1970). *Russell remembered.* London: Oxford University Press.

Cronkhite, G. (1969). *Persuasion. Speech and behavioral change.* Indianapolis, IN: Bobbs Merrill.

Crosswhite, J. (1989). Universality in rhetoric: Perelman's universal audience. *Philosophy & Rhetoric, 22,* 157–173.

Crosswhite, J. (1993). Being unreasonable: Perelman and the problem of fallacies. *Argumentation, 7,* 385–402.

Damer, T. E. (1987). *Attacking faulty reasoning* (2nd ed.). Belmont, CA: Wadsworth.

Dascal, M., Dascal, V., & Landau, E. (1987). The art of moving and the art of proving. In F. H. van Eemeren, R. Grootendorst, J. A. Blair, & Ch. A. Willard (Eds.), *Argumentation: Perspectives and approaches. Proceedings of the Conference on Argumentation 1986* (pp. 179–186). Dordrecht/Providence: Foris Publications, PDA 3A.

Dauber, C. E. (1988). Through a glass darkly: Validity standards and the debate over nuclear strategic doctrine. *Journal of the American Forensic Association, 24,* 168–180.

Dauber, C. E. (1989). Fusion criticism: A call to criticism. In B. E. Gronbeck (Ed.), *Spheres of argument. Proceedings of the Sixth SCA/AFA Conference on Argumentation* (pp. 33–36). Annandale, VA: Speech Communication Association.

Davidson, D. (1971). Mental events. In L. Forster & J. Swanson (Eds.), *Experience and theory* (pp. 79–101). Boston: Belknap.

Davidson, D. (1980). The logical form of action sentences. In D. Davidson, *Essays in actions and events* (pp. 105–122). Oxford: Oxford University Press.

Dearin, R. D. (1982). Perelman's concept of "quasi-logical" argument: A critical elaboration. In J. R. Cox & Ch. A. Willard (Eds.), *Advances in argumentation theory and research* (pp. 78–94). Carbondale, IL: Southern Illinois University Press.

Dearin, R. D. (1989). The philosophical basis of Chaim Perelman's theory of rhetoric. In R. D. Dearin (Ed.), *The new rhetoric of Chaim Perelman. Statement & response* (pp. 17–34). Lanham, MD: University Press of America.

Deimer, G. (1975). *Argumentative Dialoge. Ein Versuch zu ihrer sprachwissenschaftlichen Beschreibung* [Argumentative dialogue: An attempt at linguistic description]. Tübingen: Niemeyer.

Delia, J. G. (1970). The logic fallacy, cognitive theory, and the enthymeme. A search for the foundation of reasoned discourse. *Quarterly Journal of Speech, 56,* 140–148.

Dewey, J. (1916). *Democracy and education.* New York: Macmillan.

Dewey, J. (1909/1991). *How we think* (Reissue of 1st ed., 1909). Buffalo: Prometheus Books.

Dijk, T. A. van, & Kintsch, W. (1983). *Strategies of discourse comprehension.* New York: Academic Press.

Dolinina, I. B. (1992). Change of scientific paradigms as an object of the theory of argumentation. In F. H. van Eemeren, R. Grootendorst, J. A. Blair, & Ch. A. Willard (Eds.), *Argumentation illuminated* (pp. 73–84). Amsterdam: Sic Sat, 1.

Ducrot, O. (1980). *Les échelles argumentatives* [Argumentative scales]. Paris: Minuit.

Ducrot, O. (1984). *Le dire et le dit* [The process and product of saying]. Paris: Minuit.

Ducrot, O. (1990). *Polifonia y argumentacion* [Polyphony and argumentation]. Cali: Universidad del Valle.

Ducrot, O., Bourcier, D., Bruxelles, S., Diller, A.-M., Foucquier, E., Gouazé, J., Maury, L., Nguyen, T. B., Nunes, G., Ragunet de Saint-Alban, L., Rémis, A., & Sirdar-Iskander, Chr. (1980). *Les mots du discours* [The words of discourse]. Paris: Minuit.

Dunbar, N. R. (1986). Laetrile: A case study of a public controversy. *Journal of the American Forensic Association, 22,* 196–211.

Dunlap, D. D. (1993). The conception of audience in Perelman and Isocrates: Locating the ideal in the real. *Argumentation, 7,* 461–474.

Eco, U. (1987). Il messaggio persuasivo [The message of persuasion]. In E. Mattioli (Ed.), *Le ragioni della retorica* (pp. 11–27). Modena: Mucchi.

Ede, L. S. (1989). Rhetoric versus philosophy: The role of the universal audience in Chaim Perelman's *The new rhetoric*. In R. D. Dearin (Ed.), *The new rhetoric of Chaim Perelman. Statement & response* (pp. 141–151). Lanham, MD: University Press of America.

Eemeren, F. H. van. (1986). Dialectical analysis as a normative reconstruction of argumentative discourse. *Text, 6,* 1–16.

Eemeren, F. H. van. (1987a). Argumentation studies' five estates. In J. Wenzel (Ed.), *Argument and critical practices. Proceedings of the Fifth SCA/AFA Conference on Argumentation* (pp. 9–24). Annandale, VA: Speech Communication Association.

Eemeren, F. H. van. (1987b). For reason's sake: Maximal argumentative analysis of discourse. In F. H. van Eemeren, R. Grootendorst, J. A. Blair, & Ch. A. Willard (Eds.), *Argumentation: Across the lines of discipline. Proceedings of the Conference on Argumentation 1986* (pp. 201–216). Berlin/New York: Foris Publications, PDA 3.

Eemeren, F. H. van. (1988). Argumentation analysis: A Dutch counter-balance. In A. Fisher (Ed.), *Critical thinking. Proceedings of the First British Conference on Informal Logic and Critical Thinking* (pp. 39–53). Norwich: University of East Anglia.

Eemeren, F. H. van. (1994). The study of argumentation as normative pragmatics. In F. H. van Eemeren & R. Grootendorst (Eds.), *Studies in pragma-dialectics* (pp. 3–8). Amsterdam: Sic Sat, 4.

Eemeren, F. H. van, Glopper, K. de, Grootendorst, R., & Oostdam, R. J. (1995). Student performance in identifying unexpressed premises and argumentation schemes. *Argumentation and Advocacy, 31,* 151–162.

Eemeren, F. H. van, & Grootendorst, R. (1984). *Speech acts in argumentative discussions. A theoretical model for the analysis of discussions directed towards solving conflicts of opinion.* Dordrecht/Cinnaminson: Foris Publications, PDA 1.

Eemeren, F. H. van, & Grootendorst, R. (1987). Fallacies in pragma-dialectical perspective. *Argumentation, 1,* 283–301.

Eemeren, F. H. van, & Grootendorst, R. (1988). Rationale for a pragma-dialectical perspective. *Argumentation, 2,* 271–291.

Eemeren, F. H. van, & Grootendorst, R. (1989). A transition stage in the theory of fallacies. *Journal of Pragmatics, 13,* 99–109.

Eemeren, F. H. van, & Grootendorst, R. (1990). Analyzing argumentative discourse. In R. Trapp & J. Schuetz (Eds.), *Perspectives on argumentation. Essays in honor of Wayne Brockriede* (pp. 86–106). Prospect Heights, IL: Waveland Press.

Eemeren, F. H. van, & Grootendorst, R. (1991). Argumentation from a speech act perspective. In J. Verschueren (Ed.), *Pragmatics at issue. Selected papers of the International Pragmatics Conference, Antwerp, August 17–22, 1987. Volume I* (pp. 151–170). Amsterdam: John Benjamins.

Eemeren, F. H. van, & Grootendorst, R. (1992a). *Argumentation, communication, and fallacies. A pragma-dialectical perspective.* Hillsdale, NJ: Lawrence Erlbaum Associates.

Eemeren, F. H. van, & Grootendorst, R. (1992b). Relevance reviewed: The case of *argumentum ad hominem. Argumentation, 6,* 141–159.

Eemeren, F. H. van, & Grootendorst, R. (Guest Eds.). (1992c). *Argumentation, 6,* 137–290. Special issue on relevance.

Eemeren, F. H. van, & Grootendorst, R. (1993). The history of the *argumentum ad hominem* since the Seventeenth Century. In E. C. W. Krabbe, R. J. Dalitz, & P. A. Smit (Eds.), *Empirical logic and public debate. Essays in honour of Else M. Barth* (pp. 49–68). Amsterdam/Atlanta: Rodopi.

Eemeren, F. H. van, & Grootendorst, R. (1994a). Argumentation theory. In J. Verschueren & J. Blommaert (Eds.), *Handbook of pragmatics* (pp. 55–61). Amsterdam: John Benjamins.

Eemeren, F. H. van, & Grootendorst, R. (1994b). Writing argumentative texts: From analysis to presentation. In F. H. van Eemeren & R. Grootendorst (Eds.), *Studies in pragma-dialectics* (pp. 221–231). Amsterdam: Sic Sat, 4.

Eemeren, F. H. van, & Grootendorst, R. (1995a). Perelman and the fallacies. *Philosophy & Rhetoric, 28,* 122–133.

Eemeren, F. H. van, & Grootendorst, R. (1995b). The pragma-dialectical approach to fallacies. In H. V. Hansen & R. C. Pinto (Eds.), *Fallacies: Classical background and contemporary developments* (pp. 130–144). University Park, PA: The Pennsylvania State University Press.

Eemeren, F. H. van, Grootendorst, R., Blair, J. A., & Willard, Ch. A. (Eds.). (1992). *Argumentation illuminated.* Amsterdam: Sic Sat, 1.

Eemeren, F. H. van, Grootendorst, R., Jackson, S., & Jacobs, S. (1993). *Reconstructing argumentative discourse.* Tuscaloosa/London: The University of Alabama Press.

Eemeren, F. H. van, Grootendorst, R., & Kruiger, T. (1984). *The study of argumentation.* New York: Irvington.

Eemeren, F. H. van, Grootendorst, R., & Meuffels, B. (1984). Het identificeren van enkelvoudige argumentatie [Identifying single argumentation]. *Tijdschrift voor Taalbeheersing* [Journal of Speech Communication], *6,* 297–310.

Eemeren, F. H. van, Grootendorst, R., & Meuffels, B. (1985). Gedifferentieerde replicaties van identificatie-onderzoek [Differentiated replications of identification research]. *Tijdschrift voor Taalbeheersing* [Journal of Speech Communication], *7,* 241–258.

Eemeren, F. H. van, Grootendorst, R., & Meuffels, B. (1989). The skill of identifying argumentation. *Journal of the American Forensic Association, 25,* 239–245.

Egner, I. (1989). The role of topos in the use of a wobe particle. *Argumentation, 3,* 271–283.

Ehninger, D. (1970). Argument as method: Its nature, its limitations, and its uses. *Communication Monographs, 37,* 101–110.

Ehninger, D., & Brockriede, W. (1963). *Decision by debate.* New York: Dodd, Mead.

Eisenberg, A., & Ilardo, J. A. (1980). *Argument. A guide to formal and informal debate* (2nd ed., 1st ed. 1972). Englewood Cliffs, NJ: Prentice-Hall.

Emmet, E. R. (1960). *The use of reason.* London: Longmans, Green.

Ennis, R. H. (1962). A concept of critical thinking. *Harvard Educational Review, 32,* 81–111.

Ennis, R. H. (1989). Critical thinking and subject specificity. *Educational Researcher, 18,* 4–10.

Enos, T., & Brown, S. C. (1993). *Defining the new rhetorics.* Newbury Park, CA: Sage.

Eubanks, R. (1986). An axiological analysis of Chaim Perelman's theory of practical reasoning. In J. L. Golden & J. J. Pilotta (Eds.), *Practical reasoning in human affairs. Studies in honor of Chaim Perelman* (pp. 53–67). Dordrecht: Reidel.

Eveling, H. S. (1959). Methods and criteria of reasoning. *Philosophical Quarterly, 9,* 188–189.

Fadely, L. D. (1967). The validity of the comparative advantages case. *Journal of the American Forensic Association, 4,* 28–35.

Farrell, Th. B. (1976). Knowledge, consensus, and rhetorical theory. *Quarterly Journal of Speech, 62,* 1–14.

Farrell, Th. B. (1986). Reason and rhetorical practice: The inventional agenda of Chaim Perelman. In J. L. Golden & J. J. Pilotta (Eds.), *Practical reasoning in human affairs. Studies in honor of Chaim Perelman* (pp. 259–286). Dordrecht: Reidel.

Farrell, Th. B. (1993). *Norms of rhetorical culture.* New Haven/London: Yale University Press.

Fearnside, W. W., & Holther, W. B. (1959). *Fallacy: The counterfeit of argument.* Englewood Cliffs, NJ: Prentice Hall.

Feteris, E. T. (1987). The dialectical role of the judge in a Dutch legal process. In J. W. Wenzel (Ed.), *Argument and critical practices. Proceedings of the Fifth SCA/AFA Conference on Argumentation* (pp. 335–339). Annandale VA: Speech Communication Association.

Feteris, E. T. (1989). *Discussieregels in het recht. Een pragma-dialectische analyse van het burgerlijk proces en het strafproces* [Discussion rules in law. A pragma-dialectical analysis of civil and criminal proceedings] (with a summary in English). Dordrecht/Cinnaminson: Foris Publications.

Feteris, E. T. (1990). Conditions and rules for rational discussion in a legal process: A pragma-dialectical perspective. *Argumentation and Advocacy, 23,* 108–177.

Feteris, E. T. (1991). Normative reconstruction of legal discussions. In F. H. van Eemeren, R. Grootendorst, J. A. Blair, & Ch. A. Willard (Eds.), *Proceedings of the Second International Conference on Argumentation* (Organized by the International Society for the Study of Argumentation at the University of Amsterdam, June 19–22, 1990) (pp. 768–775). Amsterdam: Sic Sat, 1A/1B.

Feteris, E. T. (1993a). The judge as a critical antagonist in a legal process: A pragma-dialectical perspective. In R.E. McKerrow (Ed.), *Argumentation and the postmodern challenge. Proceedings of the Eighth SCA/AFA Conference on Argumentation* (pp. 476–480). Annandale VA: Speech Communication Association.

Feteris, E. T. (1993b). Rationality in legal discussions. A pragma-dialectical perspective. *Informal Logic, 15*, 179–188.

Finocchiaro, M. A. (1974). The concept of *ad hominem* argument in Galileo and Locke. *The Philosophical Forum, 5*, 394–404.

Finocchiaro, M. A. (1980). *Galileo and the art of reasoning.* Dordrecht: Reidel.

Finocchiaro, M. A. (1981). Fallacies and the evaluation of reasoning. *American Philosophical Quarterly, 18*, 13–22.

Finocchiaro, M. A. (1994). The positive versus the negative evaluation of arguments. In R. H. Johnson & J. A. Blair (Eds.), *New essays in informal logic* (pp. 21–35). Windsor: Informal Logic.

Fisher, A. (1988a). *The logic of real arguments.* Cambridge, England: Cambridge University Press.

Fisher, A. (Ed.). (1988b). *Critical thinking. Proceedings of the First British Conference on Informal Logic and Critical Thinking.* Norwich: University of East Anglia.

Fisher, W. R. (1986). Judging the quality of audiences and narrative rationality. In J. L. Golden & J. J. Pilotta (Eds.), *Practical reasoning in human affairs. Studies in honor of Chaim Perelman* (pp. 85–103). Dordrecht: Reidel.

Fisher, W. R. (1987). *Human communication as narration.* Columbia: University of South Carolina Press.

Fogelin, R. (1978). *Understanding arguments, an introduction to informal logic.* New York: Harcourt, Brace, Jovanovich.

Føllesdal, D., Walloe, L., & Elster, J. (1986). *Rationale Argumentation. Ein Grundkurs in Argumentations und Wissenschafstheorie* [Rational argumentation. An introduction in the theory of argumentation and science]. Berlin/New York: Walter de Gruyter.

Foss, S. K., Foss, K. A., & Trapp, R. (1991). *Contemporary perspectives on rhetoric* (2nd ed.). Prospect Heights, IL: Waveland Press.

Foster, W. T. (1908). *Argumentation and debating.* Boston: Houghton-Mifflin.

Fredriksson, G. (1969). *Det politiska språket* [Political language use] (1st ed. 1962). Staffanstorp: Bo Cavefors.

Freeley, A. J. (1966). *Argumentation and debate* (2nd ed.). Belmont, CA: Wadsworth.

Freeman, J. B. (1985). Dialectical situations and argument analysis. *Informal Logic, 7*, 151–162.

Freeman, J. B. (1988). *Thinking logically: Basic concepts for reasoning.* Englewood Cliffs, NJ: Prentice-Hall.

Freeman, J. B. (1991). *Dialectics and the macrostructure of arguments. A theory of argument structure.* Berlin/New York: Foris Publications, PDA 10.

Freeman, J. B. (1992). Relevance, warrants, backing, inductive support. *Argumentation, 6*, 219–235.

Frege, G. (1967). Begriffsschrift. In J. van Heijenoot (Ed.), *From Frege to Gödel* (Reprint). Cambridge, MA: Harvard University Press.

Frixen, G. (1987). Struktur und Dynamik natürlichsprachlichen Argumentierens [Structure and dynamics of everyday argumentation]. *Papiere zur Linguistik, 36*, 45–111.

Garavelli, M. B. (1990). *Manuale di retorica* [Handbook of rhetoric]. Milano: Bompiani.

Garssen, B. (1994). Recognizing argumentation schemes. In F. H. van Eemeren & R. Grootendorst (Eds.), *Studies in pragma-dialectics* (pp. 105–111). Amsterdam: Sic Sat, 4.

Geissner, H. (1978). Das handlungstheoretische Interesse an der Rhetorik, oder: Das rhetorische Interesse am gesellschaftlichen Handeln [The importance of practical theory to rhetoric, or: The importance of rhetoric to public action]. In H.F. Plett (Ed.), *Rhetorik. Kritische Positionen zum Stand der Forschung* (pp. 230–51). München: Fink.

Geissner, H. (1986a). *Sprecherziehung. Didaktik und Methodik der mündlichen Kommunikation* [Speech education. Pedagogy and methodology of oral communication]. Frankfurt am Main: Scriptor.

Geissner, H. (1986b). *Rhetorik und politische Bildung* [Rhetoric and political education]. Frankfurt am Main: Scriptor.

Geissner, H. (1987). Rhetorical communication as argumentation. In F. H. van Eemeren, R. Grootendorst, J. A. Blair, & Ch. A. Willard (Eds.), *Argumentation: Across the lines of discipline.*

Proceedings of the Conference on Argumentation 1986 (pp. 111–119). Dordrecht/Providence: Foris Publications, PDA 3.

Geissner, H. (1988a). *Mündlich: Schriftlich. Sprechwissenschaftliche Analysen 'freigesprochener' und 'vorgelesener' Berichte* [Oral communication: Written communication. Linguistic analyses of messages that are spontaneously produced or read aloud]. Frankfurt am Main: Scriptor.

Geissner, H. (1988b). *Sprechwissenschaft. Theorie der mündlichen Kommunikation* [Speech communication. A theory of oral communication]. Frankfurt am Main: Scriptor.

Genette, G. (1969). *Figure. Retorica e strutturalismo* [Figures of speech. Rhetoric and structuralism]. Torino: Einaudi.

Gerhardus, D., Kledzig, S. M., & Reitzig, G. H. (1975). *Schlüssiges Argumentieren. Logisch Propädeutisches Lehr- und Arbeitsbuch* [Sound arguing. Logical pre-school text book]. Göttingen: Vandenhoeck & Ruprecht.

Gerritsen, S. (1994). A defence of deductivism in reconstructing unexpressed premises. In F. H. van Eemeren, & R. Grootendorst (Eds.), *Studies in pragma-dialectics* (pp. 41–47). Amsterdam: Sic Sat, 4.

Glaser, E. (1941). *An experiment in the development of critical thinking*. New York: Teacher's College, Columbia University.

Golden, J. L. (1986). The universal audience revisited. In J. L. Golden & J. J. Pilotta (Eds.), *Practical reasoning in human affairs. Studies in honor of Chaim Perelman* (pp. 287–304). Dordrecht: Reidel.

Golden, J. L., & Pilotta, J. J. (Eds.). (1986). *Practical reasoning in human affairs. Studies in honor of Chaim Perelman*. Dordrecht: Reidel.

Gomez Diaz, L. M. (1991). Remarks on Jean-Blaise Grize's logics of argumentation. In F. H. van Eemeren, R. Grootendorst, J. A. Blair, & Ch. A. Willard (Eds.), *Proceedings of the Second International Conference on Argumentation* (Organized by the International Society for the Study of Argumentation at the University of Amsterdam, June 19–22, 1990) (pp. 123–132). Amsterdam: Sic Sat, 1A/B.

Goodnight, G. Th. (1980). The liberal and the conservative presumptions: On political philosophy and the foundation of public argument. In J. Rhodes & S. Newell (Eds.), *Proceedings of the [First] Summer Conference on Argumentation* (pp. 304–337). Annandale, VA: Speech Communication Association.

Goodnight, G. Th. (1982). The personal, technical, and public spheres of argument: A speculative inquiry into the art of public deliberation. *Journal of the American Forensic Association, 18,* 214–227.

Goodnight, G. Th. (1987a). Argumentation, criticism and rhetoric: A comparison of modern and post-modern stances in humanistic inquiry. In J. W. Wenzel (Ed.), *Argument and critical practices. Proceedings of the Fifth SCA/AFA Conference on Argumentation* (pp. 61–67). Annandale, VA: Speech Communication Association.

Goodnight, G. Th. (1987b). Generational argument. In F. H. van Eemeren, R. Grootendorst, J. A. Blair, & Ch. A. Willard (Eds.), *Argumentation: Across the lines of discipline. Proceedings of the Conference on Argumentation 1986* (pp. 129–144). Dordrecht/Providence: Foris Publications, PDA 3.

Goodnight, G. Th. (1991). Controversy. In D. W. Parson (Ed.), *Argument in controversy. Proceedings of the Seventh SCA/AFA Conference on Argumentation* (pp. 1–13). Annandale, VA: Speech Communication Association.

Goodnight, G. Th. (1993). Legitimation inferences: An additional component for the Toulmin model. *Informal Logic, 15,* 41–52.

Goodwin, D. (1991). Distinction, argumentation, and the rhetorical construction of the real. *Argumentation and Advocacy, 27,* 141–158.

Goodwin, D. (1992). The dialectic of second-order distinctions: The structure of arguments about fallacies. *Informal Logic, 14,* 11–22.

Göttert, K. H. (1978). *Argumentation. Grundzüge ihrer Theorie im Bereich theoretischen Wissens und praktischen Handelns* [Argumentation. Theoretical and practical characteristics of argumentation theory]. Tübingen: Niemeyer.

Gottlieb, G. (1968). *The logic of choice: An investigation of the concepts of rule and rationality*. New York: Macmillan.

Govier, T. (1980a). Review of Wellman's *Challenge and response*. *Informal Logic Newsletter, 2*, 10–15.

Govier, T. (1980b). More on inductive and deductive arguments. *Informal Logic Newsletter, 2*, 7–8.

Govier, T. (1982). Who says there are no fallacies? *Informal Logic Newsletter, 5*, 2–10.

Govier, T. (1983). Critical review of McPeck's Critical thinking and education. *Dialogue, 22*, 170–175.

Govier, T. (1985). *A practical study of argument*. Belmont, CA: Wadsworth.

Govier, T. (1987). *Problems in argument analysis and evaluation*. Dordrecht: Foris Publications, PDA 5.

Gracio, R. A. L. M. (1993). Perelman's rhetorical foundation of philosophy. *Argumentation, 7*, 439–450.

Grewendorf, G. (1975). *Argumentation und Interpretation. Wissenschaftstheoretische Untersuchungen am Beispiel germanistischer Lyrikinterpretationen* [Argumentation and interpretation. A study of interpretations of German poetry]. Kronberg: Scriptor.

Grewendorf, G. (1980). Argumentation in der Sprachwissenschaft [Argumentation in linguistics]. *Zeitschrift für Literaturwissenschaft und Linguistik, 38/39*, 129–151.

Grice, H. P. (1975). Logic and conversation. In P. Cole & J. Morgan (Eds.), *Syntax and semantics. Volume 3: Speech acts* (pp. 41–58). New York: Academic Press.

Grice, H. P. (1977). *Some aspects of reason* (Immanuel Kant Lectures, unpublished manuscript). Stanford University.

Grice, H. P. (1989). *Studies in the way of words*. Cambridge, MA: Harvard University Press.

Grinsted, A. (1991). Argumentative styles in Spanish and Danish negotiation interaction. In F. H. van Eemeren, R. Grootendorst, J. A. Blair, & Ch. A. Willard (Eds.), *Proceedings of the Second International Conference on Argumentation* (Organized by the International Society for the Study of Argumentation at the University of Amsterdam, June 19–22, 1990) (pp. 725–733). Amsterdam: Sic Sat, 1A/B.

Grize, J.-B. (1982). *De la logique à l'argumentation* [From logic to argumentation]. Genève: Librairie Droz.

Grize, J.-B. (1986). Raisonner en parlant [Reasoning while speaking]. In M. Meyer (Ed.), *De la metaphysique à la rhétorique* (pp. 45–55). Bruxelles: Editions de l'Université de Bruxelles.

Groarke, L. (1992). In defense of deductivism: Replying to Govier. In F. H. van Eemeren, R. Grootendorst, J. A. Blair, & Ch. A. Willard (Eds.), *Argumentation illuminated* (pp. 113–121). Amsterdam: Sic Sat, 1.

Gronbeck, B. E. (Ed.). (1989). *Spheres of argument. Proceedings of the Sixth SCA/AFA Conference on Argumentation*. Annandale, VA: SCA.

Gross, A. G. (1990). *The rhetoric of science*. Cambridge, MA: Harvard University Press.

Grootendorst, R. (1978). Rationele argumentatie en drogredenen. Een formeel-dialectische analyse van het *argumentum ad hominem* [Rational argumentation and fallacies. A formal-dialectic analysis of the *argumentum ad hominem*]. In *Taalbeheersing 1978. Verslagen van een symposium gehouden op 13 april 1978 aan de Katholieke Hogeschool te Tilburg* (pp. 69–83). Enschede: VIOT and TH Twente.

Grootendorst, R. (1987). Some fallacies about fallacies. In F. H. van Eemeren, R. Grootendorst, J. A. Blair, & Ch. A. Willard (Eds.), *Argumentation: Across the lines of discipline. Proceedings of the Conference on Argumentation 1986* (pp. 331–342). Dordrecht/Providence: Foris Publications, PDA 3.

Groupe μ. (1970). *Rhétorique générale*. Paris: Larousse.

Gutenberg, N. (1987). Argumentation and dialectical Logic. In F. H. van Eemeren, R. Grootendorst, J. A. Blair, & Ch. A. Willard (Eds.), *Argumentation: Perspectives and approaches. Proceedings of the Conference on Argumentation 1986* (pp. 397–403). Dordrecht/Providence: Foris Publications, PDA 3A.

Gutenplan, S. D., & Tamny, M. (1971). *Logic.* New York: Basic Books.

Guthrie, W. K. C. (1971). *The Sophists.* London: Cambridge University Press.

Haan, G. J. de, Koefoed, G. A. T., & Tombe, A. L. des. (1974). *Basiskursus algemene taalwetenschap* [Basic course in general linguistics]. Assen: Van Gorcum.

Haarscher, G. (Ed.). (1993). *Chaïm Perelman et la pensée contemporaine.* Bruxelles: Bruylant.

Haarscher, G., & Ingber, L. (Eds.). (1986). *Justice et argumentation. Autour de la pensée de Chaïm Perelman* [Justice and argumentation. On the philosophy of Chaim Perelman]. Bruxelles: Editions de l'Université de Bruxelles.

Habermas, J. (1971). Vorbereitende Bemerkungen zu einer Theorie der Kommunikativen Kompetenz [Preliminary remarks on a theory of communicative competence]. In J. Habermas & H. Luhmann, *Theorie der Gesellschaft oder Sozialtechnologie. Was leistet die Systemforschung?* (pp. 107–141). Frankfurt: Suhrkamp.

Habermas, J. (1973). Wahrheitstheorien [Theories of truth]. In H. Fahrenbach (Ed.), *Wirklichkeit und Reflexion. Festschrift für Walter Schulz zum 60. Geburtstag* (pp. 211–265). Pfullingen: Günther Neske.

Habermas, J. (1981). *Theorie des Kommunikativen Handelns* [A theory of communicative action] (Vols. I and II). Frankfurt am Main: Suhrkamp.

Habermas, J. (1991). *Moral consciousness and communicative action.* (Translation of *Moralbewusstsein un kommunikatives Handeln*, 1983, Frankfurt am Main: Suhrkamp). Cambridge, MA: MIT Press.

Hamblin, Ch. L. (1970). *Fallacies.* London: Methuen.

Hamblin, Ch. L. (1971). Mathematical models of dialogue. *Theoria, 37,* 130–155.

Hamilton, E., & Cairns, H. (Eds.). (1994). *The collected dialogues of Plato, including the Letters.* (Bollingen Series LXXI. *Euthydemus* translated by W. H. D. Rouse) (15th pr., 1st pr. 1961). Princeton, NJ: Princeton University Press.

Hample, D. (1977a). Testing a model of value argument and evidence. *Communication Monographs, 44,* 106–120.

Hample, D. (1977b). The Toulmin model and the syllogism. *Journal of the American Forensic Association, 14,* 1–9.

Hample, D. (1978). Predicting immediate belief change and adherence to argument claims. *Communication Monographs, 45,* 219–228.

Hample, D. (1979a). Motives in law: An adaptation of legal realism. *Journal of the American Forensic Association, 15,* 156–168.

Hample, D. (1979b). Predicting belief and belief change using a cognitive theory of argument and evidence. *Communication Monographs, 46,* 142–146.

Hample, D. (1980). A cognitive view of argument. *Journal of the American Forensic Association, 16,* 151–158.

Hample, D. (1981). The cognitive context of argument. *Western Journal of Speech Communication, 45,* 148–158.

Hample, D. (1992). What is a good argument? In W. L. Benoit, D. Hample, & P. J. Benoit (Eds.), *Readings in argumentation* (pp. 313–336). Berlin/New York: Foris Publications, PDA 11.

Hansen, H. V. (1990). An informal logic bibliography. *Informal Logic, 12,* 155–184.

Hardin, C. L. (1959). The uses of argument. *Philosophy of Science, 26,* 160–163.

Hardin, C. L. (1960). Methods and criteria of reasoning. *Philosophy of science, 27,* 319–320.

Harman, G. (1986). *Change in view. Principles of reasoning.* Cambridge, MA: MIT Press.

Hastings, A. C. (1962). *A reformulation of the modes of reasoning in argumentation.* Unpublished doctoral dissertation, Northwestern University, Evanston, IL.

Healy, P. (1987). Critical reasoning and dialectical argument. *Informal Logic, 9,* 1–12.

Heeney, T. (1995). Henry Johnstone's *anagnorisis: Argumentum ad hominem* as tragic trope to truth. In F. H. van Eemeren, R. Grootendorst, J. A. Blair, & Ch. A. Willard (Eds.), *Analysis and evaluation. Proceedings of the Third International Conference on Argumentation. Vol. II* (pp. 382–394). Amsterdam: Sic Sat, 5B.

Heidrich, C. H. (1982). Montague-grammars for argumentative dialogues. In E. M. Barth & J. L. Martens (Eds.), *Argumentation. Approaches to theory formation* (pp. 191–227). Amsterdam: John Benjamins.

Hendricks, V. F., Elvang-Gøransson, M., & Pedersen, S. A. (1995). Systems of argumentation. In F. H. van Eemeren, R. Grootendorst, J. A. Blair, & Ch. A. Willard (Eds.), *Reconstruction and application. Proceedings of the Third International Conference on Argumentation. Vol. III* (pp. 351–367). Amsterdam: Sic Sat, 5C.

Herbig, A. F. (1992). *'Sie argumentieren doch scheinheilig!' Sprach- und sprechwissenschaftliche Aspekte einer Stilistik des Argumentierens* ["You are arguing hypocritically!" Linguistic aspects of a stylistics of argumentation]. Bern: Peter Lang.

Heritage, J. (1984). A change-of-state token and aspects of its sequential placement. In J. M. Atkinson & J. Heritage (Eds.), *Structures of social action. Studies in conversation analysis* (pp. 299–346). Cambridge, England: Cambridge University Press.

Hintikka, J. (1968). Language-games for quantifiers. In N. Rescher (Ed.), *Studies in logical theory* (American Philosophical Quarterly Monograph Series 2, pp. 46–76). Oxford: Blackwell.

Hintikka, J. (1976). *The semantics of questions and questions of semantics: Case studies in the interrelations of logic, semantics, and syntax.* Amsterdam: North-Holland.

Hintikka, J. (1981) The logic of information-seeking dialogues: A model. In W. Becker & W. K. Essler (Eds.), *Konzepte der Dialektik* (pp. 212–231). Frankfurt am Main: Vittorio Klostermann.

Hintikka, J. (1987). The fallacy of fallacies. *Argumentation, 1,* 211–238.

Hintikka, J. (1989). The role of logic in argumentation. *The Monist, 72,* 3–24.

Hintikka, J., & Bachman, J. (1991). *What if . . . ? Toward excellence in reasoning.* Mountain View, CA: Mayfield.

Hintikka, J., & Hintikka, M. B. (1982). Sherlock Holmes confronts modern logic: Toward a theory of information-seeking through questioning. In E. M. Barth & J. L. Martens (Eds.), *Argumentation: Approaches to theory formation. Containing the contributions to the Groningen Conference on the Theory of Argumentation, October 1978* (pp. 55–76). Amsterdam: John Benjamins.

Hintikka, J., & Kulas, J. (1983) *The game of language: Studies in game-theoretical semantics and its applications.* Dordrecht: Reidel.

Hintikka, J., & Saarinen, E. (1979). Information-seeking dialogues: some of their logical properties. *Studia Logica, 38,* 355–363.

Hirokawa, R. Y., & Scheerhorn, D. R. (1985). The functions of argumentation in group deliberation. In J. R. Cox, M. O. Sillars, & G. B. Walker (Eds.), *Argument and social practice. Proceedings of the Fourth Summer Conference on Argumentation* (pp. 737–746). Annandale, VA: Speech Communication Association.

Hirsch, R. (1987). Interactive argumentation: Ideal and real. In F. H. van Eemeren, R. Grootendorst, J. A. Blair, & Ch. A. Willard (Eds.), *Argumentation: Perspectives and approaches. Proceedings of the Conference on Argumentation 1986* (pp. 434–441). Dordrecht/Providence: Foris Publications, PDA 3B.

Hirsch, R. (1989). *Argumentation, information and interaction.* Gothenborg Monographs in Linguistics 7. Department of Linguistics, University of Göteborg.

Hirsch, R. (1991). Belief and interactive argumentation. In F. H. van Eemeren, R. Grootendorst, J. A. Blair, & Ch. A. Willard (Eds.), *Proceedings of the Second International Conference on Argumentation* (Organized by the International Society for the Study of Argumentation at the University of Amsterdam, June 19–22, 1990) (pp. 591–603). Amsterdam: Sic Sat, 1A/B.

Hitchcock, D. (1983). *Critical thinking: A guide to evaluating information.* Toronto: Methuen.

Holmquest, A. H. (1989). Rhetorical gravity. In B. E. Gronbeck (Ed.), *Spheres of argument. Proceedings of the Sixth SCA/AFA Conference on Argumentation* (pp. 37–41). Annandale, VA: Speech Communication Association.

Horn, N. (1967). Zur Bedeutung der Topiklehre Theodor Viehwegs für eine einheitliche Theorie des juristischen Denkens [On the importance of Theodor Viehweg's topical theory to a general theory of judicial thinking]. *Neue Juristische Wochenschrift, 20,* 601–608.

Horn, N. (1981). Topik in der rechtstheoretischen Diskussion [The theory of topics in discussions and legal theory]. In D. Breuer & H. Schanze (Eds.), *Topik: Beiträge zur interdisziplinären Diskussion* (pp. 57–64). München: Fink.

Houtlosser, P. (1994). The speech act "advancing a standpoint." In F. H. van Eemeren & R. Grootendorst (Eds.), *Studies in pragma-dialectics* (pp. 165–171). Amsterdam: Sic Sat, 4.

Hoven, P. J. van den. (1984). *Het formuleren van een formele kritiek op een betogende tekst* [Formulating a formal criticism of an argumentative text] (With a summary in English). Doctoral dissertation, Utrecht.

Hoven, P. J. van den. (1987). The external justification of a dialectical consensus. In F. H. van Eemeren, R. Grootendorst, J. A. Blair, & Ch. A. Willard (Eds.), *Argumentation: Perspectives and approaches. Proceedings of the Conference on Argumentation 1986* (pp. 364–371). Dordrecht: Foris Publications, PDA 3A.

Hovland, C. I. (Ed.). (1957). *The order of presentation in persuasion.* New Haven, CT: Yale University Press.

Hovland, C. I., & Janis, I. L. (Eds.). (1959). *Personality and persuasibility.* New Haven, CT: Yale University Press.

Hovland, C. I., Janis, I. L., & Kelley, H. H. (1953). *Communication and persuasion: Psychological studies of opinion change.* New Haven, CT: Yale University Press.

Hovland, C. I., & Rosenberg, M. J. (Eds.). (1960). *Attitude organization and change.* New Haven, CT: Yale University Press.

Hudson, W. D. (Ed.). (1969). *The is–ought question: A collection of papers on the central problem in moral philosophy.* London: Macmillan.

Hunter, A. (Ed.). (1990). *The rhetoric of social research.* New Brunswick, NJ: Rutgers University Press.

Huth, L. (1975). Argumentationstheorie und Textanalyse [Argumentation theory and text-analysis]. *Der Deutschunterricht, 27,* 80–111.

Hynes, T. J. (1989). Can you buy cold fusion by the six pack? Or Bubba and Billy-Bob discover Pons and Fleischmann. In B. E. Gronbeck (Ed.), *Spheres of argument. Proceedings of the Sixth SCA/AFA Conference on Argumentation* (pp. 42–46). Annandale, VA: Speech Communication Association.

Ilie, C. (1994). *What else can I tell you? A pragmatic study of English rhetorical questions as discursive and argumentative acts.* Stockholm: Almqvist & Wiksell International.

Infante, D. (1981). Trait argumentativeness as a predictor of communicative behavior in situations requiring argument. *Central States Speech Journal, 32,* 265–273.

Ivie, R. L. (1987). The ideology of freedom's 'fragility' in American foreign policy argument. *Journal of the American Forensic Association, 24,* 27–36.

Jackson, S. (1983). The arguer in interpersonal argument: Pros and cons of individual-level analysis. In D. Zarefsky, M. O. Sillars, & J. Rhodes (Eds.), *Argument in transition. Proceedings of the Third Summer Conference on Argumentation* (pp. 631–637). Annandale, VA: Speech Communication Association.

Jackson, S. (1992). 'Virtual standpoints' and the pragmatics of conversational argument. In F. H. van Eemeren, R. Grootendorst, J. A. Blair, & Ch. A. Willard (Eds.), *Argumentation illuminated* (pp. 260–269). Amsterdam: Sic Sat, 1.

Jackson, S., & Jacobs, S. (1980). Structure of conversational argument: Pragmatic bases for the enthymeme. *Quarterly Journal of Speech, 66,* 251–265.

Jackson, S., & Jacobs, S. (1982). The collaborative production of proposals in conversational argument and persuasion: A study of disagreement regulation. *Journal of the American Forensic Association, 18,* 77–90.

Jackson, S., Jacobs, S., & Rossi, A. M. (1987). Conversational relevance: Three experiments on pragmatic connectedness in conversation. In M. L. McLaughlin (Ed.), *Communication Yearbook 10* (pp. 323–347). Newbury Park, CA: Sage.

Jacobs, S. (1987). The management of disagreement in conversation. In F. H. van Eemeren, R. Grootendorst, J. A. Blair, & Ch. A. Willard (Eds.), *Argumentation: Across the lines of discipline. Proceedings of the Conference on Argumentation 1986* (pp. 229–239). Dordrecht/Providence: Foris Publications, PDA 3.

Jacobs, S. (1989). Speech acts and arguments. *Argumentation, 3*, 345–365.

Jacobs, S., & Jackson, S. (1981). Argument as a natural category: The routine grounds for arguing in natural conversation. *Western Journal of Speech Communication, 45*, 118–132.

Jacobs, S., & Jackson, S. (1982). Conversational argument: A discourse analytic approach. In J. R. Cox & Ch. A. Willard (Eds.), *Advances in argumentation theory and research* (pp. 205–237). Carbondale, IL: Southern Illinois University Press.

Jacobs, S., & Jackson, S. (1983). Strategy and structure in conversational influence attempts. *Communication Monographs, 50*, 285–304.

Jacobs, S., & Jackson, S. (1989). Building a model of conversational argument. In B. Dervin, L. Grossberg, B. J. O'Keefe, & E. Wartella (Eds.), *Rethinking communication* (pp. 153–171). Newbury Park, CA: Sage.

Jason, G. (1986). Are fallacies common? A look at two debates. *Informal Logic, 8*, 81–92.

Jason, G. (1989). Fallacies are common. *Informal Logic, 11*, 101–106.

Jayez, J. (1989). Problems of context and knowledge. *Argumentation, 3*, 303–319.

Jens, W. (1983). *Von deutscher Rede* [On German speech]. München: Piper.

Johnson, R. H. (1981). Toulmin's bold experiment. *Informal Logic Newsletter, 3*, No. 2, 16–27 (Part I), No. 3, 13–19 (Part II).

Johnson, R. H. (1987). The blaze of her splendors: Suggestions about revitalizing fallacy theory. *Argumentation, 1*, 239–253.

Johnson, R. H. (1989). Massey on fallacy and informal logic: A reply. *Synthese, 80*, 407–426.

Johnson, R. H. (1990a). Hamblin on the standard treatment. *Philosophy and Rhetoric, 23*, 153–167.

Johnson, R. H. (1990b). Acceptance is not enough: A critique of Hamblin. *Philosophy and Rhetoric, 23*, 271–287.

Johnson, R. H. (1992). The problem of defining critical thinking. In S. P. Norris (Ed.), *The generalizability of critical thinking* (pp. 38–53). New York: Teachers' College Press.

Johnson, R. H., & Blair, J. A. (1977). *Logical self-defense*. Toronto: McGraw-Hill Ryerson.

Johnson, R. H., & Blair, J. A. (1980). The recent development of informal logic. In J. A. Blair & R. H. Johnson (Eds.), *Informal logic. The First International Symposium* (pp. 3–28). Point Reyes, CA: Edgepress.

Johnson, R. H., & Blair, J. A. (1993). *Logical self-defense* (3rd ed.). Toronto: McGraw-Hill.

Johnson, R. H., & Blair, J. A. (1994). *Logical self-defense* (U.S. edition). New York: McGraw-Hill.

Johnstone, H. W., Jr. (1957–1958). Methods and criteria of reasoning. *Philosophy and phenomenological review, 18*, 553–554.

Johnstone, H. W., Jr. (1958–1959). New outlooks on controversy. *Review of metaphysics, 12*, 57–67.

Johnstone, H. W., Jr. (1959). *Philosophy and argument*. University Park: Pennsylvania State University Press.

Johnstone, H. W., Jr. (1968). Theory of argumentation. In R. Klibansky (Ed.), *La philosophie contemporaine* (pp. 177–184). Firenze: La Nuova Italia Editrice.

Johnstone, H. W., Jr. (1970). *The problem of the self*. University Park: Pennsylvania State University Press.

Johnstone, H. W., Jr. (1983). Truth, anagnorisis, argument. *Philosophy & Rhetoric, 16*, 1–15.

Johnstone, H. W., Jr. (1993). Editor's introduction. *Argumentation, 7*, 379–384.

Journal of the American Forensic Association, 18 (1982), 133–160. Special forum on debate paradigms.

Jungslager, F. S. (1994). Identifying argumentation. In F. H. van Eemeren & R. Grootendorst (Eds.), *Studies in pragma-dialectics* (pp. 112–118). Amsterdam: Sic Sat, 4.

Kahane, H. (1969). *Logic and philosophy*. Belmont, CA: Wadsworth.

Kahane, H. (1971). *Logic and contemporary rhetoric. The use of reasoning in everyday life*. Belmont, CA: Wadsworth.

Kahane, H. (1973). *Logic and philosophy* (2nd ed.). Belmont, CA: Wadsworth.

Kahane, H. (1976). *Logic and contemporary rhetoric. The use of reason in everyday life* (2nd ed.). Belmont, CA: Wadsworth.

Kahneman, D., Slovic, P., & Tversky, A. (Eds.). (1982). *Judgment under uncertainty: Heuristics and biases*. Cambridge, England: Cambridge University Press.

Kalivoda, G. (1986). *Parlamentarische Rhetorik und Argumentation* [The rhetoric and argumentation of parliament]. Untersuchungen zum Sprachgebrauch des 1. Vereinigten Landtags in Berlin 1847. Frankfurt am Main: Peter Lang.

Kamlah, W., & Lorenzen, P. (1967). *Logische Propädeutik; Vorschule des vernünftigen Redens* [Logical propaedeutic: Pre-school of reasonable discourse]. Mannheim: Hochschultaschenbücher-Verlag.

Kamlah, W., & Lorenzen, P. (1973). *Logische Propädeutik; Vorschule des vernünftigen Redens* [Logical propaedeutic: Pre-school of reasonable discourse] (2nd ed.). Mannheim: Hochschultaschenbücher-Verlag.

Kamlah, W., & Lorenzen, P. (1984). *Logical propaedeutic: Pre-school of reasonable discourse* (Translation of *Logische Propädeutik; Vorschule des vernünftigen Redens*. Mannheim: Hochschultaschenbücher-Verlag, 1967). Lanham, MD: University Press of America.

Kaplow, L. (1981). Rethinking counterplans: A reconciliation with debate theory. *Journal of the American Forensic Association, 17*, 215–226.

Karon, L. A. (1989). Presence in the new rhetoric. In R. D. Dearin (Ed.), *The new rhetoric of Chaim Perelman. Statement & response* (pp. 163–178). Lanham, MD: University Press of America.

Kasher, A. (1982). Gricean inference revisited. *Philosophica, 29*, 25–44.

Keith, W. (Ed.). (1993). Rhetoric in the rhetoric of science. Special Issue of the *Southern Communication Journal, 58*, No. 4.

Kellner, H. (1989). *Language and historical representation*. Madison: University of Wisconsin Press.

Kennedy, G. A. (1994). *A new history of classical rhetoric*. Princeton, NJ: Princeton University Press.

Kienpointner, M. (1983). *Argumentationsanalyse*. Innsbruck: Verlag des Instituts für Sprachwissenschaft der Universität Innsbruck. Innsbrucker Beiträge zur Kulturwissenschaft, Sonderheft 56.

Kienpointner, M. (1987). Towards a typology of argumentative schemes. In F. H. van Eemeren, R. Grootendorst, J. A. Blair, & Ch. A. Willard (Eds.), *Argumentation: Across the lines of discipline. Proceedings of the Conference on Argumentation 1986* (pp. 275–287). Dordrecht/Providence: Foris Publications, PDA 3.

Kienpointner, M. (1992a). *Alltagslogik. Struktur und Funktion vom Argumentationsmustern*. Stuttgart/Bad Cannstatt: Frommann-Holzboog.

Kienpointner, M. (1992b). How to classify arguments. In F. H. van Eemeren, R. Grootendorst, J. A. Blair, & Ch. A. Willard (Eds.), *Argumentation illuminated* (pp. 178–188). Amsterdam: Sic Sat, 1.

Kienpointner, M. (1993). The empirical relevance of Perelman's new rhetoric. *Argumentation, 7*, 419–437.

Kindt, W. (1988). Zur Logik von Alltagsargumentationen [On the logic of everyday argumentation]. *Fachbericht 3*. Erziehungswissenschaftliche Hochschule Koblenz.

Kindt, W. (1992a). Organisationsformen des Argumentierens in natürlicher Sprache [The organization of argumentation in everyday speech]. In H. Paschen & L. Wigger (Eds.), *Pädagogisches Argumentieren* (pp. 95–120). Weinheim: Deutscher Studienverlag.

Kindt, W. (1992b). Argumentation und Konfliktaustragung in Äusserungen über den Golfkrieg [Argumentation and conflict resolution in statements on the Gulf War]. *Zeitschrift für Sprachwissenschaft, 11,* 189–215.

King-Farlow, J. (1973). Toulmin's analysis of probability. *Theoria, 29,* 12–26.

Kinneavy, J. L. (1971). *A theory of discourse.* Englewood Cliffs, NJ: Prentice-Hall.

Klein, J. (1987). *Die konklusiven Sprechhandlungen. Studien zur Pragmatik, Semantik, Syntax und Lexik von Begründen, Erklären-warum, Folgern und Rechtfertigen* [Conclusive speech acts. Studies of the pragmatic, semantic, syntactic and lexical aspects of supporting, explaining why, concluding, and justifying]. Tübingen: Niemeyer.

Klein, W. (1980). Argumentation und Argument [Argumentation and argument]. *Zeitschrift für Literaturwissenschaft und Linguistik, 38/39,* 9–57.

Kline, S. L., & Woloschuk, J. A. (1983). Moral reasoning development: An introductory review of correlates and antecedents. In D. Zarefsky, M. O. Sillars, & J. Rhodes (Eds.), *Argument in transition. Proceedings of the Third Summer Conference on Argumentation* (pp. 611–630). Annandale, VA: Speech Communication Association.

Kloosterhuis, H. (1994). Analysing analogy argumentation in judicial decisions. In F. H. van Eemeren & R. Grootendorst (Eds.), *Studies in pragma-dialectics* (pp. 238–245). Amsterdam: Sic Sat, 4.

Kluback, W. (1980). The new rhetoric as a philosophical system. *Journal of the American Forensic Association, 17,* 73–79.

Kneale, W. (1949). *Probability and induction.* Oxford: Clarendon Press.

Kneale, W., & Kneale, M. (1962). *The development of logic.* Oxford: Clarendon Press.

Kneupper, C. W. (1978). On argument and diagrams. *Journal of the American Forensic Association, 14,* 181–186.

Kneupper, C. W. (1979). Paradigms and problems: Alternative constructivist/interactionist implications for argumentation theory. *Journal of the American Forensic Association, 15,* 220–227.

Koch, H. J. (1980). Das Frankfurter Projekt zur juristischen Argumentation: Zur Rehabilitation des deduktiven Begründens juristischer Entscheidungen [The Frankfurt project on legal argumentation: Towards a rehabilitation of deductive argument for judicial decisions]. In W. Hassemer, A. Kaufmann, & U. Neumann (Eds.), *Argumentation und Recht. Archiv für Rechts- und Sozialphilosophie* (pp. 59–86). Wiesbaden: F. Steiner.

Koetsenruijter, W. (1994). A strategy for the dialectical reconstruction of the confrontation stage. In F. H. van Eemeren & R. Grootendorst (Eds.), *Studies in pragma-dialectics* (pp. 172–179). Amsterdam: Sic Sat, 4.

Komlósi, L. I. (1991). The power and fallability of a paradigm in argumentation: A case study of subversive political discourse. In F. H. van Eemeren, R. Grootendorst, J. A. Blair, & Ch. A. Willard (Eds.), *Proceedings of the Second International Conference on Argumentation* (Organized by the International Society for the Study of Argumentation at the University of Amsterdam, June 19–22, 1990) (pp. 994–1005). Amsterdam: Sic Sat, 1A/B.

Komlósi, L. I., & Knipf, E. (1987). Negotiating consensus in discourse interaction schemata. In F. H. van Eemeren, R. Grootendorst, J. A. Blair, & Ch. A. Willard (Eds.), *Argumentation: Perspectives and approaches. Proceedings of the Conference on Argumentation 1986* (pp. 82–89). Dordrecht/Providence: Foris Publications, PDA 3A.

Kopperschmidt, J. (1975). Pro und Contra im Fernsehen [Pro and contra on television]. *Der Deutschunterricht, 27,* 42–62.

Kopperschmidt, J. (1976a). *Allgemeine Rhetorik. Einführung in die Theorie der persuasiven Kommunikation* [General rhetoric. Introduction to the theory of persuasive communication]. Stuttgart: Kohlhammer.

Kopperschmidt, J. (1976b). Methode statt Appell. Versuch einer Argumentationsanalyse [Method instead of appeal. An attempt at argument analysis]. *Der Deutschunterricht, 28,* 37–58.

Kopperschmidt, J. (1977). Von der Kritik der Rhetorik zur kritischen Rhetorik [From criticism of rhetoric to a critical rhetoric]. In H. F. Plett (Ed.), *Rhetorik. Kritische Positionen zum Stand der Forschung* (pp. 213–229). München: Fink.

Kopperschmidt, J. (1978). *Das Prinzip vernünftiger Rede* [Principles of rational speech]. Stuttgart: Kohlhammer.

Kopperschmidt, J. (1980). *Argumentation* [Argumentation]. Stuttgart: Kohlhammer.

Kopperschmidt, J. (1987). The function of argumentation: A pragmatic approach. In F. H. van Eemeren, R. Grootendorst, J. A. Blair, & Ch. A. Willard (Eds.), *Argumentation: Across the lines of discipline. Proceedings of the Conference on Argumentation 1986* (pp. 179–188). Dordrecht/Providence: Foris Publications, PDA 3.

Kopperschmidt, J. (1989a). *Methodik der Argumentationsanalyse* [Methodology of argumentation analysis]. Stuttgart: Frommann-Holzboog.

Kopperschmidt, J. (1989b). Öffentliche Rede in Deutschland [Public speaking in Germany]. *Muttersprache, 99*, 213–30.

Kopperschmidt, J. (1990a). Gibt es Kriterien politischer Rhetorik? Versuch einer Antwort [Do criteria for political rhetoric exist? A tentative answer]. *Diskussion Deutsch, 115*, 479–501.

Kopperschmidt, J. (Ed.). (1990b). *Rhetorik Bd. 1: Rhetorik als Texttheorie* [Rhetoric Vol. 1: Rhetoric as a theory of text]. Darmstadt: Wiss. Buchgesellschaft.

Kopperschmidt, J. (Ed.). (1991). *Rhetorik Bd. 2: Wirkungsgeschichte der Rhetorik* [Rhetoric Vol. 2: A history of rhetoric]. Darmstadt: Wiss. Buchgesellschaft.

Kopperschmidt, J. (1995). Grundfragen einer allgemeinen Argumentationstheorie unter besonderer Berücksichtigung formaler Argumentationsmuster [Fundamental questions for a general theory of argumentation arising from an analysis of formal patterns of argumentation]. In H. Wohlrapp (Ed.), *Wege der Argumentationsforschung* (pp. 50–73). Stuttgart/Bad Cannstatt: Frommann-Holzboog.

Koren, R. (1993). Perelman et l'objectivité discursive. Le cas de l'écriture de presse en France [Perelman and discursive objectivity. The case of the French press]. In G. Haarscher (Ed.), *Chaim Perelman et la pensée contemporaine* (pp. 469–487). Bruxelles: Bruylant.

Körner, S. (1959). The uses of argument. *Mind, 68*, 425–427.

Krabbe, E. C. W. (1978). The adequacy of material dialogue-games. *Notre Dame Journal of Formal Logic, 19*, 321–330. (reprinted in Krabbe 1982a, 160–169).

Krabbe, E. C. W. (1982a). *Studies in dialogical logic*. Doctoral dissertation. Groningen: Groningen University.

Krabbe, E. C. W. (1982b). Essentials of the dialogical treatment of quantifiers. In E. C. W. Krabbe (Ed.), *Studies in dialogical logic* (pp. 249–257). Groningen: Groningen University.

Krabbe, E. C. W. (1985a). Noncumulative dialectical models and formal dialectics. *Journal of Philosophical Logic, 14*, 129–168.

Krabbe, E. C. W. (1985b). Formal systems of dialogue rules. *Synthese, 63*, 295–328.

Krabbe, E. C. W. (1986). A theory of modal dialectics. *Journal of Philosophical Logic, 15*, 191–217.

Krabbe, E. C. W. (1988). Creative reasoning in formal discussion. *Argumentation, 2*, 483–498.

Krabbe, E. C. W. (1992). Review of J. Woods, & D. Walton, Fallacies: Selected papers, 1972–1982. *Argumentation, 6*, 475–479.

Kripke, S. A. (1965). Semantical analysis of intuitionistic logic I. In J. N. Crossley & M. A. E. Dummett (Eds.), *Formal systems and recursive functions* (pp. 92–130). Amsterdam: North-Holland.

Kruger, A. N. (1975). *Argumentation and debate: a classified bibliography* (2nd ed., 1st ed. 1964 as *A classified bibliography of argumentation and debate*). Metuchen, NJ: Scarecrow Press.

Kunst-Gnamus, O. (1987). Argumentation and persuasion. In F. H. van Eemeren, R. Grootendorst, J. A. Blair, & Ch. A. Willard (Eds.), *Argumentation: Perspectives and Approaches. Proceedings of the conference on argumentation 1986* (pp. 103–109). Dordrecht/Providence: Foris Publications, PDA 3A.

Kunst-Gnamus, O. (1991). An attempt at conceptualizing the difference between pragmatic and rational argumentation. In F. H. van Eemeren, R. Grootendorst, J. A. Blair, & Ch. A. Willard (Eds.), *Proceedings of the Second International Conference on Argumentation* (Organized by the International Society for the Study of Argumentation at the University of Amsterdam, June 19–22, 1990) (pp. 653–662). Amsterdam: Sic Sat, 1A/B.

Lambert, K., & Ulrich, W. (1980). *The nature of argument.* New York/London: Macmillan/Collier-Macmillan.

Laughlin, S. K., & Hughes, D. T. (1986). The rational and the reasonable: Dialectical or parallel systems? In J. L. Golden & J. J. Pilotta (Eds.), *Practical reasoning in human affairs. Studies in honor of Chaim Perelman* (pp. 187–205). Dordrecht: Reidel.

Lausberg, H. (1969). *Elementi di retorica* [Elements of rhetoric]. Bologna: Il Mulino.

Lauth, R. (1979). *Theorie des philosophischen Arguments. Der Ausgangspunkt und seine Bedingungen* [A theory of philosophical argumentation. Starting point and conditions]. Berlin/New York: Walter de Gruyter.

Lazerowitz, M. (1958–1959). Methods and criteria of reasoning. *British Journal for the Philosophy of Science, 9,* 68–70.

Lear, J. (1980). *Aristotle and logical theory.* Cambridge, England: Cambridge University Press.

Leeman, A. D., & Braet, A. C. (1987). *Klassieke retorica: Haar inhoud, functie en betekenis* [Classical rhetoric: Form, function, and meaning]. Groningen: Wolters-Noordhoff.

Levinson, S. C. (1983). *Pragmatics.* Cambridge, England: Cambridge University Press.

Lewinski, J. D., Metzler, B. R., & Settle, P. L. (1973). The goal case affirmative: An alternative approach to academic debate. *Journal of the American Forensic Association, 9,* 458–463.

Lichtman, A., Garvin, C., & Corsi, J. (1973). The alternative-justification affirmative: A new case form. *Journal of the American Forensic Association, 10,* 59–69.

Lichtman, A. J., & Rohrer, D. M. (1980). The logic of policy dispute. *Journal of the American Forensic Association, 16,* 236–247.

Lipman, M. (1988). Critical thinking—what can it be? *Educational Leadership,* September, 38–43.

Little, J. F., Groarke, L. A., & Tindale, C. W. (1989). *Good reasoning matters.* Toronto: McLelland & Stewart.

Lo Cascio, V. (1991). *Grammatica dell'argomentare: strategie e strutture* [A grammar of arguing: Strategies and structures]. Firenze: La Nuova Italia.

Locke, J. (1690/1961). Of reason. In J. W. Yolton (Ed.), *An essay concerning human understanding, Book IV, Chapter XVII, 1690.* London: Dent.

Lorenzen, P. (1969). *Normative logic and ethics.* Hochschultaschenbücher 236. Mannheim: Bibliographisches Institut.

Lorenzen, P. (1987). *Lehrbuch der konstruktiven Wissenschaftstheorie* [Textbook of constructive theory of science]. Mannheim/Vienna/Zürich: Bibliografisches Institut Wissenschaftsverlag.

Lorenzen, P., & Lorenz, K. (1978). *Dialogische Logik* [Dialogical logic]. Darmstadt: Wissenschaftliche Buchgesellschaft.

Lorenzen, P., & Schwemmer, O. (1975). *Konstruktive Logik, Ethik und Wissenschaftstheorie* [Constructive logic, ethics and the theory of science] (2nd ed.). Mannheim: B.I.-Wissenschaftsverlag. Hochschultaschenbücher Band 700.

Lueken, G.-L. (1991). Incommensurability, rules of argumentation, and anticipation. In F. H. Van Eemeren, R. Grootendorst, J. A. Blair, & Ch. A. Willard (Eds.), *Proceedings of the Second International Conference on Argumentation* (Organized by the International Society for the Study of Argumentation at the University of Amsterdam, June 19–22, 1990) (pp. 244–252). Amsterdam: Sic Sat, 1A/B.

Lueken, G.-L. (1992). *Inkommensurabilität als Problem rationalen Argumentierens* [Incommensurability as a problem of rational argumentation]. Stuttgart/Bad Cannstatt: Frommann-Holzboog.

Lueken, G.-L. (1995). Konsens, Widerstreit und Entscheidung. Überlegungen anlässlich Lyotards Herausforderung der Argumentationstheorie [Consensus, dissent, and decision. Thoughts on Lyotard's challenge to argumentation theory]. In H. Wohlrapp (Ed.), *Wege der Argumentationsforschung* (pp. 358–385). Stuttgart/Bad Cannstatt: Frommann-Holzboog.

Lumer, Chr. (1988). The disputation: A special type of cooperative argumentative dialogue. *Argumentation, 2*, 447–464.

Lumer, Chr. (1990). *Praktische Argumentationstheorie. Theoretische Grundlagen, praktische Begründung und Regeln wichtiger Argumentationsarten* [A practical theory of argumentation. Theoretical foundations, and practical justifications, and rules for major types of argument]. Braunschweig: Vieweg.

Lundquist, L. (1980). *La cohérence textuelle: Syntaxe, sémantique, pragmatique* [Textual coherence: Syntax, semantics, and pragmatics]. Kopenhagen: Arnold Busck, Nyt Nordisk Forlag.

Lundquist, L. (1983). *L'analyse textuelle: Méthode, exercises* [Textual analysis: Methods, exercises]. Paris: CEDIC.

Lundquist, L. (1987). Towards a procedural analysis of argumentative operators in texts. In F. H. van Eemeren, R. Grootendorst, J. A. Blair, & Ch. A. Willard (Eds.), *Argumentation: Perspectives and approaches. Proceedings of the Conference on Argumentation 1986* (pp. 61–69). Dordrecht/Providence: Foris Publications, PDA 3A.

Lundquist, L. (1991). How and when are written texts argumentative? In F. H. van Eemeren, R. Grootendorst, J. A. Blair, & Ch. A. Willard (Eds.), *Proceedings of the Second International Conference on Argumentation* (Organized by the International Society for the Study of Argumentation at the University of Amsterdam, June 19–22, 1990) (pp. 639–646). Amsterdam: Sic Sat, 1A/B.

Luscher, J. (1989). Connecteurs et marques de pertinence: l'example de *d'ailleurs* [Connectives and markers of relevance: The case of *anyway*]. *Cahiers de Linguistique Française, 10*, 101–145.

Lyne, J. (1983). Ways of going public: The projection of expertise in the sociobiology controversy. In D. Zarefsky, M. O. Sillars, & J. Rhodes (Eds.), *Argument in transition. Proceedings of the Third Summer Conference on Argumentation* (pp. 400–415). Annandale, VA: Speech Communication Association.

Mackenzie, J. D. (1979a). Question-begging in non-cumulative systems. *Journal of Philosophical Logic, 8*, 117–133.

Mackenzie, J. D. (1979b). How to stop talking to tortoises. *Notre Dame Journal of Formal Logic, 20*, 705–717.

Mackenzie, J. D. (1981). The dialectics of logic. *Logique et analyse, 24*, 159–177.

Mackenzie, J. D. (1985). No logic before Friday. *Synthese, 63*, 329–341.

Mackenzie, J. D. (1989). Reasoning and logic. *Synthese, 79*, 99–117.

Mackenzie, J. D. (1990). Four dialogue systems. *Studia Logica, 49*, 567–583.

Maier, R. (1989). Natural logic and norms in argumentation. In R. Maier (Ed.), *Norms in argumentation. Proceedings of the Conference on Norms 1988* (pp. 49–65). Dordrecht: Foris, PDA 8.

Makau, J. M. (1984). The Supreme Court and reasonableness. *Quarterly Journal of Speech, 70*, 379–396.

Maneli, M. (1978). The new theory of argumentation and American jurisprudence. *Logique et Analyse, 21*, 19–50.

Maneli, M. (1994). *Perelman's new rhetoric as philosophy and methodology for the next century.* Dordrecht: Kluwer.

Manicas, P. T. (1966). On Toulmin's contribution to logic and argumentation. *Journal of the American Forensic Association, 3*, 83–94.

Markov, B. V. (1993). Philosophy and argumentation (in Russian, with a summary in English). *Journal of Speech Communication and Argumentation, 1*, 76–86.

Mason, D. (1961). The uses of argument. *Augustinianum, 1*, 206–209.

Massey, G. (1981). The fallacy behind fallacies. *Midwest Journal of Philosophy, 6,* 489–500.

Mates, B. (1953). *Stoic logic.* Berkeley: University of California Press.

Mates, B. (1967). Communication and argument. *Synthese, 17,* 344–355.

McCloskey, D. N. (1985). *The rhetoric of economics.* Madison: University of Wisconsin Press.

McKerrow, R. E. (1980). Argument communities: A quest for distinctions. In J. Rhodes & S. Newell (Eds.), *Proceedings of the [First] Summer Conference on Argumentation* (pp. 214–227). Annandale, VA: Speech Communication Association.

McKerrow, R. E. (1982). Rationality and reasonableness in a theory of argument. In J. R. Cox & Ch. A. Willard (Eds.), *Advances in argumentation theory and research* (pp. 105–122). Carbondale, IL: Southern Illinois University Press.

McKerrow, R. E. (1986). Pragmatic justification. In J. L. Golden & J. J. Pilotta (Eds.), *Practical reasoning in human affairs. Studies in honor of Chaim Perelman* (pp. 207–223). Dordrecht: Reidel.

McKerrow, R. E. (Ed.). (1993). *Argument and the postmodern challenge. Proceedings of the Eighth SCA/AFA Summer Conference on Argumentation.* Annandale, VA: Speech Communication Association.

McPeck, J. (1981). *Critical thinking and education.* Oxford: Martin Robertson.

McPeck, J. (1990). *Teaching critical thinking: Dialogue and dialectic.* New York: Routledge, Chapman & Hall.

Measell, J. S. (1985). Perelman on analogy. *Journal of the American Forensic Association, 22,* 65–71.

Mengel, P. (1991). The peculiar inferential force of analogical arguments. In F. H. van Eemeren, R. Grootendorst, J. A. Blair, & Ch. A. Willard (Eds.), *Proceedings of the Second International Conference on Argumentation* (Organized by the International Society for the Study of Argumentation at the University of Amsterdam, June 19–22, 1990) (pp. 422–428). Amsterdam: Sic Sat, 1A/B.

Mengel, P. (1995). *Analogien als Argumente* [Analogies as arguments]. Bern: Peter Lang.

Metzing, D. (1975). *Formen kommunikationswissenschaftlicher Argumentationsanalyse* [Types of communication-theoretical analyses of argumentation]. Hamburg: Buske.

Meyer, M. (1982a). *Logique, langage et argumentation* [Logic, language, and argumentation]. Paris: Hachette.

Meyer, M. (1982b). Argumentation in the light of a theory of questioning. *Philosophy & Rhetoric, 15,* 81–103.

Meyer, M. (1986a). *De la problématologie. Philosophie, science et langage* [On problematology. Philosophy, science, and language]. Brussels: Pierre Mardaga.

Meyer, M. (1986b). *From logic to rhetoric* (Translation of *Logique, langage et argumentation.* Paris: Hachette, 1982). Pragmatics and beyond VII: 3. Amsterdam: John Benjamins.

Meyer, M. (1988). The rhetorical foundation of philosophical argumentation. *Argumentation, 2,* 255–270.

Meyer, M. (Ed.). (1989). *From metaphysics to rhetoric* (Translation of *De la métaphysique à la rhétorique.* Bruxelles: Editions de l'Université de Bruxelles, 1986). Dordrecht: Kluwer.

Michalos, A. C. (1970). *Improving your reasoning.* Englewood Cliffs, NJ: Prentice-Hall.

Mickunas, A. (1986). Perelman on justice and political institutions. In J. L. Golden & J. J. Pilotta (Eds.), *Practical reasoning in human affairs. Studies in honor of Chaim Perelman* (pp. 321–339). Dordrecht: Reidel.

Mills, G. E. (1968). *Reason in controversy.* Boston: Allyn & Bacon.

Missimer, C. A. (1990). Perhaps by skill alone. *Informal Logic, 12,* 145–154.

Moeschler, J. (1982). *Dire et contredire* [Asserting and countering]. Bern: Peter Lang.

Moeschler, J. (1985). *Argumentation et conversation* [Argumentation and conversation]. Paris: Hatier.

Moeschler, J. (1989a). Pragmatic connectives, argumentative coherence and relevance. *Argumentation, 3,* 321–339.

Moeschler, J. (1989b). *Modélisation du dialogue. Représentation de l'inference argumentative* [Modelling dialogue. The representation of argumentative inference]. Paris: Hermès.

Moeschler, J. (1989c). Presentation. *Argumentation, 3,* 243–245.

Moeschler, J., & Spengler, N. de. (1982). La concession ou la réfutation interdite: Approche argumentative et conversationelle [Concessions or the prohibition of refutations: An argumentative and conversational approach]. In *Concession et consécution dans le discours.* Cahiers de Linguistique Française 4 (pp. 7–36). Genève: Université de Genève.

Montague, R. (1974). In R. H. Thomson (Ed.), *Formal philosophy.* New Haven, CT: Yale University Press.

Naess, A. (1947). *En del elementaere logiske emner* [Some elementary subjects in logic]. Oslo: Universitetsforlaget.

Naess, A. (1953). *Interpretation and preciseness. A contribution to the theory of communication.* Oslo: Skrifter utgitt ar der norske videnskaps academie.

Naess, A. (1966). *Communication and argument. Elements of applied semantics* (English translation of *En del elementaere logiske emner.* Oslo: Universitetsforlaget, 1947). London: Allen and Unwin.

Naess, A. (1978). *Elementaire argumentatieleer* (Dutch translation of *En del elementaere logiske emner.* Oslo: Universitetsforlaget, 1947). Baarn: Ambo.

Naess, A. (1992a). Arguing under deep disagreement. In E. M. Barth & E. C. W. Krabbe (Eds.), *Logic and political culture* (pp. 123–131). Amsterdam: North-Holland.

Naess, A. (1992b). How can the empirical movement be promoted today? A discussion of the empiricism of Otto Neurath and Rudolph Carnap. In E. M. Barth, J. Vandormael, & F. Vandamme (Eds.), *From an empirical point of view. The empirical turn in logic* (pp. 107–155). Gent: Communication & Cognition, part II.

Naess, A. (1993). "You assert this?" An empirical study of weight-expressions. In E. C. W. Krabbe, R. J. Dalitz, & P. A. Smit (Eds.), *Empirical logic and public debate. Essays in honour of Else M. Barth* (pp. 121–132). Amsterdam/Atlanta: Rodopi.

Natanson, M., & Johnstone, H. W., Jr. (Eds.). (1965). *Philosophy, rhetoric, and argumentation.* University Park: Pennsylvania State University Press.

Nelson, J. S., Megill, A., & McCloskey D. N. (Eds.). (1987). *The rhetoric of the human sciences: Language and argument in scholarship and public affairs.* Madison: University of Wisconsin Press.

Neumann, U. (1986). *Juristische Argumentationslehre* [A legal theory of argumentation]. Darmstadt: Wissenschaftliche Buchgesellschaft.

Newell, S. E., & Adams, K. L. (1985). Social confrontation in varying degrees of intimacy. In J. R. Cox, M. O. Sillars, & G. B. Walker (Eds.), *Argument and social practice. Proceedings of the Fourth Summer Conference on Argumentation* (pp. 634–647). Annandale, VA: Speech Communication Association.

Newell, S. E., & Rieke, R. D. (1986). A practical reasoning approach to legal doctrine. *Journal of the American Forensic Association, 22,* 212–222.

Newell, S. E., & Stutman, R. K. (1983). Interpersonal disagreement: The study of social confrontation. In D. Zarefsky, M. O. Sillars, & J. Rhodes (Eds.), *Argument in transition. Proceedings of the Third Summer Conference on Argumentation* (pp. 725–739). Annandale, VA: Speech Communication Association.

Nimmo, D., & Mansfield, M. W. (1986). The teflon president: The relevance of Chaim Perelman's formulations for the study of political communication. In J. L. Golden, & J. J. Pilotta (Eds.), *Practical reasoning in human affairs. Studies in honor of Chaim Perelman* (pp. 357–377). Dordrecht: Reidel.

Nisbett, R., & Ross, L. (1980). *Human inference: Strategies and shortcomings of social judgement.* Englewood Cliffs, NJ: Prentice-Hall.

Nølke, H. (1992). Semantic constraints on argumentation: From polyphonic micro-structure to argumentative macro-structure. In F. H. van Eemeren, R. Grootendorst, J. A. Blair, & Ch. A. Willard (Eds.), *Argumentation illuminated* (pp. 189–200). Amsterdam: Sic Sat, 1.

Norris, S., & Ennis, R. (1989). *Evaluating critical thinking.* Pacific Grove, CA: Midwest Publications.

Nuchelmans, G. (1976). *Wijsbegeerte en taal* [Philosophy and language]. Meppel: Boom.

Nuchelmans, G. (1993). On the fourfold root of the *argumentum ad hominem.* In E. C. W. Krabbe, R. J. Dalitz, & P. A. Smit (Eds.), *Empirical logic and public debate. Essays in honour of Else M. Barth* (pp. 37–47). Amsterdam/Atlanta: Rodopi.

O'Connor, D. J. (1959). The uses of argument. *Philosophy, 34,* 244–245.

Oesterle, J. A. (1952). *Logic: the art of defining and reasoning.* Englewood Cliffs, NJ: Prentice-Hall.

Öhlschläger, G. (1979). *Linguistische Überlegungen zu einer Theorie der Argumentation* [Linguistic arguments for a theory of argumentation]. Tübingen: Niemeyer.

Öhlschläger, G. (1980). Zum Explizitmachen von Voraussetzungen beim Argumentieren [On making argumentative assumptions explicit]. *Zeitschrift für Literaturwissenschaft und Linguistik, 38/39,* 152–168.

O'Keefe, B. J. (1988). The logic of message design: Individual differences in reasoning and communication. *Communication Monographs, 55,* 80–103.

O'Keefe, B. J., & Benoit, P. J. (1982). Children's arguments. In J. R. Cox & Ch. A. Willard (Eds.), *The field of argumentation. Advances in argumentation theory and research* (pp. 154–183). Carbondale, IL: Southern Illinois University Press.

O'Keefe, D. J. (1977). Two concepts of argument. *Journal of the American Forensic Association, 13,* 121–128.

O'Keefe, D. J. (1982). The concepts of argument and arguing. In J. R. Cox & Ch. A. Willard (Eds.), *Advances in argumentation theory and research* (pp. 3–23). Carbondale, IL: Southern Illinois University Press.

Olbrechts-Tyteca, L. (1963). Rencontre avec la rhétorique [Encounter with rhetoric]. In L. Olbrechts-Tyteca, *La théorie de l'argumentation. Perspectives et application* (pp. 3–18). Louvain/Paris: Editions Nauwelaerts.

Oostdam, R., Glopper, K. de, & Eiting, M. H. (1994). Argumentation in written discourse: Secondary school students' writing problems. In F. H. van Eemeren & R. Grootendorst (Eds.), *Studies in pragma-dialectics* (pp. 130–141). Amsterdam: Sic Sat, 4.

Pater, W. A. de. (1965). *Les topiques d'Aristote et la dialectique platonicienne.* Fribourg: Editions St. Paul.

Patterson, J. W., & Zarefsky, D. (1983). *Contemporary debate.* Boston: Houghton Mifflin.

Paul, R. (1982). Teaching critical thinking in the strong sense. *Informal Logic Newsletter, 4,* 2–7.

Paul, R. (1985). McPeck's mistakes. *Informal Logic, 7,* 35–43.

Paul, R. (1987). Critical thinking in the strong sense and the role of argumentation in everyday life. In F. H. van Eemeren, R. Grootendorst, J. A. Blair, & Ch. A. Willard (Eds.), *Argumentation: Across the lines of discipline. Proceedings of the Conference on Argumentation 1986* (pp. 379–382). Dordrecht/Providence: Foris Publications, PDA 3.

Paul, R. (1989). Critical thinking in North America: A new theory of knowledge, learning, and literacy. *Argumentation, 3,* 197–235.

Paul, R. (1990). *Critical thinking.* Rohnert Park, CA: Center for Critical Thinking and Moral Critique.

Peirce, Ch. S. (1992). *Reasoning and the logic of things.* (Kenneth Lain Ketner, Ed.). Cambridge, MA: Harvard University Press.

Pelsma, J. R. (1937). *Essentials of debate.* New York: Thomas Y. Crowell.

Pera, M. (1991). *Scienza e retorica* [Science and rhetoric]. Bari: Laterza.

Pera, M. (1994). *The Discourses of Science* (Translation of *Scienza e retorica.* Bari: Laterza, 1991). Chicago/London: The University of Chicago Press.

Perelman, Ch. (1963). *The idea of justice and the problem of argument.* London: Routledge & Kegan Paul.

Perelman, Ch. (1970). The new rhetoric: a theory of practical reasoning. *The great ideas today. Part 3: The contemporary status of a great idea* (pp. 273–312). Chicago: Encyclopedia Britannica.

Perelman, Ch. (1976). *Logique juridique. Nouvelle rhétorique* [Judicial logic. New rhetoric]. Paris: Dalloz.

Perelman, Ch. (1979a). La philosophie du pluralisme et la nouvelle rhétorique [The philosophy of pluralism and the new rhetoric]. *Revue Internationale de Philosophie, 127/128*, 5–17.

Perelman, Ch. (1979b). The rational and the reasonable. In Ch. Perelman, *The new rhetoric and the humanities. Essays on rhetoric and its applications* (pp. 117–123). With an introduction by Harold Zyskind. Dordrecht: Reidel.

Perelman, Ch. (1980). *Justice, law, and argument. Essays on moral and legal reasoning*. Dordrecht: Reidel.

Perelman, Ch. (1982). *The realm of rhetoric* (Translation of Perelman 1977). Notre Dame/London: University of Notre Dame Press.

Perelman, Ch., & Olbrechts-Tyteca, L. (1958). *La nouvelle rhétorique. Traité de l'argumentation* [The new rhetoric. Treatise on argumentation]. Paris: Presses Universitaires de France.

Perelman, Ch., & Olbrechts-Tyteca, L. (1966). *Trattato dell'argomentazione. La nuova retorica* [Treatise on argumentation. The new rhetoric] (Translation of Perelman & Olbrechts-Tyteca 1958). Torino: Einaudi.

Perelman, Ch., & Olbrechts-Tyteca, L. (1969). *The new rhetoric. A treatise on argumentation* (Translation of *La nouvelle rhétorique. Traité de l'argumentation*. Paris: Presses Universitaires de France, 1958). Notre Dame/London: University of Notre Dame Press.

Perelman, Ch., & Olbrechts-Tyteca, L. (1989). Act and person in argument. In R. D. Dearin (Ed.), *The new rhetoric of Chaim Perelman. Statement & response* (pp. 69–78). Lanham, MD: University Press of America.

Peters, T. N. (1989). On the natural development of public activity: A critique of Goodnight's theory of argument. In B. E. Gronbeck (Ed.), *Spheres of argument. Proceedings of the Sixth SCA/AFA Conference on Argumentation* (pp. 26–32). Annandale, VA: Speech Communication Association.

Piaget, J. (1923). *Le langage et la pensée chez l'enfant* [Language and thinking of children]. Neuchâtel: Delachaux et Niestlé.

Piaget, J., & Beth, E. W. (1961). *Epistémologie mathématique et psychologie. Essai sur les relations entre la logique formelle et la pensée réelle* [Mathematical epistemology and psychology. Study on the relation between formal logic and natural thought]. Paris: PUF, EEG XiV.

Pilotta, J. L. (1986). The concrete-universal: A social science foundation. In J. L. Golden & J. J. Pilotta (Eds.), *Practical reasoning in human affairs. Studies in honor of Chaim Perelman* (pp. 379–392). Dordrecht: Reidel.

Pinto, R. C. (1994). Logic, epistemology and argument appraisal. In R. H. Johnson & J. A. Blair (Eds.), *New essays in informal logic* (pp. 116–124). Windsor: Informal Logic.

Plett, H. (1975). *Textwissenschaft und Textanalyse. Semiotik, Linguistik, Rhetorik* [The study of text and the analysis of texts. Semiotics, linguistics, rhetorics]. Heidelberg: Quelle & Meyer.

Plug, J. (1994). Reconstructing complex argumentation in judicial decisions. In F. H. van Eemeren & R. Grootendorst (Eds.), *Studies in pragma-dialectics* (pp. 246–253). Amsterdam: Sic Sat, 4.

Pomerantz, A. (1984). Agreeing and disagreeing with assessments: Some features of preferred/dispreferred turn shapes. In J. M. Atkinson & J. Heritage (Eds.), *Structures of social action. Studies in conversation analysis* (pp. 57–102). Cambridge, England: Cambridge University Press.

Popper, K. R. (1972). *Objective knowledge. An evolutionary approach*. Oxford: Clarendon Press.

Popper, K. R. (1974). *Conjectures and refutations. The growth of scientific knowledge*. London: Routledge & Kegan Paul.

Pratt, J. M. (1970). The appropriateness of a Toulmin analysis of legal argumentation. *Speaker and Gavel, 7*, 133–137.

Prelli, L. (1989). *A rhetoric of science: Inventing scientific discourse*. Columbia, SC: University of South Carolina Press.

Primatarova-Miltcheva, A. (1987). Sequences with concessive, adversative, and restrictive sentences and clauses and the simulation of dialogical argumentation patterns in monological discourse. In F. H. van Eemeren, R. Grootendorst, J. A. Blair, & Ch. A. Willard (Eds.), *Argu-*

mentation: Perspectives and Approaches. Proceedings of the Conference on Argumentation 1986 (pp. 43–51). Dordrecht/Providence: Foris Publications, PDA 3A.

Primatarova-Miltcheva, A., & Nedeltchev, M. (1991). Restraints on the development from totalitarian propaganda towards an argumentative discourse. In F. H. van Eemeren, R. Grootendorst, J. A. Blair, & Ch. A. Willard (Eds.), Proceedings of the Second International Conference on Argumentation (Organized by the International Society for the Study of Argumentation at the University of Amsterdam, June 19–22, 1990) (pp. 859–866). Amsterdam: Sic Sat, 1A/B.

Purtill, R. L. (1972). Logical thinking. New York: Harper.

Putnam, L. L., Wilson, S. R., Waltman, M. S., & Turner, D. (1986). The evolution of case arguments in teachers' bargaining. Journal of the American Forensic Association, 23, 63–81.

Quasthoff, U. (1978). The uses of stereotype in everyday argument. Journal of Pragmatics, 2, 1–48.

Quintilian. (1920). The Institutio Oratoria of Quintilian. London: Heineman.

Quiroz, G., Apothéloz, D., & Brandt, P.-Y. (1992). How counter-argumentation works. In F. H. van Eemeren, R. Grootendorst, J. A. Blair, & Ch. A. Willard (Eds.), Argumentation illuminated (pp. 172–177). Amsterdam: Sic Sat, 1.

Rawls, J. (1971). A theory of justice. Cambridge, MA: Harvard University Press.

Ray, J. W. (1978). Perelman's universal audience. Quarterly Journal of Speech, 64, 361–375.

Reboul, A. (1988). Les problèmes de l'attente interprétative: Topoi et hypothèses projectives [Problems of interpretative expectation: Topoi and hypotheses]. Cahiers de Linguistique Française, 9, 87–114.

Reboul, A. (1989). Relevance and argumentation: How bald can you get. Argumentation, 3, 285–302.

Reboul, O. (1988). Can there be non-rhetorical argumentation? Philosophy & Rhetoric, 21, 220–223.

Reboul, O. (1990). Rhétorique et dialectique chez Aristote [Aristotle's views on rhetoric and dialectic]. Argumentation, 4, 35–52.

Reboul, O. (1991). Introduction à la rhétorique. Théorie et pratique [Introduction to rhetoric. Theory and practice]. Paris: Presses Universitaires de France.

Rees, M. A. van. (1989). Conversation, relevance, and argumentation. Argumentation, 3, 385–393.

Rees, M. A. van. (1991). Het kritische gehalte van probleemoplossende discussies [The critical quality of problem solving discussions]. In M. M. H. Bax & W. Vuijk (Eds.), Thema's in de taalbeheersing [Themes in speech communication research] (pp. 29–36). Dordrecht: ICG Publications.

Rees, M. A. van. (1992a). The adequacy of speech act theory for explaining conversational phenomena: A response to some conversation analytical critics. Journal of Pragmatics, 17, 31–47.

Rees, M. A. van. (1992b). Problem solving and critical discussion. In F. H. van Eemeren, R. Grootendorst, J. A. Blair, & Ch. A. Willard (Eds.), Argumentation illuminated (pp. 281–291). Amsterdam: Sic Sat, 1.

Rees, M. A. van. (1994a). Analysing and evaluating problem-solving discussions. In F. H. van Eemeren & R. Grootendorst (Eds.), Studies in pragma-dialectics (pp. 197–217). Amsterdam: Sic Sat, 4.

Rees, M. A. van. (1994b). Analysing and evaluating small-group decision-making discussions. In L. van Waes, E. Woudstra, & P. van den Hoven (Eds.), Functional communication quality (pp. 149–160). Amsterdam/Atlanta: Rodopi.

Rees, M. A. van. (1995a). Argumentative discourse as a form of social interaction: Implications for dialectical reconstruction. In F. H. van Eemeren, R. Grootendorst, J. A. Blair, & Ch. A. Willard (Eds.), Reconstruction and application. Proceedings of the Third International Conference on Argumentation. Vol. III (159–167). Amsterdam: Sic Sat, 5C.

Rees, M. A. van. (1995b). Functions of repetition in informal discussions. In C. Bazanella (Ed.), Repetition in discourse. Berlin/New York: Walter de Gruyter.

Rehbein, J. (1995). Zusammengesetzte Verweiswörter in argumentativer Rede [Composite anaphora in argumentative speech]. In H. Wohlrapp (Ed.), Wege der Argumentationsforschung (pp. 166–197). Stuttgart/Bad Cannstatt: Frommann-Holzboog.

Reinard, J. C. (1984). The role of Toulmin's categories of message development in persuasive communication. Two experimental studies on attitude change. *Journal of the American Forensic Association, 20,* 206–223.

Rescher, N. (1959). Methods and criteria of reasoning. *Modern Schoolman, 36,* 237–238.

Rescher, N. (1964). *Introduction to logic.* New York: St. Martin's Press.

Rescher, N. (1975). *Introduction to logic* (5th ed.). New York: St. Martin Press.

Rescher, N. (1976). *Plausible reasoning: An introduction to the theory and practice of plausible inference.* Assen: Van Gorcum.

Rescher, N. (1977). *Dialectics: A controversy-oriented approach to the theory of knowledge.* Albany: State University of New York Press.

Reve, K. van het. (1977). Hoe anders is de Sowjetmens [How different are the Soviet people]. *NRC Handelsblad,* March 11, p. 7.

Rhetorik. Ein internationales Jahrbuch [Rhetoric. An international yearbook] (1982–). (J. Dyck, W. Jens, & G. Ueding, Eds.). Tübingen: Niemeyer.

Rieke, R. D. (1986). The evolution of judicial justification: Perelman's concept of the rational and the reasonable. In J. L. Golden & J. J. Pilotta (Eds.), *Practical reasoning in human affairs. Studies in honor of Chaim Perelman* (pp. 227–244). Dordrecht: Reidel.

Rieke, R. D., & Sillars, M. O. (1975). *Argumentation and the decision-making process.* New York: Wiley.

Rieke, R. D., & Sillars, M. O. (1984). *Argumentation and the decision-making process* (2nd ed.). Glenview, IL: Scott Foresman.

Rieke, R. D., & Stutman, R. K. (1990). *Communication in legal advocacy.* Columbia, SC: University of South Carolina Press.

Rijk, L. M. de. (1962). On the twelfth century theories of fallacy. In *Logica modernorum. A contribution to the history of early terminist logic. Vol. I.* Assen: Van Gorcum.

Riley, P., Hollihan, T. A., & Freadhoff, K. D. (1987). Argument in the law: The special case of the small claims court. In F. H. van Eemeren, R. Grootendorst, J. A. Blair, & Ch. A. Willard (Eds.), *Argumentation: Analysis and Practices. Proceedings of the Conference on Argumentation 1986* (pp. 142–151). Dordrecht/Providence: Foris Publications, PDA 3B.

Rödig, J. (1976). Logik und Rechtswissenschaft [Logic and legal science]. In D. Grimm (Ed.), *Rechtswissenschaft und Nachbarwissenschaften. Band 2* (pp. 53–79). München: Beck.

Rödig, J. (1980). *Schriften zur juristischen Logik* [Cahiers on judicial logic]. Berlin: Springer.

Rodingen, H. (1977). *Pragmatik der juristischen Argumentation. Was Gesetze anrichten und was rechtens ist* [The pragmatics of legal argumentation. What laws bring about, and what is legally the case]. Freiburg/München: Alber.

Rodingen, H. (1981). Rhetorik im Recht: Ortsbestimmmung und Überblick [Rhetoric in law: orientation and overview]. *Rhetorik, 2,* 85–105.

Rorty, R. (1979). *Philosophy and the mirror of nature.* Princeton, NJ: Princeton University Press.

Roulet, E. (1989). De la structure de la conversation à la structure d'autres types de discours [From the structure of conversation to the structure of other types of discourse]. In C. Rubattel (Ed.), *Modèles du discours. Recherches actuelles en Suisse romand* (pp. 35–60). Bern: Peter Lang.

Roulet, E., Auchlin, A., Moeschler, J., Rubattel, C., & Schelling, M. (1985). *L'articulation du discours en français contemporain* [The organization of discourse in contemporary French]. Bern: Peter Lang.

Rowland, R. C. (1981). Argument fields. In G. Ziegelmueller, & J. Rhodes (Eds.), *Dimensions of argument. Proceedings of the Second Summer Conference on Argumentation* (pp. 56–79). Annandale, VA: Speech Communication Association.

Rowland, R. C. (1982). The influence of purpose on fields of argument. *Journal of the American Forensic Association, 18,* 228–246.

Ryding, E. (1980). *Att luras utan att ljuga.* Lund: Doxa.

Ryle, G. (1954). *Dilemmas.* Cambridge, England: Cambridge University Press.

Ryle, G. (1976). *The concept of mind.* (5th ed., 1st ed. 1949). Harmondsworth, England: Penguin Books.

Saarinen, E. (Ed.). (1979). *Game-theoretical semantics: Essays on semantics by Hintikka, Carlson, Peacocke, Rantala, and Saarinen*. Dordrecht: Reidel.

Sabine, G. H. (1966). *A history of political theory*. London: George G. Harrap.

Salmon, W. C. (1963). *Logic*. Englewood Cliffs, NJ: Prentice-Hall.

Salmon, W. C. (1984). *Logic* (3rd ed.). Englewood Cliffs, NJ: Prentice-Hall.

Sandig, B., & Püschel, U. (Eds.). (1992). *Stilistik. Bd. III: Argumentationsstile. Germanistische Linguistik* [Stylistics. Vol. III: Styles of argumentation. German linguistics]. Hildesheim: Olms.

Savigny, E. von. (1976). *Argumentation in der Literaturwissenschaft. Wissenschaftstheoretische Untersuchungen zu Lyrikinterpretationen* [Argumentation in literary studies. Theoretical study of the interpretation of poetry]. München: Beck.

Schagrin, M. L. (1968). *The language of logic. A programmed text*. New York: Random House.

Schanze, H. (Ed.). (1974). *Rhetorik. Beiträge zu ihrer Geschichte in Deutschland vom 16.–20. Jahrhundert* [Rhetoric. Contribution to its history in Germany from the 16th to the 20th century]. Frankfurt am Main: Athenäum Fischer Taschenbücher.

Schegloff, E. A., Jefferson, G., & Sacks, H. (1977). The preference for self-correction in the organization of repair in conversation. *Language, 53*, 361–382.

Schellens, P. J. (1979). Vijf bezwaren tegen het Toulmin-model [Five objections to the Toulmin model]. *Tijdschrift voor Taalbeheersing* [Journal of Speech Communication], *1*, 226–246.

Schellens, P. J. (1985). *Redelijke argumenten: een onderzoek naar normen voor kritische lezers* [Reasonable arguments: A study of norms for critical readers] (With a summary in English). Dordrecht: Foris.

Schellens, P. J. (1987). Types of argument and the critical reader. In F. H. van Eemeren, R. Grootendorst, J. A. Blair, & Ch. A. Willard (Eds.), *Argumentation: Analysis and practices. Proceedings of the Conference on Argumentation 1986* (pp. 34–41). Dordrecht: Foris Publications, PDA 3B.

Schellens, P. J., & Verhoeven, G. (1988). *Argument en tegenargument. Een inleiding in de analyse en beoordeling van betogende teksten* [Argument and counter-argument. An introduction to the analysis and evaluation of argumentative texts]. Leiden: Martinus Nijhoff.

Schiappa, E. (1985). Dissociation in the arguments of rhetorical theory. *Journal of the American Forensic Association, 22*, 72–82.

Schiappa, E. (1989). 'Spheres of argument' as *topoi* for the critical study of power/knowledge. In B. E. Gronbeck (Ed.), *Spheres of argument. Proceedings of the Sixth SCA/AFA Conference on Argumentation* (pp. 47–56). Annandale, VA: Speech Communication Association.

Schiappa, E. (1993). Arguing about definitions. *Argumentation, 7*, 403–418.

Schipper, E. W., & Schuh, E. (1960). *A first course in modern logic*. London: Routledge & Kegan Paul.

Schmidt, S. J. (1976). Literary science as a science of argument. *New Literary History, VII*, 467–481.

Schmidt-Faber, W. (1986). *Argument und Scheinargument. Grundlagen und Modelle zu rationalen Begründungen im Alltag* [Argument and pseudo-argument. Foundations and models of everyday rational argumentation]. München: Fink.

Scholz, H. (1967). *Abriss der Geschichte der Logik* [An historical overview of logic] (3rd ed.). München: Karl Alber Freiburg.

Schopenhauer, A. (1818–1830). Eristische Dialektik [Eristic dialectics]. In A. Hübscher (Ed.), *Der handschriftliche Nachlass. Band III* (pp. 666–695). Frankfurt am Main: Berliner Manuskripte, Waldemar Kramer.

Schreckenberger, W. (1978). *Rhetorische Semiotik. Analyse von Texten des Grundgesetzes und von rhetorischen Grundstrukturen der Argumentation des Bundesverfassungsgerichtes* [Rhetorical semiotics. The analysis of constitutional texts and of basic rhetorical patterns in the argumentation of the Supreme Court]. Freiburg: K. Alber.

Schuetz, J. (1991). Perelman's rule of justice in Mexican appellate courts. In F. H. van Eemeren, R. Grootendorst, J. A. Blair, & Ch. A. Willard (Eds.), *Proceedings of the Second International Conference on Argumentation* (Organized by the International Society for the Study of Argumentation at the University of Amsterdam, June 19–22, 1990) (pp. 804–812). Amsterdam: Sic Sat, 1A/1B.

Schwitalla, J. (1976). Zur Einführung in die Argumentationstheorie: Begründung durch Daten und Begründung durch Handlungsziele in der Alltagsargumentation [Introduction to argumentation theory: Data and action goals as a form of justification in everyday argumentation]. *Der Deutschunterricht, 28*, 22–36.

Schwitalla, J. (1987). Common argumentation and group identity. In F. H. van Eemeren, R. Grootendorst, J. A. Blair, & Ch. A. Willard (Eds.), *Argumentation: Perspectives and Approaches. Proceedings of the Conference on Argumentation 1986* (pp. 119–126). Dordrecht/Providence: Foris Publications, PDA 3A.

Scott, R. L. (1967). On viewing rhetoric as epistemic. *Central States Speech Journal, 18*, 9–17.

Scriven, M. (1976). *Reasoning*. New York: McGraw-Hill.

Scult, A. (1985). A note on the range and utility of the universal audience. *Journal of the American Forensic Association, 22*, 84–87.

Scult, A. (1989). Perelman's universal audience: One perspective. In R. D. Dearin (Ed.), *The new rhetoric of Chaim Perelman. Statement & response* (pp. 153–162). Lanham, MD: University Press of America.

Searle, J. R. (1969). *Speech acts. An essay in the philosophy of language.* Cambridge, England: Cambridge University Press.

Searle, J. R. (1979). *Expression and meaning. Studies in the theory of speech acts.* Cambridge, England: Cambridge University Press.

Secor, M. (1987). How common are fallacies? *Informal Logic, 9*, 41–48.

Seech, Z. (1987). *Logic in everyday life: Practical reasoning skills.* Belmont, CA: Wadsworth.

Seech, Z. (1993). *Open minds and everyday reasoning.* Belmont, CA: Wadsworth.

Segre, C. (1985). *Avviamento all'analisi del testo letterario* [The analysis of literary texts]. Torino: Einaudi.

Seibert, Th.-M. (1977). Argumentationsbeispiele aus dem Rechtsbereich [Examples of legal argumentation]. In M. Schecker (Ed.), *Theorie der Argumentation* (pp. 313–353). Tübingen: Narr.

Seibert, Th.-M. (1981). Topos and Status im Rahmen einer entwickelten juristischen Pragmatik [Topos and stasis in the framework of a well-developed pragmatic theory]. In D. Breuer, & H. Schanze (Eds.), *Topik. Beiträge zur interdisziplinären Diskussion* (pp. 80–92). München: Fink.

Seibert, Th.-M. (1987). The arguments of a judge. In F. H. van Eemeren, R. Grootendorst, J. A. Blair, & Ch. A. Willard (Eds.), *Argumentation: Analysis and practices. Proceedings of the Conference on Argumentation 1986* (pp. 119–122). Dordrecht/Providence: Foris Publications, PDA 3B.

Seibold, D. R., McPhee, R. D., Poole, M. S., Tanita, N. E., & Canary, D. J. (1981). Argument, group influence, and decision outcomes. In G. Ziegelmueller & J. Rhodes (Eds.), *Dimensions of argument. Proceedings of the Second Summer Conference on Argumentation* (pp. 663–692). Annandale, VA: Speech Communication Association.

Sellars, R. W. (1917). *The essentials of logic.* New York: Houghton Mifflin.

Sentenberg, I. V., & Karasic, V. I. (1993). Pseudo-argumentation: Some types of speech manipulations (in Russian, with a summary in English). *Journal of Speech Communication and Argumentation, 1*, 30–39.

Settekorn, W. (1977). Pragmatique et rhétorique discursive [Pragmatics and discursive rhetoric]. *Journal of Pragmatics, 1*, 195–209.

Sheppard, S. A., & Rieke, R. D. (1983). Categories of reasoning in legal argument. In D. Zarefsky, M. O. Sillars, & J. Rhodes (Eds.), *Argument in transition. Proceedings of the Third Summer Conference on Argumentation* (pp. 235–250). Annandale, VA: Speech Communication Association.

Sherif, M., & Hovland, C. I. (1961). *Social judgment.* New Haven, CT: Yale University Press.

Shi-Xu. (1992). Argumentation, explanation, and social cognition. *Text, 12*, 263–291.

Shi-Xu. (1995). Cultural attitudes: In contexts of argumentation and explanation. In *Argumentation*, *9*, 371–398.

Siegel, H. (1985). McPeck, informal logic and the nature of critical thinking. *Philosophy of Education: Proceedings, 41*, 61–72.

Siegel, H. (1988). *Educating reason: Rationality, critical thinking and education.* New York: Routledge.

Siegel, H. (1993). Not by skill alone: The centrality of character in critical thinking. *Informal Logic, 15*, 163–177.

Sikora, J. J. (1959). The uses of argument. *New Scholasticism, 33*, 373–374.

Sillars, M. O. (1981). Investigating religious argument as a field. In G. Ziegelmueller & J. Rhodes (Eds.), *Dimensions of argument. Proceedings of the Second Summer Conference on Argumentation* (pp. 143–151). Annandale, VA: Speech Communication Association.

Simmons, E. D. (1959). Methods and criteria of reasoning. *New scholasticism, 32*, 526–530.

Simons, H. W. (Ed.). (1990). *The rhetorical turn: Invention and persuasion in the conduct of inquiry.* Chicago: The University of Chicago Press.

Slot, P. (1993). *How can you say that? Rhetorical questions in argumentative texts.* Amsterdam: IFOTT, 2.

Slot, P. (1994). Reconstructing indirect speech acts. In F. H. van Eemeren & R. Grootendorst (Eds.), *Studies in pragma-dialectics* (pp. 188–196). Amsterdam: Sic Sat, 4.

Snedaker, K., & Schuetz, J. (1985). Storytelling in opening statements: Framing the argumentation of the trial. In J. R. Cox, M. O. Sillars, & G. B. Walker (Eds.), *Argument and social practice. Proceedings of the Fourth Summer Conference on Argumentation* (pp. 465–482). Annandale, VA: Speech Communication Association.

Snoeck Henkemans, A. F. (1992). *Analysing complex argumentation. The reconstruction of multiple and coordinatively compound argumentation in a critical discussion.* Amsterdam: Sic Sat.

Snoeck Henkemans, A. F. (1995a). *Anyway* and *even* as indicators of argumentative structure. In F. H. van Eemeren, R. Grootendorst, J. A. Blair, & Ch. A. Willard (Eds.), *Reconstruction and application. Proceedings of the Third International Conference on Argumentation. Vol. III* (pp. 183–191). Amsterdam: Sic Sat, 5C.

Snoeck Henkemans, A. F. (1995b). *But* as an indicator of counter-arguments and concessions. *Leuvense Bijdragen, 84.*

Sobota, K. (1990a). *Sachlichkeit. Rhetorische Kunst der Juristen* [Realism. The rhetorical skills of lawyers]. Frankfurt am Main: Peter Lang.

Sobota, K. (1990b). System and flexibility in law. *Argumentation, 5*, 275–282.

Sperber, D., & Wilson, D. (1986). *Relevance. Communication and cognition.* Oxford: Basil Blackwell.

Strawson, P. (1952). *Introduction to logical theory.* Oxford: Oxford University Press.

Strecker, B. (1976). *Beweisen. Eine praktisch-semantische Untersuchung* [Proving. A practical-semantic examination]. Tübingen: Niemeyer.

Struck, G. (1971). *Topische Jurisprudenz. Argument und Gemeinplatz in der juristischen Arbeit* [Topical jurisprudence. Arguments and topoi in legal practice]. Frankfurt am Main: Athenäum.

Struck, G. (1977). *Zur Theorie juristischer Argumentation* [Toward a theory of legal argumentation]. Berlin: Duncker & Humblot.

Stump, E. (1978). Dialectic in ancient and medieval logic. In E. Stump (Ed.), *Boethius's De topicis differentiis* (pp. 159–261). Ithaca, NY: Cornell University Press.

Tammelo, I. (1969). *Outlines of modern legal logic.* Wiesbaden: F. Steiner.

Tammelo, I. (1978). *Modern logic in the service of law.* Wien: Springer.

Tarello, G. (1972). Sur la spécificité du raisonnement juridique. In *Die juristische Argumentation* [On the special status of judicial reasoning] (Vorträge der Weltkongresses für Rechts- und Sozialphilosophie, Brüssel, 29. VIII–3. IX. 1971) (pp. 103–124). Wiesbaden: Franz Steiner Verlag GmbH.

Tarski, A. (1956). On the concept of logical consequence (J. H. Woodger, Trans.), In *Logic, semantics, metamathematics* (pp. 409–420). Oxford: Clarendon Press.

Thomas, S. N. (1973). *Practical reasoning in natural language.* Englewood Cliffs, NJ: Prentice-Hall.

Thomas, S. N. (1986). *Practical reasoning in natural language* (3rd ed.). Englewood Cliffs, NJ: Prentice-Hall.

Tirkkonen-Condit, S. (1985). *Argumentative text structure and translation* (Studia Philologica Jyväskyläensia 18). Jyväskylä: University of Jyväskylä.

Tirkkonen-Condit, S. (1987). Argumentation in English and Finnish editorials. In F. H. van Eemeren, R. Grootendorst, J. A. Blair, & Ch.A. Willard (Eds.), *Argumentation: Across the lines of discipline. Proceedings of the Conference on Argumentation 1986* (pp. 373–378). Dordrecht/Providence: Foris Publications, PDA 3.

Toulmin, S. E. (1950). *An examination of the place of reason in ethics.* Cambridge, England: Cambridge University Press.

Toulmin, S. E. (1958). *The uses of argument.* Cambridge, England: Cambridge University Press.

Toulmin, S. E. (1964). *The uses of argument* (2nd ed.). Cambridge, England: Cambridge University Press.

Toulmin, S. E. (1972). *Human understanding.* Princeton, NJ: Princeton University Press.

Toulmin, S. E. (1976). *Knowing and acting. An invitation to philosophy.* New York: Macmillan.

Toulmin, S. E. (1988). *The uses of argument* (9th ed.). Cambridge, England: Cambridge University Press.

Toulmin, S. E. (1990). *Cosmopolis: The hidden agenda of modernity.* New York: Free Press.

Toulmin, S. E. (1992). Logic, rhetoric and reason: Redressing the balance. In F. H. van Eemeren, R. Grootendorst, J. A. Blair, & Ch. A. Willard (Eds.), *Argumentation illuminated* (pp. 3–11). Amsterdam: Sic Sat, 1.

Toulmin, S. E., & Janik, A. (1973). *Wittgenstein's Vienna.* New York: Simon & Schuster.

Toulmin, S. E., Rieke, R., & Janik, A. (1979). *An introduction to reasoning.* New York: Macmillan.

Trapp, R. (1983). Generic characteristics of argumentation in everyday discourse. In D. Zarefsky, M. O. Sillars, & J. Rhodes (Eds.), *Argument in transition. Proceedings of the Third Summer Conference on Argumentation* (pp. 516–530). Annandale, VA: Speech Communication Association.

Trent, J. D. (1968). Toulmin's model of an argument: An examination and extension. *Quarterly Journal of Speech, 54,* 252–259.

Ueding, G., & Jens, W. (Eds.). (1992). *Historisches Wörterbuch der Rhetorik* [Historical dictionary of rhetoric]. Band 1. Tübingen: Niemeyer.

Ueding, G., & Jens, W. (Eds.). (1994). *Historisches Wörterbuch der Rhetorik* [Historical dictionary of rhetoric]. Band 2. Tübingen: Niemeyer.

Ueding, G., & Steinbrink, B. (1994). *Grundriss der Rhetorik. Geschichte, Technik, Methode* [Foundations of rhetoric. History, techniques, method]. Stuttgart: Metzler.

Ulrich, W. (1992). In defense of the fallacy. In W. L. Benoit, D. Hample, & P. J. Benoit (Eds.), *Readings in argumentation* (pp. 337–356). Berlin/New York: Foris Publications, PDA 11.

Valesio, P. (1980). *Novantiqua: Rhetorics as a contemporary theory.* Bloomington: Indiana University Press.

Vedung, E. (1982). *Political Reasoning.* Newbury Park, CA: Sage.

Vedung, E. (1987). Rational argumentation and political deception. In F. H. van Eemeren, R. Grootendorst, J. A. Blair, & Ch. A. Willard (Eds.), *Argumentation: Across the lines of discipline. Proceedings of the Conference on Argumentation 1986* (pp. 353–364). Dordrecht/Providence: Foris Publications, PDA 3.

Verbiest, A. E. M. (1987). *Confrontaties in conversaties* [Confrontations in conversations] (with a summary in English). Dordrecht: ICG Printing.

Verbiest, A. E. M. (1994). A new source of argumentative indicators? In F. H. van Eemeren & R. Grootendorst (Eds.), *Studies in pragma-dialectics* (pp. 180–187). Amsterdam: Sic Sat, 4.

Viehweg, Th. (1974). *Topik und Jurisprudenz. Ein Beitrag zur rechtswissenschaftlichen Grundlagenforschung* [Topics and jurisprudence. A contribution to the study of the foundations of law]. München: Beck.

Viskil, E. (1994). Definitions in argumentative texts. In F. H. van Eemeren & R. Grootendorst (Eds.), *Studies in pragma-dialectics* (pp. 79–86). Amsterdam: Sic Sat, 4.

Volquardsen, B. (1995). Argumentative Arbeitsteilung und die Versuchungen des Expertenwesens [The division of argumentative labor and the trial of experts]. In H. Wohlrapp (Ed.), *Wege der Argumentationsforschung* (pp. 339–350). Stuttgart/Bad Cannstatt: Frommann-Holzboog.

Völzing, P.-L. (1979). *Begründen, Erklären, Argumentieren. Modelle und Materialien zu einer Theorie der Metakommunikation* [Supporting, explaining, arguing. Models and materials for a theory of meta-communication]. Heidelberg: Quelle & Meyer.

Völzing, P.-L. (1981). *Kinder argumentieren. Die Ontogenese argumentativer Fähigkeiten* [Children argue. The development of argumentative skills]. Paderborn: Schöningh.

Völzing, P.-L. (1987). Some remarks on the development of argumentation. In F. H. van Eemeren, R. Grootendorst, J. A. Blair, & Ch. A. Willard (Eds.), *Argumentation: Perspectives and approaches. Proceedings of the Conference on Argumentation 1986* (pp. 187–195). Dordrecht/Providence: Foris Publications, PDA 3A.

Voss, J. F., Fincher-Kiefer, R., Wiley, J., & Ney Silfies, L. (1993). On the processing of arguments. *Argumentation, 7*, 165–181.

Walker, G. B., & Sillars, M. O. (1990). Where is argument? Perelman's theory of fallacies. In R. Trapp & J. Schuetz (Eds.), *Perspectives on argumentation. Essays in honor of Wayne Brockriede* (pp. 134–150). Prospect Heights, IL: Waveland Press.

Wallace, K. R. (1989). Topoi and the problem of invention. In R. D. Dearin (Ed.), *The new rhetoric of Chaim Perelman. Statement & response* (pp. 107–119). Lanham: University Press of America.

Walther, J. (1990). *Philosophisches Argumentieren. Lehr-und Übungsbuch* [Philosophical argumentation. A text book]. Freiburg/München: K. Alber.

Walton, P.-A. (1970). *ABC om argumentation* [The ABC of argumentation]. Stockholm: Almqvist & Wiksell.

Walton, D. N. (1984). *Logical dialogue games and fallacies.* Lanham, MD: University Press of America.

Walton, D. N. (1985a). *Arguer's position. A pragmatic study of ad hominem attack, criticism, refutation, and fallacy* (Contributions in Philosophy 26). Westport, CT: Greenwood.

Walton, D. N. (Ed.). (1985b). New directions in the logic of dialogue. *Synthese, 63*, 259–274.

Walton, D. N. (1987). *Informal fallacies. Towards a theory of argument criticisms.* Pragmatics & Beyond Companian Series, 4. Amsterdam: John Benjamins.

Walton, D. N. (1989a). *Informal logic. A handbook for critical argumentation.* Cambridge, England: Cambridge University Press.

Walton, D. N. (1989b). *Question-reply argumentation.* Westport, CT: Greenwood.

Walton, D. N. (1991). *Begging the question.* Westport, CT: Greenwood.

Walton, D. N. (1992a). *The place of emotion in argument.* University Park, PA: The Pennsylvania State University Press.

Walton, D. N. (1992b). *Slippery slope arguments.* Oxford: Oxford University Press.

Walton, D. N. (1992c). Types of dialogue, dialectical shifts and fallacies. In F. H. van Eemeren, R. Grootendorst, J. A. Blair, & Ch. A. Willard (Eds.), *Argumentation illuminated* (pp. 133–147). Amsterdam: Sic Sat, 1.

Walton, D. N., & Krabbe, E. C. W. (1995). *Commitment in dialogue: Basic concepts of interpersonal reasoning.* Albany: State University of New York Press.

Warnick, B. (1981). Arguing value propositions. *Journal of the American Forensic Association, 18*, 109–119.

Warnick, B., & Inch, E. S. (1989). *Critical thinking and communication: The use of reason in argument.* New York: Macmillan.

Warnick, B., & Kline, S. L. (1992). The new rhetoric's argument schemes: A rhetorical view of practical reasoning. *Argumentation and Advocacy, 29*, 1–15.

Weddle, P. (1978). *Argument. A guide to critical thinking.* New York: McGraw-Hill.

Weinberger, O. (1970). *Rechtslogik. Versuch einer Anwendung moderner Logik auf das juristische Denken* [Judicial logic. An attempt to apply modern logic to judicial thinking]. Wien: Springer.

Weinstein, M. (1990a). Towards an account of argumentation in science. *Argumentation, 4*, 269–298.

Weinstein, M. (1990b). Towards a research agenda for informal logic and critical thinking. *Informal Logic, 2*, 121–143.

Weinstein, M. (1994). Informal logic and applied epistemology. In R. H. Johnson & J. A. Blair (Eds.), *New essays in informal logic* (pp. 140–161). Windsor: Informal Logic.

Wellman, C. (1971). *Challenge and response: Justification in ethics.* Carbondale: Southern Illinois University Press.

Wenzel, J. W. (1979). Jürgen Habermas and the dialectical perspective on argumentation. *Journal of the American Forensic Association, 16*, 83–94.

Wenzel, J. W. (1980). Perspectives on argument. In J. Rhodes & S.E. Newell (Eds.), *Dimensions of argument: Proceedings of the Summer Conference on Argumentation* (pp. 112–133). Annandale, VA: Speech Communication Association.

Wenzel, J. W. (1987). The rhetorical perspective on argument. In F. H. van Eemeren, R. Grootendorst, J. A. Blair, & Ch. A. Willard (Eds.), *Argumentation: Across the lines of discipline. Proceedings of the Conference on Argumentation 1986* (pp. 101–109). Dordrecht/Providence: Foris Publications, PDA 3.

Werling, D. A., & Rieke, R. D. (1985). The path of legal reasoning in sex discrimination cases. In J. R. Cox, M. O. Sillars, & G. B. Walker (Eds.), *Argument and social practice. Proceedings of the Fourth Summer Conference on Argumentation* (pp. 445–464). Annandale, VA: Speech Communication Association.

Whately, R. (1848). *Elements of logic* (9th ed., 1st ed. 1826). London: Longmans.

Whitehead, A. N., & Russell, B. (1910–1913). *Principia mathematica* (Three vols.). Cambridge, England: Cambridge University Press.

Wiche, R. T. P. (1983). Over het belang voor logica en samenleving van een correcte interpretatie van generische uitspraken [On the importance of a correct interpretation of generic statements for logic and society]. *Filosofie en Praktijk* [Philosophy and Practice], *4*, 84–96.

Wiche, R. T. P. (1988). Over het onderscheid tussen argumentatieve en formele discussies [On the distinction between argumentative and formal discussions]. *Tijdschrift voor Taalbeheersing* [Journal of Speech Communication], *10*, 121–131.

Wiethof, W. E. (1985). Critical perspectives on Perelman's philosophy of legal argument. *Journal of the American Forensic Association, 22*, 88–95.

Will, F. L. (1960). The uses of argument. *Philosophical Review, 69*, 399–403.

Willard, Ch. A. (1976). On the utility of descriptive diagrams for the analysis and criticism of arguments. *Communication Monographs, 43*, 308–319.

Willard, Ch. A. (1978a). A reformulation of the concept of argument: The constructivist/interactionist foundations of a sociology of argument. *Journal of the American Forensic Association, 14*, 121–140.

Willard, Ch. A. (1978b). Argument as nondiscursive symbolism. *Journal of the American Forensic Association, 14*, 187–193.

Willard, Ch. A. (Guest Ed.). (1982). Special issue: Symposium on argument fields. *Journal of the American Forensic Association, 18*, 191–257.

Willard, Ch. A. (1983). *Argumentation and the social grounds of knowledge.* Tuscaloosa: The University of Alabama Press.

Willard, Ch. A. (1987). Valuing dissensus. In F. H. van Eemeren, R. Grootendorst, J. A. Blair, & Ch. A. Willard (Eds.), *Argumentation: Across the lines of discipline. Proceedings of the Conference on Argumentation 1986* (pp. 145–157). Dordrecht/Providence: Foris Publications, PDA 3.

Willard, Ch. A. (1989). *A theory of argumentation.* Tuscaloosa: The University of Alabama Press.

Willard, Ch. A. (1995). *Liberal alarms and rhetorical excursions: A new rhetoric for modern democracy.* Chicago: University of Chicago Press.

Winans, J. A., & Utterback, W. E. (1930). *Argumentation*. New York: Century.

Windes, R. R., & Hastings, A. C. (1969). *Argumentation and advocacy*. New York: Random House.

Wintgens, L. J. (1993). Rhetoric, reasonableness and ethics: An essay on Perelman. *Argumentation*, 7, 451–460.

Wisdom, J. (1957/1991). *Proof and explanation. The Virginia Lectures by John Wisdom*. (S. Barker, Ed.). Lanham, MD: University Press of America.

Wisse, J. (1989). *Ethos and pathos from Aristotle to Cicero*. Amsterdam: Hakkert.

Wittgenstein, L. (1953). *Philosophical investigations*. (G. E. M. Anscombe, Trans.). New York: Macmillan.

Wittgenstein, L. (1969). *On certainty*. (G. E. M. Anscombe & G. H. von Wright, Eds.). Oxford: Blackwell.

Wodak, R., Nowak, P., Pelikan, J., Gruber, H., Cillia, R. de, & Mitter, R. (1990). *"Wir sind alle unschuldige Täter!": Diskurshistorische Studien zum Nachkriegsantisemitismus* ["We are all innocent culprits!" Discourse-historical study of post-war antisemitism]. Frankfurt am Main: Suhrkamp.

Wohlrapp, H. (1977). Analytische und konstruktive Wissenschaftstheorie. Zwei Thesen zur Klärung der Fronten [An analytic and constructive theory of science. Two theses to clarify the positions]. In G. Patzig, E. Scheibe, & W. Wieland (Eds.), *Logik, Ethik, Theorie der Geisteswissenschaften*. Hamburg: Meiner.

Wohlrapp, H. (1987). Toulmin's theory and the dynamics of argumentation. In F. H. van Eemeren, R. Grootendorst, J. A. Blair, & Ch. A. Willard (Eds.), *Argumentation: Perspectives and approaches. Proceedings of the Conference on Argumentation 1986* (pp. 327–335). Dordrecht/Providence: Foris Publications, PDA 3A.

Wohlrapp, H. (1990). Über nicht-deduktive Argumente [On non-deductive arguments]. In P. Klein (Ed.), *Praktische Logik. Traditionen und Tendenzen* (pp. 217–235). Göttingen: Van den Hoeck & Ruprecht.

Wohlrapp, H. (1991). *Argumentum ad baculum* and ideal speech situation. In F. H. van Eemeren, R. Grootendorst, J. A. Blair, & Ch. A. Willard (Eds.), *Proceedings of the Second International Conference on Argumentation* (Organized by the International Society for the Study of Argumentation at the University of Amsterdam, June 19–22, 1990) (pp. 397–402). Amsterdam: Sic Sat, 1A/B.

Wohlrapp, H. (1995). Argumentative Geltung [Argumentative validity]. In H. Wohlrapp (Ed.), *Wege der Argumentationsforschung* (pp. 280–297). Stuttgart/Bad Cannstatt: Frommann-Holzboog.

Woods, J. (1967). Is there a relation of intensional conjunction? *Mind*, 78, 357–368.

Woods, J. (1980). What is informal logic? In J. A. Blair, & R. H. Johnson. (Eds.), *Informal logic. The First International Symposium* (pp. 57–68). Point Reyes, CA: Edgepress.

Woods, J. (1992a). Who cares about the fallacies? In F. H. van Eemeren, R. Grootendorst, J. A. Blair, & Ch. A. Willard (Eds.), *Argumentation illuminated* (pp. 23–48). Amsterdam: Sic Sat, 1.

Woods, J. (1992b). Apocalyptic relevance. *Argumentation*, 6, 189–202.

Woods, J. (1995). Fearful symmetry. In H. V. Hansen & R. C. Pinto (Eds.), *Fallacies: Classical background and contemporary developments*. University Park, PA: The Pennsylvania State University Press.

Woods, J., & Walton, D. N. (1982). *Argument: The logic of the fallacies*. Toronto: McGraw-Hill Ryerson.

Woods, J., & Walton, D. N. (1989). *Fallacies: Selected papers, 1972–1982*. Dordrecht/Providence: Foris Publications, PDA 9.

Wunderlich, D. (1974). *Grundlagen der Linguistik* [Foundations of linguistics]. Reinbek bei Hamburg: Rowohlt Taschenbuch Verlag.

Wunderlich, D. (1980). Pro und Kontra [Pro and contra]. *Zeitschrift für Linguistik und Literaturwissenschaft*, 38/39, 109–127.

Yanal, R. J. (1991). Dependent and independent reasons. *Informal Logic*, 13, 137–144.

Yaskevich, Ya. S. (1993). Scientific argumentation: Logical and communicative aspects (in Russian, with a summary in English). *Journal of Speech Communication and Argumentation, 1*, 93–102.

Yingling, J. M., & Trapp, R. (1985). Toward a developmental perspective on argumentative competence. In J. R. Cox, M. O. Sillars, & G. B. Walker (Eds.), *Argument and social practice. Proceedings of the Fourth Summer Conference on Argumentation* (pp. 619–633). Annandale, VA: Speech Communication Association.

Yoshino, H. (1978). Über die Notwendigkeit einer besonderen Normenlogik als Methode der juristischen Logik [On the necessity of a special logic of norms as a method for judicial logic]. In U. Klug, Th. Ramm, F. Rittner, & B. Schmiedel (Eds.), *Gesetzgebungstheorie, Juristische Logik, Zivil- und Prozessrecht. Gedächtnisschrift für Jürgen Rödig* (pp. 140–161). Berlin: Springer.

Yost, M. (1917). Argument from the point of view of sociology. *Quarterly Journal of Public Speaking, 3*, 109–127.

Zagar, I. Z. (1995). Argumentation in language opposed to argumentation with language: Some problems. In F. H. van Eemeren, R. Grootendorst, J. A. Blair, & Ch. A. Willard (Eds.), *Reconstruction and application. Proceedings of the Third International Conference on Argumentation. Vol. III* (pp. 200–218). Amsterdam: Sic Sat, 5C.

Zarefsky, D. (1969). The 'traditional case'-'comparative advantage case' dichotomy: Another look. *Journal of the American Forensic Association, 6*, 12–20.

Zarefsky, D. (1980). Product, process, or point of view? In J. Rhodes & S. Newell (Eds.), *Dimensions of argument. Proceedings of the Summer Conference on Argumentation* (pp. 228–238). Annandale, VA: Speech Communication Association.

Zarefsky, D. (1982). Persistent questions in the theory of argument fields. *Journal of the American Forensic Association, 18*, 191–203.

Zarefsky, D. (1995). Argumentation in the tradition of speech communication studies. In F. H. van Eemeren, R. Grootendorst, J. A. Blair, & Ch. A. Willard (Eds.), *Perspectives and approaches. Proceedings of the Third International Conference on Argumentation. Vol. I* (pp. 32–52). Amsterdam: Sic Sat, 5A.

Ziegelmueller, G., & Rhodes, J. (Eds.). (1981). *Dimensions of argument. Proceedings of the Second Summer Conference on Argumentation*. Annandale, VA: Speech Communication Association.

Zillig, W. (1982). *Bewerten. Sprechakttypen der bewertenden Rede* [Asserting. Speech act types of the assertive mode]. Tübingen: Niemeyer.

AUTHOR INDEX

SUBJECT INDEX